Y0-BDL-468

ENGLISH TEXT

System and Structure

by

J.R. MARTIN
University of Sydney

JOHN BENJAMINS PUBLISHING COMPANY
PHILADELPHIA/AMSTERDAM

1992

Library of Congress Cataloging-in-Publication Data

Martin, J.R.
  English text : system and structure / by J.R. Martin.
    p.   cm.
  Includes bibliographical references and index.
  1. English language--Discourse analysis. 2. English language--Syntax. I. Title.
PE1422.M37   1992
420'.141--dc20   92-19652
ISBN 90 272 2079 4 (Eur.) / 1-55619-115-4 (US) (Hb., alk. paper)   CIP
ISBN 90 272 2129 4 (Eur.) / 1-55619-485-4 (US) (Pb., alk. paper)

© Copyright 1992 - John Benjamins B.V.
No part of this book may be reproduced in any form, by print, photoprint, microfilm, or any other means, without written permission from the publisher.

John Benjamins Publishing Co. · P.O. Box 75577 · 1070 AN Amsterdam · The Netherlands
John Benjamins North America · 821 Bethlehem Pike · Philadelphia, PA 19118 · USA

ENGLISH TEXT

for H.A. Gleason, Jr. — metatheoretican, teacher and discourse pioneer

Table of Contents

Preface   xiii

1.   Discourse semantics: A proposal for triple articulation

1.1   A context for discourse analysis   1
1.2   System and structure   3
1.3   The metafunctional organisation of meaning   7
1.3.1   Metafunction and system   8
1.3.2   Metafunction and structure   10
1.4   Stratification   14
1.5   Discourse structure   21
1.6   Discourse systems   26
Notes   28

2.   Negotiation: Shaping meaning through dialogue

2.1   MOOD — basic resources for negotiation   31
2.2   SPEECH FUNCTION and MOOD: adjacency pairs   36
2.3   EXCHANGE STRUCTURE   46
2.4   Extending constituency — exchanges, moves and acts   50
2.4.1   Moves and acts   51
2.4.2   Move complexes   57
2.5   Replacing constituency — dependency models   60
2.5.1   Fawcett et al.'s systemic flowchart   60
2.5.2   Butler's daughter dependency approach   65
2.6   Exchange dynamics: non-adjacent pairs   66
2.6.1   Tracking   67
2.6.2   Challenging   71
2.7   Consensus and debate   76
2.8   Analysis   78
2.8.1   Classroom discourse   78

2.8.2	Service encounters	82
2.9	Envoi	90
Notes		91

3.   Identification: Reference as semantic choice

3.1	Learning to refer	93
3.2	Participant identification	95
3.3	Participant identification in English: system	98
3.3.1	Phoricity	98
3.3.2	Reference as semantic choice	102
3.3.3	Phoricity and context: retrieving presumed information	121
3.3.4	IDENTIFICATION in [3:1]	127
3.4	IDENTIFICATION and stratification	129
3.4.1	Participants and nominal groups	129
3.4.2	Grammaticalising phoricity	134
3.4.3	IDENTIFICATION and ideational grammar	136
3.4.4	Grammatical metaphor	138
3.5.	Participant identification in English: structure	140
3.5.1	Reference chains	140
3.5.2	Two texts analysed	146
3.6	Location and manner	153
3.7	IDENTIFICATION and NEGOTIATION	155

4.   Conjunction & continuity: The logic of English text

4.1	The limits of grammar	159
4.2	Conjunctive relations in English: general issues	168
4.2.1	Diversification	168
4.2.2	Logico-semantic relations	170
4.2.3	Internal and external relations	178
4.2.4	Implicit and explicit relations	183
4.3	External relations: system	184
4.3.1	External temporal relations	185
4.3.2	External consequential relations	193
4.3.3	External comparative relations	202
4.3.4	External additive relations	205
4.3.5	External locative relations	206
4.4	Internal relations: system	207

4.4.1	Internal comparative relations	207
4.4.2	Internal additive relations	218
4.4.3	Internal consequential relations	222
4.4.4	Internal temporal relations	224
4.4.5	Distinguishing internal and external relations	226
4.5	CONTINUITY	230
4.6	CONJUNCTION in English: structure	234
4.6.1	Elaborating reticula	235
4.6.2	Range	238
4.6.3	Direction of dependency	240
4.6.4	Contiguity	241
4.7	Analysis of two texts	243
4.7.1	Notational conventions	243
4.7.2	Analysis	244
4.8	Constituency, dependency and conjunctive relations	249
4.9	Grammatical metaphor and conjunctive structure	264
4.10	CONJUNCTION, IDENTIFICATION and NEGOTIATION	265
Notes		269

5.   Ideation: The company words keep

5.1	Lexical departure	271
5.2.	Describing lexis	273
5.2.1	Dictionary and thesaurus	273
5.2.2	Collocation	275
5.2.3	Lexis as delicate grammar	277
5.2.4	Lexical relations in cohesion analysis	286
5.2.5	Lexical cohesion and field	288
5.3	Lexical relations: system	290
5.3.1	The problem of units	290
5.3.2	Taxonomic relations	294
5.3.2.1	Superordination	297
5.3.2.2	Composition	303
5.3.3	Nuclear relations	309
5.3.4	Activity sequences	321
5.4.	Lexical relations: structure	326
5.4.1	Preparing the text	326
5.4.1.1	Unit of analysis	326
5.4.1.2	Experiential metaphor (nominalisation)	327

5.4.1.3   Lexical rendering   329
5.4.1.4   Lexical strings   331
5.4.2   Text analysis   332
5.4.2.1   Categories   332
5.4.2.2   Passes   333
5.4.2.3   Analysis   338
5.4.2.4   Kickball   369
5.5   Lexical relations and cohesive harmony   370
5.6   Lexical relations and discourse semantics   372
Notes   379

6.   Texture: Interleaving discourse semantics, lexicogrammar and phonology

6.1   Models of texture   381
6.1.1   Cohesion and register   381
6.1.2   Linguistic resources   382
6.1.3   Modularity and interaction   390
6.1.4   The role of grammatical metaphor   393
6.1.5   Textual meaning   401
6.1.6   Context   404
6.2   Grammatical metaphor   406
6.2.1   Ideational metaphor   406
6.2.1.1   Logical metaphor   408
6.2.1.2   Experiential metaphor   409
6.2.2   Interpersonal metaphor   412
6.2.3   Textual metaphor   416
6.3   Interaction patterns   417
6.3.1   Cohesive harmony   417
6.3.2   Method of development   434
6.3.3   Point   448
6.3.4   Modal responsibility   461
6.4   Texture and context   488
Notes   491

7.   Context: Register, genre and ideology

7.1   Context   493
7.1.1   Register theory   497

7.1.2	Communicative planes: register, genre and ideology	501
7.2	Register	508
7.2.1	Mode	508
7.2.1.1	Monologue/dialogue	510
7.2.1.2	Action/reflection	516
7.2.2	Tenor	523
7.2.2.1	Status	527
7.2.2.2	Contact	528
7.2.2.3	Affect	533
7.2.3	Field	536
7.2.3.1	Activity sequence	537
7.2.3.2	Taxonomy	540
7.2.3.3	Field agnation	542
7.3	Genre	546
7.3.1	Particle, wave and field	548
7.3.1.1	Particle	550
7.3.1.1.1	Synoptic perspectives	550
7.3.1.1.2	Dynamic perspectives	551
7.3.1.2	Prosody	553
7.3.1.3	Wave (Periodicity)	559
7.3.2	Genre agnation	560
7.3.2.1	Factual genres	562
7.3.2.2	Narrative genres	564
7.3.2.3	Genre as system	569
7.3.3	Genre and register	571
7.4	Ideology: discursive power	573
7.4.1	Coding orientation: ideology as system	576
7.4.2	Contratextuality: ideology as process	581
7.4.3	Prejudice	585
7.4.4	Naturalisation (inertia)	586
Notes		588
References		591
Index		613

Preface

In this book I have attempted to document the stage my work has reached since I first became interested in discourse analysis in 1968. I was a first year student at the time, in Michael Gregory's English department at Glendon College in Toronto. Gregory began our course by introducing us to Hallidayan linguistics (grammar, register theory and stylistics) and hired Waldemar Gutwinski to join the department to teach "American" linguistics. It was Gutwinski who first introduced me to discourse structure, and I have been shunting between clause grammar and cohesion analysis ever since.

Gutwinski was a student of Al Gleason's, and after finishing my BA at Glendon I enrolled in an MA at the University of Toronto to study discourse analysis with him. After my MA I went to Essex to begin a PhD with Michael Halliday, returning to Toronto for 18 months to work with Gleason before finishing my degree in Sydney in 1977; Halliday had founded a new Department of Linguistics there the previous year. I began teaching in that department in 1978; *English Text* is the result of lecture courses in discourse semantics that I began in 1979.

My debt to Al Gleason, and to Michael Halliday and Ruqaiya Hasan will be more than obvious to readers of this book. Readers familiar with systemic grammar will perhaps forgive me if I refer to Gleason as my meta-Theme and Halliday and Hasan as my meta-New. My thanks to them for all of the kindness they have shown me over the years.

In addition I would like to thank the hundreds of students in our undergraduate programme and MA programme in Applied Linguistics who have had to learn these analyses to earn their degrees. Their contribution has been inestimable, both in terms of their frustrations and what I have helped them achieve. I would like to thank two of my former students in particular, Eija Ventola and Joan Rothery, who applied these analyses over many years to extended bodies of text and complained loudly when things didn't work. The few improvements I have managed to make in response to their queries have helped tremendously. I am also indebted to my colleagues Christian Matthiessen and Clare Painter who commented on parts of the manuscript, especially on Chapters 1 and 5.

Beyond the confines of my own Department, I would like to thank the many colleagues who have supported my work over the years, particularly in the fields of social semiotics and educational linguistics which have provided the main contexts for this research: members of the Newtown Semiotic Circle, the Literacy and Education Research Network (LERN), the Disadvantaged Schools Programme in the Metropolitan East Region of Sydney, participants in the series of Language in Education conferences anchored by Fran Christie, and my systemic colleagues across Australia and overseas who I see at national and international systemic workshops/conferences/congresses (whatever they now happen to be called). Of these, Michael Halliday and Christian Matthiessen deserve special mention, both again, for the invaluable grammar of English they have designed and taught me to use.

Most of all I would like to thank my wife, Anne Cranny-Francis, whose care has made it possible for me to live what I think (like write this book for example, and many many things more).

I would like to dedicate this book to H.A. Gleason, Jr., who taught me to model text structure.

1. Discourse semantics

A proposal for triple articulation

1.1 A context for discourse analysis

English Text is an introduction to discourse analysis within the framework of systemic functional linguistics. Its aim is to provide a comprehensive set of discourse analyses which can be used to relate any English text to the context in which it is used. Readers familiar with Halliday and Hasan's seminal *Cohesion in English* will find in *English Text* an elaboration of their work, in ways that have been influenced by Gleason's stratificational approach to discourse structure (Gutwinski 1976:36-63) and by almost 20 years of research by systemic linguists since *Cohesion in English* was first circulated in manuscript form.

Like *Cohesion in English*, *English Text* uses systemic functional grammar to ask questions about text structure, and complements the grammar by developing additional analyses which focus on text rather than the clause (Chapters 2-6 below). *Cohesion in English* organises this division of labour as the opposition between grammar and cohesion (between structural and non-structural resources for meaning). *English Text* organises this division of labour in a different way — stratally, as an opposition between grammar and semantics (between clause oriented and text oriented resources for meaning). Because a semantics of this kind focusses on text-size rather than clause-size meanings, it will be referred to as **discourse semantics**. The question of stratifying the content plane in this way will be a recurrent theme throughout the volume.

Halliday's *Introduction to Functional Grammar* (1985a) outlines the grammar of English which realises the discourse semantics developed in *English Text* (for a very useful elaboration of this grammar, see Matthiessen 1992). As Matthiessen and Halliday (in press) point out, in functional linguistics semantics is **naturally** (not arbitrarily) related to grammar. It follows from this point that functional approaches to discourse systems and structures will be enriched to the extent that they are able to draw on comprehensive, semantically oriented grammars which interface in a responsible way with textual considerations. *English Text* evolved in tandem with the richest extant English grammar of this kind, as developed by Halliday, and later Matthiessen, in the Department of Linguistics at the University of Sydney. For many linguists, the richness of Halliday and Matthiessen's grammar has appeared excessive (see for example Huddleston's (1988) dismissal of Halliday (1985a)). It is important to stress here however that what might appear extravagant from the point of view of "syntax" is more often than not fundamental to the point of parsimony from the perspective of discourse analysis (see Matthiessen (1989) for an alternative perspective on Halliday (1985a) and Matthiessen and Martin (1991) for a reply to Huddleston (1988)). *English Text* has been designed to complement in a solidary way a non-parsimonious grammar of this kind. It has been designed in other words to be grammatically responsible, interfacing with a grammar that is equally responsible to textual considerations.

There are any number of uses to which the analyses presented here can be put. In Australia they have evolved in two main contexts: (i) as a means of exploring the relation between text and context — between text and register, genre and ideology (see Chapter 7 below); and (ii) as one foundation for the development of an educational linguistics, which has been used in particular to focus on literacy development (e.g. Painter and Martin 1986, Hasan and Martin 1989). From the start, this work has been pursued within the framework of critical linguistics (inspired by Fowler et al. 1979, Kress and Hodge 1979, Chilton 1985, Kress 1985/1989, Fowler 1987, Fairclough 1989) — a linguistics which "deconstructs" texts in such a way as to draw attention to the semiotic systems they instantiate, with a view to critically evaluating the ideologies they construe. Observational, descriptive and explanatory adequacy aside, this means that *English Text* has been written as a contribution to the linguistics envisioned by Halliday (1985e:5) as "an ideologically committed form of social action." For this reason it needs in part to be read in the context of projects oriented to de-naturalising hegemonic discourses and, concomitantly, facilitating intervention in political processes (e.g. Poynton 1985/1989, Martin 1985b/1989, Threadgold et al. 1986, Christie 1991, Giblett and O'Carrol 1990, and the new journal *Social Semiotics*).

1.2 System and structure

As noted above, the model of language assumed and being developed here is a systemic functional one. Its critical texts centre around the work of M.A.K. Halliday and his colleagues and are critically reviewed in Butler (1985a); for a sympathetic introduction, see Matthiessen and Halliday (in press). The model's fundamental assumptions can be characterised in broad terms as follows:

Language as a resource (modalization) -
(i)   Language is a network of relationships.
(ii) Description shows how these relationships are inter-related.
(iii) Explanation reveals the connection between these relationships and the use to which language is put.

These assumptions can be usefully contrasted with those associated with formal grammar, particularly that influenced by Chomsky:

Language as a system of rules (modulation) -
(i)   Language is a set of sentences.
(ii) Description shows which sentences are in the set and which out.
(iii) Explanation reveals why the line between in and out falls where it does in terms of an innate neurological speech organism.

The basic contrast here is between the conceptualisation of language as a resource for meaning (functional linguistics) and the conceptualisation of language as a system of rules (formal linguistics). One of the main advantages of a functional grammar over a formal one is that it allows us to reason grammatically. To illustrate this point consider the relation of the grammatical systems of MODALIZATION (epistemic modality in formal semantics) and MODULATION (deontic modality in formal semantics) to the assumptions just outlined (for further discussion of MODALIZATION and MODULATION see Chapter 6 below). Following Halliday (1970c, 1985a), MODALIZATION is the system that mediates degrees of probability and usuality in propositions (e.g. *maybe, probably, certainly*); MODULATION on the other hand mediates degrees of obligation and inclination in proposals (e.g. *allowed to, supposed to, required to*). Reasoning grammatically then, functional linguistics is a linguistics oriented to MODALIZATION; it is concerned with choice — with what speakers might and tend to do (see Nesbitt and Plum 1988 on modelling usuality). Formal linguistics on the other hand is a linguistics oriented to MODULATION; it is concerned with restrictions — with what speakers are neurologically required not to do (for further discussion of this and related oppositions see Halliday 1974, 1977b, 1984c). Reasoning grammatically in this way is very important for understanding the relationship between grammar and text and we will return to this dialectic again and again throughout this book.

Systemic linguistics has its roots in Firthian linguistics, and so not surprisingly it is a type of system structure theory. Unlike Firth however, who gave equal status to the concepts of system and structure in his model, systemic linguistics gives priority to system. Following Hjelmslev (1961), paradigmatic relations are mapped onto potential and syntagmatic relations onto actual; thus **system** is described in terms of paradigmatic oppositions, **process** in terms of syntagmatic structure. System and process are related through the important concept of **realisation**.

This type of model can only be briefly illustrated here, beginning with MOOD (which will be taken up again in Chapter 2; for an excellent extended introduction see Matthiessen and Halliday in press). The structures used are taken from Halliday (1985a), the systems from Halliday (1976b); for more on system, process and realisation see Matthiessen (1985), Kasper (1988) and Matthiessen (1992).

As noted above systemic linguistics is especially concerned with system — with relationships between linguistic units of various kinds. This means that it tends to reason about proportionalities (rather than about structures as in formal linguistics). This can be illustrated for MOOD by considering the following examples, arranged in proportions. Throughout this book ":" represents "is to", and "::" represents "as" in displays of this kind (so the examples should be read as "*Ford has arrived* is to *Has Ford arrived?* as *Marvin is leaving* is to *Is Marvin leaving?*" and so on).

> Ford has arrived:Has Ford arrived?::
> Marvin is leaving:Is Marvin leaving?::
> Zaphod will go:Will Zaphod go?
>
> Has Ford arrived?:Who has arrived?::
> Is Marvin leaving?:Who is leaving?::
> Will Zaphod go?:Who will go?

Systemic linguistics has been designed to investigate the **interrelationships** reflected in proportionalities of this kind. It uses system networks to model their **valeur**. The valeur reflected in the oppositions just considered is presented in Fig. 1.1; each system is concerned with one kind of opposition and

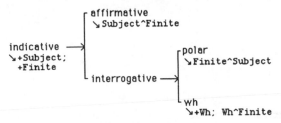

Fig. 1.1. Basic MOOD systems

the systems are ordered along a scale of **delicacy** from left to right — if [indicative] is chosen, then either [declarative] or [interrogative] must be; if [interrogative] then [polar] or [wh]. The square brackets with horizontal arrows pointing into them mean "or".

System networks such as those in Fig. 1.1 represent language as a resource, rather than as a set of rules. As noted above, system is related to process through the concept of realisation — realisation formalises the **instantiation** of system in process. The realisation statements which specify the manifestation of MOOD options in structure are listed underneath features in the network in Fig. 1.1, just after the realisation arrows slanting down-ward to the right. In these realisation statements "+" means "insert" and "^" means "sequence". These realisation statements relate system to structure; the statements in Fig. 1.1 are summarised and then glossed to clarify their reading in Table 1.1.

Based on these realisation statements, if the features [indicative, interrogative, polar] are selected from the network in Fig. 1.1, then the MOOD structure in Fig. 1.2 can be derived (one relevant feature, i.e. [major], was not included in Fig. 1.1; the feature [major] accounts for the presence of a Predicator — see Fig. 1.4 below). Fig. 1.2 represents the clause as a bundle of features, realised by the structural sequence Finite^Subject^Predicator.

Table 1.1. The instantiation of system in structure in Fig. 1.1

FEATURE	REALISATION	GLOSS ON REALISATION
[indicative]	+Subject; +Finite	(insert Subject; insert Finite)
[declarative]	Subject^Finite	(sequence Subject before Finite)
[polar]	Finite^Subject	(sequence Finite before Subject)
[wh]	+Wh; Wh^Finite	(insert Wh; sequence before Finite)

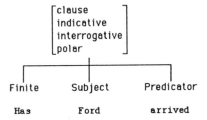

Fig. 1.2. MOOD structure for a polar, interrogative, indicative clause

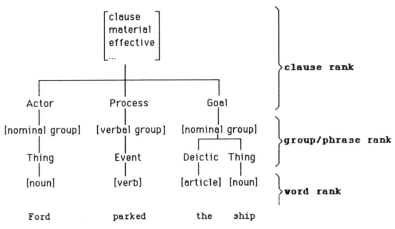

Fig. 1.3. Experiential structure for an effective material clause

Note that structures of this kind contain both function (e.g. Finite; initial upper case) and class labels (e.g. clause; lower case, enclosed in square brackets). These structures, like the systems which underlie them, are further organised along a scale of rank, which reduces the number of levels between clause and morpheme required in analysis (see Hudson 1967/ 1981). Making use of a different set of functions (from Halliday 1985a), implying a different set of options, this labelling and bracketing is further illustrated in Fig. 1.3. Three ranks are included (i.e. clause, group and word), but word structure is not shown.

The concepts of system and structure and of rank have been applied extensively to both phonology and grammar within systemic theory for more than three decades (for applications at the level of discourse by the

Table 1.2. Ranks deployed in English grammar and phonology

CONTENT FORM	EXPRESSION FORM
(grammar)	(phonology)
clause	tone group
group/phrase	foot
word	
morpheme	syllable
	phoneme

Birmingham School, see Chapter 2 below). For English, a phonological rank scale consisting of tone group, foot, syllable and phoneme has been proposed (for work on tone group and foot see for example Halliday 1967c; 1970b; van Leeuven 1982; El-menoufy 1988; for work across languages on syllable and phoneme see Mock 1985, Prakašam 1987). For introductions to English clause, group/phrase and word structure see Halliday (1985a), Fawcett (1980), Matthiessen (1992), Matthiessen & Bateman 1991. Adopting Hjelmslev's terminology, the scaffolding for this research by rank and strata is outlined in Table 1.2.

1.3 The metafunctional organisation of meaning

Functional grammatical descriptions in systemic grammar have been developed well beyond a simple re-labelling of grammatical classes (such as that used in tagmemics or Huddleston's 1984 outline of English syntax). Two complementary descriptions of English clause structure have already been introduced: Finite^Subject^Predicator for *Has Ford arrived?* and Actor^ Process^Goal for *Ford parked the ship*. These descriptions derive from Halliday's (1985a) multi-tiered perspective on the English clause (cf. the tiers of

Marvin	is	parking	the ship	**Perspective**:
Actor	Process		Goal	**experiential**
Subject	Finite	Predicator	Complement	**interpersonal**
Theme	Rheme			**textual**

phonological structure suggested in Goldsmith 1976, 1990) and reflect an interpersonal and experiential perspective respectively. A third perspective, the textual, is added in the analysis of *Marvin is parking the ship* above.

This means that grammatical classes at group/phrase rank (i.e. nominal group, verbal group and nominal group) are bracketed in three different ways at clause rank. *Is parking* for example is multiply labelled as Finite^Predicator, Process and part of the Rheme. The reason for this is that the clause enters into different systems of valeur depending on the type of meaning considered, and the layered function structures are designed to reflect these divergent oppositions. These different kinds of meaning are exemplified in the following proportionalities:

Experiential proportions -
Trillian is cooking dinner:Dinner is cooking::
Zaphod is marching the troops:The troops are marching::
Ford is boiling the kettle:The kettle is boiling

Interpersonal proportions -
Trillian is cooking the dinner:Cook the dinner::
Zaphod is marching the troops:March the troops::
Ford is boiling the kettle:Boil the kettle

Textual proportions -
Trillian is cooking the dinner:The dinner is being cooked by Trillian::
Zaphod is marching the troops:The troops are being marched by Zaphod::
Ford is boiling the kettle:The kettle is being boiled by Ford

In the first set, the valeur is concerned with the construction of experience in terms of acting on or happening. In the second, the clauses are opposed with respect to their function in dialogue: giving information or demanding a service. In the third, information flow is being manipulated with adjustments made to the clause's beginning and end. Halliday refers to these different types of meaning as metafunctions — the experiential, the interpersonal and the textual respectively, and has argued that they are systematically coded into the content plane from the point of view of both system (Halliday 1969; 1970a; Martin 1984) and structure (Halliday 1984a; Matthiessen 1989; Matthiessen and Halliday in press).

1.3.1 *Metafunction and system*

Systemic arguments for metafunctional diversity refer to the relative independence of experiential, interpersonal and textual systems in networks

formulating paradigmatic relations at clause rank. Partial networks underlying the experiential, interpersonal and textual proportionalities noted
above are outlined in Fig. 1.4. In the grammar of the English clause, the
system of TRANSITIVITY organises experiential oppositions, MOOD organises
interpersonal oppositions, and THEME textual ones. Critically, these three
systems cross-classify the clause, which selects relatively independently for
TRANSITIVITY, MOOD and THEME.[1] The network suggests that all clauses are
[material], [mental] or [relational] at the same time as they are [indicative]
or [imperative] at the same time as they are [theme marked] or [theme
unmarked]. It is for this reason that the network encloses all three systems
with a brace whose logical meaning in system network is "and" (as opposed
to square brackets, which mean "or"). The [affirmative/interrogative]
opposition on the other hand is dependent on the MOOD feature [indicative];
it combines freely with the features [material/mental/relational] and with
[theme marked/theme unmarked] clauses, but not with [imperative]. For
further discussion of the paradigmatic motivation for metafunctional
organisation in functional grammar see Martin (1991a).

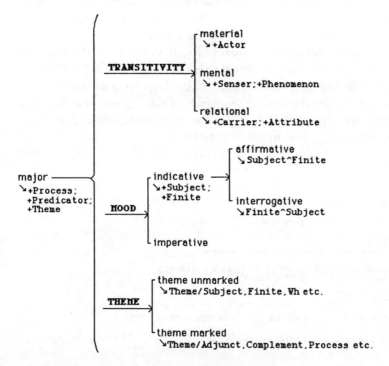

Fig. 1.4: Basic TRANSITIVITY, MOOD and THEME systems

1.3.2 *Metafunction and structure*

Structural arguments for metafunctional diversity are of particular relevance here in light of the proposals for discourse structures to be developed in Section 1.5 below. Halliday's (1979a) suggestion is that experiential meanings predispose particulate forms of realisation, interpersonal meanings prosodic ones and textual meanings periodic[2] ones. He relates this suggestion to Pike's construal of language as particle, wave and field, arguing, with Pike (e.g. 1982), that the same linguistic phenomena usually have to be viewed from a number of complementary angles in order to be fully understood.

Again, Halliday's suggestions can only be briefly reviewed here. To begin, experiential meaning tends to construct experience as inter-related parts of a whole. At clause rank for example it construes the world as goings on consisting of a nuclear process and participant, additional participants, and circumstances. This type of organisation lends itself to constituency analysis, and tree diagrams can be used to represent the relation of parts to wholes (tree notation has been elaborated to capture the notion of nuclearity below). This experiential construal of reality at clause rank is outlined in Fig. 1.5 for clauses such as *Marvin left the ship in the parking lot, The ship was left by Marvin in the parking lot, It was in the parking lot that Marvin left the ship, Did Marvin leave the ship in the parking lot?* and so on. Experiential meaning at clause rank, unlike interpersonal and textual meaning, is not usually realised by sequence; in this respect tree diagrams overdetermine the representation of process, participant and circumstance relations by presenting them in left to right order.

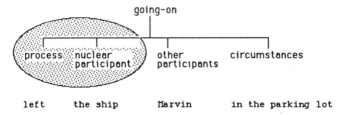

Fig. 1.5. Experiential (part/whole) structure for the clause

This form of representation is much less effective for interpersonal meanings whose realisation spreads across a clause or group, especially where these meanings are amplified. Halliday (1985a) does represent interpersonal meaning in similar terms, in order to facilitate the mapping of experiential and interpersonal layers of structure onto each other. Note however that the negative attitude colouring the whole of a clause like *That stupid bloody cretin is really giving me the bloody shits* is not captured in a part/whole representation of this kind. For non-discrete realisation of this type we need a more prosodic form of representation.

By drawing on prosodic analysis, as developed by Firth and his colleagues (see Palmer 1970), we can extend Halliday's (1985a) interpretation, adding a prosody of Negative attitude to the analysis as outlined in Fig. 1.6. Note that the prosody is realised continuously, amplifying attitude wherever the potential for expressing attitudinal meaning is made available: in the Epithet (*stupid bloody*) and Thing (*cretin*) of the Subject nominal group, in the intensifying Modal adjunct (*really*) following the Finite, in the metaphorical 'process' (*give someone the shits*[3]) and in the nominal group Complement provided by this metaphor (Epithet: *bloody*, Thing: *shits*).

Thirdly, constituency representation is also poorly adapted to textual meaning, which tends to structure clauses and groups in such a way as to highlight first and last position. The English clause for example uses first position to highlight the speaker's angle on the experience being constructed while last position is hearer oriented, highlighting information that is in some respect new. The systems of THEME and INFORMATION can thus be seen as assigning peaks of prominence to the beginning and end of the English clause; this textual patterning assigns a periodic texture to English discourse as it unfolds. Halliday's analysis of THEME and INFORMATION structure is presented in Fig. 1.7, followed by a more iconic form of representation highlighting clause texture as a rhythmic pulse.

Negative attitude ⟶					
Subject	Finite	Mood Adjunct	Predicator	Complement	Complement
That stupid bloody cretin	is	really	giving	me	the bloody shits

Fig. 1.6. Negative affect as a clause prosody

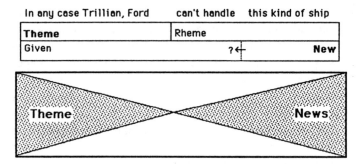

Fig. 1.7. Textual meaning as a wave (peaks of prominence)

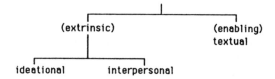

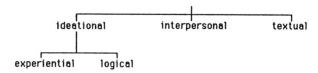

Fig. 1.8. Halliday's metafunctions (paradigmatic grouping)

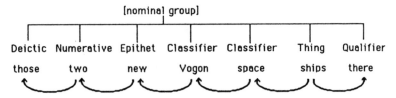

Fig. 1.9. Logical (part/part) and experiential (part/whole) structure in the English nominal group

In addition to the experiential, interpersonal and textual metafunctions just considered, Halliday has in addition proposed a fourth metafunction, the logical. Systemically the logical metafunction comprises recursive systems (such as TENSE, PROJECTION and AGENCY in English; see Halliday 1985a), which tend to be associated across languages with experiential meaning. Structurally logical meaning is realised as another kind of particulate structure — but this time as part/part rather than part/whole. Because of these systemic and structural associations with experiential meaning, Halliday (e.g. 1974:95) groups the experiential and logical metafunction together under the heading ideational. This organisation is outlined in Fig. 1.8.

The difference between experiential and logical structure can be illustrated using Halliday's (1985a) description of the English nominal group. Halliday argues that a nominal group like those *two new Vogon space ships there* can be treated in two ways. Experientially it is a constituent structure, with modifiers playing a number of different roles with respect to the Thing — Deictic, Numerative, Epithet, Classifier and Qualifier. Logically however, the nominal group is better considered as a word complex, with *ship* as Head, and with modifiers as regressive or progressive dependents. These complementary perspectives are outlined in Fig. 1.9.[4]

The relationship between the metafunctions, realisation principles and types of structural is summarised in Table 1.3. We will return to the question of metafunction and types of structure in Section 1.5 below when a preliminary cartography for discourse semantics is introduced. But before mapping out a new stratum, reasons for stratifying the content plane need to be specifically addressed.

Table 1.3. Metafunctions, realisation and types of structure

Metafunction	REALISATION	TYPE OF STRUCTURE
ideational:	particulate:	
logical	part/part	interdependency (univariate)
experiential	part/whole	constituency (multivariate)
interpersonal	prosodic	prosody
textual	periodic	wave

1.4 Stratification

As noted in section 1 above, *English Text* proposes establishing a discourse semantics stratum to complement the metafunctionally organised grammatical descriptions just outlined. This raises the important issue of stratification in systemic functional models, about which there has been considerable uncertainty over the years (cf. Butler 1985:77-81). It is thus important to be as explicit as possible about the motivation for and nature of the stratification proposed. The strategy adopted here will be to review the arguments for distinguishing content and expression form, before pursuing the problem of stratifying the content plane.

To begin, consider a language called *phonese*, in which there is a one to one relation between sounds and meanings, such as that "spoken" by animals and young humans in the proto-language phase[5] (Halliday 1975, Painter 1984). In such a language we have a very simple system of signs. Formulated systemically, it consists of a system with a list of features. The labelling of features in a system of this kind is a moot point; since content and expression are fused, either "semantic" or "phonetic" labels can be used.[6] In Fig. 1.10 fused labels interfacing with both content and expression substance are employed; the language modelled there consists of six signs, with a bi-unique relation between meaning and sound.

Fig. 1.10. Phonese — language as a system of (6) signs

What are the limitations of a semiotic system of this kind as far as sustaining a recognizably human culture are concerned? The main problem lies in the inordinately large number of sounds it would require humans to distinguish orally in production and aurally in reception. This situation could be marginally improved by using our hands instead of our tongues and our eyes instead of ears (as in Chinese writing or the sign language of the deaf). But this would still not provide us with anywhere near enough meanings to go round.[7]

The solution, referred to by Hjelmslev (1961) as the essential genius of human language, involves combining sounds in sequence to distinguish meanings. This immediately provides a stratified model with two ranks in the phonology, phoneme (distinct sounds) and syllable (distinct combinations of sounds) and one in grammar, the word (distinct meanings). At this point a second language can be proposed, *lexese*, in which there is a one to one relation between meanings and words.

As far as we know, evolved systems on the model of lexese do not occur. Once again, their limitations are obvious. They would require humans to remember an inordinately large number of words; and they have the further important limitation that no-one could mean something they hadn't already heard. The logical way out of systems of this kind is once more a combinatorial one — adding on a grammar than organises sequences of words. This brings us to something more closely resembling human language, at least as it is modelled in Hjelmslevian terms — a two strata system, with a minimum of two ranks on each stratum and an non-bi-unique (and therefore in principle arbitrary) relation between sound and meaning. This kind of two strata system is outlined in Fig. 1.11.

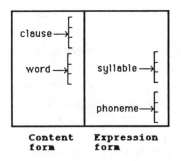

Fig. 1.11. A minimal stratified linguistic system

As we know, human languages[8] elaborate these two strata in various ways: removing their experiential bias by adding foot and tone group ranks to the phonology, enabling the periodic and prosodic patterning characterising textual and interpersonal meaning; incorporating metafunctional layering in the grammar, of the different types discussed above; systematizing combinations of words (groups) and reduced clauses (phrases) giving rise to an intermediate rank of group/phrase in the grammar (see Halliday 1985a:159); introducing morphology (eg. Hudson 1973), adding a rank below the word; providing for clause linkage (see Chapter 4) and so on. This raises the question of the point at which the grammar and phonology become saturated? When is stratification necessary within the content plane, especially given the extravagant approach to grammar pursued by systemic linguists as outlined above?

Extravagant as systemic functional grammars are, they do run out of steam. Three of their limitations will now be briefly reviewed.

First, there is the question of semantic motifs running through the grammar which cannot be generalised at that level because of their diverse structural realisations. The following proportionalities can be used to illustrate this point:

Ford is smiling because Trillian arrived:	[behavioural]
It pleases Ford that Trillian has arrived:	[mental]
Ford is happy that Trillian has arrived::	[relational]
Ford is frowning because Trillian has left:	[behavioural]
It disturbs Ford that Trillian has left:	[mental]
Ford is unhappy that Trillian has left::	[relational]
Ford is trembling because Trillian is missing:	[behavioural]
It terrifies Ford that Trillian is missing:	[mental]
Ford is shattered that Trillian is missing	[relational]

Following Halliday (1985a), the first clause in each set is behavioural, the second mental and the third relational — fundamentally different process types. At the same time all three clauses construct a relatively uniform, and not unfamiliar disposition for Ford. One way[9] to generalise across these various realisations of the same disposition is to stratify the content plane, setting up an attitude network realised across process types (with realisations extending into other areas of the grammar as well; for example adverbial and nominal groups). Semantic diffusions of this kind permeate the grammar (for examples see Halliday 1985a: tense and temporal adjuncts p. 182; modal verbs and adverbs p. 85-89; nominal group p. 163-165 and relational clauses p. 112-114; the synoptic summary of expansion p. 306-307; and variations on a causal theme p. 378-384), and focus attention on one of the limitations of operating with an unstratified content plane.

Second, there is the process of grammatical metaphor, whereby the content plane derives structures requiring more than one level of interpretation. The following proportionalities illustrate phenomena of this kind:

Ford was unhappy so Trillian left:	[congruent]
Ford's unhappiness led to Trillian's departure::	[metaphorical]
Zaphod was delighted so Trillian celebrated:	[congruent]
Zaphod's delight resulted in Trillian's celebration::	[metaphorical]
Marvin was bored and so became miserable:	[congruent]
Marvin's boredom engendered his misery	[metaphorical]

It is the second member of each set that concerns us here. Each is "literally" a circumstantial relational clause with a causal verb (i.e. *led to*, *resulted in* and *engendered*) relating two nominalisations. At the same time each clause codes a "figurative" or "transferred" meaning closely related to the meaning literally coded in the first member of each set. Halliday (1985b) relates multiply coded structures such as these to the evolution of writing in English, describing them as **grammatical metaphors**. They contrast with the **congruent** structures typifying spoken English, for which a single layer of coding provides an adequate interpretation.[10]

Stratifying the content plane provides one mechanism for handling semantic layering of this kind. The level of grammar can be used to provide an interpretation of the "literal" meaning of metaphorical structures and the meaning of congruent ones; the level of semantics can then be deployed to construct additional interpretations for metaphorical expressions (their "figurative" or "transferred" meaning). Note that it is not being suggested here that a semantics be set up to generate meanings which are then expressed congruently or metaphorically in grammatical forms (see Martin 1991a for further discussion). Rather, taking semantics as point of departure, choosing an metaphorical realisation means encoding additional layers of meaning; it is not just a question of choosing an untypical means of expression. The grammar makes meaning, irrespective of whether it constitutes, or participates as one level, in the content plane. Grammatical metaphor is further explored in Chapters 2 to 6 below, especially Chapter 6.

Third there is the problem of text. This is really a question of limits. As far as experiential structure is concerned the most embracing grammatical unit is the clause; and the grammar extends its scope by combining clauses in logical interdependency structures referred to in Halliday (1985a) as clause complexes. But even extended in this way, the grammar provides only a partial account of textual patterns. At issue are proportionalities of the following kinds:

As soon as the Vogon began his poem, Ford yawned:	taxis
The Vogon began his poem. Immediately Ford yawned::	cohesion

Table 1.4. Function/rank matrix for lexicogrammatical systems (Halliday 1973:141)

function \ rank	IDEATIONAL Experiential	IDEATIONAL Logical	INTERPERSONAL	TEXTUAL
CLAUSE	TRANSITIVITY types of process participants & circumstances (identity clauses) (things, facts & reports)	condition addition report	MOOD types of speech function modality (the WH-function)	THEME types of message (identity as text relation) (identification, predication, reference, substitution)
Verbal GROUP	TENSE (verb classes)	POLARITY catenation secondary tense	PERSON ('marked' options)	VOICE ('contrastive' options)
Nominal GROUP	MODIFICATION epithet function enumeration (noun classes) (adjective classes)	classification sub-modification	ATTITUDE attitudinal modifiers intensifiers	DEIXIS determiners 'phoric' elements (qualifiers) (definite article)
Adverbial (incl. prepositional) GROUP	'MINOR PROCESSES' prepositional relations (classes of circum-stantial adjunct)	narrowing sub-modification	COMMENT (classes of comment adjunct)	CONJUNCTION (classes of discourse adjunct)
WORD (incl. lexical item)	LEXICAL 'CONTENT' (taxonomic organization of vocabulary)	compounding derivation	LEXICAL 'REGISTER' (expressive words) (stylistic organization of vocabulary)	COLLOCATION (collocational organization of vocabulary)
INFORMATION UNIT			TONE intonation systems	INFORMATION distribution & focus

HYPOTACTIC COMPLEXES OF CLAUSE, GROUP & WORD

PARATACTIC COMPLEXES (all ranks)
co-ordination
apposition

COHESION ('above the sentence': non-structural relations)
reference; substitution & ellipsis; conjunction;
lexical cohesion

Because the poem was appalling, Trillian frowned:	taxis
The poem was appalling. Consequently Trillian frowned::	cohesion
The Vogon poem was awful whereas Zaphod's was inspiring:	taxis
The Vogon poem was appalling. But Zaphod's was inspiring	cohesion

Each of these oppositions represents the line drawn by Halliday and Hasan (1976; Halliday 1973; 1985a:288) between grammar (in this case the clause complex) and cohesion, with grammar focussing on structural resources for realising text and cohesion on non-structural ones. This complementarity clearly set out in Halliday's (1973:141) function/rank matrix (Table 1.4), where cohesion is treated as the non-structural component of the textual metafunction. In *Cohesion in English* terms, structure is concerned with relationships within the sentence, cohesion with relationships between them.

Halliday and Hasan do recognise that "cohesion within the sentence need not be regarded essentially as distinct phenomena" (1976:9), but argue that in the description of a text "it is the intersentence cohesion that is significant, because that represents the variable aspect of cohesion, distinguishing one text from another" (1976:9). In a sense, the line they draw between cohesion and grammar is justified descriptively rather than theoretically. The main problem with this treatment is that it fails to bring out the continuity between the structural (i.e. *as soon as, because, whereas*) and nonstructural (i.e. *immediately, consequently, by contrast*) resources. In essence, the amount of cohesion in a text varies according to mode: the more spoken the text, the less cohesion, since clause complexes are longer in speech than in writing (Halliday 1985b) and cohesion is only measured between clause complexes. The alternative developed in *English Text* will be to pursue Halliday and Hasan's definition of text as a semantic unit by setting up a level of discourse semantics stratified with respect to lexicogrammar on the content plane. This will permit generalisations to be made across structural and non-structural textual relations.

The impetus for stratification provided by semantic motifs, grammatical metaphor and cohesion gives rise to a model in which the discourse semantics both generalises across grammatical resources and accounts for relations between as well as within clause complexes. The discourse semantics is thus more abstract than, and deals with larger units than, lexicogrammar. Stratification of this kind can be usefully compared with expansions of descriptive power in other models where an increase in abstraction need not involve a focus on larger units (e.g. the syntax, semantics, pragmatics

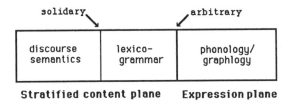

Fig. 1.12. Stratification of the content plane, as proposed in English Text

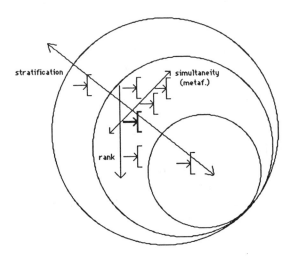

Fig. 1.13. Rank, metafunction and stratification as deployed in English Text

stratification associated with formal syntax, truth functional semantics and speech act theory; see Levinson 1983) or where a focus on larger units may not involve an increase in abstraction (eg. extending the scale of rank at the level of grammar to include units larger than the clause as in tagmemics; see for example Longacre 1976, 1979). The model developed to this point is outlined in Fig. 1.12. The solidary (or "natural") relationship between discourse semantics and lexicogrammar is noted in the model and contrasted with the experientially[11] arbitrary relationship between content and expression form.

An alternative projection (from Martin and Matthiessen 1991[12]) of these three strata, incorporating the additional axes of rank and metafunction is outlined in Fig. 1.13. There, the strata are presented as concentric circles, which helps to capture the sense in which discourse semantics addresses patterns of lexicogrammatical patterns and lexicogrammar in turn addresses patterns of phonological ones.[13] Within strata, description is further organised through layering (simultaneous metafunctions) and constituency (ranks). This projection also has the advantage of backgrounding the content/expression duality deriving from Hjelsmlev and underpinning Fig. 1.12. Somewhat more sympathetic then to Firth than to Hjelmslev, the model can be read as three meaning making levels, with the meanings made by smaller circles progressively recontextualised by larger ones.

1.5 Discourse structure

In Section 1.3.2 above three highly generalised types of structure were introduced, the particulate, prosodic and periodic, and correlated with the ideational, interpersonal and textual metafunctions respectively. Particulate, prosodic and periodic realisation is an important motif, and one that will be taken up in various places throughout *English Text*, especially in Chapters 6 and 7. At this point however it is necessary to return to earlier work by Halliday (1981b) on univariate and multivariate structure.

In this work Halliday is concerned to distinguish the kinds of structure generated by the logical metafunction (univariate structures) from those realising experiential, interpersonal and textual meaning (multivariate structures). **Univariate** structures as defined as structures involving a single variable, which recurs one or more times. **Multivariate** structures on the other hand involve more than one variable, with each variable occuring only once. This is the distinction between open ended projecting structures such as *Ford thought Marvin wanted Zaphod to tell Trillian that ...* (α 'β 'γ

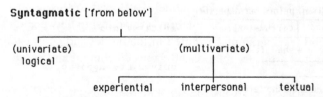

Fig. 1.14. Regrouping of metafunctions with respect to univariate and multivariate structure

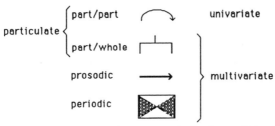

Fig. 1.15. The tension between particulate/prosodic/periodic realisation and univariate/ multivariate representation

"δ — univariate) and closed structures such as *Ford bored Marvin* (Phenomenon^Process^Senser — multivariate). Note that from a syntagmatic perspective this amounts to another grouping of metafunctions, complementary to that in Fig. 1.8 above; in Fig. 1.14 the logical metafunction is opposed to the three others (as in Halliday 1978a:131).

The tension between Fig. 1.8 and Fig. 1.14 as far as realisation is concerned is summarised in Fig. 1.15. Throughout his work on English grammar Halliday has used univariate structure to model logical meaning and multivariate structures to model experiential, interpersonal and textual meaning (the problems prosodic and periodic realisation cause for interpersonal and textual multivariate representations notwithstanding). In fact, only experiential meaning is ideally suited to multivariate representation.

Halliday recognises two types of univariate structure, hypotactic and paratactic. With hypotaxis, the recurring variables have unequal status; with parataxis they have equal status. The contrast between multivariate and these two types of univariate structure is exemplified below, following Halliday (1985a):

Ford   met   Trillian before her departure

Actor	Process	Goal	Circumstance

multivariate

Ford met Trillian before she left

α	β

univariate:hypotactic

Ford met Trillian and then she left

1	2

univariate:paratactic

Univariate structure at the rank of clause brings us to a grammatical frontier — the distinction between the clause complex and cohesion discussed in Section 1.4 above. As noted, Halliday and Hasan refer to relationships beyond this frontier as non-structural; and from the perspective of lexicogrammar, this is just what they are — semantic relationships which transcend grammatical structure.

From the perspective of discourse semantics however, these relationships can be construed as "structural", although clearly involving structure of a non-grammatical kind. This construal is important in order to understand the sense in which the discourse semantics unit text instantiates discourse semantics systems. In taking this step however it is important to clarify just how discourse structures differ from grammatical ones. IDENTIFICATION and IDEATION structures will be considered here.

First IDENTIFICATION. Consider the following proportionalities:

> There was a robot : It looked bored ::
> There was a robot : The android looked bored ::
> There was a robot : This model looked bored

The relevant opposition here is between introducing a participant (*a robot*) and presuming one (*it, the android, this model*). In the examples *it, the android* and *this model* assume that identity is recoverable from context, while *a robot* does not. A comprehensive account of these and related oppositions will be presented in Chapter 3.

Introducing/presuming oppositions of this kind are one resource for constructing discourse structure in text (for producing what Halliday and Hasan refer to as cohesive ties). Read as texts, the proportionalities reviewed above display three structures of this kind:

```
a robot      a robot       a robot
  ↑            ↑             ↑
  it       the android   this model
```

What kind of structures are these? If we try to relate structure of this kind to those we are famliar with from grammar, then they are more closely related to univariate structures than multivariate ones. They are open ended, with the same type of relation between elements potentially occurring over and over again; a cohesive chain such as *a robot-the android-it-it-the robot...* in other words is more like a clause complex than a clause. It is (semantic) inter-dependency that is relevant here, not constituency.

Within univariate structures, the analogy is with hypotaxis. Presuming items are semantically dependent on the information they presume, with presumed information functioning as a kind of Head. A semantic structure of this kind can be modelled by drawing a dependency arrow between items. Typically in grammar, dependency structures are represented with an arrow pointing towards the Dependent, away from the Head. Here however, the dependency will be modelled with the arrow pointing towards the Head, in the direction of presumed information. This makes it possible to use the arrow notation to capture the location of presumed information, which may precede (anaphora) or follow (cataphora) the Dependent (for details see Chapter 3 below).

Note that in cohesive chains, presuming items may themselves be presumed, thereby taking on the role of Head as the text develops as outlined below:

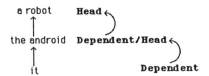

It is in this respect that discourse structures differ most strongly from phonological and grammatical ones; with IDENTIFICATION structures, an item which is dependent is typically itself depended on as the text unfolds, dependents becoming Heads in their turn.[14]

With IDEATION, a different type of discourse structure is found. Consider the following proportionalities:

> I'm a little tired of this **robot**:
> but I'd love to try that **android**::
>
> I'm not pleased with this **robot**:
> but that **model** looks fine

In these examples a semantic relationship is established between *robot* and *android* and between *robot* and *model*; but it is not one that depends on identity of reference as above (in both examples the related items refer to different participants). Rather the cohesive tie is one that depends on taxonomic relations among machines which behave in important respects like humans: *android* is a hyponym of *robot* in the first example; and *model*

is a superordinate of *robot* in the second. This type of semantic relation is
more analogous with parataxis: the items related are mutually expectant —
android is no more dependent on *robot* in the first example than *robot* is on
android. With ideational semantic relations of this kind, there is no need to
propose a discourse Head. Consequently the relationship between expectant items will be modelled with an arrow-less inter-dependency line as outlined below (the taxonomic relations linking items have been noted as valences on these dependency lines; for details see Chapter 5 below):

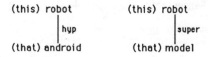

As with "hypotactic" semantic structures, these "paratactic" relationships
may extend over any number of mutually expectant items to form lexical
strings:

Following Lemke (1985), discourse semantics structures of this kind will
be referred to as covariate. Covariate structures are those in which a semantic
interdependency is constructed between items (which may or may not be
grammaticalised) and in which dependent items have the potential to themselves be depended on. These structures are the principle resource used by
the discourse semantics for constructing text (although multivariate and
univariate structures are also found and will be further considered in Chapter 2). A summary of the types of structure considered to this point and
their association with different strata is outlined in Fig. 1.16. In this model,
covariate structures in which one item presumes another are referred to as
phoric[15] (see Chapter 3 below); covariate structures in which information is
not so presumed are referred to as expectant.

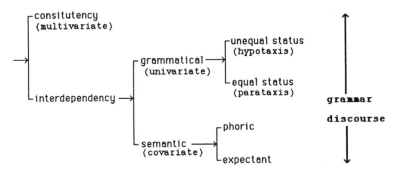

Fig. 1.16. Types of grammatical and discourse structure

1.6 Discourse systems

The chapters which follow are organised in the following way. Chapters 2, 3, 4 and 5 deal with the four central discourse systems constituting the discourse semantic stratum proposed: NEGOTIATION, IDENTIFICATION, CONJUNCTION and IDEATION respectively. These chapters are organised by metafunction: NEGOTIATION considers the discourse semantics of interpersonal meaning, IDENTIFICATION the discourse semantics of textual meaning, CONJUNCTION the discourse semantics of logical meaning, and IDEATION the discourse semantics of experiential meaning. Chapter 6 then looks at the ways in which the discourse structures generated by these systems interact systematically with lexicogrammatical structures (the question of **texture**). Finally, in Chapter 7, a model of context will be built up by sketching in the connotative semiotics of register, genre and ideology. The purpose of these descriptions is to enhance, not supplant, those offered in *Cohesion in English; English Text* functions for the most part to recontextualise Halliday and Hasan's conception of cohesion from the perspective of discourse semantics. Their very rich descriptions of texture in English will not in general be recapitulated, but rather presumed. This is particularly true with respect to SUBSTITUTION and ELISIPIS, which will barely be touched on at all (see Chapter 6 below for further discussion).

NEGOTIATION is an interpersonal system concerned with discourse as dialogue. Given an exchange such as that presented below, an account will be developed which shows how a sequence of speech acts which we might gloss informally as question, nomination, answer and validation are syntagmatically related to each other and systemically related to other types of exchange. This work takes as its point of departure the work on classroom discourse developed by the Birmingham school (Sinclair and Coulthard 1975).

What is it? Ford?	question & nomination
– It might be a Range.	answer
– Right, it is.	validation

IDENTIFICATION is a textual system concerned with tracking participants in discourse. At issue here is the way in which people, places and things are introduced in text and potentially referred to again once introduced (e.g. *a robot...the android* below). This work is based on Gleason's analysis of discourse structure within a stratificational framework (Gleason 1968) and Halliday and Hasan's (1976) description of referential cohesion.

| There was a robot. | presumed information |
| It looked bored. | anaphoric pronoun |

CONJUNCTION focuses on logical meaning — on relations of addition, time, cause and comparison between messages, as these are variously realised through paratactic, hypotactic and cohesive conjunctions (or metaphorically within a clause; see Chapter 4 for details). Once again, this analysis is inspired by Gleason (1968) and by Halliday and Hasan (1976).

| The Vogon began his poem. | preceding event |
| **Immediately** Ford yawned. | succeeding event |

Finally IDEATION attends to a variety of experiential relations among "lexical" items — hyponymy, antonymy, synonymy, meronymy and so on (the semantics of collocation if you will). The major influence on this chapter is once again Halliday and Hasan.

| There was a **robot**. | superordinate |
| The **android** looked bored. | hyponym |

Before going on to explore these systems it perhaps needs to be stressed that like *Cohesion in English, English Text* does **not** equate cohesion with coherence. Hasan's methodology for measuring coherence, cohesive harmony, will be introduced in Chapter 6, alongside other analyses which focus on patterns of interaction among discourse semantics systems and across strata. It is only by the end of Chapter 6 then that something approximating a comprehensive analysis of texture will have been achieved.

Beyond this, as Halliday and Hasan note, the concept of cohesion is not in itself sufficient to define a text. Context is also critical and it is for this reason that Chapter 7 has been included in this volume to contextualise the work on discourse semantics developed in Chapters 2 through 6. Needless to say only a brief sketch of a model of the contexts in which English is used is provided at that stage. Since they have so often been misunderstood in this regard, we will close this introductory chapter with the following quotation from Halliday and Hasan (for further discussion of this point see Chapters 6 and 7 below).

> The concept of COHESION can therefore be usefully supplemented by that of REGISTER, since the two together effectively define a TEXT. A text is a passage of discourse which is coherent in these two regards: it is coherent with respect to the context of situation, and therefore consistent in register; and it is coherent with respect to itself, and therefore cohesive. Neither of these two conditions is sufficient without the other, nor does the one by necessity entail the other. (Halliday and Hasan 1976: 23)

NOTES

1. The realisation statements for the THEME options are not complete. The realisation of marked and unmarked Themes depends on MOOD; see Matthiessen (1992) for details.

2. Halliday (1979) actually refers to **periodic** structures as **culminative** ones; the term periodic is preferred here because of the misleading association between culmination and final position.

3. A grammatical metaphor in Australian English for the mental process of affection *(x) shits (me)*. Compare the North American *(x) pisses (y) off*.

4. Halliday's own notation for hypotactic interdependency of this kind involves Greek letters, with α as Head. Using this notation the logical structure of *those two new Vogon space ships there* would be ζ ε δ γ β α β.

5. Halliday, but not Painter, actually models the proto-language phase as a two strata system; Painter's mono-stratal characterisation is preferred here.

6. In traffic-light-ese this is the problem of labelling terms as [stop/speed up/go] or [red/yellow/green].

7. Young children give up a system of this kind at a point where they distinguish several dozen signs; but as Halliday and Painter point out, running out of distinctions is not the reason they move on.

8. Languages differ of course in the elaborations they pursue; the number of ranks distinguished is one variable (e.g. no distinction between word and morpheme ranks in Vietnamese).

9. An alternative solution is explored in Martin and Matthiessen (1991) who suggest complementing systemic typology with a topological perspective.

10. Interpersonal meaning has been backgrounded to simplify the discussion here; it is important to note however that certain types of interpersonal metaphor are much more common in speaking than writing (see Chapter 2 and 6 below).

11. Interpersonally and textually of course the relationship is far from arbitrary: the systems of TONALITY, TONICITY and TONE, alongside phonaesthesia, are all meaning making resources which stand in a natural relationship with interpersonal and textual systems in lexicogrammar; see also the discussion of TONE SEQUENCE, TONE CONCORD and logical meaning in Chapter 4.

12. The concentric circle projection was initially designed by Halliday.

13. What Lemke (1984) generalises as the principle of **metaredundancy**.

14. For an intriguing discussion of this pattern in the grammar, where it is anomalous, see Plum (1988:119-122) on janus structures in the clause complex.

15. Conjunctive structures would be treated as phoric in this system, since clauses containing conjunctions presume clauses the conjunction links them to; see Chapter 4 below.

2. Negotiation

Shaping meaning through dialogue

2.1 MOOD — basic resources for negotiation

This chapter is concerned with the semantics of MOOD in English (the grammatical description of MOOD proposed in Halliday 1976b:105-110 and Halliday 1985a will be assumed). Its basic concern will be to interpret MOOD from a discourse perspective as a resource for negotiating meaning in dialogue.

To begin, consider two central MOOD systems, which classify English clauses as three basic types of interact (Fig. 2.1):

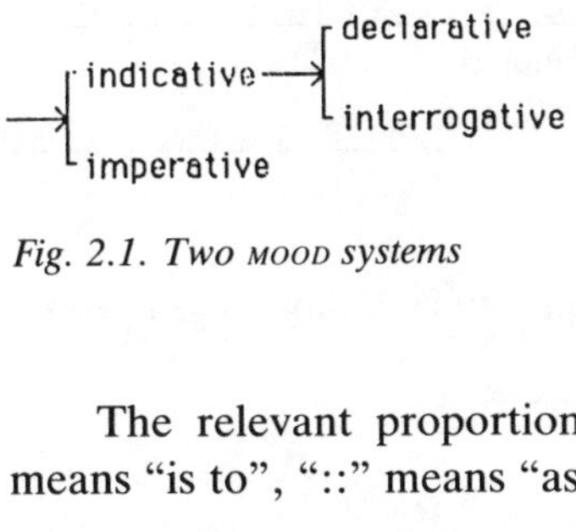

Fig. 2.1. Two MOOD systems

The relevant proportionalities are as follows (as in Chapter 1, ":" means "is to", "::" means "as"):

> [indicative vs imperative]
> He found it/Did he find it?:Find it::
> He has it/Does he have it?:Have it::
> He'll get it/Will he get it:Get it
>
> [declarative vs interrogative]
> He found it:Did he find it?::
> He has it:Does he have it?::
> He'll get it:Will he get it?

Feature by feature, the appropriate structural realisations are:

[declarative]   Subject ^ Finite ^ Predicator...
[interrogative]   Finite ^ Subject ^ Predicator...
[imperative]   Predicator...

Traditionally, these systems and structures have come to be viewed as formal ones — the basic *syntax* of the English clause. Halliday (1984a, 1985a) on the other hand suggests that these systems and structures require a richer interpretation, beyond form, in spite of the fact that the content of the terms is less than transparent (largely because of their antiquity; see Halliday 1984b/1988 on the ineffability of linguistic categories). Rather, the systems engender two fundamental oppositions: *information* as opposed to *goods and services* (indicative vs imperative) and *giving* (declarative) as opposed to *demanding* (interrogative). He accordingly proposes a semantic perspective on the grammatical labels along the following lines, fleshing out the paradigm with an additional category which is not grammaticalised in MOOD at the very general level of delicacy outlined above (the Offer), as in Table 2.1.

Table 2.1. Semantic interpretation of central MOOD systems

	GIVING	DEMANDING
GOODS & SERVICES	Offer	Command
INFORMATION	Statement	Question

Offers and Commands are grouped together by Halliday as *proposals*, Statements and Commands as *propositions*:

PROPOSALS:
Offer   Can I get you a drink?
Command   Get me a drink, would you?

PROPOSITIONS:
Statement   There's lots of beer.
Question   Is there any Tooheys?

Semantically oriented labels of this kind highlight the meaning of the grammatical terms (in this case, their typical function in dialogue) and are used throughout Halliday (1985a) to focus on the grammar as a functionally organised meaning making resource (rather than as a syntax, or set of forms). No attempt is made to distinguish stratally between grammar and meaning; rather the grammar in infused with meaning, and a stratal distinction between grammar and semantics systematically blurred.

In this book however, an attempt will be made to unpick the boundary between grammar and semantics in a systemic functional interpretation of English and Halliday's relabelling provides a point of departure for stratifying the content plane, along the lines suggested in Chapter 1. This is an important step as far as interpreting dialogue is concerned since there is no simple relation between general grammatical classes and the role they play in structuring a conversation. The most commonly discussed example of this is the realisation of demands for goods and services (see for example Butler 1988 on the semantics of modalised directives). Each class considered so far for example, imperative, declarative and interrogative MOOD, can be used to code a Command [throughout this chapter a dash will be used to signal the beginning of a new turn — that is, a change of interlocutor]:

> Get me the new one, please. — Allright, I will.:
> I'd like the new one, please. — Allright.:
> Can I have the new one, please? — Allright.

Evidence for the fact that the different grammatical classes are performing a related discourse function comes from their context: from their co-text — the inclusion of *please* and the reply *allright*; and from the context of situation, where one might well observe goods being exchanged.

Furthermore, as can be seen from the examples above, the relevance of the co-text is also grammaticalised in English. The relevant systems have to do with clause ellipsis and substitution and are described in detail in Halliday and Hasan (1976). There are two major patterns to be considered. The first can be established with respect to the more general MOOD functions Mood (including Subject, Finite and Mood Adjuncts) and Residue (including Predicator, Complement and other Adjuncts) and illustrated as follows:

> Get me the new one, please. — Allright, I'll get it for you.
> Get me the new one, please. — Allright, I will ~~Residue~~.
> Get me the new one, please. — Allright ~~Mood Residue~~.

The first response (*Allright, I'll get it for you.*) is full, though potentially elliptical. The second (*Allright, I will.*) ellipses the Residue. The third (*Allright.*) ellipses both Residue and Mood functions. Alternatively, the Mood and Residue functions together may be substituted with *so* or *not*.

> Will he make it? — Maybe **so**.
> Will she win it? — Perhaps **not**.

The second pattern is found in the environment of wh interrogatives of both the first order and second order (echo) types; again, both elliptical and potentially elliptical structures are found:

> Which is the new one? — This one's the new one.
> Which is the new one? — This one.
>
> This is the new one. — Which one's the new one?
> This is the new one. — Which one?

As before, there is no one to one relation between grammatical class and discourse function. Responses may be either elliptical or not, as illustrated. In addition, elliptical clauses may initiate dialogue, with ellipsed information typically recoverable from the non-verbal context (for tone analysis used see Halliday 1967c; 1970b; 1985a; El-Menoufy 1988 — tone 2 is rising, tone 1 falling in the examples below):

> //2 Coming? // — Yes, I am.
> //1 Leaving now. // — Oh, are you?

Following Halliday (1984a) the semantic inventory of interacts outlined above can now be expanded into four pairs, which will be referred to provisionally, following work in ethnomethodology (e.g. Schegloff & Sacks 1973), as "adjacency pairs":

Offer	Can I get you a drink?
Acknowledge Offer	— Yes, thanks.
Command	Get me a drink, will you?
Response Offer to Command	— Allright, I will.
Statement	The match is at 2pm.
Acknowledge Statement	— Oh, is it?
Question	What time's the match?
Response Statement to Question	— At 2pm.

The grammar then makes available resources for tying an initiation to a response (ellipsis and substitution) and for orienting the exchange to goods and services or information and to giving or demanding (declarative, interrogative and imperative). These resources do not however stand in any biunique relation with a particular move in dialogue, so two levels of analysis are needed to relate system and text. The MOOD systems considered to this point are outlined below (Fig. 2.2), along with the SPEECH FUNCTION network underlying them (Fig. 2.3). This is the bare bones of the stratified approach to interpreting dialogue to be developed in this Chapter.

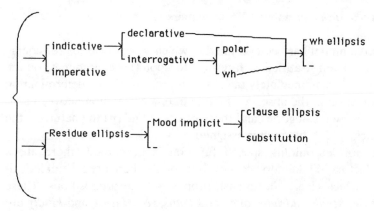

Fig. 2.2. MOOD — *key systems*

For discussion of these and related systems interpreted as part of an explicit structure producing device, see Mann & Matthiessen 1985, Matthiessen 1985, Matthiessen & Bateman 1991; in general throughout this book the generative interpretation of Halliday's grammar designed by Mann and Matthiessen at the Information Sciences Institute and referred to as Nigel will be assumed wherever the issue of explicit realisation is relevant.

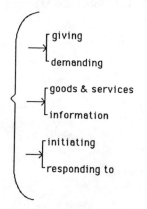

Fig. 2.3. SPEECH FUNCTION — *key systems*

2.2 SPEECH FUNCTION and MOOD: adjacency pairs

To this point a model has been outlined in which SPEECH FUNCTION (discourse semantics) has been stratified with respect to MOOD (lexicogrammar) on the content plane. This immediately raises two questions: (i) the determination of speech function in the absence of a one to one correlation between general SPEECH FUNCTION categories and those of MOOD; and (ii) the nature of the units to which speech function is assigned.

As far as determining speech function is concerned, there are a number of factors to take into account. First of all, there are several indexical markers which clearly distinguish proposals from propositions. These include *please, kindly, allright, okay* and *thank-you*. *Please* and *kindly* are found in Commands, *allright* and *okay* in Response Offers to Commands and *thank-you* in responses to Offers or Commands.

> Could I have a midi of Coopers, **please**?
> — **Okay**.
> — **Thanks**.

Beyond this, it is difficult to find unique grammatical criteria for recognizing very general categories such as Offer, Command, Statement and so on. However, when a more delicate categorisation is considered much more specific statements of realisation can be made. Interesting work in this area has been undertaken by Butler (1988), who looks at non-imperative realisations of Commands which contain a modal verb, demonstrating their relation to politeness phenomena; and by Fawcett et al. (1988:132-133) who

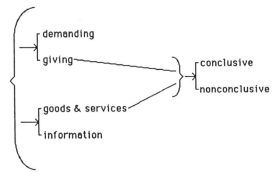

Fig. 2.4. Further delicacy for Offers — following Hasan

provide a very delicate categorisation of speech function (unfortunately without specifying realisation rules). Beyond this, the most significant work in the area has been undertaken by Hasan (forthcoming), working on the category of Offer. Her strategy is to extend the SPEECH FUNCTION network in delicacy to the point where it makes more categorical predictions about the realisation of discourse semantics in lexicogrammar.

As a first step Hasan adds the system [conclusive/nonconclusive] to the SPEECH FUNCTION systems noted above. This allows her to distinguish between Offers which accompany the handing over of goods or performance of a service (*proffers*) and Offers which foreshadow such (*pre-offers*). The contrast can be illustrated using her examples as follows (Offers in bold face):

PROFFER [conclusive]

Karen	Could you get me a drink?
Mother	— Please.
Karen	— Please.
	Lemonade, lemonade, please.
Mother	— **Here you are**...

PRE-OFFER [nonconclusive]

Christine	Mummy, can I play with one of your old skirts?
	Can you show me?
Mother	— **In a few minutes I'll get you one**.

This distinction enables the specification of lexicogrammatical realisations to be narrowed down considerably. Proffers select declarative MOOD, have exophoric circumstances of location in space as marked Themes (e.g. *Here*), tend to refer exophorically to the beneficiary (*you*) and phorically to any goods exchanged (the goods were elided in *Here you are*.); the realisation of proffers in effect verges on the idiomatic: *Here you are, There you are, Here you go, There you go* etc.

Similar specifications cannot be made for pre-offers without taking several more steps in delicacy (see Hasan's paper for the details of these). But it is clear that the realisation relationship between discourse semantics and lexicogrammar has been considerably clarified simply by taking one step — subclassifying [giving/goods & services] exchanges as [conclusive/nonconclusive]. This is essentially the strategy that needs to be pursued to respond to Levinson's (1983:289-294) critique of what he refers to as discourse analysis where he casts doubt on the possibility of delimiting a set of interacts and deriving them reliably from their realisations in text. It provides a

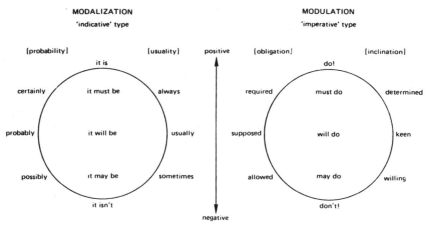

Fig. 2.5. Relation of modality to polarity and MOOD *(Halliday 1985a: 335)*

mechanism for systematically relating SPEECH FUNCTION to MOOD, and at the same time establishes a set of SPEECH FUNCTION classes that is clearly limited, and at the same time indefinitely extendable (through the scale of delicacy).

A second set of evidence relevant to determining speech function is evidence from the co-text, either through the presence of one of the indexical markers noted above in an adjacent interact, or through the expression of gradations within probablity, usuality, inclination and obligation. Halliday (1985a:335) associates degrees of MODALIZATION (probability and usuality) with propositions and degrees of MODULATION (inclination and obligation) with proposals; and within proposals, inclination is associated with Offers and Response Offers to Commands and obligation with Commands and Acknowledge Offers.

Examples of this grading in the context of the adjacency pairs considered to this point are provided below.

> OFFER ^ ACKNOWLEDGE OFFER (obligation)
> Shall I mark them then?
> — You're required/supposed/allowed to.
>
> COMMAND ^ RESPONSE OFFER TO COMMAND (inclination)
> Get me a drink, would you?
> — I'm willing/keen/determined to.
>
> QUESTION ^ RESPONSE STATEMENT TO QUESTION (probability)
> Will she win then?
> — Possibly/probably/certainly she will.

STATEMENT ˆ ACKNOWLEDGE STATEMENT (usuality)
She wins then.
— Sometimes/usually/always[1] she does.

The presence of realisations along these scales (with positive and negative polarity as outer poles), including their metaphorical variants (see Halliday 1985a:336), provides additional evidence for assigning speech function to grammatical classes. The metaphorical realisation of inclination *I'd love to* in the following pair, clearly associates it with exchanging goods and services, not information:

Why don't you get us a beer?
— I'd love to.

Similarly the scale of usuality associates the first pair below with the negotiation of propositions, while that of inclination implies the negotiation of a service.

Can you open this window?
— Sometimes/usually/always.

Can you open this window?
— I'm willing/keen/determined to.

The one clause type to which the notion of negotiation through grading does not transparently apply is the wh interrogative. One might argue that in an adjacency pair like the following, the response simply supplies the missing experiential meaning; grading is not an issue:

What do you reckon would be good for a five-year-old kid?
— Fairy tales.

Note however that the elliptical response does take over the degree of probability coded in the wh interrogative; it's full form is She **would** like *fairy tales*, with modality probable, as opposed to possible or certain. The actual answer to this question is taken up in 2.8 below (text 2) and demonstrates that interlocutors are prepared to negotiate modality in the context of wh interrogatives where they feel uncomfortable with what an elliptical response might imply: — *She'll like fairy tales, does she?* The non-ellipitical reply enables its speaker to adjust modality in the tag.

The final set of factors to be taken into account when determining speech function are considerations of context. *Can you open this window?* when inspecting a property is likely to be heard differently than when sitting in a stuffy room. Field, mode, tenor, genre and ideology are all relevant as participating levels of semiosis; it is not possible simply to map speech function directly from 'words on the page'. The systematic relevance of these contextual variables will be taken up again in Chapter 7.

It should also be noted in passing that in the model being developed here both grammar and discourse semantics make meaning. Levinson (1983:290) comments that the first move in the following text is both "a question and an offer, as indicated by the response".

> Would you like another drink?
> — Yes, I would, thank-you, but make it a small one.

This is just what would have been predicted by the model developed to this point. Grammatically the first move is a demand for information (interrogative) while semantically it offers goods (Offer); both MOOD and SPEECH FUNCTION contribute a layer of meaning to the clause. Typically, where both levels are responded to (the *Yes, I would* and *thank-you* in the above), the grammar is responded to first (*Thank-you, yes, I would* is unlikely).

The question of how many layers of meaning to recognize raises the problem of units: just what unit is it to which speech function is being assigned? Is for example the response *Yes, I would, thank-you, but make it a small one.* one speech act or two (or more)? Given what has been stressed to this point about the grammar making available resources for structuring dialogue the most appropriate unit would appear to be a *clause selecting independently for MOOD*. This rules out the embedded and hypotactically dependent clauses illustrated below:

> They loved the team **that won**. (defining relative)
> They defeated **whoever they met**. (nominalised wh clause)
> They watched **Manly winning**. (act)
> It pleased them **that Balmain lost**. (fact)
> They wondered **if they'd win**. (hypotactic projection)
> They won, **which surprised them**. (hypotactic expansion)

But it does admit paratactically dependent clauses, which do select independently for MOOD. Note the variation in MOOD possible after *but*, showing that the *but* is introducing a new move:

> Yes, I would, thank-you, but make it a small one.
> Yes, I would, thank-you, but I'd like a small one.
> Yes, I would, thank-you, but could you make it a small one?

The MOOD network underlying this definition is presented below, along with examples of realisations for terminal features. [Ventola's 1988a criticisms of the unit proposed will be taken up in 2.3 below.]

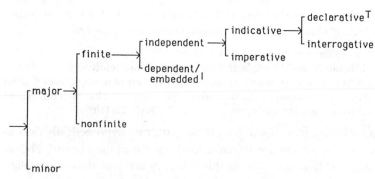

Fig. 2.6. MOOD *in English: systems relevant to unit of analysis*[2]

SAMPLE REALISATIONS:

[declarative]	I'd like a small one.
[interrogative]	Could you make it a small one?
[imperative]	Make it a small one.
[dependent]	I was wondering **if you could make it a small one**.
[nonfinite]	I noticed **you making a small one**.
[minor]	Hey!

These classes can be interpreted semantically as follows. Independent clauses negotiate MODALIZATION and MODULATION — speakers typically work towards consensus as far as grading probability, usuality, inclination and obligation are concerned. Dependent and embedded clauses on the other hand code meanings as already negotiated — the responses in the following example are to the main clause, not the clause embedded in it (*Did you love the beer*? not *Did you try the beer*?):

> I loved the beer I tried last time.
> — Did you?

Hypotactically dependent clauses may turn out to be better taken from a discourse perspective as an intermediate case (between embedded and independent clauses) — quantative studies might well show them to be more negotiable than embedded clauses, though less likely to be responded to than independent ones. Note in this connection that when projection is used to express modality metaphorically (Halliday 1985a:336), it is the structurally dependent clause that is in fact being negotiated:

> I think he'll be there. (meaning 'maybe he'll be there'.)
> — Will he? (more likely than *Oh, do you?*)

This need not of course block the 'sardonic' interlocutor from negotiating the projecting clause as if it deserved a congruent reading:

> "I'm inclined to think---" said I.
> "I should do so," Sherlock Holmes remarked impatiently.
> I believe that I am one of the most long-suffering of mortals; but I'll admit that I was annoyed at the sardonic interruption. "Really, Holmes," said I severely, "you are a litle trying at times." (Doyle 1981:769)

Pending quantitative investigation of these patterns, hypotactically dependent clauses will be grouped with embedded ones as in the network above. The most negotiable clause type in this category involves dependent elaboration as these clauses can be tagged:

> α   Sherlock put Watson down,
> $^=$β   which was mean, wasn't it?

With nonfinite clauses, meaning is presented not so much as having been negotiated as non-negotiable: the clauses have been nominalised, and thereby taken out of the realm of potential interacts and into that of things (cf. *They watched **Manly winning/the game/their favorite player***).

Minor clauses lack Subject, Finite and Predicator functions, so the question of negotiating MODALIZATION and MODULATION does not directly arise. This raises the question of the function of minor clauses as interacts. For one thing, minor clauses are used to initiate two types of adjacency pair: Greetings and Calls. Greetings (subsuming leave-takings) are found at the beginning and end of conversations, making way for or closing down negotiations:

> Greeting   G'day.
> Response to Greeting   — G'day.

Calls summon the attention of potential negotiators where this attention has not been secured or has wandered:

> Call   Bill.
> Response to Call   — What?

Both Calls and Greetings can be realised through major clauses, although these are for the most part lexicalised formulas: *How's it going?*, *Nice weather we're having!*, *We'll be seeing you.*, *Got a minute?*, *Listen to this.* etc.

Minor clauses are also commonly used to react, coding a speaker's attitude. These may or may not function as a comment on preceding co-

text; some of the most taboo for example are more commonly spoken with
no-one else around:

Exclamation	Damn!

Spoken as a comment on co-text, an interlocutor or in the presence of a
potential interlocutor, Exclamations commonly precipitate dialogue. What
is precipitated however often has the form and function of an initiating
interact, not a responding one, especially where the Exclamation is purely
expressive:

Exclamation	Damn!
Question	What's wrong?
Response Statement to Question	— Nothing.

Where Exclamations comment, grading is negotiable, and pair parts scaling
the attitude are found. There are various formulas for expressing solidarity
(e.g. *I'll say/You're not wrong/You're not kidding* etc.) and intensifiers that
adjust the attitude by degree (e.g. *quite/rather/sort of/absolutely* etc.).

Exclamation	What an idiot!
Response to Exclamation	— Quite so.

The expression of attitude in English is of course not restricted to minor
clauses. Attitude may also be coded in negotiating interacts — through syst-
tems oriented to comment and evaluation at both clause (e.g. *regrettably*)
and group (e.g. *can't stand* and *silly bugger*) ranks:

Regrettably I **can't stand** the **silly bugger**.

And one major clause type, the exclamative, focusses explicitly on attitude:

What a silly bugger he is!

Responses to exclamatives may grade with respect to either MODALIZATION
(*certainly/sometimes*), or to the intensity of the reaction (*rather*):

What a silly bugger he is!
— He **certainly** is/He is **sometimes**/Yes he is **rather**.

This raises the question of how to draw the line between Exclamations
and Statements. On the one hand, exclamatives have affirmative syntax
(Subject^Finite) and so are definitely negotiable; at the same time, declarative clauses may encode reaction through attitudinal adjuncts (e.g. *regrettably*) or through group rank systems (e.g. *can't stand* and *silly bugger*). The
strategy developed here will be to treat attitudinal minor clauses and
exclamatives as Exclamations:

Exclamation [minor/exclamative]   **What a fool!/What a fool** he's been!
Response to Exclamation   — Quite so.

and to include other MOOD classes only where attitude is explicitly graded in a response:

Statement [declarative]   He's been **such a fool**.
Acknowledge Statement   — Oh, has he?

But:

Exclamation [declarative]   He's been **such a fool**.
Response to Exclamation   — **Absolutely**.

The relevant section of the MOOD network needs to be adjusted as follows, incorporating the feature [exclamative] and adding the feature [affirmative]

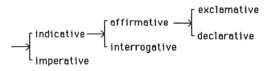

Fig. 2.7. MOOD revised to include an exclamative option

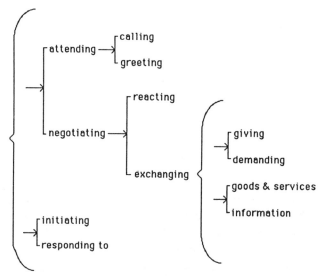

Fig. 2.8. SPEECH FUNCTION — systems underlying basic adjacency pairs

to generalise across the Subject^Finite stucture in both exclamative and declarative clauses.

Significantly, attitude is not realised through the Mood function in English, unlike MODALIZATION and MODULATION which can be expressed through modal verbs and adjuncts. For this reason ellipsis in English does not facilitate the negotiation of attitude — the attitude to be graded is commonly realised in the Residue itself. It thus follows from the grammar that how a speaker feels is less commonly negotiated through pair parts in dialogue than is inclination, obligation, probability and usuality and that where it is negotiated, MODALIZATION and MODULATION are typically being negotiated as well since the Mood element is normally present (cf. *Yes he is rather* above).

The SPEECH FUNCTION network can now be elaborated as in Fig. 2.8, giving rise to the seven adjacency pairs which follow.

Call [attending:calling/initiating]
John.
Response to Call [attending:calling/responding to]
— Huh?

Greeting [attending:greeting/initiating]
See you.
Response to Greeting [attending:greeting/responding to]
— Bye-bye.

Exclamation [negotiating:reacting/initiating]
Utter rubbish!
Response to Exclamation[negotiating:reacting/responding to]
— Absolutely.

Offer [negotiating:exchanging:giving/goods & services//initiating]
Let me get you a beer.
Acknowledge Offer [negotiating:exchanging:giving/goods & services//
responding to]
-Please do.

Command [negotiating:exchanging:demanding/goods & services//initiating]
Get me a beer.
Response Offer to Command [negotiating:exchanging:demanding/goods &
services//responding to]
— I'd love to.

Statement [negotiating:exchanging:giving/information//initiating]
He's won.
Acknowledge Statement [negotiating:exchanging:giving/information//
responding to]
— Oh, has he?

Question [negotiating:exchanging:demanding/information//initiating]
Has he won?
Response Statement to Question [negotiating:exchanging:demanding/information//responding to]
— *Certainly.*

2.3 EXCHANGE STRUCTURE

To this point a stratified approach to the function of interacts has been proposed, with MOOD and SPEECH FUNCTION each contributing one layer of meaning on the content plane (cf. Butler 1987:215 who argues for the importance of recognising three strata rather than two: syntax, semantics and illocutionary force; the difference follows from his interpretation of syntax as a set of forms whose 'literal' meanings are important, but which do not themselves contribute a layer of meaning to the dialogue). It was further noted that through ellipsis and the grading systems associated with MODALIZATION, MODULATION and attitude the grammar is structured in such a way as to pair off the interacts, giving rise to the seven basic adjacency pairs suggested above. The major limitation of the description to this point is that it is not explicit about how in dialogue this pairing takes place. Both MOOD and SPEECH FUNCTION classify individual interacts, not sequences. It is to the question of sequencing interacts that this section now turns.

Work on sequencing has developed within two major traditions, referred to by Levinson (1983) as discourse analysis (including the Birmingham school) and conversational analysis (ethnomethodology). The work of the Birmingham school will be developed at this point (see especially Sinclair & Coulthard 1975; Coulthard & Montgomery 1981). The basic strategy of this school is to treat sequences of interacts as multivariate stuctures, positing a

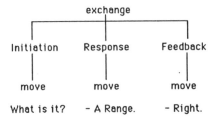

Fig. 2.9. Birmingham school exchange structure

rank scale at the level of discourse. The ranks which are relevant to the discussion at this point are the move and the exchange, where an exchange is set up as a three part structure, consisting (potentially) of three moves: Initiation ^ (Response) ^ (Feedback) as in Fig. 2.9.

Structures of this kind immediately call into question the notion of adjacency **pairs**. Clearly a given interact can give rise to more than one other — exchanges consisting of up to five moves will be proposed below. Note however that there is a strong tendency for exchanges to begin with non-elliptical major clauses, continue with elliptical major ones and close with minor clauses as in the example above (see Berry 1981a:142-145). Minor clauses thus function as a kind of closure in exchanges just as they do in conversations themselves (the leave-takings discussed above).

Working within the scale and category model of language developed in Halliday (1961), Sinclair and Coulthard proposed 5 classes of move realizing 2 major classes of exchange. Berry (1979, 1981a, 1981b, 1981c) has considerably elaborated this framework within a systemic functional paradigm and it is this work that will be taken as point of departure here. Expressed as a structure potential Berry's analysis for the exchange is as follows:

$$((Dx1) \; ^\wedge \; X2) \; ^\wedge \; X1 \; ^\wedge \; (X2f)$$

This formula circumscribes exchanges as consisting of one obligatory move (the X1) and three optional ones (Dx1, X2, X2f). In order to illustrate these it is useful to re-invoke the grammar's opposition of goods and services to information (of action to knowledge in Berry's terms). Both types of exchange can begin in any of three ways, and may or may not follow up the obligatory move:

INFORMATION (KNOWLEDGE)		GOODS & SERVICES (ACTION)	
Dk1	What is it?	Da1	Can I get you a beer?
K2	— A Range.	A2	— Yes please.
K1	— Right.	A1	— Here you go.
K2	Are you coming?	A2	Get me a beer, will you?
K1	— Yes, I am.	A1	— Here you go.
K1	I'll be there at six.	A1	Have a beer.
K2f	— Oh.	A2f	— Thanks.

This model thus expands the pairs notion to allow for one, two, three and four move exchanges. This needs to be expanded by one move to handle follow-up sequences such as the following (for attested examples see Ventola 1987:100):

K1	I'll be there at six.	A1	Have a beer.
K2f	— You will.	A2f	— Thank-you.
K1f	— Yes.	A1f	— You're welcome.

The distinction between X1 and X2 slots in the exchange has to do with what Berry refers to as primary and secondary knowers and actors. The primary knower is defined as the person "who already knows the information" (Berry 1981a:126) and the primary actor as the person who "is actually going to carry out the action" (Berry 1981c:23). Exchanges can be initiated by either party; Berry 1981a classifies exchanges initiated by the primary knower or actor as A-event and exchanges initiated by the secondary knower or actor as B-event following Labov's (Labov 1972a:301; Labov & Fanshel 1977) distinction between A events (about which A knows but B does not) and B events (about which B knows but A does not).

Berry (1981c) formulates her description in systemic functional terms, thereby extending the descriptive power of the model beyond the limitations of the scale and category approach adopted by the Birmingham school. Her network has been elaborated below to include the extra follow-up move noted above and as well to include the distinction between immediate and postponed action (see Ventola 1987:101). The point here is that when goods are handed over or a service performed, the obligatory A1 move may not be verbally realised; but when there is a delay between an A2 move and handing over goods or performing a service the A1 move must be realised verbally, as a kind of promissory note. Compare:

A2	Can you get me that book?
A1	— NV (handing over book)
A2f	— Thanks.

A2	Can you get me that book?
A1	— I'll get it tomorrow.
A2f	— Thanks.

Ventola 1987 reformulates Berry's network including these distinctions in Fig. 2.10.

It remains to expand this network to handle calling, greeting and reacting sequences. Calling and greeting exchanges are realised as adjacency pairs; reacting exchanges may consist of one or two moves, depending on whether attitundinal grading is negotiated, as outlined above. The options in the immediately preceding network follow on from the feature [exchanging] in Fig. 2.11.

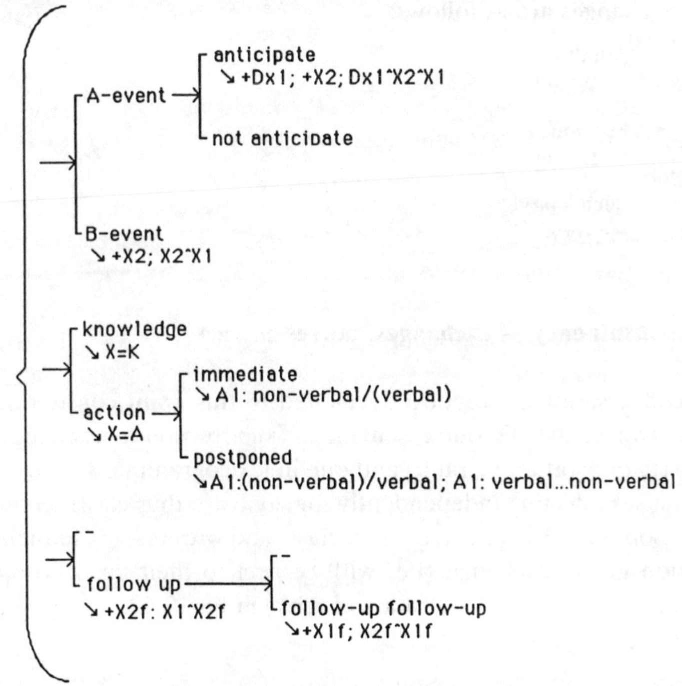

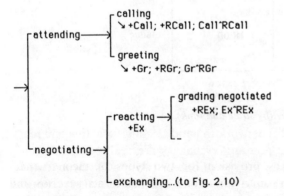

Fig. 2.10. NEGOTIATION: *Extending Berry 1981c*

Fig. 2.11. NEGOTIATION — *primary delicacy*

The additional exchanges are as follows:

Call	John?
RCall	— What?

Gr	See you.
RGr	— Bye-bye.

Ex	Such a pity!
REx	— Very.

2.4 Extending constituency — exchanges, moves and acts

The model of conversational structure developed to this point consists of three networks, two in the discourse semantics (NEGOTIATION at exchange rank and SPEECH FUNCTION at move rank) and one in lexicogrammar (MOOD at clause rank). Clauses selecting independently for MOOD are thus classified in three ways: by MOOD class, by SPEECH FUNCTION class, and with respect to their structural function in the exchange (i.e. with respect to their NEGOTIATION class). The picture is presented, by strata and rank, in Fig. 2.12.

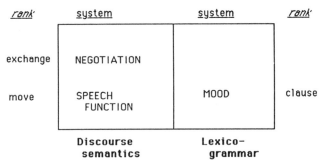

Fig. 2.12. Resources for dialogue (by strata and rank)

The model thus makes provision for two types of incongruence: between NEGOTIATION and SPEECH FUNCTION and between SPEECH FUNCTION and MOOD. While it is unusual to find both types of incongruence in text, Ventola's category of linguistic service (1987:115-117) functions semantically as both an action and a knowledge exchange, and can be initiated with an interrogative as in the example below:

> Can you tell me your name?
> — Yes, allright, John Smith.

The responding move in this example picks up on the grammar (*Can you...Yes*), the SPEECH FUNCTION (*tell me...allright*) and the exchange structure (*your name...John Smith*). This can be captured by analysing the exchange structure as K2^K1 (since the exchange can only be successfully completed by providing the appropriate information), with the K2 realised by a demand for services, which is in turn coded through the grammar as a modalised polar interrogative. Note that linguistic services of this kind thus demonstrate that Berry's (1981a:40) suggestion that the exchange be viewed as a lexicogrammatical rank consisting of clauses cannot be maintained since such a model could not show that *Can you tell me your name?* is initiating an exchange of information as a service.

The rank scale at the level of discourse proposed originally by Sinclair and Coulthard included three additional ranks, two above the exchange (lesson and transaction) and one below (the move). Considerations at the ranks of lesson and transaction will be handled under the heading of genre in this book and will be taken up again in Chapter 7, along with a discussion of why genre is treated as as underlying connotative semiotic rather than a higher rank at the level of discourse semantics (it follows that *framing* and *focussing* exchanges, which are relevant to lesson boundaries, will not be followed up in this Chapter, which is concerned in other words with *conversational* exchanges). But the Birmingham school's proposals for move structure are relevant here.

2.4.1 *Moves and acts*

Sinclair and Coulthard's model involved extending the notion of multivariate structure to handle constituency within moves. This meant setting up a further rank, the act, whose classes function as elements of move structure. Burton (1980; 1981) developed Sinclair and Coulthard's model in the context of dramatic and conversational text. Her categorisation was slightly revised by Butler (1985b), whose interpretation is taken as point of departure here (and again in part in 2.5 below). Butler focusses in particular on moves negotiating goods and services, and the discussion of moves and acts will be limited to his interpretation of this type of exchange.

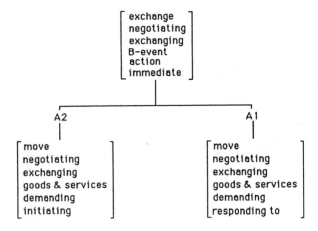

Fig. 2.13. Exchange structure: English Text *(two ranks)*

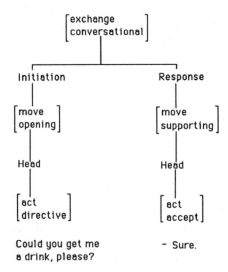

Fig. 2.14. Exchange structure: Burton (three ranks)

To begin, it is useful to compare Burton's analysis of a basic action exchange with that developed in 2.3 above. The *English Text* analysis developed to this point is presented first, with full feature specifications at exchange and move rank. Then Burton's analysis is shown, including the additional rank of act. The feature specifications in Burton's description are simpler, reflecting the scale and category theory she employs; the focus on paradigmatic relations is much less delicate than in a systemic functional description.

A2   Could you get me a drink, please?
A1   — Sure.

The advantage of introducing move structure is to allow for expansions of the A2 and A1 moves. Butler (1985b:224) recognises two classes of Pre-Head act in the A2 move, *starter* and *preface*. The starter is defined as "directing attention towards some area in order to facilitate the hearer's response to a coming initiation", the preface as "signalling reintroduction of a diverted topic, or an interruption, or a personal viewpoint on what is to come" (Butler 1985b:221). For example:

A2   preface   About that drink you mentioned,
          directive   could you get me a beer, please?

Two classes of Post-Head are also proposed: *comment* and *prompt* (surprisingly, at the same time both Burton (1981:77) and Butler (1985b:222) define comments as appearing after informative acts or other comments, which in fact rules them out of action exchanges where they follow directives and either accepts or reacts). The comment "expands, justifies or provides additional information to a preceding informative or comment" while the prompt "reinforces a preceding directive or elicitation" (Butler 1985b:222). For example, the A2 move under consideration can be further expanded as follows:

A2   preface   About that drink you mentioned,
          directive   could you get me a beer, please?
          comment   It's getting late.

Pre-Head and Post-Head acts are also suggested for the A1 move; for Post-Head, comment, as defined above, and for Pre-Head, *accept*, whose function is "to indicate that the speaker has heard and understood the previous utterance and is compliant" (Burton 1981:77). In this model the Head of an A1 move is always a non-verbal action, with what were treated as verbal realisations of the A1 above analysed as accept acts in Pre-Head position;

strangely, this means that in postponed action exchanges, the A1 move has no Head.

```
A1    accept    — Sure.
      react     (hands over drink)
      comment   Nice and cold.
```

To take this just one step further, all opening moves can be preceded by a *marker* or *summons* filling what Burton terms the Signal function. The marker "signals a discourse boundary, and shows speaker has a topic to introduce"; the summons "indicates speaker wants to get hearer's attention in order to introduce a topic" (Butler 1985b:222). Taking up this potential effects the following exchange:

```
(A2)  Signal      summons     John,
      Pre-Head    preface     about that drink you mentioned,
      Head        directive   could you get me a beer, please?
      Post-Head   comment     It's getting late.

(A1)  Pre-Head    accept      — Sure.
      Head        react       (hands over drink)
      Post-Head   comment     Nice and cold.
```

The complete structural analysis is presented in Fig. 15.

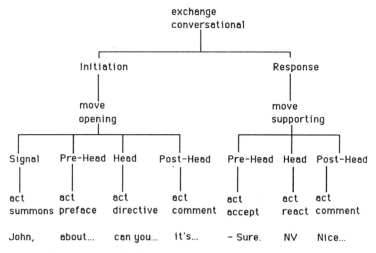

Fig. 2.15. An expanded action exchange — following Burton

For various reasons this multivariate approach to move structure will not be pursued here. These reflect in general the modular approach to text structure underlying *English Text*, which can be illustrated in part with respect to the exchange just considered.

To begin, as currently formulated in Halliday (1985a), the grammar itself provides adequate descriptions of the vocative *John* and the circumstance of matter *about that drink you mentioned*, both of which appear in thematic position. Halliday's Theme ^ Rheme analysis would be as follows:

John,	about that drink you mentioned,	can you get me a beer, please?
Theme		Rheme
interpersonal vocative	topical marked	

Where grammar is conceived as making meaning, there is no need to add an extra layer of interpretation to the semantics to simply re-label these functions. This is not to argue that vocatives cannot function as interacts on the discourse level — Call ^ Response to Call sequences of moves were recognised above. And clearly the topical orientation realised through the circumstance of matter above can be coded as an independent clause:

> John, you mentioned a drink awhile ago.
> Can you get me one?

But the point is that once the topical orientation enters the discourse as an independent clause, it is itself negotiable, and more appropriately analysed as an interact initiating an exchange of information. What is being suggested here is that the first pair of exchanges below is much more likely than the second:

> John, you mentioned a drink a while ago.
> — Oh, yes I did.
> — Could you get me one?
> — Right away.

> John, about that drink you mentioned...
> — Oh, did I?
> — could you get me one.
> — Sure.

The general point here is that if the grammar, or phonology for that matter (cf. Burton and Butler's treatment of silent stress as an act!), does the work, so be it. The model developed here does not dualise meaning and form and so does not have to re-state the contributions made by phonology and lexicogrammar to text structure at the level of semantics.

Equally important, as far as modularity is concerned, is the fact that negotiation provides just one of four perspectives on text structure elaborated in the model of discourse semantics presented here. As an example of a starter act, functioning as a Pre-Head in move structure, Butler re-presents the following example from Sinclair and Coulthard:

| starter | These three then are for you to sort out for yourselves. |
| directive | Can you translate...can you be an Egyptologist and translate the names from this chart? |

And clearly the starter and directive are cohesively related. As far as reference is concerned, there are two chains: *you-yourselves-you-you* and *these three-the names*. Lexically, *translate* is tied hyponymically to *sort out*, and there is a strong collocation pattern running through the *sort out-translate-Egyptologist-translate* string. Furthermore there is an implicit internal conjunctive relationship of cause relating the two acts: "**since** these are here for you to sort out, I asking that you pretend you're an Egyptologist and translate the names from the chart". In a model of discourse structure such as that proposed by the Birmingham school, all aspects of text structure have to be incorporated into a single rank scale such as act-move-exchange-transaction-lesson. This naturally puts a great deal of pressure on move structure to capture cohesive relations as multivariately structured act sequences. Here on the other hand, identification, conjunction and ideation will be treated separately from negotiation as discourse structures in their own right. Most significantly this avoids the embarrassments experienced by the Birmingham school when refocussing their attention on monologic text (see Coulthard and Montgomery 1981:1-38 for discussion of anxieties in this respect).

Burton (1981:67) comments on integrating cohesion into the move and act framework following Montgomery as follows:

> Where there are long passages of informatives offered in the text it seems inadequate to give one label of informative to the whole passage, or even to label the first clause inform and all subsequent units comment...In coding my data I have found the following categories useful: additive, adversative and causal items; repeat, restate and qualify items; where it seems to

me the first three are sub-categories of informative, and the second three are sub-categories of comment.

Fawcett et al. (1988:132) considerably elaborate this framework, recognizing 16 classes of act based on the conjunctive relationship holding between them and a preceding move. For a comprehensive discussion of these conjunctive relations interpreted as a independent component of discourse structure see Chapter 4 below.

The same type of response holds for comments as for the starter just considered (and for at least the following of Burton and Butler's acts: marker, preface, metastatement, conclusion, prompt, evaluate): they are cohesively related to other acts in an exchange, but these relations are better dealt with comprehensively when non-dialogic aspects of text structure are reviewed instead of trying to push them into a dialogic mould.

2.4.2 *Move complexes*

Ventola (1987;1988a) is also concerned with the analysis of "complex" moves. Her suggestions however involve univariate, not multivariate structure. At issue is the analysis of texts such as the following, which given the model presented to this point needs to be taken as two exchanges:

K2   Have you ever heard of Baron Munchhhausen?
K1   No, I've never heard about them.

K1   It's the first time I've heard of them.

Clearly the two K1 moves are paraphrases — experientially they are in fact identical. The difference lies in their interpersonal and textual structure: Subject *I* vs *It* and unmarked Theme *No, I* vs marked Theme *the first time* (for predicated Theme see Halliday 1985a:60). But since a move has been defined as a clause selecting independently for MOOD, and their MOOD structure differs, they are taken as separate moves, implying two exchanges.

Ventola proposes using Halliday's logico-semantic relations of expansion (elaboration, extension and enhancement) as the basis for recognising a new discourse unit, the move complex. Moves or move complexes could then be taken as filling structural slots in the exchange. The simple move is defined as realised by a clause selecting independently for MOOD as above (incorporating hypotactic clause complexes); the move complex is defined as realised by a paratactic clause complex. Using an arched line to link moves in a move complex, Ventola re-analyses the two exchanges considered above as one; Halliday's (1985a) clause complex notation is included to show the relationship of elaboration between the second and third interacts:

K2	Have you ever heard of Baron Munchhausen?	
⌐K1	No, I've never heard about them.	1
⌐K1	It's the first time I've heard of them.	=2

This analysis is attractive, and could obviously be used to treat a large number of the act to act relations within moves analysed from a multivariate perspective by the Birmingham school. The preface, directive and comment in the following could be taken as a move complex realising the A2 move:

⌐A2	You mentioned a drink a while ago —	1	preface
⌐A2	how about getting me one;	x2	directive
⌐A2	it's awfully hot in here.	x3	comment

The major problem with this suggestion lies in what is to be treated as a paratactic clause complex. The sequence *No, I've never heard about them.* ^ *It's the first time I've ever heard of them.* was not in fact transcribed as such, but as two sentences (*Talking Shop: demands on language* 1978). With paratactic elaboration the line between dependent and independent clauses is admittedly not very clear. But the last move complex considered can be re-coded in a way which makes a paratactic interpretation very unlikely:

> You mentioned as drink awhile ago, didn't you?
> Well, how about getting me one.
> My reason for asking is that it's awfully hot in here.

In this example the conjunctive links are realised cohesively, between sentences, rather than within the clause complex (congruently through the cohesive conjunction *well*, and metaphorically through the nominalisation *my reason for asking*). From the point of view of conversational structure one might want to argue that whether realised cohesively or not, the interacts are functioning in the same way to negotiate an exchange of goods and services. But Ventola's definition of a move complex cannot be applied to the cohesively realised example (for a further example of a response which is not interpretable as a single move complex see the discussion of [4:2] in Chapter 4 below).

Halliday's (1985b) notion of *congruence* bears on the problems encountered here. Just as one can argue that there is an unmarked relationship between grammar and phonology whereby tone groups are associated with a single clause, so one might suggest that a similar unmarked relationship holds between a move and the clause complex: generally speaking a move in the exchange will be realised by a clause and its dependents. Whether or not to include paratactic dependents as suggested by Ventola can then be taken as an empirical question, subject to quantitative analyses of exchange structure. From the point of view of grammar, paratactically dependent clauses can select independently for MOOD; knowing just how often they do so would bear critically on whether or not to include them in the definition of the unmarked realisation of a move. One advantage of proceding along this tack would be to capture the sense in which the cohesive, three sentence realisation of the A2 move just considered reads as someone talking like a book.

Retreating somewhat then from the position adopted above, a move will be defined as a discourse unit whose **unmarked** realisation is as a clause selecting independently for MOOD. This admits as unmarked realisations the first and second examples below; in the first the reason for asking is reduced to a phrase through nominalisation, whereas in the second it is realised as a hypotactically dependent enhancement (notationally $^{x}\beta$). The third example can then be left open to textual interpretation. In contexts where the reason for asking is not itself negotiated, it can be taken as dependent on the demand for goods and as part of the A2 move. In contexts where it is negotiated (in light of the grammar presenting it as negotiable), it can be taken as an independent K1 move.

A2   Can you get me a beer in light of my impending death from thirst?

A2   Can you get me a beer   α
        before I die of thirst? $^{x}\beta$

A2   Can you get me a beer?
(K1?)   I'm dying of thirst.

The point is that seen as process, any dialogue is an on-going site of textual dynamism. There is nothing to prevent an interlocutor digging in and negotiating information presented as non-negotiable: *my impending death from thirst* is not presented for grading in the first example above; but one can imagine contexts in which it is contested, light-heartedly or not. Because of this dynamism it is not possible to define discourse units as categorically as grammatical ones. There is a system, but its potential for ongoing re-contextualisation means that there will always be rough edges for the analyst. Analysis in other words will inevitably involve interpretation.

2.5 Replacing constituency — dependency models

In Section 2.4 above it was seen that a degree of consenses at the rank of exchange begins to break down when considering the internal structure of moves. The Birmingham school's mulitvariate extension to the rank of act was contrasted with Ventola's univariate expansion of the move complex. A much more radical departure is found in the work of Fawcett et al. (1988), which replaces a constituency perspective with a dependency one. Unfortunately this shift is partially obscured by the representation of structures Fawcett et al. claim their system to generate.

2.5.1 *Fawcett et al.'s systemic flowchart*

Fawcett et al.'s basic strategy is to forego paradigmatic description at the rank of exchange and start instead with a network which at primary delicacy subclassifies initiating moves (into five classes). Their network, which they describe as a systemic flowchart, then opens up options in a subsequent supporting move, depending on the class of initiating move chosen; these choices in turn lead on to options realised in a third move and so on. The relevant network in reproduced below.

In order to generate what was described above as a A2ˆA1ˆA2fˆA1f exchange, one would first select [influence action], then [support] (e.g. NV comply), then [support] (e.g. gratitude), then [support] (e.g. disclaim difficulty). The perspective on exchange structure is thus a dynamic one (see Martin 1985a): the network works through the exchange move by move. The choices available depend on the point that has been reached. This is an important perspective on exchange structure, and on the structure of text in general (see Ventola 1984; 1987 for a dynamic perspective on generic structure). But the critical question here is whether it is the only perspective necessary as Fawcett et al. imply.

The kind of structure actually generated by Fawcett et al.'s network is a dependency one. The initiating act in the exchange is taken as Head, which is followed by a number of Post-Head moves. Using dependency notation, their flowchart suggests a structure of the following kind (Fig. 2.17) for the choices worked through above (using their example *Bring me some water. — (brings water) — Thanks. — You're welcome.*).

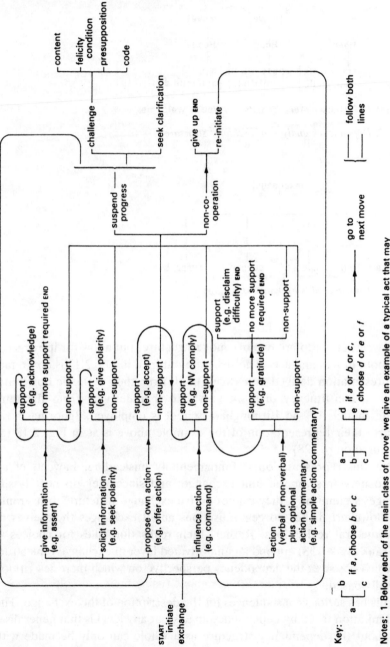

Fig. 2.16. *Systemic flowchart for moves in exchanges. Reproduced from R.P. Fawcett and D. Young [eds] New Developments in Systemic Linguistics, Vol.2: theory and application, 1988, by permission of Pinter Publishers Ltd, London.*

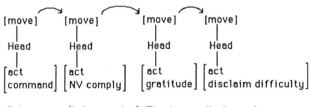

Fig. 2.17. Dependency analysis of exchange structure

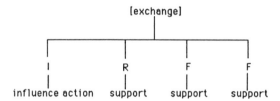

Fig. 2.18. Fawcett et al.'s exchange structure

Fawcett et al. do not explore move structure, but allow for it by recognizing both moves and acts. The structure outlined in Fig. 2.17 is not in fact the representation derived by Fawcett et al. from their systemic flowchart. Instead, a constituency diagram very like that deriving from the multivariate models of the Birmingham school is employed. Ignoring move structure, their representation of the example above is as in Fig. 2.18 (as represented on p. 128).

But this representation is fundamentally misleading. Fawcett et al. have no networks for the unit exchange; and since they do not classify exchanges systemically, they cannot derive exchange structure at this rank. Their flowchart makes no generalisations about exchanges themselves or their structural realisations. Rather, their realisation rules for choices at move rank (1988:138) append an unmotivated layer of exchange rank structure which obscures the dependency perspective on which their description is actually based.

This has serious consequences for the description of the exchange. The basic limitation faced by dependency analysis at any level is that generalisations about the dependency structure as a whole can only be made with respect to its Head. In the exchange there are two main candidates for Head: the obligatory X1 move and the initiating move. Fawcett et al. choose the latter. This means that exchanges are classified with respect to their opening move, giving five classes of exchange according to how the exchange begins:

1.	give information	It's mine.
2.	solicit information	Is it mine?
3.	propose own action	Shall I get you some water.
4.	influence action	Bring me some water.
5.	action (plus optional commentary)	(brings water) Here you are.

This contrasts with the classification of exchanges developed here in which, following Berry, action exchanges are opposed to knowledge ones, and then, exchanges initiated by the primary actor/knower are opposed to those initiated by the secondary actor/knower. The NEGOTIATION network in other words groups 1 and 2 together as opposed to 3, 4 and 5; and it groups 3 and 5 together, as opposed to 4. It further claims that action and knowledge exchanges are proportional in this respect. And critically, this classification is reflected in the structural descriptions generated by the negotiation network:

A-event: anticipate   Dx1 ˆ X2 ˆ X1
" "   : not anticipate   X1

B-event   X2 ˆ X1

Fawcett et al. in other words classify exchanges with respect to the function of their first move; *English Text* classifies exchanges with respect to structural configurations of move functions. Alternatively, Fawcett et al. could have subclassified the Head move with respect to what followed, using the [A-event/B-event] and [anticipate/not anticipate] features; sister dependency rules could then have been formulated to produce the appropriate sequences. But this would mean that the actual discourse function of the first move would have to be specified at act rank; and more seriously that the dynamic representation with which Fawcett et al. are very much concerned would have to be sacrificed. Sequent moves would no longer be dependent on immediately preceding moves, but on the Head.

As their description stands, since they take the initiating act as Head, Fawcett et al. are not able to show that the X1 move plays the same role in each exchange. In action exchanges for example the A1 is variously taken as I(nititation), R(esponse to Initiation) and R(esponse to Response), with I(nitation) realised by a propose own action move and R(esponse) by a NV comply + compliance marker or verbal comply move. Their structural representations for action exchanges are as follows:

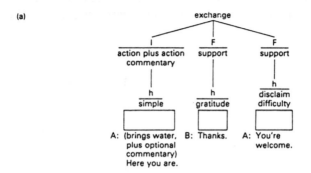

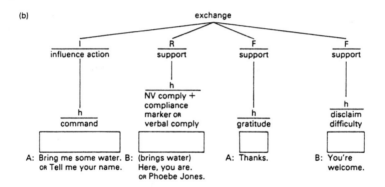

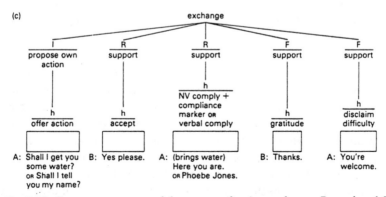

Fig. 2.19. Common structures of three types of action exchange. Reproduced from R.P. Fawcett and D. Young [eds] New Developments in Systemic Linguistics, Vol.2: theory and application, 1988, by permission of Pinter Publishers Ltd, London.

The only way to capture the relevant generalisations here is to have what *English Text* describes as the A1 move realised by the same class of act. But Fawcett et al. are clearly reluctant to pursue this course, since the way in which the A1 is realised is sensitive to its position in the exchange. This problem is even clearer in knowledge exchanges. The realisation of K2 and K1 moves differs radically depending on whether the exchange is anticipated or not:

[anticipate]		[not anticipate]	
Dk1	*What is it?*	K2	*What is it?*
K2	*— A Range.*	K1	*— A Range.*
K1	*— Right.*	K2f	*— Oh.*
K2f	*— Oh.*		

Fawcett et al. would have to treat the K2 move which initiates an exchange differently from that following a Dk1 move (a "teacher question"): as I(nitiation) realised by solicit information and R(esponse to Initiation) realised by a give polarity, give new content, try out new content or give choice of given content act. This obscures the parallel roles of the second-ary and primary knower in the exchange.

It can thus be seen that dependency models run into serious difficulties as far as making generalisations about classes of exchange structure are concerned. This amounts to say that the multivariate approach underlying the work of the Birmingham school provides a useful perspective on dialogic aspects of discourse structure, which needs to be seriously addres-sed before abolishing the rank of exchange as a level at which systemic analysis is pursued.

2.5.2 *Butler's daughter dependency approach*

Butler (1985b) develops an approach which involves both constituency and dependency, drawing on Hudson's daughter dependency model of clause structure (Hudson 1976; 1987). His model recognises constituency relations between exchanges, moves and acts as well as dependency ones. His struc-tural representation for *John, could you just hold this spanner for me a minute? I seem to need three hands. — Sure.* (takes spanner) is presented in Fig. 2.20 (in daughter dependency grammar function labels play a minor role; the description is constituted wholly by class labels here).

This kind of representation allows generalisations to be made both with respect to relations between constituents and their constitute (via

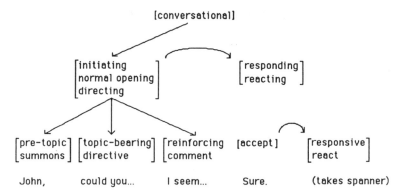

Fig. 2.20. Butler's daughter dependency exchange structure

daughter dependency rules), and between units without implying a constitute (sister dependency rules), and so could be used to overcome the difficulties encountered in a pure dependency description such as those
exemplified above. The model is however articulated from a synoptic
perspective; it does not generate in anything approximating real time, and
so choices cannot be consistently shown to depend on what has already
been generated as in Fawcett et al. It is to this dynamic perspective that the
chapter now turns.

2.6 Exchange dynamics: non-adjacent pairs

In 2.3 it was noted that one basic problem with the adjacency pair notion
was that interacts do not always come in pairs. This section is concerned
with the further problem that they are not always adjacent either. This
phenomenon can be illustrated as follows:

A2	Let's go to a movie.	A2	Let's go to a movie.
	— A what?		— I'm not keen.
	— A movie.		— C'mon.
A1	— Okay.	A1	— Oh, allright.

In these examples the A2^A1 exchange is interrupted by an additional adjacency pair. In the example on the left this has the function of clarifying the
experiential meaning of what has been proposed; in the example on the

right the interruption focusses on interpersonal meaning — on the inclination of the primary actor to participate. Interruptions focussing on experiential meaning will be dealt with first, under the heading *tracking*. Then interpersonal suspensions will be considered under the heading *challenging*.

2.6.1 *Tracking*

Clearly, in order to negotiate interpersonal meaning, interlocutors have to agree on what they negotiating about. Consequently, any comprehensive treatment of conversational structure must include discussion of the resources used to ensure that the experiential meaning under consideration is shared. One common signal of this is the back-channel (bch), which is used to monitor the dialogue, reassuring interlocutors that negotiation is proceeding smoothly (this phenomenon is most prominent in telephone conversations). These are realised paralinguistically (*hm*, *mm* etc.) and by polarity items (e.g. *yes*, *yeah*, *no*). They typically occur during another speaker's turn and do not appear to be sensitive to phonological, grammatical or discourse boundaries. In this they differ from follow-up moves, with whose realisation they partially overlap. This makes it difficult to distiguish between back-channelling and follow-up moves at the end of exchanges; for coding purposes, ambiguous moves can be taken as follow-ups at the end of an exchange unless they overlap with another speaker's turn. Ventola (1987:106-107) illustrates back-channel moves as follows:

K1	Server:	Say it you're looking at fourteen days,
bch	Client:	Hm.
K1	Server:	at Sanyor Beach,
bch	Client:	Yes.
		(2 seconds pause — S leafing through brochure)
K1	Server:	depending on which departure you wanted,
bch	Client:	Hm.
		(4 seconds pause — S keeps turning pages over)
K1	Server:	so all you have to do...

Back-channel moves contrast with other tracking moves, all of which have a potential response. This is because other moves occur where there is some doubt as to the experiential meaning being negotiated. This doubt may be on the part of the current speaker. Ventola's above example continues as follows:

| check | Server: | //2 fourteen days, right// |
| rcheck | Client: | Uhm. |

Here the Server checks on information included in the first clause of what is becoming a long clause complex to make sure two weeks is what the Client intends. Other tracking moves involve a change of turns.

These can be divided into those which explore experiential meaning coded in the previous turn and those which elaborate upon it. Simplifying slightly, Ventola's example of clarifying moves, which elaborate experiential meaning, is as follows:

K2	Client:	What time flights then go to Sydney tomorrow?
cl	Server:	//2 er morning or afternoon now//
rcl	Client:	Uh, mid-morning, early afternoon.
K1	Server:	Uh well, you've got a 9:30 and 10:15...

Clarifications then take the experiential meaning of a previous turn and elaborate it in specific ways. From the point of view of logico-semantic relations in the clauses complex (Halliday 1985a) clarifications can in principle be fleshed out to form a elaborating paratactic clause complex with the turn they clarify:

1	What time do flights go to Sydney tomorrow:
⁼2	what time do they go to Sydney tomorrow morning?

The rest of the tracking moves simply explore that experiential meaning that has already been made. Where this meaning has been completely missed, interlocutors request a complete replay, using items such as *what*, *pardon*, *huh*, *sorry*, *eh*, *I beg your pardon* and so on:

K2	Does she have Peter Pan?
cf	— What?
rcf	— Does she have Peter Pan?
K1	— Yes.

Where single elements of structure alone have been missed, second order wh questions (echo questions) are used to probe the preceding move; these may focus on either a major clause constituent, or the Head of a group:

K1	I found the book.
cf	— You found what?
rcf	— The book.
K2f	— Oh.

K1	I've got a cold.
cf	— A what?
rcf	— A cold.
K2f	— //1 Do you//

Finally, an interlocutor may replay experiential meaning, on a falling or rising tone, by way of confirmation. The rising tone signals less certainty, and so is more likely to receive a response; the response may include an expression of polarity, or a further repetition of the experiential meaning in question, or both:

```
K2    Does she have Peter Pan?
cf    — //2 Peter Pan//
rcf   — Yes.
K1    — No.

K1    She's already got Peter Pan.
cf    — //2 Peter Pan//
rcf   — //1 Peter Pan//
K2f   — Oh, she has, has she?
```

Where this repetition shows that in fact the experiential meaning of the preceding move has been misheard, it will be replayed, giving rise to sequences such as the following:

```
K2    Do you have Snow White?
cf    — The Snow Queen.
rcf   — No,
rp    Snow White.
rrp   — Oh.
K1    No.
```

These options are outlined below along with the appropriate realisation rules in Fig. 2.21.

Tracking moves are found at any point in exchange structure, although the more experiential meaning a given move makes explicit, the more likely it is to be misunderstood and so tracking is more common at the beginning of an exchange than at the end. Further restrictions should be noted. For example, partial confirmations realised through wh echo questions are only possible after major clauses; and repetitions are extremely unlikely after follow-up moves since by this point interlocutors are selecting from closed classes of items which are extremely predictable in terms of what has gone before. The general point is that the kind of tracking possible depends on the structure of the move that is being tracking (typically the immediately preceding one). Tracking options in other words depend on the point reached in the sequential unfolding of the moves in the exchange; they are not sensitive to exchange classes *per se*.

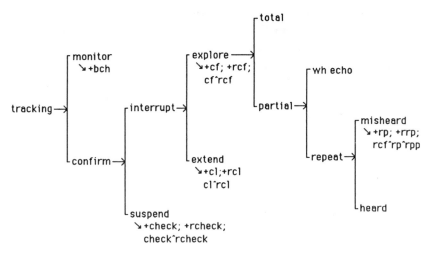

[**Key**:
bch = backchannel;
ch = check;
rcheck = response to check;
cl = clarification;
rcl = response to clarification;
cf = confirmation;
rcf = response to confirmation;
rp = replay;
rrp = response to replay]

Fig. 2.21. Tracking moves: clarifying experiential meaning

For this reason a multivariately based constituency model is inappropriate for tracking moves. Tracking is a feature of the dyanmic as opposed to the synoptic structure of the exchange (see Martin 1985a for discussion of synoptic and dynamic perspectives on semiosis). Tracking moves will consequently be treated as dependent on the moves they track, rather than as constituents of the exchange. No attempt will be made to formulate a dynamic potential for tracking moves here. This would involve making use of flowchart models (such as that suggested by Fawcett et al. 1988), transition networks (as outlined in Winograd 1983) or some such notation which makes choices available in terms of what has already been syntagmatically determined. System networks and realisations rules as developed for grammar are not appropriate since choices are made independently of text time.

For a hint of what one type of dynamic model for the exchange might resemble, see Martin (1985a).

In modelling exchanges, constituency relations will be shown to the left of the moves, and dependency to the right (following Ventola 1987). This gives rise to exchange structures such as the following, for exchanges including both synoptically and dynamically generated moves.

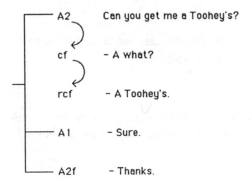

A2	Can you get me a Toohey's?
cf	– A what?
rcf	– A Toohey's.
A1	– Sure.
A2f	– Thanks.

2.6.2 Challenging

The second type of interruption to be considered is interpersonally, rather than experientially oriented and not only has the potential to suspend, but in fact to abort the exchange. The term challenging is taken from Burton (1980; 1981), but is being redefined here (some of her challenging moves have already been considered under the heading tracking above).

Aborting moves will be considered first. These function to extricate interlocutors from an exchange. With calls and greetings, they refuse attention:

Gr   Hi.
ch   – Piss off.

Call   John.
ch   – (ignore)

With negotiating exchanges, escape strategies are sensitive to what is being exchanged. Where this is an opinion, the interlocutor must refuse to grade, thereby avoiding a sympathising reaction:

Ex   A pity.
ch   – None of my business.

With goods and services, it is necessary to stop the primary actor accomplishing the non-verbal action which may accompany (proffer) or follow from (promise) the A1 move. In order to do this interlocutors typically frustrate the modulation projected by the initiating interact with a contradictory one. Following a Da1 move, this involves the secondary actor refusing to oblige the primary actor by expressing disinclination:

```
Da1 ⌐   Shall I get you a drink?
ch  ⌐    - No thanks.
```

After an A2 move, it is necessary for the primary actor to refuse to be obliged, either through disinclination or disability:

```
A2 ⌐   Get me a drink, will you?
ch ⌐    - No, I won't/Ican't.
```

Refusals in both environments strongly predict justifying moves (for discussion of the internal conjunctive relationship involved see Chapter 4 below):

```
Da1 ⌐   Shall I get you a drink?
ch  ⌐    - No thanks.
just⌐    I'm driving.
```

```
A2  ⌐   Get me a drink, will you?
ch  ⌐    - No,
just⌐    I'm too tired.
```

Commonly, the justification itself appears, **implying** the relevant modulation; these can usefully be coded by conflating challenge with justification:

```
Da1      ⌐   Shall I get you a drink?
ch/just⌐      - I'm driving.
```

With information exchanges the situation is more complex; it is not simply a matter of introducing a contradictory modality because these either function as or to negotiate the K1 move. Consider:

```
⌐K2    Is John coming?
⌐K1    - No.
```

```
⌐K1    John might be coming later.
⌐K2f   - No, he isn't.
⌐K1f   - Oh really.
```

Rather, as with exclamations, interlocutors have to avoid grading probability or usuality completely. The easist way to do this following a Dk1 or K2 move is to claim ignorance:

Dk1 ⌐ Is it a Range?
ch ⌐ – I've no idea.

K2 ⌐ What's that one?
ch ⌐ – I don't know.

This leaves the problem of what to do when an exchange is initiated with an A1 or K1 move and the secondary knower or actor does not want to be implicated. This involves undoing the service performed, possibly rejecting goods where this is possible:

A1 ⌐ Here you go.
ch ⌐ – I don't want anymore.

With initiating K1 moves, the relevance of their experiential meaning can be denied.

K1 ⌐ John might be coming over.
ch ⌐ – So what?

Alongside being aborted through the strategies outlined above, exchanges are also subject to interruptions that negotiate degrees of attitude, probability, usuality, obligation and inclination. As formulated above, the exchange allows some scope for negotiations of this kind:

⌐ A2 Finish it then.
└ A1 – I have to.

⌐ K2 Will you finish it?
└ K1 – Maybe.

But these negotiations may in fact be prolonged while interlocutors query the degree of authority invested in preceding moves. The exchange cannot proceed towards closure until some consensus is reached. Action exchanges arbitrate inclination:

⌐ Da1 ⌐ Shall I get you a beer?
│ ch ⌐ – Could you/ would you/must you?
│ rch ⌐ – I'm willing/ keen to/determined to.
├ A2 – Fine.
├ A1 – Here you are.
└ A2f – Thanks.

⌐ A2 ⌐ Get me a beer, will you?
│ ch ⌐ – May I/will I/must I?
│ rch ⌐ – You could/should/have to.
├ A1 – Allright.
└ A2f – Thanks.

Information exchanges probe modalization:

Dk1	So what is it?
K2	- //2 A Range//
ch	- Well, is it?
rch	- Probably.
K1	- It is one.
K2f	- Right.

K1	I reckon it's a Range.
ch	- Are you sure?
rch	- It could be.
K2f	- I guess so.

With exclamations, degrees of attitude are adjudicated, although as noted in section 2.2 above, the realisation of attitude outside the Mood function does not lend itself to prolonged negotiation:

Ex	He's such an idiot.
ch	- Kind of.
rch	- A complete imbecile!
ch	- Not quite.
rch	- Unmitigated!
Rex	- Oh allright.

In general however, negotiations may in principle be indefinitely prolonged:

K1	It's a Range.
ch	- No it isn't.
rch	- It is.
ch	- Are you certain?
rch	- Absolutely.
ch	- Really?
rch	- Yes.
K2f	- Alright then.

As illustrated in the examples of challenges querying authority, the orientation (Halliday 1985a:336) can be subjective or objective and explicit or implicit. This can be illustrated with respect to a modalization of probability as follows:

subjective: explicit	I reckon it's a Range.
"　　　　implicit	It would be a Range.
objective: implicit	It's probably a Range.
"　　　　explicit	It's likely it's a Range.

K1	It's a Range.
ch	- Is it?
rch	- I reckon/it would be/probably/it's likely.

In addition, both MODALIZATION and MODULATION have an indefinitely large range of metaphorical realisations. (Halliday 1985a:334) for example lists as just a few metaphorical examples of certainty:

> it is obvious that...
> everyone admits that...
> it stands to reason that...
> it would be foolish to deny that...
> the conclusion can hardly be avoided that...
> no sane person would pretend that...not...
> commonsense determines that...
> all authorities on the subject are agreed that...
> you can't seriously doubt that...

Because of these incongruent extensions, the category of challenge is a relatively open-ended one in the analysis of exchange structure. Grading with respect to attitude, MODALIZATION and MODULATION can be used to set parameters with respect to which a challenge can be mounted. But the more metaphorical the realisation of the challenge, the more it takes on the function of an independently negotiable move. For this reason challenges which might at first appear designed simply to suspend an exchange while consensus is negotiated often function to abort:

```
A2      Get me a beer, will you?
ch      - Do I have to?
rch     - Yes.
ch      - I can't see any reason why I should.
rch     - I'm more tired than you are.
ch      - You aren't.
rch     - I've been out all day.
ch      - So have I...
```

The point at which the interlocutors stop negotiating a protest to an A2 move and start negotiating K1 moves is far from clear. Abortion is even more likely when grading is implicated rather than explicitly manifest:

```
A2      Get me a beer, will you?
ch      - It's too hot.
rch     - No it isn't.
ch      - It's 30 degrees.
rch     - Rubbish.
```

It is thus hard to draw the line suggested by Berry (1981a:136) between less (queries) and more (challenges) serious disruptions to the exchange. However her analysis of queries delaying the appearance of predicted moves underlies the discussion of challenges presented here.

As with tracking, challenging depends on the meaning made by preceding moves, and so is best modelled dynamically. Dependency notation
has been used to relate challenges to the moves they apprehend. As with
tracking, no attempt will be made to model challenging as a dynamic system.

2.7　Consensus and debate

Before illustrating the analytical framework outlined above with respect to
three texts, it is important to re-contextualise the model. To begin, as will
be obvious to the reader, the discussion is systematically incomplete in at
least three major respects. First, it has ignored work on speech act theory,
which is clearly relevant to a more delicate categorisation of NEGOTIATION
and SPEECH FUNCTION and their realisation in lexicogrammar (see however Fawcett et al. 1988, Hasan 1988; forthcoming for relevant bridge-
building in this area). Second, it has not dealt with conversational analysis
as practised by the ethnomethodologists, and so is especially weak in the
area of turntaking (although less so in other areas as will be pointed out
below). And thirdly it has dealt only minimally with intonation; whether
this is treated as a meaning making resource in its own right following El-
Menoufy (1988), as most delicate MOOD following Halliday (1967c), or as a
direct encoding of discourse structure following Brazil (1981), this omission
is a serious one. By way of apology one can only point out that *English Text*
is being written as a reasonably comprehensive model of discourse semantics within the framework of systemic functional linguistics, and so could
not afford to devote more than a single chapter to conversational structure.

General questions of scholarship aside, one unfortunate aspect of these
limitations has to do with degrees of convergence between what Levinson
(1983) dismisses as discourse analysis (288-294) and extolls under the heading conversational analysis (294-366). Similarities include:

(i) a concern with the semantics of the core MOOD systems [indicative/
imperative] and [declarative/interrogative], whether explicitly acknowledged as in discourse analysis or not as in conversational analysis; compare
Levinson's (1983:336) table correlating content and format in adjacency
pair seconds with the treatment of SPEECH FUNCTION above:

Table 2.1. Levinson's correlations of content and format in adjacency pair seconds

FIRST PARTS:	Request	Offer/Invite	Assessment	Question	Blame
SECOND PARTS:					
preferred	acceptance	acceptance	agreement	expected answer	denial
dispreferred	refusal	refusal	disagreement	unexpected answer or non-answer	admission

(ii) An interest in [minor] pairs: e.g. greeting, calling and boundary exchanges vs openings, closings and turn-taking in general.

(iii) Recognition that dialogue is not built up simply out of pairs: e.g. five move exchange structure vs pre-sequences (pre-invitations, pre-requests, pre-arrangements, pre-announcements etc.).

(iv) Recognition that pairs can be interrupted: e.g. tracking and challenging moves vs repairs, side sequences and insertion sequences.

(v) The notion of markedness: e.g. congruence between discourse semantics and lexicogrammar vs preferred and dispreferred seconds.

At the same time it is important not to lose sight of the ideological predispositions which distinguish *English Text* from work in ethnomethodology. These have mainly to do with an orientation to linguistics as social action. This means that analyses presented here are designed to be useful in practical contexts, which means in turn that they must be comprehensive, not partial. That is to say they are designed to account at one level of delicacy for whole texts rather than focus anecdotally on interesting pair parts here and there.

There is no reason in principle why these macro- and micro-perspectives should not complement each other and in time converge. For this synthesis to occur however it would be necessary for conversational analysts to make more explicit their position on a number of key issues:

a. MODULARITY — how many components will the model of conversation have?; and what role will language play in this modularity?

b. REALISATION — how are these different components related (by rank, strata, plane, metafunction etc.)?

c. TYPE OF STRUCTURE — what kinds of structure are adjacency pairs: univariate, multivariate or other?; is constituency or dependency representation appropriate?

d.   ROLE OF GRAMMAR — will this be viewed as a meaning making module?; or will it be preferred to invoke the conduit metaphor (Reddy 1979)?

Unless some attempt is made to address these and similar questions, convergence will be slow. And it is doubtful whether ethnomethodologists would involve themselves in such an undertaking given their general resistance to deploying English resources for technicality as these have evolved in scientific discourse (see Halliday 1988b).

2.8 Analysis

To close the chapter, three texts will be analysed, using the descriptive framework outlined above.

2.8.1 Classroom discourse

The first text is from Butler (1984) (borrowing data here from Linda Gerot):

[2:1:1]	Teacher:	What's number six.
[2:1:2]		Um, Richard Best.
[2:1:3]	Richard:	— Yes.
[2:1:4]	Teacher:	— Look at question six.
[2:1:5]		Can you tell us the answer to that please?
[2:1:6]	Richard:	— Not care.
[2:1:7]	Teacher:	— Pardon?
[2:1:8]	Richard:	— Generally do not care for their young.
[2:1:9]	Teacher:	— Good.
[2:1:10]		Generally do not care for their young.

At exchange rank, the *English Text* analysis for this text is given in Fig. 2.22.

In his discussion of this example, Butler lists 13 facts for which discourse analysis should provide some account. The first 6 refer to a simplified sequence *Can you tell us the answer to question six please? — Generally do not care for their young. — Good.*

Fact 1:   The teacher's first utterance is a request for information; however:

Fact 2:   It is unlike most requests for information in many other registers

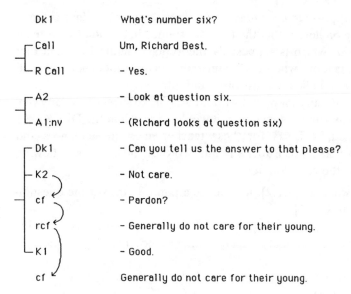

Dk 1	What's number six?
Call	Um, Richard Best.
R Call	– Yes.
A2	– Look at question six.
A1:nv	– (Richard looks at question six)
Dk 1	– Can you tell us the answer to that please?
K2	– Not care.
cf	– Pardon?
rcf	– Generally do not care for their young.
K1	– Good.
cf	Generally do not care for their young.

Fig. 2.22. English Text *analysis of Butler's text (exchange rank)*

(for example casual conversation) in that the teacher himself knows the answer.

Fact 3: The pupil's utterance is a response to the teacher's request, giving what he thinks is the required information; however:

Fact 4: Confirmation or rejection by the teacher is expected in such sequences. The rising intonation of the pupil's reply may be an explicit indication of this expectation.

Fact 5: The further comment which seems to be expected by the pupil is given in the teacher's second utterance.

Fact 6: This piece of dialogue, like the original authentic subtext, is a coherent unit.

To begin, it is clear that these facts go well beyond common sense observations about the text. The dialogue has already been theoretically digested, as borne out by the technicality of the language coding what Butler calls "facts": e.g. *utterance, register, casual conversation, rising intonation, subtext, coherent, unit.* And in any case, everyday language is itself a theory of the world, in this case, a theory of conversation: *teacher, request, information, answer, pupil, response, confirmation, rejection, sequence, reply, expectation, comment, dialogue, authentic*. What actually seems to be going on here is that the facts are framed in a kind of semi-technical *lingua franca*, which is supposedly theoretically neutral enough that students of conversation, whether discourse or conversational analysts, will suspend credulity and allow discussion to unfold.

Suspending credulity then, and without wishing to subscribe in any way to the epistemology Butler is invoking, it would appear that the Dk1^K2^K1 structure suggested by Berry for these teacher question sequences and adopted above covers all of Butler's points. To these he adds the following facts, referring to the complete text:

Fact 7: The teacher, in [2:1:2], nominates a pupil to answer the question he asks in [2:1:1].

Fact 8: The pupil, however, in [2:1:3], takes the nomination as a call for attention, presumably because he has not heard the question properly.

Fact 9: The teacher repeats the question in [2:1:5] (actually in a reformulated version).

Fact 10: He prefaces this with an act [2:1:4] whose purpose is to direct the pupil's attention to the written question to be answered.

Fact 11: The teacher does not hear the pupil's reply in [2:1:6], and so produces [2:1:7] which requests repetition.

Fact 12: The pupil recognises the request and repeats the answer (in an expanded form) in [2:1:8]

Fact 13: As well as evaluating the reply, in [2:1:9], the teacher repeats it [2:1:10].

These facts include a number of register specific observations, at least three of which require comment (for discussion of register specificity and socio-semantic networks see Turner 1985; 1987). The first has to do with facts 7 and 8: in classrooms there is a teacher who initiates almost all exchanges and a number of students who take turns in reply; and the teacher chooses who will reply. This means that for this register the calling system needs to be revised. The move by which teachers select pupils to respond will be referred to functionally as a Summons (adapting the Birmingham term for one class of act with a closely related function); this may be preceded by a Bid if pupils initiate the attention exchange, inviting selection — realised non-verbally through raised hands (or even in some classrooms by calling out: *Miss, Sir, Me* etc.). Fortunately for the *English Text* analysis presented above the pupil responds to what was intended as a Summons as if it was a Call, probably because, as Butler speculates, he was not paying attention.

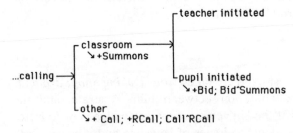

Fig. 2.23. Revised [calling] systems for classroom registers

The next issue has to do with the analysis of *Look at question six* as an A2 move unrelated to the following Dk1. This move would have been treated as a starter act functioning in Pre-Head position in an opening move functioning as Initiation in a conversational exchange in the Birmingham model. As is typical of starter acts, *Look at question six* is strongly related cohesively to *Can you tell us the answer to that please*? Referentially, *that* refers anaphorically to *question six*; lexically, *question* is the converse of *answer*; and conjunctively, the first move is the internal means to the second. As noted above, in general *English Text* prefers to distribute descriptive responsibility for text structure across phonology, lexicogrammar and the four different systems comprising the discourse semantics. There is nothing in the model however to block a register specific extension of the exchange-move framework developed above to include the rank of act if incorporating the relationship between *Look at question six* and *Can you tell us the answer to that please*? into the description of conversational structure itself seemed desirable.

Finally, there is the treatment of the teacher's repetition of the pupil's elaborated answer as a dependent tracking move. This is again a distinctive feature of the register; teachers consistently replay answers to Dk1 moves, partly by way of making sure all the class has an opportunity to hear them, and partly by way of providing an opportunity for reformulation into slightly more technical or abstract language where this is appropriate. The confirming function of these moves is so similar to that of tracking experiential meaning in other contexts, that there seems to be little gain in reanalysing them here. But again, if it seemed desirable, the rank scale proposed above could be extended to allow for two act K1 moves, consisting of both an evaluation (*Good*) and an accept (*Generally do not care for their young*) as in Coulthard (1977:106).

2.8.2 Service encounters

The final two texts to be considered are taken from *Talking Shop: demands on language* (1978), a collaboration between Film Australia and the Department of Linguistics at the University of Sydney with a view to introducing secondary school students to issues of language and register. Both are service encounters; for a detailed introduction to this genre see Ventola (1987). Text [2:2] takes place in the book department of a large inner city store, between a young salesperson and a prospective customer, the latter role being played by a professional actor (overlapping speech in bold).

[2:2:1]	Server:	Can I help you, sir?
[2:2:2]	Client:	— Um...I'm looking for a book on Baroness Munchhausen.
[2:2:3]	Server:	— Baroness Munch**hausen**.
[2:2:4]	Client:	— **It's a** new — it's a new Golden Book.
[2:2:5]	Server:	— Oh yeah.
[2:2:6]		**Maybe you'll find it** in here.
[2:2:7]	Client:	— **Have you seen the book**?
[2:2:8]	Server:	— Baroness Munchhausen.
[2:2:9]		What's it on?
[2:2:10]		**Is it** just **a little** fairy tale?
[2:2:11]	Client:	— **It's** — **it's** — uh...well, she was the first woman's fibber.
[2:2:12]	Server:	— Oh yeah.
[2:2:13]	Client:	— Have you heard of Baron Munchhausen?
[2:2:14]	Server:	— No, I've never heard about them.
[2:2:15]		**It's the first** time I've heard of them.
[2:2:16]	Client:	— **Well, he was a** — well, he was a very famous liar.
[2:2:17]	Server:	— Oh yeah.
[2:2:18]	Client:	— I thought you'd know all about it.
[2:2:19]	Server:	— No.
[2:2:20]		I've started here today.
[2:2:21]	Client:	— Oh.
[2:2:22]		Maybe I'll get something else while I'm here.
[2:2:23]		Do you — **What do you reckon** would be good for a five-year-old kid?

[2:2:24]	Server:	— **What for?**
[2:2:25]		A five year old.
[2:2:26]		She'll like fairy tales, does she?
[2:2:27]	Client:	— Well, fairy tales, anything like that, yeah.
[2:2:28]		Um...well let's have a...
[2:2:29]	Server:	— **Peter Pan?**
[2:2:30]	Client:	— **Train to Timbuctoo.**
[2:2:31]	Server	— Has she got Peter Pan?
[2:2:32]	Client:	— Yeah.
[2:2:33]		But we'll tell you what we haven't got: Train to Timbuctoo.
[2:2:34]		Where's Timbuctoo?
[2:2:35]	Server:	— Timbuctoo?
[2:2:36]	Client:	— Yeah.
[2:2:37]	Server:	— It's in Canada isn't it...somewhere up **there**...in the timber.
[2:2:38]	Client:	— **Canada.**
[2:2:39]		Well, I don't know about...
[2:2:40]		Timbuctoo.
[2:2:41]		No.
[2:2:42]		I think it's — I think it's in Algeria somewhere or another.
[2:2:43]	Server:	— Algeria.
[2:2:44]	Client:	— (??????)
[2:2:45]	Server:	— Oh yeah.
[2:2:46]		**Algeria.**
[2:2:47]	Client:	— **Uh...allright, I'll take that then**.
[2:2:48]	Server:	— Okay.
[2:2:49]		Just take it over to the cashier, please.
[2:2:50]	Client:	— Okay.
[2:2:51]	Server:	— **Okay.**
[2:2:52]	Client:	— **Thanks**.
[2:2:53]	Server:	— Thanks a lot.

Text [2:2] will now be considered, exchange by exchange. It begins with a Da1 move, which opens the service encounter. The client does not explicitly reply to this move, and the rest of the text could be interpreted following Ventola (1987:118) as a linguistic service filling the obligatory A1 slot in the exchange.

> Da1   Can I help you, sir?

The text continues with three knowledge exchanges, each beginning with a K1 move; the first is tracked and the second followed up:

> K1   Um...I'm looking for a book on Baroness Munchhausen.
>
> cf   - Baroness Munchhausen.

K1   - It's a new - it's a new Golden Book.

K2f   - Oh yeah.

K1   Maybe you'll find it in here.

This is followed by four more knowledge exchanges, each beginning with a K2 move. The first is tracked; the second and third explore the book's subject matter and genre. The client begins a potentially elliptical reply to the third (*It's — it's*) which he then reformulates by identifying Baroness Munchhausen. If responses are defined interpersonally, as potentially elliptical sequent acts, then this would have to be ruled out as a K1 move; experientially however it does relate to the book's subject matter and so will be counted as a reply here, which is then followed up. The fourth K2 move receives two replies, each of which reformulates the question in the same way by reconstructing *Baron Munchhausen* through reference as *them* (meaning both Baron and Baroness Munchhausen). The second reply simply reformulates the first thematically and so the two together will be taken as a move complex following Ventola's (1988a) suggestion.

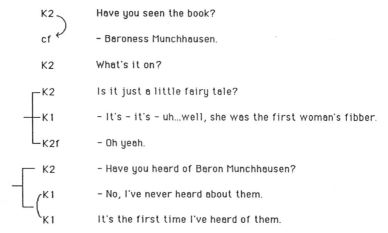

K2   Have you seen the book?

cf   - Baroness Munchhausen.

K2   What's it on?

K2   Is it just a little fairy tale?

K1   - It's - it's - uh...well, she was the first woman's fibber.

K2f   - Oh yeah.

K2   - Have you heard of Baron Munchhausen?

K1   - No, I've never heard about them.

K1   It's the first time I've heard of them.

These questions are followed by four knowledge exchanges beginning with K1 moves, the first three of which are followed up. The third K1 move is causally related to the negative reply preceding — a kind of justification. As noted above conjunctive relations will be treated separately in Chapter 4, rather than incorporated into the analysis of conversational structure here.

K1   Well, he was a - well he was a very famous liar.

K2f   - Oh yeah.

```
 ┌─K1          – Uh...I thought you'd know all about it.
─┤
 └─K2f         – No.

 ┌─K1          I've started here today.
─┤
 └─K2f         – Oh.

   K1          Maybe I'll get something else while I'm here.
```

The client then asks for advice; his K2 move is tracked twice, first with a wh echo and then partially repeated. This insertion sequence is followed by reply which like that in [2:2:11] is not potentially elliptical: the appropriate response to the wh question, fairy tales, is itself subjectively modalised, and then tagged as if not modalised at all. Halliday (1985a:340) glosses its meaning as "I think it likely she likes fairy tales; is that the case?" which he contrasts with *She'll like fairy tales, will she?* meaning "do you agree that it's likely?" Again, on the basis of its experiential relation to the K2 move, this will be treated as a response. The follow-up elaborates the experiential meaning of the K1, adjusting *fairy tales* to *fairy tales, anything like that.*

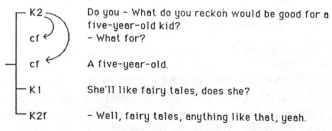

```
 ┌─K2          Do you – What do you reckon would be good for a
─┤             five-year-old kid?
 │  cf         – What for?
─┤
 │  cf         A five-year-old.
 │
 ├─K1          She'll like fairy tales, does she?
 │
 └─K2f         – Well, fairy tales, anything like that, yeah.
```

This is followed by the beginning of an A2 move which is simultaneously interrupted by both the client and server. The server replays his K2 move, to which the client replies, following on with an initiating K1 move.

```
    A2         Um...well, let's have a...

    K2         – Peter Pan?

    K1         – Train to Timbuctoo.

 ┌─ K2         – Has she got Peter Pan?
─┤
 └─ K1         – Yeah.

    K1         But I'll tell you what we haven't got: Train to
               Timbuctoo.
```

The client then questions the location of Timbuctoo; his K2 move is tracked, then answered. The answer is then tracked, challenged, tracked again, challenged again and finally replaced with the client's own suggestion; the client in other words takes over the role of primary knower with respect to the negotiation of the location of Timbuctoo (which incidentally is in Mali).

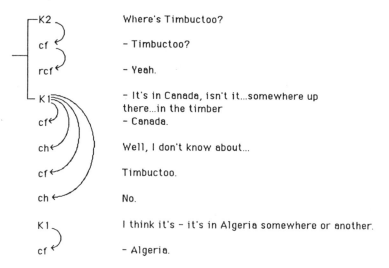

K2	Where's Timbuctoo?
cf	– Timbuctoo?
rcf	– Yeah.
K1	– It's in Canada, isn't it...somewhere up there...in the timber
cf	– Canada.
ch	Well, I don't know about...
cf	Timbuctoo.
ch	No.
K1	I think it's – it's in Algeria somewhere or another.
cf	– Algeria.

Move [2:2:44] is unfortunately unintelligible, which makes the exact discourse function of [2:2:45] (*Oh yeah.*) and [2:2:46] (*Algeria.*) uncertain. [2:2:45] may be following up on either [2:2:44] or [2:2:42] before; similarly [2:2:46] may be tracking either [2:2:42] or [2:2:44].

The text then approaches closure with pair of action exchanges. In the first the client offers to buy the book, to which the server agrees. The client is then guided in a further exchange on how to carry through the A1 move. Note that the first of these exchanges begins with what the Birmingham school would refer to as a marker, *allright*, which signals that the exchange is functioning to close the genre. It may in fact better to interpret the *Okay* move coded as A2f below in this light as a direct realisation of generic rather than exchange structure.

| Da1 | Uh..alright, I'll take that then. |
| A2 | – Okay. |

$$\left\lceil \begin{array}{ll} \text{A2} & \text{Just take it over to the cashier, please.} \\[2mm] \text{A1} & \text{- Okay.} \\[2mm] \text{A2f} & \text{- Okay.} \end{array} \right.$$

Finally the service encounter is brought to a close with an exchange of thanks. These have been coded as a greeting (leave-taking) sequence [cf. Ventola (1987) who treats similar pairs as finishing attention, a subclass of calling move; trading items of the same class is however more characteristic of greeting pairs (e.g. *Hi. — Hi.*) than calling ones (cf. *John. — What?*), and so the greeting classification will be preferred here].

$$\left\lceil \begin{array}{ll} \text{Gr} & \text{- Thanks.} \\[2mm] \text{RGr} & \text{- Thanks a lot.} \end{array} \right.$$

Text [2:3] presents a second service encounter text from *Talking Shop*. It will be analysed for NEGOTIATION, SPEECH FUNCTION and MOOD [no attempt will be made to assign SPEECH FUNCTION to tracking moves as the system built up in 2.2 above was based primarily on the semantics of major MOOD classes].

[2:3:1]	Client:	That's pretty.
[2:3:2]		Can you tell me how many cups that would hold?
[2:3:3]	Server:	— Em...about five or six, I think.
[2:3:4]	Client:	— Five or six?
[2:3:5]	Server	— Yeah.
[2:3:6]		Doesn't say.
[2:3:7]		Looks like it'd hold about five.
[2:3:8]	Client:	— Mhmm.
[2:3:9]		Who's the manufacturer, do you know?
[2:3:10]	Server:	— Em...not unless it says on it.
[2:3:11]	Client:	— Does the tray go with the set?
[2:3:12]	Server:	— It says it does, I think.
[2:3:13]		Yes.
[2:3:14]	Client:	— It does?
[2:3:15]	Server:	Yeah.
[2:3:16]	Client:	— It's all part of the same thing.
[2:3:17]		Is it made by Grosvenor, or whom do you think?
[2:3:18]	Server:	— You ever heard of Hacker?
[2:3:19]	Client:	— Hacker?
[2:3:20]	Server:	— Yeah.
[2:3:21]	Client:	— No.
[2:3:22]		Is that the manufacturer?

[2:3:23]	Server:	— That's what it's made by, yup.
[2:3:24]	Client:	— Oh, I see.
[2:3:25]		Well, let me think about it and maybe come back.
[2:3:26]	Server	— Okay.
[2:3:27]	Client	— Good.

Text [2:3] begins with a K1 move, congruently realised as a declarative. It follows this with a request for a linguistic service. This needs to be coded as K2 in exchange structure, since the exchange can only reach closure through provision of the relevant information. As far as SPEECH FUNCTION is concerned, this move can be taken as a demand for goods and services (a Command) since it could have included *please* and its reply could be prefaced with *allright*. Grammatically, this is a modulated polar interrogative projecting a wh question; the grammar and discourse semantics are thus incongruent with respect to the type of question being asked as well. The reply to the K2 move is itself tracked. Two K1 moves follow, the second of which is followed up; both elide their Subjects, whose referents are recoverable exphorically.

[In the analysis, the first column presents NEGOTIATION structure, the second SPEECH FUNCTION where appropriate, the third MOOD and the fourth the text itself.]

K1	statement	[declarative]	That's pretty.
K2	command	[interrogative]	Can you tell me how many cups...
K1	response offer to command	[elliptical declarative]	– Em...about five or six, I think.
cf			– Five or six?
rcf			– Yeah.
K1	statement	[declarative]	Doesn't say.
K1	statement	[declarative]	Looks like it'd hold about five.
K2f	acknowledge statement	(paralinguistic)	Mhmm.

Two further information exchanges follow, both beginning with K2 moves. The first is an information question, with a grammatically projecting tag: *do you think?* Its reply responds to the grammar of the projection, since the server does not in fact know who the manufacturer is. The second question is about polarity and realised congruently in the grammar as a polar interrogative. It receives two replies, the first less definite than the second; these will be taken as a move complex realising the K1 slot in the exchange. The K1 is then followed up, and the follow-up followed up, as the interlocutors negotiate the appropriate modality on which to close the exchange. What seems to have been resolved is then summed up by the client in a K1 move.

K2	question	[interrogative]	Who's the manufacturer, do you...
K1	response statement to question	[declarative – substitution]	– Em...not unless it says on it.
K2	question	[interrogative]	– Does the tray go with the set?
K1	response statement to question	[elliptical declarative]	– It says it does, I think.
K1	response statement to question	[elliptical declarative]	Yes.
K2f	acknowledge statement	[elliptical declarative	– It does?
K1f	acknowledge statement	[elliptical declarative]	– Yeah.
K1	statement	[declarative]	– It's all part of the same thing.

The next part of text [2:3] begins with a K2 move, which is once again is realised in such a way as to solicit both polarity and information; this time a paratactic group complex *Grosvenor or whom* is projected by *do you think?* The server responds to this with a question of her own, which is tracked and then responded to. This diversion prompts the client to ask again about the manufacturer, getting a direct answer this time round, which is followed up.

K2	question	[interrogative]	Is it made by Grosvenor...
K2	question	[interrogative]	– You ever heard of Hacker?
cf		[minor]	– Hacker?
rcf		[minor]	– Yeah.
K1	response statement to question	[elliptical declarative]	– No.
K2	question	[interrogative]	Is that the manufacturer?
K1	response statement to question	[declarative]	– That's what it's made by, yup.
K2f	acknowledge statement	[elliptical declarative]	– Oh, I see.

The service encounter then closes with an action exchange; the client offers to think it over and return, to which the server agrees. The A2 move *Okay* ellipses both Mood and Residue functions and so could be taken either as declarative (i.e. *Okay, I will.*) or imperative (*Okay, do.*) MOOD. The Da1 move includes a marker *Well*, signalling that the genre is winding down as with the *allright* in [2:2:47] above.

```
┌─ Da1    offer          [imperative]      Well, let me think about it...

├─ A2     acknowledge    [eliptical        - Okay.
│         offer          declarative/
│                        imperative]

└─ A1     response       [minor]           - Good.
          offer to
          command
```

2.9 Envoi

In this Chapter a general framework for analysing conversational structure has been proposed. Its focus was on the discourse semantics of MOOD, and so the discussion was restricted in several places to interpersonal meaning, setting aside as far as possible the logical, textual and experiential metafunctions. This is in accordance with the modular strategy to building up a picture of discourse semantics adopted in *English Text*. In subsequent chapters, a complementary focus on these other metafunctions will be developed, setting aside the problem of integration until Chapter 6, and the problem of context until Chapter 7.

As is apparent, modularity poses problems of explicitness even within the interpersonal perspective adopted throughout Chapter 2. Investigating the complex interrelationships between the systems of TONE, MOOD, SPEECH FUNCTION and NEGOTIATION is a major task which has barely been broached here. It may be wise to pursue this initially on a register specific basis. The generality across contexts of the descriptions proposed here mitigates strongly against more detailed statements of realisation, both congruent and metaphorical, across ranks and strata. What has been proposed will hopefully however provide a point of departure for this important work.

NOTES

1. *Always* would of course be realised between Subject and Finite (i.e. *she always does*).

2. The I/T superscript notation shows that dependent/embedded clauses are declarative by default; according to this network projected proposals have both nonfinite (*I asked **him to come***) and dependent (*I asked him **if he could come***) realisations.

3. Identification

Reference as semantic choice

3.1 Learning to refer

Chapter 2 began by looking at some of English's basic grammatical resources for structuring dialogue and worked towards an account of conversational structure by interpreting the discourse semantics of these. Chapter 3 begins on the other hand with a focus on text, not system. Consider then [3:1], written by a 7 year old in Sydney, Australia, after a class trip to the city zoo:

> [3:1] at the zoo
>   One day I went to the zoo and I saw Rhinocerous I moved to a Hippopotamus I touched him and he is hand and he is big and so I went on and I saw the tiger and this man was feeding him it was eating it up Mum tod me mv on and next came then a gorilla. I had a baby gorilla. My mum tod me to move on. I saw a watch. It was 5 ock.

This is a representative text from a young writer at a stage when spelling, punctuation and handwriting itself are still hard work. These struggles account for much of what is not English in [3:1]; for example, *I saw Rhinocerous*, with the article before *Rhinocerous* missing, or *he is hand* for whatever was intended there (possibly "he is hard"?). Beyond this the writer is still learning to manage the discourse semantics of written text. As far as CONJUNCTION is concerned the text makes use of "spoken" rather than "written" sentences; e.g. the "run-on" sentence *I touched him and he is hand and he is big and so I went on and I saw the tiger and this man was feeding him* (see Halliday 1985b on grammatical intricacy in spoken language). In addition, with respect to IDENTIFICATION some of the characters in [3:1] are introduced as if the reader already knew who they were; for example *the tiger*, *this man* and *it*. Of course the reader the writer may have in mind, the teacher, probably knows very well who and what the writer is referring to. The teacher has after all been on the class trip to the zoo. But

Table 3.1. First and subsequent mention of participants in text [3:1]

PARTICIPANT	FIRST MENTION	SECOND MENTION
'the writer'	I	I, I, I, I, I, me, my, me, I
'the zoo'	the zoo	the zoo
'the rhinocerous'	Rhinocerous	-
'the hippotamus'	a Hippotamus	him, he, he
'the tiger'	the tiger	him, it
'the man'	this man	-
'the food'	it	-
'Mum'	Mum	my mum
'the gorilla'	a gorilla	I (It intended?)
'the baby gorilla'	a baby gorilla	-
'the watch'	a watch	-

reference of this kind is not really appropriate in written mode, where context independency is functional across most contexts.

All in all, the writer refers to 11 people, places and things in her text: the writer herself, the zoo, the rhinocerous, the hippotamus, the tiger, the man, the tiger's food, the writer's mother, the gorilla, its baby gorilla and the watch. The ways in which the participants are introduced in [3:1] and referred to subsequently is outlined in Table 3.1.

What light does Table 3.1 shed on the system the child is using to get her characters into the text and refer to them once there? As far as subsequent mention is concerned, there is a clear tendency towards pronominal reference: 15 out of 17 second mentions are pronouns. Of the other 2 second mentions, one makes use of the definite article (***the*** *zoo*); the other uses a possessive deictic followed by a noun (***my*** *mum*). With first mentions, the picture is less clear. These are grammaticalised as follows:

indefinite article	a Hippotamus, a gorilla, a baby gorilla, a watch
definite article	the zoo, the tiger
pronoun	I, it
demonstrative	this man
proper name	Mum
no deixis	Rhinocerous

Some of these realisations seem appropriate; others do not. As suggested above, *the tiger*, *this man* and *it* seem to assume knowledge on the part of a general reader that s/he could not have. Yet the tiger is realised in the same way as the zoo (*the* + noun); and the food is realised in the same way as the writer (pronominally). Why is *the zoo* appropriate, but *the tiger* not? Why *I* but not *it*? Clearly the answer is not a grammatical one as with Rhinocerous, which is not a well formed nominal group. In the remainder of this chapter an attempt will be made to analyse the way in which participants are identified in English which gives a text-based answer to these questions. As with NEGOTIATION and MOOD, the focus will be on how English is structured to refer to participants, not simply on how it is used to do so.

3.2 Participant identification

Participant identification is the term introduced by the Hartford stratificationalists to refer to the strategies languages use to get people, places and things into a text and refer to them once there. A useful introduction to the work of this school is provided by Gutwinski (1976:41-53; see also Gleason 1968/1973, Taber 1966, Cromack 1968, Stennes 1969). Inspired by Gleason, these linguists were the first to give a strong discourse orientation to work on semantics. Their model has been very influential on the conception of discourse semantics being developed in *English Text* and so will be reviewed briefly here.

Working within a stratificational framework (see Lockwood 1972 for a basic introduction and Makkai & Lockwood 1973 for a collection of key papers) Gleason's proposals for a discourse oriented semology involved setting up semantic structures for texts referred to a **reticula**. These consisted of events and the connections between them (an **event-line**) and participants and the roles they play in events. The typical semological structure of a narrative, showing the event-line and participants only, is represented in Fig. 3.1. (following Gleason 1968:50)

Reticula such as these enabled the Hartford stratificationalists to focus on the way in which discourse structure conditioned the realisation of participants, sequences of actions (or **event clusters**; see Taber 1966) and role relations in grammar. The same participant for example would be identified in different ways (nominally, pronominally, zero anaphora), depending on context (see Gleason 1968 on Kâte). The same event cluster might be realised as a paratactic or hypotactic clause complex (*A man came home and ate supper* vs *After he came home, the man ate supper*; Cromack 1968:44). Or the same role relation might be realised as Subject or Object (*John likes opera* vs *Opera pleases John*; Gleason 1968:51). In systemic terms, reticula focussed on IDENTIFICATION, CONJUNCTION and TRANSITIVITY.

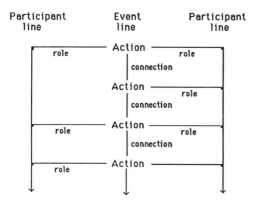

Fig. 3.1. Typical semological structure of a narrative (Hartford School)

One major difference between this model of semantic structure and that being developed here has to do with role relations. Unlike stratificational models, which typically dualise meaning and form, the systemic functional model assumed here treats grammar as a meaning making resource. Consequently case relations are handled at the level of lexicogrammar and mapped onto interpersonal and textual structures at that level. Another difference has to do with the greater emphasis placed on system, alongside structure, as far as IDENTIFICATION and CONJUNCTION are concerned. The work of the Hartford school remained at a very programmatic stage as far as semotactics was concerned.

The Hartford stratificationalists were particularly concerned to examine the ways in which discourse structures were realised variously across languages. Gleason 1968 focusses in particular on the way in which IDENTIFICATION and CONJUNCTION are realised in Kâte, discussing in some detail its somewhat exotic switch reference and conjunction system (see Martin 1983a for a more detailed discussion of participant identification in English, Tagalog and Kâte). The narrative reticulum exemplified above for example is realised differently in English and Tagalog, as the following text illustrates. At issue here are differences having to do with the way in which participants are tracked.

[3:2]   *H-in-alik-**an** ng babae   ang bata*
        kissed   woman TM child
        'The woman kissed the child'

pero t-**um**-*ulog* *pa* *siya;*
but slept still s/he
'but s/he still slept';

kaya **na**-*masdan* *siya* *nang* *kaunti*
so observed her/him little
'so she observed her/him awhile'

at *pagkatapos* **um**-*alis.*
and after left
'and then left.'

The basic contrast between English and Tagalog as far as participant identification is concerned is illustrated in the first clause: *Hinalikan ng babae ang bata* 'The woman kissed the child'. In English the roles of the woman and the child are marked by the word order (Subject ˆ Finite/Predicator ˆ Complement) at clause rank and by active voice in the verbal group. In Tagalog on the other hand word order in the clause does not realise experiential meaning. What marks the role relationships are the markers *ang* and *ng* in conjunction with focus affixes on the verb. In the first clause of [3:2], *ang* marks the child as Theme and *ng* marks the woman as not Theme; the suffix *-an* shows that the Theme is acted on. The Tagalog role marking system interacts with participant identification in that the Theme is almost always "definite" — and so translated into English as *the*.

This means that what at a first glance might look like definite and indefinite articles in the Tagalog system (*ang* and *ng*) are really case markers; and it turns out that Tagalog does not have a [definite/indefinite] article system as part of its grammatical resources for tracking participants. Like English it does have demonstratives, pronouns and proper names (each with their own distinctive case forms; and like English it employs ellipsis (clauses 3 and 4 in [3:2]) when the participant in question is recoverable from the context (much more frequently than English does in fact, since MOOD distinctions do not depend on the presence of a Mood function). And unlike English, the Theme in Tagalog is almost always definite.

The means that the work of identifying participants in English is done mainly through the nominal group, whereas in Tagalog the process is undertaken through co-operating clause and nominal group systems (which contrasts again with Gleason's account of Kâte where nominal groups and clause complexes are involved). In the remainder of this chapter English resources for participant identification will be outlined. To begin the discourse semantics of 'definiteness' will be presented, followed by a review of the implications of stratifying discourse semantics and nominal group systems. Subsequently two texts will be analysed and the chapter will conclude with a comparison of IDENTIFICATION and NEGOTIATION as far as discourse structure is concerned.

3.3 Participant identification in English: system

3.3.1 *Phoricity*

As noted in Section 3.2 above, one of the relative peculiarities of English as far as grammatical resources for identifying participants is concerned is its definite/indefinite article system. This system fleshes out nominal group structure to the point where every time a participant is mentioned, English codes the identity of that participant as explicitly recoverable from the context or not. This contrasts with the situation in Tagalog where in [3:3] neither participant is so marked; Tagalog's grammar need not assign definiteness, as is reflected in the ambiguity of the English gloss.

> [3:3]   *ka-pa-pasok ng babae   sa tindahan*
>   just entered   woman   store
>   'A/the woman has just entered a/the shop.'

Thus in text [3:1] above, aside from *Rhinocerous*, which is not a grammatical English nominal group, every participant is marked by the grammar as "given" or "new". Basically, indefinite nominal groups code the identity of the participant being realised as not recoverable, whereas pronouns, demonstratives, the definite article and proper names signal that the participant's identity is in some sense known. Reorganising Table 3.1 with respect to this semantic opposition (identity recoverable or not as opposed to first or subsequent mention), the realisation of participants in [3:1] can be outlined as in Table 3.2.

The basic discourse opposition organising Table 3.2 has to do with **phoricity** (from endo*phoric*, exo*phoric*, homo*phoric*, ana*phoric*, cata*phoric*; see 3.3.3 below). The nominal groups in [3:1] have been organised semantically into *phoric* and *non-phoric* classes according to whether their grammar signals the identity of the participant they realise as recoverable or not. Comparing Tables 3.1 and 3.2, it can be noted that

Table 3.2. Coding recoverability in [3:1]

IDENTITY NOT RECOVERABLE	IDENTITY RECOVERABLE
indefinite article:	**pronoun**: I, I, I, I, I, I, I, me, me, my mum him, it ['the tiger']
a Hippopotamus............................	he, he, him
a gorilla.....................................	I(t)
a baby gorilla	
a watch	
	demonstrative: this man
	definite article: the zoo, the zoo the tiger
	proper name: Mum

there are correlations between phoric and non-phoric groups and first and subsequent mention: all non-phoric groups for example are associated with first mention. But several participants in [3:1] are realised phorically at first mention: e.g. the writer (*I*), the zoo (*the zoo*), the tiger (*the tiger*) and the mum (*Mum*). A number of these are perfectly appropriate and will be taken up in 3.3.3 below (for a thorough discussion of the correlations between phoric/non-phoric items and first/subsequent mention in a related narrative context, see Du Bois 1980).

By definition then, phoric items require that information be recovered from the context. There are three main types of information that need to be recovered, and nominal groups may depend on their context with respect to any one, or any combination of the three. The first type, *reminding* phoricity, has been illustrated in the IDENTITY RECOVERABLE column of Table 3.2. It signals that the identity of the participant being realised is recoverable [throughout this chapter the phoric items under focus will be underlined in examples and the information they depend on dotted underlined; most of the examples are based on the narrative analysed as [3.87] below]:

REMINDING PHORICITY ('you know my identity')
[3:4]   The little boy had a frog in a jar.
        It ran away.

The second type, *relevance* phoricity, signals that the identity of one or more participants related to the participant being realised is recoverable. In nominal groups this is realised through comparative and superlative constructions (for nominal group structure see Halliday 1985a:159-169):

RELEVANCE PHORICITY ('you know the identity of related participants')
[3:5]   The boy found the frog.
          There was another frog too.

Finally, redundancy phoricity is concerned not with tracking the identity of participants but with signalling (in the context of nominal groups) that experiential meaning needs to be recovered from the context. This is realised through substitution and ellipsis (for a full account see Halliday & Hasan 1976:91-111 & 147-166):

REDUNDANCY PHORICITY ('you know my experiential content')
[3:6]   The boy found his frog
          and brought home a baby one too.

English nominal groups not only code all three types of phoricity, but combine them freely; for example:

the bigger frog   reminding + relevance
the big one   reminding + redundancy
a bigger one   relevance + redundancy
the bigger one   reminding + relevance + redundancy

This means that in principle a nominal group may depend on three distinct aspects of its context, as in [3:7].

[3:7]   The boy found two frogs.
          One was smaller than the other.
          The boy took the smaller one home.

There, *the smaller one* depends on *two frogs* for the recovery of the experiential content of its Head (redundancy phoricity); it as well depends on *the other* for recovery of the participant compared to it in terms of size (relevance phoricity); and it depends on *one* where the identity of the smaller frog was first established (reminding phoricity).

Aside from nominal groups, systems depending items on their context in terms of recoverable information are found throughout the grammar, and can be itemised as follows (at clause rank, as noted in Chapter 2, substitution and ellipsis signal interpersonal, and thereby experiential meaning as recoverable):

Reminding phoricity -

CIRCUMSTANCE OF LOCATION (see Section 6 below):

[3:8] The boy reached the pond.
       There he found his frog.

FACTS (Halliday 1985a:243-248):

[3.9] The boy couldn't find his frog.
       It worried him that he couldn't.

Relevance phoricity -

CIRCUMSTANCE OF MANNER & EXTENT (see Section 6 below):

[3:10] The boy ran quickly for a few yards;
        but his dog ran farther and faster.

CONJUNCTION (see Chapter 4 below):

[3:11] The frog ran away
        so the boy went to find it.

CONTINUITY (see Chapter 4 below):

[3:12] The boy felt worried
        and his dog did too.

Redundancy phoricity -

VERBAL SUBSTITUTION & ELLIPSIS (see Halliday & Hasan 1976):

[3:13] Has he found his pets?
        — He has done his dog,
        but I don't think he's found his frog.

CLAUSE SUBSTITUTION & ELLIPSIS (see Chapter 2 above):

[3:14] Has he found his pets?
        — I think so.

TONICITY (see Halliday 1967c):

[3:15] Did he bring home a frog?
        — //1 He brought home a **baby** frog//

Halliday and Hasan (1976) describe phoric items as presupposing information from their context; and where this information is found in the co-text, the link between presupposing and presupposed constitutes a cohesive tie. As the term presupposition is more generally understood in linguistics to refer to what remains true of an utterance when it is negated (e.g. Keenan 1971:45), it will be replaced here with the term *presumption*. Phoric items will thus be described as *presuming* information from their context. Note that this definition of presumption in terms of phoric systems approaches in its textual orientation, but is by no means equivalent with what Levinson (1983:29) refers to as pragmatic presupposition, "defined in terms of assumptions the speaker makes about what the hearer is likely to accept without challenge" (Givón 1979:50). Givón's definition appears

oriented to both interpersonal and textual considerations; here interpersonally oriented assumptions made by interlocutors about what can be assumed
and what is negotiable in dialogue were introduced in Chapter 2 above and
will be taken up again in Chapter 6 when discussing the meaning of Subject.

3.3.2 *Reference as semantic choice*

As far as particpant identification is concerned the central oppositions have
to do with reminding and relevance phoricity. With nominal groups, redundancy phoricity has to do with recovering experiential meaning, not participant identity, and so can be set aside here. The core reference paradigm is
thus:

	[presenting]	[presuming]
[comparison]	a smaller frog	the smaller frog
[-]	a frog	the frog

Formulated systemically as in Fig. 3.2 this gives the simultaneous systems [presenting/presuming] and [comparison/-]. Presenting reference signals that the identity of the participant in question cannot be recovered from
the context; presuming reference signals that it can. Presenting reference is
thus strongly associated with first mention and presuming reference
categorically associated with second mention. The [comparison/-] system
makes reference to the identity of related participants optional.

The realisation of the [presenting/presuming] system and the probability of phoric options being chosen is very much affected by a third system,
[generic/specific], which cross-classifies [presenting/presuming] and [com-

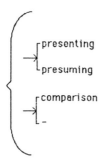

Fig. 3.2. Two central IDENTIFICATION *systems*

parison/-]. Generic reference is selected when the whole of some experiential class of participants is at stake rather than a specific manifestation of that class. This type of reference is typical of scientific report writing and is illustrated in [3:16]. There the world's deserts are referred to generically six times: *deserts, the true hot deserts, they, they, They, cool deserts* (bold in text). The text then turns to specific manifestations of this class: *five major hot desert belts, the largest hot desert, this, the great Sahara* (small caps in text).

[3:16] Fifteen per cent of the world's land area consists of **deserts**. **The true hot deserts** straddle the Tropics in both hemispheres. **They** are found on all continents between the latitudes of approximately 15 to 30 degrees, and **they** extend inland from the west coasts to the interiors of these continents. **They** are never found on east coasts in these latitudes as all east coasts receive heavy rains from either on-shore trade winds or monsoons.

Cool deserts are found further polewards in the deep interiors of large continents like Eurasia or where mountains form rain-shadows, which keep out rain bearing winds that might otherwise bring wet conditions.

There are FIVE MAJOR HOT DESERT BELTS in the world...THE LARGEST HOT DESERT extends from the west coast of North Africa eastwards to Egypt and the Red Sea — THIS is THE GREAT SAHARA that covers 9 million square kilometres...(Sale et al. 1980:45-46).

Text [3:16] shows that generic reference can be phoric: *they* refers generically to hot deserts, which information has to be recovered from the cotext. But [3:16] also shows that generic participants can be introduced either definitely or indefinitely: *the true hot deserts* vs *cool deserts*. Significantly, it does not seem to matter whether definite or indefinite deixis is used. The text can be re-written reversing the definiteness (i.e. *true hot deserts...the cool deserts*) without any apparent effect on the meaning; and *true hot deserts...cool deserts* or *the true hot deserts...the cool deserts* would have been possible too (cf. text [4:2:k] in Chapter 4 below: *With the Dachshund, a Dachshund is tabled*). The reason for this is that with generic reference definiteness does not matter; as long as the experiential content of a generic nominal group is understood, it is clear which participant is being identified. Generic groups in other words do not depend on their context in the way specific groups do; unless their realisation involves demonstratives or pronouns (e.g. *they* and *these desert water-tanks* in [3:17] below), their context is in effect simply that of knowledge of the language being used.

For similar reasons generic groups may neutralise number. Note that in [3:17] a *thick waterproof covering* could be replaced with *thick waterproof coverings* without necessarily implying that cacti have more than one layer or kind of covering to protect their pulpy cells. Similarly *animals* can be substituted with *an animal* (or to return to the question of definiteness *the animals* for that matter) without significantly affecting the meaning of the text.

[3:17] The cacti have extensive root systems spreading in all directions — sideways and downwards — to soak up as much water as possible when it rains. They are able to swell to store water, and they then use this water over long periods of drought. *A thick waterproof covering* protects these desert water-tanks with their soft pulpy cells, and their leaves are often reduced to thorns to cut down on water-loss and protect the plant from *animals* that might otherwise eat it for its moisture (Sale et al. 1980:59).

These neutralisations affect the nature of cohesive patterns in texts oriented to generic classes of participant; pronouns and demonstratives are commonly used to presume generic participants, but *the* is not phoric in generic contexts. This has the effect of breaking up the participant line into a number of short generic reference chains. This point will be taken up again in 3.5 below. Note that when qualified, pronouns can themselves be used generically: **He who hesitates** *is lost*. These pronouns simply point forward to their Qualifier and do not in themselves presume generic participants.

Because adjectives typically have a classifying rather than a descriptive function in generic nominal groups (realising Classifier rather than Epithet in Halliday's 1985a:163-165 terms), relevance phoricity is less commonly realised than in specific groups. However it is possible; the second paragraph in text [3:16] for example could have been extended as follows, with *flatter terrain* presuming the identity of the relevant participant mountains (cf. *the Dachshund...the bigger breeds of dog...the smaller breeds of dog* in [4:2] in Chapter 4 below).

[3:18] *Flatter terrain* would allow the rains in, which would lead to a very different type of ecosystem.

To this point three simultaneous reference systems have been proposed; these are represented as a network in Fig. 3.3.

Various types of [presenting] and [presuming] reference will now be reviewed, beginning with the feature [presenting]. Where specific reference is co-selected with presenting, the question of how many members of a class is relevant, giving rise to a [total/partial] opposition. The pronominal and

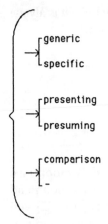

generic
specific

presenting
presuming

comparison
-

Fig. 3.3. Three central IDENTIFICATION *systems*

nominal realisations of these features are displayed in the following paradigm (throughout this section *sm* will be used to refer to unstressed *some*; using foot notation /ˌsome/).

	PRONOMINAL	NOMINAL
TOTAL	everything everyone everybody	every bee every boy
PARTIAL	something someone somebody	a bee/sm bees a boy/sm boys
	anything anyone anybody	any bee/bees any boy/boys

Both the [presenting/presuming] and the [total/partial] oppositions are neutralised with the interrogative pronouns *who* and *what* as can be seen in the range of answers possible to the questions in [3:19] and [3:20]:

[3:19] Who did you see?
— Everyone/someone//John.

[3:20] What did you see?
— Everything/something//the cat.

When it functions as a Deictic however, the interrogative *what* is selective;

in [3:21] partial reference is strongly predicted in the reply [*which* is always phoric and will be taken up under presuming reference below].

[3:21] What books did you bring?
— Just a few I needed/the ones I like. (cf. — ??All of them.)

		PRONOMINAL	NOMINAL
TOTAL:	HUMAN	who	-
	NONHUMAN	what	-
PARTIAL:	HUMAN	who	what boys
	NONHUMAN	what	what bees

Note that when participating in the prosodic realisation of negation (see Matthiessen 1988a:160-161) *anyone, anybody, anything, any* + noun and *nothing* do not realise participants. Thus the contrast between [3:22] and [3:23]: *anyone* provides a referent for *them* in the interrogative example, but not in the negative.

[3:22] Did you find anyone?
— Yes, they're waiting outside.

[3:23] I didn't find anyone.
— *Bring them in.

The IDENTIFICATION network has now been expanded as follows:

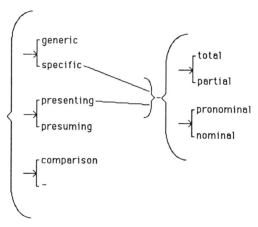

Fig. 3.4. IDENTIFICATION — expanding [specific/generic]

These options do not distinguish within partial pronominal reference between *somebody/someone/something* and *anybody/anyone/anything*. The contrast is between [restricted] reference to a particular member of a class and [unrestricted] reference to any of its manifestations. With partial nominal reference the picture is a more complicated one. The following paradigm provides a discourse oriented interpretation of the function of indefinite deixis where this is not conflated with the Head of a nominal group, but realised separately through the Deictic function in nominal group structure (for which see Halliday 1985a:160-162).

	MARKED:		UNMARKED:	
	SINGULAR	PLURAL/ MASS	SINGULAR	PLURAL/ MASS
UNRESTRICTED	any	any	a	/ˆ sm /
NONPARTICULAR	/some/	Ø	"	"
PARTICULAR	one	/some/	"	"
MAJOR ROLE	this, a certain	these, certain	"	"

This paradigm grades Deictics in relation to the importance to a text of the participant they introduce. There are various ways of measuring the centrality of a participant in discourse. The more central the participant the more likely it is to be Theme, the more likely to be Agent or Medium (see Halliday 1985a:144-154) rather than Circumstance, the more likely it is to provide a referent for a phoric item and so on. And in some languages the significance of the role a participant plays is grammaticalised. Stennes (1969) noted that in Adamawa Fulani phoric reference to focussed major, unfocussed major and minor participants was grammatically distinct. What is being suggested here is that for English the centrality of a participant conditions probabilistically the way in which it will be introduced.

Unfortunately there is only a little textual evidence supporting this claim. One piece of which the author is aware derives from research reported in Rochester and Martin (1979). Unpublished analyses undertaken in conjunction with this research showed that mass and plural nouns lacking an indefinite article (e.g. *frogs*, *grass*) provided referents for other nominal groups three times less often than when an indefinite article was present (e.g. *some frogs*, *some grass*). Further to this Du Bois (1980:220) suggests on the basis of his analysis of the English Pear Stories that "for humans, the zero-form plural is not used to mark non-identifiable referents. In contrast with characters, initial mentions of objects as zero-form plurals were not uncommon." Given that humans tend to play more important roles in narrative than non-humans, this lends additional support to the grading proposed above.

What is perhaps best treated as a hypothesis then is that English uses the unmarked realisations *a* and /ʌsm/ when it does not wish to comment on the centrality of the participant being introduced. However, if it does wish to comment, it scales deictics along the following cline:

LEAST CENTRAL

He asked <u>any guy</u> he met there. (pl. — any guys)
He asked /<u>some</u>/ guy he met there. (pl. — guys)
He asked <u>one guy</u> he met there. (pl. — /some/ guys)
He asked <u>this guy</u> he met there. (pl. — these guys)

MOST CENTRAL

The outer poles of this scale involve the features [unrestricted] and [major role]. The option [unrestricted] is realised by *any*, as it is with specific presenting pronominal groups (i.e. *anyone, anybody, anything*), and signals that it does not matter which member of the experiential class in question is being referred to. At the other end of the scale, the feature [major role] is realised by the demonstratives *this/these* in more "spoken" registers and *a certain/ certain* in more "written" ones. Needless to say, the demonstratives *this/these* are not phoric in this usage; rather, they signal that one participant in particular is focal at this point in the text. The contrast is between [3:24] and [3:25] below.

[3:24] So he looked under **any log** he could;
        but there was nothing to be found.

[3:25] So he looked under **this log**;
        but it was slippery
        and he couldn't hang onto it.
        The log slipped out of his hand
        and rolled away towards his dog...

In between these outer poles is the contrast between [nonparticular] and [particular] reference. This opposition predicts that the relevant deixis in [3:26] and [3:27] codes participants less central to the text than those in [3:28] and [3:29].

NONPARTICULAR:
[3:26] The boy passed **/some/ rock** (or other) and then went down to the pond.

[3:27] The boy looked around and saw **trees, bees and grass,** but no frog.

PARTICULAR:

[3:28]   There was **one frog** there (in particular) that the boy liked...

[3:29]   There were **/some/ frogs** there (in particular) that the boy liked...

This scale is in certain respects a natural development in a language like English which has developed definite/indefinite articles the way it has. Prior to the development of this system there was no need to mark every nominal group as "given" or "new". But "newness" could be made explicit, as it can be in many languages (see Martin 1983a:60-62 for discussion), with the cardinal *one* or, in the plural, a quantifier like *some*. In Tagalog for example *isa* 'one' and *ilan* 'few' can even be used to over-ride the very strong association of Theme with definiteness noted above in 3.2. The use of related items to realise [particular] reference in English reflects this pattern.

According to the *Oxford English Dictionary*, *any* was typically used in Old English in interrogative, hypothetical or conditional clauses, where the participant referred to has a speculative existence. So it seems a natural development for this item to extend its meaning to take over the dismissive 'it doesn't matter who' reference referred to as [unrestricted]. Finally, there is a kind of iconicity involved in selecting proximate demonstrative reference to refer to central participants which might be glossed as 'near in importance to the speaker' (cf. the interpretation of proximate as 'strongly associated with' below). These suggestions need to be checked across a range of languages before firm hypotheses can be developed; but some kind of reinterpretation of cardinals, quantifiers and proximate demonstratives in terms of the importance of a participant when first introduced in text is likely to be critical to be an interpretation of indefinite reference in many languages. Presenting reference will not be considered in more detail here; the IDENTIFICATION network has now been extended as in Fig. 3.5.

To this point the systems used to introduce specific participants have been considered in some detail. The next step is to develop the feature [presuming], taking into account phoric options.

As noted in 3.1 above, English resources for signalling that the identity of a participant is recoverable include proper names, pronouns and the definite article and demonstratives. Choosing among these resources depends in part on how much experiential meaning needs to be made explicit to identify the participant in question. Proper names and pronouns are very restricted in the forms of experiential modification they allow (see

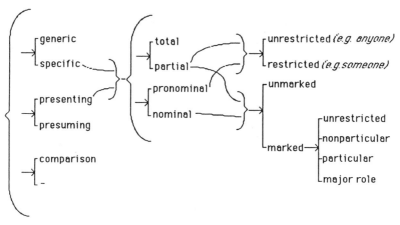

Fig. 3.5. Expanded IDENTIFICATION *network*

Halliday 1985a:168) and so can only be selected when next to no experiential meaning is required. However, interpersonal considerations are also critical; referring to participants by name opens up an important set of interpersonal resources particularly sensitive to tenor and ideology which unfortunately cannot be pursued here. For discussion of the interpersonal semantics of naming see Poynton (1984, 1985/1989, 1990a).

Referring to participants by name involves making use of signs which have been assigned to individuals in a community to uniquely identify them. There are obviously more participants than names to go round in most communities and the system is only functional as long as participants in a given context can be named differently. Texts assign names to unfamiliar participants where necessary, making use of elaborating structures — for example the identifying clause in [3:30]:

[3:30] There was a little boy. His name was **Tommy**.

Names are phoric and when the identity of the participant to which they refer is not recoverable participant identification breaks down. Note the attested repair in [3:31] as the speaker realises her addressee is not a member of the community that can uniquely identify *John* (data from Guenter Plum; see Plum 1988):

[3:31] ...Friends of my parents had a beagle and **John** hadn't seen a beagle (that's my husband) so he went and looked at one...

[Note that names can be used as common nouns: *the Smith we knew back in Perth, a young Smith I hadn't yet met, a few of the Smiths who came*. In addition there are marked realisations in which *a* means 'with whom you wouldn't be familiar' (e.g. *a Mrs. John Smith*) and stressed *the* (with "spelling pronunciation" /ðiy/) means 'the famous one you will have heard of' (e.g. / *not* / *the* / *Michael* / *Halli* / *day* /). The point is however that names do not require a definite article to be "definite".]

Where names are either not available or inappropriate, signs will be selected that have not been tagged for specific individuals. Where number, gender and case are sufficient to identify the participant in question, personal pronouns will be used (excluding the generalised pronoun *one*, which is not phoric): *I, me, mine, my; we, us, ours, our; you, yours, your; he, him, his; she, her, hers, her; they, them, theirs, their; it, its*. For systemic interpretations of this system see Halliday and Hasan (1976:44), Halliday (1985a:168), Fawcett (1988a). Here a simple distinction will be made between interlocutor (1st and 2nd person) and non-interlocutor (3rd person) roles.

Where more experiential meaning is required, a common noun will be selected as Thing, and Numerative, Epithet, Classifier and Qualifier elements added as appropriate (for systemic interpretations of nominal group structure see Fawcett 1980; Halliday 1985a:159-175). The choices that are relevant to the discussion at this point have to do with the Deictic function. If the interlocutor/non-interlocutor opposition is relevant to identifying the participant in question then demonstrative reference will be selected (see Halliday 1985a:160 who notes this connection between person and demonstratives; this relationship is even clearer in languages like Tagalog which distingush as well with demonstratives between proximity to the speaker and proximity to the addressee). This opposes participants near (in the sense of what Halliday 1985a:160 calls "associated with") the interlocutors (*this/these*) to those less proximate (*that/those*). Where "proximity" to the interlocutors is not relevant the definite article *the* can be used to mark the identity of participants as recoverable.

This subclassification of presuming reference is formulated systemically in Fig. 3.6. below. Naming is referred to as [unique] reference and opposed to [variable]; within variable reference [pronominal] and [nominal] are contrasted; then nominals are subclassified into those with demonstratives [directed] and those without [undirected]; finally directed reference is broken down into [proximate] and [distant].

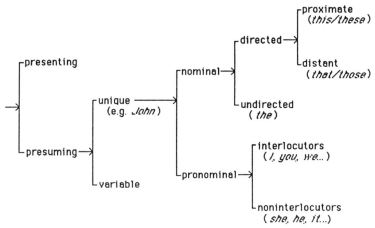

Fig. 3.6. Expanding [presuming] reference

The final set of distinctions relevant to presuming reference covers the
of these have the function of combining relevance with reminding phoricity
in the context of [undirected] groups. The classes of item in question are:

phoric Deictics:	both, either, neither, each, which
ordinative Numeratives:	first, second, third etc.; next, last etc.
superlative Epithets:	biggest, most enormous etc.

Each of these items has the function of referring to a group of participants
relevant to the participant being identified by virtue of including it as a
member. So, within undirected reference there is a contrast between presuming the identity of the participant being realised and optionally presuming the identity of group of participants to which it belongs. This opposition
is illustrated in the difference between [3:32] and [3:33]:

[3:32] The boy took the frog home.

[3:33] The boy took the smallest frog home.

In [3:32] *the frog* signals that the identity of the frog is recoverable; but in
[3:33] *the smallest frog* signals not only that the identity of the frog the boy
took home is recoverable (reminding phoricity), but that the identity of the
group of frogs from which it was selected is presumed as well (relevance
phoricity).

The general phoric question word involving reference to a superset is
which. *Which* questions are responded to either by using an Epithet or

Numerative to select the relevant member of the superset or by using a Deictic that says it doesn't really matter. This opposition is illustrated in [3:34]:

[3:34] Which one would you like?
NON-SELECTIVE — Both/either/neither/ each.
SELECTIVE — The <u>first</u> one/the <u>next</u> one/the <u>biggest</u> one etc.

The [non-selective] Deictics distinguish between individuated (*each*) and dual (*both, either, neither*) reference. Within dual, inclusive *both* contrasts with alternative *either/neither*.

For selective Deictics the basic distinction has to do with selection on the basis of order, as realised through ordinative Numeratives and selection on the basis of quality, as realised through superlative Epithets. Order is realised through ordinal numerals (*first, second, third* etc.) or position in time and space (e.g. *next, last, final, ultimate, penultimate* etc.). Quality is realised through superlative adjectives, where these are not simply attitudinal; note that in *He made **the dumbest moves*** the superlative morphology is not phoric if *the dumbest moves* simply means 'some very dumb moves worth exclaiming about'. The opposition between order and quality is illustrated in [3:35]:

[3:35] Which one will we take?
ORDER — The <u>next</u> one/the <u>last</u> one/the <u>penultimate</u> one etc.
QUALITY — The <u>biggest</u> one/the <u>flattest</u>/the <u>reddest</u> one etc.

Phoric reference to supersets presumed on the basis of quality is recursive in the sense that where more than one quality is relevant to isolating one participant from the set, two or more superlative Epithets can be used. Note that this does not mean that extra supersets are being presumed. The holiday is [3:36] is isolated along three dimensions within the same superset:

[3:36] What are you hoping for?
— The <u>longest, most relaxing, most refreshing</u> holiday ever.

This subclassification of undirected reference is outlined systemically in Fig. 3.7. Reference to a [superset] is made optional; then [selective] reference to a particlar member of the superset is contrasted with [non-selective] reference; the remaining options break down selective and non-selective reference as these have just been described (the recursivity of the [quality] feature is not shown).

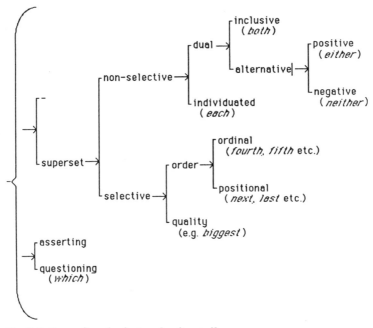

Fig. 3.7. Expanding the feature [undirected]

The description is now in a position to review the following proportionalities between presenting and presuming superset Deictics (taken from Hudson 1974). Note that /θ/ and /tʃ/ are strongly associated with phoric Deictics in English: *which, each, either, neither, both, the, this, that, these, those* (for *such, other; there, then* see below) — the phonaesthesia perhaps deriving from the iconicity of pointing with the tongue.

PRESENTING: PRESUMING SUPERSET::
what/who:which::
every:each::
any:either::
no:either::
all:both

The final set of options to be developed is also associated with relevance phoricity — but of a comparative rather than a superlative kind. Comparative reference differences from superset reference in that it combines freely with both presenting and presuming groups: *a/the larger frog, a/the more attractive option*. Presenting groups on the other hand do not presume supersets in English. In apparent counterexamples to this principle such as [3:37] the superlative adjective functions as a Classifier, not an Epithet, and does not presume a group of prizes of which the participant in question is the second (similarly *A **First Book** in German*, i.e. 'a primer'):

> [3:37] What's this one then?
> — It's just <u>a second prize</u> I picked up at the Easter Show.

This explains both the oddity and the rhetorical effect of Sachs, Schegloff and Jefferson's *A **simplest systematics** for the organisation of turn-taking for conversation* which presumes a set of turn-taking systematics without in fact claming that theirs is uniquely identifiable among this set as simpler than the others (the effect is not the same as writing *one of the simplest systematics*; cf. Halliday and Hasan 1976:81 who suggest that *a latest notion* means 'one of the latest notions' — implying that they would prefer to crossclassify the [presenting/presuming] system with both comparison and superset reference, rather than making superset reference dependent on the feature [undirected]).

For these reasons then the [comparison/-] system is simultaneous with the options [presenting/presuming] and [generic/specific]. And where both types of relevance phoricity are selected (via comparison and superset), the superset reference will be realised first, isolating a participant among the class made relevant through comparison: *the biggest greener frog*. So while there can be a number of greener frogs, of which one is the biggest, there cannot be a number of biggest frogs, among which one is greener: **the greener biggest frog*.

Comparison is realised through Post-Deictics (which precede Numeratives, if any), Numeratives and Epithets (which follow Numeratives, if any) in nominal group structure (realisations taken from Halliday and Hasan 1976:76; for nominal group structure see Halliday 1985a:162-169).

POST-DEICTIC   (an)other, same, different, identical , similar

NUMERATIVE   more, fewer, less, further, additional;
so/as + quantifier [much, many, little, few etc.],
equally + quantifier ["   "   "   "   "]

EPITHET   such, (an)other/else, same, different, identical, similar; bigger;
so/as/more/less/such + adjective,
similarly/identically/equally + adjective

Comparison is also realised through comparative Attributes in intensive attributive relational clauses (see Halliday 1985a:115):

[3:38] This one was   bigger/more enormous.
        Carrier   Process   Attribute

As with superset reference, the nature of the experiential relevance of the presumed participant may or may not be specified. It is **not** specified when *other, same, different, identical* and *similar* function as Post-Deictic or when the same items or *such* realise the Epithet; it **is** specified when comparative quantifiers and adjectives are deployed. This opposition is illustrated below.

GENERAL -   the   other   four   frogs
                     Deictic Post-Deictic Numerative Thing

                     the   four   other   frogs
                     Deictic Numerative Epithet   Thing

EXPERIENTIALISED -

QUALITY: the   four   bigger   frogs
                     Deictic Numerative Epithet   Thing

                     the   four   equally big   frogs
                     Deictic Numerative Epithet (β α)   Thing

QUANTITY: fewer   frogs
                     Numerative   Thing

                     equally many   frogs
                     Numerative (β α) Thing

Similarly, as with superset reference, comparison in terms of quality is recursive, so that a relevant participant can be presumed with respect to an indefinite number of qualities. Again, this does not mean that each comparison presumes an additional relevant participant. If *a smaller, lighter coloured, cuter frog* in [3:39] is qualified, it is qualified with respect to another or another set of participants, not three different participants, one bigger, one darker and a third less cute: *a smaller, lighter coloured, cuter frog than the one(s) I saw.*

[3:39] It was a smaller, lighter coloured, cuter frog.

As far as the nature of the comparison itself is concerned, this may be on the basis of similarity or difference. With general comparison this is the contrast between *such, same, equal, similar, identical* realising [semblance] and *other, different, else* realising [difference]. Where the comparison is experientialised, [difference] is realised either through the comparative morpheme *-er* or through submodification of a two or more syllable adjective with *more* or *less*; [semblance] is always realised through submodification in this context:

> so/as/such/equally/similarly/identically + adjective.

The following paradigm exemplifies this crossclassification.

	QUANTITY	QUALITY
DIFFERENCE	fewer frogs	bigger frogs
SEMBLANCE	as many frogs	such big frogs
	β α	β α

The feature [semblance] could be further subclassified, into [identity] and [similarity]. This makes it possible to note the way in which the features [presenting] and [presuming] condition its realisation; *such* occurs only in the context of presenting reference, *same* only in the context of presuming reference.

	PRESENTING	PRESUMING
SIMILARITY	a similar frog; such a frog	the similar frog;
IDENTITY	an identical frog; an equal amount	the identical frog; the equal amount; the same frog/amount

The distinction between [similarity] and [identity] also accounts for the difference between *so* and *that* where they realise comparison in Attributes. Both are colloquial in register. *So* realises similarity and points to the non-verbal context, often to an iconic measuring gesture:

> [3:40]   The frog was about <u>so big</u>.

That realises [identity] and depends on information recoverable from either the verbal or non-verbal context; it is exclamatory in intensity:

> [3:41]   You mean he was <u>that stupid</u>!

The final comparison system to be considered relates participants to relevant proposals (see Halliday 1985a:235-247) and is realised by *too* and *enough*. These items assess quantity or quality with respect to the amount or degree necessary to enable a presumed proposal; this function is perhaps clearest when the proposal is embedded in the same nominal group as in [3:42] and [3:43]:

> [3:42]   The boy was <u>too</u> upset [[to eat his breakfast]].

> [3:43]   The boy had <u>enough</u> time [[to finish it]].

Too realises [difference]; [3:42] means that the boy was upset to a degree **different** from that required to eat his breakfast. *Enough* on the other hand realises [semblance]; [3:43] means that the boy had the amount of time **identical** to that he needed to finish.

Where the proposal presumed is not structurally embedded as a Qualifier, it has to be recovered from the context. This is illustrated in [3:44] to [3:45]. *Enough* functions as a Numerative as far as assessing quantity is concerned, whereas *too* submodifies:

[3:44] He promised that he would pay
        if he had enough money.

[3:45] He asked them to water the garden
        if there was too little time.

Both *too* and *enough* function as submodifiers when assessing quality:

[3:46] The boy felt the need to take the frog home;
        but it was too young.

[3:47] His brief was to find his frog;
        but was he clever enough?

Comparison systems are formulated systemically in Fig. 3.8. The feature [comparison] is cross-classified with respect to two systems: the [general/ experientialised] comparison system which distinguishes between making the dimensions of quantity or quality explicit or not, and the [semblance/

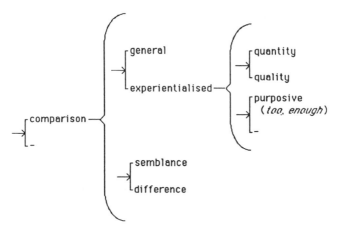

Fig. 3.8. Comparison systems

difference] system which opposes comparison in terms of how participants are alike to comparison in terms of how they are unalike. The feature [experientialised] is then itself cross-classified according to whether the dimension of quantity or quality is relevant and whether another participant or a proposal is presumed (again, the recursivity of the [quality] feature is not shown).

This completes the development of the reference network to the level of delicacy under focus here. Before briefly reviewing its principal systems however, two ways of avoiding the options discussed above need to be taken into account. One has to do with "the grammar of little texts" (Halliday 1985a:372-377), as found in headlines, telegrams, titles, labels, diagrams, instructions, notices, billboards, notes and so on. In these registers requirements of space may mean that parts of the grammar which are not absolutely essential will actually be turned off. Where this includes turning off deixis in nominal group structure, the network of proportionalities systemicised above will simply not be relevant. The only Deictic found in the following list for example is *the*, which cannot be left out of *flash in the pan*, and because of the idiom is not in fact phoric (formatting as in original small texts):

> **Flash in the pan fizzles**
> **agenda planning diary**
> Home address:
> Blood type:
> Doctor:
> **METRIC SYSTEM: DEMYSTIFICATION**
> COMMON MARKET: FREE TRADE AREA
> **Curbs to be eased on loan sharks**

The second way of avoiding the reference systems outlined above is to use [generalised] reference (Halliday & Hasan 1976:53-54). Halliday and Hasan list its realisations, gloss their meanings and exemplify this type of reference as follows:

you/one	'any human individual' You never know.
we	'a group of individuals with which the speaker wishes to identify' (including royal and editorial we) We don't do that sort of thing here.
they	'persons unspecified' They're mending the road out there.
it	'universal meteorological operator' It's snowing.

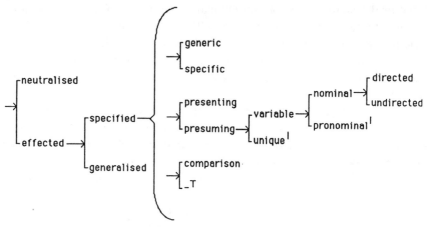

Fig. 3.9. IDENTIFICATION - *primary delicacy*

The relationship of these "out" options to the principal reference systems is formulated systemically in Fig. 3.9. For more delicate realisations of the features [presenting], [undirected] and [comparison] see the networks presented in the course of developing the description above.

This network contrasts the [neutralised] reference of little texts with that in registers where deixis is fully effected; then [effected] reference is broken down into [generalised] reference to no one in particular and [specified] reference to classes or participants or their members. The feature [specified] open up options in three simultaneous systems: the [generic/specific] opposition, the [presenting/presuming] opposition which makes reminding phoricity available and the [comparison/-] one which opens up the possibility of relevance phoricity as well. Then a break-down is provided for [presuming] reference leading through the features [variable], [nominal] and [undirected] to the possibility of presuming a superset, invoking relevance phoricity once again.

Since proper names and pronouns are not modified with comparative adjectives or quantifers in English, the feature comparison cannot be co-selected with them. The $^{I/T}$ superscript notation is used to block this combination. In the next section the ways in which phoric items depend on their context will be addressed.

3.3.3 *Phoricity and context: retrieving presumed information*

Phoricity systems, as defined above relate phoric items to their context by way of presumed information. The ways in which they do this depends on the type of phoricity involved and within different systems on the particular options selected. Halliday and Hasan (1976:145) point out for example that redundancy phoricity is essentially a textual relation: it exists primarily as an anaphoric (or occasionally cataphoric) device, and in its rare exophoric use it tends to give an effect of "putting the words in the other person's mouth".

Predispositions to different aspects of context have already been noted in 3.3.2 above with respect to reminding and relevance phoricity as far as participant identification is concerned. Demonstratives for example point to the non-verbal context more regularly than does the definite article which has evolved from them. Similarly, interlocutor (i.e. 1st and 2nd person) pronouns more typically refer outside the text than in; and it would be very unusual to find the attributive *so* + adjective presuming information from the co-text. Proper names differ from all of these in that they are commonly used to refer to participants that are present in neither the co-text nor the immediate situation; they simply assume that interlocutors know who is being referred to, whether they are around in any material sense or not. These phoric orientations to different aspects of the context are set out below.

	OUTSIDE TEXT	INSIDE/OUTSIDE TEXT
SITUATION	this, that, these, those	the
	I/you/we...	she/he/it...
	Attribute: so + adjective	Attribute: that + adjective
COMMUNITY	proper names	

These orientations can be systematised as follows. Adapting Malinowki's terms, a distinction can be drawn between context of culture and context of situation. Context of situation refers here to relevant information that can be perceived (seen, heard, felt, tasted, smelled), including text; context of culture embraces relevant information which cannot be perceived, but which can be assumed because of shared knowledge among interlocutors deriving from their membership in some definable community. As noted above, proper names regularly depend on information retrievable from the context of culture. The definite article is commonly phoric in this way as well, presuming information available through membership in communities of any size. Some typical examples are presented below, scaled with respect to the size of community involved.

EXAMPLES OF REFERENCE TO THE CONTEXT OF CULTURE (HOMOPHORA)

[community]	[homophoric nominal group]
English speakers	the sun, the moon
nations	the president, the governor
states	the premier, the Department of Education
businesses	the managing director, the shareholders
offices	the secretary, the photo-copier
families	the car, the baby, the cat

Technically, reference of this kind is referred to as **homophora**. It is used when interlocutors' membership in a particular community means that certain participants can be treated as inherently "given".

Where participants are not inherently given, reference must be made to the context of situation, which can be divided into two parts: verbal (co-text) and non-verbal. Technically reference to the co-text is referred to as **endophora** and reference to the non-verbal context as **exophora**. These different types of reference to the context are illustrated in [3:48] to [3:50] below. Note that it is endophoric reference which is cohesive.

HOMOPHORA
[3:48] Is the cat in?

EXOPHORA
[3:49] Pass me that knife, will you?

ENDOPHORA
[3:50] Once upon a time there was a little girl.
          She lived with her mother and father in the woods.

The analysis being presented here needs to be contrasted with that of Halliday and Hasan (1976:71-74) who treat homophoric reference as a type of exophora, and who classify generic reference realised by *the* as a kind of homophora. Homophora is distinguished from exophora/endophora here because its realisation includes the class of proper names, which class is not used exophorically or endophorically; in other respects the realisation of homophora, exophora and endophora overlaps. Generic reference is not treated as a type of homophora because definite and indefinite articles function as alternative realisations (cf. the discussion of the realisation of deserts in [3:16] above); generic reference depends on knowledge of the language and culture as a whole, not knowledge of the relevant cultural context. Note the contrast between [3:51] and [3:52]: generic reference does not presume the identity of the manager of a particular company the way homophoric reference does.

GENERIC

[3:51] The/a manager functions as a kind of supervising executive...

HOMOPHORIC

[3:52] Will you please put me through to the manager right away?

Endophoric reference typically involves presuming information from the preceding co-text (**anaphora**) or from the following co-text. Where presumed information follows, it usually appears quickly, either within the structure of the same nominal group, or in the same or an adjacent clause complex — otherwise participant identification would break down. As Halliday and Hasan (1976:72-73) point out, *the* always points forward structurally, to information in modifying elements within the same nominal group, typically the Qualifier. This forward reference within the same nominal group will be referred to as **esphora**, adapting slightly a term from Ellis (1971). Esphora is a very common way of introducing participants to a text; note the contrast between the presenting first mention in [3:53] and the esphoric strategy in [3:54]:

[3:53] We met some people there
and they wanted to get something to eat...

[3:54] The people we met there wanted to get something to eat...

Du Bois (1980:224-225) suggests that this strategy is used when the Qualifier gives enough information to identify a participant and when that information is "not particularly noteworthy" (i.e. not worth negotiating and so embedded; see Chapter 2 above).

Forward reference between groups is cohesive and will be referred to as **cataphora**, narrowing Halliday and Hasan's (1976:72) definition in order to oppose the term to esphora. This cohesive cataphora is realised by proximate demonstratives (*this/these*) and presumes text, not participants:

[3:55] This is what bothers me -
you can't trust them.

These distinctions among homophoric, endophoric, exophoric, anaphoric, cataphoric and esphoric reference are summarised in Fig. 3.10.

To this point the examples of endophoric reference given have all involved presuming information that has been made explicit in the co-text.

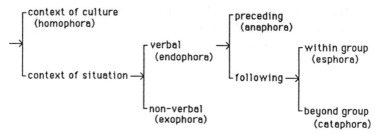

Fig. 3.10. Types of phora

However, as Haviland and Clark (1974) point out, phoric nominal groups may presume information that is implied rather than directly retrievable (see also Clark & Haviland 1977). Consider [3:56] below:

[3:56] He bumped into a branch;
        he hadn't noticed the tree at all.

In [3:56] the identity of the tree has to be established with respect to one of its parts — the branch realised in the preceding clause. Haviland and Clark referred to indirect reference of this kind as **bridging** and carried out experiments indicating that it may be more difficult for interlocutors to recover presumed information of this kind (see also Clark & Haviland 1977, and Rochester & Martin 1979 who found that this type of reference was avoided by non-thought disordered schizophrenic speakers).

Bridging depends on experiential connections between presuming and presumed which facilitate the recovery of an implied identity. The relevant lexical relations are taken up in detail in Chapter 5. Implicational relations between parts and wholes or among parts are very common:

PRESUMING	PRESUMED
the tree	a branch
the floor	the room
the door	the window
the top	the roof
the water	a pond

Similarly subclasses may be bridged from classes:

[3:57] He brought some flowers;
        the roses in particular looked great.

But note that when a more general class picks up a subclass, the reference is direct; *the plants* and *the things* in [3:58] refer to the same participant, the roses, that *them* and *the roses* do (see Halliday and Hasan 1976:278-279):

[3:58]   He planted <u>some roses</u>;
         The insects loved <u>them</u>/<u>the roses</u>/<u>the plants</u>/<u>the things</u>.

Alongside these taxonomy focussed examples, bridging may depend on experiential relationships of various kinds:

PRESUMING	PRESUMED
the seeds	sowing the fields
the weight	carrying a heavy load
the snow	it snowed all night
the bus	set off to work
the reindeer	Santa
the drover	the cattle

At times the information presumed by phoric nominal groups may not be retrievable from the context, verbal or non-verbal. Where this is confusing, interlocutors may interrupt through one or other of the tracking options described in Chapter 2 (cf. [3:30] above):

[3:59]   John hadn't seen a beagle...
         — Who?
         — My husband, John.
         Anyway, so he went and looked at one...

More commonly interlocutors interlocutors simply process the phoric item as a first mention; Haviland and Clarke refer to this strategy as **addition**.

Finally, it may be that more than referent is available, rendering a phoric group **ambiguous**:

[3:60]   The boy put <u>his hat</u> and <u>coat</u> on;
         <u>it</u> was black.

These additional options, covering bridging, addition and ambiguous reference are added to the IDENTIFICATION network in Fig. 3.11.

Although presented in network form as if the different types of phoric reference do not combine, as Halliday and Hasan (1976:73-74) point out, phoric items may well point in more than one direction at once. Participants which are homophoric or exophoric at first mention, can be interpreted as either of these plus anaphoric on subsequent mention:

[3:61]   <u>The sun</u>'s hot;
         <u>it</u>'s starting to burn me.

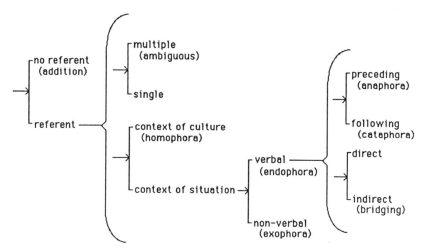

Fig. 3.11. Retrieval network

[3:62]   Look at that yacht;
         it's a beauty.

Anaphora and esphora is another common combination:

[3:63]   We saw some tall ships in the harbour;
         the boats we saw were here for the Bicentennial.

Where the focus is on cohesive relations, homophora, exophora and
esphora can be set aside after first mention, thereby biassing the reference
analysis to intra-textual relations (see 3.5 below). But where some measure
of contextual dependency is the issue (as in Hawkins 1977, Rochester and
Martin 1979, Martin 1983c) the disadvantages of introducing such a bias
have to be carefully considered.

As with the tracking and challenging options presented in Chapter 2,
these retrieval categories broach upon a dynamic as opposed to a synoptic
perspective on participant identification (see Martin 1985a). The choices
reviewed are relevant to both decisions a speaker must make when selecting phoric or non-phoric items and to processes the listener must go
through to recover any information which is presumed. And it is the particular point that has been reached in the syntagmatic unfolding of a text
that is critical to any decisions made. No attempt will be made to model
IDENTIFICATION as a dynamic system here. For a study of participant identifi-

cation processes in the context of schizophrenic discourse, see Martin and Rochester (1979); Goodman (1987) presents an application of the framework developed here in miscue analysis.

3.3.4 IDENTIFICATION in [3:1]

In this section the analyses developed in 3.3.2 and 3.3.3 will be applied to text [3:1], partly by way of exemplification, and partly to specify what it is that shows the text to be that of an immature writer. The nominal groups in [3:1] are listed below. Each is coded for the IDENTIFICATION choices made and the type of reference to the context where these choices are phoric. The analysis will be annotated for purposes of discussion, rather than presented in detail.

NOMINAL GROUP	REFERENCE (terminal features)	RETRIEVAL (where phoric)
one day	presenting...particular	-
I	presuming...interlocutor	anaphoric[i]
the zoo	presuming...undirected:-	homophoric
I	presuming...interlocutor	anaphoric
Rhinocerous[ii]	neutralised	-
I	presuming...interlocutor	anaphoric
a Hippoptoamus	presenting...unmarked	-
I	presuming...interlocutor	anaphoric
him	presuming...noninterlocutor	anaphoric
he	presuming...noninterlocutor	anaphoric
he	presuming...noninterlocutor	anaphoric
I	presuming...interlocutor	anaphoric
I	presuming...interlocutor	anaphoric
the tiger	presuming...undirected:-	bridging[iii]
this man	presenting...major role[iv]	-
him	presuming...noninterlocutor	anaphoric
it	presuming...noninterlocutor[v]	anaphoric
it	presuming...noninterlocutor	bridging[vi]
Mum	presuming:unique	homophoric[vii]
me	presuming...interlocutor	anaphoric
a gorilla	presenting...unmarked	-
I(t)[viii]	presuming...noninterlocutor	anaphoric
a baby gorilla	presenting...unmarked	-
my (mum)[ix]	presuming...interlocutor	anaphoric
I	presuming...interlocutor	anaphoric
a watch	presenting...unmarked	-
it[x]	-	-

i.   Anaphoric to the writer's name, which was written at the top of
     her story; pronominal references to the writer could in addition be
     coded as exophoric throughout [3:1] (the writer's name itself was
     homophoric, identifying the writer to her teacher and the class).

ii. Deixis omitted, presumably because of attention lapsing due to
     handwriting struggles; not an appropriate selection for this con-
     text.

iii. The identity of the tiger can be taken as implied by the field — the
     zoo, Rhinocerous and the Hippopotamus mentioned earlier in the
     text; however the writer is inconsistent, bridging the tiger here,
     but introducing the Hippopotamus, gorilla and baby gorilla with
     presenting groups; a more mature writer would probably have
     introduced the tiger with a presenting group as well.

iv. Since the man does not actually play an ongoing role in the story,
     taking *this man* as the realisation of [major role] is perhaps gener-
     ous here; it should perhaps be alternatively analysed as [presum-
     ing...directed:proximate] and involving addition.

v.   Note the gender switch in referring to the tiger — first *he* and then
     it; higher order animals may of course be endowed with human
     consciousness (especially in writing for, and therefore by, chil-
     dren), though consistently so endowed or not throughout a text in
     mature writing.

vi. Possibly bridged from *feeding* (although pronouns are not com-
     monly used to refer to implied participants since they contain only
     a little experiential content which can be followed up when bridg-
     ing).

vii. As a name, *Mum*, is homophoric within a family unit; and this is
     interpretable as the community at risk here; compare with *mum* as
     a common noun in note ix below.

viii. The writer's *I* is being interpreted as *It*; few children have baby
     gorillas, but gorillas commonly do (note the importance of going
     beyond the experiential meaning of a particular group to recon-
     struct the reference relation here)!

ix. *My mum*, like other nominal groups with a possessive Deictic,
     realises two participants (see discussion in 3.4.1 below); however
     the possessive functions as the deixis for the participant it mod-
     ifies, and so reference and retrieval are coded only once, for *my*.

x.   *It* does not realise a participant; see 3.4.1 below.

Notes ii, iii, iv, v, vi and viii index the text as that of a young writer. The problems referred to in ii and viii are almost certainly graphological in origin; but the others point to immature use of the IDENTIFICATION system, given the genre (recount of personal experience; see Martin 1985b:3-5) and mode (written — see Chapter 7 below).

3.4 IDENTIFICATION and stratification

As with SPEECH FUNCTION and MOOD in Chapter 2, IDENTIFICATION has been stratified with respect to nominal group structure here. This raises a number of issues concerning the way in which descriptive responsibility is distributed across the two strata and how interaction between the strata should be interpreted. These will be taken up under four headings below. The relationship between participants and nominal groups will be considered first.

3.4.1 *Participants and nominal groups*

The entry condition for the IDENTIFICATION network developed in section 3.3 was participant, where this can be defined as a person, place or thing, abstract or concrete, capable of functioning as Agent or Medium in TRANS-ITIVITY (for Agent and Medium see Halliday 1985a:144-155). Defined in this way, it can be argued that all participants are realised through nominal groups; but not all nominal groups realise participants and some nominal groups realise more than one. This incongruence will now be explored in more detail, first taking into account nominal groups not realising partici-pants (referred to by Du Bois 1980:209-217 as *non-referential* uses of nomi-nal groups). The review will proceed as follows:

i.   structural *it*
ii.   idioms
iii.   negation
iv.   Attribute
v.   Range
vi.   Extent
vii.   Role
viii   possessive Deictics
ix.   Pre-Deictic, Pre-Numerative, Pre-Epithet, Pre-Classifier

One of the most common classes of nominal group not realising a par-ticipant is structural *it*, which appears where English needs a Subject to show

MOOD but for various reasons has no appropriate participant around to fill this grammatical function. Theme predication and impersonal projection both make use of *it* in this way; *it* is "structurally cataphoric" in both examples below:

THEME PREDICATION (Halliday 1985a:59-61)
[3:64] It was the frog he lost.

IMPERSONAL PROJECTION (e.g. Halliday 1985a:153, 245)
[3:65] It's likely he's lost his frog.

Meteorological *it* was included, following Halliday and Hasan (1976), under [generalised] reference above; it is however a borderline case, and could just as well be treated as not realising a participant at all, parallel to the examples in [3:64] and [3:65].

An example of an idiom containing a nominal group not realising a participant was introduced among the examples relevant to [neutralised] reference above: *flash in the pan fizzles*. The idiom preserves the Deictic *the* precisely because it is collocationally frozen; the nominal group is not relevant to participant identification because "the pan" is not a participant in the text.

Indefinite nominal groups under the scope of negation were also considered above, where it was pointed out that they do not provide referents for presuming groups. The reason for this is that they do not introduce participants to a discourse:

[3:66] He didn't see anyone there.

In addition there are four TRANSITIVITY functions, typically realised by nominal groups, which do not necessarily realise participants: Attribute, Range and Circumstances of Extent and Role. Attributes describe or classify participants; they are realised by adjectives, indefinite nominal groups or attitudinal superlatives. Their indefinite deixis in contexts where they are decribing participants that have already been introduced gives away the fact that they are not realising a participant themselves:

[3:67] He   was   silly/a silly man/the silliest thing
        Carrier Process Attribute

Ranges functioning as nominal realisations of a process present a further category of nominal group not realising a participant (see Halliday's process Range, 1985a:135); note the following proportionalities:

        dance:do a dance::
        bath:take a bath::

dine:have dinner::
talk:give a talk::
sing:sing a song::
play:play tennis::
ask:ask a question
etc.

The discourse function of Halliday's entity Range (1985a:134) is less deter-
minate and these present another borderline case of nominal groups which
may or may not be best interpreted as realising a participant: *cross the field*,
climb the mountain, *play the piano* etc. This indeterminacy however gener-
ates a prediction that Ranges are less likely to provide referents for presuming nominal groups than Goals:

PROCESS ˆ RANGE	PROCESS ˆ GOAL
play tennis	play the puck
drive the car	drive the ball
serve dinner	serve the ball
make a move	make a doll
take a dive	take your friend
fake an illness	fake a Picasso
etc.	

Some Circumstances of Location are perhaps best treated along these
lines, as subclassifying the Process with respect to direction rather than
introducing a participant (see Chapter 5, section 5.3.3 for further discussion);
note the lack of deixis in the nominal groups of destination in *ride to work*,
come to school, *go to theatre* (medicine), *return home* etc. (cf. the single
process translations into Tagalog: *pasok* 'go to work/school', *uwi* 'return
home').

Circumstances of Extent are realised through nominal groups realising
measurement: yards, laps, rounds, years etc. (Halliday 1985a:137-138). It is
unlikely that they would be presumed by a phoric nominal group:

[3:68] She swam 40 laps.
Actor Process Circumstance: extent

The last transitivity role to be considered is Circumstance of Role,
which like the Attribute, simply functions to classify participants, not introduce them (Halliday 1985a:142):

[3:69] She arrived as Dracula.
Actor Process Circumstance: role

Finally the problem of realising more than one participant in a nominal
group needs to be addressed. Clear cases involved nominal groups embed-

ded in the Deictic and Qualifier functions and can be passed over qucikly here; for example three participants, John, Mary and the friend, are realised in a group like *John's friend who Mary had never met.*

Possessive pronouns in Deictic position, function like embedded nominal groups to realise a participant different from that coded through the Numerative ˆ Epithet ˆ Classifier ˆ Thing structure. Like embedded groups, these possessive pronouns function in place of the deixis that would otherwise be associated with the group. This raises the problem of how to interpret the phoricity of the participant realised through the Thing in possessive groups like *his frog, John's friend* and so on. Halliday and Hasan (1976:70) and Halliday (1985a:160) treat possessive pronouns as a type of specific deixis, alongside *the, this, that, these* and *those* (see diagram below).

This seems to imply that the identity of the frog and the friend in *his frog* and *John's friend* is being coded as recoverable, alongside the identity of *his* and *John. His frog* in other words does not mean 'a frog of his' nor does *John's friend* mean 'a friend of John's'; where the latter meanings are intended then the expressions *one of his frogs* or *one of John's friends* would have to occur. Du Bois (1980:243) concurs, arguing that "*his* is similar to *the* in that it demands (presupposes) identifiability, but different in that it supplies some extra information that may help make the identification possible".

The issue then is whether possessive Deictics **are** the deixis of the participants they possess. Is the possessed participant identified through its possessor, or does the possessive Deictic neutralise this participant's phoricity (as with neutralised reference in the grammar of little texts)? Du Bois' data indicates that *a frog of his* or *a friend of John's* do not alternate with

Table 3.3. Specific Deictics (Halliday 1985a:160)

	Determinative			Interrogative
Demonstrative	this these	that those	the	which(ever) what(ever)
Possessive	my his their one's	your her	our its	whose(ver)
	[John's] [my father's] etc.			[which person's] etc.

his frog or *John's friend* to introduce participants (1980:243-245); pending further investigation this suggests that the interpetation of possessive Deictics as the deixis of the participants they possess is correct. Accordingly, possessive nominal groups will only be coded once for phoricity below, even though they realise two participants. This is after all literally what the grammar of the English nominal group argues: "recover the identity of the possessed participant here through its possessor".

Another way in which nominal groups can expand their structural potential to realise more than one participant is through embedding in Pre-Deictic, Pre-Numerative, Pre-Epithet and Pre-Classifier positions (for the first two of these see Halliday 1985a:174-175). This can be exemplified as follows (embedded groups in bold face; see Martin 1988a for further discussion):

Pre-Deictic:	**the top** of the mountain
Pre-Numerative:	**a pair** of boots
Pre-Epithet:	**the tallest** of the mountains
Pre-Classifier:	**that kind** of gear

Their structure is outlined in Fig. 3.12, taking *of* as a structure marker (i.e. not as a constituent):

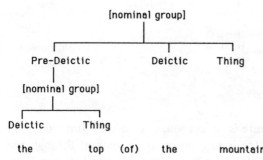

Fig. 3.12. Embedded nominal group in Pre-Deictic function

In a sense these structures take a single participant and split it in two. Pre-Deictics to this by focussing on some facet of the whole: back, side, face, front, back, top etc. Pre-Numeratives parcel off a measurement: jar, bunch, pack, carton, slice etc. Pre-Epithets provide distinct nominal groups for both the participant being differentiated (e.g. *the tallest*) and the group out of which (superlative; e.g. *the mountains*) or with respect to which (comparison) it is being distinguished (cf. the discussion of relevance phoricity above). Pre-Classifiers bring the class, breed, kind, type, species etc. of Thing to nominal attention (see Chapter 5, Section 5.3.2.1).

There may be good experiential reasons for doing this. Pre-Numeratives for example make mass nouns countable (e.g. *three boxes of jam*) and count nouns "massable" (e.g. *a flock of geese*). And having split participants in two, independent deixis selections may be taken up in each nominal group: **some** boxes of **that** jam I like, **a** flock of **those** geese we saw. Where deixis is made explicit in both nominal groups, they are best taken as realising two participants and coded twice for phoricity; where deixis is not coded in the second group and the group is presumed as a single participant, this is hardly necessary (e.g. *a strong cup of tea*, *this kind of beer* etc.).

The incongruence between participants, nominal groups and the explicit realisation of deixis is summarised in the following table.

	#NOMINAL GROUPS	#PARTICIPANTS	PHORICITY MARKED
structural *it*	1	-	-
idioms	1	-	-
indefinite negation	1	-	-
Attribute	1	-	-
Range	1	0/1	-/once
Extent	1	-	-
Role	1	-	-
possessive Deictics	1/2	2	once
Pre-D/N/E/C	2	1/2	once/twice

3.4.2 *Grammaticalising phoricity*

As far as nominal group structure is concerned, phoric items function in all places except the Classifier. Reminding phoricity is realised through the Deictic and Thing; relevance phoricity is realised through Deictic, Post-Deictic, Numerative and Epithet — with supersets presumed by the Deictic, Numerative and Epithet and relevant sets by the Post-Deictic, Numerative and Epithet. The relevant items and structures are sumarised below with respect to each element of structure:

DEICTIC   the, this, that, these, those;
my, your, our, his, her, its, their;
each, either, neither, which, both

POST-DEICTIC	same, similar, identical, different, other
NUMERATIVE	first, second etc.; next, last, final, ultimate etc.
EPITHET	comparative; superlative
THING	pronoun; proper name
QUALIFIER	else, comparative [e.g. something else/bigger]

In addition, redundancy phoricity is operative, with *one/ones* substituting for the Thing, or with ellipsis presuming elements of structure left-wards from the Thing. Substitution is exemplified in the second clause of [3:70], ellipsis in the third.

[3:70]   Do you have any other woks?
— We have those other two large aluminum **ones**.
— **Those two** would be nice.

Setting aside the Qualifier, the range of the different types of phoricity across elements of nominal group structure is outlined in Fig. 3.13.

This distribution of phoric items across different elements of nominal group structure makes it very difficult to capture the relevant textual generalisations at the level of grammar. The structure of pronominal, proper and common nominal groups is very divergent (cf. *he, Professor Emeritus J C Smith, that fellow I met last week*), for good experiential and interpersonal reasons. But all three types of group may be presuming in the same way and need to be classed together as far as textual meaning is concerned. The same point can be made with respect to relevance phoricity: Deictics, Numeratives and Epithets are generated by quite different nominal group systems, but from the point of view of textual meaning all can presume supersets.

In theory, the IDENTIFICATION network developed above could be viewed as cross-classifying other nominal group systems much as THEME at clause

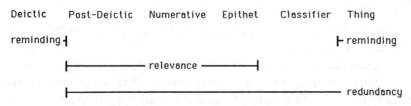

Fig. 3.13. Realisational domains of phoricity types

rank cross-classifies TRANSITIVITY and MOOD. But the interdependence between textual and other nominal group options is so great that a tremendous amount of correlative marking (see Martin 1987) or negative conditioning in realisation (see Fawcett 1980) would be required; IDENTIFICATION options would not in other words combine relatively freely with other nominal group ones in a way characteristic of simultaneous systems at the same rank on the same stratum. The relationship between IDENTIFICATION and nominal group systems displays much more clearly the interlocking diversification (Lockwood 1972) characteristic of inter- rather than intra-stratal relations. Setting aside then the question of discourse structure, to be taken up in 3.5 below, there are sound systemic reasons for stratifying IDENTIFICATION and nominal group oppositions (cf. the critical discussion of Halliday's (1976b) DEIXIS network in Martin 1987).

3.4.3 IDENTIFICATION and ideational grammar

To this point participant identification has been approached from the point of view of discourse semantics, with a focus on the nature of phoric items and the work interlocutors must do to track down presumed information. But it is important not to overlook the role that grammar plays in participant tracking. For one thing, identifying structures (Halliday 1985a:112-128) may grammaticalise the relation between presuming and presumed. This happened in [3:31] above, where the Token *that* (referring to *John*) was explicitly assigned the Value *my husband*.

> [3:31]   ...Friends of my parents had a beagle and <u>John</u> hadn't seen a beagle (<u>that's my husband</u>) so he went and looked at one...

Apposition is also used in this way; [3:31] might have been spoken as follows, with the nominal group complex *John, my husband* doing the work of the Token ˆ Value structure above:

> [3:71]   ...Friends of my parents had a beagle and **John, my husband**, hadn't seen a beagle so he went and looked at one...

This kind of identification is referred to by Hasan (1984a, 1985b) as one kind of *instantial* reference.

Grammar also plays a role in transforming the identity of a participant. The Attributes referred to above as not themselves realising participants are commonly used to add qualities to and/or classify a participant in a new way. The Attribute in [3:72] serves both functions:

[3:72] The woman went off to visit her step-sister, who was **an old potter** who lived in the woods.

Attributes extend the ways in which a participant can be identified; the grandmother can be referred to as *the potter*, *the old lady*, *the older woman* and so on as well as *her step-sister* in text following [3:72].

Material processes are also commonly involved in transforming participants. Renovation of this kind is exemplified in Halliday and Hasan's (1976:2) example, reproduced as [3:73] below. Obviously the process of washing and coring apples transforms their identity, and the participant presumed by *them* is not experientially identical to that referred to with *six cooking apples*; this would be even more radically the case had the recipe suggested *wash and chop* instead of *wash and core*.

[3:73] Wash and core six cooking apples.
Put them into a fireproof dish.

Such examples demonstrate one of the respects in which textual meaning provides only a partial account of text structure and the importance of taking the contribution a meaning making grammar makes to discourse structure into account. Certainly, as Brown and Yule (1983:204) suggest, a "account of textual relations produced as a *post hoc* analysis of the structure of a completed text should not necessarily be revealing about how a processor working 'on-line' as the discourse unfolds experiences that discourse."

Finally it has to be noted, as implicated in 3.4.3 above, that the grammar may be actively involved in creating participants in discourse. Once the decision for example has been made to realise a process as a Process + Range structure (e.g. *have a bath*), then the fact that the process has been nominalised potentialises it as a participant; and a text can pick it up and develop it along these lines:

[3:74] Where have you been?
— Oh, I had a bath;
in fact it was quite a splendid one.
There was plenty of hot water;
so I just luxuriated in it for hours.

Similarly the nominal groups realising Circumstances of Extent, or filling Pre-Deictic, Pre-Numerative, Pre-Epithet or Pre-Classifier positions may be taken up as participants in a discourse, although the textual motivation for selecting a nominal group realisation may not have been to introduce a new participant in the first place. This is illustrated with respect to Pre-Numeratives in [3:75].

[3:75] I got two jars of mulberry jam.
        — Let's see them/I hate it.

The role of the grammar in creating new participants will be further explored with respect to gramatical metaphor in 3.4.4 below.

3.4.4 *Grammatical metaphor*

Certainly the major resource as far as the grammar creating participants is concerned is nominalisation. Through this resource the grammar is able to turn a range of non-participant meanings into participant-like ones (see Halliday 1985a:321-332 on ideational metaphor). Typical examples include:

MEANING	UNMARKED GRAMMATICAL CLASS	NOMINALISED FORM
'quality'	adjective: literate	literacy
'process'	verb: implement	implementation
'assessment'	modal verb: must	commitment
'logical relation'	conjunction: so	effect

High levels of nominalisation characterise abstract written English, especially in the context of science, the humanities and administration. These texts typically involve generic rather than specific reference and so few of the nominalised participants play a role in long reference chains; esphoric *the* is common in these participant creating nominal groups (e.g. **the** *implementation of key targets as operational components of the new strategy — and hence also of **the** process of negotiation*). The following text, villified as "superb balderdash" by Tarzie Vittachi (1989:11), creates numerous generic participants of this kind (nominalised processes in bold face). None of the participants the grammar constructs are presumed in [3:76], but all have the potential to provide referents for subsequent phoric nominal groups.

[3:76] The **implementation** of key targets as **operational** components of the new **strategy** — and hence also of the **process** of **negotiation** — may be conceived in the time frame of a decade but only in the form of a dynamic **process**, with different time frames for different components, and with an inbuilt and effective **mechanism** for **review** and **reappraisal**, leading to **adjustments** and **correctives** whenever the **strategy** is seen to deflect from the **goals** and **objectives** of **development** for which it was devised. It should be in the form not of a '**plan** of **action**' but rather of a **manifesto**, which provides the framework of a sustained **commitment** to, and **implementation** of, **developmental goals** and their **operational** components, and embodies institutional **mechanisms** for continuous **negotiation**, **monitoring**, **appraisal**, **criticism** and **modification**.

Alongside these grammatical resources for constructing participants, discourse semantics can also be used to turn non-participant meanings into things. It does this by using *it, this* and *that* to refer to text. This is discussed by Halliday and Hasan (1976:52-53, 66-67) under the headings of extended reference (to text as act) and text reference (to text as projection). They point out that this is the main use made of demonstratives in most registers of English. Instead of nominalising non-participants to treat them as participants, *it, this* and *that* simply construct them as such by referring to them. To illustrate this consider the range of responses possible in [3:77]:

		PRESUMED AS:
[3:77]	She saw them building a new school.	
i.	— If you say <u>so</u>. — Do you think <u>so</u>?	locution/idea
ii.	— Who told you <u>that</u>? — I can't believe <u>that</u>.	locution/idea
iii.	— <u>That</u>'s impossible/<u>It</u>'s not possible.	fact
iv.	— <u>That</u>'s hard work/<u>It</u>'s hard work.	act
v.	— <u>That</u>'s what we needed/<u>It</u>'s what we needed.	thing

Response v illustrates the pattern considered to this point: reference between participants — *that* and *it* presume a phenomenon, realised earlier as *a new school*. In response iv however, *that* and *it* presume a macro-phenomenon — the act of building a new school; to make response iv explicit, *building a new school* would have had to be embedded in the Subject (i.e. *[[Building a new school]] is hard work*). Response iii takes this one step further, presuming a metaphenomenon — the fact that she saw them building a new school: cf. *It's not possible [[that she saw them building a new school]]*. In ii *that* also presumes *she saw them building a new school* as a metaphenomenon — but this time as a projected locution or idea, not a fact. *That* contrasts with *so* in i; as Halliday (1985a:234) points out, with verbal processes the distinction is between quoting (*that*) and reporting (*so*), whereas with mental processes the opposition is between assertion (*that*) and postulation (*so*).

The responses in [3:77] can be read as scaled according to the degree of "participanthood" the reference items entail. *So* respects clausehood; but in reconstructing the meanings made in *She saw them building a new school* as reported locutions or ideas, facts and acts *that* and *it* are transforming text into thing. This is another instance of grammatical metaphor, this time functioning as a kind of discourse process. This point will be taken up again below in connection with internal conjunction (Chapter 4) and metalinguistic lexis (Chapter 5).

3.5 Participant identification in English: structure

3.5.1 *Reference chains*

In Chapter 2, conversational structure was approached from a multivariate perspective, with a view to applying notions of constituency as these had evolved for grammatical description to dialogue. This approach had to be abandonned once dynamic moves were taken into account, and dependency structures were introduced to handle tracking and challenging moves. Here, with reference structures, it is the dependency approach that will be pursued.

The reason for this is that reference structures are essentially covariate ones. Where endophoric, phoric items depend semantically on the items they presume, but need not be grammatically related to them. And presuming items can themselves be presumed. The covariate structures deriving from phoric options in the IDENTIFICATION system will be referred to as **reference chains** (closely related to Hasan's identity chains; see Hasan 1984a, 1985b).

At its simplest, a reference chain consists of two items, one presuming, one presumed. For display purposes, the nominal group realising a given participant in a text will be used to to name that realisation of the participant in the reference chain. Thus for [3:78] participant identification can be modelled with a dependency arrow showing the presumed nominal group to be dependent on the presuming one.

[3:78] There was a frog in a jar
        and it escaped.

For longer texts, these chains can simply be extended, with presuming items shown to be as well presumed; these then form the systemic equivalent of the "participant lines" in the Hartford stratificationalists' reticula:

[3:78] There was a frog in a jar
        and it escaped;
        the boy saw it was missing
        and went to find it.
        In the end he found the frog in a pond.

The basic descriptive strategy underlying chains formed in this way is to take each phoric item back once to the item which last realised or presumed the information that needs to be recovered. It is according to this principle that the third *it* in [3:78] is shown as dependent on the second *it*, not *the frog*, or on both *the frog* and the preceding *it*. The rationale for this is that in order to understand the second *it*, the information it presumed would have had to be recovered and is thus immanent for recovery by the subsequent link in the chain.

Chains may both split, and conjoin again. In [3:79] two distinct participants are introduced and then referred to as one in a single nominal group. The text then picks them apart again. Again, the dependency relations in the chain are worked out in accordance with the principle that anaphoric items are related backwards once to the item last realising or presuming the information they presume; thus *the boy* in the fifth clause and *the dog* in the sixth are shown to presume *they* in the fourth.

[3:79] The boy and the dog woke up
        and saw that the frog was missing.
        with the boy leading the way
        They headed off for the woods,

with the boy leading the way
and the dog following behind him.

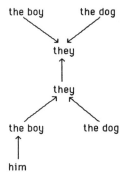

As noted in 3.1 above, first mentions of participants in discourse are commonly phoric. Exophoric and homophoric first mention is quite common; parts and possessions are typically introduced via possessive Deictics; and bridging is favoured where the identity of a participant can be indirectly presumed. As Du Bois (1980:254) comments, "the definite article is the unmarked member of the pair. When consciousness is not focussed on the task of introducing characters, it is the unmarked *the* which is uttered, whether or not the initial mention is in fact identfiable." It may be that Du Bois' data has been biassed in this way by its re-telling context — that of speakers recounting the plot of a short film they have just seen. But it is certainly true that the principle of introducing participants phorically where possible is a very general one across a wide range of English texts.

Where chains are initiated exophorically or homophorically this raises the question of how to analyse subsequent mentions of the same participant. The most economical strategy is to code the first member of the chain as exophoric or homophoric and subsequent realisations as anaphoric. It then follows from the way the chain initiating item is coded that the rest of the realisations in the chain are interpretable as both anaphoric and exophoric or homophoric as well. This strategy is illustrated for [3:80] and [3:81] below.

[3:80]   Pass me that one, will you?
          — Here, take it.
          You've been drooling over it for more than an hour.

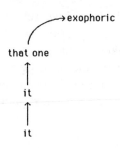

[3:81] Is the cat in?
— Yes, she's upstairs;
get her dinner out, will you?

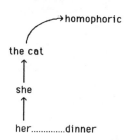

With esphoric and cataphoric reference, the presumed information follows the phoric item, and so the dependency arrow needs to point to succeeding, not preceding text. With esphoric reference, participants can be entered as single nominal groups in participant chains, to distinguish it from cataphoric reference between nominal groups and co-text outside the structure of the phoric group. Cataphoric reference almost always presumes text, rather than participants; this can be entered into the participant chain where room is available, or simply indexed to the relevant portion of the text being analysed. This is illustrated for [3:82] below:

[3:82] Then the guy we saw shouting came up
and screamed at us like this:
"You bloody stupid pommie bastard..."

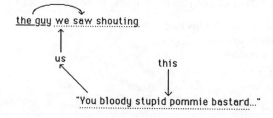

It remains to propose a notation for distinguishing relevance from reminding phoricity and direct presumption from bridging. Reminding phoricity and direct presumption can be taken as the unmarked cases, requiring no special notation; relevance phoricity and bridging can then be marked as valences on the dependency line connected presuming to presumed. This is illustrated below with RL marking relevance phoricity and BR bridging:

[3:83]   The boy saw his frog with another one,
         sitting on a log in the middle of a pond;
         but the water was very deep.

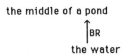

Note that redundancy phoricity is not taken as contributing to the structure of reference chains, since it is not concerned with presuming the identity of participants, but simply with presuming some aspect of their experiential meaning. Substitution and ellipsis at group rank is thus more appropriately treated as an aspect of lexical cohesion (see the discussion of lexical strings in Chapter 5 below and Hasan 1984a, 1985b on similarity chains).

Finally instantial reference needs to be considered. Where the ideational resources of the grammar (identifying clauses or nominal group apposition) are used to identify participants, the dependency line connecting them in reference chains can be assigned the valence INST. Instantial reference often has the effect of conjoining chains, as in [3:84] below.

[3:84]   The boy was looking for his frog
         he eventually found one
         but he didn't realise
         it was his frog.

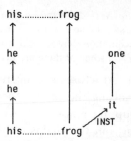

The reference chains developed above have been organised to reflect the sequential unfolding of a text, with succeeding items listed below preceding ones. Except for structural cataphora (esphora), the chains are neutral with respect to grammatical structure; semantic dependency is noted between items irrespective of clause or sentence boundaries. The analysis of reference contrasts in this respect with that exemplified in Halliday and Hasan (1976:340-355), which looks only at cohesive ties between, not within, sentences. Here, as far as participant identification is concerned, the discourse structure of [3:85], [3:86] and [3:87] is treated as identical.

[3:85] The boy was tired.
However, he kept looking.

[3:86] Although the boy was tired,
he kept looking.

[3:87] The boy kept looking in spite of his fatigue.

the boy

he/his

Finally, a comment on generic chains. The second paragraph of [3:16] above has been extended to illustrate the way in which these chains are effectively re-initiated each time a non-phoric nominal group is used to realise the generic participant in question. The group *cool deserts* does this twice in the extended version of [3:16]. Recalling that *the* is not phoric in generic groups, this is a common textual pattern.

[3:16] ...Cool deserts are found further polewards in the deep interiors of large continents like Eurasia or where mountains form rain-shadows, which keep out rain bearing winds that might otherwise bring wet conditions....[For much of the year they may not look like deserts because they are lightly covered with snow. But the snow is not very deep and because it does not melt and run off gives a false impression of how wet cool deserts are. In winter they simply save whatever precipitation they get. Cool deserts can in fact be every bit as dry as the Sahara and some of them are even drier.]

This means that as far as reference structure is concerned, [3:16] includes three independent chains, all realising the same generic participant. Since *cool deserts* is not a phoric group, it cannot be shown to depend on previous realisations of this participant; but the chains can be aligned directly under one another by way of showing that the same participant is being realised, though not continuously presumed. This strategy brings out the experiential similarity between generic and specific chains alongside their textual differences.

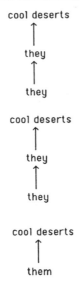

3.5.2 *Two texts analysed*

The approach to reference structure just outlined will now be illustrated with respect to two texts. Both are drawn from research into the development of children's narrative reported in Martin (1983c). The first text is a oral re-telling by a 10/11 year old girl of a story she has just learned by looking through the picture story *Frog, where are you?* by Mercer Mayer (1974). The text, divided into ranking clauses, is presented below; phoric items have been underlined.

[3:88] i.   Tommy was laying at the bottom of his bed,
        ii.   looking at his pet frog with his dog.
        iii.   While he was asleep
        iv.   with the dog on his bed
        v.   the frog tried to get out of the glass jar.
        vi.   The next morning they saw the frog had gone,
        vii.   so they looked out the window,
        viii. and the dog had a glass on his head.
        ix.   The dog fell out the window
        x.   and smashed the glass
        xi.   and Tommy came out
        xii.   and held the dog
        xiii. and the dog licked his face
        xiv.   and they called for him.
        xv.   They went down to the woods
        xvi.   and there was a swarm of bees coming out of a bee-hive.
        xvii. He went to the top of a rock
        xviii. and the next minute he was on top of a reindeer.
        xix.   The dog went behind the rock
        xx.   and the next thing they knew the reindeer was running after the dog
        xxi.   with Tommy on his head.
        xxii. They fell into the water off a cliff-top
        xxiii. and Tommy saw a hollow tree,
        xxiv. so they both went over the tree
        xxv.   and Tommy told his dog
        xxvi. to be quiet
        xxvii. and they saw his pet frog and another frog and lots of baby frogs.
        xxviii. Tommy took one of the baby frogs home with him.

The reference structure of [3:88] is presented in Fig. 3.14. To simplify
the diagram, bridging and esphoric dependencies have been omitted; bridging is taken up in notes below. The two participants in possessive nominal
groups are aligned with their respective chains with a dotted line showing
that the identity of the participant realised in the Thing is recoverable via
the participant by which it is possessed (e.g. *his bed* in [3:88:i]). Where the
Thing participant has already been identified (as with *his pet frog* in
[3:88:xxvii]), it is shown as well as presuming preceding items in its chain.
Note that these analyses of reference structure consist only of phoric items
and any non-phoric items they presume; non-phoric items which are not
presumed are not included since they do not enter into semantic dependencies related to participant identification. In [3:88] only four minor participants chains, the glass, the rock, the reindeer, and the baby frogs are introduced non-phorically.

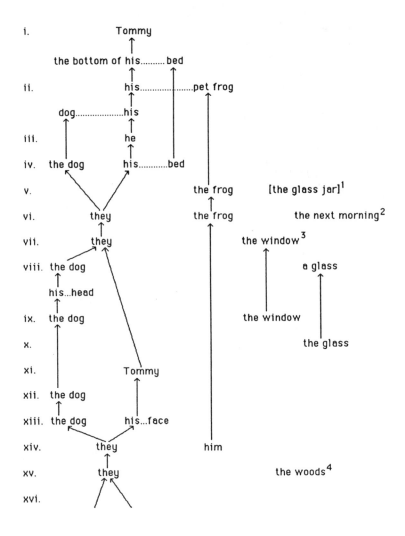

i.   Tommy

        the bottom of his.........bed

ii.   his.................pet frog

              dog...................his

iii.   he

iv.   the dog   his...........bed

v.   the frog   [the glass jar]¹

vi.   they   the frog   the next morning²

vii.   they   the window³

viii. the dog   a glass

        his...head

ix.   the dog   the window

x.   the glass

xi.   Tommy

xii.   the dog

xiii. the dog   his...face

xiv.   they   him

xv.   they   the woods⁴

xvi.

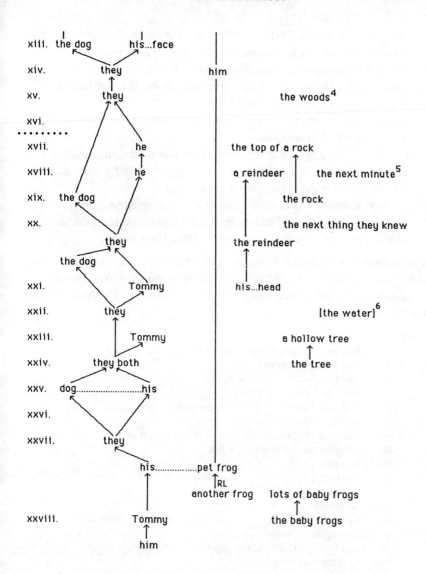

Fig. 3.14. Reference chains in text [3:88]

1. *the glass jar* — the first example of addition in the text; the presumed information is neither directly recoverable nor implied.
2. *the next morning* — in narrative, setting in time often involves relevance phoricity of this kind, bridging from the setting in time implied here by lying in bed asleep.
3. *the window* — bridged from *laying at the bottom of his bed*, implying a room with a window.
4. *the woods* — apparently bridged from *came out*; introducing this participant non-phorically was not felt appropriate by most children (cf. *there was a woods out the back and...*)
5. *the next minute* — setting in time bridging as in note 2 above.
6. *the water* — the second example of addition in the text; the identity of this participant is not recoverable from the co-text.

The second text is drawn from the same research. This time the story is told by another 10/11 year old female who is recounting an adapted version of the Aesop fable, which has just been read to her. Phoric items are again underlined.

[3:89]
i. There was once a donkey
ii. and he was carrying some sacks of sugar on his back
iii. and it was a very hot day
iv. and the donkey was very tired.
v. Soon he came to a stream
vi. and to get home
vii. he had to cross the stream;
viii. but at the bottom of the stream it was very muddy,
ix. so when the donkey stepped in
x. he sank;
xi. but then he decided to have a little rest
xii. and when he got up
xiii. he found
xiv. that the sacks were very much lighter than they were before,
xv. so that didn't bother him,
xvi. and that's because all the sugar had melted in the steam
xvii. so there was none left.
xviii. Another time the donkey had some sponges in th.. in the sacks
xix. and again he had to cross the stream,
xx. so he thought:
xxi. "Last time he went in the stream
xxii. the sacks got lighter,"
xxiii. so he thought
xxiv. he'd do it again on purpose;

xxv.   so he stepped in
xxvi.   and when he...and after a short while when he got up again
xxvii.   he found
xxviii. that the sacks were very heavy
xxix.   and that's because all the sponges collected water
xxx.   and he found
xxxi.   that he couldn't walk very well,
xxxii.   and so that's what happens
xxxiii. if you don't know the difference between sponges and sugar.

The reference chains in [3:89] are outlined in Fig. 3.15. Esphoric groups have been omitted: *the bottom of the stream, lighter than they were before, last time he went in* and *the difference between sponges and sugar*. Information presumed through text reference and extended reference is not shown in the diagram, but is taken up in the following notes; information indirectly presumed by *another time, last time* and *lighter* (in [3:89:xxii]) is similarly treated. In this text all major participants are introduced non-phorically: *a donkey, some sacks of sugar, a stream* and *some sponges*.

1. Both of the potential participants (the sacks and the sugar) in this Pre-Numerative structure are presumed in [3:89].
2. *that* presumes the projection *that the sacks were much lighter than they were before* as a fact (text reference).
3. *that* again presumes the same projection as a fact (text reference).
4. *Another time* is another setting in time marker, presuming the previous episode via bridging.
5. *Last time* — again, setting in time, bridging from the previous episode.
6. *lighter* — than they were in xviii; involving bridging as the relevant information about the sacks' weight was implicit there.
7. *it* presumes *he went in the stream* as an act (extended reference).
8. *that* presumes the projection *that the sacks got very heavy* as a fact (text reference).
9. *that* presumes an indefinite amount of information here as a fact — minimally clauses xxxii through xxv, but probably the whole story, especially if xxxii and xxxviii are taken as Coda as far as narrative structure is concerned (see Chapter 7 below).

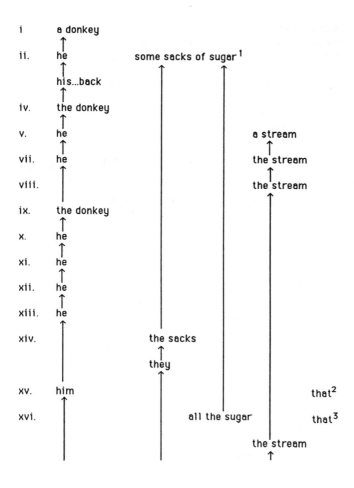

i.   a donkey

ii.   he   some sacks of sugar[1]

        his...back

iv.   the donkey

v.   he   a stream

vii.   he   the stream

viii.   the stream

ix.   the donkey

x.   he

xi.   he

xii.   he

xiii.   he

xiv.   the sacks

                        they

xv.   him   that[2]

xvi.   all the sugar   that[3]

                                        the stream

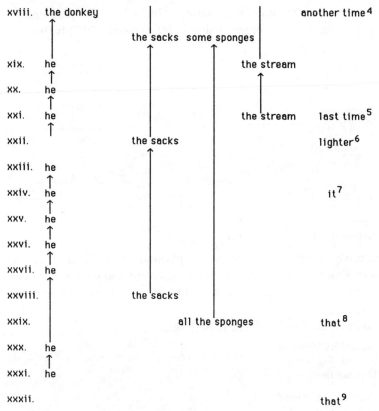

Fig. 3.15. Reference chains in text [3:89]

3.6 Location and manner

Because the point of departure for this chapter has been participant identification, closely related IDENTIFICATION systems realised through demonstrative and comparative adverbs have not yet been considered. The
demonstrative adverbs function as Circumstances of Location in clause
structure (e.g. *Come here.*) or as Qualifiers in nominal groups (e.g. *that guy*
there; they are realised by *here*, *there*, *now* and *then*. Each involves reminding phoricity, presuming location in space or time. They function both
exophorically and endophorically; and where endophoric *here* and *there*

may presume text (see Halliday and Hasan 1976:74-75). The paradigm of oppositions is a simple one, exemplified in [3:90] through [3:93] below.

	PROXIMATE	DISTANT
TIME	here	there
SPACE	now	then

[3:90] I'm at work;
        bring it here.

[3:91] He's a bit off.
        — You're right there.

[3:92] It's past noon;
        do it now.

[3:93] I got a computer in 88;
        writing was harder before then.

Comparative adverbs realise relevance phoricity; they function as Circumstances of Extent and Manner in clause structure and presume events. Both relevant events and supsersets of events are presumed. The network of oppositions is outlined in Fig. 3.16; typical realisations are shown in the network and illustrated in [3:94] through [3:99].

Extent [quantity:difference]
[3:94] Ben ran five miles;
        Carl ran farther.

Manner [quality:semblance]
[3:95] Ben ran very fast;
        Carl didn't run as fast.

Extent [quantity:difference:superset]
[3:96] The runners ran long distances;
        Carl ran farthest.

Manner [quality:difference:supserset]
[3:97] The sprinters ran fast heats;
        Ben didn't run fastest.

Extent [quantity:purposive]
[3:98] You had to set a record to place;
        Ben ran fast enough.

Manner [quality:purposive]
[3:99] You had to run a record time to win;
        Carl ran too slow.

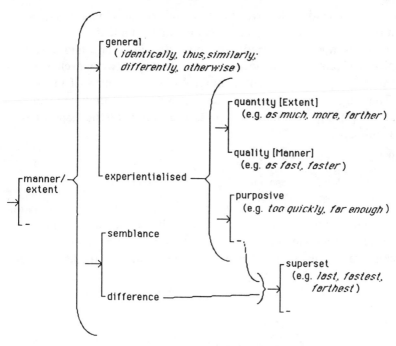

Fig. 3.16. Phoric circumstances of extent and manner

3.7 IDENTIFICATION and NEGOTIATION

Before moving on to a consideration of CONJUNCTION in Chapter 4, some of the differences between NEGOTIATION and IDENTIFICATION as discourse systems will be reviewed.

First, metafunction. NEGOTIATION is an interpersonal system; it focusses on the discourse semantics of MOOD. IDENTIFICATION on the other hand is a textual system; it focusses on the discourse semantics of nominal DEIXIS. It is for this reason that the entry conditions to the two systems differ. NEGOTIATION takes as point of origin the move and the exchange, where an exchange is defined as consisting of one or more moves and a move is defined as a discourse unit whose unmarked realisation is a clause selecting independently for MOOD. IDENTIFICATION has the semantic entity participant as its entry condition; its unmarked realisation is a nominal group and the people, places and things this encodes all have the potential to participate as Agent or Medium in clause structure at some point or other in a text.

NEGOTIATION was approached from both a multivariate and covariate perspective in Chapter 2. The notion of constituency between exchange and move was developed to account synoptically for sequences of up to five moves. These moves are mutually predicting as set out in their constituency structures. In [3:100] the initiation expects a response and the response presumes its initiation:

[3:100]   ┌─ K2   Who won?
            ─┤
                └─ K1   – Ben did.

In addition, dependency structures were introduced to account for tracking and challenging moves which are not strongly predicted by initiations; indeed, interlocutors may formulate interacts so as to avoid them. So while the tracking move in [3:101] depends on the interact it tracks, it is not expected by it.

[3:101]   ┌─ K1 ⟍   Ben won.
                │
            ─┤ cf ⟨   – Who?
                │
                │ rcf ⟋   – Ben Johnson.
                │
                └─ K1f   – Wow!

Reference structures make use of semantic dependency structures of this kind. Phoric items depend on the co-text they presume, but are not themselves predicted by it. Given a nominal group realising a participant in a text, there is no way of knowing whether or not it will be presumed, aside from the occasional selection of presenting reference marking certain participants as central to a discourse (signalled through *this*, *these*, *a certain* and *certain*). The dependency relationship between presuming and presumed is thus very like that between a tracking or challenging move and the move on which it depends.

[3:102]   Ben won.   Ben
            – He did?   ↑
                                he

Finally the major limitation on the acount of participant identification in this chapter needs to be acknowledged — that is, it's lack of attention to the **process** of identifying participants. This is reflected in the concentration on textual relations at the expense of their interaction with experiential ones and the lack of a procedural orientation to determining what would be appropriate to identifying a participant at a particular place in the unfolding of a text and how exactly interlocutors might go about retrieving presumed information. The account thus falls far short of the specificity required for computer implementation and text generation.

4. Conjunction & continuity

The logic of English text

4.1 The limits of grammar

One of the central concerns in Chapters 2 and 3 has been the relationship between discourse structures and grammatical ones. Having stratified the content plane and grounded description on Halliday's (1985a) formulation of lexicogrammar as a meaning making resource, the nature of the complementarity between grammar and discourse is naturally a focal issue. This is especially true with conjunctive relations, since it is in this area that Halliday (1985a:192-251) has elaborated his grammatical description to the point where very long passages of spontaneous spoken monologue are netted in. His clause complex analysis has in other words pushed grammatical description to new frontiers, and it is to the limits of these that this chapter first turns.

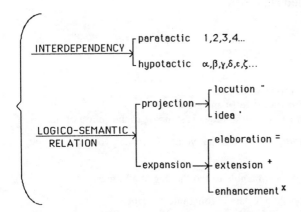

Fig. 4.1. Halliday's (1985a) description of clause complex relations

Halliday's (1985a:197) paradigm for clause complex relations is formulated systemically as Fig. 4.1, along with notational conventions for analysing the dependency relations involved. The network distinguishes both the type of interdependency (paratactic or hypotactic) and the kind of logico-semantic relation involved (projection or expansion).

This analysis is illustrated for text [4:1] below (taken from the research reported in Plum 1988). The text consists of 8 clauses, forming a single clause complex (in written English the clause complex coincides with the graphological unit sentence and [4:1] has been transcribed in these terms). Indentation is used to reflect the scope of the relations; expressed with bracketing the anlaysis is as follows:

$$1 \ (1 \ ^{+}2 \ (\alpha \ ^{x}\beta)) \ ^{x}2 \ (\alpha \ ^{'}\beta \ (\alpha \ ^{x}\beta \ (1 \ ^{+}2 \ (\alpha \ ^{x}\beta)))).$$

[4:1]	a.	1 1		Usually then he feels down the neck, along its body,
	b.	$^{+}2$	α	and he can sort of feel conformation
	c.		$^{x}\beta$	by doing this,
	d.	$^{x}2$	α	so you're hoping all the time
	e.		$^{'}\beta \ \alpha$	that your dog will stand nice and steady
	f.		$^{x}\beta \ 1$	so the judge can do this
	g.		$^{+}2 \ \alpha$	and it doesn't hamper him
	h.		$^{x}\beta$	handling the dogs.

Text [4:1] is in fact just part of a much longer response to an interview question designed to elicit a procedural text (see Chapter 7 below; Martin 1985b:5-6). The full response is presented as [4:2] below, divided into ranking clauses and clause complexes; embedded clauses are enclosed in double brackets (thus: [[embedded clause]]).

[4:2] Question:
     1.a.   What do you have to do in the showing area,
       b.   with the dog on the lead?

Response:
     2.c.   Well, you always walk
       d.   with the dog on the left-hand side,
       e.   the reason being is [[the judge is standing in the centre of the ring]].

     3.f.   So, therefore, you need to get yourself between your dog and the judge.

     4.g.   The dog (!) must be able to see the dog at all times.

     5.h.   So, usually when a class is going into the ring,
       i.   the first thing it does is:
       j.   the judge is standing in the centre of the ring,

k.	the people sort of walk the ring, with their dogs,
l.	and then...we sort of wait.

6.m.	With the Dachshund, a Dachshund is tabled.

7.n.	That's [[because it's a low dog]],
o.	and the judge goes over that.

8.p.	With the bigger breeds of dog, they're stood on the ground,
q.	because it's easier [[for the judge to handle them]].

9.r.	With the smaller breeds of dog such as Corgis, all the Toy-breeds, Dachshunds and this type of thing we — as our turn comes,
s.	we stand our dog on the table,
t.	we stand it in show stance,
u.	with the lead, the lead held up,
v.	hoping
w.	that our dog will stand like a nice statue,
x.	so as the judge can come.

10.y.	The judge handles it,
z.	and this is [[where I'm telling you, temperament plays a big part]].

11.aa.	The judge has to be able to look into the dog's mouth
bb.	to see
cc.	that it's teeth are perfect.

12.dd.	Usually then he feels down the neck, along its body,
ee.	and he can sort of feel conformation
ff.	by doing this,
gg.	so you're hoping all the time
hh.	that your dog will stand nice and steady
ii.	so the judge can do this
jj.	and it doesn't hamper him
kk.	handling the dogs.

13.ll.	After the judge has handled and gone over the dog,
mm.	then, you really do [[whatever the judge tells you]].

14.nn.	Basically it is always the same.

15.oo.	He usually says,
pp.	or she usually says,
qq.	"Walk your dog in a triangle."

16.rr.	Now, as I told you already,
ss.	the dog is always walked on the left-hand side.

17.tt.	So, if your judge is standing here,
uu.	we walk away from him that way.

18.vv.   That is [[so the judge can get the hind movement of your dog]].

19.ww.   Then we usually walk sideways like that
xx.   so as he can see [[the dog moving all over]]
yy.   and then we walk back to the judge
zz.   so as he can see the front movement.

20.aaa.   After that he usually tells you
bbb.   to wait over there.

21.ccc.   He proceeds to do that with every dog.

22.ddd.   Then he will say,
eee.   "Line your dog up."
fff.   or "Get the best out of your dog."
ggg.   and he will sum them all up
hhh.   and put them in first, second or third.

As reflected in the numbering and punctuation, [4:2] has been divided into 22 clause complexes. This number could have been reduced by 3 had the *so*'s introducing clauses f, h and tt not been taken as cohesive conjunctions introducing a new clause complex (they were so taken because each *so* was spoken on its own separate tone group); and the number might have been reduced again by further liberalising one's criteria for clause complex boundaries (e.g. the treatment of *then* in clauses dd, ww and ddd). But most analysts would probably be hard pressed to reduce the response to a single clause complex (or a single move complex filling a K1 response to a K2 move for that matter; see Chapter 2, section 2.4.2 above). The following clauses in particular do not make use of clause complex resources to encode causal or temporal relations:

n.   That's because it's a low dog.
vv.   That is so the judge can get the hind movement of your dog.
aaa.   After that he usually tells you...
ccc.   He proceeds to do that with every dog.

Each of these uses a combination of IDENTIFICATION and TRANSITIVITY to make the necessary logical connections between parts of the text. The first two are causal and involve text reference; anaphoric *that* functions as Carrier in an attributive relational clause with cause and purpose clauses embedded in the Attribute (for attributive processes see Halliday 1985a:112-128). *That* has been replaced with an embedded enhancement in the related identifying clauses below to help focus explicitly on the connection being made. The proportionalities are as follows:

ATTRIBUTIVE (text reference):IDENTIFYING (embedded enhancement)::

That's [[because it's a low dog]]:
The reason [[why a Dachshund is tabled]] is (the fact) [[that it's a low dog]]::

That is [[so the judge can get the hind movement of your dog]]:
The purpose [[of walking away from the judge]] is (the need) [[for him to get the hind movement of your dog]]

The temporal examples also make use of *that*, but in the context of extended rather than text reference. In *After that*, *that* functions as part of a Circumstance of Location in time, with the temporal connection coded as a preposition. In the last example, *that* functions as a Range for the general process *do* and temporal succession is coded through the process *proceed*.

The point is that while examples such as these make use of resources other than the clause complex to mark logical relations between parts of a text, there is a sense in which the alternative realisations are all variations on the same theme — namely that of relating one part of a text to another in terms of the natural logic of time, cause, comparison and addition (see Halliday 1985a:378-384 for variations on a causal theme). So not only does the clause complex need to be supplemented as far as a consideration of logical relations is concerned, but it needs to be abstracted from as well so that a more general treatment can be pursued, taking the clause complex into account as just one of its manifestations. It is for this reason of course that logical relations will be interpreted from the perspective of discourse semantics, rather than that of lexicogrammar here.

What then of the range of alternative realisations for logical relations in English text? To begin, consider the kinds of explicit connection between clause complexes in [4:2]. These include two of what Halliday and Hasan (1976:267) call continuatives, *well* and *now*; and seven instances of other cohesive conjunctions, realised by three items, *therefore*, *so* and *then* (as noted, *so* and *then* may also realise paratactic dependency within the clause complex, most clearly when accompanied by *and*). Temporal succession is also realised through a resumptive β clause supplementing *then* in clause complex 13: *after the judge has handled and gone over the dog, then...*; closely related to this pattern is the Circumstance of location in time noted above, with succession coded through a preposition rather than a hypotactic conjunction and the reference item *that* presuming the relevant acts: *after that*. Finally, as discussed above, there are two causal Attributes (introduced by *that's because...* and *that's so...*) and the process *proceeds* coding temporal succession as phase in a verbal group complex. These various realisations are listed below, scaled according to the degree to which the information being logically connected is experientially integrated within a single clause structure (from least integrated *well, now* to most integrated *proceeds*).

EXPLICIT CONNECTIONS:

continuative:	well [1-2], now [15-16]
cohesive conjunction:	therefore [2-3];
	so [2-3], so [4-5], then [11-12],
	so [16-17], then [18-19], then [21-22]
resumptive β clause:	after...then [10...12-13]
Circumstance of location:	after that [19-20]
circumstantial Attribute:	that's because... [6-7], that's so...[17-18]
phase (verbal group complex):	proceeds to do that [10...20-21]

In addition there are a number of connections that are not made explicit but which have to be filled in to make sense of [4:2]. The least implicit of these is the comparison between clause complexes 6...7 and 8 and between 8 and 9; clause complexes 8 and 9 are both introduced with Circumstances of Matter functioning as marked Themes which contain comparative reference between generic groups. The reference chain runs as follows:

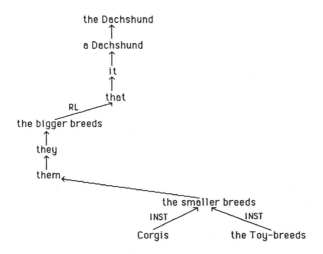

Fig. 4.2. Reference chains in [4:2:6-9]

The rest of the connections listed below have to be inferred from the experiential meaning of the clause complexes involved. The important point to note at this stage is that simply putting clauses next to each other suggests some logical connection between them, whether or not this is made explicit through the various linking resources the grammar provides.

IMPLICIT CONNECTIONS:
comparison: with the bigger breeds of dog [6..7-8]
            with the smaller breeds [8-9]
causal [3-4], [10-11]
temporal [9-10]
elaboration [14-15]
comment [13-14]

Alongside these "cohesive" (i.e. inter-sentence relations in Halliday and Hasan's 1976 sense of the term) relations between clause complexes, text [4:2] exhibits a variety of grammatical dependencies inside clause complexes. The conjunctive items used are as follows:

PARATACTIC	and, so, or, and then
HYPOTACTIC: FINITE	when, because, so as, as, if, after...then
HYPOTACTIC: NON-FINITE	with, by

There are also implicit paratactic and hypotactic dependencies. The hypotactic ones are marked by non-finite processes: imperfective *hoping* [v], *handling* [kk] and perfective *to see* [bb]. The implicit paratactic examples are of the elaboration type, which is usually not marked with a conjunction (see Halliday 1985a:204); within this category t clarifies s:

r	$^{x}\beta$	...as our turn comes,
s	α 1	we stand our dog on the table,
t	$^{=}2\,\alpha$	we stand it in show stance,
u	$^{=}\beta$	with the lead held up

This leaves the two anomalous structures in [4:2], clauses e and i to be considered. Both clauses involve grammatical metaphor, realising cause as a noun (*reason*; cf. *so, because*) and temporal succession as a superlative Numerative (*first*; cf. *initially, firstly*). Clause e (*the reason being is the judge is standing in the centre of the ring*) starts off as a hypotactically dependent non-finite clause, predicting something like the following:

c. Well, you always walk
d. with the dog on the left-hand side,
e. the reason being the judge is standing in the centre of the ring.

But after *being* the clause changes ground, switching into a finite identifying process; working backwards from the end of the clause, the sequence c, d, e might be predicted to have unfolded as follows, with two clause complexes, not one:

    c.   Well, you always walk
    d.   with the dog on the left-hand side.

    e.   The reason is the judge is standing in the centre of the ring.

This kind of dynamic reformulation is not at all uncommon in spontaneous monlogue (for a considered discussion see Plum 1988:94-124).

    Clause i starts off in the opposite direction, as a finite identifying clause; the kind of text it predicts is as follows:

    h.   So, usually when a class if going into the ring,
    i.   the first thing it does is walk the ring,
    j.   and then it waits.

But instead of the embedded clause [[*walk the ring*]], the speaker introduces a ranking clause with a new Subject: *the judge is standing in the centre of the ring* and develops a paratactic clause complex from this. In both cases the dynamic shift seems prompted by the need to make the position of the judge in the ring clear, in order to make the behaviour of the trainers and their dogs in the showing area interpretable to an outsider.

    To this point the limitations of Halliday's clause complex analysis have been explored with respect to the variety of of ways in which logical relations can be realised, between clause complexes or within and marked through conjunctions, TRANSITIVITY and IDENTIFICATION or simple juxtaposition. It is also important to note that clause complex analysis is somewhat biassed towards local relations between pairs of adjacent clauses and that certain texts, especially abstract written ones, may have a global rhetorical organisation requiring a different analytical perspective. This kind of organisation is exemplified in [4:3] below (example taken from Halliday 1985a:100).

    [4:3] 1.a. Governments were committed to inflation
           b. because they were themselves part of the system which required it.

          2.c. Modern capitalism thrives on expansion and credit,
           d. and without them it shrivels.

          3.e. Equally however it requires the right context,
           f. which is an expanding world economy:

g. a national economy is distinct and severable from other national economies in some senses but not all.

4.h. If the total economy of which it is a part does not expand,
  i. then the inflation in the particular economy ceases to be fruitful
  j. and becomes malignant.

5.k. Furthermore, the more the particular economy flourishes,
  l. the more dependent is it upon the total economy to which it is directing a part of its product,
  m. and the more dangerous is any pause in it alimentation -
  n. the easier it is to turn from boom to bust.

6.o. Finally, any government operating within such a system becomes overwhelmingly committed to maintaining it,
  p. more especially when symptoms of collapse appear -
  q. as they did in the last decade of our period
  r. when governments felt compelled to help out not only lame ducks but lame eagles too.

7.s. All this was inflationary.

This text has been organised by its author, Peter Calvocoressi, into seven clause complexes (orthographic sentences). Of interest here is the rhetorical structure of the argument he is developing. Basically, clause complexes 2, 3, 4, 5 and 6 provide supporting argumentation for the thesis advanced in clause complex 1; and 7 sums up the impact of 2 through 6. In all, four arguments are presented: clause complexes 3 and 4 form a single argument alongside those in 2, 5 and 6 — and what Halliday and Hasan (1976:241) as *internal* conjunctions are used to organise them (*equally*, *furthermore* and *finally*). The structure of the text is as follows:

	Thesis	(clause complex 1)
	Argument 1	(clause complex 2)
equally	Argument 2	(clause complexes 3 & 4)
furthermore	Argument 3	(clause complex 5)
finally	Argument 4	(clause complex 6)
	Conclusion	(clause complex 7)

This kind of global rhetorical structure is well beyond the scope of clause complex analysis. It represents the organisation of text taken as a whole and divided into stages rather than as a combination of clauses put together two by two — the perspective required is a "top-down" one, complementing interpretation from the "grammar up". This problem will be taken up in detail below when internal as opposed to external conjunctive relations are considered.

4.2 Conjunctive relations in English: general issues

4.2.1 *Diversification*

As annotated above for [4:2], in spontaneous spoken monologue the semantic system CONJUNCTION tends to be realised through paratactic and hypotactic relationships within the clause complex, and through 'cohesive' conjunctions relating clause complexes to each other. Texts produced in this mode foreground realisations of CONJUNCTION as logico-semantic relations between processes. In other modes however, these relations may tend to be realised within, rather than between processes — as Circumstances in any process type, within the structure of relational clauses (especially of the circumstantial variety) and even within the structure of nominal groups. A more systematic account of this diversification will now be developed. The account will be exemplified through temporal relations, taking [4:2:k-l] as point of departure; for a parallel account of causal relations see Halliday (1985a:378-384).

[4:2]   k.   The people sort of walk the ring, with their dogs,
        l.   **and then**...we sort of wait.

As a relationship **between** these two processes, the meaning can be structured as follows:

COHESIVE CONJUNCTION
[4:4]   We walk the ring with our dogs. **Afterwards** we just wait.

PARATACTIC CONJUNCTION
[4:5]   We walk the ring with our dogs **and then** we just wait.

HYPOTACTIC CONJUNCTION (finite)
[4:6]   **After** we walk the ring with our dogs we just wait.

HYPOTACTIC CONJUNCTION (non-finite)
[4:7]   **Subsequent to** walking the ring with our dogs we just wait.

Alternatively, the temporal relation can be realised **within** a process. This involves nominalising to some degree one or both of the processes of walking and waiting, at least weakly as an embedded clause or more strongly as a nominalisation. The possibilities are as follows (as above, the realisation of the temporal relation is in boldface; any accompanying embedding is enclosed in double brackets and nominalised processes are in italics):

CIRCUMSTANCE OF LOCATION
[4:8]   **After** our *tour* of the ring, we just wait.

ATTRIBUTIVE (Attribute: phrase)
[4:9]   Our *tour* of the ring   is   **prior to** our **wait**.
         Carrier   Process   Attribute/Circumstance
Attribute/Circumstance

ATTRIBUTIVE (Attribute: clause)
[4:10]   Our *tour* of the ring   is   [[**before** we wait]].
         Carrier   Process   Attribute/Circumstance

IDENTIFYING (Token or Value/Circumstance)
[4:11]   Our *tour* of the ring   is   the **antecedent** of our *wait*.
         Token   Process   Value/Circumstance

IDENTIFYING (Process:circumstantial)
[4:12]   Our *tour* of the ring   **precedes**   our *wait*.
         Token   Process:circumstantial   Value

It is in fact possible to spread the realisation of the relation over two identifying clauses, by coding the temporal succession in a phoric Numerative, modifying a general noun:

[4:13]   The **first** thing [[we do]] is [[tour the ring with our dogs]];
         the **next** thing [[we do]] is [[we wait]].

Finally the temporal relation may be expressed within the structure of a nominal group, with one process nominalised as Thing and the other functioning as Qualifier; in this case the temporal relation is expressed as a preposition or conjunction introducing the Qualifier:

[4:14]   our *tour* of the ring **prior** to our *wait*
         our *tour* of the ring **preceding** our *wait*
         our *tour* of the ring **before** we wait
         etc.

Note that if an event is repeated, temporal succession may be expressed in the Numerative, through a phoric reference item, either presuming or not presuming the subsequent event esphorically; but this is not possible with two distinct events such as walking and waiting in the examples above:

our **previous** *tour* of the ring to this one
our **previous** *tour* of the ring

These divergent patterns of realisation are summarised in Fig. 4.3. Expressing logical relations within a process depends on grammatical metaphor; one or both of the processes involved must be "thing-ized" to

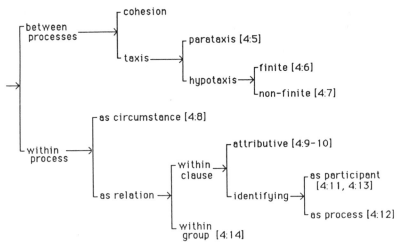

Fig. 4.3. Divergent grammaticalisations of CONJUNCTION

some extent — via embedding or nominalisation. These realisations of log-ical relations can be taken as metaphorical and are more characteristic of written than spoken text (see the discussion of mode in Chapter 7 below; Halliday 1985b).

4.2.2 *Logico-semantic relations*

The problem of just how to classify the logico-semantic relations that can be realised through the diversified realisations outlined above is a difficult one. A large number of classifications have been proposed, including Beekman & Callow (1974), Longacre (1976), Halliday & Hasan (1976), Martin (1983b), Halliday (1985a) and Mann & Thompson (1986) to name just a few of the more comprehensive. Some of these are universalist in orienta-tion, gathering together an "etic" pool of relations which might be gram-maticalised from one language to another (eg. Beekman & Callow, Lon-gacre and Mann & Thompson); others focus on particular languages, look-ing at relations realised there (eg. Halliday & Hasan, Martin and Halliday on English or Martin 1981 on Tagalog). Another source of divergence among the classifications has to do with what type of realisation is taken as point of departure for the analysis. Halliday & Hasan for example focus on cohesive relations between clause complexes, Martin (1983b) bases his clas-sification on hypotactic conjunctions and Halliday (1985a) develops a categorisation for paratactic and hypotactic relations within the clause complex. Given the different oppositions as one moves from one of these types of realisation to another, not to mention the problem of universalist vs particularist schemes, it is hardly surprising that the classifications that have been proposed are divergent in many respects.

In order to explore this indeterminacy, a comparison will be made among the classifications proposed within systemic theory for English: Halliday and Hasan (1976), Martin (1983b) and Halliday (1985a). Halliday and Hasan's (1976:242-243) Summary Table of Conjunctive relations is reproduced here as Table 4.1 below. This table is organised around two axes: four types of logico-semantic relation — additive, adversative, casual, temporal and the external/internal opposition passed over above (to be taken up in 4.2.3 below).

Halliday's (1985a:306-307) synoptic summary of expansion is reproduced as Table 4.2. This paradigm takes a different set of logico-semantic relations as one axis — elaboration, extension and enhancement and their subclasses and the diversification of the realisation of these categories throughout the grammar as the other. Martin's classification will be introduced in the course of making a few points about Tables 4.1 and 4.2; an overview is then presented in Table 4.3 below.

Before looking at differences among the schemes, similarities should be noted. All three classifications set up very comparable additive, temporal and consequential categories for the meanings clustering around the "proto-typical" *and*, *then* and *so*. These do not correspond exactly, but they do have a large number of relations in common. Indeterminacy on the other hand seems to arise in the area of Halliday and Hasan's adversative, Halliday's elaborating and Martin's comparative relations.

Two main factors would appear to underlie the divergent classifications in this area. One was noted above and has to do with the type of grammaticalisation linguists take as point of departure for their scheme. Halliday and Hasan for example focus on "cohesive" relations between clause complexes, and set up additive, adversative, causal and temporal as kinds of logico-semantic relation at primary delicacy — with the items *and*, *yet*, *so* and *then* "typifying these four very general conjunctive relations" (1976:239). Martin (1983b) on the other hand starts with hypotactic relations, and splits up the adversative category into concession (typified by *although*) and contrast (typified by *whereas*); concession is then related to causals under a general consequential heading and contrast is grouped with similarity under a new heading of comparison.

Table 4.1. Types of conjunction. Reproduced from M.A.K. Halliday and R. Hasan, Cohesion in English. London (1976), Longman.

	External/internal	Internal (unless otherwise specified)		
Additive	Additive, simple: Additive *and, and also . . .* Negative *nor, and . . . not* Alternative *or, or else*	Complex, emphatic: Additive *furthermore, in addition, besides* Alternative *alternatively* Complex, de-emphatic: After-thought *incidentally, by the way*	Apposition: Expository *that is, I mean, in other words* Exemplificatory *for instance, thus*	Comparison: Similar *likewise, similarly, in the same way* Dissimilar *on the other hand, by contrast*
Adversative	Adversative 'proper': Simple *yet, though, only* Containing 'and' *but* Emphatic *however, nevertheless, despite this*	Contrastive: Avowal *in fact, actually, as a mater of fact* Contrastive (external): Simple *but, and* Emphatic *however, on the other hand, at the same time*	Correction: Of meaning *instead, rather, on the contrary* Of wording *at least, rather, I mean*	Dismissal: Closed *in any case, in either case, whichever way it is* Open-ended *in any case, anyhow, at any rate, however it is*

	External/internal	Internal (unless otherwise specified)		
Causal	Causal, general: Simple — so, then, hence, therefore Emphatic — consequently, because of this Causal, specific: Reason — for this reason, on account of this Result — as a result, in consequence Purpose — for this purpose, with this in mind	Reversed causal: Simple — for, because Causal, specific: Reason — it follows, on this basis Result — arising out of this Purpose — to this end	Conditional (also external): Simple — then Emphatic — in that case, in such an event, that being so Generalized — under the circumstances Reversed polarity — otherwise, under other circumstances	Respective: Direct — in this respect, in this regard, with reference to this Reversed polarity — otherwise, in other respects, aside from this
Temporal	Temporal, simple (external only): Sequential — then, next, after that Simultaneous — just then, at the same time Preceding — previously, before that Conclusive: Simple — finally, at last Correlative forms: Sequential — first ... then Conclusive — at first ... in the end	Complex (external only): Immediate — at once, thereupon Interrupted — soon, after a time Repetitive — next time, on another occasion Specific — next day, an hour later Durative — meanwhile Terminal — until then Punctiliar — at this moment	Internal temporal: Sequential — then, next, secondly Conclusive — finally, in conclusion Correlative forms: Sequential — first ... next Conclusive — ... finally	'Here and now': Past — up to now, hitherto Present — at this point, here Future — from now on, henceforward Summary: Summarizing — to sum up, in short, briefly Resumptive — to resume, to return to the point

Table 4.2. Halliday's (1985a) synoptic summary of expansion

type of expansion		functional relationship with which expansion is combined	COHESION between clause complexes (non-structural)	INTERDEPENDENCY between clauses in a clause complex		
				paratactic	hypotactic	
(ii) ELABORATION	opposition	expository exemplificatory	In other words For example	that is	which, who	non-finite clause
					NON-DEFINING RELATIVE CLAUSE	
	clarification	various types	Or rather, Anyway, Actually &c.	at least		
(+) EXTENSION	addition	positive negative adversative	Also Neither However	and nor but	while whereas	besides without
	variation	replacive subtractive alternative	On the contrary Otherwise Alternatively	only or	except that if not then	instead of other than
(x) ENHANCEMENT	spatio-temporal place	extent point(s)	There	there	as far as where(ver)	
	spatio-temporal time	extent point(s) prior subsequent various complex types	Throughout Simultaneously Previously Next Finally, At once, Meanwhile &c.	now then	while when(ever) before, until after, since as soon as &c.	while, in when, on before, until after, since
	manner	means quality comparison	Thus Likewise	so	as, as if	by like, as if
	causal-conditional cause	reason result purpose insurance	Therefore Consequently To that end	so, for thus	because in order that in case	with, by as a result of (so as) to, for in case of
	causal-conditional condition	positive negative concessive	In that case Otherwise Nevertheless	then otherwise though	if, as long as unless although	if, in event of without despite*
	matter	respective	In that respect			
class of item { that is being related: by which relationship is realized			clause(complex): prepositional phrase or adverb	independent clause: conjunction	finite or non-finite dependent clause: conjunction, preposition, or relative (noun)	

EMBEDDING of clause as Modifier in nominal group	CIRCUMSTAN-TIATION in clause (as process)	PHASE, CONATION &c. in verbal group complex (TENSE, VOICE in verbal group)		ATTRIBUTION or IDENTIFICATION as relational process in clause
which, who; [non-finite / clause] that — DEFINING RELATIVE CLAUSE	as — ROLE	PASSIVE VOICE — is [v^n]	PHASE / (a) TIME — start, keep / (b) REALITY — seem, turn out	INTENSIVE 'is' — (=)
whose, of which — DEFINING RELATIVE CLAUSE (POSSESSIVE)	with, including without — ACCOMPANIMENT / instead of except (for)	PAST TENSE — has [v^n] / OBLIGATION — has to [v^o]	CONATION & POTEN-TIALITY — try; succeed; can; learn	POSSESSIVE 'has' — (+)
DEFINING RELATIVE CLAUSE (CIRCUMSTANTIAL) / (a) CIRCUMSTANCE AS HEAD — place (where/that) time (when/that) reason (why/that) &c. / (b) CIRCUMSTANCE AS MODIFIER — [HEAD noun] where/at which when/on which for which about which &c.	for at, in — PLACE / for at, on before after during &c. — TIME / by, with [adverb] like — MANNER / because of for in case of — CAUSE / in the event of in default of despite / about — MATTER	PRESENT TENSE — is (at) [$v^ŋ$] / EXPECT-ATION — is to [v^o]	MODULA-TION / (a) TIME — begin by / (b) MANNER — venture, hesitate / (c) CAUSE — happen, remember	CIRCUMSTANTIAL 'is at' / (a) CIRCUMSTANCE AS PROCESS — occupies, follows, causes concerns &c. / (b) CIRCUMSTANCE AS PARTICIPANT — is at, in, on, before, like, because of, about &c. / (×)
finite or non-finite rankshifted clause: relative (noun, adverb, or prepositional phrase)	prepositional phrase: preposition	verbal group: auxiliary	verbal group complex: verb	nominal group: verb or preposition

Table 4.3. Contrasting typologies of relations in Martin (1983b) and Halliday and Hasan (1976)

MARTIN (1983b)	HALLIDAY & HASAN (1976)
additive 'besides'	additive 'and'
comparative: contrast 'whereas' 　　　　　　similarity 'like'	adversative 'but'
consequential: concession 'although' 　　　　　　cause 'because' 　　　　　　etc.	causal 'so'
temporal 'after'	temporal 'then'

The fact that in English *but* neutralises the distinction between contrast and concession as far as relations between clause complexes are concerned is probably one factor influencing the difference between the classifications. The general point is that oppositions among cohesive conjunctions are different from those among hypotactic ones, and that in any attempt to generalise a framework for logico-semantic relations across these and other realisations some indeterminacy is bound to arise.

The second factor underlying the differences in categorisation has to do with the essential indeterminacy of some of the relations themselves. The problem of alternation (*or*) and contrast (*whereas*) is a case in point. Both relations imply a system of terms (a taxonomy of some kind; see Chapter 5 below) — for example tea or coffee as hot after-dinner drinks.

$$\text{after-dinner drinks} \longrightarrow \begin{cases} \text{tea} \\ \text{coffee} \end{cases}$$

The terms themselves can then be viewed in two ways. One way is to view them as available alternatives, which combine in text like additives:

A OR B:A AND B::
We have tea or coffee: we have tea and coffee::
Get tea. — Or coffee?:Get tea — And coffee?::
They drink either tea or coffee:They drink both tea and coffee::
Have tea, or coffee instead:Have tea, and coffee as well

Another way of looking at the terms is to consider how they are similar (as a result of subclassifying after-dinner drinks) and how they differ (since they are oppositions in the same system). Looked at in this way not A but B contrasts with A similarly B:

A WHEREAS B:
A LIKE B::

Tea doesn't taste bitter to me whereas coffee does:
Tea tastes just as bitter to me as coffee does::

I take tea with milk but coffee without:
I take tea with milk as I do with coffee::

So you have tea in the morning while she takes coffee:
So you have tea in the morning just as she does

Since the relationship between such terms can be looked at in different ways, classifying the relevant hypotactic conjunctions becomes problematic (e.g. *while, whereas, apart from, without, except that, instead of, rather than, other than*). Halliday (1985a) groups them with additives under the heading extension, emphasising the relationship between alternation ('or') and addition ('and'); Martin (1983b) on the other hand focusses on the idea of opposition ('whereas'), grouping them with similarity ('like') under the general heading of comparison. Because of the indeterminacy of the relations themselves, neither categorisation is completely satisfactory.

These problems are not isolated. Halliday (1985a) for example subclassifies enhancing relations on the basis of his categories for types of Circumstance in the system of TRANSITIVITY. Thus *likewise* comes out as enhancing:manner and *in that respect* as enhancing:matter. This contrasts with the *Cohesion in English* analysis which groups *likewise* among the additives (extension:addition for Halliday 1985a) and *in that respect* among causals (enhancing:causal-conditional for Halliday 1985a). Since the prepositions realising circumstantial relations organise the world differently from conjunctions, this divergence is not surprising.

It would appear then that apart from the general criteria of utility and comprehensiveness, all that can be demanded of a particular classification at this stage is that its point of departure be made clear and the lines it draws between categories be as explicit as possible. For suggestions concerning the way in which historical evidence might be used to clarify some of these issues see Traugott (1978, 1982).

In this chapter, following Martin (1983b), four main types of logico-semantic relation will be recognised: additive, comparative, temporal and consequential. And CONJUNCTION will be developed as a system of oppositions at the level of discourse semantics, in an attempt to generalise across the diverse realisations of logical relations reviewed through this section. This has two important implications for the classification scheme. First, the distinction between internal and external conjunction will be taken as fundamental (following Halliday and Hasan 1976); this has repercussions for the grammar based categorisation developed in Halliday (1985a) and reproduced as Table 4.2 above (see 4.2.3 below). Second, as far as possible CONJUNCTION will be set up in such a way that it can be inter-related with other discourse systems. The opposition of similarity to difference is an important aspect of NEGOTIATION (comply/resist), IDENTIFICATION (semblance/difference) and IDEATION (synonym/antonym) and will accordingly be given more prominence in the analysis presented here than in Haliday and Hasan (1976) or Halliday (1985a).

A synoptic preview of this classification is presented below as Table 4.4, which can be usefully compared at this point with Tables 4.1 and 4.2. Examples of representative conjunctions are provided, limited with respect to notes 1-4 below.

4.2.3 *Internal and external relations*

As noted in 4.1 with respect to text [4:3] some kinds of relations between clause complexes are more "rhetorical" than experiential. *Equally* there coded the arguments it connects as equal in status; *furthermore* indicated that there was another argument to be considered; and *finally* signalled that the last in a series of arguments was being presented. At the same time it is clear that *equally* is a kind of comparative conjunction — it marks the "similarity" in status between the arguments; similarly *furthermore* is additive, monitoring the "accumulation" of evidence; and *finally* is temporal — the argument it introduces is the "ultimate" one.

The rhetorical nature of these conjunctions can be brought out by comparing them with three experientially oriented conjunctive relations in the same text:

SIMILARITY
l.   **the more** the particular economy flourishes,
m.   **the more** dependent is it upon the total economy to which it is directing a part of its product,

Table 4.4. Classification of logico-semantic relations in English Text

	Distinctive Internal[1]	External/internal: "Cohesive"[2]	Paratactic[3]	Hypotactic[4]
Additive				
addition:	Moreover, In addition	And	and	besides
alternation:	Alternatively	Or	or	if not...then
Comparative				
similarity:	Equally, That is	Likewise	soˆ Finite	like, as, as if, like when
contrast:	On the other hand	In contrast, Instead	but	whereas, except that
Temporal				
simultaneous:	At the same time	Meanwhile, Throughout	and meanwhile	while, when, as long as
successive:	Finally, At first	Previously, Thereupon	then	after, since, now that
Consequential				
purpose:	To this end	To this end	modulation + so	so that, lest, so as, in case
condition:	Then	Then, Otherwise	modality + so	if, even if, unless
consequence:	In conclusion, After all	Therefore, For	so	because, as, since
concession:	Nevertheless, Admittedly	However, Yet	but	although, in spite of
manner:	In this way	Thus	and thus	by, thereby

1. Examples of conjunctions which cannot be external are given where possible (exceptions: *in this way, then, to this end*)
2. Examples of "cohesive" (i.e. inter-sentence) conjunctions limited to those which can be clause complex initial.
3. Examples of paratactic conjunctions limited to those which allow a branching structure (i.e. ellipsis within the clause complex: *John arrived but Mary didn't.*)
4. Examples of hypotactic conjunctions limited to those introducing clauses that can be either Theme or Rheme in the clause complex.

ADDITION

c.   Modern capitalism thrives on expansion and credit,

d.   **and** without them it shrivels.

SIMULTANEOUS

q.   as they did in the last decade of our period

r.   **when** governments felt compelled to help out not only lame ducks but lame eagles too.

The correlative structure linking l with m realises a genuine comparison between the rate at which an economy flourishes and the rate at which it becomes dependent on the world economy, not simply a comparison between the status of two arguments. Similarly, the *and* linking c to d links two comments on modern capitalism, without accumulating them as rhetorical extensions to the text. And the *when* linking q to r relates the events as occurring at the same time in history, as opposed to the time taken for the text itself to unfold.

Halliday and Hasan (1976:239-241) refer to what have been characterised as rhetorical relations here as *internal*; these relations obtain in the organisation of the text itself rather than the organisation of the world the text describes. The experiential relations are referred to as *external*, oriented to what is going on outside the text, rather than within (Van Dijk 1977b:208ff) opposes semantic to pragmatic connectives along the same lines). The underlying opposition in their terms is that of text vs "reality":

> The essential fact here is that communication is itself a process, albeit a process of a special kind; and that the salient event in this process is the text. It is this that makes it possible for there to be two closely analogous sets of conjunctive relations: those which exist as relations between external phenomena, and those which are as it were internal to the communication situation. (1976:240)

Internal relations in other words structure semiosis; external ones code the structure of the world.

A less materialist interpretation, drawing on the semiotic approach to context to be developed in Chapter 7, could be framed along the following lines. This would treat external relations as by and large oriented to field — they encode the institutional organisation of our culture. Internal relations on the other hand are oriented to genre (including the conversational structure realising genre in dialogic modes) — they encode the organisation of text as it is formulated to construct our culture.

The distinction between external and internal is probably clearest with temporal relations. External relations are used to display the activity sequences in which people engage as members of various institutions. Internal relations on the other hand attend to text-time — time in relation to what is being said, not what is being done. In certain registers, especially those where language accompanies what is going on institutionally, text time and field time are so much in tune that the internal/external distinction is not that important. The temporal relations in the following recipe excerpt can be read either as external ('after you've done that, do this') or internal ('now I've told you that, I'll tell you this') without really affecting the meanings made (recipe adapted from Solomon 1976:56); this is because the text is perfectly iconic with its field:

[4:15] a. Hard boil the eggs,
     b. cool under running water,
     c. chill
     d. and set aside.
     e. **Next**, extract the coconut milk
     f. as described on page 11,
     g. and keep the first extract or thick milk, and the second extract, or thin milk, separate.
     h. **Then** heat the ghee
     i. and fry onion, garlic, ginger, chillies and curry leaves on low heat
     j. until the onions are done.
     ...

In other modes, where language is constitutive of what is going on as in [4:3] above, the distinction between external and internal relations is vital. The temporal organisation of such texts will be quite different from that of the institutional events to which they refer and internal relations will prove critical in signalling this textual organisation.

Because of their orientation to text-time, internal relations are found most commonly in two syntagmatic environments. One was noted above in connection with [4:3]; the role of internal relations there was to organise the argument. More generally, across genres, the role of internal relations is to scaffold the schematic structure of a text (see Chapter 7 below). The other environment is that of the exchange, particularly exchange dynamics. Both challenges to moves and links between exchanges are commonly marked with internal conjunctions; two examples from [2:2] were:

[2:2]	31.	Server:	⎡ K2	Has she got Peter Pan?
	32.	Client:	⎣ K1	– Yeah.
	33.		K1	**But** we'll tell you what we haven't got...

37. Server: K l   It's in Canada, isn't it...somewhere up there...
38. Client: cf   – Canada.
39.   ch   **Well,** I don't know about...

The following texts exemplify the four major categories of logico-semantic relation about to be developed here, first in their external, then in their internal reading.

ADDITIVE
[4:16] external   Ben came in
                   and sat down.

[4:17] internal   Ben was tired.
                   Moreover he hadn't slept the night before.

COMPARATIVE
[4:18] external   Ben runs
                   like Carl does.

[4:19] internal   Ben runs well;
                   like you should see his start.

TEMPORAL
[4:20] external   Ben came in
                   and then had a drink.

[4:21] internal   Ben wasn't ready.
                   First he hadn't studied;
                   and **second**, he'd been up all night.

CONSEQUENTIAL
[4:22] external   Ben was getting hungry
                   because he could smell dinner.

[4:23] internal   Is Ben getting hungry -
                   because dinner's ready.

The centrality of the internal/external distinction to an adequate account of the discourse semantics of logical relations is the main factor distinguishing Halliday's (1985a) classification of expansion from that being developed here (the difference between Tables 4.2 and 4.3 above). The internal/external opposition does not play a part in Halliday's (1985a) discussion because his focus is on the clause complex in relation to the rest of the grammar, rather than in relation to cohesion and text structure. In particular, a good deal of his elaboration category is reinterpreted here as simply the internal face of comparative similarity rather than as a major logico-semantic category in its own right. This issue will be taken up again when internal comparison is considered in detail below.

The distinction between internal and external relations, although clear in principle, is in some cases hard to draw, either because it doesn't matter as in [4:15] above, or because certain relations, such as the concessive, are themselves interpersonal enough in orientation that they fudge the distinction being drawn between organising text and constructing field. This problem will be taken up in 4.5 after external and internal relations have been presented in detail.

4.2.4 Implicit and explicit relations

In reviewing the links between clause complexes in [4:2] above it was noted that several of these relationships were implicit — not overtly marked by a conjunctive relation. This raises the question of when implicit links are to be recognised, and when no links at all. Halliday and Hasan (1976:329-355) code only for explicit connections; and Halliday (1985a:308-309) cautions against reading too much into a text. Nevertheless it is hard to see how texts like [4:2] can be interpreted unless implicitly realised connections are made. An example each of an implicit temporal, consequential and comparative connection from [4:2] is given below (the implicit connection is "rendered" in bold face).

[4:2] TEMPORAL SUCCESSION
  t. we stand it in show stance,
  u. with the lead, the lead held up,
  v. hoping
  w. that our dog will stand like a nice statue,
  x. so as the judge can come.
      ['then']
  y. The judge handles it,
  z. and this is where I'm telling you, temperament plays a big part.

CONSEQUENTIAL CASUAL
  f. So, therefore, you need to get yourself between the dog and the judge.
      ['because']
  g. The dog (!) must be able to see the dog at all times.

COMPARATIVE CONTRAST
  p. With the bigger breeds of dog, they're stood on the ground,
  q. because it's easier for the judge to handle them.
      ['whereas']
  r. With the smaller breeds of dog such as Corgis, all the Toy-breeds, Dachshunds and this type of thing we — as our turn comes...

As a test for the presence of an implicit connection it can be required that the connection could have been explicit; thus a conjunction like *then* could have been used to relate x to y, *because* to relate d and e and *whereas* to link p and q without affecting the logical relationship between the processes (other than to make it explicit). This test works well with external comparative, temporal and consequential relations. Problems arise with additives however, since it is possible to insert *and* between almost any pair of independent clauses in many texts (and in some spoken modes this is very nearly what happens: recall text [3:1] above — *I touched him and he is hand and he is big and so I went on and I saw the tiger and this man was feeding him*). Internal relations pose a similar problem in that it is generally possible to treat the movement from one ranking clause to another in a text as a "rhetorical" one, and to make it explicit with an appropriate internal conjunction. The following passage from text [2:3] above is fleshed out in this way below (appended material in square brackets; conjunctions in bold face):

[2:3]	1.	Client	That's pretty.
	2.		[**So**] can you tell me how many cups that would hold?
	3.	Server	- [**Well**] em...about five or six, I think.
	4.	Client	- Five or six?
	5.	Server	- [**Well**] yeah.
			['**Cos** it] doesn't say.
			[**But** it] looks like it'd hold about five.

Accordingly, with the exception of internal comparison (Halliday's category of elaboration) which is often unmarked but crucial to an interpretation of the generic organisation of text, implicit additive and implicit internal relations will generally be passed over without comment in the analyses undertaken below.

4.3 External relations: system

As in Martin (1983b) the point of departure for the analysis presented here will be the hypotactic clause complex. It is in this area that English makes the most delicate experiential distinctions as far as logico-semantic relations between clauses are concerned. The coverage of the networks will be limited to those clause complexes which allow dependent clauses to be realised in first or second position (setting aside for example apparently hypotactic conjunctions such as *whereupon*, *thereby*, temporal *as long as*, resultative *so that* and so on). A complete specification of the diversification of the realisations of each type of conjunctive relation is beyond the scope of this chapter. However, where possible, an example of a "cohesive" and a metaphorical realisation of the features established will be provided at the end of each section below (for a very useful discussion of diversified realisations of conjunctive relations see Winter 1977).

4.3.1 *External temporal relations*

External temporal relations are strongly oriented to the activity sequences constituting fields (see Chapters 5 and 7 below). Most of these relations (excepting co-extensive simultaneous ones) have the experiential structure Anterior˙Posterior, where Anterior names the event which begins before the Posterior.

At primary delicacy the opposition is between [successive] relations, where the Anterior does not continue beyond the beginning of the Posterior, and [simultaneous] relations, where the two events overlap to some extent. This is the opposition between *after* and *while* in [4:24] and [4:25]:

SUCCESSIVE
[4:24] **After** we walk the ring with our dog,
        we just wait.

SIMULTANEOUS
[4:25] **While** the judge is handling the dog,
        we hope that it will stand nice and steady.

When the β clause encodes a punctiliar event, then simultaneity is realised by *when*; it does not matter whether the two events go on for exactly the same amount of time as in [4:26], or simply overlap to some extent as in [4:27]. Where the two events overlap, the α clause makes use of a secondary [present in past] TENSE selection to envelop the β (for TENSE see Halliday 1985a:179-184).

SIMULTANEOUS:COEXTENSIVE (β clause punctiliar)
[4:26] **When** the dog barked
        the judge started.

SIMULTANEOUS:OVERLAPPING (β clause punctiliar)
[4:27] **When** the judge arrived,
        we *had been waiting* for several minutes
        and he kept us standing around for a few more.

If the β clause is durative on the other hand, either *when* or *while* can be used:

SIMULTANEOUS:COEXTENSIVE (β clause durative)
[4:28] **When/while** we were waiting,
     we felt confident.

SIMULTANEOUS:OVERLAPPING (β clause durative)
[4:29] **When/while** the judge was handling the dog,
     it barked.

Expressed as a paradigm the distribution is as follows:

Table 4.5. Cross-classifying simultaneous temporal relations

	β CLAUSE PUNCTILIAR	β CLAUSE DURATIVE
COEXTENSIVE	when	when, while, (as)
OVERLAPPING	when	when, while

Alongside *when* and *while*, the conjunction *as* can be used when the events are overlapping as long as the β clause is both durative and non-stative. If the β clause is stative, then *as* is read consequentially: *As we were confident, we handled our dogs well.*

SIMULTANEOUS:OVERLAPPING (β clause durative & non-stative)
[4:30] As we were entering the ring,
     my dog barked.

As long as has not been included as a realisation in the network for an external temporal relations below because it cannot appear first in a temporal clause complex. Like *as*, it must introduce a non-stative durative clause to get a temporal reading (contrast the temporal *We stayed as long as our competitors did* with consequential *We were happy as long as the judge was*; the β clause can precede the α on the consequential reading). *As long as* (like *as soon as* below) could in any case be interpreted as involving embedded comparison, from which it is obviously derived:

Carl didn't run fast:
Carl didn't run as fast [[as Ben did]]::

Carl didn't last long:
Carl didn't last as long [[as Ben did]]

The network for simultaneous relations is presented as Fig. 4.4.

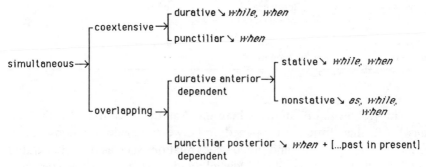

Fig. 4.4. Hypotactic simultaneous temporal relations

With successive relations there is less overlap among the realisations. The two main factors to consider are: i. whether the Posterior follows the Anterior immediately, or simply follows; and ii. whether the Posterior or Anterior clause is made dependent. The opposition between following and following immediately is illustrated in [4:31] and [4:32].

FOLLOWING
[4:31] **After** we table the dogs
          the judge comes to handle them.

FOLLOWING IMMEDIATELY
[4:32] **As soon as** we table the dogs
          the judge comes to handle them.

The opposition between a dependent Anterior and a dependent Posterior is illustrated in [4:33] and [4:34].

FOLLOWING (β/Anterior)
[4:33] **Since** we won that competition
          we've won several more.

FOLLOWING (β/Posterior)
[4:34] **Before** we won that competition
          we'd won several others.

The intersection of these oppositions is outlined in the paradigm below:

Table 4.6. Cross-classifying successive temporal relations

	ANTERIOR/β	POSTERIOR/β
FOLLOWING	after, since, now that	before
FOLLOWING IMMEDIATELY	once, as soon as	until

With [following] relations, where the Anterior is conflated with the β clause, a further distiction is opened up between [deictic] relations tied to the moment of speaking, and [nondeictic] relations such as those illustrated in [4:31] and [4:33] above. With [deictic] relations there is a choice between extending the Anterior to the present (*since*) or extending the Posterior from the present (*now that*).

FOLLOWING...DEICTIC:EXTENSION TO PRESENT
[4:35] **Since** we started competing
        we've only won three awards.

FOLLOWING...DEICTIC:EXTENSION FROM PRESENT
[4:36] **Now that** we've started competing again
        we expect to win several awards.

Finally, with [following immediately] relations where the Anterior event is dependent, the conjunction *once* contrasts with *as soon as* to indicate a sense of relief that the Posterior is getting under way. Where the β clause is Posterior, *until* is used.

FOLLOWING IMMEDIATELY...RELIEF UNMARKED (β/Anterior)
[4:37] **As soon as** we left the ring,
        John arrived.

FOLLOWING IMMEDIATELY...RELIEF (β/Anterior)
[4:38] **Once** we'd left the ring
        we felt better.

FOLLOWING IMMEDIATELY (β/Posterior)
[4:39] **Until** he arrived,
        we weren't sure what to do.

The network comprising these successive oppositions is presented as Fig. 4.5.

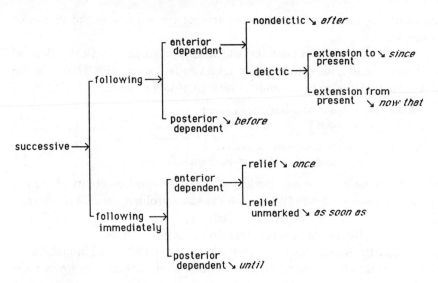

Fig. 4.5. Hypotactic successive temporal relations

There are a number of variations on *as soon as*, which shade into diversified realisations involving Circumstances and IDENTIFICATION (as with *after that* in [4:2:aaa] above). These include *the moment that, the minute that, the second that* and so on. This borderline area of realisation between the systems of IDENTIFICATION and CONJUNCTION will not be pursued here. Halliday & Hasan (1976:230-231) and Halliday (1985a:308) suggest incorporating the "circumstantial" realisations into the account of CONJUNCTION to bring out proportionalities such as the following:

instead:instead of that::
as a result:as a result of that::
in consequence:in consequence of that
etc.

But pursuing this is really a question of perspective. From the point of view of IDENTIFICATION these expressions are phoric and combine with experiential clause systems to link clauses in a text; from the point of view of CONJUNCTION they are only minimally distinct from realisations involving conjunctions alone. It may be that Halliday and Hasan and Halliday are suggesting many of the realisations involving IDENTIFICATION are now congruent (that is, no longer processed as grammatical metaphors); this would be one reason for including them as part of the system of CONJUNCTION in the discourse semantics.

There are two conjunctions which appear to hypotactically depend Posterior events, but which cannot then conflate them with Theme in the clause complex: *whereupon* and /ˌ *when*/ (non-salient *when*):

> [4:40] The judge looked in the dog's mouth,
> **whereupon** it jumped at him.

> [4:41] We were walking into the ring,
> /ˌ **when**/ suddenly an Alsatian leapt over the wall.

These might be taken as paratactic because of the unacceptability of the rising dependency sequence (β ˆ α); but the same problem arises with *thereby* clauses in 4.3.2 below, which are clearly hypotactic in light of their nonfinite process (*He started barking, **thereby** ruining our chances*).

The distinction drawn between [following] and [following immediately] relations makes it necessary to point out that conjunctions set a lower limit on the logico-semantic relation obtaining between two processes, but that they do not exhaust these relations. The sequence of clauses in both [4:31] and [4:32] for example could be used to refer to the same sequence of events, one immediately following on from the other. But in [4:31] *after* signals simply that the Posterior event followed the Anterior; the fact that it followed immediately is only made explicit through *as soon as* in [4:32]. The potential immediacy in other words is left implicit in [4:31].

This lower limit principle is very important when it comes to interpreting conjunctive relations between clauses. It entails for example that [4:42] be taken simply as additive as far as explicit conjunctive relations are concerned:

> [4:42] We table the dogs
> **and** the judge comes to handle them.

Additional implicit relations can then be recognised where appropriate (i.e. where they can be made explicit and are necessary to interpret the text). This strategy avoids the problem of having to recognise several types of *and* — an additive, temporal or causal version depending on the co-text. Conjunctions, then, make explicit those logico-semantic relations which have to be recognised; but they do not set an upper limit on those that might as well obtain implicitly.

The complete network for hypotactic external temporal relations is presented as Fig. 4.6. Where plausible examples can be found, "cohesive",

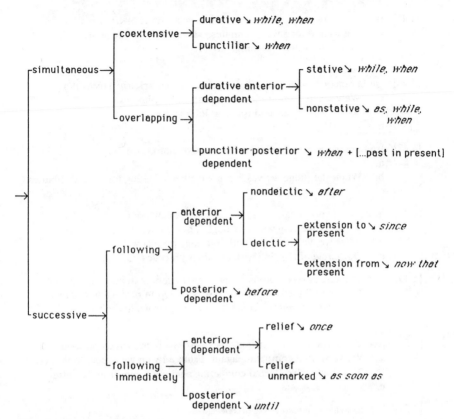

Fig. 4.6. Hypotactic external temporal relations in English

hypotactic and metaphorical realisations of its terminal features are illustrated in [4:43-54].

[4:43] [SIMULTANEOUS:COEXTENSIVE:DURATIVE]
    a.   We stand and wait. **Throughout** the judge handles the dogs.
    b.   **While** we stand and wait the judge handles the dogs.
    c.   -

[4:44] [SIMULTANEOUS:COEXTENSIVE:PUNCTILIAR]
    a.   The dog barked. **Simultaneously** the judge sneezed.
    b.   **When** the dog barked, the judge sneezed.
    c.   -

[4:45]   [SIMULTANEOUS:OVERLAPPING:DURATIVE ANTERIOR DEPENDENT:STATIVE]
     a.   We waited for several minutes. **Meanwhile** the judge arrived.
     b.   **While** we waited the judge arrived.
     c.   -

[4:46]   [SIMULTANEOUS:OVERLAPPING:DURATIVE ANTERIOR DEPENDENT:NONSTATIVE]
     a.   We walked around the ring. **Meanwhile** John left.
     b.   **As** we walked around the ring John left.
     c.   -

[4:47]   [SIMULTANEOUS:OVERLAPPING:PUNCTILIAR POSTERIOR DEPENDENT]
     a.   -
     b.   **When** the judge arrives, we'll have been waiting for several minutes.
     c.   -

[4:48]   [SUCCESSIVE:FOLLOWING:ANTERIOR DEPENDENT:NONDEICTIC]
     a.   We walk the ring with our dogs. **Then** we just wait.
     b.   **After** we walk the ring with our dogs we just wait.
     c.   Our circle of the ring with our dogs **precedes** our wait.

[4:49]   [SUCCESSIVE:FOLLOWING:ANTERIOR DEPENDENT:DEICTIC:EXTENSION TO PRESENT]
     a.   We entered the competition last year. **Up to now** we haven't won.
     b.   **Since** we entered the competition last year we haven't won.
     c.   -

[4:50]   [SUCCESSIVE:FOLLOWING:ANTERIOR DEPENDENT:DEICTIC:EXTENSION FROM PRESENT]
     a.   We've started competing again. **From now on** we expect to do better.
     b.   **Now that** we've started competing again, we expect to do better.
     c.   -

[4:51]   [SUCCESSIVE:FOLLOWING:POSTERIOR DEPENDENT]
     a.   The judge handled the dogs. **Previously** we'd tabled them.
     b.   **Before** the judge handled the dogs we'd tabled them.
     c.   Our tabling the dogs was **followed** by the judge handling them.

[4:52]   [SUCCESSIVE:FOLLOWING IMMEDIATELY:ANTERIOR DEPENDENT:RELIEF]
     a.   We were finally able to leave the ring. **Then at last** we felt better.
     b.   **Once** we were finally able to leave the ring we felt better.
     c.   -

[4:53]   [SUCCESSIVE:FOLLOWING IMMEDIATELY:ANTERIOR SUBORDINATE:RELIEF UNMARKED]
     a.   The judge looked in the dog's mouth. **Immediately** it barked.
     b.   **As soon as** the judge looked in the dog's mouth it barked.
     c.   -

[4:54]   [SUCCESSIVE:FOLLOWING IMMEDIATELY:POSTERIOR DEPENDENT]
     a.   -
     b.   We waited **until** the judge told us to get the best out of our dogs.
     c.   -

4.3.2 *External consequential relations*

Like temporal relations, external consequential relations are oriented to the activity sequences constituting fields; but the connections between events are "modulated" in such a way that one event is seen as *enabling* or *determining* the other rather than simply preceding it. All consequential relations have the experiential structure Cause · Effect. Within consequential relations the basic opposition is. between **how** and **why**.

MANNER (sufficient conditions)
[4:55] *How* did you win?
-**By** training hard.

CAUSE (necessary conditions)
[4:56] *Why* did you win?
-**Because** we trained hard.

With [manner] relations, the relationship between events is modulated through "potentiality"; *we won by training hard* means that the Cause (preparing well) enabled the Effect (winning). With other consequential relations the connection between events is modulated through "obligation": *we won because we trained hard* means that the Cause determined the Effect. This is the "natural logic" of the distinction between sufficient and necessary conditions:

we won by training hard (among other things):
we trained hard enough to win (but we lost)::

we won because we trained hard:
we trained hard enough **to make sure** we won

Alongside being modulated through obligation, causal relations may be modalised. With both condition and purpose the relation between Cause and Effect is a contingent one; and in both cases the Effect is irrealis — there is a possibility, a probability or a certainty that it will be determined by the Cause, but as the meanings are made it has not yet ensued. This is the opposition between [4:57] and [4:58-9].

CONSEQUENCE (Effect realis)
[4:57] Cause   **Because** we trained hard,
        Effect   we won.

CONDITION (Effect irrealis)
[4:58] Cause   **If** we'd trained hard,
        Effect   we'd have won.

PURPOSE (Effect irrealis)
[4:59]   Cause   We trained hard
         Effect   **so that** we'd win.

The distinction between condition and purpose has to do with modulation again. Purposives contain an additional modulation of inclination, associated with the Effect (the Effect is desired). This can be brought out by comparing hypotactic and paratactic realisations of the purposive relation; these proportionalities also reveal another peculiarity of purposive relations, namely that desire for the Effect commences before the Cause — wanting to win, get there on time and give the opposition a chance are the **motivation** for, not the results of, training hard, driving fast and skating slowly in the examples below (with all other consequential relations the Cause is temporally anterior):[1]

> we trained hard **so that** we'd win:
> we *wanted* to win, **and so** we trained hard::
>
> we drove fast **in order to** get there on time:
> we were *keen* to get there on time **and so** we drove fast::
>
> we skated slowly **to** give them a chance:
> we were *willing* to give them a chance **and so** we skated slowly

The relationship between modalization and modulation and the basic types of consequential relation (manner, consequence, condition and purpose) is outlined below.

Table 4.7. MODALIZATION, MODULATION and consequential relations

		MODULATION	MODALIZATION (Effect irrealis)
MANNER (thus, by)		potentiality	-
CAUSE:	CONSEQUENCE (so, because)	obligation	-
	CONDITION (then, if)	obligation	probability
	PURPOSE (so that)	obligation & inclination	probability

Expressed systemically, the oppositions reviewed thus far are as presented in Fig. 4.7.

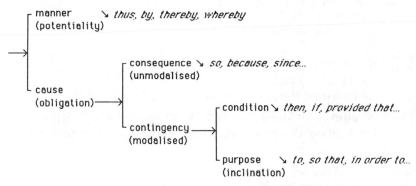

Fig. 4.7. Basic consequential options

Contingent relations make a distinction between conjunctions incorporating negative polarity (*unless* and *lest*) and those which don't. The proportionalities and relevant paradigm are as follows:

UNLESS:IF...NOT::
LEST:SO THAT...WILL + NOT

unless Ben plays you'll lose:
if Ben doesn't play you'll lose::

Ben'll play **lest** you lose:
Ben will play **so that** you **won't** lose

But the opposition between "positive" and "negative" values has a different meaning in the context of conditional relations from that in purposives. With conditionals, the opposition is between exclusion and inclusion (or non-exclusive to be precise). *Unless* means 'if and only if not'; *if* on the

Table 4.8. POLARITY and purposive relations

	CONDITION	PURPOSE
"POSITIVE"	if	so that
"NEGATIVE"	unless	lest

other hand does not preclude the possibility of additional modalised
Causes:

EXCLUSIVE
[4:60]   **Unless** you go that way ['as long as you don't']
         you'll be there by six.
         (It's the only way you can go wrong.)

INCLUSIVE
[4:61]   **If** you go that way
         you'll be there by six.
         (But you could also go the back way.)

With purposives the opposition is between [desire] and [fear]. *So that*
encodes an inclination to achieve the Effect, *lest* an inclination to avoid it:

DESIRE
[4:62]   He went that way
         so that he'd get there by six.

FEAR
[4:63]   He went that way
         lest he lose his way (less archaicly: **for fear of** losing his way)

Just as [following] and [following immediately] successive relations can
be used to connect the same sequence of events, conditionals can be used in
contexts where purposive relations are understood. So [4:64] might be used
in the same context of situation as [4:65].

[4:64]   **If** you go that way,
         you'll get there by six.

[4:65]   Go that way
         in order to get there by six.

But with conditionals, the Effect may or may not be desirable; *if* and *unless*
do not code it as one or the other:

[4:66]   **If** you go that way
         you'll get there by six/you'll get lost.

[4:67]   **Unless** you go that you
         you'll get there by six/you'll get lost.

Purposives on the other hand always code the Effect as desired or feared.
In [4:68] Ben will be read as wanting to get lost, and as not wanting to get
there by six in [4:69].

[4:68] Ben went that way
so that he'd get lost.

[4:69] Ben went that way
for fear of getting there by six.

In other words, fear and desire are implicit in [4:66] and [4:67], but can be read in where the context indicates they are needed to make sense of the conditional meanings made explicit. Fear and desire on the other hand are grammaticalised in [4:68] and [4:69].

Inclusive conditionals can be further divided into factual and counterfactual; with counterfactuals the β clause an additional secondary [past] tense.[2]

COUNTERFACTUAL
[4:70] **If** we **had** prepared well,
we would have won.

Factual conditionals choose among high, median and low modalization, according to the probability of the Cause taking place:

FACTUAL:MODALITY POSSIBLE
[4:71] **If** we enter
we'll win.

FACTUAL:MODALITY PROBABLE
[4:72] **Provided** we enter
we'll win.

FACTUAL:MODALITY CERTAIN
[4:73] **As long as** we enter
we'll win.

Degrees of probability are also possible with purposives, but there are only two values, high/median and low:

PURPOSIVE:DESIRE:MODALITY POSSIBLE
[4:74] We'll enter
in case we win.

PURPOSIVE:DESIRE:MODALITY CERTAIN/PROBABLE
[4:75] We'll enter
so that we'll win.

The network for contingent consequential relations is as follows:

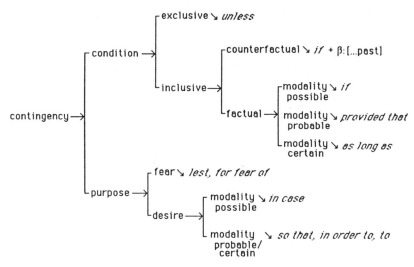

Fig. 4.8. Hypotactic external consequential contingent relations

Both manner (*whereby*, *thereby*) and consequence (/ˌ *so that/*) have realisations which apparently make the Effect dependent, but which do not allow the β clause to be realised first in a clause complex:

MANNER
[4:76]   We prepared well,
         thereby managing to win.

CONSEQUENCE
[4:77]   We prepared well,
         /ˌ**so that/** in the end we won.

Consequence is also commonly realised referentially, through esphoric comparison as in [4:78]:

[4:78]   We prepared **so** well [[**that** we won]].

It remains to consider concessive relations, which will be taken here as crossclassifying manner, consequence, condition and purpose rather than as a fifth consequential category (cf. Longacre 1976:149-158 on what he calls frustration). The reason for this is that concessives function as a kind of "anti-modulation", cancelling the potentiality or obligation which would otherwise enable or determine the consequential relation between events.

The opposition is illustrated for manner relations in [4:79] and [4:80]; in [4:79] entering the right shows was enough to win, but in [4:80] the enablement is cancelled — entering the right shows was not sufficient to win.

MANNER
[4:79] **By** entering the right shows,
        we won.

MANNER/CONCESSION
[4:80] **Even by** entering the right shows,
        we didn't win.

The concessive and non-concessive realisations of the major categories of consequential relations are illustrated below for hypotactic and non-hypotactic relations:

Table 4.9. Concessive and non-concessive consequentials

	NON-CONCESSIVE	CONCESSIVE
MANNER	by	even by
	thus	but
CONSEQUENCE	because	although/even though
	so/therefore	but/however
CONDITION	if	even if
	then	even then
PURPOSE	in order to	without[3]
	so + inclination	even so

The hypotactic proportionalities can be exemplified as follows:

NON-CONCESSIVE:CONCESSIVE::
Ben improved his time **by** training hard:
Ben didn't improve his time **even by** training hard::

Ben improved his time **because** he trained hard:
Ben didn't improve his time **even though** he trained hard::

Ben will improve his time **if** he trains hard:
Ben won't improve his time **even** if he trains hard::

Ben can train hard **in order to** improve his time:
Ben can train hard **without** improving his time

Concessive conditionals can be further subclassified according to the universality of the contingency denied. Single, alternative and universal concessive contingency is illustrated below:

CONDITIONAL/CONCESSIVE:SINGLE

[4:81] **Even if** we get that judge again
we'll win.

CONDITIONAL/CONCESSIVE:ALTERNATIVE

[4:82] **Whether** we get that judge again or not
we'll win.

CONDITIONAL/CONCESSIVE:UNIVERSAL

[4:83] **Whichever** judge we get
we'll win.

[*Even* does not combine with additive or comparative relations; but it does with some temporals: eg. *even when, even while, even before, even after*. With these its meaning is counter-aspectual and there is an implicit consequential relation present which is undone as well — *Ben was upset even after he left* means 'Ben left, and **so** he shouldn't **still** have been upset, **but** he was' (cf. the discussion of CONTINUITY in 4.5 below).]

The relationship between the concessive opposition and other consequential systems is outlined below; for further delicacy see the networks developed above. Note that in attributive clauses concession may be realised hypotactically by making the Attribute a marked Theme and concatenating it with *though/as* ˆ Subject ˆ Finite: *Crazy though/as it it seems, Ben didn't think he'd be caught* (cf. *although it seems crazy...*; see [4:199b] below).

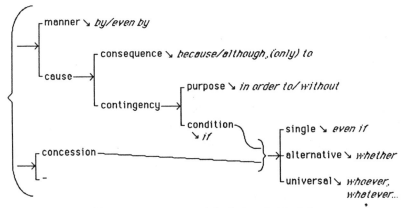

Fig. 4.9. External hypotactic consequential relations in English

Where plausible illustrations can be found, "cohesive", hypotactic and metaphorical realisations of non-concessive relations are illustrated below.

[4:84] [manner]
    a. We mated two champions. **Thus** we won a lot of prizes.
    b. **By** mating two champions, we won a lot of prizes.
    c. Mating two champions **enabled** our winning a lot of prizes.

[4:85] [cause:consequence]
    a. We arrived late. **So** we didn't have much time to prepare.
    b. **Because** we arrived late, we didn't have much time to prepare.
    c. Our late arrival **led** to us having little preparation time.

[4:86] [cause:contingency:condition:exclusive]
    a. Our dog had to stand nice and still. **Otherwise** we wouldn't have won.
    b. **Unless** our dog had stood nice and still, we wouldn't have won.
    c. Our dog standing nice and still was a **necessary condition** of our win.

[4:87] [cause:contingency:condition:inclusive:counterfactual]
    a. He **might** have arrived on time. **Then** he would have won.
    b. **If** he'd arrived on time he would have won.
    c. **Not** arriving on time as **predicted precluded** his win.

[4:88] [cause:contingency:condition:inclusive:factual:modality possible]
    a. We **might** go. **Then** we'll win.
    b. **If** we go, we'll win.
    c. Going will **open up** the **possibility** of winning.

[4:89] [cause:contingency:condition:inclusive:factual:modality probable]
    a. We'll **probably** turn up. **Then** we'll win.
    b. **Provided that** we turn up we'll win.
    c. Just turning up will **make** a win **likely.**

[4:90] [cause:contingency:condition:inclusive:factual:modality certain]
    a. We'll **certainly** show up. **Then** we'll win.
    b. **As long as** we show up, we'll win.
    c. Just showing up will **ensure** (the **certainty** of) a win.

[4:91] [cause:contingency:purpose:fear]
    a. We **didn't want** to lose. **So** we didn't enter.
    b. We didn't enter **for fear** of losing.
    c. Our **fear** of losing **prevented** us from entering.

[4:92] [cause:contingency:purpose:desire:modality possible]
    a. We **wanted** to win and had a **chance**. **So** we entered.
    b. We entered **in case** we won.
    c. The **chance** of winning **encouraged** us to enter.

[4:93] [cause:contingency:purpose:desire:modality probable/certain]
    a. We **wanted** to win and had a **good chance**. **So** we entered.

> b. We entered **so that** we would win.
> c. The **prospect** of winning **led** us to enter.

4.3.3 *External comparative relations*

Within the framework of systemic functional approaches to discourse, comparative relations are the most controversial category to be developed here; as Tables 4.1 and 4.2 above indicate, they are not treated as a major category of logical relation by either Halliday and Hasan or Halliday. To explore this question, it will be useful to return to text [4:2].

> [4:2] p. With the bigger breeds of dog, they're stood on the ground,
> q. because it's easier for the judge to handle them.
> r. With the smaller breeds of dog such as Corgis, all the Toy-breeds, Dachshunds and this type of thing we — as our turn comes,
> s. we stand our dog on the table...

As noted in Section 4.1 above, there is a clear relationship of contrast between p-q and r-s. This is coded through the comparative reference (*bigger* vs *smaller*) and the lexical cohesion (most clearly *ground* vs *table* — see Chapter 5 below); and the contrast is highlighted by the marked Themes in p and r. As noted in 4.2.4 above the contrast could have been made explicit in [4:2] with a conjunction such as *but*.

Consider now a modified version of this part of the interview:

> [4:94] a. With the bigger breeds of dog, they're stood on the ground.
> b. With the smaller breeds such as Dachshunds, they're stood on the table.
> c. Likewise breeds with similar stature like the Corgis, all the Toy-breeds and this type of thing are tabled,
> d. so as the judge can handle them more easily.

This text focusses on similarity as well as difference. Lexical cohesion (the co-hyponymy of *Dachshunds* with *Corgis* and *Toy-breeds* and the repetition of table (*table, tabled*), comparative reference (*similar stature*) and an explicit conjunction (*likewise*) make the comparison clear.

Halliday and Hasan (1976) treat the contrastive relation in [4:94:a-b] as closely related to concession (under their general adversative category) and the similarity in [4:94:b-c] as a kind of additive. Halliday (1985a) on the other hand treats contrast as related to additive relations under the heading extension and similarity as closely related to temporals and causals under the heading enhancement. The different analyses are outlined below:

Table 4.10. Divergent treatments of contrast and similarity in Halliday and Hasan (1976) and Halliday (1985a)

	Halliday & Hasan (1976)	Halliday (1985a)
"contrast"	adversative:contrastive	extension:addition
"similarity"	additive:comparison	enhancement:manner: comparison

These interpretations fail to bring out the very similar ways in which IDEN-TIFICATION and IDEATION participate in the realisation of both contrast and similarity (as exemplified in [4:84] above; see also Hoey 1983:107-133 for a very pertinent discussion of matching patterns). Taking into account these textual patterns and the fact that a similar/different opposition is basic to all other discourse semantic systems, comparison will be set up as a major category of conjunctive relation here. The congruence of the like/unlike opposition across discourse systems is shown below.

Table 4.11. Contrast and similarity across discourse semantics systems

	"LIKE"	"UNLIKE"
CONJUNCTION	similarity	contrast
IDENTIFICATION	semblance	difference
IDEATION	synonymy	antonymy
NEGOTIATION (Halliday 1985a:69)	accept undertake acknowledge answer	reject refuse contradict disclaim

The external comparison network is a small one; the basic opposition is between [contrast] and [similarity]:

CONTRAST

[4:95] **Whereas** usually we win
this time we lost.

SIMILARITY

[4:96] **As** usually happens,
we won.

In addition to the kind of contrast illustrated in [4:95], there are replacement and exception categories to consider. With replacives (e.g. *instead of*, *in place of*) the blurry line between contrast and alternation discussed in 4.2.2 above is hardest to draw:

EXCEPTION
[4:97] We had a good day,
        except for losing the Best of Show award.

REPLACEMENT
[4:98] We won Best of Show
        instead of missing out as usual.

The network for external comparison is as follows:

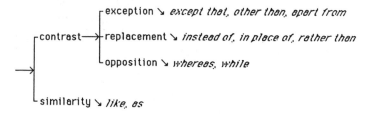

Fig. 4.10. External hypotactic comparative relations

There are two variations on [similarity], one conditional and one temporal, where apparently hypotactically dependent clauses cannot appear initially in the clause complex:

SIMILARITY (conditional)
[4:99] Ben looked
        as if he'd just won the Best of Show.

SIMILARITY (temporal)
[4:100] Ben looked
        like when he won Best of Show.

'Cohesive', hypotactic and incongruent realisations are as follows:

[4:101] [contrast:exception]
        a.   We enjoyed the show. **Only** we lost the final event.
        b.   We enjoyed the show **except that** we lost the final event.
        c.   Our loss in the final event **marred** our enjoyment of the show.

[4:102] [contrast:replacement]
    a. We should have gone to the show. **Instead** we stayed home.
    b. **Instead of** going to the show we stayed home.
    c. Going to the show was **replaced** by staying home.

[4:103] [contrast:opposition]
    a. We won with the Corgis. **But** we lost with the Dachshunds.
    b. **While** we won with the Corgis, we lost with the Dachshunds.
    c. Our win with the Corgis **contrasted** with our loss with the Dachshunds.

[4:104] [similarity]
    a. We won with the Corgis. **Similarly** we came first with the Dachshands.
    b. We won with the Corgis, just **as** we did with the Dachshunds.
    c. Our win with the Corgis was **parallelled** by our first with the Dachshunds.

4.3.4 *External additive relations*

External additive relations, like external comparative ones, form a small resource compared with temporals or consequentials. The basic distinction is between addition and alternation. With addition, there is a positive/negative system opposing *and* to *nor*, in spite of morphological appearances which make it look like a negative realisation of *or* (*Our Corgi didn't win nor did the Dachshund* means that 'the Corgi didn't win **and** that the Dachshund didn't either'). All additive relations have correlative paratactic realisations.

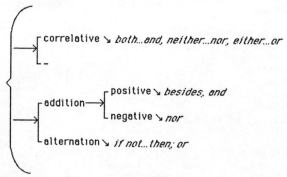

Fig. 4.11. External additive relations

[4:105] [addition:positive]
    a.   Our Dachshund performed well. **And** she looked splendid on the day.
    b.   **Besides** peforming well our Dachshund looked splendid on the day.
    c.   -

[4:106] [addition:negative]
    a.   She didn't move at all well in the ring. **Nor** did she stand still when tabled.
    b.   **Alongside** not moving well in the ring, she didn't stand still when tabled.
    c.   -

[4:107] [alternation]
    a.   You could go down to Melbourne. **Or** you could go in the Easter Show.
    b.   **If** you **don't** go down to Melbourne, you could go in the Easter Show.
    c.   -

4.3.5 *External locative relations*

Finally, there is a small set of locative relations, all of which could be analysed in other than conjunctive terms. These include the phoric adverbs *here*, *there* and *elsewhere*, esphoric *as far as* and clauses introduced with *where* (see 4:187f below) or *wherever*. The close relationship between spatial and temporal categories noted by Halliday (1985a:137-139) as far as circumstantial relations are concerned does not really extend to logico-semantic relations between clauses and clause complexes.

[4:108] Look at the problem on page 34;
    here we see something of what bothered the systemicists.

[4:109] So it's actually multivariate.
    — **There** you're mistaken.

[4:110] He treats MODULATION as interpersonal in the IFG.
    Elsewhere Halliday has argued for its experiential nature.

[4:111] Actually I haven't read
    as far as I'd have liked.

[4:112] He took us around,
    wherever we wanted to go. [cf. to whichever places...]

4.4 Internal relations: system

Internal relations differ from external ones in ways that affect the strategy of presentation adopted here. First, additive and comparative relations are a much richer resource internally than externally and so will be considered first. Second, while the great majority (if not all) of external conjunctions discussed in 4.3 above can be used internally, there are a large number of internal conjunctions that are only or in other cases, generally, used to code internal relations. To simplify the presentation only those conjunctions which are used internally most or all of the time will be considered here; and circumstantial realisations involving IDENTIFICATION will not be explicitly considered (eg. *in this* way, *in that respect* etc.). Third, internal relations are basically "cohesive", functioning as connections between clause complexes; so the point of departure here will be "cohesive", rather than hypotactic conjunctions.

4.4.1 *Internal comparative relations*

Internal comparative relations are a resource for organising meanings with respect to similarity and difference. The comparison involved is a textual one; it is not oriented to how meanings are alike or unlike with respect to field. One way to see this is to take the same experiential meaning and recast it internally as in [4:113] and [4:114] below. In [4:113] a text is developed in which Dr. Metherell's conservative politics are presented in opposition to his interest in 'reforming' education — the text is organised to challenge the idea that conservatives don't in fact turn back the clock. In [4:114] on the other hand a text is presented in which Dr. Metherell's reforms are presented as an elaboration of his conservative nature — the text takes it for granted that reactionary Ministers of Education will undo liberal reforms.

INTERNAL SIMILARITY
[4:113] Dr. Metherell's a conservative;
he wants to preserve the status quo.

On the other hand he does want education to change,
and his approach has alienated many parents and teachers.

INTERNAL DIFFERENCE
[4:114] Dr. Metherell's a conservative;
he wants to preserve the status quo.

> **That is**, he does want education to change,
> and his approach has alienated many parents and teachers.

The internal conjunction in these two texts codes different ideologies — different attitudes to what conservative governments do; but as far as external relations are concerned, what Dr. Metherell is up to experientially in the two texts remains the same.

Internal similarity will be developed first. The following conjunctions are commonly used to make these relations explicit:

REFORMULATION:
that is, in other words, i.e., for example, for instance, e.g.;
in short, in brief, in general, generally, in particular, particularly;
in fact, actually, at least, indeed

COMPARISON:
likewise, similarly, in the same way, equally, correspondingly, by the same token;
again

These can be usefully divided into two main groups, as above, according to whether they mark the fact that a text is **reformulating** meaning in order to clarify what is meant, or whether they signal that something is the **same** about the way in which distinct meanings are being organised. This is the contrast between *that is* and *similarly* in [4:115] and [4:116] below.

REFORMULATION
[4:115] *The riot began* shows that *riot* is a process term, even though it is in nominal form.

> **That is**, the fact that *riot* is a noun does not mean that it cannot represent an action as its colligation with *began* shows.

COMPARISON
[4:116] *The riot began* shows that *riot* is a process term, even though it is in nominal form.

> **Similarly**, *the violence ended suddenly* marks *violence* as a process term even though it has no corresponding verb form. (Trew 1979:123)

Invoking the conduit metaphor (*pace* Reddy 1979), one might argue that [reformulation] is about different ways of saying the same thing, while [comparison] is about similarities between ways of saying different things. But since reformulations are not in any useful sense "synonymous", this formulation is somewhat misleading (as ever when content and form are so dualised in functional linguistics). It would be better to say that with [reformulation], the first formulation and the second have almost all their meaning in common; a little fine tuning is all that's required. With [comparison] on the other hand, the meanings compared are different; but the way in which they are presented is in some respect the same (for a useful discussion of reformulation see Hoey 1983:143-167 on general-particular patterns).

Internal and external comparison are not always easy to separate. Text [4:116] above for example does have an external reading in which phasing processes like *began* and *ended* are argued to unveil metaphorical processes in the same way. The following example is more clearly internal; the comparison is between two lines of argument and interpretation, not between experiential meanings:

> [4:117] Thirdly there is the question of the relation of language to culture, on which we have little information in the reports on the north-west Amazon referred to above, but on which we can make some safe guesses. For instance, it would be surprising if any of the languages concerned lacked a word for 'long-house' or 'tribe', and we might reasonably expect a word for 'phratry' (though such higher-level concepts often lack names, as we shall see in 3.3.4).
>
> **Similarly**, we may predict that most concepts relevant to the culture will have words in each language to express them, and that most words in each language will express cultural concepts, definable only in terms of the culture concerned. (Hudson, 1980:10)

With [reformulation], the basic distinction is between reworking a meaning in order to clarify it and adjusting it in order to get it right. This is the opposition between [4:115] above (repeated below) and [4:118]. In [4:115] *that is* does not imply that anything was wrong with the first formulation; its experiential meaning is simply restated by way of clarification. In [4:118] on the other hand *in fact* does imply that something was not quite right the first time round; in this example the implication is that the first formulation was not strong enough.

REFORMULATION:REWORK:ABSTRACTION:EXHAUST
> [4:115] *The riot began* shows that *riot* is a process term, even though it is in nominal form.
>
> **That is**, the fact that *riot* is a noun does not mean that it cannot represent an action as its colligation with *began* shows.

REFORMULATION:ADJUST
> [4:118] *The riot began* shows that *riot* is a process term, even though it is in nominal form.

In fact, *riot* would have to be classified lexically as an action word.

Reworking to clarify takes a number of different forms. There are two basic strategies. One is to shift the level of abstraction at which the meanings are formulated; the other is to shift generality. This is the contrast between [4:115] and [4:119]. In [4:115] the reformulation spells out in a more concrete way why *riot* is a process term (the first formulation may be more or less abstract than the second, with no apparent effect on the conjunctions used):

Table 4.12. Reformulation in text [4:115]

	FIRST FORMULATION (more abstract)	REFORMULATION (more concrete)
"NOUN FORM"	in nominal form	is a noun
"INCONGRUENCE"	is a process term	represent an action
"EVIDENCE"	the riot began	it's colligation with began

In [4:119] on the other hand the second formulation is on the same level of abstraction but more general than the first — the specific example *the riot began* is generalised to a comment on one recognition criteria for the metaphorical realisation of processes.

> REFORMULATION:REWORK:GENERALITY...GENERALISE
>
> [4:119] *The riot began* shows that *riot* is a process term, even though it is in nominal form.
>
> **In general**, nominals which function as Mediums for processes which characterise them as having beginnings and ends are in fact realising actions.

Table 4.13. Reformulation in text [4:19]

FIRST FORMULATION (more specific)	REFORMULATION (more general)
riot	nominals
began	processes which...ends
the riot began	function as Mediums
riot is a process term	nominals are...realising actions

This is in effect the distinction between identification (Token Value) and attribution (Carrrier Attribute) in intensive relational clauses (see Halliday 1985a:114-115). Compare the following relational clauses from [4:115]:

IDENTIFYING ('is a manifestation of')
it (riot) cannot represent an action
Token Process Value [difference in abstraction]

ATTRIBUTIVE ('is a member of the class of')
riot is a process term
Carrier Process Attributive [difference in generality]

Within the "identifying" mode, both relational clauses and internal conjunction make a distinction between "exhaustive" and "exemplicatory" (i.e. non-exhaustive) manifestation. In this respect [4:115] contrasts with [4:120].

REFORMULATION:REWORK:ABSTRACTION:EXEMPLIFY
[4:120] When a clause shows that an idea encoded as a noun has a temporal beginning or end, this stands as evidence that the "idea" is an action.

For example, *the riot began* shows that *riot* is a process term, even though it is in nominal form.

Unlike intensive attributive clause relations, internal reformulation can work either from particular to general as in [4:119] above, or from general to particular as in [4:121] (intensive attributive clauses can only assign subclasses to classes; it is for this reason that possessive relationals are so commonly used in science to subclassify — *Mammals include monotremes, marsupials and placentals*) and has distinct conjunctions for moving in one direction or the other.

REFORMULATION:REWORK:GENERALITY...PARTICULARISE
[4:121] The text has a number of actions encoded as nouns which colligation clearly shows to be actions.

In particular certain of these occur as Mediums with verbs indicating they have a beginning and end, which concepts apply only to actions.

The final reformulation option to be noted has to do with the summative generalisation realised through *in short, in brief, in summary, to sum up* and so on. This relation ranges retrospectively across an accumulation of more specific meanings which are brought together by way of summary.

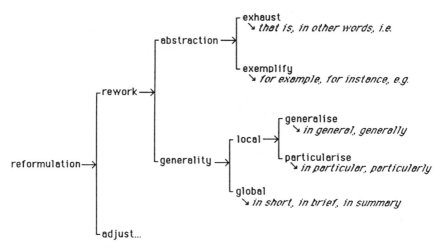

Fig. 4.12. Reformulation: rework systems

REFORMULATION:REWORK:GENERALITY:GLOBAL

[4:122] The riot began shows that riot is a process term, even though it is in nominal form. Similarly, the violence ended suddenly marks violence as a process term even though it has no corresponding verb form.

In short, several colligations in the text show that many nominals are encoding actions, not things.

The reformulation systems which rework meanings along the lines just discussed are presented in Fig. 4.12 (in informal spoken English the somewhat stigmatised *like* can be used to realise any of these reformulations, and in a sense makes explicit their function as the internal face of comparison).

Reformulations introduced by *in fact*, *actually*, *at least*, *indeed* and so on carry the implication that the original formulation was not quite right; it needs more than rephrasing in other words — it has to be adjusted to tune in accurately to the meaning being made. The difference between *at least* and *indeed* has to do with whether the reformulation is toned up or down. In [4:123] the first formulation is something of an overstatement and needs to be played down; in [4:124] on the other hand the first formulation understates and needs to be amplified:

REFORMULATION:ADJUST...DIMINISH

[4:123] The way in which Liz addresses Mary is also significant: she feels perfectly free to use her first name, whereas Mary does not once use Liz's name.

At least Mary does not use Liz's name when actually addressing her. She does use it once when quoting something an former client had told her about Mary.

REFORMULATION: ADJUST...AUGMENT

[4:124] The way in which Liz addresses Mary is also significant: she feels perfectly free to use her first name, whereas Mary does not once use Liz's name.

Indeed Mary does not adress Liz at all, by name or otherwise.

Where an understatement or overstatement has been made, but a speaker wishes to adjust the meaning without specifying whether too much or too little was meant, then conjunctions such as *in fact* or *actually* can be used. These can be substituted for either *at least* or *indeed* (for example in [4:123] and [4:124] above), and so neutralise the [augment/diminish] system just introduced. In [4:125] *in fact* is used in a context where *indeed* could have been used to make the understatement in the first formulation explicit.

REFORMULATION: ADJUST: CORRECT

[4:125] The way in which Liz addresses mary is also significant: she feels perfectly free to use her first name, whereas Mary does not once use Liz's name.

In fact, Mary does not address Liz by any name. (Kress & Fowler 1979:67)

In fact often has a concessive "flavour", occurring in the environment of an explicit or implicit concessive relation as in [4:126]. But as [4:125], and [4:127] below demonstrate, it is not concessive in its own right; it is not possible to make a concessive relation explicit in [4:125] or [4:127] with a conjunction like *but* because counterexpectation is not part of the meaning.

[4:126] Commonly the term theory is used for the clearly articulated "models" that are part of the sciences — like the model of the atom as a stucture of particles orbiting about a nucleus of particles, or of light as waves, or the model of society as a conflict between contending forces. The models are meant to represent the reality of things underlying what we perceive. They are used to locate the phenomena we perceive in a network of causality whose laws and connections are those of the model, and to transfer by analogy the reasoning known to apply to the models to the field in question.

But in fact all description, and not only the kind found in scientific discourse, involves theory, that is, systems of concepts involved in explaining things, in connecting events with other events, in pacing them in the context of patterns and structures and causes. (Trew 1979b:95-96)

[4:127] An obvious difference between the reports is that *The Times* report is in the passive form, and the *Guardian* one in the active, although the content is very similar in the two cases. The contrast is repeated in the headlines. Using the passive form puts the (syntactic) agents of the killings, "police", in less focal position. By itself this may not seem very important — but as

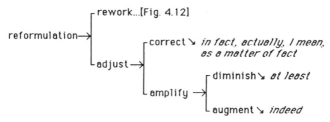

Fig. 4.13. Reformulation: adjust systems

> the first step in a process that goes further the next day, it does become important.
>
> **In fact** there is an indication of how this could develop further, in *The Times* report. Not only is it in the passive, but the syntactic agent is deleted... (Trew 1979b:98)

The network for adjusting reformulations and their relationship to reworking ones is outlined in Fig. 4.13.

Turning from reformulation to comparison, the concern of internal comparative relations is not with fine tuning a meaning that has just been made but with noting similarities in lines of argument or interpretation. Where the similarity is between adjacent portions of a text, conjunctions such as *likewise, similarly, correspondingly, in the same way, by the same token* and *equally* are used, the number of which indicates that a more delicate anlaysis might be justified in this area. A good example of comparison of this kind was provided in [4:3] above, where *equally* marked the second argument in support of the thesis as of the same significance as the first:

COMPARISON:CONTIGUOUS

[4:3]   1.a. Governments were committed to inflation
        b. because they were themselves part of the system which required it.

        2.c. Modern capitalism thrives on expansion and credit,
        d. and without them it shrivels.

        3.e. **Equally** however it requires the right context,
        f. which is an expanding world economy:
        g. a national ecnomy is distinct and severable from other national economies in some senses but not all.

Where similar lines of argumentation and interpretation are for some reason separated from each other, then the conjunction *again* is used to pick up the thread as it were. *Again* is one of the two conjunctions in English that regularly connects non-adjacent material in text (the other is *still*; see the discussion of temporals below). Text [4:116] is repeated below and then elaborated in such a way as to separate the two arguments compared in [4:128] in order to illustrate the function of this "resumptive" *again*.

COMPARISON:CONTINGUOUS

[4:116] *The riot began* shows that *riot* is a process term, even though it is in nominal form.

Similarly, *the violence ended suddenly* marks *violence* as a process term even though it has no corresponding verb

COMPARISON:INTERRUPTED

[4:128] *The riot began* shows that *riot* is a process term, even though it is in nominal form. It is a general fact about human language that while actions are congruently realised as verbs and things as nouns, the relation between meaning and form is not bi-unique. Actions can be realised through nominals and often particular colligations in a text will draw attention to this incongruence. Such incongruence can be exploited by the media for ideological purposes.

Again *the violence ended* suddenly marks *violence* as a process term even though it has no coresponding verb form.

The final internal comparative systems to be considered have to do with difference rather than similarity. Within this group [converse] relations in which two aspects of a message trade roles can be contrasted with those in which role reversal of this kind is either not present, or not explicitly drawn to attention.

DIFFERENCE:CONVERSE

[4:129] The most general and important point that has come out of this chapter is probably the close connection between data and theory. Until the data on quantitative variations on linguistic variables became available through the work of Labov, it was unnecessary to take seriously the need for quantitative statements in a linguistic theory,

and **conversely** the lack of a place for such statements in linguistic theory prevented most linguists from bothering to look for the relevant data. (Hudson 1980:190)

DIFFERENCE:OPPOSITION

[4:130] The lack of a place for quantitative statements in linguistic theory prevented linguists from bothering to look for the relevant data.

On the other hand it could be argued that the relevant data could not be interpreted in any case since the tools for its collection and statistical analysis were not readily available.

Within opposition, the distinction is between retraction and contrast. With retraction, a "straw message" is set up, often involving a negative realisation of some kind; this message is then retracted and another put in its place as in [4:131]. With contrast the first message is not set up rhetorically in order to be opposed; internal contrastive relations may select the correlative realisation *on the one hand...on the other (hand)*.

DIFFERENCE:OPPOSITION:RETRACTION

[4:131] It would certainly be wrong to dismiss the results of such asocial linguistics as simply false.

Rather, we can see it as incomplete, in the same way that linguists of the 1970s find earlier grammars incomplete because they had little to say about syntax and even less about semantics or pragmatics. (Hudson 1980:19)

DIFFERENCE:OPPOSITION:CONTRAST

[4:132] **On the one hand** we could view such grammars as false, or at least as politically irresponsible.

On the other it might be preferable to see them as incomplete; this is the more comforting liberal view.

At this point it is possible to consider grading internal comparative relations according to the degree of difference coded between formulations of a message. If *in fact* is substituted for *rather* in [4:131] then seeing asocial linguistics as incomplete is recoded as adjusting its assessment rather than replacing it. Taking this one step further, had *in other words* been used in place of *in fact* then the second formulation would be read not as adjusting the first, but simply as reworking it to make its meaning clear. Again, the same experiential content can be internally connected in different ways, depending on the way in which internal comparison is used to rhetorically construct the meanings being made. This scaling according to degrees of internal difference is outlined below:

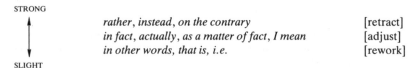

STRONG

rather, instead, on the contrary	[retract]
in fact, actually, as a matter of fact, I mean	[adjust]
in other words, that is, i.e.	[rework]

SLIGHT

The complete network for internal comparative relations is presented below.

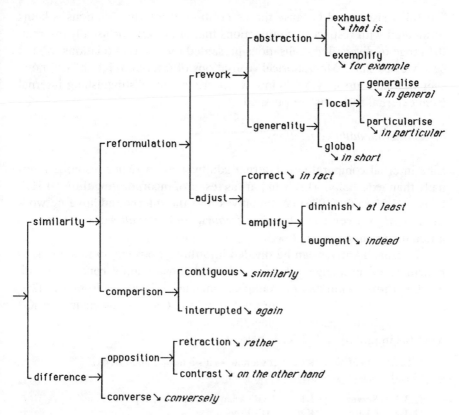

Fig. 4.14. Internal comparative relations

Internal relations are generally interpretable as "cohesive", obtaining between clause complexes rather than within. Even where conjunctions that are externally hypotactic are used, the nature of the internal and external dependency is not the same. The externally connected clause complex in [4:133] below for example is reversible, whereas the internally related clauses in [4:134] are not.

EXTERNAL EXCEPTION
[4:133] Dinner's ready
    except that the rice isn't quite done.

INTERNAL EXCEPTION
[4:134] You could call people to dinner,
    except that they're not all here.

For this reason, and because the description of internal relations is being formuated with respect to conjunctions that are always or usually internal, the range of diversified realisations presented for external relations will not be reviewed here. Metaphorical realisations of internal relations will however be taken up in 4.4.5 below when criteria for distinguishing internal from external relations are pursued.

4.4.2 *Internal additive relations*

Like internal comparatives, internal additives are a richer resource internally than externally. This is in part as result of incorporating three of Halliday and Hasan's (1976) continuatives into the internal additive network (*now, well, anyway*); two others, *of course* and *after all* will be treated as internal consequentials below.

Internal additives can be divided into those whose main function is to punctuate an exchange (*oh* and *well*) and those mainly concerned with building turns. A number of examples containing *oh* and *well* from texts [2:2] and [2:3] in Chapter 2 are represented below. *Oh* is found mainly in K2f moves, explicitly acknowledging that the information being received is news (as in [2:2:5] and [2:3:24] below).

[2:2:4]	Client	⌐K1	It's a new — it's a new Golden Book.
[2:2:5]	Server	└K2f	- **Oh** yeah.
[2:3:23]	Server	⌐K1	That's what it's made by, yup.
[2:3:24]	Client	└K2f	- **Oh** I see.
[2:3:25]		⌐Da1	**Well**, let me think about it
		└Da1	and maybe come back.

Between moves in an exchange, *well* introduces a response to information; if tonic, then the response is marked as a considered one as in [2:2:27] and [2:2:39] below. *Well* appears where there is some doubt about the information responded to, either because it is in the form of a question (typically an exchange initiating K2 move) or a statement which has been modalised, or tagged as with the K1 moves preceding *well* in the following examples.

[2:2:23]	Client	⌐K2	Do you — What do you reckon would be good for a five-year-old kid?
[2:2:24]	Server	cf	- What for?
[2:2:25]		cf	A five-year-old.
[2:2:26]	Server	⊢K1	She'll like fairy tales, does she?
[2:2:27]	Client	└K2f	- **Well**, fairy tales, anything like that, yeah.
[2:2:28]		A2	Um...**well**, let's have a...

[2:2:34]	Client	K2	Where's Timbuctoo?
[2:2:35]	Server	cf	- Timbuctoo?
[2:2:36]	Client	rcf	- Yeah.
[2:2:37]	Server	K1	- It's in Canada, isn't it...
			somewhere up there...in the timber?
[2:2:38]	Client	cf	- Canada.
[2:2:39]		ch	**Well**, I don't know about...

When used in initiating moves, *well* introduces explanatory comments as in
[2:2:16] below.

[2:2:13]	Client	K2	Have you ever heard of Baron Munchhausen?
[2:2:14]	Server	K1	- No, I've never heard about them.
[2:2:15]		K1	It's the first time I've heard of them.
[2:2:16]	Client	K1	- **Well**, he was a — **well**, he was a very famous liar.

Well is also used to mark a new stage in the development of a genre, as
in [2:2:28] and [2:3:25] above. In this function it would be treated as a
marker act, often introducing a framing or focusing move in a boundary
exchange by the Birmingham school (see Burton 1981:74-76). In [2:3:25]
the Client uses it to introduce her leave-taking; and in [2:2:28] it marks the
beginning of a new phase in the Client's search for an appropriate book.

Used to demarcate stages in a text, *well* needs to be grouped with items
such as *now, allright, okay, incidentally, by the way, anyway, anyhow* and
so on. These all have the function of organising discourse on a global level.
These can be subclassified according to whether they are oriented to genre
or field. *Well, now, okay* and *allright* frame a text generically, with respect
to its schematic structure (see Chapter 7 below). They may mark for example the opening and closing of a step in a lecture:

TURN BUILDING:STAGING:FRAMING
[4:135] **Now**, we can solve this particular problem by letting *John*, the old Z element, be a constituent of both clauses. So we'll conflate the function
Receiver in this clause with that of Actor in the projected one, introducing
double motherhood, like so. This gets us around having to start John off in
one clause and raise it into the other one. **Okay**.

Now, what about the logical structure here? ...

Conjunctions like *incidentally, by the way, anyway* and *anyhow* are more
oriented to field than genre. They signal a change of topic, with *incidentally*
or *by the way* marking a departure from what has gone before and items
like *anyway* or *anyhow* marking a return.

TURN BUILDING:STAGING:SIDETRACKING
[4:136] Are you coming tonight? I can give you a lift.
  - Sure.
  - **Incidentally** I saw Ben this morning and he was looking well.
  Guess he's recovered from his flu. I'd been a little worried about him, get-
  ing sick so often and all.
  - Yeah, me too.
  - **Anyway**, I'll see you around eight then.
  - Okay...

These staging conjuctions contrast with developing additives that accumulate messages locally, on topic or within a stage, usually within the same turn. As with external relations the basic opposition is between addition and alternation:

TURN BUILDING:DEVELOPING:ADDITION:SIMPLE
[4:137] We could go to dinner;
    as well we could try and see a movie.

TURN BUILDING:DEVELOPING:ALTERNATION
[4:138] We could eat at seven.
    Or won't you be hungry then?

The following examples bring out the continuity between alternation and retracting or contrastive opposition depending on whether alternatives are viewed as one **or** the other, one **instead of** the other or one as **opposed to** the other.

[ALTERNATION]
[4:139] We might argue that it's a Range.   'a or b'
    Or it might be a Goal.

[RETRACTION]
[4:140] We might argue that it's a Range.   'a in place of b'
    Instead, it might be a Goal.

[CONTRAST]
[4:141] We might argue that it's a Range.   'a different from b'
    In contrast, it might be a Goal.

Simple additive relations realised through *in addition, as well, additionally, besides* which are used to extend a text can be opposed to cumulative ones like *further, furthermore* and *moreover* which build it up to something. Cumulative conjunctions are typically found in the context of an argument (as in [4:2] above; see *furthermore* in [4:2:5:k]), conjoining messages causally supporting a thesis. *Furthermore* seems more common when more than two such arguments are being conjoined, *moreover* being the unmarked form when only two arguments are used.

TURN BUILDING:DEVELOPING:ADDITION:CUMULATIVE:EXTENDING

[4:142] Processes like *laugh* and *cry* really ought to be treated as behavioural ones. Their typical tense selection for ongoing action is [present in present] and they take a conscious Medium. They cannot project; *I laughed that he lost* is very unlikely.

Furthermore, they are agnate to mental processes of reaction, being the physical manifestation of strongly liking and disliking (*thrill, please, upset, destroy* etc.).

TURN BUILDING:DEVELOPING:ADDITION:CUMULATIVE:AMPLIFYING

[4:143] Processes like laugh and cry are not mental ones. Their typical tense selection for ongoing action is [present in present] (**Why do you cry?*).

Moreover, they cannot project (**He laughed that he'd got it wrong.*).

The network for internal additive relations is presented below.

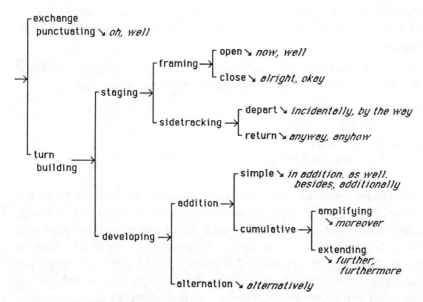

Fig. 4.15. Internal additive relations

4.4.3 *Internal consequential relations*[4]

As far as non-concessive consequential relations are concerned, distinctively internal resources are very limited; for the most part the same conjunctions are used to code internal and external relations. A few unmodalised causals are regularly internal: *consequently*, *hence* and *in conclusion*. And there is one conjunction, *after all*, which is only used internally; it introduces reasons which are so obvious as to require a mild apology for being mentioned.

> [4:144] It might be objected that people could not possibly remember information about all the social contexts for individual linguistic items, given that the term includes lexical items as well as constructions and more general patterns.
>
> **After all**, even a monoglot must know tens of thousands of linguistic items, so the burden on his memory would be very great. (Hudson 1980:232)

Concessive consequential relations on the other hand are realised through a number of distinctively internal conjunctions. *Nevertheless*, *nonetheless* and *still* function as the concessive counterparts of *consequently*, *hence* and *in conclusion*. In addition there is a set of internal concessives oriented to objections which may be conceded (*admittedly*, *of course* and *needless to say*) or dismissed (*in any case*, *at any rate*, *anyhow* and *anyway*).

By way of introducing the concessive internals, compare [4:145] and [4:146], the second of which anticipates the challenge in the first.

> [4:145] Dinner's ready.
> - **But** I'm not hungry.

> [4:146] Dinner's ready.
> **But** you may not be hungry.
> - No, I'm not.

As will be taken up in 4.4.5 below, changing the taxis as far as the realisation of internal relations is concerned helps to focus on their meaning. Paraphrasing the *but* in [4:145] along these lines produces: 'although you've called me to dinner, I'm not hungry.'; the paraphrase for [4:146] is more elaborate: 'although I've just called you to dinner I suspect you might not be hungry and am conceding a possible objection.' Some internal concessives in other words are designed to anticipate challenges.

Depending on the probability of the objection that is pre-empted, a choice opens up among *admittedly* (objection possible), *of course* (objection probable) and *needless to say* (objection certain). The median and low values are illustrated in [4:147] and the high value in [4:148]:

CONCESSIVE:OBJECTION:CONCEDE:MODALITY POSSIBLE & PROBABLE

[4:147] Moreover, most linguists would probably say the same about linguistic differences between *individual* speakers: if there are differences between the grammar of two people, there is no way of knowing which has the higher prestige in society simply by studying the grammars.

Admittedly there are individuals who clearly have *inherently* imperfect grammars, such as children, foreigners and the mentally retarded, but these deviations are easy to explain and predict, and leave intact the claim that all normal people are equal with regard to their grammars.

Of course, there is no shortage of differences between grammars, whether of individuals or whole communities, but there are no purely linguistic grounds for ranking any of the grammars higher than the others. (Hudson 1980:191)

CONCESSIVE:OBJECTION:CONCEDE:MODALITY CERTAIN

[4:148] We might get around this problem by saying that child language is the domain of a branch of psychology rather than sociology, and that psychology can provide general principles of language acquisition which will allow us to predict every respect in which the language of children in this society deviated from the language of adults. If psychology were able to provide the necessary principles, then there would be a good deal to say about language in relation to individual development, but nothing about language in relation to society.

Needless to say, no psychologist would dream of claiming that this was possible, even in principle. (Hudson 1980:6)

There is another set of internal concessives which dismiss objections rather than anticipate them. One of these is illustrated in [4:149]; the hypotactic paraphrase is something like 'I objected I wasn't hungry; but **even if** I was hungry it doesn**'t matter** because I'm going out to eat.'

CONCESSIVE:DISMISS

[4:149] Dinner's ready.
  - But I'm not hungry.
  In any case, I'm going out.
  Sorry I forgot to tell you.

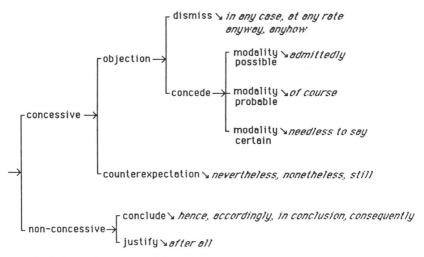

Fig. 4.16. Internal consequential relations

The network for these distinctively internal consequential oppositions is presented as Fig. 4.16. All of the realisations specified are concessive, except for *after all*, *consequently*, *hence*, *accordingly* and *in conclusion*.

4.4.4 *Internal temporal relations*

There are even fewer distinctive internal temporal conjunctions than consequentials, and so the discussion here will be very brief. Simultaneous text-time is realised through *at the same time* which connects messages that are rhetorically overlapping:

> [4:150] One of the main questions we must again ask concerns the balance between the social and the individual. For *language*, in the sense of knowledge of the linguistic items and their meanings, the balance is in favour of the social, since people learn their language by listening to others.
>
> **At the same time**, each individual's language is unique, since no two people have the same experience of language. (Hudson 1980:106)

In addition the conjunction *still* is used to signal that non-contiguous information remains relevant (*still* resembles *again* in its ability to connect non-adjacent messages):

[4:151] Don't you think that the transformation is really an inappropriate concept here. I mean it implies directionality and change where in fact we're looking at texts generated once from a set of option in their context of culture.

- Well, we don't mean to imply process or change. It's just a way of showing the marked and unmarked forms of certain relations. When we say *the police killed the rioters* is transformed into *rioters shot*, we're simply pointing out the ideological transformation that has taken place.

- But **still**, you're implying that something has changed in the text. In fact nothing has changed; though the text is agnate to others in the culture where the Agent is specified. And surely no text is ideologically neutral. All texts encode some ideology as you yourselves argue. So is there really any need for a concept of markedness, however represented?

Successive internals either enumerate a list of arguments or mark the end of some rhetorical sequence. These are illustrated in [4:152] (*pace* Halliday 1985a:136).

[4:152] There are a number of criteria for distinguished Ranges from Goals.

First, the Range cannot be probed by *do to* or *do with*, whereas the Goal can.

Second, since nothing is being "done to" it, a Range element can never have a resultative Attribute added within the clause, as a Goal can: we can say *they trampled the field flat* meaning 'with the result that it became flat', where *the field* is Goal, but not *they crossed the field flat*, where *the field* is Range, even though the flattening may have resulted from their continual crossing of it.

Next, the Range cannot be a personal pronoun, and it cannot normally be modified by a possessive.

Finally, a Range element (other than one with an "empty" verb like *have* or *do*) can often be realised as a prepositional phrase, and under certain conditions it has to be: *she climbed steadily up the mountain, he plays beautifully on the piano, I'm playing Mary at tennis.*

The network for distinctive internal termporal relations is presented below. It is perhaps important to stress again at this stage that the internal networks developed in 4.4.1-4.4.4 do not cover internal uses of conjunctions that are regularly external; nor have realisations including phoric reference items been considered. The treatment is thus partial and needs to be developed in the direction of integrating distinctively internal with other types of conjunctive realisation.

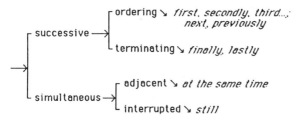

Fig. 4.17. Internal temporal relations in English

4.4.5 *Distinguishing internal and external relations*

Since many of the same conjunctions are regularly used to code internal and external relations, problems may arise in determining whether an internal or external reading is appropriate. The best test for determining the appropriate reading is to change the dependency relationship between the messages in question (from hypotactic to paratactic or "cohesive" or vice versa); with internal relations this will commonly involve projecting one of the related messages with a verbal process.

Consider for example [4:153] which allows either an internal or an external interpretation. If internal [4:153] means that the interlocutor is saying Ben is present because he has spoken with him and so knows he is around; if external [4:153] means that the interlocutor has spoken to Ben and perhaps told him to come, which is the reason for Ben showing up.

[4:153] Ben came,
        because I spoke to him.

Paraphrasing [4:153] with *so* brings out the different readings. The internal paraphrase projects the fact that Ben is present: *I'm telling you that...*[5]; the external paraphrase does not have to rely on a verbal process to make the meaning clear.

INTERNAL PARAPHRASE
[4:154] I saw Ben;
        so *I'm telling you that* he came.   [verbal process added:
                                           'that's why I'm saying...']

EXTERNAL PARAPHRASE
[4:155] I saw Ben;
        so he came.   ['that's why he came']

A move in the opposite direction, from a "cohesive" link to a hypotactic one is illustrated in [4:155] and [4:156]. Once again the paraphrase makes explicit reference to the conversational structure (cf. [4:2y-z] *The judge handles it, and this is where **I'm telling you**, temperament plays a big part* in which the interlocutor prefers the verbal process paraphrase to an internal conjunction like *so*; i.e. *We stand our dog on the table hoping that it will stand like a nice statue. **So** temperament plays a big part.*).

INTERNAL "COHESIVE" RELATION
[4:156] Let's go out for dinner.
    - **So** you finally got paid!

HYPOTACTIC PARAPHRASE
[4:157] Let's go out for dinner.
    - **Since** *you're asking me* (to go out for dinner)
      you must have finally got paid!

While verbal processes are the most common way of explicitly con-tructing text as part of the world as it were, behavioural and relational pro-cesses may be used as well. The following proportionalities between the verbal process realisation in [4:145], [4:154] and [4:157] and a closely related behavioural illustrate one aspect of this alternation.[6]

VERBAL PROCESS:
BEHAVIOURAL PROCESS::

since you're **asking** me to go out for dinner:
since you've **talking** about going out for dinner::

so I'm **telling** you that he came:
so I'm **discussing** him coming::

although you've **said** that dinner's ready:
although you've **called** me to dinner

With consequential relations the paraphrase test may involve projection in the context of a relational rather than a verbal or behavioural process. Note the following variations on [4:156]:

[4:158] Let's go out for dinner.
    - **So** you finally got paid/
    - You're **confirming** you finally got paid/
    - That **confirms** you finally got paid.

The last response in [4:158] can be read as an identifying process with an additional feature of agency (Halliday 1985a:153-164), meaning 'the fact

that you are inviting me out for dinner confirms that the fact that you finally
got paid is a fact'.

The fact that you're inviting me out	confirms	the fact that you got paid	to be	a fact
Assigner	Process	Token	Process	Value

The projection on this reading is a fact, and consequentiality is realised
through the agentive relational process *confirm* (other processes functioning in this way include *prove, show, indicate, imply, demonstrate, confirm,
substantiate, predict, illustrate, attest*; all of these can also function as verbal
processes, from which the agentive relational meanings have been derived).

What is actually going on here is that the paraphrases of the internal
relations are transforming them into external ones by reconstructing the
rhetorical structure of the text in experiential terms. Verbal and
behavioural, or in some cases the relational processes just noted, are used
to treat text itself as part of the experiential world. These experiential paraphrases of internal relations are another instance of the process of grammatical metaphor which has been introduced on a number of occasions
above. It is interesting to note that when realised as processes, external
relations favour circumstantial identifying relationals whereas internal relations rely on projection. The proportionalities are illustrated in Table 4.14
below; for a discussion of the evolution of these patterns of realisation in
scientific English see Halliday (1986b).

In spite of the usefulness of the paraphrase test to tease out incongruent
realisations for internal connections, distinguishing internal from external
additive, comparative and concessive relations can be difficult, since with
these relations the difference between contructing text and constructing
field is not always clear.

With additives, one useful rule of thumb is to check whether the second of the messages involved in the relation is potentially "branched". If
so, the relation can be taken as external. Thus [4:159] can be read as external, because of the missing Subject and Finite elements; there is no possibility of paratactic ellipsis of this kind in [4:160], which can accordingly be
taken as internal (this reading is reinforced by the clause complex initial
position of *and*).

Table 4.14. Congruent and metaphorical realisation of external and internal conjunctive relations

external	internal
CONGRUENT:METAPHORICAL::	CONGRUENT:METAPHORICAL::
CONJUNCTION:CIRCUMSTANTIAL	CONJUNCTION:VERBAL PROCESS + LOCUTION;
IDENTIFYING	BEHAVIOURAL PROCESS + ACT;
RELATIONAL PROCESS	IDENTIFYING RELATIONAL PROCESS
	+ ASSIGNER + FACT
by:**enable**::	in this way:through **pointing out** all that::
because:**cause**::	in conclusion:since I've **written** all this::
if:**condition**:	anyhow:even if I **said** all that::
before:**follow**::	finally:I'll finish by **noting**::
while:**overlaps**::	at the same time:simultaneously I'll **add**::
whereas:**contrasts with**::	on the other hand:while I just **suggested**::
like:**resembles**	similarly:like I just **argued**

EXTERNAL ADDITIVE (paratactic ellipsis)
[4:159] Such assumptions are embedded in language, learnt through language, **and** reinforced in language use. (Kress & Hodge 1979:5)

INTERNAL ADDITIVE (no branching possible)
[4:160] Language fixes a world that is so much more stable and coherent than that we actually see that it takes its place in our consciousness and becomes what we think we have seen.

And since normal perception works by constant feed-back, the gap between the real world and the actually constructed world is constantly being reduced, so that what we do 'see' tends to become what we can say. (Kress & Hodge 1979:5)

With comparatives and concessives, internal relations are clearest when lines of argumentation are being compared, contrasted or conceded. These relations often range retrospectively over a number of clauses in a text and the hypotactic paraphrase has the form *although/whereas/as I have argued that x, y, z...* . Note that there is no single message in [4:161] which can be compared externally with *Similarly, a plural object affects the status of the statement*; it is the same point that is being made and this is what the internal relation is about:

INTERNAL COMPARATIVE
[4:161] Now there are innumerable hand-to-hand fights going on with this fearsome loaf. Plurals have a kind of imprecision that singulars do not. Take

> Bugner fights Ellis tonight.
> Bugner and Ellis fight tonight.

In the first there must be a single action (the singular imposing unity on what could otherwise be regarded as many related action). In the second they may be fighting each other, at the same time, or they may be fighting different opponents, in different bouts, at different times, perhaps even in different continents.

Similarly a plural object affects the status of the statement: Shirley fights seventeen three-bob loaves. (Kress & Hodge 1979: 88-89)

4.5 CONTINUITY

Before turning to the question of conjunctive structures in text, an additional set of meanings, closely related to CONJUNCTION in certain respects, will be brought into the picture. This system will be referred to as CONTINUITY and is realised through *already, still, yet, anymore, any longer, finally, at last, only, just, even, also, as well, too, either* and *neither*. Negative and interrogative realisations of this system will not be pursued in any detail here (e.g. *yet, anymore, any longer*; see Young 1987 for a useful discussion of *already, yet, still* and *any longer* in these environments).

Unlike CONJUNCTION, which is typically realised as textual Theme in clause initial position, CONTINUITY is realised rhematically. Since all CONTINUITY items except *already* can also function as conjunctions, this difference in realisation proves useful in focussing on the differences between the two systems. Some of these are illustrated in the examples below which contrast the relevant items functioning first as conjunctions, and then as continuity items (for a discussion of the difference between CONJUNCTION and CONTINUITY in Tagalog see Martin 1981).

[4:162] CONJUNCTION   Ben is here.
                         Still I wonder if Flo is coming.

         CONTINUITY   Ben has left.
                         But Flo is **still** here.

[4:163] CONJUNCTION   The results are significant.
                         Finally let me consider the question of applicability.

         CONTINUITY   Ben trained for hours
                         and by eleven he'd **finally** finished.

[4:164] CONJUNCTION   Ben left early.
                         Yet he felt a little tired.

	CONTINUITY	Ben has left; But Flo hasn't **yet** arrived.
[4:165]	CONJUNCTION	Ben will run **even** if I have to drag him there.
	CONTINUITY	Ben beat Lindley. He **even** beat Carl.
[4:164]	CONJUNCTION	He felt like relaxing, **only** he was upset about the race.
	CONTINUITY	No, I'm not busy. I was **only** reading.
[4:167]	CONJUNCTION	You have to consider the aspect. **Also** the question of polarity comes into it.
	CONTINUITY	Ben beat Lindley and he **also** beat Carl.
[4:168]	CONJUNCTION	**Either** Ben didn't want to compete or he couldn't.
	CONTINUITY	Ben couldn't pass the test and Lindley couldn't **either**.

Alongside this structural difference in realisation, CONTINUITY differs from CONJUNCTION in that five of the fundamental oppositions associated with CONJUNCTION are not relevant. First, the messages related through CONTINUITY are not reversible (**Ben beat Lindley too. He beat Carl.*). Second, messages so related can only enter into covariate semantic dependency; hypotactic and paratactic realisations are not available. Third, the internal/external opposition is not relevant. Fourth, CONTINUITY cannot be implicit: *Ben beat Lindley and he beat Carl* does not mean 'Ben beat Lindley and he even beat Carl'. And finally, CONTINUITY cannot be realised metaphorically as a process.

It is also not necessary that the information presumed by CONTINUITY items be in an adjacent message:

[4:169] <u>Ben had always wanted to win in Rome.</u>
He'd trained hard for years
and the thought of coming second in the previous Olympics still rankled him.
Of course he wanted to win in Seoul <u>too</u>.

CONTINUITY items can be divided into three groups, those involving counterexpectation (e.g. *already*, *finally*, *still*, *only* and *even*), those involving parallel MOOD structure (e.g. *too*, *also*, *as well*) and *again* which codes experiential repetition. The three types combine freely as in [4:170]:

[4:170] Ben beat Lindley.
   And he's **already** beaten Carl **again too**.

With counterexpectation, there is a set of aspectual continuity items (e.g.
already, *finally* and *still*) which are opposed to a set which are not concerned with unexpected starts and finishes (e.g. *just* and *even*). The contrast
betwen *just* and *even* corresponds to that between *at least* and *indeed* among
the internal comparatives. *Just* signals that too much has been implied, *even*
that too little has.

DIMINISH
[4:171] Is Ben training?
   - No, he's **only** reading.

AUGMENT
[4:172] Is Ben training?
   - Yeah, he's **even** doing wind-sprints.

The aspectual continuity markers are illustrated below. Inceptives (e.g.
already, *finally* and *at last*) are opposed to continuatives (e.g. *still*); and
inceptives are divided into those signalling that something has begun sooner
than expected (*already*) and those coding that it has begun later than
expected (*finally* and *at last*).

FRUITION:PRECEDENCE
[4:173] Is Ben coming?
   - He's **already** here.

FRUITION:ENDURANCE
[4:174] Has Ben shown up?
   - He's **finally** arrived.

CONTINUATION
[4:175 Has Ben left?
   - No, he's **still** here.

The items *too*, *also* and *as well* are sensitive to parallels between the
Mood ^ Residue structures of proposals or propositions. They signal that
either the Mood or the Residue is the same:

NEW MOOD
[4:176] Ben won the race,
   but later Carl did **too**.

NEW RESIDUE
[4:177] Ben won in Rome
   and he won in Seoul **too**.

Where the Mood changes, but the Residue is constant, the realisation *so^* Finite ^ Subject is possible:

NEW MOOD
[4:178] Ben won the race,
   but later **so did** Carl.

The use of *so* and *too* to hold the Residue constant underlies their function in polarity focussed arguments such as the following where they resemble the clause substitutes *not* and *so*; *so* and *too* are always tonic in this function (tonic syllable in bold face):

[4:179] Ben won really.
   - // He did **not**.//
   - //He did **so**.//
   - //He **did**n't.//
   - //He did **too**.//

Under scope of negation, these MOOD parallels are realised through *either* or through *neither^*Finite^Subject.

Again is used to mark the recurrence of a Process ˙ Medium nucleus at some later date:

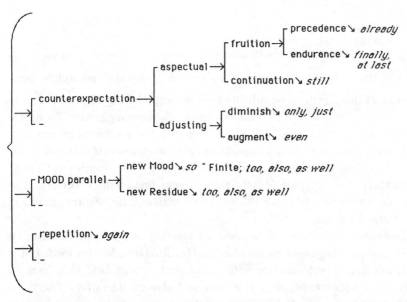

Fig. 4.18. CONTINUITY systems

REPETITION
[4:180] Ben beat Carl in Rome
and Carl lost **again** in Seoul.

The network for CONTINUITY is presented in Fig. 4.18; negative and inter-rogative realisations have not been specified (i.e. *either, neither, yet, any longer* etc.]

4.6 CONJUNCTION in English: structure

Conjunctive structures in English, like reference chains, are covariate ones. The semantic dependency between the messages related may or may not be grammaticalised; and a dependent message may itself be depended on. Thus in [4:181] the second message is the reason for the first, and is itself caused by the third; and this consequentiality has not been gram-maticalised, though it could have been — the text can be recoded as a clause complex ([4:182]) or a single clause ([4:183]).

[4:181] Ben was tired.
He hadn't slept all night.
This race was just too important.

[4:182] Ben was tired
since he hadn't slept all night
as this race was just too important.

[4:183] Ben's fatigue was **caused** by lack of sleep **due to** the importance of the race.

The work of the Hartford stratificationalists on modelling discourse depen-dencies of this kind was presented in Chapter 3; their suggestion for narra-tive structure is represented below. Recall that these reticula incorporate TRANSITIVITY relations (roles), conjunctive relations (connections) and REFER-ENCE chains (the participant lines). Their notation for "participant lines" was elaborated in Chapter 3; here their "event line" will be reworked to handle CONJUNCTION, including the range of semantic distinctions noted in 4.2, 4.3 and 4.4 above.

Extensions are required because of typological differences between English and the languages focussed on at Hartford (see Martin 1983a); it is also important to reformulate reticula in such a way that they can be applied to a wide range of genres, not just spoken narrative. The main changes have to do with the following factors:

(i) the distinction between external and internal relations.

(ii) the fact that messages may be related to more than one other.

(iii) the fact that related messages need not be contiguous

(iv) the fact that messages may depend on those which follow as well as those which precede.

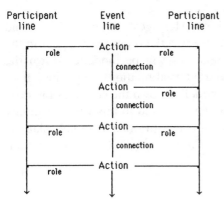

Fig. 4.19. *Typical semological structure of a narrative*

4.6.1 *Elaborating reticula*

The Hartford school modelled conjunctive relations between actions, more or less equivalent to the TRANSITIVITY function Process in systemic theory. Since TRANSITIVITY relations are treated as part of lexicogrammar in the model developed here, an appropriate discourse semantics unit needs to be found. The unit message will be adopted here, where this is realised as a ranking clause that is neither a projection, nor a hypotactically dependent elaborating clause. This means that locutions and ideas, elaborating β clauses and all embedded clauses will be treated as part of messages rather than as conjunctively related units in their own right. The following grammatical items (bold in the examples) will thus be treated as message parts, not as messages in their own right:

locution	He said **he'd won**.
idea	He thought **he'd won**.

=β	He said he'd won, **which he had**.
[[fact]]	It pleased him **that he'd won**.
[[act]]	I saw **him win**.
[[relative clause]]	The guy **who won** ended up losing.
[[wh clause as Head]]	**Whoever won** ended up losing.

None of these units enter into the additive, comparative, temporal and consequential oppositions outlined above; the clauses listed involve two processes, but no conjunctive relations.

Reticula will be organised as follows. Messages will be numbered and listed vertically down the centre of the page in the order they appear in the text under consideration. External relations will be modelled down the right hand side of this "event line" and internal relations down the left — except that external additives will be modelled down the centre of the message line, between messages. Additives are treated in this way to simplify the representation since they often combine with other external relations (e.g. *and so, and then, and thus* etc.) and are extremely frequent in certain modes.

Table 4.15. Summary of CONJUNCTION *resources modelled in reticula*

	External: explicit	implicit	Internal
temporal: simultaneous successive			
consequential: manner consequence condition purpose (concessive)			
comparative: similarity contrast			
additive: addition alternation		■	

[4:184] EXPLICIT EXTERNAL SUCCESSIVE
    a.   Ben walked into the room.
    b.   **Then** he had two beers.

[4:185] EXPLICIT INTERNAL EXEMPLICATORY[7]
    a.   Ben's a fantastic sprinter.
    b.   **Like** you should see his start.

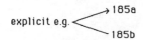

[4:186] EXPLICIT EXTERNAL ADDITIVE
    a.   Ben was tired
    b.   **and** he felt dehydrated.

```
        186a
          ↑
explicit additive
          │
        186b
```

In these examples, succeeding moves are shown to depend on preceding ones; the arrow points to the information presumed by the message containing the conjunction.

Implicit relations will be modelled in reticula where they could have been made explicit in the text under consideration and are necessary for its interpretation. Implicit additives will not be modelled, nor will implicit internals, except where these need to be recognised to make sense of the text (see discussion in 4.2.4 above).[8] A text with a simultaneous internal and external structure, including an implicit internal consequential is illustrated below.

[4:187] a.   Ben was unlucky.
       b.   He had to take steriods for his injured hamstring
       c.   **and**[9] **then** they introduced more sophisticated tests.

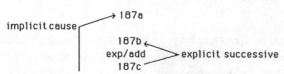

4.6.2 *Range*

As illustrated in [4:187] messages can be related conjunctively to more than one other; [4:187b] and [4:187c] are both justifications for expressing the attitude in [4:187a]. A single message may also depend on more than one other as in [4:188]. The ranging dependency arrow in the reticulum reflects what could be represented through bracketing in a clause complex analysis: (1 $^+$2) ^{x}3. The point is that "nesting" is a feature of conjunctive relations whether they are expressed through a clause complex dependency structure or not.

[4:188] a. Ben was thirsty
    b. **and** couldn't procude a specimen
    c. **so** he had two beers.

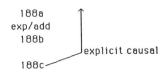

It follows that more than one message can be related to more than one other. This pattern, along with a notation for expressing nesting of additive relations is presented for [4:189] below.

[4:189] a. **Either** Ben had been up all night
    b. and hadn't slept
    c. **or** he was ill
    d. **and** and felt tired.
    e. **In any case** he looked awful.

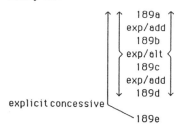

Although clear in the examples presented above, the scope of conjunctive relations is not always well defined. As an analytical strategy it is useful to keep in mind that in the unmarked case conjunctive relations obtain between two contiguous messages. The range of a relation should be extended only where necessary to make sense of a text. Following this principle, temporal successive relations for example can simply be modelled between contiguous messages; there is no need to depend each successive message backwards on all preceding ones. The first representation below will thus be preferred to the second, which is in any case clearly implied by the first. The paratactic ellipsis throughout [4:190] will be taken as making the additive relation explicit.

[4:190] a. Ben went into the room,
     b. sat down,
     c. drank two beers
     d. **and** waited for the results.

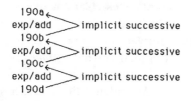

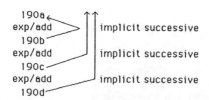

    With internal relations the principle that in the unmarked case conjunctive relations obtain between two contiguous messages does not hold. Internal conjunction is commonly used to organize groups of messages with respect to each other. Consequently the minimalist interpretation suggested above for external relations is not appropriate. Typical internal range is illustrated in 191.[10]

[4.191] a. Ben was unlucky.
     b. For one thing he had a hamstring injury.
     c. For another, they introduced more sophisticated tests.
     d. On top of all that he won his race
     e. **and so** had to be tested.

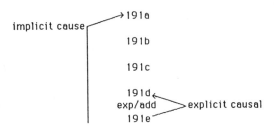

4.6.3 *Direction of dependency*

In all of the examples considered so far, messages have been shown to depend retrospectively on preceding ones. Conjunctive structures have been treated in other words as typically anaphoric, as are reference chains. Conjunctions do sometimes point forward however. This hapens in correlative paratactic structures like that in [4:189] where *either* predicts an ensuing alternative just as *or* predicts a preceding one. This was modelled by putting a arrow at both ends of the dependency line connecting dependent messages in the covariate conjunctive structure. A small number of internal conjunctions operate in this way; for example *first* and *on the one hand*. In [4:192] *first* predicts a succeeding argument, just as *second* presumes a preceding one.

> [4:192] a. I'd say it's a material process.
> b. **First**, the tense is [present in present].
> c. **Second**, the Agent is not conscious.
> d. **Finally**, this process can't project.

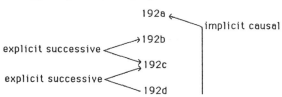

With these examples, the messages involved have been mutually presuming; the first points to the second and the second back to the first. The only context in which messages can be prospectively dependent without being retrospectively depended on at the same time is in hypotactic clauses complexes in which a dependent clause functions as a marked Theme. This is illustrated in [4:193] below.

> [4:193] a. **Once** it was all out in the open
> b. Ben felt better.

193a

193b explicit successive

No special notation will be proposed for hypotactically dependent clauses which interrupt their α; e.g. *Ben, after he'd lost, felt sad*. These could be enclosed in angled brackets in reticula, following Halliday's (1985a) notation if required. They are simply treated as if they followed their α in the analyses below.

4.6.4 *Contiguity*

The suggestion that in the unmarked case CONJUNCTION relates a message backwards in a text to the preceding one has now been qualified in two respects: more than two messages may be involved, and conjunctions can refer forward. The final qualification has to do with adjacency. In the course of presenting internal relations above, it was noted that two conjunctions, *again* and *still* are regularly used to connect non-adjacent messages, and need to be treated as exceptions. The principle of contiguity, like that of retrospective dependency, can also be over-ridden by TAXIS in clause complexes where a dependent clause is a marked Theme. This is illustrated in [4:194], where the reason for drinking two beers interrupts sitting down and having them.

[4:194] a. Ben sat down.
     b. **Because** he was dehydrated
     c. he **then** had to drink two beers.

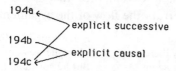

194a

194b explicit successive

194c explicit causal

At times internal reformulation leads to texts which could be treated as involving discontinuity between related messages. But since in cases like [4:195] it would be arbitrary to choose one formulation or the other as related to ensuing messages it seems appropriate to simply let the dependency arrow range over both formulations.

[4:195] a. Ben's very fast.
     b. **Like** you should see his starts.
     c. **So** he won't lose
     d. **even if** he races against Carl.

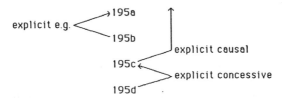

Where a series of exemplifications are given however, it seems important to relate each back to the original formulation; this may produce a series of discontinuous internal relations in a text, one for each additional formulation.

[4:196] a.   Ben trains very carefully.
       b.   He spends three hours in the gym.
       c.   He's also very selective about his diet.
       d.   He even goes to bed at nine every night.

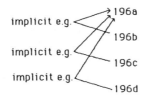

Finally, "parenthetical" messages needs to be considered. A number of these are in fact the "cohesive" realisations of elaborating β clauses; they may be explicitly punctuated as such with parentheses and create discontinuity in reticula. The fact that parentheses are used reflects the strength of the adjacency principle, which also underlies the use of footnotes in "learned" texts so as not to interrupt the flow of the argument.

[4:197] a.   Ben escaped in Rome.   α   Ben escaped in Rome,
       b.   (He was rather lucky there.)   =β   where he was rather lucky.
       c.   **But** he got caught in Seoul.   **But** he got caught in Seoul.

Similar "descriptive" interludes are common in many genres. The time line in a narrative may be interrupted as characters are commented on or described. An example of discontinuity of this kind is presented below.

[4:198] a.   Ben walked in.
       b.   He was still wearing his track suit.

    c.   His mother rushed over
    d.   and gave him a hug.

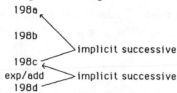

These problems of range and contiguity will be taken up again in 4.8 below when Mann and Thompson's (1985, 1986, forthcoming a, b) description of relational propositions in terms of nucleus and satellite is reviewed.

4.7 Analysis of two texts

In order to prepare for the discussion in 4.8 below, the analyses developed above will be illustrated for two texts, both taken from Mann and Thompson (1986).

4.7.1 *Notational conventions*

The following conventions will be observed for reticula. All conjunctive relations will be marked as implicit (**imp**) or explicit (**exp**) according to whether or not they are explicitly realised between clauses.

    In addition types of logico-semantic relation will be noted, up to the following points in delicacy (further delicacy can of course be derived from the networks presented above if required for particular analyses and interpretations):

temporal:	simultaneous	**simul**
	successive	**succ**
consequential:	manner	**man**
	consequence	**consq**
	condition	**cond**
	purpose	**purp**
comparative:	similarity	**simil**
	contrast	**contr**
additive:	addition	**add**
	alternation	**alt**
locative:		**loc**

In addition, consequentials will be marked as concessive (**conc**) whenever they involve counterexpectation.

Finaly, two very common types of internal comparative will be distinguished: exhaustive (**i.e.**) and exemplifying (**e.g.**) reformulation.

4.7.2 *Analysis*

Text [4:199], divided into conjunctively relatable units (or messages) is presented below (from Mann & Thompson 1986).

[4:199] a. I don't believe that endorsing the Nuclear Freeze initiative is the right step for California CC.
b. Tempting as it may be,
c. we shouldn't embrace every popular issue that comes along.
d. When we do so
e. we use precious limited resources
f. where other players with superior resources are already doing an adequate job.
g. Rather, I think we will be stronger and more effective
h. if we stick to those issues of governmental structure and process, broadly defined, that have formed the core of our agenda for years.
i. Open government, campaign finance reform, and fighting the special interests and big money — these are our kinds of issues.
j. Let's be clear: I personally favour the initiative
k. and ardently support disarmament negotiations to reduce the risk of war.
l. But I don't think endorsing a specific freeze proposal is appropriate for CCC.
m. We should limit our involvement in defense and weaponry to matters of process, such as exposing the weapons industry's influence on the political process.
n. Therefore, I urge you to vote against a CCC endorsement of the nuclear freeze initiative.

[Recall that projection is not treated as a conjunctive relation, and so the clause complexes in a, g, l and n are treated as single messages. In addition, *Let's be clear* in j is taken as an incongruent expression (in a clause) of internal reformulation, and thus not treated as a separate unit: compare *let me put this another way, let's be clear, that is to say, in other words, that is, i.e.*]

Generically, [4:199] is an example of hortatory exposition — it sets out to persuade readers that California Common Cause should not support the Nuclear Freeze initiative. Seen from the point of view of grammar, [4:199]

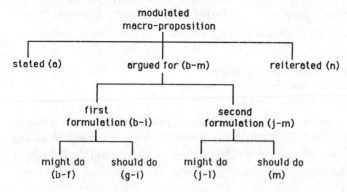

Fig. 4.20. Internal[11] structure of the argument in [4:199]

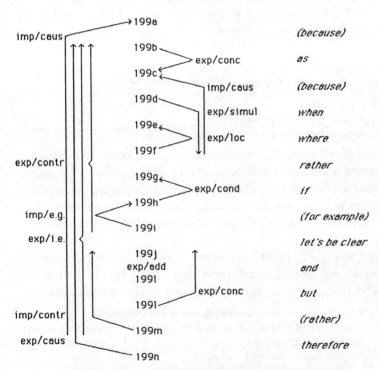

Fig. 4.21. Reticulum for conjunctive relations in [4:199]

is a modulated macro-proposition (Martin 1985b; Martin & Peters 1985). Its rhetorical structure, as coded through internal conjunction is basically as follows:

[4:199a]   presents a modulated proposition
[4:199b-m] present arguments in favour of the proposition
[4:199n]   reiterates the proposition

The supporting argument is presented first in [4:199b-i], then reformulated in [4:199j-m]. Within both formulations what CCC might be tempted to do ([4:199b-f and 4:199-j-l]) is contrasted with what CCC should do ([4:199g-i and 4:199m]). The structure of the argument is outlined in constituent terms in Fig. 4.20.

Expressed as a reticulum, the argument, including external relations, is presented in Fig. 4.21 (an external locative relation is marked between [4:198e] and [4:198f] — loc); the explicit conjunctions used to mark the relations are included to the right of the reticulum:

Externally, both formulations of the argument ([4:199b-i] and [4:199j-m]) contain parallel concessive relations:

[4:199b-c]
'although it's tempting
we shouldn't embrace every popular issue that comes along'

[4:199jk-lm]
'although I personally favour the initiative...
endorsing a specific freeze proposal is not appropriate for CCC...'

In addition, the first formulation contains a number of local external consequential temporal and locative relations. Note that since external relations never cross internal boundaries, the constituency metaphor used to represent the rhetorical structure of the argument above could have been extended to include external relations as constituents of internal ones (see 4.8 below).

In contrast to [4:199], [4:200] is a macro-proposal. It tries to get readers to buy goods, not just change the way they think. Text [4:200] is presented below, divided into messages (from Mann & Thompson 1986).

[4:200] a.   What if you're having to clean floppy heads too often?
        b.   Ask for SYNCOM diskettes, with burnished Ectype coating and dust-absorbing jacket liners.
        c.   As your floppy disk writes or reads
        d.   a Syncom diskette is working in four ways
        e.   to keep loose particles and dust from causing soft errors, dropouts.
        f.   Cleaning agents on the burnished surface of the Ectype coating actually remove build-up from the head,

g. while lubricating it at the same time.
h. A carbon additive drains away static electricity
i. before it can attract dust or lint.
j. Strong binders hold the signal carrying oxides tightly within the coating.
k. And the non-woven jacket liner (...) provides thousands of tiny pockets to keep what it collects.
l. (more than just wiping the surface)
m. To see which Syncom diskette will replace the ones you're using now,
n. send for our free "Flexi-Finder" selection guide and the name of the supplier nearest you.
o. Syncom, Box 130, Mitchell, SD 57301. 800-843-9862; 605-996-8200.

The rhetorical structure of [4:200] is not as fully developed through internal conjunction as that of [4:199]. The relationship between [4:200b] and [4:200c], [4:200l] and [4:200m] and [4:200n] and [4:200o] cannot be made explicit with internal conjunctions that fit naturally into the text. The nature of these relations will be explored in Chapter 7 when generic structure is discussed. Nevertheless, [4:200c] through [4:200l] display a very common internal structure; and [4:200a] and [4:200b] are internally related as well.

The internal relation connecting [4:200a] and [4:200b] is conditional and can be paraphrased as follows:

[4:188a-b] 'you **might** be having trouble with your floppy disk drive heads, **so** we're advising you to ask for SYNCOM diskettes.'

In the next section, [4:200c-l], four examples are given of the way in which Syncom diskettes can help:

[4:188c-e]	Syncom diskette is working in **four ways...**	
[4:188f-g]	cleaning agents...	EXAMPLE 1
[4:188h-i]	carbon additive...	EXAMPLE 2
[4:188j]	strong binders...	EXAMPLE 3
[4:188k-l]	non-woven jacket-liner...	EXAMPLE 4

The fourth example is connected to the others with an explicit internal additive conjunction (*And*). This example includes an internal relation of its own, which is on the borderline of additive and comparative relations: *more than just wiping the surface*. It has been treated as more closely related to *indeed* than *moreover*; *more than* makes explicit the augmentation. It has thus been taken as realising internal similarity rather than addition.

In addition there are a number of local temporal and consequential relations. One which may be worth commenting on here is the successive relation between [4:200h] and [4:200i]. This is simply a conservative coding oriented to the lower limit principle discussed in 4.3.2 above; *before* makes temporal succession explicit — other relations, if felt to be present, are implicit. A case could possibly be made for an implicit purposive relation as well, which might have been made explicit through conjunctions like *lest* and *for fear of* or the more periphrastic *in order to avoid*.

The reticulum dislaying the conjunctive structure of [4:200] is presented as Fig. 4.22.

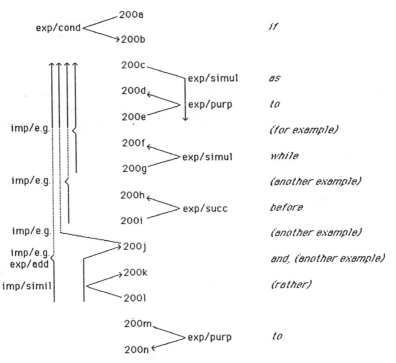

Fig. 4.22. Reticulum for conjunctive relations in [4:200]

The analyses presented by Mann and Thompson for [4:199] and [4:200] differ in a number of respects from those presented here. They use a different inventory of logico-semantic relations; they do not make a distinction between internal and external relations (however see Matthiessen & Thompson 1988, who distinguish relations pertaining to rhetorical acts from those keying on subject matter); they recognise implicit relations, but to not require that a relation be potentially explicit to be analysed; and trivially, they simply read the conjunctive relations in [4:199] and [4:200] differently in a few cases. The issues of inventory, internal/external relations and implicit/explicit realisations are closely inter-related but will not be pursued here. Instead, 4.7 below will focus on a more fundamental thoeretical difference between *English Text*'s approach to CONJUNCTION and Rhetorical Structure Theory — namely Mann and Thompson's suggestion that a text is very much more like a hypotactic clause complex in its structure than is reflected in the reticula developed here.

4.8 Constituency, dependency and conjunctive relations

As far as conjunctive relations are concerned, how then is a text like a clause (various analogies are explored in Halliday 1982b)? One suggestion, which neither *English Text* nor Rhetorical Structure Theory have pursued is that conjunctive relations effect multivariate structures, best modelled through constituency. As noted above, the constituency representation of internal relations in [4:199] could have been extended to include external ones. This would have lead to a constituency diagram like the following, with the text divided into layers of parts and conjunctions in bold face showing the relationships between them.

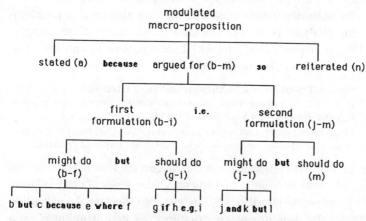

Fig. 4.23. Constituency representation of conjunction in [4:199]

But using bold-face conjunctions to show the relationships involved is of course cheating are far as multivariate structures are concerned; these need to be replaced with function labels in a pure constituency representation. The top layer of structure for example, *stated* **because** *argued for* **so** *reiterated*, would have to be reworked as Fig. 4.24.

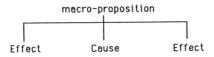

Fig. 4.24. Multivariate top layer for [4:199]

And this is where problems for the constituency approach begin to arise. As far as CONJUNCTION is concerned, the arguments are both the reasons for the thesis and the cause of the reiteration. But the multivariate representation above does not explicitly show which Effect the Cause is the cause of. It could be bracketed with one or the other by adding a layer to the tree; but it could not be bracketed with both. And if valences are added to the tree to mark the appropriate relationships, the model stops being a pure constituency one.

The sandwich structure effected by internal consequential relations in [4:199] is more typical of global "top level" relations than more local "bottom level" ones. But the fact that messages entering into conjunctive relations are usually both depending and depended on also creates problems for a multivariate analysis. Note for example that the multivariate interpretation of [4:199g-i] requires that [4:199h] function both as the Effect of [4:199g] and the Generalisation to [4:199i].

[4:199] g. Rather, I think we will be stronger and more effective
         h. if we stick to those isues of governmental structure and process, broadly defined, that have formed the basis of our agenda for years.
         i. Open government, campaign finance reform, and fighting the influence of special interests and big money — these are our kind of issues.

The functions Effect and Generalisation can be conflated as in the diagram above, treating [4:199h] as a janus constituent. Constituents of this kind have certainly been proposed in constituency analysis, but they are the exception to the rule. Generally in multivariate structures, each constituent plays a

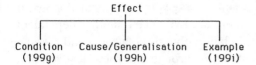

Fig. 4.25. Multivariate intepretation of [4:199:g-i]

single role. But as far as conjunctive relations are concerned, janus constituents would turn out to be the norm. Units entering into conjunctive relations usually play more than one role in the logical structure of a text.

It is for reasons of this kind that constituency has not always been favoured as far as the representation of conjunctive relations is concerned (but see Longacre 1976, 1979). Dependency treatments on the other hand have proved promising; but among these there are various approaches to follow up.

Mann and Thompson (1985, 1986, forthcoming a; Matthiessen & Thompson 1988) have developed an analysis of relational propositions in discourse which suggests that rhetorical structures are very much like clause complex ones. Two types of rhetorical dependency relation are recognised: List and Nucleus-Satellite. These can be illustrated as follows, using a text and diagrams from Matthiessen and Thompson 1988.

[4:201] a. Sanga-Saby-Kursgard, Sweden, will be the site of the 1969 International Conference on Computational Linguistics, September 1-4.

b. It is expected that some 250 linguists will attend from Asia, West Europe, East Europe including Russia, and the United States.

c. The conference will be concerned with the application of mathematical and computer techniques to the study of natural languages, the development of computer programs as tools for linguistic research, and the application of linguistics to the development of man-machine communication systems.

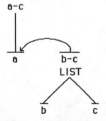

Fig. 4.26. List and Nucleus-Satellite relations illustrated

The List relation holding between messages b and c is analogous to parataxis in the clause complex — there are two nuclei, neither dependent on the other. The Nucleus-Satellite relation obtains between a and b-c, the arrow showing b-c to be dependent on a through the rhetorical relation *elaboration*; this relationship is analogous to hypotaxis in the clause complex.

The difficulty multivariate analysis faced with messages being both depending and depended on is handled in Rhetorical Structure Theory by adding layers of dependency structure. One of Matthiessen and Thompson's examples is simplified as [4:202] below to illustrate this point:

> [4:202] a. Peter Moskowitz has been with KUSC longer than any other staff member.
>   b. He volunteered to work at the station as a classical music announcer.
>   c. That was in 1970.

In [4:202] b-c are treated by Matthiessen and Thompson as satellites of [4:202a]; and [4:202b] is in turn depended on by [4:202c]. The relational analysis is shown in Fig. 4.27.

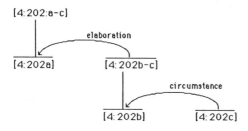

Fig. 4.27. Rhetorical relations in [4:202]

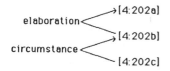

Fig. 4.28. Reticulum presentation for rethorical relations in Fig. 4.26.

Reconsidered in clause complex terms, this means that Rhetorical Structure Theory prefers α β (α β) to α β γ. This gives rhetorical structure diagrams many more layers of conjunctive structure than are modelled in reticula, where, pursuing the clause complex analogy, α β γ is preferred. Compare the reticulum presentation of Matthiessen and Thompson's analysis of [4:202] above (treating their elaboration and circumstance relations as internal for this analysis) as outlined in Fig. 4.28.

Mann and Thompson (1986) analyse [4:199] purely in terms of the Nucleus-Satellite relation. Their rhetorical structure is presented below. Mann and Thompson's division of the text into units for analysis differs slightly from that presented above. They treat [4:199d-e] as a single unit, possibly because they do not recognise locative relations (*we use precious limited resources **where** other players are already doing an adequate job*); Matthiessen and Thompson do note that these may need to be taken into account, especially for certain languages. And their segmentation of [4:199j-k] has *Let's be clear* as one unit and *I personally favour the initiative and ardently support disarmament negotiations to reduce the risk of war* as another. The treatment of *Let's be clear* may simply be due to the fact that incongruent realisations of conjunctive relations have not yet received much attention in Rhetorical Structure Theory. It is unclear why the rest of the sentence is treated as one nucleus rather than a list of two (possibly because for some reason additive relations do not figure prominently among rhetorical relations).

As can be seen from this analysis, Mann and Thompson's claim is that Nucleus-Satellite dependency relations can be motivated independently of their realisation. The following sections from [4:199] illustrate this point:

[4:199] (excerpts)
  b. Tempting **as** it may be,
  c. we shouldn't embrace very popular issue that comes along.
  j. Let's be clear: I personally favour the initiative.
  k. and ardently support disarmament negotiations to reduce the risk of war.
  l. **But** I don't think endorsing a specific freeze proposal is appropriate for CCC.

The concessive relation between [4:199b] and [4:199c] is grammaticalised through hypotaxis while that connecting [4:199j-k] to [4:199l] is realised through a "cohesive" conjunction. But Mann and Thompson recognize [4:199c] and [4:199l] as the nucleus in each case, with [4:199b] and [4:199j-k] as satellites.

Similarly, the internal relationships of contrast in [4:199] are treated as Nucleus-Satellite ones, although they are realised "cohesively". *Rather*

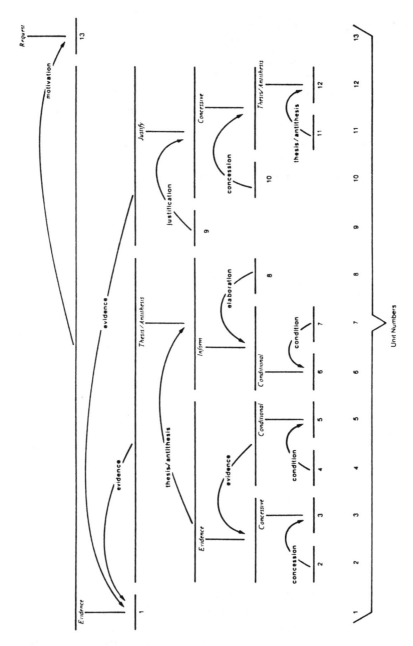

Fig. 4.29. Mann and Thompson's RST analysis of [4:199]

[4.199] — Mann and Thompson's units:

1. I don't believe that endorsing the Nuclear Freeze Initiative is the right step for California CC.

2. Tempting as it may be,

3. we shouldn't embrace every popular issue that comes along.

4. When we do so

5. we use precious, limited resources where other players with superior resources are already doing an adequate job.

6. Rather, I think we will be stronger and more effective

7. if we stick to those issues of governmental structure and process, broadly defined, that have formed the core of our agenda for years.

8. Open government, campaign finance reform, and fighting the influence of special interests and big money, these are our kinds of issues.

9. (New paragraph)   Let's be clear:

10. I personally favor the initiative and ardently support disarmament negotiations to reduce the risk of war.

11. But I don't think endorsing a specific nuclear freeze proposal is appropriate for CCC.

12. We should limit our involvement in defense and weaponry to matters of process, such as exposing the weapons industry's influence on the political process.

13. Therefore, I urge you to vote against a CCC endorsement of the nuclear freeze initiative.

makes the connection between [4:199d-f] and [4:199g-h] explicit, while the relation between [4:199l] and [4:199m] is an implicit one:

[4:199] (excerpts)

    d.   When we do so

    e.   we use precious limited resources

    f.   where other players are already doing an adequate job.

    g.   **Rather**, I think we will be stronger and more effective

    h.   if we stick to those issues of governmental structure and processes, broadly defined that have formed the core of our agenda for years.

    l.   But I don't think endorsing a specific freeze proposal is appropriate for CCC.

    m.   We should limit our involvement in defense and weaponry to matters of process, such as exposing the weapons industry's influence on the political process.

Again, though no grammatical dependency is signalled, [4:199g-h] (and [4:199i] as well) and [4:199m] are taken as nuclear to their dependent satellites, [4:199d-f] (and [4:199b-c] as well) and [4:199l].

These examples demonstrate that the Nucleus-Satellite relation in Rhetorical Structure Theory cannot be reduced to a question of TAXIS. Nor is it a question of THEME; Mann and Thompson treat the whole of [4:199] up to and including unit [4:199m] as dependent on [4:199n], at the same time as [4:199b-m] is dependent on [4:199a]. So the Nucleus may precede or follow its Satellite. And Nucleus-Satellite cannot be derived from experiential structure either (with say Causes always taken as satellites of Effects); Mann and Thompson (1986) distinguish between two rhetorical relations, Reason and Cause, which differ precisely with respect to whether the Cause or the Effect is nuclear.

Pursuing then this difference between *English Text*'s reticulum for [4:199] and Mann and Thompson's rhetorical structure for the same text, the following Nucleus-Satellite relations can be established (extrapolating slightly from Mann and Thompson's presentation in order to make the division of the text into units the same as that presented for [4:199] above). Note that none of this information is provided by the reticulum for conjunctive relations in the text.

NUCLEUS	SATELLITE
[4:199n]	[4:199a-m]
[4:199a]	[4:199b-i & j-m]
[4:199g-i]	[4:199b-f]
[4:199g-h]	[4:199i]
[4:199g]	[4:199h]
[4:199b-c]	[4:199d-f]
[4:199c]	[4:199b]
[4:199e]	[4:199d]
[4:199l-m]	[4:199j-k]
[4:199m]	[4:199l]

Using clause complex notation, these dependencies can be re-expressed as follows (with η representing nuclei, ζ satellites, and i, ii, iii... for listed nuclei; clause complex notation has to be avoided in order not to confuse the discourse dependencies at issue with grammatical ones). Halliday's elaboration, extension and enhancement superscripts are employed in place of rhetorical relations; Matthiessen and Thompson (1988) point to generalising rhetorical relations along these lines.

[4:199a]   χζ   η
[4:199b]   χζ   ι   +ζ   η   χζ
[4:199c]   η
[4:199d]   χζ   χζ
[4:199e]   η   η
[4:199f]   χζ
[4:199g]   η   η   η
[4:199h]   χζ
[4:199i]   =ζ
[4:199j]   +υ   +ζ   ι
[4:199k]   +υ
[4:199l]   η   +ζ
[4:199m]   η
[4:199n]   η

Re-expressed in tree notation, the Nucleus-Satellite structure for [4:199] is presented in Fig. 4.30.

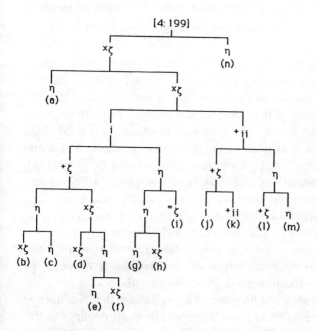

Fig. 4.30. Rhetorical relations in [4:199] expressed as a clause complex

Unfortunately, having distanced Nucleus-Satellite and Listing rhetorical structures from TAXIS, Rhetorical Structure Theory provides no independent semiotic criteria for distinguishing Nucleus from Satellite. Matthiessen and Thompson appeal to a general cognitive tendency to chunk elements and relate this to work in gestalt psychology on the way in which perceptual input is sorted into central and non-central structure. Rhetorical Structure Theory thus offers no substantial arguments against *English Text*'s suggestion that conjunctive structures are basically Head-less ones at the level of discourse semantics (i.e. covariate, not hypotactic and paratactic).

There are on the other hand good reasons for believing that Rhetorical Structure Theory as presently articulated is inadequate as a representation of conjunctive structure. These have to do with:

    i.   sandwich structures in which an initiating message is replayed to culminate a logical sequence.

   ii.   simultaneous conjunctive structures.

  iii.   the dynamics of text as process, especially in the spoken mode.

The first problem is in fact illustrated in [4:199] in which [4:199a] presents a thesis, [4:199b-m] present arguments in favour of this position and [4:199n] reiterates the thesis (for another sandwich argument see the reconsideration of [4:3 below]). Rhetorical Structure Theory analysts have to treat this top layer of structure as involving one or more nuclei. Since the thesis reiterated in [4:199n] is the same as that realised in [4:199a], a list structure with two nuclei is not appropriate. Consequently one of these must be arbitrarily selected as nucleus for the text as a whole. Mann and Thompson opt for [4:199n], which they treat as motivated by [4:199a-m]; [4:199a] is in turn supported by two pieces of evidence, [4:199b-i] and [4:199j-m]. However plausible this analysis for [4:199], the point here is that Rhetorical Structure Theory demands that text be analysed as formed around one or more Heads. With sandwich structures (e.g. *for several reasons...first...second...third...for these reasons; generalisation...that is...for example...in short* etc.) this forces an arbitrary choice between the initiating message and its recapitulation as Nucleus for the text.

Equally serious is Rhetorical Structure Theory's claim that conjunctive relations in text can be reduced to a single chain. The short-comings of this position can be demonstrated with respect to [4:3 above]. Consider first the relationship between clause complexes 2 and 3:

[4:3] 2.c.   Modern capitalism thrives on expansion and credit,
      d.   and without them it shrivels.

3.e. **Equally however** it requires the right context,
  f. which is an expanding world economy:
  g. a national ecnomy is distinct and severable from other national economies in some senses but not all.

These are simultaneously related through internal comparison and concession. The third clause complex is assigned the same status in the argument as the second through the internal comparative conjunction *equally*, at the same time as it is related to it by *however*: 'although I've just argued that modern capitalism thrives on expansion and credit and without them it shrivels, it is equally important to say that it requires the right context, which is...'. Rhetorical Structure Theory could be elaborated to recognize more than one rhetorical relation at a time between nucleus and satellite. However the problem of simultaneous rhetorical relations is compounded when the relations inter-connect the same messages in different ways. To illustrate this point, [4:3] needs to be reconsidered as a whole:

[4:3]   1.a. Governments were committed to inflation
        b. because they were themselves part of the system which required it.

        2.c. Modern capitalism thrives on expansion and credit,
        d. and without them it shrivels.

        3.e. Equally however it requires the right context,
        f. which is an expanding world economy:
        g. a national economy is distinct and severable from other national economies in some senses but not all.

        4.h. If the total economy of which it is a part does not expand,
        i. then the inflation in the particular economy ceases to be fruitful
        j. and becomes malignant.
        5.k. Furthermore, the more the particular economy flourishes,
        l. the more dependent is it upon the total economy to which it is directing a part of its product,
        m.and the more dangerous is any pause in it alimentation -
        n. the easier it is to turn from boom to bust.

        6.o. Finally, any government operating within such a system becomes overwhelmingly committed to maintaining it,
        p. more especially when symptoms of collapse appear -
        q. as they did in the last decade of our period
        r. when governments felt compelled to help out not only lame ducks but lame eagles too.

        7.s. All this was inflationary.

As noted earlier in the chapter, this text presents four arguments in support of the proposition that governments were committed to inflation. Taking Mann and Thompson's analysis of [4:199] as a model, these would presumable be taken as four dependent pieces of evidence, as in Fig. 4.31.

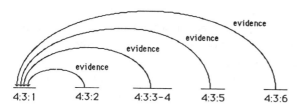

Fig. 4.31. Evidence in [4:3]

But these pieces of evidence are at the same time related to each other through internal addition (*furthermore*), comparison (*equally*) and temporal succession (*finally*). Whether this internal accumulation would be treated as listed Nuclei, or as a set of interdependent Nucleus-Satellite relations is unclear. The critical point is that because it is so closely modelled on clause complex interdependency, Rhetorical Structure Theory cannot at present handle simultaneous conjunctive structures in text (the same problem arises in [4:200] where the fourth example of the way in which Syncom diskettes work is internally related to the other three by *And*). Since internal and external conjunction very commonly assign simultaneous layers of structure to a text (as in [4:3] and [4:200]), much as experiential and interpersonal metafunctions in the grammar do for the clause, this short-coming is a very serious one indeed.

The final set of problems to be considered follows from the very strong preference in Rhetorical Structure Theory for Nuclear-Satellite relations over Listing ones (involving the claim that a text is much more like a hypotactic clause complex than a paratactic one) and the general neutrality of Nucleus and Satellite with respect to Theme. Rhetorical Structure Theory's preference for "hypotactic" dependency and α β(α β(α β(α β... chains leads to multilayered rhetorical structures of considerable "depth". And the fact that satellites can precede the nucleus means that rhetorical structures may be in large part regressive ("branching" downwards to the left).

As noted, Mann and Thompson analyse [4:199] totally in terms of Nucleus-Satellite relations; and 5 of the nuclei in [4:199] follow their satellites, including 3 out of the 4 top level nuclei. The result is a text structure in which the text's second and penultimate messages are among the 8 "deepest" in the text, and the first and last messages are the two "shallowest". In addition the text's least dependent nucleus [4:199n] comes last, and its third and fourth least dependent nuclei are [4:199g] and [4:199m], both of which occur well into the text.

The text is repeated below to highlight the significance of regressive dependency and depth in RST analysis. Note for example that the second message, *Tempting as it may be*, is a satellite to [4:199c], which is in turn part of a satellite to [4:199g-i], which is in turn part of a satellite to [4:199n]. Before this clause could be generated in other words the text would have to be processed backwards from its end message to one of its deepest points.

[4:199] a. I don't believe that endorsing the Nuclear Freeze initiative is the right step for California CC.
   b. Tempting as it may be,
   c. we shouldn't embrace every popular issue that comes along.
   d. When we do so
   e. we use precious limited resources
   f. where other players with superior resources are already doing an adequate job.
   g. Rather, I think we will be stronger and more effective
   h. if we stick to those issues of governmental structure and process, broadly defined, that have formed the core of our agenda for years.
   i. Open government, campaign finance reform, and fighting the special interests and big money — these are our kinds of issues.
   j. Let's be clear: I personally favour the initiative
   k. and ardently support disarmament negotiations to reduce the risk of war.
   l. But I don't think endorsing a specific freeze proposal is appropriate for CCC.
   m. We should limit our involvement in defense and weaponry to matters of process, such as exposing the weapons industry's influence on the political process.
   n. Therefore, I urge you to vote against a CCC endorsement of the nuclear freeze initiative.

among "DEEPEST" CLAUSES	b, m	
"SHALLOWEST" CLAUSES	a, n	
KEY NUCLEI (scaled)	n,	NOT DEPENDENT
	a,	ONCE DEPENDENT
	g & m	TWICE DEPENDENT
	c	THRICE DEPENDENT
	etc.	

It would perhaps be unfair to suggest that RST analysis treats [4:199] as a text which unfolds backwards from its end instead of working forwards from its beginning. The picture is in fact more complex than this, involving both progressive and regressive dependencies. However, it is clear that Rhetorical Structure Theory is not at all concerned with the way in which text unfolds as a process, with what has been realised taken as point of departure for what comes next. Somewhat ironically, given the similarity between RST interpretation and clause complex analysis, rhetorical structures are very synpotic in orientation. They account for text as a finished, pre-conceived, edited product. The model has been developed mainly in the context of providing an account of written texts (see Matthiessen and Thompson 1988), so this development is hardly surprising.

Consequently it is important to conclude this critique of Rhetorical Structure Theory by looking briefly at the dynamic nature of conjunctive relations as these unfold in spontaneous spoken monologue. A number of passages from [4:2] will be reviewed; some of these were commented on in 4.1 above because they cause problems for the clause complex analysis, in spite of the fact that Halliday's system was specifically designed to handle the dynamics of clause combining.

The first two examples illustate a shift between multivariate and uni-variate structure. Message [4:2e] starts off as a hypotactically dependent non-finite clause (*the reason being*) and changes into a finite relational identifying one (*the reason is the judge is standing in the centre of the ring*). Clause complex 5 works in the oppositive direction; message [4:2i] initiates a relational identifying clause (*the first thing it does is*) but the text then shifts gears into a paratactic sequence beginning with *the judge is standing in the centre of the ring*.

[4:2]   2.c. Well, you always walk
              d. with the dog on the left-hand side,
              e. the reason being is [[the judge is standing in the centre of the ring]].

         5.h. So, usually when a class is going into the ring,
              i. the first thing it does is:
              j. the judge is standing in the centre of the ring,
              k. the people sort of walk the ring, with their dogs,
              l. and then...we sort of wait.

The next excerpt illustrates three points. Early on it includes a paren-thetical explanatory remark (*That's because it's a low dog*) which interrupts what would otherwise have been a straight-forward paratactic sequence:

With the Dachshund, a Dachshund is tabled and the judge goes over that.
Interpolations of this kind are strong markers of the on-going nature of text
production.

[4:2] 6.m. With the Dachshund, a Dachshund is tabled.
   7.n. That's [[because it's a low dog]],
    .o. and the judge goes over that.
   8.p. With the bigger breeds, of dog, they're stood on the ground,
      q. because it's easier [[for the judge to handle them]].
   9.r. With the smaller breeds of dog such as Corgis, all the Toy-breeds,
      Dachshunds and this type of thing we — as our turn comes,
      s. we stand our dog on the table,
      t. we stand it in show stance,
      u. with the lead, the lead held up,
      v. hoping
      w. that our dog will stand like a nice statue,
      x. so as the judge can come.
  10.y. The judge handles it,
      z. and this is where I'm telling you, temperament plays a big part.

This passage also provides a spoken example of the "sandwich" structures
discussed in [4:3] and 4:199] above. First a contrast is made between tabling
Dachshunds — [4:2m-o] and [4:2p-q]; then the same point is made by contrasting [4:2p-q] with [4:2r-x]. From a synoptic perspective it seems redundant to repeat the point, but dynamically there is nothing unusual about
presuming messages being themselves presumed.

Finally [4:2] as well contains an illustration of what happens when a
speaker runs out of steam. There is no real reason why [4:2y] could not
have been tactically related to [4:2x], thereby extending clause complex 9:
e.g. *...so as the judge can come and handle it and...* . But the speaker stops,
and initiates a new clause complex; it is probably not an accident that the
preceding clause complex was one of the two longest in the text.

Summarising these observations as discourse maxims one might come
up with the following:

i.   **Sort out what you've said** (worry about what's next as it comes).
ii. **Keep surfacing** (don't get too embedded or too deeply dependent).

Whatever the moral drawn or how framed, there is abundant evidence that
texts are produced progressively by speakers who constantly monitor what
they say as they say it and for the most part make retrospective connections
between new messages and what has already been said. The deep regressive
structures proposed by Rhetorical Structure Theory are thus inappropriate

as a model of the dynamics of text production and need to be complemented by a more process oriented account. The flatter, covariate structures proposed by *English Text* on the other hand seem more promising as a first step in the development of dynamic representations.

This means that at present choosing between reticula and rhetorical structures as models of conjunctive relations will be largely influenced by mode — RST diagrams should in principle work better for writing than speaking (assuming that the problems of sandwich and simultaneous conjunctive structures can be solved). The issue of conjunctive nuclei will be taken up again in 4.9 below. The next section will look briefly at the problems caused by grammatical metaphor for the analysis of conjunctive relations in both models.

4.8 Grammatical metaphor and conjunctive structure

The realisation of conjunctive relations within clauses causes problems for the definition of messages provided in 4.6 above where ranking, non-projected clauses were proposed as constituting the event-line in reticula. The following messages from [4:199] can be used to illustrate the problem (nominalisations in bold-face).

> [4:199] j.   Let's be clear: I personally favour the **initiative**
> k.   and ardently support **disarmament negotiations** to reduce the **risk** of **war**.

This can be translated into a more "spoken" text by removing the nominalisations; the result is a longer clause complex with fewer lexical items per clause:

> [4:203] (= SPOKEN PARAPHRASE of [4:199j-k])
> a.   1   Let's be clear:
> b. $^=$2 1 α   I'm happy
> c. ^{x}β   when people get going about about nuclear arms
> d. $^+$2 ^{x}β α   and if people want to negotiate
> e. ^{x}β   so that they can disarm
> f. ^{x}γ   so that we won't end up fighting each other
> g.   α   then I strongly support them.

It may be argued that the conjunctive relations in [4:199j-k] are too deeply buried to worry about. But this objection will not hold for [4:204] where they are explicitly realised through circumstantial relations (*through* and *resulting from*) in clause structure. The text is reporting on what its author describes as a "sustained orgy of animalism over three nights" by "as many as 50 of the 300" of Queensland's rugby playing police attending a football carnival in Toowoomba in March 1989 (the lamented figurehead had already been suspended from duty pending the outcome of corruption charges).

[4:204] a.   Government and police sources agreed that the force's problem is lack of morale **through** a lack of discipline **resulting from** the absence of a strong figurehead. (Robbins 1989:24)

The projection in this text is just a clause long in its written form, but can be unpacked into a three message clause complex as follows:

[4:205] (= SPOKEN PARAPHRASE of the projection in [4:204])
   a.   the police force has problems
   b.   because they aren't being disciplined
   c.   because the force doesn't have a strong commissioner.

As can be seen from these examples, unpacking the grammatical metaphors characteristic of written text will have dramatic consequences for any text's conjunctive structure. But not unpacking them means that a good deal of the logical structure of many texts will be missed. The safest course would appear to be to first analyse a text as it has been grammaticalised into messages (i.e. ranking non-projected clauses); this is certainly critical to an understanding of genre — a significant part of the motivation for incongruent realisations of CONJUNCTION in the first place is after all to allow internal conjunction to scaffold a text's schematic structure (as in [4:3] above). Subsequently, the text could be unpacked and further analyses undertaken which might enhance an understanding of the text's ideology, field, tenor or mode (se Chapter 7 below). Certainly unpacking of this kind was a key tool in the development of critical linguistics at East Anglia (see Fowler et al. 1979; Kress & Hodge 1979).

As suggested above, Rhetorical Structure Theory does not appear to have addressed this issue. In practice, relational propositions which are realised within clauses through TRANSITIVITY relations are simply ignored.

4.9 CONJUNCTION, IDENTIFICATION **and** NEGOTIATION

In this chapter, an account of a third major discourse system, CONJUNCTION, has been presented; in addition the relatively minor system of CONTINUITY was briefly reviewed. CONJUNCTION represents the discourse semantics of clause complex relations, much as IDENTIFICATION underlies nominal group DEIXIS and NEGOTIATION underlies MOOD. The association of these discourse systems with metafunctions and their unmarked realisation in lexicogrammar is summarised in Table 4.16.

Table 4.16. Discourse systems, metafunction and grammaticalisation

(DISCOURSE SYSTEM)	METAFUNCTION	GRAMMATICALISATION
CONJUNCTION	logical	clause complex: LOGICO-SEMANTICS & INTERDEPENDENCY
IDENTIFICATION	textual	nominal group: DEIXIS
NEGOTIATION	interpersonal	clause: MOOD

Like reference chains, conjunctive structures were interpreted as covariate ones. Just as participants are commonly presuming and presumed, so messages depend conjunctively on preceding ones and are themselves depended on. Similarly, like participants, messages were shown to typically depend on preceding messages rather than following ones — "cataphoric" dependency being highly marked. These parallels are brought out in the structural representation of these relations as follows (note that the dependency arrow points to the information presumed, which is thus treated as a kind of "phoric" Head):

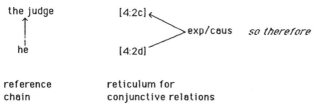

Fig. 4.32. IDENTIFICATION and CONJUNCTION structures compared

A further parallel has to do with the distinction between reference to participants as opposed to text reference and external as opposed to internal conjunction:

TEXT REFERENCE: INTERNAL CONJUNCTION: :

PARTICIPANT REFERENCE: EXTERNAL CONJUNCTION

Both text reference and internal conjunction construct text as part of rather than as an interpretation of the world. A whole set of what could be taken as internal conjunctions (which were not explicitly considered in 4.4 above) are in fact a combination of these two text organising resources: *for this reason, with this in mind, in this way, arising out of this, to this end, in that case, that being so, in this respect, with reference to this, aside from this, at this point, returning to that point* etc.

Turning to differences between IDENTIFICATION and CONJUNCTION, whereas IDENTIFICATION involves both reminding and relevance phoricity, CONJUNCTION always involves relevance phoricity: through CONJUNCTION messages presume relevant, not the same information, where relevance is specified in terms of additive, comparative, temporal and consequential relations. In these respects IDENTIFICATION and CONJUNCTION contrast with NEGOTIATION where responding moves typically involve redundancy phoricity, realised though clause substitution and ellipsis. The association of different types of phoricity with these discourse systems is summarised in Table 4.17.

Although very different from NEGOTIATION in a number of respect (covariate vs multivariate structure; relevance vs redundancy phoricity and so on), CONJUNCTION is similar in that it relates discourse units whose

Table 4.17. Discourse systems, phoricity and realisation

(DISCOURSE SYSTEM)	PHORICITY	REALISATION
IDENTIFICATION	reminding	definite article & demonstratives; pronoun; proper name
	relevance	comparative; superlative
CONJUNCTION	relevance	explicit conjunction
NEGOTIATION	redundancy	Residue ellipsis — *Did he?* clause ellipsis — *Possibly.* substitution — *Maybe not/so.*

unmarked realisation is a ranking clause. Moves and messages are typically realised through the same grammatical unit, which means that clauses may be related to each other simultaneously through both systems. The most typical environment for this is the challenge:

[4:206] a.   K1 ⌐   It's a Nucleus.
       b.   ch ⌡   -**But** can you be sure?

This is the source of what might be viewed as the over-determination of conjunctive relations in the work of the Birmingham school who have attempted to elaborate exchange structure to handle CONJUNCTION in terms of logical relations between moves (see Chapter 2.4.1 above).

Note that a certain amount of over-determination is inevitable since conversational structure can be used as an incongruent expression of conjunctive relations (just as there is no escaping the overlap between CONJUNCTION and IDENTIFICATION in realisations such as *after this, in the same way, on the other hand, in that respect* and so on). *Let's be clear* was taken as an incongruent realisation of internal reformulation in [4:199] above. And the internal conditional relation opening text [4:200] was in fact realised through an adjacency pair:

[4:200] a.   ⌐K2   What if you're having to clean floppy heads too often?
       b.   ⌊K1   Ask for SYNCOM diskettes, with burnished Ectype
                      coating and dust-absorbing jacket liners.

Perhaps the main point to stress at this stage is that the modular approach to discourse structure being developed here means that no one component is responsible for accounting comprehensively for textual relations. Models which adopt a more singular perspective on text structure on the other hand require a more elaborate apparatus. It is because of this for example that the work of the Birmingham school includes ranks and classes of exchange, move and act which were not covered in Chapter 2. If CONJUNCTION is to be subsumed under NEGOTIATION, then NEGOTIATION will obviously have more work to do. Similarly, Rhetorical Structure Theory attributes much more structure to a text than does the conjunction analysis proposed here (i.e. the Nuclear-Satellite dependencies reviewed above). This will probably turn out to be because it is subsuming a number of aspects of discourse structure under conjunctive relations which would be dealt with differently here. Certainly the fact that generic structure (see Chapter 7 below) is seen to complement conjunctive structure makes a difference as far as top-level structure is concerned. And the discussion of the way in which the discourse systems proposed here interact with each other and with lexicogrammar in Chapter 6 below bears critically on readers' intuitions about nuclearity, especially as far as Theme and method of development are concerned. The ramifications of adopting a comprehensive modular approach are wide-spread, especially where taken in the context of a meaning making functional grammar. This have to be kept constantly in mind.

In closing it might be noted that CONJUNCTION is in many respects the most upward-looking system in the discourse semantics. Internally, its relations range over much larger portions of a text than is characteristic of NEGOTIATION or IDENTIFICATION (with the exception of extended and text reference). And its logico-semantic relations are very senssitive to the staging structure of a genre, not surprisingly since both types of structure have a strong ideational orientation. From the perspective of text in context then, CONJUNCTION can be interpreted as the gate-way to the discourse semantics much as the clause is the gate-way mediating relations between discourse semantics and lexicogrammar. It is thus a useful place to start whenever the structure of whole texts is under consideration and an interpretation of their relationship to ideology, genre and register is what is required.

NOTES

1. Note that *we wanted to win, we were keen to get there on time* and *we were willing to give them a chance* are treated as Effects in this analysis, in order to bring out their agnation to **effected** results in non-purposive relations: e.g. *we trained hard so that we'd win: we trained hard with the result that we won.*

2. Compare the "present" conterfactual *If we **were** well prepared we would win.*

3. Compare the realisation with *only to: We arrived early **(only) to** find them gone.*

4. Manner has the distinctive internal realisation *in this way*, which has not been incorporated into the discussion here.

5. Or alternatively, using a mental process, *I saw Ben so I **believe** he's here.*

6. Behavioural/mental/relational proportionalities are also important; note *since you're **asking** me to go out for dinner: since you're **thinking** about going out for dinner: since you've **got** going out to dinner on your mind.*

7. Exemplification and restatement are such common and rhetorically significant internal relations that internal comparison: similarity relations will be treated with greater delicacy, notated *e.g.* (exemplification) and *i.e.* (restatement).

8. An exception to this principle is internal reformulation (especially i.e. and e.g. relations) which is typically implicit but needs ot be recognised when deconstructing the rhetorical structure of abstract text.

9. For reasons of space the notation for additive relations has been abbreviated in this and following examples (including the omission of dependency arrows).

10. The incongruent internal addition (*for one thing, for another, on top of all that*) has not been represented in the reticulum.

11. Because [4:199:a] and [4:199:n] both involve projections (*I don't believe...; I urge...*) the causal relations which sandwich the rest of the text could be interpreted as external; Fig. 4.21 however treats both projections as interpersonal metaphors (high modalization and high modulation respectively), taking the reasoning as internal.

5. Ideation

The company words keep

5.1 Lexical departure

To this point, the point of departure for exploring discourse systems has been a grammatical one: general MOOD classes (realising NEGOTIATION), closed system nominals (tracking participants) and clause complex structures (used extensively to code conjunctive relations in spontaneous spoken monologue). In this chapter on the other hand the point of departure is lexis. It is the contribution made by open system items to discourse structure that is under consideration. This is an ambitious undertaking, in at least two respects. First, lexis has received less attention in functional linguistics than has grammar, and so there is less to build on (however see Matthiessen forthcoming a for a comprehensive survey of lexical description from a systemic perspective). And second, the scope of the experiential meaning coded through lexis in any language is vast, which fact alone makes it harder to bring under analytical control. Nevertheless, lexical relations have an important role to play in discourse structure. And any comprehensive account of discourse semantics has at least to open up discussion in this area.

Something of the role played by lexical relations is illustrated in [5:1] below. A mother is talking with her 10 year old son about his experiences at school earlier in the day. Towards the end the mother realises that she may have misinterpreted the field, and interrupts to clarify the situation. It is the lexical cohesion that has been misread, not the NEGOTIATION, IDENTIFICATION or CONJUNCTION.

[5:1] A a You know what?
          b In s...kickball we have two captains, right?
          c And um...Ca...Kevin is the best kid in the whole class.
          d He can beat up everybody in the whole class, Kevin,
          e and he...he can kick real real real far,

	f	so whoever gets picked first is Kevin.
	g	But Kevin was captain,
	h	and he picked uh...some junk guy like George,
	i	and then...um...Randall picks Carl.
	j	He's second best really -
	k	he can beat...he's...he can beat up everybody second, everybody else -
	l	he can beat up everybody in class except Kevin.
	m	And then they pick...(sigh)...um..Kevin picks W...um...Hey,
	n	and then...um...they pick someone else like -
	o	and then...um...they pick Sandra, a girl,
	p	and then they say "Well, well, Paul."
	q	and then...they all clap real loud.
	r	I was the only one that cla...I got a clap for.
	s	Yo...you...they wanted me to be second...on our team,
	t	but James was second.
	u	Everybody um...wanted me to be second
	v	but...Randall didn't agree.
	w	He wanted James
	x	and I was after James.
	y	I got a home run today.
B	z	Is this for soccer or baseball?
	aa	I was picturing this for soccer.
	bb	It was for baseball, huh?
A	cc	I got a home run.
B	dd	Wa...the teams that you were just telling me about were being picked, was that for baseball?
A	ee	Kickball.
B	ff	Oh, kickball.
A	gg	And I s...I hop off the base[1]
		...

An interpretation of the nature of this misunderstanding will be offered in 5.4.3.3 below. Meanwhile it suffices to comment that it is relations between lexical items, not lexical items per se that have been misunderstood. And the misreading of these relations is in fact a misreading of the text's field. Expectations have been set up which have not been fulfilled, and so the recount has to be interrupted to sort things out. This means that although considerations of register have been set aside as far as possible in Chapters 2, 3 and 4, with lexical cohesion the register variable field needs to be brought more clearly into the picture. Consequently this chapter will bridge in a number of places to the discussion of context in Chapter 7 below.

5.2 Describing lexis

5.2.1 *Dictionary and thesaurus*

The two traditional approaches to the study of lexis in western scholarship are well known: the dictionary and the thesaurus. The main difference between these two resources has to do with their method of organisation. The dictionary is organised around a semantically arbitrary listing of lexical items; it purports to unpack their "meaning" by means of paraphrase and exemplars. The thesaurus on the other hand is organised around meaning; it purports to display the wordings through which meanings can be aptly expressed.

The folk-conception of a dictionary entry as a "form" and the definition as its "meaning" is of course a misleading one. In fact the relationship between words and definitions is not stratal (i.e. words are not being associated with the semantic primes they realise). All that is going on is that one wording is being reformulated as another. This process reaches a kind of closure as reformulations exhaust the words associated with a particular lexical field. Pursuing the reformulations of an item such as *yacht* in the *Oxford English Dictionary* illustrates the circularity inherent in closure of this kind.

WORD	DEFINITION (reformulation)
yacht	a light, fast sailing ship
ship	a large sea-going vessel
vessel	a craft or ship of any kind
craft	vessels or boats
boat	a small open vessel

The relationship between words and ideas in a thesaurus is not a stratal one either. Rather, words are classified notionally, by means of a system which Roget describes as one which would "conduct the inquirer most readily and quickly to the object of his search" (Dutch 1966:xxvi). At primary delicacy, Roget's system divides ideas into Abstract Relations, Space, Material World, Intellect, Volition and Sentient and Moral Powers; Space is then broken into Space in General, Dimensions, Form and Motion; and Motion is subclassified as General, Degrees of Motion, Conjoined with Force and With Reference to Direction. Fig. 5.1 outlines this part of Roget's system.

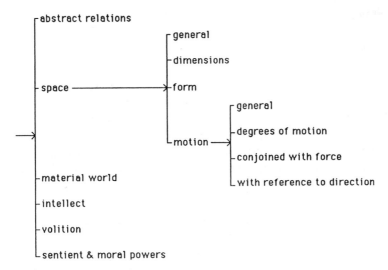

Fig. 5.1. A systemic formulation of initial delicacy in Roget

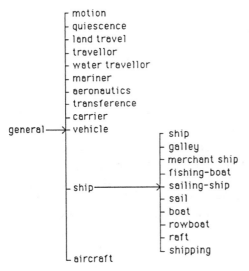

Fig. 5.2. Subclassification of General motion in Roget

Roget's system develops the idea of general motion up to the category sailing-ship (as outlined in Fig. 5.2) and then lists some fifty lexical items under this heading; one of these is the lexical item *yacht*. This strategy reinforces the notion/wording duality invoked by Roget in introducing his work; but all that is really going on is that his classification is being arrested at a certain point in delicacy. There is no reason why his system could not be extended until lexical items are given a unique classification.

Yacht appears among the following items under the "idea" sailing-ship (note that Roget's punctuation imposes one further level of classification on this list): *sailboat, sailing vessel, sailer; wind-jammer, clipper, ship, tall s., full-rigged s., square-rigged s., fore-and-aft-rigged s., schooner-rigged s., lateen-rigged s.; four-masted ship, three-masted s., three-master, bark, barque, barquentine; two-masted ship, brig, hermaphrodite-b., cutter-b., brigantine, schooner, pinnace, snow, grab; frigate, sloop, corvette, warship; cutter, ketch, yawl, dandy, lugger; xebec, felucca, tartane, saic, caique, dhow, gallivat, junk, lorcha, sampan; sailing barge, smack, gabbard, hoy, hooker, nobby, bawley; yacht, skiff.*

Because it is organised according to meaning, a thesaurus provides a more appropriate model of lexical description for functional linguistics than a dictionary does (see Matthiessen forthcoming a for discussion of this point in the context of computational linguistics). This point will be taken up again in 5.2.3 below.

5.2.2 *Collocation*

Amongst other dualities, Firth (1957b/1968) naturally rejected the word/meaning dichotomy invoked by dictionary and thesaurus makers and many linguists to explain their work. For Firth, the purpose of a linguistic description was to make statements of meaning. And he approached lexical meaning from two perspectives: context and collocation. He defined contextual meaning as "the functional relationship of the sentence to the processes of a context of situation in the context of culture" (1957b/1968:195). This was his alternative to the referentially based theories of word meaning passed over above. In addition Firth insisted that it was important to consider syntagmatic aspects of a lexical item's meaning potential. He described collocational meaning as follows: "One of the meanings of *night* is its collocability with *dark*, and of *dark*, of course, collocation with *night*" (1957b/1968:196). This interest in mutual expectancy betwen lexical items was one aspect of Firth's interest in the notion of predictability in discourse:

> The moment a conversation is started, whatever is said is a determining condition for what, in any reasonable expectation, may follow. What you say raises the threshold against most of the language of your companion, and leaves only a limited opening for a certain likely range of responses. This sort of thing is an aspect of what I have called contextual elimination. (1935/1957a:31-32)

Firth's interest in collocation was taken up by a number of his students and developed within the framework of scale and category linguistics (Halliday 1961, 1966b; McIntosh 1961/1966; Sinclair 1966). Halliday (1961) set up lexis as a distinct level within lexicogrammar, concerned with open as opposed to closed system items, making the point that word and lexical item were not necessarily co-extensive units (*round the twist* for example patterns lexically as a single item agnate to *crazy, mad, insane, bonkers* etc., but is composed of three words). More importantly, lexical items enter into patterns which not predicted by grammar and are to some extent independent of both grammatical structure and a lexical item's formal scatter. Thus (*pace* Carter 1987:53) *fat* and *obese* make different predictions about attendant lexical items. One finds *fat man, fat woman, fat belly, fat baby, fat chicken, fat salary, fat wad of notes, fat book* and *obese man, obese woman, obese belly*; but *obese baby, obese chicken, obese salary, obese wad of notes, obese book* are unlikely. Moreover, the same expectancy relations hold for different grammatical structures: *the man was obese* but not *the book was obese*; they are not strongly affected by an item's morphological scatter: *the fat/fatter/fattest man* but not *obesity in books/being an obese book*; and they obtain as well between items that are not grammatically related: *Consider men for example. Obesity is a real problem.* but not *Consider books for example. Obesity frustrates editors.*

Sinclair et al. (1970) report on a research project at Edinburgh and Birmingham during the period 1963-1969 which made an initial inquiry into collocational relations in English. A large corpus was examined by focusing on selected items (*nodes*) and optimizing a *span* of four items on either side of the node to determine the extent to which nodes predicted certain items and not others. The aim was to produce a *cluster* of items predicted by the node within this span, and eventually by comparing clusters to establish *lexical sets* composed of items which collocate in similar ways. The results at this stage were disappointing — only a small percentage of open system items in the corpus appeared with any frequency, and even for those that did, few items recurred often enough in their span for interesting statistically significant lexical sets to be established. Fortunately computer technology advanced rapidly to the point where this research was taken up again, both at Birmingham (Reed 1977, 1984, Sinclair 1987, 1988) and Toronto (Benson et al. 1986, Benson and Greaves 1992, forthcoming) and the kind of collocational thesaurus envisioned by Halliday (1966b:160) no longer seems out of reach.

Sinclair (1987) in fact suggests on the basis of progress in this research that collocation (the idiom principle) is a far better model of text production than grammatical derivation (the open choice principle), amplifying Firth's comments on contextual elimination: "All the evidence points to an underlying rigidity of phraseology, despite a rich superficial variation" (1987:331). He suggests as well that collocation patterns may map more closely onto contextual ones than caution might first have led linguists to expect: "there is a great deal of overlap with semantics, and very little reason to posit an independent semantics for the purpose of text description" (1987:331). One of the main purposes of this chapter is to propose a model of the discourse semantics of lexical relations which could be used to test this challenge.

5.2.3 *Lexis as delicate grammar*

Alongside laying the groundwork within systemic theory for exploring lexical meaning from a syntagmatic perspective, Halliday (1961) also outlined what he referred to as the grammarian's dream. Instead of the traditional domain of syntax being invaded by lexical hordes as a result of collocation studies (as forecast by Sinclair 1988:87), grammar would be extended in delicacy to the point of dissolving lexis. Reformulating this perspective in (1966b), Halliday writes:

> ...the grammar attempts, both progressively and simultaneously, to reduce the very large class of formal items, at the rank at which they can be most usefully abstracted (for the most part generally as words, but this is merely a definition truth from which we learn what 'word' means), into very small sub-classes. No grammar has, it is believed, achieved the degree of delicacy required for the reduction of all such items to one member classes, although provided the model can effectively handle cross-classification it is by no means absurd to set this as the eventual aim: that is, a unique description for each item by its assignment to a 'micro-class', which represents its value as the product of the intersection of a large number of classificatory dimensions. (Halliday 1966b:149)

Halliday's suggestion here is that looked at from the perspective of grammar lexis is not different in kind, but simply different in generality: the grammar of a language makes more general meanings, while lexis makes more specific ones. The contrast here is with the bricks and mortar view inherited from traditional grammar by formal linguistics, where one either starts with structures and adds on words (transformational approaches), or starts with words and adds on structures (lexicalist approaches).

Berry (1977b:62) and Fawcett (1980:153 & 218) illustrate the way in which extending the grammar to the point in delicacy where features are realised by lexical items rather than structures might proceed. As Butler (1985a:134) points out however, Fawcett makes no attempt to justify his delicate systems. The most important study in this area therefore is Hasan (1987) which focusses on just nine material processes: *gather*, *collect*, *accumulate*; *scatter*, *divide*, *distribute*; *strew*, *spill*, *share*. Her analysis is unfortunately too complex to outline here; but the kinds of arguments she draws on to extend the grammar are significant. Where Halliday (1985a) justifies his process types largely on the basis of configurations of Agent, Process and Medium, Hasan additionally draws the Beneficiary role into the picture. She argues for example that whereas *gathered* may or may not involve a Beneficiary as in [5:2] and [5:3], *divide* always implies one ([5:4]) and *strew* never can ([5:5]):

BENEFICILE:POTENTIAL:-BENEFACTIVE
[5:2]   Ben gathered some flowers.

BENEFICILE:POTENTIAL:+BENEFACTIVE
[5:3]   Ben gathered **them** some flowers.

BENEFICILE:INHERENT
[5:4]   Ben divided **us** an apple.

NON-BENEFICILE
[5:5]   *Ben strewed **them** some breadcrumbs.

Hasan also argues on the basis of circumstantial roles — for example Halliday's (1985a) Circumstance of cause:behalf (which she refers to as Ultimate Client). Along these lines Circumstance of location might have been drawn on to independently motivate the distinction between *gather* (Hasan's acquisition) and *divide* and *strew* (Hasan's deprivation) since sources are only compatible with processes of acquisition; unlike *from the garden* in [5:6], the prepositional phrases in [5:7] and [5:8] can only be interpreted as Qualifiers in their respective nominal groups — they are not Circumstances functioning at clause rank. It is only in [5:6] that the Medium (i.e. *some flowers*) is in motion away from a location in space.

MATERIAL:ACTION:DISPOSAL:ACQUISITION
[5:6]   Ben gathered them some flowers **from the garden**.

MATERIAL:ACTION:DISPOSAL:DEPRIVATION
[5:7]   Ben divided us an apple from the garden.

MATERIAL:ACTION:DISPOSAL:DEPRIVATION
[5:8]   Ben strewed some clothes from the shop.

Working from the grammar end, this perspective on lexis as delicate grammar will be illustrated here by following through some of Halliday's (1985a) related work on process types. At initial delicacy these can be divided into processes of action, signification and being, with each of these broken down into two main subclasses. These distinctions and the inherent participant roles associated with these options are outlined in Fig. 5.3; a further system has been added for relational processes, which have been subclassified according to VOICE[2] (attributive for middle relationals, identifying for effective ones).

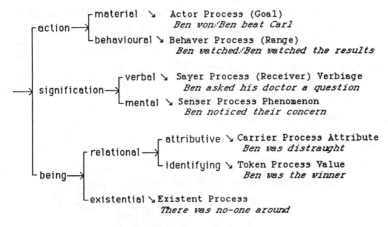

Fig. 5.3. Process types in English

Halliday (1985a) cross-classifies the [attributive/identifying] opposition with the [intensive/possessive/circumstantial system]. Possessive and circumstantial relationals will be set aside in the discussion here.

Relational identifying processes can be extended in delicacy along the following lines. Unfortunately space does not permit elaboration of the argumentation involved (Hasan after all spends 25 pages on just nine items); the sketch is intended for the purpose of illustration only. Identifying clauses can first be divided into those with an additional agent and those without. This additional agent may have the function of assigning Token to Value[3] (*make, call, name, christen, dub, elect, vote — They voted her chairperson*) or of proving a fact (the *confirm, prove, show, indicate, imply, demonstrate, confirm, substantiate, predict, illustrate, explain, attest* set discussed in 4.4.5 above). Where an additional agent is not present, the verb *be* is the most common verb used. But a large number of other processes are available and can be used to make more delicate distinctions explicit as far as the relationship between Token and Value is concerned. The most basic distinction is between exemplifying and exhausting processes. Exemplifying processes typically have an indefinite Value and resemble attributive processes, but they are reversible: *Cricket's a good sport to watch/a good sport to watch is cricket*.

Exhausting processes typically have definite Values. Three major classes are proposed below. In order to pursue a delicate lexical analysis of this kind it must be assumed either that the listing of relevant lexical items is exhaustive or that missing lexical items are synonymous with those considered. The latter, overly optimistic assumption, will be tendered here.

EQUALITY
> *equal, add up to, make, come out as/at, amount to;*
> *translate, render, paraphrase, reformulate, transliterate*

SIGNIFICATION
> *signify, realise, code, encode, express, expound;*
> *spell, write, transcribe, read;*
> *mean, denote, connote, define;*
> *call, name;*
>
> *symbolise, represent, stand for, refer to, imply, index, express, reflect, personify;*
>
> *indicate, suggest, betoken, connote, smack of, evoke, evince, betray, reveal*

ROLE
> *play, act, act as, function as, portray;*
> *typify, personify*

Exhausting processes can be divided into three major classes. With [equality] either some quantity or wording is identified as the same:

AMOUNT
[5:9]   That equals the highest score ever made on this ground:
        That is **the same as** the highest score ever made on this ground

WORDING
[5:10] *Pangulo* translates *president*:
        Pangulo means **the same as** *president*

With [role] an actor is assigned to a part:

ROLE
[5:11] Mel Gibson plays Mad Max:
        Mel Gibson plays **the role** of Mad Max

    The largest class has to do with processes of signification. These can be
grouped into three sets. One deals with realisation relationships within
semiotic systems; a second handles relationships between non-semiotic
manifestations and their meanings; and the third has to do with meanings

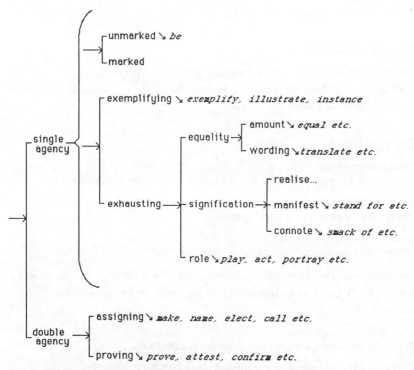

Fig. 5.4. Intensive identifying processes in English

that are suggested rather than denoted:

REALISE
[5:12]   C-A-T **spells** *cat.*

MANIFEST
[5:13]   The red **stands for** the blood that's been shed.

CONNOTE
[5:14]   His behaviour **smacked** of jealousy.

The network for intensive identifying processes developed to this point is presented in Fig. 5.4.

The discussion will now be limited to the semiotic options subclassifying the feature [realise]. These can be divided into a general set which do not specify which strata or ranks are being related and a set which is specific to either the semantics/grammar interface or the grammar/phonology (including grammar/graphology) one:

GENERAL
[5:15]   *Signify* **realises** the feature [general].

STRATUM SPECIFIC
[5:16]   /šip/ **transcribes** *ship*

Both interfaces make a distinction between encoding and decoding, depending on whether the Token is treated as closer or further away from expression substance than the Value.

GRAMMAR/PHONOLOGY:ENCODING
[5:17]   N-G **spells** *ng.*

GRAMMAR/PHONOLOGY:DECODING
[5:18]   But it actually **reads** *the dog must be able to see the dog at all times.*

SEMANTICS/GRAMMAR...ENCODING
[5:19]   *Spell* **means** 'to represent graphically as.'

SEMANTICS/GRAMMAR...DECODING
[5:20]   'To represent graphically as' **defines** *spell.*

In addition the semantics/grammar interface allows for a naming option, typically used to assign names to participants or to establish technical terms.

SEMANTICS/GRAMMAR:NAMING
[5:21]   A hill with steep sides and a flat top **is called** a butte.

The options just reviewed are outlined systemically in Fig. 5.5.

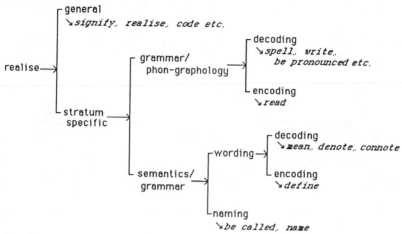

Fig. 5.5. Semiotic identifying processes in English

This brings us to the point where two lexical items have been uniquely classified (*define* and *read*) and a step or two in delicacy would isolate several others (e.g. *call, name, mean, denote, connote, spell, write, transcribe*). This serves to illustrate the fundamental continuity between grammar and lexis within a systemic functional model envisioned by Halliday. It does not illustrate the kind of argumentation that might be used to justify lexical systems, for which see Hasan (1987).

Halliday (1966b:149) suggested that for the grammarian's dream to be realised it would be necessary to allow for cross-classification in the description. A strictly taxonomic approach, such as that just pursued for identifying processes, would not be sufficient. One aspect of this has in fact been illustrated above. The [encoding/decoding] system had to be repeated for both semiotic interfaces. This portion of the network could have been re-expressed as Fig. 5.6, departing from strictly taxonomic subclassification:

The componential approach is certainly more economical than the taxonomic one, although harder to read and thus inappropriate for some display purposes (for discussion see Fawcett 1988b). But formulated systemically, the strictly taxonomic and componential networks are notational variants (see Martin 1987). A more substantive issue has to do with whether lexical realisation is allowed for non-terminal features. The verb *be* for

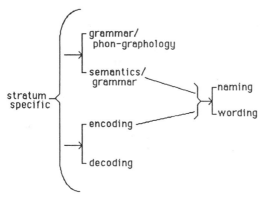

Fig. 5.6. Componential approach to stratum specific processes

example can be used to realise all single agency identifying processes. This was networked above by setting up a [marked/unmarked] system simultaneous with the [exemplifying/exhausting] opposition; this was more economical than repeating the system for each subclass of exhausting or exemplfying process as in what Fawcett (1988b) calls a "displayed network".

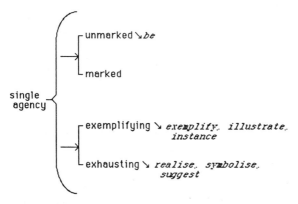

Fig. 5.7. Be *as an unmarked option*

Alternatively, *be* could have been specified as an optional lexicalisation of the feature [single agency], which if taken up would have to be interpreted as foreclosing choices in more delicate systems. The network could then have been simplified as in Fig. 5.8, with the choice between [exemplifying] and [exhausting] dependent on [single agency] not being realised through *be*:

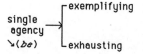

Fig. 5.8. Optional lexicalisation realisation operator

As a general strategy for handling superordination relations this approach would considerably simplify systemic formulations of lexis as delicate grammar. With nominal taxonomies in particular, several hyponymic steps between general and specific lexical items are common: e.g. *platypus-monotreme-mammal-vertibrate-animal*. The parentheses around lexical items realising non-terminal features would have to be taken as a new type of realisation operator, arresting delicacy as far as building up a selection expression was concerned.

Along these lines the paradigm in Table 5.1 is reformulated systemically as Fig. 5.9, incorporating the additional information that *dog* and *cow* are unmarked as far as both maturity and sex are concerned.

Table 5.1. Cross-classification by sex and species

MATURE:		CANINE	BOVINE
	MALE	dog	bull
	FEMALE	bitch	cow
IMMATURE		puppy	cow

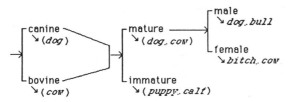

Fig. 5.9. Network illustrating non-terminal lexicalisation

5.2.4 *Lexical relations in cohesion analysis*

Alongside the collocational and componential/taxonomic approaches to lexical relations outlined above, a third perspective on lexical relations emerged from work on textual cohesion. Both stratificational (Gutwinski 1976) and systemic (Halliday and Hasan 1976) models of cohesion acknowledged the importance of lexical ties and proposed basic classificatory systems. Gutwinski, reporting in 1976 on the work of the Hartford stratificationalists in the late 1960's, made use of the following categories when analysing lexical cohesion (Gutwinski 1976:57):

1. repetition of item
2. occurrence of synonym or item formed on same root
3. occurrence of item from same lexical set (co-occurrence group)

The repetition category takes into account the fact that lexical items tend to expect themselves; if an item is realised once in a text, it is likely to appear again. The second category grouped together synonymy and morphological variations on a given item. This means that the relationship between items like *craft* and *vessel* is classified in the same way as that between *vessel* and *vessels*:

SYNONYM:SYNONYM::
DERIVED/INFLECTED FORM:DERIVED/INFLECTED FORM
craft:vessel::   big:large::   jump:leap::
vessel:vessels   larger:larger   jumps:jumping

This proportionality does not sit easily within models which make a distinction between word and lexical item. For this reason systemic linguists have generally treated the recurrence of words from a lexical item's formal scatter under the heading repetition.

Where Gutwinski's first category is based on formal repetition and his second on near repetition of meaning, his third focusses on collocation. His example of a co-occurrence group is a notional lexical set: *train, track, baggage-car, rails* (Gutwinski 1976:82). As collocational thesauri were not available to provide operational definitions of such sets, analysis of items belonging to the same co-occurrence group proceeded on an intuitive basis.

Halliday and Hasan (1976), documenting research roughly contemporary with that of the Hartford school, present a slightly more developed list:

1. same item
2. synonym or near synonym (including hyponymy; 1976:338)
3. superordinate
4. 'general' item
5. collocation (including antonymy and meronymy;[4] 1976:285)

As forecast above, they treated items formed on the same root as repetitions. Gutwinski's category of synonymy was extended to include one further semantic relation, hyponymy (grouping *trunk/boot* and *flower/rose* under the same heading). In addition Halliday and Hasan introduce the categories of superordination and general item. These raises a number of difficulties.

For one thing, the distinction between hyponymy (part of synonymy) and superordination is by no means clear. Halliday and Hasan may have in mind a cline such as *rose-flower-plant-thing*, reserving hyponymy for relations between an item and its immediate superordinate (e.g. *rose-flower*) and using superordination for more distant relations (e.g. *rose-plant*). Their most general category along this cline, general item, can be formally distinguished in that its exponents (e.g. *thing, person, stuff, creature, business, move, place, location* etc.) are not tonic when cohesive, unless strongly contrastive; it would be very marked for *place* to carry the tonic in [5:22], even though it is the last salient sylable in the tone group.

> [5:22] //5 Melbourne's a **ter**rible place //;
>   it actually hailed on me!

Although easily distinguished, the problem with the category of general item it that it is hard to see how it is lexically cohesive. General words certainly do participate with phoric reference items to identify participants as Halliday and Hasan (1976:280) exemplify (*the elm-the tree-that old* **thing**). But as non-phoric groups, general items like *thing, person* and *stuff* are so close to being closed system items that their probability of co-occuring with specific clusters of closed system items is likely to be very low — so low that their contribution to lexical cohesion is arguably quite negligible. In light of these difficulties Halliday and Hasan's hyponymy, superordination and general item categories will be collapsed below.

Halliday and Hasan also include the category of collocation, although in the context of cohesion analysis this is semantically rather than probabilistically defined in terms of some "recognizable lexico-semantic (word meaning) relation" (1976:285).

As part of her work on children's narrative in the late sixties and early seventies, Hasan further elaborated these categories. As reported in Halliday and Hasan 1985[5] her general categories are as follows:

1. repetition   leave, leaving, left
2. synonymy   leave, depart
3. antonymy   leave, arrive
4. hyponymy   travel-leave; rose-tulip (as co-hyponyms)
5. meronymy   hand, finger; finger-thumb (as co-meronyms)

In this framework, hyponymy is separated from synonymy, and apparently collapsed with superordination and general item under the heading hyponymy. In addition, antonymy and meronymy, included under collocation in Halliday and Hasan, are established as distinct categories in their own right. Hasan also makes it clear that relations between co-hyponyms and co-meronyms are to be included under headings 4 and 5 respectively.

Interestingly, the category of collocation has been discarded. This reflects a general move among cohesion analysts towards breaking down the category of collocation by pulling out and defining relations that had previously been glossed over under the lexicogrammatical notion of mutual expectancy. The point of this is to make cohesion analysis more reliable in the absence of collocational thesauri. Further developments along these lines will be presented in 5.3 below.

Finally, mention should be made of Halliday (1985a:310-312), who maintains repetition and collocation as distinct categories, and groups together synonymy, antonymy, meronymy and hyponymy under a general heading of synonymy.

5.2.5 *Lexical cohesion and field*

One critical consideration which has been set aside in the discussion of lexical relations to this point is that of field specificity. In general cohesion .analysts have tended not to be very specific about this point. Categories tend to be illustrated with examples from core vocabulary, which are kept as field neutral as possible: verbs, adverbs and adjectives are favoured over nouns, and "commonsense" nouns are used rather than technical ones. It is no accident that Hasan chooses action verbs in exploring the grammarian's dream; fields tend to differentiate themselves nominally, through technical lexis, rather than through verbs, adjectives and adverbs (see Martin 1989; 1990b). But even with verbs, the question of field slips in. The analysis of semiotic identifying processes above for example drew in part on the field of linguistics for its interpretation of of processes such as *expound, realise, code* and *transcribe*.

This raises the question as to what extent lexis can be treated as most delicate grammar while maintaining a lexicogrammar that is essentially neutral with respect to field. Certainly progress can be made with core vocabulary (see Carter 1982, 1986, 1987:33-46 for a useful introduction to the notion of core vocabulary), and with the less specialised word classes of verb, adjective and adverb. One way of keeping the grammar neutral would be to locate specialised taxonomies in the register variable field, allowing the grammar to focus on field neutral oppositions. This would mean for example that the similarity between *morphology* in linguistics and geology could be brought out in lexicogrammar and the differences between them in field taxonomies; similarly for *cover* in yachting and sleeping. And analysts could make a principled decision as to whether they were analysing lexical cohesion with respect to lexicogrammatical taxonomies or field ones, depending on the purposes for which the analysis was designed.

For the remainder of this chapter it will be assumed that lexical cohesion will be analysed with respect to field oppositions, and that lexical relations can approached from four different perspectives within a systemic functional model. These perspectives are:

    i. from the point of view of mutual expectancy in lexicogrammar (**collocation**)
    ii. from the point of view of more delicate options in lexicogrammatical networks (**the grammarian's dream**)
    iii. from the point of view of semantic relations between lexical items in text (**lexical cohesion**)
    iv. from the point of view of register specific oppositions (**field taxonomies**)

An overview of these perspectives is provided in Table 5.2. The relations underlying lexical cohesion will be elaborated next in section 5.3.

Table 5.2. Lexical relations across planes and strata

Context	Language	
	DISCOURSE SEMANTICS	LEXICOGRAMMAR
field specific taxonomies	lexical relations (cohesion)	field neutral taxonomies (as delicate grammar)
		collocation patterns (lexical sets)

5.3 Lexical relations: system

5.3.1 *The problem of units*

The problem of semantic units has been a recurrent one throughout Chapters 2, 3 and 4. Stratifying the content place makes it possible to distinguish move or message from clause, and participant from nominal group, although in a functional grammar, semantic units will obviously be founded on grammatical ones. The issue arises once again here, with respect to the nature of the discourse semantic units lexical cohesion is analysed between.

As the term lexical cohesion implies, Gutwinski, Halliday and Hasan, Hasan and Halliday have all been concerned with cohesive ties between lexical items. The distinction within a systemic model between lexical item and word means that in principle cohesion analysis is not tied to orthographic word boundaries. Phrasal verbs for example can be taken as single lexical items. And frozen collocations such as *round the twist* or *kick the bucket* could also be netted in. Halliday and Hasan's (1976) treatment of phrases like *in that respect* or *instead of this* as conjunctions implies a similar stance.

Just how far this notion of lexical item could be pushed however, remains unclear. Matthiessen forthcoming a reports on the following categorization of lexical phrases by Becker (1975) (see Sinclair 1987:321-322 for elaboration of this list; see also Carter 1987:60 reporting on Alexander 1984):

i.	polywords	(blow up)
ii.	phrasal constraints	(by pure coincidence)
iii.	deictic locutions	(for that matter)
iv.	sentence builders	([A] gave [B] a (long) song and dance about [C])

v. situational utterances   (How can I ever repay you?)
vi. verbatum texts   (Better late than never.)

The problem is that if strong mutual expectancy is used to define lexical items, where does one stop? If phrasal verbs are treated as single items, then what about Process Range structures:

> take a bath:bathe::
> have dinner:dine::
> make progress:progress::
> sing a song:sing::
> play the guitar:strum::
> score a goal:score::
> shoot the puck:shoot

And if Process Range structures, such as these, what about Process and Medium:

> cook + meal, beakfast, lunch, dinner, food, rice, curry, pasta etc.
> drive + car, Mazda, motorcycle, Honda, boat, bus, train, truck etc.
> shoot + animal, deer, duck, goose, enemy, soldier, terrorist etc.

Or Process and Circumstance (of location, with deixis-less destinations):

> go to + work, school, theatre, training, practice, footy, hockey, lunch etc.

The point is that the distinction between word and idiom is a gradient one, and that distingushing word from lexical item does not determine where the line between the two is drawn. If as Sinclair (1987, 1988) implies we can move beyond Becker and treat whole texts as mutually expectant, then collocation will not function as the most effective criteria on which to base the units lexical cohesion is analysed between.

As an alternative to approaching the problem simply from the perspective of grammar and lexis, one can turn to the level of context, and ask questions about appropriate units based on the structure of the register variable field. Field is unfortunately a relatively underspecified construct in systemic theory and will be further developed in Chapter 7 below. Nevertheless, an outline of the range of its concerns can be developed briefly here. Halliday (1985c:12) defines field of discourse as follows:

> The FIELD OF DISCOURSE refers to what is happening, to the nature of the social action that is taking place; what is it that the participants are engaged in, in which the language figures as some essential component.

This is a useful starting point for interpreting the contextual semantics of experiential meaning in functional linguistics because the perspective is a social one, and because of the emphasis placed on language as action; field is not specifically tied to subject matter or topic, notions through which it can be discussed only in certain modes (it makes little sense for example when watching and listening to a rugby league training session to ask what the topic is; the appropriate question is "What is going on?").

Halliday's notion of field will be developed here by defining fields as sets of activity sequences oriented to some global institutional purpose. Examples include: linguistics, tennis, cooking, wine making, gardening, dog breeding, film, architecture, sewing, car racing, philosophy, sailing, building, chess, war, politics, religion and so on. This listing should not be taken as implying that the concept of delicacy is not critical. Obviously there are fields within fields, and subfields within these: yachting for example is a type of sailing which can in turn be subsumed under sport. Nor does the listing imply that a given text cannot mix fields; it is quite common in reflective modes for more than one field to be drawn on, although typically one dominant institutional focus will be clear (see Martin 1986a for an interpretation of texts in these terms). Finally it should be stressed that as with all semiotic categories, boundaries are fluid and unclear; this is essential for meaning to evolve — there would be no social semiotics in Australia today if linguistics, semiotics, philosophy, sociology, marxism, feminism, structuralism, post-structuralism and so on hadn't leaked (it goes without saying however that the presence of fuzzy boundaries does not mean that categories do not exist!).

A given institution comprises a large number of different activity sequences, where these are realised linguistically through temporally ordered chains of Process and Medium with their attendant participant and circumstantial roles. Tennis for example includes, among other activity sequences, playing, coaching, commenting, analysing, viewing, training, club meetings, tournament presentations, interviews, grading and so on. The participants and processes in these are overlapping, not identical. At the same time, each of these activities participates in an overall institutional focus — that of making it possible for people to enjoy in diverse ways a game played with strung raquets and a furry hollow ball.

As a first approximation, these activity sequences can be broken down as follows:

    i.   taxonomies of actions, people, places, things and qualities
    ii. configurations of actions with people, places, things and qualities and of people, places and things with qualities.
    iii. activity sequences of these configurations

This can be illustrated from the field of tennis as follows:

    i. TAXONOMY — part/whole relations among *game-set-match*
   ii. CONFIGURATION — Agent Process Medium structure *player-serve-ball*
  iii. ACTIVITY SEQUENCE — *player serve-opponent return-player volley*

On the basis of this characterisation of field, the discourse semantic unit underlying lexical item and entering into cohesive lexcial relations can be set up. Since it is an experientially defined unit, it will be referred to as a **message part**, to bring out its metafunctional relationship with CONJUNCTION. For a given field, the message part realises (i) one of the features taxonomising people, places and things, or (ii) one of the actions configuring with people, places and things and entering into activity sequences, or (iii) one of the qualities associated with people, places, things and actions. The message part may or may not be realised by a single lexical item; congruent and incongruent realisations are exemplified in Table 5.3.

Table 5.3. *Simple and complex lexicalisation of message part*

MESSAGE PART	CONGRUENT (1 lexical item)	INCONGRUENT (1+ lexical items)
'person'	champion	tournament winner
'place'	court	playing area
'thing'	draw	playing schedule
'quality'	outstanding	first class
'action'	smash	hit an overhead
'quality'	well	out of sight

The network for lexical relations developed below will be organised around these three different aspects of the contextual structure of activity sequences. The examples and analysis illustrated will be strongly biased towards texts in which the language gives an iconic account of what is going on. For texts where language is more reflectively constitutive of field, the concepts of technicality and abstraction need to be introduced; discussion of these variables will be delayed until Chapter 7 below.

    Taxonomically based relations are in general better understood than those having to do with configurations (hereafter **nuclear** relations) or activity sequences because of the long tradition of scholarship invested in them (see Lyons 1977:174-229 for useful synopsis; his terminology will be fol-

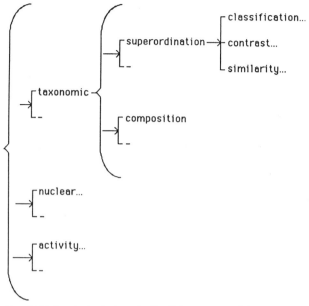

Fig. 5.10. Lexical relations in English: primary delicacy

lowed where possible in the analyses presented below). The lexicogrammatical realisation of nuclear relations has been the focus of more recently evolved accounts of transitivity (cf. Fillmore 1968, Halliday 1967a, 1968, 1976c, 1985a, Starosta 1988). And activity sequences have been discussed from the point of view of temporal conjunction, especially in narrative genres (e.g. Labov & Waletzky 1967, Hasan 1984b); work in artificial intelligence on frames and scripts is also relevant (see Brown and Yule 1983:237-250 for an introduction). However, the presentation of lexical relations below is considerably circumscribed by the relatively recent history of work on nuclear structures and sequences. At primary delicacy, the system for lexical relations is presented as Fig. 5.10.

5.3.2 *Taxonomic relations*

Following on from what has just been said, taxonomic relations can be opposed to nuclear and activity ones. Taxonomic relations are of two main types, depending on the kind of taxonomy they reflect. Superordination

Table 5.4. Examples of superordination and composition

	SUPERORDINATION	COMPOSITION
'people'	player-first seed	team-player
'places'	line-service line	court-line
'things'	official-referee	racquet-strings
'actions'	hit-volley	-
'quality'	excellent-agile	-

relations reflect taxonomies based on subclassification (the "is a" relation); composition relations reflect taxonomies based on the relation of parts to wholes (the "has a" relation). People, places and things are usually organised with respect to both types of taxonomy in a given field. Actions can also be thought of as related through superordination (although with generally shallow taxonomies) or composition; but the part/whole perspective amounts to viewing actions as parts of activity sequences, and so will be taken up under that heading below. Qualities are organised by superordination (again with shallow taxonomies), but not by composition. Some examples are presented in Table 5.4.

Superordination taxonomies then are built up around the principle of subclassification. An informal illustration is presented below from the field of music. Field taxonomies such as these reflect the extent to which their designers participate in the field in question. The classification presented in Fig. 5.11 has been prepared from the point of view of a listener, record buyer and occasional reader of popular music magazines. The less delicate systems situate popular music within the more general field of the performing arts.

Modern music is subsequently broken down as in Fig. 5.12 with a view to the kinds of music that can be heard in clubs or on the radio and watched on video in the western cities which function as the main market for the music industry. More delicacy could obviously be provided by keen listeners in any of the fields outlined; and experts in the field might well question the nature of the categorisation as a whole. The point of this network is simply to illustrate superordination from the point of view of a field specific taxonomy which would underlie statements like *Cool is a kind of American improvised modern popular music performed in jazz clubs in New York and Los Angeles in the late 50's and early 60's.*

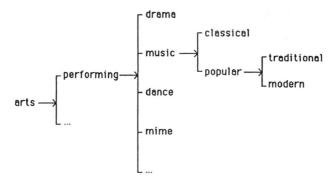

Fig. 5.11. Illustrative superordination taxonomy for performing arts

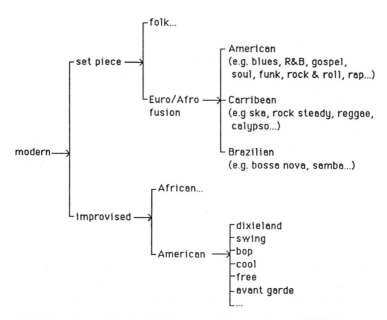

Fig. 5.12. Illustrative superordination taxonomy for modern popular music

Composition taxonomies organise people, places and things in a given field with respect to part/whole rather than class/subclass relations. An illustrative taxonomy is outlined in Fig. 5.13, drawing once again on the field of music. The less delicate systems focus on the organisation of the swing bands that toured North America by bus and train before, during and after the second world war. The taxonomy is again designed with the casual listener rather than the jazz buff in mind.

The more delicate systems break down the players into sections as they were typically organised on stage. This means for example that flutes are placed in the sax section, since they tended to be played occasionally by tenor players (the fingering for tenor and soprano sax and flute being very much the same). A superordination taxonomy for instruments (rather than a composition one for players) would of course treat flutes very differently from saxophones; its embouchure and method of playing is more like that for horns, although it's keyboard is sax-like in design.

Note that for both the taxonomies illustrated, some options are realised by single lexical items, and others by multiple ones (in Classifier ˙ Thing structures; see below). Thus one finds the *horns* and the *reeds*, but the *rhythm section*, not the *rhythm*. And where specific features are lexicalised, there is always a Classifer ˙ Thing structure available as an alternative: e.g. *modern American improvised music* and *jazz*. It is this alternation between lexical items and Classifer ˙ Thing structures that underlies the phylogenetic uncertainty that often surrounds the status of certain realisations as compound words, hyphenated words or distinct lexical items (cf. *airplane, seaplane, jet plane*).

5.3.2.1 *Superordination*

Now that superordination and composition field specific taxonomies have been illustrated, the taxonomic systems for lexical relations will be presented in detail, starting with systems oriented to superordination. The focus of these systems is on message parts which share most of their meaning.

A number of technical terms have evolved to name relationships among classes and subclasses; these include hyponymy, hyperonymy, cohyponymy and superodination. Taking as an example the system subclassifying saxophones (Fig. 5.15), these can be illustrated as follows:

  i. *soprano* is a **hyponym** of *saxophone*
  ii. *saxophone* is a **hyperonym** or **superordinate** of *soprano*
  iii. *soprano, alto, tenor* and *baritone* are **co-hyponyms**

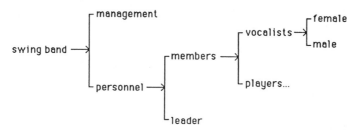

Fig. 5.13. Illustrative composition taxonomy for swing band

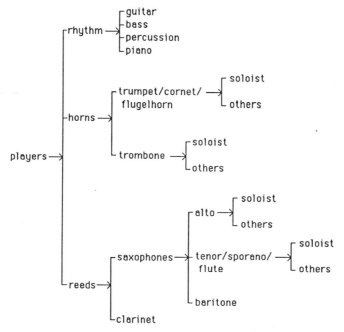

Fig. 5.14. Illustrative composition taxonomy for players in swing band

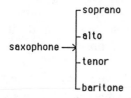

Fig. 5.15. Classification of saxophones

Depending on the field the relationship between hyponym and hyperonym has different names. These are commonly realised through Pre-Classifier structures (for which see Martin 1988a): *a **class** of noun, a **make** of car, a **breed** of dogs* etc. And they are use cohesively as well: *Like my new car? — Yes, what **make** is it?* A cohesive relationship between one of these items and the hyponym it relates to a hyperonym will be referred to as **relational hyponymy/hyperonymy**. Typical realisations include: *class, kind, type, form, breed, make, sort, style, species, order, family, variety, genre, grade, brand, caste, category*.

As far as lexical cohesion is concerned, the term hyponymy can be used for relations in which the subclass follows its class (e.g. *sax-alto*), and the term hyperonymy for the converse sequence where the subclass appears first (e.g. *alto-sax*). The term superordination is synonymous with

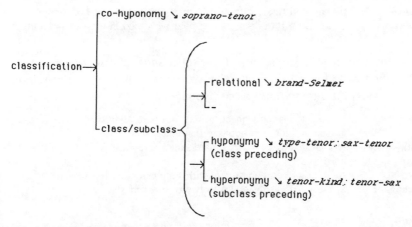

Fig. 5.16. Classification systems in English

hyperonymy; it will be used here simply as the name of the feature distinguishing relations oriented to superordination taxonomies from those oriented to composition. The classification oppositions presented to this point are outlined in Fig. 5.16.

Closely related to hyponymy is the category of synonymy. Indeed, synonyms might well be defined as co-hyponyms for which differences in meaning do not matter. Returning to Roget's **sailing-ship** entry for example, it is clear that Roget stops classifying and starts listing items as the differences in meaning between them get quite small:

> **sailing-ship**, sailboat, sailing vessel, sailer; wind-jammer, clipper, ship, tall s., full-rigged s., square-rigged s., fore-and-aft-rigged s., schooner-rigged s., lateen-rigged s.; four-masted ship, three-masted s., three-master, bark, barque, barquentine; two-masted ship, brig, hermaphrodite-b., cutter-b., brigantine, schooner, pinnace, snow, grab; frigate, sloop, corvette, warship; cutter, ketch, yawl, dandy, lugger; xebec, felucca, tartane, saic, caique, dhow, gallivat, junk, lorcha, sampan; sailing barge, smack, gabbard, hoy, hooker, nobby, bawley; *yacht*, skiff.

Sailing-ship, *sailboat*, *sailing vessel* and *sailer* are apparently offered as synonyms; and it is hard to distinguish among them on the basis of dictionary definitions (although their collocation patterns are very likely to differ). The *Concise Oxford Dictionary* (1964 edition used for definitions given below) can be used on the other hand to differentiate *cutter*, *ketch*, *yawl*, *dandy* and *lugger*; but one has to read closely to see the difference between *ketch* and *yawl* (i.e. the contrast between *forward* and *abaft*):

ketch	two-masted vessel with mizzen-mast stepped forward of rudder
yawl	two-masted fore-&-aft sailing-boat with mizzen-mast stepped abaft the rudder post

Among the two-masted ships, *brig*, *brigantine*, *snow* and *schooner* can be distinguished as follows; but only active participants in the field of sailing would be able to use these items as co-hyponyms.

brig	two-masted square-rigged vessel, but with additional lower fore-&-aft sail on graff and boom to main mast
brigantine	two-masted vessel with square-sailed fore-mast & fore-&- aft main mast
snow	small brig-like sailing vessel with supplementary trysail mast
schooner	fore-&-aft-rigged vessel with two or more masts

The difference between synonyms and co-hyponyms is in other words largely a question of delicacy with respect to a particular field. One additional factor that needs to be taken into account is the difference between experiential and interpersonal meaning. Items that might be treated as synonyms experientially, often differ with respect to the attitudinal meaning they code (*pace* Carter 1982:40-41; 1987:41-42):

> EXPERIENTIAL:EXPERIENTIAL + ATTITUDE::
> beat:trounce::
> walk:stroll::
> overweight:obese::
> thin:slim::
> house:home::
> conservative:fascist
> ...

Setting aside the fact that for many texts these fine differences in meaning do not matter, it could be argued that the only true synonymy is repetition, including a lexical item's formal scatter (e.g. *defeat, defeats, defeated, defeating*). But even here, an item's derivational scatter gives one pause. Looked at from the point of view of repetition, the difference between synonymy and co-hyponymy can be thought of an a kind of scale, graded along the following lines:

SAME MEANING

defeat:defeat	repetition
defeat:defeats	inflectional difference
defeating:defeat	derivational difference
defeat:down	synonym
defeat:trounce	attitudinal difference
defeat:subjugate	co-hyponym

ANOTHER MEANING

The oppositions having to do with similarity in meaning can be outlined systemically as in Fig. 5.17.

One further category that needs to be brought in here is antonymy. Whereas synonyms are co-hyponyms for which differences in meaning may not matter, antonyms are co-hyponyms for which they must — because the

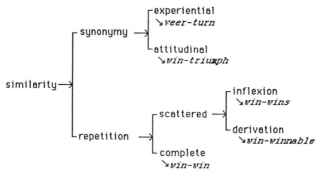

Fig. 5.17. Similarity systems in English

items in question are **opposed** in meaning rather than complementing each other; further to this antonyms always come in pairs:

> win:lose::
> happy:sad::
> employed:out of work::
> winner:runner-up::
> quickly:slowly
> ...

Closely related to antonyms are converses (Lyons 1977:279-280). As Lyons points out these are predominantly associated with reciprocal social roles (e.g. *employer-employee*), kinship relations (e.g. *sister-brother*) and location in time and space (e.g. *before-after, on top of-underneath*). A number of processes are also related in this way (e.g. *learn-teach, give-receive, say-hear*). Converses involve a role reversal of some kind; note that clauses in the following proportionalities imply each other:

> Ben is Ian's **tutor**:
> Ian is Ben's **student**::
>
> Ben is Jan's **brother**:
> Jan is Ben's **sister**::
>
> Ben's **behind** Jan:
> Jan is **in front of** Ben::
>
> Ben **gave** Jan the book:
> Jan **recevied** the book from Ben

Related to converses and antonyms are contrasts which involve non-binary oppositions. Lyons (1977:289) divides these into cycles and series. Series have outmost members (e.g. *high distinction-distinction-credit-pass-fail*) whereas cycles simply order members between two others (e.g. *Monday-Tuesday-Wednesday-Thursday-Friday-Saturday-Sunday*). The difference is that while *Sunday* is to *Monday* as *Monday* is to *Tuesday*, a *pass* is not related to a *high distinction* as a *high distinction* is to a *distinction*. The "poles" placed on days of the week are arbitrary ones, since time is a cycle which has no real beginning or end.

Antonyms and series may involve gradable or non-gradable oppositions where they involve qualities of people, places and things. The test for gradability has to do with whether an item can be intensified or compared (see Martin 1992 for a review of grading and interpersonal meaning). Thus one can ask *how new/old* something is, but not how *dead/alive*; or one can query *how hot/warm/tepid/cool/cold* something is, but not *how Monday* or *how credit*. Lyons refers to the gradable series as scales, and the non-gradable series as ranks. In addition he reserves the term antonym for gradable oppositions, introducing complementarity for gradable ones.

Table 5.5. Scales, ranks, antonyms and complementaries

	GRADABLE	NONGRADABLE
BINARY	**complementarity**	**antonym**
	big/small	present/absent
NON-BINARY	**scales:**	**ranks**
	excellent-	field marshall-
	good-	general-
	fair-	...
	poor-	corporal-
	awful	private

The network for contrastive lexical relations is presented in Fig. 5.18; Lyons' (1977) terminology is included in paretheses following the relevant systemic feature.

5.3.2.2 Composition

The second type of hierarchical organisation noted above had to do with composition rather than superordination. The relevant technical terms are

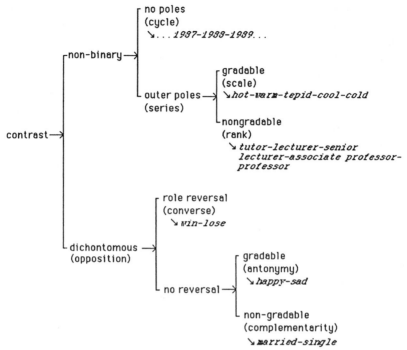

Fig. 5.18. Contrast systems in English

meronymy and **co-meronymy** (there is nothing corresponding to the hypo/ hyper- opposition noted above for class/subclass relations; the term meronymy was coined by Jeff Ellis and was first presented in Halliday and Hasan (1980:48), then taken up in Hasan (1984a, 1985b)). Given a composition system such as that for *chair* in Fig. 5.19, *arm* would function as a meronym of *chair*, and *arm* and *leg* would be co-meronyms.

Fig. 5.19. Decomposition of chairs

As with hyponymy, the relationship between part and whole may be named. Thus *a kind of chair* is proportional with *a part of the chair*, but with the name of the relational filling a Pre-Numerative (Halliday 1985a:174) rather than a Pre-Classifier position. The relational items may function cohesively between clauses, as in *The chair's broken. — Which **part**?* The following items are among those realizing **relational meronymy**:

> part, content, ingredient, fitting, member, constituent, stratum, rank, plane, element, factor, component, faction, excerpt, extract, selection, piece, segment, section, portion, measure

Alongside this set, there are two groups of items which function in what Halliday (1985a:174) calls Pre-Deictic and Pre-Numerative position. Those in Pre-Deictic position name components with respect to their location in time or space (e.g. *the **top** of the wall*): *top, inside, side, bottom, edge, middle, inside, outside, environs, start, finish, beginning, end*. These items may function "cohesively" in text: *We played well that set. — Not at the **start***. Those in Pre-Numerative position measure out some portion of the whole (e.g. *a **sip** of beer*): *jar, bottle, schooner, glass, midi, jug, can, loaf, mouthful, spoonful, pound, ounce, kilo, yard, metre*. These are also used "cohesively": *Would you like a beer? — Just a **midi** thanks*.

A further distinction can be drawn between alienable and inalienable part/whole relations. These are not grammatically distinguished in English possessive constructions (e.g. *the front garden's trees* and *the car's boot*). But when the whole is realised as a qualifier, inalienable possessives favour the preposition *of*, whereas alienable ones are more likely to be introduced with locative prepositions such as *in, inside, within* etc.

Table 5.6. Alienable and inalienable possession

ALIENABLE (the tree in the garden)	INALIENABLE (the boot of the car)
garden:tree::	tree:boot::
room:chair::	room:wall::
stream:fish::	fish:gills::
car:spare tire::	car:boot::
cup:coffee	cup:handle
...	...

These constitution systems are outlined systemically and exemplified in Fig. 5.20.

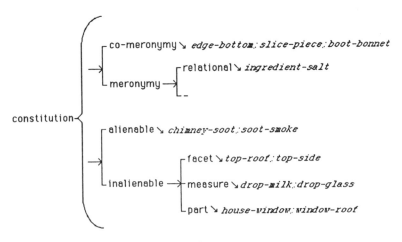

Fig. 5.20. Constitution systems in English

There are two further types of compositional relationship to be noted. One has to do with the meaning 'composed/consists in/be made up of' and relates material to the object it constitutes. Examples include *knife-steel, lake-water, fence-wood, water-H2O, ring-gold, window-glass, plate-perspex, sweater-wool*. This relationship will be termed **consistency**.

The second has to do with what Lyons (1977:315) refers to as **collectives**. There are two types, both of which have the function of treating collections of individual participants as aggregates. One set functions in Pre-Numerative position, as with the measure meronymy introduced above. But here their function is to group together individuals rather than separate them out by parts (thus *a member of the flock* contrasts with *a flock of geese*). Seen from the perspective of English's number system, their function is to reconstruct count nouns as a mass. Like other items functioning in Pre-Numerative structures, they can be used cohesively between clauses: *Did you see the ships? — I visited the whole **squadron***. This set includes *flock, herd, family, group, pod, gaggle, squadron, convoy, flotilla, team, deck, anthology, school, clutch, brace, pride*.

The second type cannot function as Pre-Numerative: *a cattle of cows and calves* or *a furniture of chairs and sofas* are nonsense. These items do nevertheless assemble a potentially heterogenous collection of individuals into a single group. They function "cohesively" in examples like *Ben put the cutlery, glasses and plates into the sink and washed up the **dishes***. This set includes *cattle, clergy, furniture, dishes, cutlery, beverages, parts of speech, shrubbery, collection, constellation, galaxy, solar system, compilation, assembly, company, conference, stable, troupe, orchestra, band, conglomeration, portfolio*.

An overview of constitution systems is presented in Fig. 5.21.

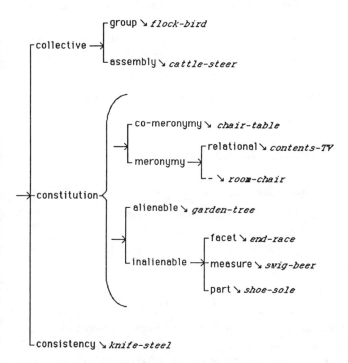

Fig. 5.21. Composition relations in English

Before turning to a discussion of nuclear relations in 5.3.3 below, the question of how many steps apart in a taxonomy items may be and still be treated as cohesive needs to be addressed. For example, *rose* and *flower* are more closely related taxonomically than *rose* and *plant*; and *mosquito* is closer to *insect* than to *invertebrate*. Are *rose-flower* and *rose-plant*, or *mosquito-insect* and *mosquito-invertebrate* equally cohesive? Similarly, a *door-knob* is part of a *door*, which is in turn part of a *house*; but it would be very odd to speak of *the house's door-knob* or even to say that *the house has a door-knob*. Should this be taken as evidence that *door-knob* and *house* are not lexically cohesive?

One way of resolving the question of how taxonomic distance affects cohesion is to make use of IDENTIFICATION and test items to see whether they are experientially close enough for one to have been presumed by the other. Along these lines, *the flower* straightforwardly presumes a *rose*, as *the insect* presumes *a mosquito*. Hyponyms do not directly presume their superordinates, but they may presume them indirectly through bridging. The reason for this difference is that superordinates contain less information than their hyponyms, while hyponyms encode all of the experiential meaning of their superordinates. This asymmetry is reflected in definitions:

rose   a beautiful & usually fragrant *flower* usually of red or yellow or white

In the following examples hyponyms are bridged from their superordinates:

BRIDGING: HYPONYM FROM HYPERONYM
[5:23] Ben admired his flowers, especially the roses.

BRIDGING: HYPONYM FROM HYPERONYM
[5:24] Ben hated the insects there, especially the mosquitos.

Bridging is also possible with parts and wholes, working in either direction:

BRIDGING: PART FROM WHOLE
[5:25] Ben walked into the stadium to look at the track.

BRIDGING: WHOLE FROM PART
[5:26] Ben saw a chimney. He was close to the cottage now.

With part/whole relations however, the distance between items in a composition taxonomy is important. It is possible to bridge between *a book-case* and *a room*, but not so easily between *a book-case* and *a house*; and bridging between *a book-case* and *a station* (in the sense of an Australian ranch) is highly unlikely.

[5:27] Ben walked int the room. The book-cases were full.
[5:28] Ben walked into the house. The book-cases were full.
[5:29] *Ben walked onto the station. The book-cases were full.

This interaction between IDENTIFICATION and IDEATION provides a criterion for determining when relations between lexical items are cohesive. They can be treated as such where one item codes sufficient experiential meaning to be presumed by another, either directly, or indirectly through bridging. Nominalisation can be used to create a context for this test when lexical relations between processes or qualities are in doubt:

> Ben **raced** well, **tacking** brilliantly:
> The race went well; the tacking was brilliant

5.3.3 *Nuclear relations*

Nuclear relations reflect the ways in which actions, people, places, things and qualities configure as activities in activity sequences. The following Process Medium structures from the field of tennis illustrate the kind of relations involved. In this field players *serve aces* and *volley winners*, but they do not **serve lobs* or **volley double-faults*.

serve + ace	*hit + ace
smash + overhead	*smash + volley
put away + volley	*put away + serve
hit + winner	*hit + loser
net + passing shot	*net + lob
intercept + volley	*intercept + serve
drop + shot	*drop + lob
lob + return	*lob + approach shot
volley + winner	*volley + ace

In previous approaches to lexical cohesion, nuclear relations have been handled under the heading collocation. An attempt will be made to unpack these relations here in order to identify more precisely the semantic relations involved. What this amounts to is a foray into the discourse semantics of experiential grammar, which is in itself a daunting task. It is however an essential one, since the lexical relations under consideration here cannot be explained simply by appealing to grammatical structure. The relation between *serve* and *ace* for example is not limited to the Process Medium structure itself; the elements configured may be in different clauses — *Ben serves...That's his fifth ace of the match.* And the configuration may be realised metaphorically — *Ben's serve produced very few aces today.*

The basic strategy used here will be to apply Halliday's general logico-semantic relations of expansion to clause, nominal group and verbal group meanings in order to produce a more abstract level of interpretation. These relations were introduced in 4.1 above in connection will Halliday's (1985a) treatment of the clause complex. Halliday's description of each relation, and examples of their realisation between clauses are reviewed below:

Elaboration (=)

In ELABORATION, one clause elaborates on the meaning of another by further specifying or describing it. The secondary clause does not introduce a new element into the picture, but rather provides a further characterization of one that is already there, restating it, clarifying it, refining it...

That clock doesn't go; it's not working.
She wasn't a show dog; I didn't buy her as a show dog.
Each argument was fatal to the other: both could not be true.
(Halliday 1985a:203)

Extension (+)

In EXTENSION, one clause extends the meaning of another by adding something new to it. What is added may just be an addition, or a replacement, or an alternative...

I breed the poultry and my husband looks after the garden.
I said you looked like an egg, sir; and some eggs are very pretty, you know.
(Halliday 1985a:207)

Enhancement (x)

In ENHANCEMENT one clause enhances the meaning of another by qualifying it in one of a number of possible ways: by reference to time, place, manner, cause or condition...

It's the Cheshire cat: now I shall have somebody to talk to.
The three soldiers wandered about for a minute or two, and then quietly marched after the others.
(Halliday 1985a:211)

Halliday himself projects these relations across the grammar in his Synoptic summary of expansion table (1985a:306-307), reproduced as Table 4.2. This projection will be slightly revised and extended here so that action and signifying processes, and the experiential structure of nominal and verbal groups are brought into the picture. To begin, relational processes, which Halliday does consider, will be set aside.

First, elaboration. Elaboration has to do with specifying, restating, clarifying or refining meaning and was considered in some detail in Chapter 4 with respect to internal reformulation. This meaning is grammaticalised through Process˙Range (e.g. *have lunch*) structures in the clause, Classifier ˙Thing (e.g. *morning tea*) structures in nominal groups and Event˙Particle (e.g. *put up with*) structures in verbal groups.

With clauses, elaboration is through Process˙Range:process (as opposed to Range:entity) structures (Halliday 1985a:134-137). These are of two kinds. One type makes use of a general verb such as *do, make, take* etc. and expresses the experiential meaning of the process as a Range: e.g. *do work*. The Range in effect elaborates on the general verb by specifying the meaning involved. The other type makes use of a more specific verb which the Range function then subclassifies; the verbs *play* and *tell* are commonly specified in this way. From the point of view of field, *playing tennis, playing monopoly, playing rummy* and so on are all hyponyms of *play*. As Halliday (1985a:135) points out, "Tennis is clearly not an entity; there is no such thing as tennis other than the act of playing it."

> play = tennis/football/cards/monopoly/chess/rummy...
> tell = joke/story/anecdote/news/answer/solution...

Table 5.7 illustrates a number of these Process˙Range constructions. Note the way in which they contrast with the Process˙Medium structures in parentheses. From the point of view of field, the Process˙Range:process structure involves just one meaning (which is realised through two lexical items, one elaborating the other; the Process˙Medium structures on the other hand involve two meanings, an action and the participant that action is mediated through).

Table 5.7. Elaboration and extension in the clause

Clause

PROCESS	=	RANGE:PROCESS	(PROCESS + MEDIUM)
play		tennis	(play + the ball)
sing		song	(sing + her x to sleep)
score		run	(score + some dope)
ask		question	(ask + Mary x to tea)
tell		story	(tell + him off)
take		bath	(bathe + the baby)
do		dance	(dance + her x over)
make		friend	(befriend + John)

A similar process of elaboration is found in Classifier˙Thing structures in nominal groups (Halliday 1985a:164-165). These realise taxonomic features which cannot be manifested through a single lexical item (e.g. *red wine*) or

Table 5.8. Elaboration and extension in the nominal group

Nominal group			
CLASSIFIER	=	THING	(EPITHET + THING)
frying		pan	(frying + fish)
spectator		fleet	(visiting + fleet)
deciding		race	(good + race)
nominal		group	(difficult + group)
red		wine	(nice + wine)
brick		wall	(green + wall)
first		prize	(lousy + prize)
tenor		saxophone	(new + saxophone)

which need not be (e.g. *Chinese frying pan/wok*). The Classifier functions to specify the relevant subclass of Thing; several may be required to complete the elaboration, as in *visiting American linguistics professor*. A number of examples are presented in Table 5.8 and contrasted with descriptive Epithet˙Thing structures in parentheses. Note that a *frying fish* is not usually a kind of fish, but rather a fish that is frying.

A related pattern is found in English verbal group, where phrasal verbs adjust the meaning of their main verb. From the point of view of field only a single event is involved, and most phrasal verbs can be paraphrased with single lexical items (though these are typically less spoken in register). Phrasal elaborations of the verb *look* are exemplified below. Alternative non-phrasal lexicalisations are presented in Table 5.9 (in bold face), and

Table 5.9. Phrasal and non-phrasal processes

PHRASAL VERB	PROCESS X CIRCUMSTANCE OF LOCATION
look=at/**examine** it closely	look x in that direction
look=after/**protect** your child	look x after my arrival
look=over/**check** the manuscript	look x over the wall
look=up/**visit** John	look x up the pipe
look=through/**peruse** the book	look x through the microscope
look=around/**window-shop** in town	look x around the corner
look=out/**take care** (it's hot)	look x out the window
look=up=to/**admire** Ben	look x up to the top
look=in=on/**visit** John	look x in the basket/look x on the shelf

Table 5.10. Elaboration in the verbal group

Verbal group

EVENT	=	PARTICLE	(MEDIUM)
sum		up	(the problem)
beat		up	(the class)
line		up	(the dogs)
see		through	(the disguise)
meet		up with	(a friend)
look		into	(the matter)
talk		over	(the issue)
run		away with	(the game)

the phrasal verbs are contrasted with examples in which the same verb and preposition realise a Process˙Circumstance of location structure.

Further examples are introduced in Table 5.10; the relevant Medium is provided in parentheses to clarify the phrasal interpretation.

Having taken this step, a number of related grammatical structures present themselves for treatment along similar lines. At clause rank, there is a class of locative phrases which can be interpreted as subclassifying the Process whose ritual destination they provide. These are associated with verbs of motion (especially *go* and *come*); their destination is realised through an unmodified nominal head (e.g. *come to **tea***). A number of these "locative Ranges" are listed below:

go/come = to/from work/school/class/uni/theatre/daycare;
to/from training/practice/football/hockey;
to/from dinner/tea/lunch/breakfast/supper;
to/from bed

The same verbs are similarly elaborated at group rank. The verbal group complexes involved specify types of coming and going with respect to leisure activities:

go/come = swimming, skiing, snorkelling, jogging, running, sailing,
handgliding, surfing, drinking etc.

With nominal groups, one further set of elaborations to consider are realised through Pre-Deictic, Pre-Numerative, Pre-Epithet and Pre-Classifier structures. The first three of these code part/whole relations and the last class/subclass ones. Like Classifier˙Thing structures, from the point of view of field these function simply as grammatical resources for isolating particular parts or classes of people, places and things.

Pre-Deictic	the top of = the ridge, the back of = the garden
Pre-Numerative	a herd of = buffalo, a mouthful of = food
Pre-Epithet	the last of = the questions, the biggest of = the melons
Pre-Classifier	that kind of = beer, this sort of = thing

Finally, possessive Deictics can be taken as elaborating where the relationship between the participant realised through the Deictic and that realised through the Thing are in a part whole relation rather than an ownership one: *the train's passengers* or *its wheels* but not *his passengers* or *its kittens*.

These pre-nominal structures contrast with qualifying ones in which facet, measure, isolation and type are coded as distinct participants; the latter can be treated as involving two message parts:

ONE MESSAGE PART:TWO MESSAGE PARTS::
the top of the ridge:the ridge x on the top::
a herd of buffalo:buffalo x in the herd::
the biggest of the melons:the melons x that were the biggest::
that kind of beer:beer x of that kind
the train's passengers:the passengers x on the train

As far as analysing lexical cohesion with specific fields in mind is concerned, all of the elaborating structures discussed above can be taken as realising single message parts. This is the main source of incongruence between message part and lexical item as these units are being defined here.

Next, extension. With extension distinct meanings are combined. The contrast between Process˙Range:process and Process˙Medium structures in the clause, and Classifier˙Thing and Epithet ˙ Thing structures in the

Table 5.11. Extension in the clause

Clause

PROCESS	+	RANGE:ENTITY	PROCESS	+	MEDIUM
climb		mountain	shoot		terrorist
play		piano	hug		friend
cross		court	cook		rice
like		tennis	please		crowd (it pleased them that...)
see		play	strike		me (it struck me that...)
consider		text	convince		audience (it convinced them...)

nominal group has already served to illustrate the difference between elaboration and extension at issue here. Where Range:processes elaborate a Process, Range:entities (Halliday 1985a:134-135) and Mediums (Halliday 1985a:144-154) extend them as outlined in Table 5.11.

Similarly, whereas Classifiers elaborate the Thing, Epithets add qualities. These may be of an experiential or an attitudinal kind:

Table 5.12. Extension in the nominal group

Nominal group			
EPITHET +	THING	EPITHET + (ATTITUDINAL)	THING
red	car	ugly	car
big	lunch	chauvinist	pig
round	ball	pleasant	spot
speeding	bullet	beautiful	shot
hungry	puppy	greedy	kitten

As implied above, possessive Deictics realising ownership rather than composition can be taken as extending.

With verbal groups, extension combines events. Halliday (1985a:255-269) categorises a wide variety of verbal group complexes with respect to both expansion and projection. He reserves the category of extension for conation: *try to do, try and do, attempt to do, avoid doing, succeed in doing, manage to do, get to do, fail in doing, learn to do, practise doing* etc. This analysis has the advantage of bringing out the relationship between verbal group complexes and clause complex ones:

VERBAL GROUP COMPLEX:CLAUSE COMPLEX::
he wants to go:he wanted John to go::
he asked to go:he asked Ben to go::
he pretended to have done it:he pretended that he'd done it::
he claimed to have done it:he claimed he had done it
etc.

For purposes of lexical cohesion analysis however, all verbal group complexes will be treated as involving extension here, in order to bring out proportionalities of the following kind:

ELABORATION:EXTENSION:ENHANCEMENT::
(phrasal verb:verbal group complex:event x quality::)
look into:keep looking:look carefully::
run into:attempt to run:run quickly::
see through:happen to see:see clearly::
go over:promise to go:go reluctantly
etc.

Finally, enhancement. With enhancement, one meaning qualifies another with respect to the circumstantial categories of Extent, Location, Manner, Cause and Matter (Halliday 1985a:137-144). With clauses, the relationship between enhancing clauses and Circumstances is clear, since conjunctive relations can be realised incongruently through circumstantial roles. The relevant proportionalities are as follows:

ENHANCING BETA ($^x\beta$):CIRCUMSTANCE::
Ben left after beating Carl:Ben left **after his win**::
The crowd cheered while Ben ran:the crowd cheered **during his run**::
Ben cried because he lost:Ben cried **because of his loss**::
Ben smiled although he'd lost::Ben smiled **in spite of his loss**::
Ben runs like Carl does:Ben runs **like Carl**

Adverbial realisations of manner are probably better treated as enhancements of events (at verbal group rank) rather than of processes (clause rank). This brings out the semantic continuity at group rank between modifying nouns and modifying verbs:

EPITHET^THING:EVENT^MANNER ADVERB::
careful player:play carefully::
hungry child:eat hungrily::
fast track:run fast::
intense pressure:write intensely
etc.

It is sometimes argued that Manner adverbs should be treated as circumstances in light of the fact that they all have alternative prepositional phrase realisations. Note however that in order to be expressed as a prepositional phrase, these qualities of events must be nominalised, making the circumstantial realisation the marked one (see Matthiessen forthcoming a):

MANNER ADVERBS:INCONGRUENT PREPOSITIONAL PHRASES::
Ben ran **quickly**:Ben ran with considerable speed::
Ben won **easily**:Ben won with ease::
Ben slept **fitfully**:Ben slept in fits and starts::
Ben winced **painfully**:Ben winced in great pain

The prepositional realisations will be taken here as enhancing Processes, and the adverbial realisations as enhancing Events.

The same prepositional phrases used to enhance Processes can also be used to enhance Things, functioning as Qualifiers in nominal groups:

CIRCUMSTANTIAL QUALIFIERS
the restaurant **at the end of the universe**
the race **through the galaxy**
the noise **from the engine room**
the ship **like Ford's**
the present **for Zaphod**
the story **about Trillian**

This interpretation of the semantics of experiential grammar in terms of the general logico-semantic relations of elaboration, extension and enhancement is summarised in Table 5.13.

Table 5.13. *Elaboration, extension and enhancement across clauses and groups*

Elaboration	**Extension**	**Enhancement**
PROCESS = RANGE	PROCESS + MEDIUM +RANGE:ENTITY	PROCESS X CIRCUMSTANCE
take shot	shoot deer	shoot field
(take a shot)	(shoot the deer)	(shoot in the field)
CLASSIFIER = THING	EPITHET + THING	THING X QUALIFIER
parking lot	new car	car park
(a parking lot)	(a new car)	(the car in the park)
EVENT = PARTICLE	EVENT + EVENT	EVENT X QUALITY
shoot up	try shoot	shoot carefully
(shoot up)	(try to shoot)	(shoot carefully)

At clause rank, the TRANSITIVITY roles which have not been considered are Agent and Beneficiary (including Client, Recipient and Receiver). These roles are intermediate between extensions and enhancements, and are accordingly realised both with and without prepositions in clause structure:

Agent: + preposition The ship was stolen **by Ford**.
    − preposition **Ford** stole the ship.

Client: + preposition He bought the present **for Trillian**.
    − preposition He bought **Trillian** the present.

Recipient: + preposition He gave the drink **to Zaphod**.
           − preposition He gave **Zaphod** the drink.

Receiver: + preposition He told the story **to Arthur**.
        − preposition He told **Arthur** the story.

In line with the proposals developed above, the prepositional realisations of these intermediate roles can be taken as enhancing and the non-prepositional realisations as extending.

Matthiessen (1922) sums up the semantic continuity between participants and circumstances as outlined in Fig. 5.22, which also brings out their nuclearity with respect to the Process:

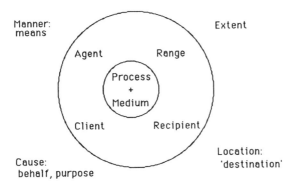

Fig. 5.22. Nuclearity: participants and circumstances (following Matthiessen 1992)

The elaboration, extension and enhancement analysis presented above provides an alternative perspective on peripherality. Matthiessen's diagram can be amended in line with this perspective by treating Process˙Range:process structures as more nuclear than Process˙Medium ones. Range:entities could be left as more peripheral than Mediums since like Agent and Beneficiaries they have both prepositional and non-prepositional realisations (Halliday 1985a:149): *Carl won **the long jump**/Carl won **at the long jump**. The notion of peripherality is extended to nominal and verbal groups in Table 5.14.

Table 5.14. An alternative model of nuclearity

CENTRE	NUCLEUS	MARGIN	PERIPHERY
Process = Range:process	+ Medium + Range:entity	+x Agent +x Beneficiary	x Circumstance
Classifier = Thing	+ Epithet	(+x Numerative?)	x Qualifier
Event = Particle	+ Event (event complex)	(+x causative?)	x Manner adverb

It remains to consider relational clauses, which function to instantiate (Hasan 1985b:82) the relationships of elaboration, extension and enhancement just considered; with relational clauses the grammar works to positively construct the relationships involved rather than simply realising them. Halliday (1985a:307) treats intensive relationals as elaborating, possessives as extending and circumstantials as enhancing:

	ATTRIBUTIVE	IDENTIFYING
=	Ben is a champion	Ben is the champion
+	Ben has the gold medal	Ben's is the gold medal
x	Ben is in the starting blocks	Ben occupies the starting blocks

This interpretation can be adopted here with two reservations. First, descriptive intensive attributive clauses need to be distinguished from classifiying ones:

DESCRIPTIVE:CLASSIFYING::
Ben is fast:Ben is a champion::
Ben isn't vain:Ben isn't a Jamaican now::
Ben was eager:Ben was a go-getter::
Ben is guilty::Ben's just a victim

The descriptive type will be treated as extending here, since they assign qualities to participants in the same way that Epithet˙Thing structures do. The classifying type relates subclasses to their superordinates and is better left as elaborating since its function is similar to that of Classifier˙Thing structures in the nominal group.

Second, possessive clauses which have to do with part/whole relations rather than ownership will be treated as elaborating because of their taxonomic focus. Their function is similar to that of the classifying inten-

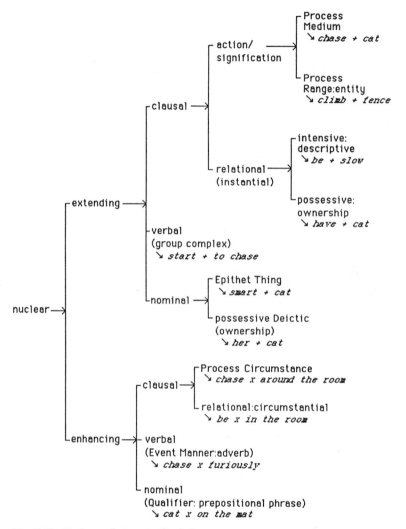

Fig. 5.23. Nuclear relations in English

sives in that they assign parts to wholes, building up composition taxonomies for a given field. In this respect they resemble the Pre-Deictic, Pre-Numerative and possessive Deictic structures discussed above.

OWNERSHIP $(+)$:COMPOSITION $(=)$::
Ben has a dog:Ben has strong legs::
Ben has a house:the house has ten rooms::
Ben owns a car:the car has four doors::
the suit belongs to Flo:the suit has only one leg

The network for nuclear relations is presented as Fig. 5.23 (the category of instantial relations was introduced in Chapter 3; see Hasan 1984a, 1985b).

5.3.4 *Activity sequences*

The final major category of lexical relations to be considered has to do with expectancy relations between activities in activity sequences. These relations are based on the way in which the nuclear configurations outlined above are recurrently sequenced in a given field. A *point* in tennis for example is constituted by a sequence of *shots* within the parameters defined by the game. The joy participants in this field take from the game derives from the way in which players push against these limits. A typical sequence of activities from the activity sequence named point is as follows:

    player + serves
    opponent + returns
    player + volleys
    opponent + lobs
    player + smashes
    opponent + retrieves
    player + smashes
    opponent + misses

The activity sequences in a field are themselves organised into composition taxonomies. A *point* for example has one or more *shots* as its parts. The point (or *rally* if more than one shot is involved) is itself part of a *game*, which is part of a *set*, which may be part of a *match*, which may be part of a *round* in a *tournament*. Depending on the degree of involvement of participants in the field, this taxonomy can be extended further in both directions. With coaching, a shot can be broken down into parts (i.e. treated as an activity sequence in its own right); and tournaments are part of an activity sequence resulting in a player's professional *ranking* or amateur *grading*. Beyond this, one probably has to move from the field of tennis to that of sport in general at the top end of the scale, and from tennis to sport physiology at the bottom.

[professional ranking/amateur grading]
tournament
round
match
set
game
point/rally
shot
[coaching needed to break shot into an activity sequence]

In Chapter 4 (Table 4.7) it was noted that relations between messages can be both modulated and modalised; the resulting consequential relations were outlined as in Table 5.15. Seen in this light, consequential conjunctions can be interpreted as interpersonal interventions by interlocutors as far as logical relations between messages are concerned.

Table 5.15. Modulation and modalization of consequential relations

		MODULATION	MODALIZATION (Effect irrealis)
MANNER (*thus, by*)		potentiality	-
CAUSE:	CONSEQUENCE (*so, because*)	obligation	-
	CONDITION (*then, if*)	obligation	probability
	PURPOSE (*so that*)	obligation & inclination	probability

But whether or not interlocutors use consequential conjunctions to intervene interpersonally in activity sequences, expectancy relations between activities are generated by a field and do obtain. The probability of one activity following another is not usually made explicit. The most common conjunction relating activities in an activity sequence is *and*, alongside the much more occasional realisation of temporal succession (as in text [2:1] above; see discussion in 4.2.4). Conversely, when an unexpected activity occurs, its improbability usually is made explicit; the concessive conjunctions introduced as cancelling causal modulations in Chapter 4 (Table 4.9) are used for this purpose (Table 5.16).

Table 5.16. Concessive and non-concessive consequential relations

	NON-CONCESSIVE	CONCESSIVE
MANNER	by	even by
	thus	but
CONSEQUENCE	because	although/even though
	so/therefore	but/however
CONDITION	if	even if
	then	even then
PURPOSE	in order to	without
	so + inclination	even so

The concessive relation in [5:30] below for example marks the fact that Becker's double faulting was unexpected in the field. In this way it is concessive relations, rather than temporal or consequential ones that provide the main textual evidence for the presence of expectancy relations between activities in activity sequences deriving from a given field.

[5:30] Becker served for the match in the third set
but double faulted three times
to level the set.

For purposes of analysing scientific English it is useful to draw a distinction between expectancy relations and implicational ones. Whereas in most fields probability modalises the relation between activities (one is **likely** to follow another), in science an attempt is made to construct reality in such a way that one activity implies another (the relationship between the two is causally modulated). In the following text for example, one activity follows another by law; in scientific discourse this relation is made explicit through conditional consequential conjunctions (typically *if/then*).

[5:31] We saw that **leaching** was a very prominent process in all hot, wet, forest lands; in deserts because the rainfall is so low, it hardly occurs at all. Instead a reverse process may develop called **calcification**. Water may soak into the ground after rains and dissolve mineral salts in the usual way, but as the surface dries out, this water is drawn upwards like moisture rising through blotting paper. The salts then accumulate in the surface soil as this moisture evaporates; thus desert soils are often rich in mineral salts, particularly calcium, sodium and potassium. Provided the salts are not too concentrated (and their concentration is reduced under irrigation), they contain a plentiful supply of plant foods and can therefore be considered as *fertile soils*. (Sale et al. 1980:55)

The logical structure of the activity sequence calcification outlined here is as follows (from Martin 1989:39):

i.   **If** water soaks into the ground
ii. **then** it will dissolve mineral salts.
iii. **If** it does, **then if** the surface dries out
iv. **then** the water is drawn upwards.
v.   **If** it is, **then if** the water evaporates
vi. **then** salts accumulate in the surface soil.

Accordingly, as far as lexical relations between activities are concerned, a distinction will be drawn between expectancy and implicational relations according to whether one activity is probably followed by another (modalization; activity *a* probably followed by activity *b*) or is absolutely determined by the other (modulation; activity *a* necessarily followed by activity *b*) as in the scientific explanation discussed above (see Fig. 5.24).

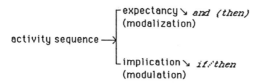

Fig. 5.24. Activity sequence relations

Before moving on to consider the discourse structure of lexical relations in 5.4 below, the terminology being developed for ideational meaning will be reviewed. The description of ideational meaning has now been pursued on three levels: lexicogrammar, discourse semantics and field. At its most basic level a field consists of activity sequences, which are in turn composed of activities, which are themselves made up of actions configuring with people, places and things, all four of which components may be configured with qualities. Activity sequences stand in an unmarked relation to temporally sequenced clauses complexes in lexicogrammar; the grammatical functions (based on Halliday 1985a) which correspond most closely to the field categories just reviewed are outlined in Table 5.17.

Table 5.17. Ideational labelling across levels

FIELD	DISCOURSE SEMANTICS	EXPERIENTIAL GRAMMAR
activity sequence	(unnamed)	clause complex (temporal)
activity	message	Process (& TRANSITIVITY roles)
activity	message part	Event
people & things	message part	Thing
place	message part	Circumstance
quality	message part	Epithet; Manner adverb

The level of discourse semantics is the least differentiated as far as ideational meaning is concerned. This is mainly due to the fact that the description developed here has focussed on relationships between experiential meanings, rather than the experiential meanings themselves. So while it was found important to distinguish between message parts and lexical items, no formal distinctions were drawn among message parts. As work on discourse semantics continues, particularly with respect to grammatical metaphor, it will prove necessary to differentiate technically among the different meanings at this level. As far as *English Text* is concerned, the distinctions made at the levels of field and lexicogrammar are rich enough to carry the burden of the text analyses presented below.

These ideational units at the level of discourse semantics are brought into relation with the interpersonal and textual units proposed in Table 5.18.

Table 5.18. Discourse semantics: units proposed in English Text

INTERPERSONAL	TEXTUAL	IDEATIONAL: logical	experiential
exchange			
move		message	
	participant		message part

5.4 Lexical relations: structure

5.4.1 *Preparing the text*

5.4.1.1 *Unit of analysis*

As has just been reviewed, lexical cohesion is being developed here as an analysis of relations between message parts. A message part is realised congruently as a lexical item and incongruently through one of the elaborating structures defined above. These are reviewed in Table 5.19.

Table 5.19. Congruent and incongruent realisations of message parts

	MULTIPLE LEXICAL ITEMS (incongruent)	SINGLE LEXICAL ITEM (congruent)
CLAUSE	Process = Range:process *act = a role* Process = ritual Location *go = to work*	Process *act* *go*
VERBAL GROUP	Event = Particle *think = over* Event = Leisure event *go = skating*	Event *consider* *skate*
NOMINAL GROUP	Classifier = Thing *skating = rink* Pre-Deictic = Thing *the edge of = the rink* Pre-Numerative = Thing *a pair of = skates* Pre-Epithet = Thing *the largest of = the rinks* Pre-Classifier = Thing *that kind of = rink* Deictic (possessive) = Thing *her = foot*	Thing *rink* *the rink* *the skates* *the rink* *the rink* *the foot*

Separate message parts will be recognized where the grammar itself does the work of constructing elaborations. The following relational clause types will thus be interpreted as instantially connecting two message parts:

RELATIONAL:ATTRIBUTIVE:CLASSIFYING/ INTENSIVE
[5:32]   **Ben** is a **sprinter**.

[4:2:7.n.] That's [[because **it**'s **a low dog**]],

RELATIONAL:ATTRIBUTIVE:COMPOSITION/POSSESSIVE
[5:33]   **The court** has **lines**.

At group and word rank instantial relations are constructed through apposition:

[4:2:9.r.] With the **smaller breeds of dog** such as **Corgis, all the Toy-breeds, Dachshunds and this type of thing** we — as our turn comes,

[5:34]   I met **Ben**, a **friend** of mine from Toronto.

[5:35]   Ben **stroked** (i.e. **lobbed**) the ball over Flo's head.

The analysis of lexical relations in two texts presented below will show some of the ways in which this characterisation of the differences between message parts and lexical items needs to be extended in order to present a full account of experiential cohesion in text.

5.4.1.2 *Experiential metaphor (nominalisation)*

Derivational variants were classified as repetitions in 5.3.2 above, alongside inflexional members of a lexical item's formal scatter. This implied that congruent and incongruent realisations of a particular message part would be treated under this heading. Accordingly, both the verb *stand* and the noun *table* in [4:2:6] would be treated as a repetition of the verb *tabled* in [4:2:6], both of which are antonyms of *ground* (taking *tabled* as metaphorical variant of *stand on the table*).

[4:2]   6.m.   With the Dachshund, a Dachshund is **tabled**.
          8.p.   With the bigger breeds of dog, they're **stood** on the **ground**,
          9.s.   we **stand** our dog on the **table**,

This procedure suggests that grammatical metaphor can be safely passed over as far as lexical cohesion is concerned, by simply unpacking metaphorical realisations of message parts in a text. However, the problem is not as straight-forward as this. *Hind movement, moving all over* and *front movement* for example could be taken as co-hyponyms in the following excerpts from [4:2], given that two of the lexicalisations are elaborating Classifier = Thing structures (*hind movement* and *front movement*) grammatically constructing movement of two different types.

[4:2]   18.vv.   That is [[so the judge can get the **hind movement** of your dog]].
          19.xx.   so as he can see [[the dog **moving all over**]]
            zz.   so as he can see the **front movement**.

Alternatively, *moving all over*, the congruent lexicalisation, could be taken as the base line. Unpacking *hind movement* and *front movement* would mean analysing cohesion among *moving from the back, moving all over* and *moving from the front*, yielding two lexical strings, one built up around repetition (of *moving*) and the other around opposition (*front-all over-back*). This would contrast sharply with the co-hyponymy analysis based on the nominalisations suggested above. The two analyses are displayed in Fig. 5.25.

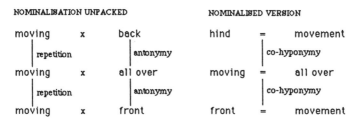

NOMINALISATION UNPACKED   NOMINALISED VERSION

moving   x   back   hind   =   movement
  | repetition | antonymy | co-hyponymy
moving   x   all over   moving   =   all over
  | repetition | antonymy | co-hyponymy
moving   x   front   front   =   movement

Fig. 5.25. Analysis of original nominalised and unpacked versions of [4:2:18-19]

What can be seen from examples such as these is that experiential metaphor is a process that can be used to reconstrue lexical relations in text. Below, nominalisations will be analysed as such when taxonomic relations are considered and unpacked for the interpretation of nuclear structures and expectancy sequences. In this way the taxonomy building contribution of nominalisations to a text can be captured at the same time as the activities they realise are brought into focus with respect to field.

One of the main functions of nominalisation is in fact to build up technical taxonomies of processes in specialised fields (see Chapter 7 below). Once technicalised, these nominalisations are interpretable as things (for example *leaching* and *calcification* in [5:31] above). *Hind movement* and *front movement* may not have reached the status of technical terms in the passage quoted above; their relationship with the embedded clause *moving all over* in [4:2] shows that as grammatical metaphors they are still alive. This is less obvious however with *show stance* in [4:2:9]:

[4:2]   9.t.   we **stand** it in **show stance**,
            w.   that our dog will **stand like a nice statue**,
          12.hh.   that your dog will **stand nice and steady**

The problem here is whether to treat in *show stance, like a nice statue* and *nice and steady* as co-hyponyms, or to treat *show stance* as a technical term naming a particular activity in the field of dog showing, which is then descriptively characterised by *like a nice statue* and *nice and steady*. The decision as to whether *show stance* is a "live" grammatical metaphor or a technical term depends on expert knowledge which is not available to the author. Whichever analysis is most appropriate here, the important point is that technical terms have been nominalised with the creation of field specific superordination and composition taxonomies in mind and should not therefore be unpacked in a synchronic analysis of lexical relations.

The problem of grammatical metaphor and technicality will be taken up again during the analysis of texts in 5.4.2 below.

5.4.1.3 *Lexical rendering*

Another type of "rendering" which needs to be reviewed has to do with substitution and ellipsis and pronominal reference. The issue here is that the more of these phoric items a text has, the less lexical cohesion it will display; and texts have more or less substitution, ellipsis and pronominal reference depending on mode — dialogic texts accompanying a social process will turn out to have far fewer lexical relations than reflective monologic ones (this is of course reflected in their lexical density; see Halliday 1985b/ 1989). This means that some texts may have next to no lexical cohesion at all; and this makes it difficult to measure coherence (through cohesive harmony analysis as developed by Hasan 1984a) or to analyse the text for field. Accordingly, Hasan (1985b:87; 1984a) has developed a technique known as **lexical rendering**, whereby phoric pronouns, substitutes and ellipses are filled in prior to measuring cohesive harmony. The technique is illustrated below for six clauses from text [4:2]. The items rendered are underlined in the original text and the taxonomic lexical relations in each text are displayed to illustrate the kind of difference in lexical cohesion a rendering of this kind effects.

[4:2]   ORIGINAL TEXT
11.aa. The judge has to be able to look into the dog's mouth
   bb. to see
   cc. that **it**'s teeth are perfect.
12.dd. Usually then **he** feels down the neck, along its body,
   ee. and **he** can sort of feel conformation
   ff   by doing **this**,

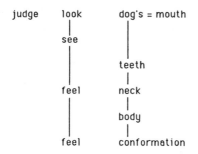

[4:2]   LEXICALLY RENDERED
11.aa   The judge has to be able to look into the dog's mouth
    bb.   to see
    cc.   that the **dog**'s teeth are perfect.
12.dd.   Usually then the **judge** feels down the neck, along the **dog**'s body,
    ee.   and the **judge** can sort of feel conformation
    ff.   through the **judge feeling** down the **neck**, along the **dog**'s **body**,

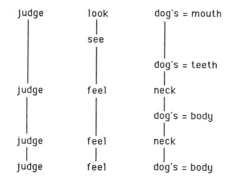

As with the unpacking of grammatical metaphors discussed above, this procedure radically changes a text's mode. This makes it inappropriate for register analysis which attends to contextual dependency. It is however an essential technique when focusing on field or measuring coherence. In most cases analysing a text in its original and in its rendered form provides the richest interpretation. Below a compromise procedure related to that suggested for experiential metaphors above will be pursued. Texts will be analysed in the original when taxonomic relations are considered; then when nuclear and expectancy relations are analysed, a lexically rendered version of the text will be used. This helps to bring the anlaysis of nuclear relations more closely in line with Hasan's work on cohesive harmony (see discussion in 5.5 below). These unpacking and rendering strategies for different types of lexical analysis are summarised in Table 5.20 below.

Table 5.20. Unpacking and rendering strategies adopted by English Text

	EXPERIENTIAL METAPHORS UNPACKED	LEXICAL RENDERING
TAXONOMIC RELATIONS	no	no
NUCLEAR RELATIONS	yes	yes
ACTIVITY RELATIONS	yes	yes

5.4.1.4 *Lexical strings*

All of the discourse structures introduced to this point have been covariate ones, with the exception of the multivariate intrepretation of the exchange introduced in Chapter 2. But even there the multivariate approach presented only a partial picture; covariate tracking and challenging structures had to be developed to fill out the picture. Lexical relations are also covariate structures — message parts depend semantically on each other, and depending message parts are themselves depended on.

The other trend which has been noted is for cohesive items to depend retrospectively on preceding ones. It is exceptional for phoric reference items and conjunctions to point forward in text; "anaphora" is far and away the unmarked relation. The exception once again is exchange structure; questions for example predict following answers, just as answers predict preceding questions. The prospective and retrospective nature of these "adjacency pair" relations was captured through the multivariate analysis ot the exchange which set up mutually expectant exchange functions (e.g. Da1^A2^A1^A2f).

Lexical relations resemble conversational ones more than reference or conjunctive structures. Like moves, and unlike most messages and participants, message parts are not phoric (unless they are ellipsed or substituted for). When lexicalised, they simultaneously depend on preceding message parts and predict ensuing ones. For this reason the dependency line representing the semantic dependency between message parts in text analysis will point neither forward nor backward in the text; the arrows which might have been added to each end of the line to capture the mutual expectancy will omitted to simplify the presentation:

[4:2]   12.dd. Usually then he feels down the **neck**, along its **body**,

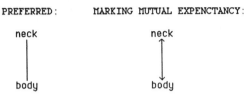

The type and directionality of the dependency structures associated with each of the four major discourse semantic systems proposed in *English Text* are summarised in the following Table 5.21.

Table 5.21. Type of structure and direction of dependency for discourse systems

	STRUCTURE	DIRECTION OF DEPENDENCY
NEGOTIATION	multivariate & covariate	prospective & retrospective
IDENTIFICATION	covariate	retrospective (occasionally cataphoric)
CONJUNCTION	covariate	retrospective (occasionally cataphoric)
IDEATION	covariate	prospective & retrospective

5.4.2 *Text analysis*

5.4.2.1 *Categories*
The texts considered below will be analysed for lexical relations up to the point in delicacy reflected in the following categories. Hyponymy (abbreviated **hyp**) for example will be used for all class-subclass relations (including hyponymy and hyperonymy whether relational or not). The

categories used and the subclasses of relation they range over are outlined
in Table 5.22.

Table 5.22. Categories used for analysis of lexical relations

TAXONOMIC		(INCLUDING)
hyp	hyponymy	(hyponymy, hyperonymy/+ − relational)
cohyp	cohyponymy	
contr	contrast	(cycle, scale, rank, converse, opposition)
syn	synonymy	(attitudinal, experiential)
rep	repetition	(inflexional, derivational, complete)
mer	meronymy	(collective, consistency, constitution/+ − relational)
comer	comeronymy	
NUCLEAR		
+	extension	
x	enhancement	
ACTIVITY		
^	expectancy	

5.4.2.2 *Passes*

Reflecting the break-down of lexical relations into taxonomic, nuclear and
activity relations in 5.3 above, lexical cohesion will be analysed in three passes, one oriented to each of these components. The taxonomic pass will be
restricted to relations associated with people, places, things and qualities,
setting aside taxonomic relations between actions for consideration alongside nuclear relations. As with IDENTIFICATION, message parts will be taken
back once to the nearest taxonomically related message part in the text.
The resulting structures will be referred to as **lexical strings**.

This procedure produces the two string analysis illustrated below for
lexical relations in the first five clauses of text [4:2]. The type of taxonomic
relation depending one message part on the other is marked as a valence on
the dependency line connecting the message parts. The lexicalisations of
the relevant message parts are used to refer to these in the strings. Note
that elaborations are included as single message parts (as with *the centre of*
= *the ring*).

> [4:2]   1.a. What do you have to do in the showing area,
>   b. with the dog on the lead?

2.c. Well, you always walk
    d. with the dog on the left-hand side,
    e. the reason being is [[the judge is standing in the centre of the ring]].

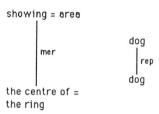

With instantial relations, the elaboration marker = will be used as a valence, classifying the relation as one between message parts rather than within:

[4:2] 9.r. With the smaller breeds of dog **such as** Corgis, all the Toy-breeds, Dachshunds and this type of thing we — as our turn comes,

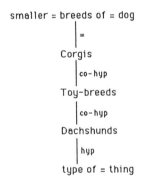

As noted in 5.4.1 above, texts will neither be unpacked as far as experiential metaphor is concerned, nor lexically rendered when taxonomic relations are considered.

The procedure whereby message parts are taken back once to the nearest related message part involves a very particulate view of lexical cohesion. A more field-like perspective (see Pike 1982 on particle, wave and field) can be introduced by depending messages parts on all the preceding message parts deemed relevant. Taking just clause [4:2:9r] in text [4:2] as an example, the lexical string illustrated above can be converted into the following **lattice** in Fig. 5.26.

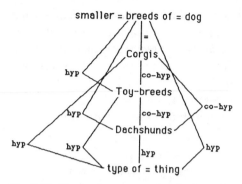

Fig. 5.26. Maximal representation for lexical relations

Whatever the theoretical desirability of this complementary perspective, it is obvious that after just a few clauses the lattice becomes impossible to read as the two dimensional display is saturated, and that after a few clauses more it becomes next to impossible to deconstruct a text accurately without the assistance of a computer to keep track of relations. The "localist" strategy which obtains in the particulate analysis will thus be pursued here. This brings the analysis of lexical relations in line with that of other discourse structures, where retrospective pairing of adjacent items is the norm. Sinclair, Jones and Daley's (1970) optimization of a span of four words on either side of a node provides some indirect empirical support for this particulate interpretation.

Taxonomic relations between actions will be included in the analysis of nuclear relations. This helps simplify the display of lexical strings produced in the taxonomic pass and also helps prepare for the interpretation of cohesive harmony. Accordingly nuclear relations will be grouped into strings based on taxonomic relations among the actions they realise. The following excerpt from text [4:2] has been analysed in this way, producing three strings of nuclear relations: standing the dog, the owners hoping and the judge handling.

The nuclear structures are displayed horizontally across the page, with extension and enhancing relations marked between the relevant message parts. Taxonomically related nuclear structures are listed under each other, with valences marking the taxonomic relation involved. The analysis presented assumes a lexical rendering of the items underlined in the text. In addition, non-finite clauses with missing participants and circumstances are fleshed out, enclosing the rendered material in parentheses to distinguish it from renderings associated with substitution, ellipsis and pronominal reference (e.g. *to see* is rendered *so that the judge can see*; this is an extension to Hasan's proposals for lexical rendering). Group rank extensions and enhancements are included in the analysis and marked between the relevant parts of message parts (e.g. *nice + statue*); the related parts are placed on separate lines in the analysis to distinguish them from clause rank extensions and enhancements.

[4:2]   9.r.   With the smaller breeds of dog such as Corgis, all the Toy-breeds, Dachshunds and this type of thing we — as our turn comes,
       s.   **we** stand **our** dog on the table,
       t.   **we** stand **it** in show stance,
       u.   with the lead, the lead held up,
       v.   hoping
       w.   that **our** dog will stand like a nice statue,
       x.   so as the judge can come.
    10.y.   The judge handles **it**,
       z.   and this is where I'm telling you, temperament plays a big part
   11.aa.   The judge has to be able to look into the dog's mouth
     bb.   to see
     cc.   that **it**'s teeth are perfect.
   12.dd.   Usually then **he** feels down the neck, along **its** body,
     ee.   and **he** can sort of feel conformation
     ff.   by **doing this**,
     gg.   so **you**'re hoping all the time
     hh.   that **your** dog will stand nice and steady
     ii.   so the judge can **do this**
     jj.   and it doesn't hamper **him**
     kk.   handling the dogs.

s.	handler	+	stand	+	dog + handler	x	table
			rep				
t.	handler	+	stand	+	dog	x	show = stance
			rep				
w.			stand	+	dog + handler	x	nice + statue
			rep				
hh.			stand	+	dog + handler	x	nice, steady

v.   (handler) +   hoping
                          |
                          | rep
gg.   handler   +   hoping

y.   judge   +   handles   +   dog
                         |
                         | mer
aa.   judge   +   look   x   dog's = mouth
                         |
                         | syn
bb.   judge   +   see
                         |
                         | co-mer
dd.   (judge)   +   feels   x   neck, body
                         |
                         | syn
ee.   judge   +   feel = conformation
                         |
                         | mer
ff.   (judge)   +   feel   x   neck, body
                         |
                         | co-mer
ii.   judge   +   look   x   dog's = mouth
          judge   +   see
          judge   +   feel   x   neck, body
                         |
                         | mer
kk.   (judge)   +   handling   +   dog

As suggested in 5.4.1 above, for this analysis, and for that of expectancy relations below, the text has been lexically rendered; grammatical metaphors were not an issue in the example considered, but these too would have been unpacked where relevant to the analysis of nuclear relations.

The third pass focusses on expectancy relations. There are two sets of these in the excerpt analysed for nuclear relations above, one a sub-part of the other. The encompassing activity sequence relates the owners tabling the dog to the judge coming and handling it. Then the judge's handling is broken down into looking in the mouth to check its teeth and feeling down its neck and along its body. The two sets of nuclear relations entering into these expectancy relations are outlined below.

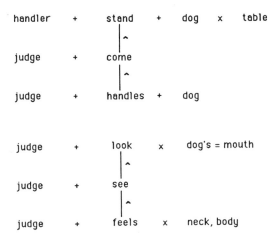

Looking at the text from these three different perspectives compensates in part for the particulate strategy of analysis adopted in each since lexical relations are being analysed simultaneously from three different angles. Interpretations of lexical relations and other aspects of discourse structure from the points of view of wave and field however need to be articulated to complement this perspective. The notions of wave and field will be taken up again in Chapter 6 below when the interaction of discourse semantic and lexicogrammatical structures is considered.

5.4.2.3 *Analysis*

The first text to be considered is text [4:2] which was the point of departure for the CONJUNCTION analyses developed in Chapter 4. The text is a relatively iconic one, focussing step by step on the showing area activity sequence in the field of dog showing. Generically, the text is a procedure; its function is to explain how things are done in a given field. The text is represented below, followed by an analysis of taxonomic relations. To simplify the labelling in this analysis, the category of repetition will be left unmarked.

Taxonomic relations of superordination and composition are included in the same string. Thus the sequence *class-handler-dogs-Dachshund* form part of a single string even though *handlers* and *dogs* are co-meronyms of *class* and *Dachshund* as a hyponym of *dogs*. The decision between recognizing superordination or composition relations between message parts is in many cases an arbitrary one; *handlers* and *dogs* in the above sequence could just as well be treated as types of participant in the ring (co-hyponyms) as members of a class (co-meronyms). Including both types of relation in the same string means that the decision made in these contexts is simply one about the valence assigned rather than one about whether the items belong in separate strings. This minimizes the impact of arbitrary coding decisions on the lexical cohesion analysis.

[4:2]   Question:
    1.a.   What do you have to do in the showing area,
    b.   with the dog on the lead?
    Response:
    2.c.   Well, you always walk
    d.   with the dog on the left-hand side,
    e.   the reason being is [[the judge is standing in the centre of the ring]].
    3.f.   So, therefore, you need to get yourself between your dog and the judge.
    4.g.   The dog (!) must be able to see the dog at all times.
    5.h.   So, usually when a class is going into the ring,
    i.   the first thing it does is:
    j.   the judge is standing in the centre of the ring,
    k.   the people sort of walk the ring, with their dogs,
    l.   and then...we sort of wait.
    6.m.   With the Dachshund, a Dachshund is tabled.
    7.n.   That's [[because it's a low dog]],
    .o.   and the judge goes over that.
    8.p.   With the bigger breeds, of dog, they're stood on the ground,
    q.   because it's easier [[for the judge to handle them]].
    9.r.   With the smaller breeds of dog such as Corgis, all the Toy-breeds, Dachshunds and this type of thing we — as our turn comes,
    s.   we stand our dog on the table,
    t.   we stand it in show stance,
    u.   with the lead, the lead held up,
    v.   hoping
    w.   that our dog will stand like a nice statue,
    x.   so as the judge can come.
    10.y.   The judge handles it,
    z.   and this is [[where I'm telling you, temperament plays a big part]]
    11.aa.   The judge has to be able to look into the dog's mouth
    bb.   to see
    cc.   that it's teeth are perfect.
    12.dd.   Usually then he feels down the neck, along its body,

ee.   and he can sort of feel conformation
ff.   by doing this,
gg.   so you're hoping all the time
hh.   that your dog will stand nice and steady
ii.   so the judge can do this
jj.   and it doesn't hamper him
kk.   handling the dogs.
13.ll.   After the judge has handled and gone over the dog,
mm.   then, you really do [[whatever the judge tells you]].
14.nn.   Basically it is always the same.
15.oo.   He usually says,
pp.   or she usually says,
qq.   "Walk your dog in a triangle."
16.rr.   Now, as I told you already,
ss.   the dog is always walked on the left-hand side.
17.tt.   So, if your judge is standing here,
uu.   we walk away from him that way.
18.vv.   That is [[so the judge can get the hind movement of your dog]].
19.ww.   Then we usually walk sideways like that
xx.   so as he can see [[the dog moving all over]]
yy.   and then we walk back to the judge
zz.   so as he can see the front movement.
20.aaa.   After that he usually tells you
bbb.   to wait over there.
21.ccc.   He proceeds to do that with every dog.
22.ddd.   Then he will say,
eee.   "Line your dog up."
fff.   or "Get the best out of your dog."
ggg.   and he will sum them all up
hhh.   and put them in first, second or third.

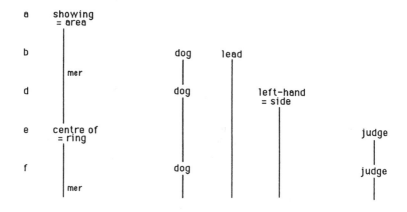

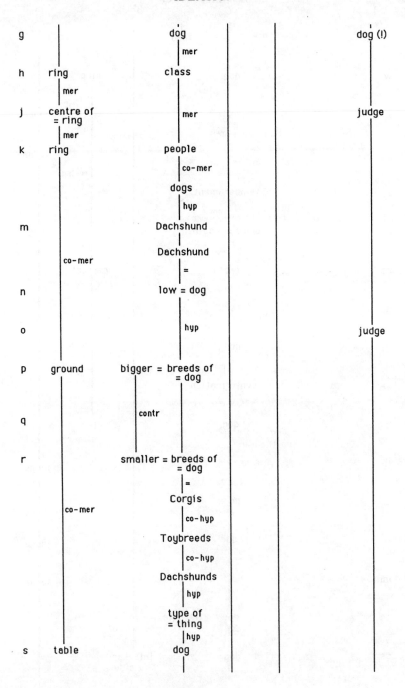

g   dog   dog (!)
                                │ mer
h   ring   class
        │ mer
j   centre of   mer   judge
        = ring
        │ mer
k   ring   people
                               │ co-mer
                              dogs
                               │ hyp
m   Dachshund

                           Dachshund
        │ co-mer   │ =
n   low = dog

o   │ hyp   judge

p   ground   bigger = breeds of
                           = dog

q   │ contr

r   smaller = breeds of
                           = dog
                           │ =
                          Corgis
        │ co-mer   │ co-hyp
                          Toybreeds
                           │ co-hyp
                          Dachshunds
                           │ hyp
                          type of
                          = thing
                           │ hyp
s   table   dog

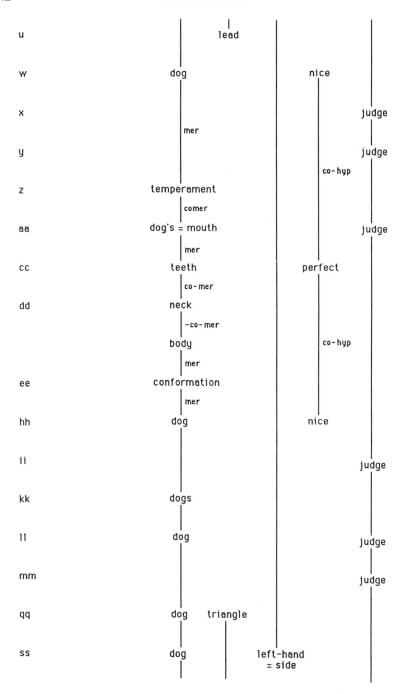

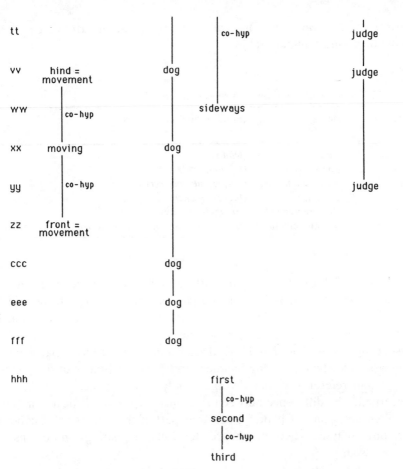

Fig. 5.27. Taxonomic relations in text [4:2]

As can be seen from the analysis of taxonomic relations the text consists of three main lexical strings and a number of minor ones. Of the major strings the judge string is constructed purely out of repetition relations (except for referring to the judge as the dog in [4:2q]; note that it is the nuclear config-uration which insists that this lexicalisation be treated as a slip of the ton-gue). The showing area string on the other hand is built up around meronymy relations. The most complex string is that dealing with the class in the ring. This is developed through meronymy relations in the first part of the text (a-k), switching to hyponymy as breeds of dog are discussed (l-s) and then back to meronymy with respect to the judge examining the various parts of the dogs on show. The realisations of the minor strings are included in the following summary table.

Table 5.23. *Major and minor lexical strings in text [4:2]*

MAJOR STRINGS	MINOR STRINGS	(minor string realisations)
ring	lead	(*lead* x2)
class	dog's position	(*left-hand side* x2)
judge	positive qualities	(*perfect-nice-perfect*)
	class sizes	(*bigger-smaller*)
	class movement	(*triangle-sideways*)
	dog movement	(*front movement-moving all over-hind movement*)

Text [4:2] illustrates nicely the difference between reference chains and lexical strings. They may be co-extensive, as with the judge string in [4:2]; every lexicalisation of the judge is this text refers to the same generic participant, which is also realised through the phoric pronouns *he* or *she*. The class string on the other hand lexicalises a number of different participants: the class as a whole, the dog handlers and different breeds of dog; lexical strings and reference chains diverge widely as far as these meanings are concerned. The difference between reference chains and lexical strings will be taken up again in Chapter 6 below as part of the discussion of cohesive harmony analysis, where procedures for collapsing strings and chains will be discussed.

Nuclear relations are outlined in Fig. 5.28. In addition to rendering participants inherent but not made explicit in non-finite clauses, the Subject of imperative clauses and the Agent of agentless passive clauses have been added to the analysis. These additional renderings are included in parentheses to distinguish them from renderings of substitutes, ellipses and phoric pronouns. Repetition valences will once again be omitted to simplify the presentation. Nuclear structures whose actions do not enter into taxonomic relations with other processes are not included in the analysis.

Moving

a	handler	+	do				in the showing = area	
			mer					
c	handler	+	walk					
			hyp					
f	handler	+	need to + get	+	handler	x	between handler + dog & judge	
			syn					
h	class	+	going			x	into the ring	
			hyp					
k	handler	+	walk			x	the ring	x with handler + dogs
			contr					
l	handler	+	wait					
			contr					
qq	(handler)	+	walk	+	handler + dog	x	in a triangle	
ss	(handler)	+	walk	+	dog	x	on the left-hand = side	
uu	handler	+	walk			x	away from the judge	x that way
ww	handler	+	walk			x	sideways	x like that
yy	handler	+	walk			x	back to the judge	
aaa	handler	+	walk			x	away from judge	x that way
						x	sideways	x like that
			contr			x	back to judge	
bbb	(handler)	+	wait			x	over there	

Handling

g	judge	+	see	+	dog	x at all times
			co-mer			
o	judge	+	goes = over	+	Dachshund	
			syn			
q	judge	+	handle	+	bigger + breeds of = dog	x more easily
			co-mer			
x	judge	+	come			
			co-mer			
y	judge	+	handles	+	handler + dog	
z	judge	+	handles	+	handler + dog	
			mer			
aa	judge	+	look			x into dog's = mouth
			syn			
bb	(judge)	+	see			
			co-mer			
dd	judge	+	feels			x down the neck, along dog's = body
			syn			
ee	judge	+	feel = conformation			
			syn			
ff	(judge)	+	feeling			x down the neck, along dog's = body
			mer			
ii	judge	+	look,			x into dog's = mouth
	judge	+	see,	+	[teeth + perfect]	
	judge	+	feel			x down the neck, along dog's = body
			mer			
kk	judge	+	handling	+	dogs	
			syn			
ll	judge	+	handled & gone + over	+	dog	
			co-mer			
vv	judge	+	get	+	[hind = movement + [dog + handler]]	
			syn			
xx	judge	+	see	+	[dog + moving x all over]	
zz	judge	+	see	+	[front = movement]	

Directions

mm	judge	+	tells	+	handler	
nn	judge	+	tells	+	handler	
oo	judge	+	says			
pp	judge	+	says	+	handler	+ [walk + dog x in a triangle]
aaa	judge	+	tells	+	handler	+ [wait x over there]
ccc	judge	+	proceeds + says,			+ [walk + dog x in a triangle]
	judge	+	tells			+ [wait x over there]
ddd	judge	+	say			+ [[line = up] + dog] + ['get best out of' + dog]

Judging

ggg	judge	+	sum = up co-mer	+	dogs	
hhh	judge	+	put	+	dogs	x in first, second or third

Tabling

m	(handler)	+	stood	+	Dachshund	x on the table
p	(handler)	+	stood	+	bigger + breeds of = dog	x on the ground
s	handler	+	stand	+	handler + dogs	x on the table
t	handler	+	stand	+	dog	x in show = stance
w			stand	+	handler + dogs	x like nice + statue

|
hh   stand   +   handler   x   nice & steady
                              + dogs
                |
jj   dog + stand   +   judge

Lining up

eee   (handler) +   line = up   +   dog
                        |co-hyp
fff   (handler) +   'get the best +   handler
                        out of'   + dog

Dog's position

b   dog   x   on the lead

d   dog   x   on the left-hand
                                            = side

Dog's movement

vv   (dog)   +   moving   x   from the back
                     |
xx   dog   +   moving   x   all over
                     |
zz   (dog)   +   moving   x   from the front

Judge's position

e   judge   +   standing   x   centre of = ring
                     |
j   judge   +   standing   x   centre of = ring
                     |
tt   handler +   standing   x   here
        + judge

Fig. 5.27. Nuclear relations in [4:2]

Notes on the analysis:

(i)   Four exophoric references to an imaginary map of the ring (drawn on the coffee table according to the interviewer Guenter Plum) invoked from tt-bbb have not been rendered as their precise experiential meaning is not recoverable to the analyst: tt *here*, uu *that way*, ww *like that*, aaa *over there*.

(ii)   Text and extended reference have been rendered: z *this*, ff *doing this*, ii *do this*, nn *it*, aaa *after that*, ccc *do that*.

(iii) The non-finite relational processes b *with the dog on the lead* and d *with the dog on the left-hand side* have not been rendered; the Process *be* simply verbalises an enhancing valence in these circumstantial clauses.

(iv)   The activities functioning as Ranges of mental and verbal processes are enclosed in square brackets: bb-cc *see* [*that it's teeth are perfect*] , vv *get* [*the hind movement of your dog*], xx *see* [*the dog moving all over*], zz *see* [*the front movement*], pp-qq *says* [*"Walk your dog in a triangle"*], aaa-bbb *tells* [*you to wait over there*], ddd-fff *say* [*"Line your dog up"*], [*"Get the best out of your dog"*].

(v)   *get the best out of* in fff has been treated as an idiom (i.e. collocationally frozen elaboration) realising a single action, agnate to lexicalisations like *show = off*.

The actions in [4:2] have been organised into four main strings: handlers moving around the ring and tabling their dogs, and the judge handling the dogs and directing handlers. In addition there are five minor strings. The major and minor action strings according to which the display of nuclear relations has been arranged are outlined in Table 5.24.

Table 5.24. Major and minor action strings in text [4:2]

MAJOR ACTION STRINGS	MINOR ACTION STRINGS
handler moving	handler lining up dogs
handler tabling dogs	dog's position
judge handling dogs	dog's movement
judge directing handler	judge's position
	judge judging dogs

One of the chronic problems associated with analysed taxonomic relations between processes is the decision whether to treat the relation as one of superordination or of composition. All of the actions in the handling string can for example be taken either as types of judging or as parts of what a judge does in the ring. *See* and *feels* could for example be analysed either as co-hyponyms (types of handling) or as co-meronyms (parts of handling). The meronymy option has been chosen where available in the analysis presented above; this means that the action strings are oriented towards activity sequences in field, with actions taken as steps in activity sequences. This bias is balanced in part by the interpretation of processes as delicate experiential subclasses of clause in lexicogrammar.

It remains to consider expectancy relations. These are strongly foregrounded in [4:2] since the function of a procedural text is to give a generalised account of goings on with respect to an activity sequence in a particular field. As was noted for the field of tennis in 5.3.4 above, activity sequences are themselves organised into composition taxonomies; in [4:2] for example the judge checking the dog's teeth and feeling conformation are parts of the handling sequence which is itself part of the showing sequence. These part/whole relations are reflected in the episodic structure of [4:2]. This structure is signalled in part through thematic temporally enhancing β clauses which function to introduce episodes:

h	when a class is going into the ring
r	as our turn comes
ll	after the judge has handled and gone over the dog

At the same time text reference may be used to close them:

ff	by doing **this**
ii	so the judge can do **this**
aaa	after **that**
ccc	he proceeds to do **that** with every dog

One or the other or both of these markers in used to signal episodes in [4:2]. The activity sequence presented is broken into four parts in the analysis presented below, each consisting of several activities. Because of the texts' mode (spontaneous spoken monologue) the text is somewhat less iconic as far as expectancy relations are concerned than procedures found in recipe books or instruction manuals. And because of the dialogic potential inherent in the interview situation, the text is punctuated at several points with explanatory comments breaking up the activity sequence presented.

Walking the ring

when a class is going into the ring
^

the handlers sort of walk the ring with their dogs
^

and **then** the handlers sort of wait
^

Handling

as the handler and dog's turn comes
^

the handler stand the handler's dog on the table
^

so as the judge can come
^

the judge handles the dog: the judge has to be able to look into the dog's mouth
^

                                  then he feels down the neck, along the body
^

Movement

[**after** the judge has handled...**then** you do...]

the judge says "Walk your dog in a triangle."
^

handler and dog walk away from the judge like that
^

then the handler and dog walk sideways like that
^

and then the handler and dog walk back to the judge
^

after that the judge usually tells the handler to wait over there
^

the judge **proceeds** to do that with every dog
^

Evaluation

Then the judge will say "Line your dog up" or "Get the best out of your dog."
^

and the judge will sum all the dogs up
^

and the judge will put the dogs in first, second or third

Fig. 5.29. Activity relations in text [4:2]

The second text to be considered, text [5:36] is *The Sydney Morning Herald*'s account of Australia's historic victory in the 1983 America's Cup. Generically, [5:36] is a recount rather than a procedure or news story; its function is give an account of what happened during the deciding race of the series (not to explain how to win deciding races as in a procedure nor to focus on the results as in a news story, which would have begun with the end of the race, not the beginning). The text is accompanied by the diagram outlining the structure of the race course and the position of the yachts at the end of each leg. The text is a more technical one than [4:2], requiring more "inside" knowledge for its interpretation; this again reflects the text's function which is not that of explaining what happens to an outsider (as was the case in [4:2]). It is also more lexically dense and more abstract (i.e. makes more use of experiential metaphor).

[5:36]   **Race 7**
         Tension right to the end
a   With a spectator fleet of 2,000 assembled under a cloudless sky
b   to watch the deciding race of the America's Cup,
c   the cup tension was at its highest point in 132 years -
d   then the wind shifted.

e   The light northerly breeze turned 20 degrees to the east three
         minutes before the start of the race
f   and the race was delayed.

g   As the yachts waited for the breeze to steady,
h   it faded altogether
i   and the race was postponed.
j   A lay day followed,
k   the last available to either team.
l   The race got under way at last three days later with a 10-knot wind.

m   The two boats followed each other closely through the pre-race
         manoeuvres,
n   Liberty crossing the line eight seconds ahead of Australia II.
o   They separated,
p   the Australians tacking left
q   and the Americans right.

r   It was not known which was leading
s   until they crossed after 30 minutes:
t   Australia II was ahead by about one boat-length.
u   Liberty veered left this time,
v   left free to move by the Australians.

w   When the boats next crossed, at the first mark,
x   Liberty was ahead by 29 seconds.

y   At the second mark the Americans had increased their lead to 46 seconds.
z   This was cut to 23 seconds at the third mark
aa   after the Australians hoisted a larger spinnaker.

bb   Over the next two legs the yachts were at the mercy of the breeze,
cc   their booms set square to their hulls.

dd   Liberty surged ahead
ee   when she caught a puff on the third leg,
ff   but relinguished the lead on the fourth.
gg   She struck a windless hole
hh   which cut her lead to a couple of boat lengths.

ii   The faster yacht prevailed.
jj   When they crossed about two-thirds down the leg
kk   Australia II was leading by the same margin.
ll   She was 21 seconds ahead around the fifth mark.

mm   Australia II blocked the Americans for the rest of the race.
nn   Had the Australians conceded their covering advantage,
oo   Liberty would almost certainly have surged ahead.

pp   The Australians followed every move the Americans made,
qq   tacking with them 45 times in the last leg.

rr   As a last, desperate measure, Conner tacked far to the right,
ss   scattering the spectator fleet

tt   But it was to no avail -
uu   Australia II finished 41 seconds in front of Liberty.

vv   Although Conner was in tears after the race,
ww   there were no protests.
xx   He conceded graciously.

yy   He said:
zz   "Today Australia II was just the better boat
aaa   and they beat us.
bbb   We have no excuses."

ccc   The American syndicate head, however, was not as sportmanlike.
ddd   Mr Ed du Moulin said:
eee   "I still believe Dennis Conner is the best 12-metre skipper in the world, with
the best crew and the best non-peculiar 12-metre."
(The Sydney Morning Herald, Special Edition — 4 Page lift-Off Souvenir
Wednesday September 28, 1983. p. 4)

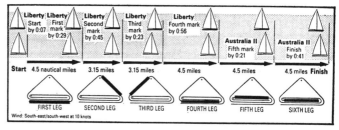

RACE 7

Tension right to the end

With a spectator fleet of 2,000 assembled under a cloudless sky to watch the deciding race of the America's Cup, the cup tension was at its highest point in 132 years — then the wind shifted.

The light northerly breeze turned 20 degrees to the east three minutes before the start and the race was delayed.

As the yachts waited for the breeze to steady, it faded altogether and the race was postponed. A lay day followed, the last available to either team. The race got under way at last three days later with a 10-knot wind.

The two boats followed each other closely through the pre-race manoeuvres, Liberty crossing the line eight seconds ahead of Australia II. They separated, the Australians tacking left and the Americans right.

It was not known which was leading until they crossed after 30 minutes: Australia II was ahead by about one boat-length. Liberty veered left this time, left free to move by the Australians.

When the boats next crossed, at the first mark, Liberty was ahead by 29 seconds.

At the second mark the Americans had increased their lead to 46 seconds. This was cut to 23 seconds at the third mark after the Australians hoisted a larger spinnaker.

Over the next two legs the yachts were at the mercy of the breeze, their booms set square to their hulls.

Liberty surged ahead when she caught a puff on the third leg, but relinquished the lead on the fourth. She struck a windless hole which cut her lead to a couple of boat lengths.

The faster yacht prevailed. When they crossed about two-thirds down the leg Australia II was leading by the same margin. She was 21 seconds ahead around the fifth mark.

Australia II blocked the Americans for the rest of the race. Had the Australians conceded their covering advantage, Liberty would almost certainly have surged ahead.

The Australians followed every move the Americans made, tacking with them 45 times in the last leg.

As a last, desperate measure, Conner tacked far to the right, scattering the spectator fleet.

But it was to no avail — Australia II finished 41 seconds in front of Liberty.

Although Conner was in tears after the race, there were no protests. He conceded graciously.

He said: "Today Australia II was just the better boat and they beat us. We have no excuses."

The American syndicate head, however, was not as sportsmanlike. Mr Ed du Moulin said: "I still believe Dennis Conner is the best 12-metre skipper in the world, with the best crew and the best non-peculiar 12-metre."

Reproduced by permission from The Sydney Morning Herald, September 28, 1983.

Taxonomic relations in [5:36], again excluding actions, are outlined in Fig. 5.30. The three strings dealing with people (the competing teams), places (the race course) and things (the boats; but not the weather conditions which are handled below) are handled first; then minor strings are considered. The lexical density of this text is such (compared with [4:2]) that it is difficult to include all of its lexical strings on a single page. The repetition valence has again been omitted as unmarked; in addition, the co-hyponym valence connecting numerals has been set aside.

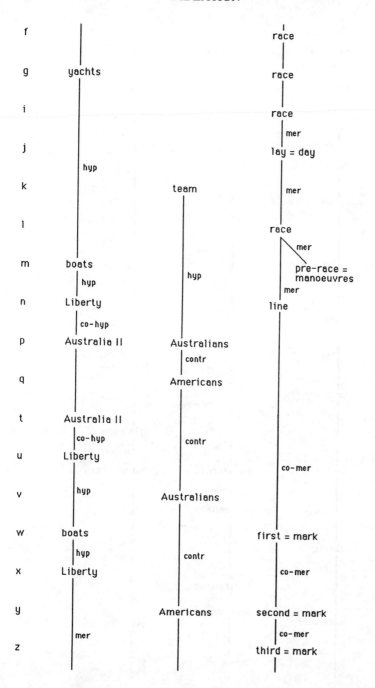

f			race
g	yachts		race
i			race
			mer
j			lay = day
	hyp		
k		team	mer
l			race
			mer
m	boats	hyp	pre-race = manoeuvres
	hyp		mer
n	Liberty		line
	co-hyp		
p	Australia II	Australians	
		contr	
q		Americans	
t	Australia II		
	co-hyp	contr	
u	Liberty		co-mer
v	hyp	Australians	
w	boats		first = mark
	hyp	contr	
x	Liberty		co-mer
y		Americans	second = mark
	mer	co-mer	co-mer
z			third = mark

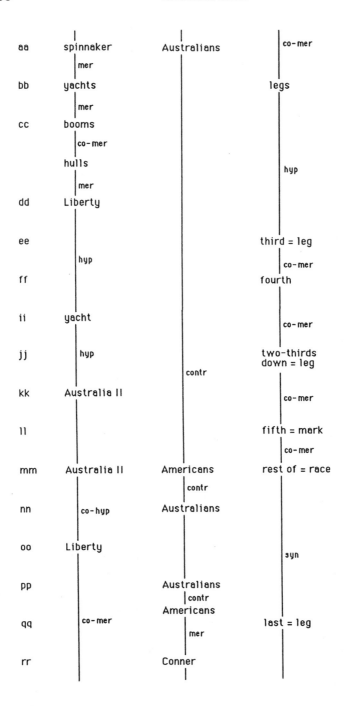

			co-mer
aa	spinnaker	Australians	
	mer		
bb	yachts		legs
	mer		
cc	booms		
	co-mer		
	hulls		hyp
	mer		
dd	Liberty		
ee			third = leg
	hyp		co-mer
ff			fourth
ii	yacht		co-mer
jj	hyp		two-thirds down = leg
		contr	
kk	Australia II		co-mer
ll			fifth = mark
			co-mer
mm	Australia II	Americans	rest of = race
		contr	
nn	co-hyp	Australians	
oo	Liberty		syn
pp		Australians	
		contr	
		Americans	
qq	co-mer		last = leg
		mer	
rr		Conner	

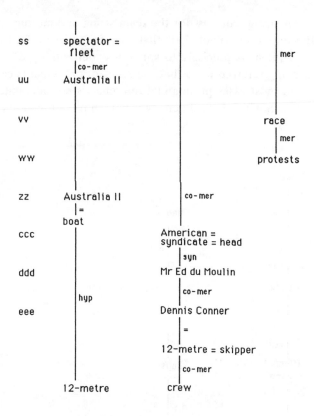

Fig. 5.30. Taxonomic relations in [5:36]: major strings

The three string could have been arranged in different ways. The teams string could have been split into one for the Australian and another for the American team and the boat string could have been divided up yacht by yacht (Liberty and Australia II); conversely the team string could have been added to the boat string via meronymy relations, taking the crew as part of their boat. The distinction between the different boats and crews would however be brought out clearly in a IDENTIFICATION analysis and so need not be invoked criterially here. The people, places and things division complements this perspective and is additionally motivated by the different types of relation predominating in the different strings: hyponymy and meronymy for the boat string, contrast for the team string and meronymy for the race itself. It is important to note here that one of the reasons for the high lexical density in [5:36] is precisely to sort out experientially which crews and boats are being referred to so that the relevant participants can be clearly identified; in most cases pronominal reference is not adequate. This illustrates one way in which lexical density is not simply a function of mode.

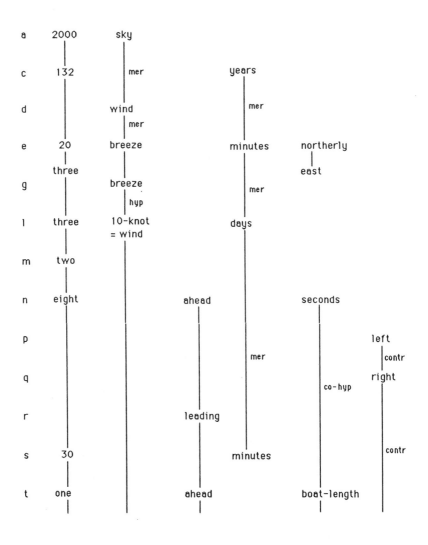

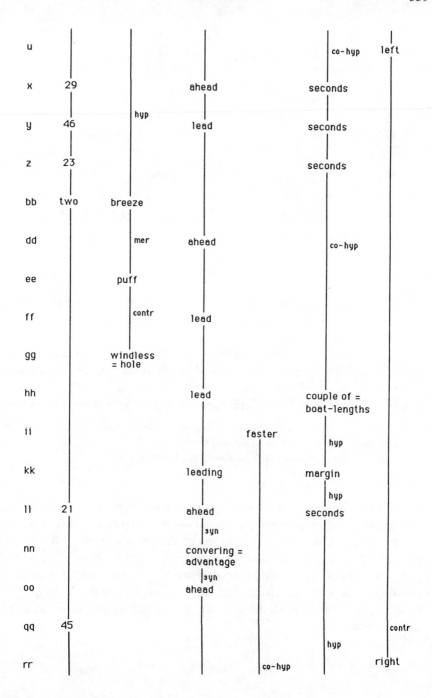

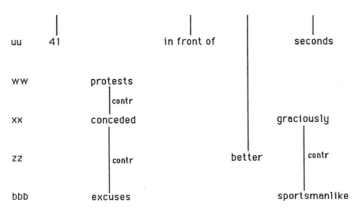

Fig. 5.31. Taxonomic relations in [5:36]: remaining strings

The major remaining strings focus on measurement. There is a long string of numerals running through the text which combines grammatically first with location in time (*in 132 years, three minutes before the start, three days later, after 30 minutes*) and then with the extent of one or the other yacht's lead: *eight seconds ahead, ahead by about one boat length, ahead by 29 seconds, increased their lead to 46 seconds* and so on. The lead string ranges across a number of different grammatical classes and lexical items:

preposition	**ahead of** Australia (n), **in front of** Liberty (uu)
adjective	was **ahead** by about one boat-length (t)
noun	their **lead** (y), their covering **advantage** (nn)
adverb	surged **ahead** (dd)
verb	was **leading** (kk)

These have all been treated simply as repetitions here; but the diversification creates problems for the analysis of nuclear relations — just how many of these realisations are to be treated as the **process** of one boat leading another? The TRANSITIVITY structures associated with each are quite varied, as the nuclear relations summarised below show. Both material and relational processes are involved; and the relationship 'being in front of' is realised as a Process, as Medium, as Range and as Circumstances of manner and location:

Table 5.25. Diversified realisations of 'leading' in [5:36]

Medium	**leading**		Manner:*by* amount
Medium	*be*	Range:**ahead**	Manner:*by* amount
Medium	*surge*		Manner:**ahead**
Agent	*cut/increase*	Medium:**lead**	Location:*to* amount
Agent	*relinquish*	Medium:**lead**	
Agent	*concede*	Medium: *covering* **advantage**	
Agent	*cross*	Medium:*line*	Location:**ahead of**
Medium	*finish*		Location:**in front of**

This diversification reflects the fundamental semantic continuity between processes and prepositions (minor processes) in English as realisations of relationships between entities. Halliday (1985a:189-191) analyses prepositions as minor processes, reflecting proportionalities between prepositions and non-finite verbs of the following kind:

PREPOSITION:NON-FINITE PROCESS::
near the house:adjoining the house::
without a hat:not wearing a hat::
about that essay:concerning that essay::
with Ben:including Ben::
due to bad weather:resulting from bad weather:
before the storm:preceding the storm::
for Ben:to help Ben
behind Ben by one second:following Ben by one second::
ahead of Liberty by 21 seconds:**leading** Liberty by 21 seconds

The semantic continuity among the various realisations of 'being in front of' are outlined as a scale in the following examples. Text [5:36] makes use of most of these to describe the lead changing hands in the final race of the America's Cup.

the boat **ahead of** Liberty	MINOR PROCESS: qualifying phrase
the boat was **ahead of** Liberty	MINOR PROCESS: attributive phrase
the boat was **ahead**	QUALITY OF THING: attributive word
the boat got **ahead**	QUALITY OF THING: phased relational
the boat surged **ahead**	QUALITY OF PROCESS: material
the boat was **leading**	MAJOR PROCESS: middle
the boat was **leading** Liberty	MAJOR PROCESS: effective
the boat had a **lead** on Liberty	NOMINALISED: possessive Attribute

the boat took the **lead** on Liberty	NOMINALISED: Range
the boat relinquished its **lead**	NOMINALISED: Medium
their **lead** won them the Cup	NOMINALISED: Agent

This diversification suggests that the notion of incongruence between message part and lexical item needs to be extended beyond the notions of elaboration and experiential metaphor introduced above. Similar problems arise in the interpretation of other strings:

WINNING

ii   The faster yacht **prevailed**
uu   Australia II **finished 41 seconds in front of** Liberty
aaa they **beat** us

CONVERING

v   **left free to move** by the Americans
mm Australia II **blocked** the Americans for the rest of the race
nn   Had the Australians **conceded their covering advantage**
pp   The Australians **followed every move** the Americans made

CONCEDING

ww there were **no protests**
xx   He **conceded graciously**
bbb We have **no excuses**
aaa The American syndicate head however was not as **sportsmanlike**

It is probable that some kind of componential analysis will have to be invoked to capture the various realisations of semantic motifs of this kind. This unfortunately is beyond the scope of the present volume.

Nuclear relations in [5:36] are outlined in Fig. 5.32. Once again the problem of how to split up or conjoin strings arises. In doubtful cases the way in which a class of actions is extended or enhanced can be used criterially to arrange the display. In [5:36] for example the actions of the yachts during the race are divided into three main strings: manoeuvering, covering and leading. Proto-typically, the manoeuvering actions are extended by a Medium and enhanced by a Circumstance of direction, the covering actions are extended by and Agent and a Medium, and the leading actions are extended by a Medium and enhanced by a Circumstance of measure. These configurations are outlined below.

MANOEUVERING

p   Medium:*Australians*   Process:*tacked*   Circumstance:*left*

COVERING

mm Agent:*Australia II*   Process:*blocked*   Medium:*Americans*

LEADING
kk   Medium:*Australia II*   Process:*leading*   Circumstance:*by a couple of boat lengths*

By dividing up the action strings in this way with extension and enhancements, the ways in which the taxonomic strings associated with people, places, things and qualities analysed in the first pass interact with action strings can be clearly illustrated.

Grammatical metaphors have been unpacked in the following analysis; the metaphors themselves are enclosed in square brackets below the unpacking at the points where this has been done; e.g. *was not as sportsmanlike* was unpacked to *behaved unsportingly* in order to relate du Moulin's behaviour to Conner's. The taxonomic relations noted take into account any group rank extensions or enhancements associated with the action; thus *conceded* x *graciously* is taken as contrasting with *was not sportsmanlike* (unpacked as *behaved* x *unsportingly*).

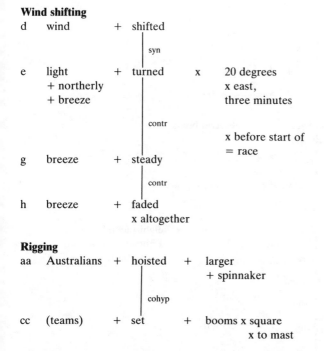

Wind shifting

d   wind   +   shifted

| syn

e   light   +   turned   x   20 degrees
    + northerly   x east,
    + breeze   three minutes

| contr
                       x before start of
                       = race

g   breeze   +   steady

| contr

h   breeze   +   faded
                  x altogether

Rigging

aa   Australians   +   hoisted   +   larger
                                      + spinnaker

| cohyp

cc   (teams)   +   set   +   booms x square
                                     x to mast

Catching wind

ee   Liberty   +   caught   +   puff of   x   on third = leg
                                     = wind

                       | contr

gg   Liberty   +   struck   +   windless
                                  = hole

Race starting

f   race   +   delayed

            | cohyp

i   race   +   postponed

            | contr

l   race   +   got = under way   x   three days later,
                                    with 10-knot
                                    = wind

Fleet assembling

a   spectator   +   assembled   x   under cloudless
    = fleet   + sky
    x 2000 | contr

rr   spectator   +   scattering   +   Conner
    + fleet

Boats manoeuvering

m   two boats   +   followed   +   two boats
                   x closely

                   | hyp

     two boats   +   manoeuvering   x   before race

                   | comer

n   Liberty   +   crossing   +   line   x   eight seconds
                                         x ahead of
                   | comer   Australia II

o   two boats   +   separated

                   | cohyp

p   Australians   +   tacking   x   left

q	Americans	+	tacking		x	right

cohyp

s	two boats	+	crossed		x	after 30 minutes

cohyp

u	Liberty	+	veered		x	left

cohyp

w	boats	+	crossed		x	at first = mark
jj	boats	+	crossed		x	two-thirds down = leg

cohyp

qq	(Australians)	+	tacking		x	with Americans, 45 times x last = leg

rr	Conner	+	tacked		x	far to right

Covering

v	Australians	+	left free to x move	+	(Liberty)

contr

mm	Australia II	+	blocked	+	Americans x for rest of = race

contr

nn	Australians	+	stopped + covering [conceded covering advantage]	+	Americans

contr

pp	Australians	+	covered ['followed every move']	+	Americans

Boats leading

r	boat	+	leading
t	Australia II	+	leading [was ahead]	x	by about one boat-length

x   Liberty   +   leading   x   by 29 seconds
                        [was ahead]

y   Americans   +   leading   x   to 46 seconds,
                        [increased lead]   at second
                                                 = mark

                          | contr

z   (Australians) +   losing   x   to 23 seconds,
                        [cut lead]   at third = mark

                          | contr

dd   Liberty   +   leading
                        x more & more
                        [surged ahead]

                          | contr

ff   Liberty   +   leading   x   on the fourth
                        x less & less
                        [relinquished lead]

                          | contr

hh   Liberty   +   leading   x   by couple of
                        [cut lead]   = boat-lengths

                          | hyp

kk   Australia II +   leading   x   by couple of
                                                 = boat-lenghts

                          |

ll   Australia II +   leading   x   by 21 seconds
                        [was ahead]

                          | hyp

oo   Liberty   +   leading
                        [surged ahead]

                          | hyp

uu   Australia II +   leading   x   by 41 seconds
                        x at finish
                        [finished in front of]

Victory
ii   faster   +   prevailed
      + yacht

                          | hyp

aaa   Australians   +   beat   +   Americans

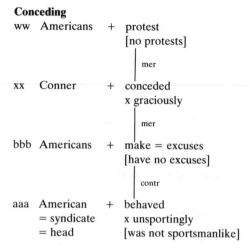

Conceding

ww   Americans   +   protest
                     [no protests]

|
mer

xx   Conner   +   conceded
                  x graciously

|
mer

bbb Americans +   make = excuses
                    [have no excuses]

|
contr

aaa American   +   behaved
     = syndicate   x unsportingly
     = head   [was not sportsmanlike]

Fig. 5.32. Nuclear relations in [5:36]

Because of the text's genre, recount rather than procedure, the realisation of activity sequences (see Fig. 5.33) is more fragmented than in text [4:2]; and some of the expectancy relations which are recursive in the field (for example tacking and covering) are realised more than once without this being felt as a repetition (cf. [4:2ccc] *He proceeds to do that with every dog* above). The only activity sequence which is realised at any length is that having to do with delaying the start of the race which involves five nuclear configurations. One of the field's expectancy relations is explicitly countered concessively in the clause complex [5:36vv-ww]. **Although** *Conner was in tears after the race, there were no protests.* The countered expectancy makes the ideological stance of the recount rather clear.

Spectators gathering
a   a spectactor fleet of 2,000 assembled under a cloudless sky
    ^
b   to watch the deciding race of the America's Cup

Delay
d   the wind shifted
    ^
f   the race was delayed
    ^

g   the yachts waited
     ^

h   the breeze failed altogether
     ^

i   the race was postponed

Starting
l   the boats jockeyed for position
     [the pre-race manoeuvres]
     ^

m   the race got under way
     ^

n   Liberty crossing the line eight seconds ahead of Australia II

Tacking
o   the boats separated, the Australians tacking left and the Americans
     right
     ^

s   the boats crossed

u   Liberty veered left this time
     ^

w   when the boats next crossed

Not covering
v   (Liberty was) left free to move by the Australians
     ^

u   Liberty veered left this time

nn   Had the Australians stopped covering
     [Had the Australians conceded their covering advantage]
     ^

oo   Liberty would almost certainly have surged ahead

Covering
jj   when the boats crossed about two-thirds down the leg
     ^

mm   The Australians blocked the Americans for the rest of the race

pp   Every time the Americans moved
     ^

     the Australians followed
     [The Australians followed every move the Americans made]

rr   As a last desperate measure, Conner tacked far to the right
     ^

qq   the Australians followed
     [The Australians followed every move the Americans made]

Chasing wind

ee   Liberty caught a puff on the third leg
      ^

dd   Liberty surged ahead

gg   Liberty struck a windless hole
      ^

hh   windless hole cut Liberty's lead to a couple of boat lengths

Conceding

vv   Although Conner was in tears after the race
      ^

ww   Conner did not protest
      ^

xx   Conner conceded graciously

Fig. 5.33 Activity relations in text [5:36]

5.4.2.4 *Kickball*

At this point it is possible to return to text [5:1] and be quite explicit about the nature of the misunderstanding that has occurred. Up to message [5:1y],

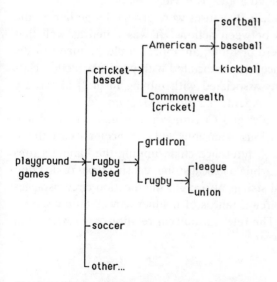

Fig. 5.34 Field taxonomy for playground games

lexical relations in [5:1] can be read as realising either of two fields — kickball or soccer. However, in [5:1y] a nuclear configuration occurs which cannot realise a soccer activity: I + got = (a home = run). The mother then intervenes to negotiate the correct interpretation in messages [5:1z-ff]. The misreading shows the importance of treating fields themselves as taxonomically related, with kickball and baseball as co-hyponyms — subfields of one type of school playground sport.

5.5 Lexical relations and cohesive harmony

The approach to lexical relations developed here represents one of two major extensions of the analysis of lexical cohesion as it was outlined in Halliday and Hasan (1976). The other has been developed by Hasan in her work on cohesive harmony (1984a, 1985b). The two approaches have different goals. The intepretation of lexical relations developed here is an attempt to refine lexical cohesion analysis in the direction of the register variable field. Hasan on the other hand has been concerned with developing a measure of coherence across texts. In spite of these different goals there is considerable convergence across the two approaches, especially with respect to what were treated above as nuclear relations.

As was noted above, nuclear structures were grouped together on the basis of taxonomic relations between actions. It was noted as well that where different groupings were possible, an appeal could be made to the kinds of extension and enhancement associated with particular action classes. For example, the actions associated with tabling in [4:2] above are canonically extended through Agent: 'handler', Medium: 'dog', Circumstance of location: 'ground/table' and Circumstance of manner: 'nice and steady' configurations. The various extensions and enhancements are themselves taxonomically related. A reference chain uniting the handlers runs through the Agent extension, while a lexical string realising types of dog runs through the Medium. Lexical strings also unite the location circumstances (*ground* and *table*) and the circumstances of manner as well (*show stance, nice statue, nice and steady*). The relevant nulcear relations are reviewed in Fig. 5.35.

Tabling

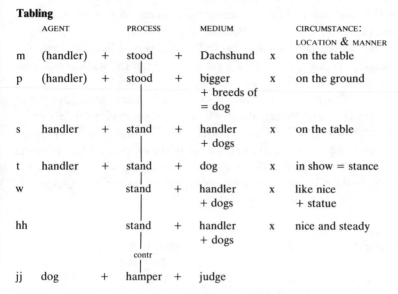

	AGENT		PROCESS		MEDIUM		CIRCUMSTANCE: LOCATION & MANNER
m	(handler)	+	stood	+	Dachshund	x	on the table
p	(handler)	+	stood	+	bigger + breeds of = dog	x	on the ground
s	handler	+	stand	+	handler + dogs	x	on the table
t	handler	+	stand	+	dog	x	in show = stance
w			stand	+	handler + dogs	x	like nice + statue
hh			stand contr	+	handler + dogs	x	nice and steady
jj	dog	+	hamper	+	judge		

Fig. 5.35. Nuclear structures for 'tabling' in text [4:2]

Whenever two or more members of the same string or chain stand in the same TRANSITIVITY relations to two or more members of another string or chain, Hasan's decribes the strings and chains as **interacting**. And she argues that the amount of chain interaction in a text is a function of its coherence. Cohesive harmony analysis will be taken up in more detail in Chapter 6 below. The main point to note at this stage is that the analysis of nuclear relations can be used as the basis for measuring chain interaction in text.

The main differences between nuclear relations and cohesive harmony analysis is that Hasan's approach is based on lexical items rather than message parts and built up around TRANSITIVITY relations rather than extending and enhancing ones. This is because nuclear relations obtain at the level of discourse semantics in the model being developed here, with message parts realised by one or more lexical items and the elaboration, extension, enhancement analysis stratified with respect to TRANSITIVITY and group rank experiential grammar.

The major advantage of the stratified approach is related to the problem of grammatical metaphor. Being less tied to lexicogrammar, the nuclear relations analysis is freed to recognise semantic continuities across a diversified range of realisations. Because the TRANSITIVITY structures are so varied, cohesive harmony analysis would give a very different account of chain interaction among the following messages than the nuclear relations analysis re-presented in Fig. 5.36. Australia II is an Actor in [5:36kk] but a Carier in [5:36ll]; similarly the Americans are a Medium in [5:36y] but an Agent in [5:36dd]; and 'being ahead of' is variously realised as a Process [5:36kk], Attribute [5:36ll], Goal [5:36y] and Circumstance [5:36dd]. So while the convergence between the cohesive harmony and nuclear relations analyses are instructive, the differences are as significant — particularly with respect to the arguments for triple articulation presented in Chapter 1.

Boats leading

kk	Australia II	+	leading	x	by couple of = boat-lengths
ll	Australia II	+	leading [was ahead]	x	by 21 seconds
y	Americans	+	leading [increased lead]	x	to 46 seconds, at second = mark
dd	Liberty	+	leading x more & more [surged ahead]		

Fig. 5.36. Nuclear structures for 'leading' in text [5:36]

5.6 Lexical relations and discourse semantics

This chapter concludes the presentation of the four major discourse systems developed in this book. Lexical relations represent the discourse semantics of experiential meaning. The association of discourse systems with metafunctions and their unmarked realisations in lexicogrammar can now be summarised as in Table 5.26.

Like reference chains and conjunctive structures, lexical strings were treated as covariate structures; messages parts are typically both depending and depended on. However, it was pointed out that lexicalised message parts are not phoric and that the retrospective dependency that charac-

Table 5.26. Unmarked realisations for discourse semantics systems in lexicogrammar

(DISCOURSE SYSTEM)	METAFUNCTION	LEXICOGRAMMATICALISATION
IDEATION	experiential	TRANSITIVITY; group rank experiential grammar; lexis as delicate grammar; collocation
CONJUNCTION	logical	clause complex: LOGICO-SEMANTICS & INTERDEPENDENCY
IDENTIFICATION	textual	nominal group: DEIXIS
NEGOTIATION	interpersonal	clause: MOOD

terised phoric reference items and conjunctions was not relevant. Rather message parts enter into relationships of mutual expectancy in text, fulfilling predictions deriving from preceding text at the same time as they create expectancies about what will follow. In this respect lexical relations are more field-like than particulate in nature, and it was suggested in 5.4.1.6 above that they might be better modelled as a kind of lattice rather than as a string if the relevant technology were available for keeping track of all the interdependencies involved and making them accessible once determined.

While message parts are not in themselves phoric, they may be realised phorically, through the systems of SUBSTITUTION and ELLIPSIS at group rank in lexicogrammar. These systems have been presented in detail in Halliday and Hasan (1976) and their discussion has been assumed throughout *English Text*. It is important to review here however the continuity between nominal and verbal ellipses and substitutes and the taxonomic cline from general superordinate to more specific hyponymic items. This grading is outlined in Table 5.27 and illustrated for nominal and verbal realisations of message parts below (see especially Halliday and Hasan 1976:106 & 129). Hasan (1985b:74) generalises these relationships under the heading co-classification.

Table 5.27. General to specific grading of substitution, ellipsis and taxonomic relations

	NOMINAL	VERBAL
ellipsis	-	-
substitution	one, ones	do, do so
pro-noun/verb	one, thing	do, happen
general noun/verb	thing, person, stuff etc.	do, take, make etc.
superordinate	ship (air/space/sailing)	attack
↑	boat	race
	sail-boat	sail
↓	yacht	manoeuvre
hyponym	12-metre	tack

Verbal scale

ELLIPSIS

[5:37]   Will they tack now?
           - They may.

SUBSTITUTION

[5:38]   Do they tack often enough?
           - I don't believe they **do**.

PRO-VERB

[5:39]   What are they **doing**?
           - Tacking.

GENERAL VERB

[5:40]   Will they tack?
           - They should **make** a move now.

SUPERORDINATE

[5:41]   Will they tack?
           - They should **attack** now.

[5:42]   Should they tack right?
           - It'd be wise to **race** over there now.

[5:43]   Should they tack left now?
           - They ought to **sail** there, yes.

HYPONYM

[5:44]   Did they tack right?
           - Great **manoeuvering**!

Nominal scale

ELLIPSIS
[5:45] He's skippered one winning 12-metre;
and he'd like to skipper another.

SUBSTITUTION
[5:46] He's skippered one winning 12-metre;
he'd like to skipper another **one**.

PRO-NOUN
[5:47] He's skippered one winning 12-metre;
the **thing** he needs is another one.

GENERAL NOUN
[5:48] He's skippered one winning 12-metre;
he's in love with the silly **thing**.

SUPERORDINATE
[5:49] He's skippered one winning 12-metre;
he'd hate a losing **ship**.

[5:50] He's skippered one winning 12-metre;
and he needs a new **boat**.

[5:51] He's skippered one winning 12-metre;
now he'll try a smaller **sail-boat**.

HYPONYM
[5:52] He's skippered one winning 12-metre;
it was a winged-keel **yacht**.

The discourse system of lexical relations then is like NEGOTIATION in that message parts, like moves, are not in themselves phoric; both systems are however associated with redundancy as opposed to relevance or reminding phoricity because of the way in which both message parts and moves may be realised through SUBSTITUTION and ELLIPSIS in lexicogrammar.

One type of lexical relation which has not received sufficient attention here is that whereby message parts either predict subsequent discourse patterns or refer backwards to what has already been written or said. Winter (1977) proposes a set of 108 Vocabulary 3 items which predict ensuing discourse patterns, especially conjunctive relations. Winter's point is that using an item like *convergence* in a sentence predicts that some kind of comparison will follow. This Vocabulary 3 item was used in section 5.5 above to introduce the discussion of cohesive harmony in relation to nuclear relations: *In spite of these different goals there is considerable* **convergence** *across the two approaches, especially with respect to what were treated above as nuclear relations.* Carter (1987:75) gives the following examples from Winter's list.

PROSPECTIVE
Examples from Winter (Vocabulary 3)

action	event	reason
cause	expect	result
compare	fact	situation
conclude	kind	solution
condition	manner	specify
contrast	point	thing
differ	problem	way

The predictive function of Vocabulary 3 items is illustrated in [5:53] below, with *methods* forecasting the presentation of alternative methods of decorating glass which follows:

[5:53] a Two **methods** of decorating glass were commonly employed on Federation houses.

b In leadlight, the design was created by the shape of the various pieces of coloured glass

c and delineated the H-shaped strips of glass called cames.

d The cames formed the framework that held the glass in position.

e Large leadlight panels required the support of iron crossbars screwed to the door or window frames.

f The alternative method of decorating 'lights', as the glass in doors or windows was called, was to set panels of stained glass into the normal leadlight framework.

g An artist painted the required scene onto glass,

h which was then fired in a kiln.

i Typical scenes might include native birds, rural views or seascapes.

j The finished pane of painted or 'stained' glass was often cut into a circular or oval shape

k and then set into its leadlight background. (Evans 1986:53)

Carter also reports on Francis's (1985) study of what she terms anaphoric nouns (A-nouns). These are used in conjunction with anaphoric reference items to refer to preceding discourse. The nominal group *the discussion of cohesive harmony in relation to nuclear relations* was used in this way in *This Vocabulary 3 item was used in section 5.5 above to introduce* **the discussion of cohesive harmony in relation to nuclear relations** (in the preceding paragraph). Carter (1987:80) lists the following examples of Francis's A-nouns. All, it can be noted, are grammatical metaphors, reflecting the fact that congruent English reconstructs discourse as a rhetorical process, not as a product or thing.

RETROSPECTIVE
Examples from Francis (A-nouns)

accusation	consideration	interpretation	report
admission	criticism	judgement	repudiation
allegation	declaration	observation	retort
answer	definition	point	revelation
argument	denial	prediction	statement
assumption	description	proposal	stipulation
belief	diagnosis	proposition	suggestion
challenge	estimate	reading	threat
complaint	evidence	reasoning	theory
conclusion	examination	reference	viewpoint
confession	hypothesis	refusal	

Predicting and referring to discourse is not simply a function of lexical items. Nuclear configurations are also used in this way; for example:

> Before I begin, let me say...
> I'll stop here for questions...
> I'll conclude by summarising...
> Before going on to Chapter 6...
> etc.

This use of messages and message parts in a kind of meta-discursive relation to preceding and subsequent meanings in text is not unlike the function of text reference or that of internal conjunction. Indeed, meta-message relations often work in conjunction with demonstratives and closely resemble text reference; and internal conjunctive relations are often realised through what Francis calls A-nouns.

TEXT REFERENCE
[5:54]   Ben lost in straight sets; **it** really upset him.

A-NOUN
[5:55]   Ben lost in straight sets; that **result** really upset him

INTERNAL CONJUNCTION
[5:56]   Ben lost in straight sets; **in that respect** I hardly recognised him.

The proportionalities among these "external" and "internal" aspects of IDEATION, IDENTIFICATION and CONJUNCTION are as follows:

ORGANISING FIELD: ORGANISING TEXT::
message part relation: meta-message relation::
participant reference: text reference::
external conjunction: internal conjunction

Throughout this chapter, much more attention has had to be paid to register variables than in Chapter 2, 3 and 4. The discussion of IDEATION was undertaken with a view to textually mediating the realisation of field in lexicogrammar. During any such consideration of the realisation of one level of meaning in another, it needs to be kept in mind that as a theoretical construct realisation is not directional. As noted in Chapter 1, to say that A realises B is to say: (i) A manifests B (i.e. makes B material); (ii) A constitutes B (i.e. makes B come to be); (iii) A reconstitutes B (i.e. continually renovates B, however gradually); and (iv) A symbolises B (i.e. is a metaphor for B). Unfortunately the grammar of English can focus on only one aspect of this realisation spectrum at a time, and the part which has usally been grammaticalised in this chapter is realisation i. A (lexicogrammar) manifests B (field).

It should go without saying however with respect to the system/process model developed here that points (ii), (iii) and (iv) are always relevant. Clearly this chapter has meant a number of things that have never been meant before; it has been involved in constructing the field of lexical relations (point (ii) above) as much as realising immanent meanings that have been previously construed. It has also attempted to renovate (point (iii) above) linguists' interpretation of grammar and meaning by configuring the grammar as Agent in a material process with meaning as the Medium produced: *grammar makes meaning* (cf. *learning how to mean, making meaning, meaning making resource* etc.). Finally (point (iv) above) lexicogrammar has been taken as naturally related to field, and thus as a resource of metaphors for interpreting this register variable. The concept of taxonomy was derived from Carrier‘Attribute and Classifier‘Thing structures; the notion of nuclear configurations was abstracted from TRANSITIVITY and experiential grammar at group rank; and the idea for activity sequences was taken from entending and enhancing clause complexes.

Realisation then is a technical concept embracing all these meanings. Grammaticalising the concept through Token‘Value structures such as *field* **is realised** *through the ideational resources of lexicogrammar* should not be taken as delimiting in any way the meaning of realisation as outlined above. Technically it may in the long run prove helpful to replace the term realisation with a less directional term like *redound* (cf. Halliday in Thibault 1987:619: "it shows just how the context of situation 'redounds with' (construes and is construed by) the semantic system."

The interaction of discourse semantic and lexicogrammatical stuctures will be taken up in Chapter 6 below in an attempt to underline the way in which the two strata contribute independently, dependently and interdependently to the process whereby meanings are made as text.

NOTES

1. I am indebted to Merle Stetser for this text.

2. The distinctions are nicely illustrated in the following text from the *Syndey Morning Herald's* Column 8, 7/4/89: Tim Stack, telling the story of Goldilocks to four year old Nathan got to the point of "And Mother Bear's porridge was t-o-o cold — but **baby bear's was just right**." Nathan's eyes lit up — "I thought **it was porridge**?"

3. Thus, again from Column 8, 7/4/89: Jessica Holloway, 4, of Rose Bay thanks her father for **naming her Jessica**, "because **everyone else calls me Jessica**, too."

4. Jeff Ellis's proposal for part/whole relations; first used in Halliday and Hasan (1980).

5. References to Halliday and Hasan (1980/1985/1989) will be to the (1985) Deakin edition.

6. Texture

Interleaving discourse semantics, lexicogrammar and phonology

6.1 Models of texture

6.1.1 *Cohesion and register*

In their introduction to *Cohesion in English* Halliday and Hasan propose the following definition of text:

> The concept of COHESION can therefore be usefully supplemented by that of REGISTER, since the two together effectively define a text. A **text** is a passage of discourse which is coherent in these two regards: it is coherent with respect to the context of situation, and therefore consistent in register; and it is coherent with respect to itself, and therefore cohesive. (1976:23)

They stress that neither of these two perspectives is sufficient without the other: "**Texture** results from the combination of semantic configurations of two kinds: those of register and those of cohesion" (1976:26). It is abundantly clear from comments such as these that the term cohesion was never intended by Halliday and Hasan as a synonym for coherence.

Halliday and Hasan supplement this definition of text and texture with a broader consideration of a culture's text-forming resources in Chapter 7. This brings the **intra**sentential resources of THEME and INFORMATION into the picture alongside the **inter**sentential resources of COHESION referred to above:

> Texture involves much more than merely cohesion. In the construction of text the establishment of cohesive relations is a necessary component; but it is not the whole story.

In the most general terms there are two other components of texture. One is the textual structure that is internal to the sentence: the organization of the sentence and its parts in a way which relates it to its environment. The other is the 'macrostructure' of the text, that establishes it as a text of a particular kind — conversation, narrative, lyric, commercial correspondence and so on. (1976:324)

Halliday (1985a) assumes the same tri-partite perspective on text forming resources, breaking down the linguistic resources as follows (1985a:313):

A. STRUCTURAL
1 thematic stucture: Theme & Rheme
2 information structure and focus: Given & New

B. COHESIVE
1 reference
2 ellipsis and substitution
3 conjunction
4 lexical cohesion

And he goes on to note that the way in which these resources are deployed is determined by register:

For a text to be coherent, it must be cohesive; but it must be more besides. It must deploy the resources of cohesion in ways that are motivated by the register of which it is an instance (1985a:318).

6.1.2 *Linguistic resources*

Hasan (1985b) uses the term texture more narrowly to refer to semantic relations realised through the intra- and intersentential text forming resources outlined by Halliday under A and B above (it is this meaning of the term that will be adopted in *English Text*); texture in this narrower sense is opposed to **text structure**, which she derives from register variables (Hasan 1977, 1979, 1984b, 1985a). Taken together, texture and text structure are the sources of **textual unity**: "The unity of any text...is of two major types: unity of structure (and) unity of texture" (1985b:52). The terms used by Hasan and Halliday are reviewed in Table 6.1.

Hasan's more delicate classification of texture creating resources is summarised in Table 6.2 (Table 5.1 from Hasan 1985b:82). Grammatical parallelism is added to Halliday's structural resources, alongside THEME and INFORMATION systems. In addition, cohesive resources are re-organised along a number of dimensions:

Table 6.1. Terms for coherence in the work of Hasan and Halliday

Halliday & Hasan (1976:23-6)	Halliday & Hasan (1976:324)	Halliday (1985a:318)	Hasan (1985b:52)
Texture	**Texture**	**Coherence**	**Textual unity**
register	macrostructure	register & text structure	text structure (predicted by register)
cohesion	cohesion	TEXTURE: cohesion	TEXTURE: cohesion
	theme, information	theme, information	theme, information, parallelism

(i) **organic** relations between messages are distinguished from **componential** relations between parts of a message;[1]

(ii) **conjunctives** are distinguished from **continuatives** (not unlike the CONJUNCTION and CONTINUITY distinction in Chapter 4 above, but involving a different use of the term continuative from that in Halliday and Hasan 1976);

(iii) the category of **adjacency pairs** is included alongside conjunctive relations;

(iv) **lexical** devices are distinguished from **grammatical** ones;

(v) the category of **instantial** relations is proposed and included in the lexical group;

(vi) componential devices are classified as involving **co-reference**, **co-classification** or **co-extension** (see Hasan 1985b:73-74).

Hasan's table provides a very useful point of comparison for the model of text forming resources proposed in *English Text*. These resources are outlined by strata in Table 6.3. The fact that *English Text* assumes a stratified content plane accounts for most of the difference in categorization. Hasan's adjacency pairs and *English Text*'s NEGOTIATION cover similar ground; as do Hasan's continuatives and *English Text*'s CONTINUITY. The only additions to Hasan's table are the systems of TONE CONCORD and TONE SEQUENCE (see Halliday and Hasan 1976:271-273; Halliday 1985a:285-286; van Leeuven 1982) and collocation; and the only omission, her category of structural parallelism.

Table 6.2. Summary of cohesive devices. Reproduced from M.A.K. Halliday and R. Hasan Language, Context and Text. © *Deaking University Press.*

NON-STRUCTURAL COHESION

	COMPONENTIAL RELATIONS		ORGANIC RELATIONS
	Device	Typical tie relation	
GRAMMATICAL COHESIVE DEVICES	A: **Reference** 1. Pronominals 2. Demonstratives 3. Definite article 4. Comparatives	} co-reference	A: **Conjunctives** e.g. causal tie concession tie ...
	B: **Substitution & Ellipsis** 1. Nominal 2. Verbal 3. Clausal	} co-classification	B: **Adjacency pairs** e.g. Question (followed by) answer; offer (followed by) acceptance; order (followed by) compliance ...
LEXICAL COHESIVE DEVICES	A: **General** 1. Repetition 2. Synonymy 3. Antonymy 4. Meronymy	} co-classification or co-extension	**Continuatives** (e.g. still, already...)
	B: **Instantial** 1. Equivalence 2. Naming 3. Semblance	} co-reference or co-classification	

STRUCTURAL COHESION

A: **Parallelism**
B: **Theme-Rheme Development**
C: **Given-New Organisation**

Table 6.3. English Text*'s organisation of text forming resources in English*

Discourse Semantics	Lexicogrammar	Phonology/Graphology
NEGOTIATION	SUBSTITUTION & ELLIPSIS	INFORMATION
IDENTIFICATION	THEME	
CONJUNCTION & CONTINUITY		TONE CONCORD & TONE SEQUENCE
IDEATION	COLLOCATION	

Hasan's componential/organic, grammatical/lexical and co-reference/ co-classification/co-extension oppositions do not conflict with *English Text*'s proposals, but simply represent a more delicate consideration of the categorisation of text forming resources at issue here. The componential/ organic opposition is reflected in the discourse semantic units proposed by *English Text*, with NEGOTIATION and CONJUNCTION linking moves and messages respectively, and IDENTIFICATION and IDEATION linking participants and message parts. These units are reviewed in Table 6.4, repeated here from Chapter 5.

Table 6.4. Discourse semantics — units proposed in English Text

| INTERPERSONAL | TEXTUAL | IDEATIONAL: | |
		LOGICAL	EXPERIENTIAL
exchange			
move		message	
	participant		message part

As noted above, the differences between Hasan's model and that proposed by *English Text* relate to collocation, sequences of tone and structural parallelism. Collocation has been included as a text forming resource in the *English Text* model in order to allow for the possibility that there are inherent expectancy relations among lexical items at the level of lexicogrammar which make a contribution to texture independent of the semantic relations predicted by field. Hasan's position is apparently that field exhaustively predicts these expectancy relations, while Sinclair (1987) posits the contrary position that collocation studies make the articulation of an independent semantics unnecessary for the purpose of text description. Given that there is no way of predicting the outcome of this debate at this time, the *English Text* model has been designed to encourage investigation of lexical relations from both the perspectives of collocation studies and of field.

The cohesive function of intonation is dealt with briefly by Halliday and Hasan (1976:271-273) who oppose the cumulative meaning of tones 1 and 3 to the contrastive meaning of tone 4. Halliday (1985a:285-286) introduces the systems of TONE CONCORD and TONE SEQUENCE. TONE CONCORD he introduces as the phonological realisation of paratactic elaboration (apposition); and TONE SEQUENCE relates unmarked sequences of tone to interdependency — cohesion, parataxis and hypotaxis. These suggestions are summarised in Table 6.5; van Leeuven (1982) adds a number of ranks above the tone group in a much more comprehensive study of this phenonenon in the context of radio announcing.

Table 6.5. Summary of TONE *as a text forming resource*

COHESION		INTERDEPENDENCY:	
tone 1	cumulative	tone 1-tone 1	cohesive
tone 3	,,	tone 3-tone 1	paratactic
tone 4	contrastive	tone 4-tone 1	hypotactic
		α tone-α tone	'apposition'

Grammatical parallelism will be passed over here as better considered under the heading of the Prague School concept of de-automatization (see Halliday 1971,1982a, Martin 1985c), which cannot be pursued in any detail here. De-automatization is the process whereby a particular linguistic stratum makes meaning which is not predicted by its context (i.e. the next higher level in the realisation model assumed here). The most familiar example of this process is the artistic deployment of rhythm, rhyme or alliteration in phonology; in poetry these contribute a layer of meaning beyond that required to turn a poem's lexicogrammatical structure into sound. Grammatical parallelism is the grammatical correlate of this process; it is exploited rhetorically in contexts where strictly speaking it is not needed to realise the meaning at hand. The result is an "surfeit" of cohesive harmony as in the following example (treated in Martin 1986a:234).

[6:1] a. What will killing 3 million kangaroos a year do for us as human beings?
       b. What sort of Australians can shrug off that kind of brutality?
       c. And what are the implications for the rest of nature, for the bush, for the land, for other animals, for our fellow human beings, when our prime wildlife is killed on this scale?
       d. In the end we are talking about our own perception of ourselves as Australians.
       e. Our nationhood, our identity, our national pride and self respect.
       f. Our humanity.

Foregrounding of this kind is also found in pathological contexts, where the grammar is de-automatized, but not for any apparent rhetorical purpose (a passage of thought disordered schizophenic discourse from Rochester and Martin (1979:94) is presented as [6:2] below; see Martin (1985c) for a discussion of the different ways de-automatization functions in pathological discourse as opposed to representations of madness in literature):

[6:2] a. What sorts of things make you angry?
       b. - When people tell you what to do,
       c. when you know what to do to keep yourself healthy and happy.
       d. Who cares about money?
       e. I sure as hell don't.
       f. You see a wino on the street corner
       g. and you think he needs it to keep himself warm in winter.
       h. Maybe there's something else I can do to help him.
       i. I like to help people.
       j. It's not a sad thing.
       k. It's not a funny thing.
       l. I'm bonkers.
       m. I'm crazy.
       n. I'm half-way insane.
       o. But not all the time — just when I let my old panties show.

Halliday (1971 and 1982a) shows how semantic patterns can be foregrounded against context in a similar way. For reasons of space de-automatization cannot be pursued here, in spite of the fact that it is a concept fundamental to the interpretation of verbal art and pathological discourse and in addition bears critically on any interpretation of the role played by the concept of realisation in semogenesis.

Compared with Halliday and Hasan (1976) the organisation of text forming resources in *English Text* reviewed above raises two questions. One has to do with the treatment of SUBSTITUTION and ELLIPSIS at the level of lexicogrammar on the content plane; the other relates to the introduction of NEGOTIATION as a discourse semantics system. The following comparison between core chapter topics in *English Text* and *Cohesion in English*, repeated here from Chapter 1, highlights these concerns.

Table 6.6. Comparison of discourse systems and types of cohesion

English Text (discourse systems)	*Cohesion in English* (types of cohesion)
NEGOTIATION	REFERENCE
IDENTIFICATION	SUBSTITUTION
CONJUNCTION	ELLIPSIS
IDEATION	CONJUNCTION
	LEXICAL COHESION

First, SUBSTITUTION and ELLIPSIS. Like the discourse semantics systems of IDENTIFICATION and CONJUNCTION, these systems can be used to presume information which is not grammatically related to presuming items. Substitutes and ellipses make explicit almost none of the experiential or interpersonal meaning they presume, treating it as redundant (thus the term redundancy phoricity, as opposed to reminding and relevance phoricity). As Halliday and Hasan point out, this redundancy is typically exploited in the context of repudiation. The second response in [6:3] illustrates this function. The Thing *drink* is presumed from the offer by the substitute *one*; this allows the unmarked tonic to fall on *small*, which is contrastive in this environment.

[6:3]   Would you like a drink?   a drink
        — //13 A small gin and **tonic thanks** //   ↑
        — //13 Just a **small** one **thanks** //   one
        — //13 Just the **small**er one **thanks** //

Note the absence of repudiation in the first response, where *gin and tonic* is realised explicitly, proposed as a hyponym of *drink*. The third response illustrates the difference between repudiation and comparison; *one* presumes the Thing *drink* as in the second response, but in addition **small**er presumes a set of bigger drinks which are not identified in the second.

In spite of the fact that SUBSTITUTION and ELLIPSIS are used to link items cohesively between clause complexes, *English Text* has not treated them as a discourse semantic system. There are two reasons for this. One is that there is nothing in the grammar to stratify them with respect to. Unlike NEGOTIATION, IDENTIFICATION, CONJUNCTION and IDEATION they are not a semantic resource with diversified lexicogrammaticalisations — there is no such thing as incongruent (i.e. metaphorical) SUBSTITUTION and ELLIPSIS, nor is there a semantic motif running through the grammar which disperses their realisation. The second reason is that SUBSTITUTION and ELLIPSIS presume grammatical functions, not meanings. At clause rank they have be defined interpersonally, with respect to Mood and Residue; at group rank specific nominal and verbal group experiential functions are similarly presumed. The difference between presuming grammatical items and presuming meanings is illustrated in [6:4] and [6:5] below. *The lengthy monograph* in [6:4bi] does not refer to any particular grammatical unit in [6:4a]; it simply presumes a meaning that was there implied:

[6:4]   a.   It took several months of writing
           b.i.   but in the end **the lengthy monograph** was complete/
           ii. ??but in the end **the lengthy one** was complete.

But replacing *the lengthy monograph* with *the lengthy* **one** as in [6:4bii] does not work, because there is no relevant Thing around in [6:4] for *one* to presume. Similarly, *that* in [6:5bi] presumes a meaning — the fact that it took several months of writing; alternatively, a response like *Did it* presumes the Residue (i.e. Predicator:*take* ^ Complement:*several months of writing*). The difference is outlined in Fig. 6.1.

[6:5]   a. It took several months of writing
        b.i. and that surprised her/
         ii. — Did it θ?

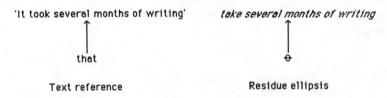

'It took several months of writing'   *take several months of writing*

                that   θ

        Text reference   Residue ellipsis

Fig. 6.1. Text reference and Residue ellipsis compared

What this argument amounts to saying is that it is more economical to leave SUBSTITUTION and ELLIPSIS in the grammar, generating cohesive ties with respect to grammatical functions defined on that stratum. Since text forming resources are distributed across all three strata in the meaning making model of language assumed by *English Text*, there is nothing remarkable in this. As far as realisation across strata is concerned, at clause rank SUBSTITUTION and ELLIPSIS redound with NEGOTIATION while at group rank they redound with IDEATION (cf. Hasan's category of co-classification above).

The other main difference between *English Text* and *Cohesion in English* has to do with the recognition of NEGOTIATION as a linguistic text forming resource. Halliday and Hasan treat this system as an aspect of the "macrostructure" of text, alongside generic structure — as a feature of register rather than of language (1976:324 & 327). Halliday's (1984a) interpretation of SPEECH FUNCTION as the semantics of MOOD however is preferred here. The relationship of SPEECH FUNCTION to MOOD mediated by interpersonal metaphor is precisely parallel to that between CONJUNCTION and the clause complex as mediated by ideational metaphor. Because of this it was possible to present a register neutral description of the semantics of dialogue in Chapter 2, just as it was possible to produce a register neutral description of conjunctive relations in Chapter 4. Both of these types of organic relation are essential components of English text forming resources and need to be interpreted systematically as semantic systems in language, not as register specific features of context.

6.1.3 *Modularity and interaction*

Each of the presentations of linguistic text forming resources considered above adopted a modular perspective. As far as *English Text* is concerned this has two main dimensions: stratification, and within strata, metafunction. A synopsis of these two axes is presented in Table 6.7, setting aside expression form.

Table 6.7. Metafunctional organisation of discourse systems

Metafunction	Discourse semantics	Lexicogrammar
interpersonal	NEGOTIATION	clause: MOOD; ELLIPSIS; MODALIZATION; MODULATION POLARITY; TAGGING; VOCATION
textual	IDENTIFICATION	nominal group: DEIXIS; pronouns; proper names; comparison
logical	CONJUNCTION	clause complex LOGICO-SEMANTICS & INTERDEPENDENCY
experiential	IDEATION	clause: TRANSITIVITY (including lexis as delicate grammar); group rank experiential grammar; collocation

Within grammar, the problem of mapping different systems onto each other is handled by realisation. Structures deriving from different metafunctional components are conflated and preselect options from constituent ranks until lexicogrammatical options are exhausted. For an introduction to this process see Halliday (1969), Mann and Matthiessen (1985), Matthiessen and Halliday (in press); for an exploration of its problems see Matthiessen (1988a).

Within discourse semantics, the ways in which systems co-operate in the process of making text is much less well understood. It is clear that discourse systems are interdependent in various ways, a number of which were introduced in Chapters 2, 3, 4 and 5 above. Some examples of these interdependencies are presented below (cf. Matthiessen & Halliday in press on metafunctional harmony). A more explicit account of this co-operation is clearly an urgent research goal; *English Text* has been concerned not so much with addressing this goal as with making it addressable by proposing four relatively independent discourse modules to beg the question (see Hoey 1983 for work on the interaction of CONJUNCTION and IDEATION). The point is that integrating meanings deriving from different metafunctions is not a task that can be left to lexicogrammar alone.

NEGOTIATION (challenging) & INTERNAL CONJUNCTION
[6:6]   Can you do it?
         — **But** it's not my turn.

NEGOTIATION (tracking) & IDEATION (taxonomic & nuclear)
[6:7]   It's a Range.
         — A **what**?
         — A **Range**.
         — Oh.

[6:8]   Grammar makes meaning.
         — **What**?
         — I said **grammar makes meaning**.
         — Oh.

CONJUNCTION (comparison) & IDEATION (taxonomic)
[6:9]   It's not **difficult**;
         in fact it's quite **easy**.

CONJUNCTION (comparison) & IDENTIFICATION (comparison)
[6:10]   The **congruent** text is easy
         whereas the **less congruent** one is quite hard.

CONJUNCTION (temporal & consequential) & IDEATION (activity)
[6:11]   He had an open goal
         but he missed.

CONJUNCTION & IDENTIFICATION (text reference)
[6:12]   Flo had nothing left to win;
         because of that she retired.

IDENTIFICATION (presuming) & IDEATION (taxonomic & nuclear)
[6:12]   **The woman** was delighted;
         she leaped high into the air.

[6:13]   The children saw **some tigers**;
         they growled.

IDENTIFICATION (comparison) & IDEATION (taxonomic)
[6:14]   Carl ran a **great** race
         but Ben ran the **better** one.

The modularity imposed by stratification is also an important issue. Discourse systems generate structures which in principle cut across grammatical and phonological ones. But the intersection of discoursal, grammatical and phonological syntagms is not random. In Chapter 5 for example the way in which the "horizontal" syntagms of TRANSITIVITY intersect with the "vertical" syntagms of discourse semantics was outlined as in Fig. 6.2; as Hasan (1984a) has suggested, the kind of interaction displayed is directly relevant to readers' intuitions about coherence in discourse.

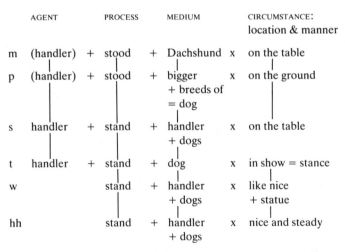

	AGENT		PROCESS		MEDIUM		CIRCUMSTANCE: location & manner
m	(handler)	+	stood	+	Dachshund	x	on the table
p	(handler)	+	stood	+	bigger + breeds of = dog	x	on the ground
s	handler	+	stand	+	handler + dogs	x	on the table
t	handler	+	stand	+	dog	x	in show = stance
w			stand	+	handler + dogs	x	like nice + statue
hh			stand	+	handler + dogs	x	nice and steady

Fig. 6.2. Intersection of lexicogrammatical (TRANSITIVITY) and discourse semantics (IDENTIFICATION and IDEATION) syntagms

As far as lexical strings and reference chains are concerned, this interaction across strata is better understood than that among discourse systems themselves. Fries (1981), Hasan (1984a), Halliday (1985a) and Plum (1988) have all done pioneering work in this area (see also Martin 1991b). Systematic interaction between discoursal, grammatical and phonological structures will be referred to here as **interaction patterns**. Four main patterns will be considered in detail below, representing the intersection of lexical strings and reference chains with experiential grammatical functions (cohesive harmony), with Theme (method of development), with Subject (modal responsibility) and with New (point). These interaction patterns are outlined by strata in Table 6.8.

Table 6.8. Some principle patterns of interaction across strata

INTERACTION PATTERN	DISCOURSE SEMANTICS	LEXICOGRAMMAR	PHONOLOGY
cohesive harmony	chains & strings	experiential functions	
method of development	chains & strings	Theme	
modal responsibility	chains & strings	Subject	
point	chains & strings		New

6.1.4 *The role of grammatical metaphor*

English grammar, like all grammars, is designed to allow considerable flexibility as far as the interaction of chains, strings and grammatical syntagms is concerned. This flexibility has to do with choice of Subject, choice of Theme and choice of New. In English, the Medium typically conflates with Subject in middle clauses and the Agent in effective ones (Halliday's 1985a:144-157 ergative perspective on TRANSITIVITY is assumed here); but the "passive" can be used to over-ride this unmarked pattern. The Range (in middle clauses), The Medium (in effective clauses), the Beneficiary (in middle or effective clauses) and the Range function in a prepositional phrase (in middle clauses) are all candidates for conflation with Subject, weaving their strings and chains through this grammatical function rather than through Complement or Adjunct.

ACTIVE:
PASSIVE::
[6:16] They had a good time: Medium/Subject:
        A good time was had by all::   Range/Subject::

[6:17]	Ben won the chicken:	Agent/Subject:
	The chicken was won by Ben::	Medium/Subject::
[6:18]	Ben bought a present for Adele:	Agent/Subject:
	Adele was bought a present by Ben::	Beneficiary/Subject::
[6:19]	Ben trained in that gym:	Medium/Subject:
	That gym's been trained in by Ben	phrasal Range/Subject

Subject conflates with unmarked topical Theme in English, and so weaving strings and chains through the Subject function typically has the effect of weaving them through Theme as well. However marked Themes are also possible; this pattern involves realising Complement (e.g. [6:33m] and [6:34dd] below), Adjunct or Residue before the Subject:

MARKED & UNMARKED THEME

Flo won that medal in Seoul	Subject/Theme	UNMARKED
In Seoul Flo won that medal	Adjunct/Theme	MARKED
That medal Flo won in Seoul	Complement/Theme	"
...and **win** it she did[2]	Residue/Theme	"

Realising meanings in first position has repercussions for what comes last in the clause, in the unmarked position for New (the grammatical unit whose last salient syllable is tonic in the tone group). But New can be conflated with a number of other clause and group functions, simply by making their final salient syllable tonic. A range of possibilities are illustrated below (tonic syllable in bold face).

MARKED AND UNMARKED TONICITY

// Carl won the 100 metres in **Rome** //	UNMARKED TONICITY	
// Carl won the 100 **met**res in Rome //	MARKED TONICITY	
// Carl won the **100** metres in Rome //	"	"
// Carl **won** the 100 metres in Rome //	"	"
// **Carl** won the 100 metres in Rome //	"	"

English's PROCESS TYPE system itself is not a flexible resource as far as weaving strings and chains through different participant and circumstance roles is concerned. Converses are found, but these are isolated as delicate options in just a few process types, and are not productive: e.g. *give/receive*, *borrow/lend*, *talk/listen*, *teach/learn*, *realise/encode*. Only mental processes of affection:reaction display substantial paradigms in this area, alternately conflating Phenomenon with Agent or Range; this alternation also has the effect of conflating Phenomenon or Senser with Subject, without affecting the voice of the verb.

PHENOMENON/AGENT:PHENOMENON/RANGE & PHENOMENON/SUBJECT:SENSER/SUBJECT::
He pleases her:she likes him::
She frightens him:he fears her::
He terrifies her:she dreads him::
He concerns her:she doubts him::
She inspires him:he depends on her::
She appals him:he detests her::
He disgusts her:she loathes him::
He amuses her:she gets a kick out of him::
She impresses him:he admires her::
He titillates her:she desires him::
He shits her:she dislikes him::
She unnerves him:he mistrusts her::
He worries her: she distrusts him
etc.

In addition, effective mental processes have relational attributive agnates which conflate Senser with Subject; examples involving projection are listed below, with discontinuous Subjects: *It...that...* . Note that the attributive realisations of reaction can all be graded as qualities: *a bit* nervous, **very** unhappy, **rather** impressed, **somewhat** disgusted, **more than a little** concerned, **extremely** unhappy.

MENTAL EFFECTIVE:RELATIONAL ATTRIBUTIVE::
It unnerves him that she's coming:he's nervous that she's coming::
It shits her that he's coming:she's unhappy that he's coming::
It impressed him that she went:he was impressed that she went::
It disgusted her that he came:she was disgusted that he came::
It concerned him that she left:he was concerned that she left::
It pleased her that he left:she was happy that he left
etc.

The resources for weaving strings and chains through different grammatical functions just reviewed are important ones; but they provide only a very partial picture of the way in which meanings are packaged for grammatical realisation. The real gatekeeper is grammatical metaphor. The best way to illustrate this is to contrast texts which do and do not make use of grammatical metaphor to organise information. Text [6:20] below is an example of a text which does not. It was written by a 16-year-old geography student in Year 10 of junior secondary school and is not untypical of the writing produced at this level in inner city Sydney schools with a high density migrant population.

[6:20]   (ORIGINAL "SPOKEN ENGLISH" VERSION; "writing as you speak")
    a. I think Governments are necessary
    b. because if there wasn't any
    c. there would be no law
    d. people would be killing themselves.
    e. They help keep our economic system in order for certain things.
    f. If there wasn't no Federal Government
    g. there wouldn't have been no one to fix up any problems that would
       have occured in the community.
    h. Same with the State Government
    i. if the SG didn't exist
    j. there would have been noone to look after the school,
    k. vandalism fighting would have occured everyday.
    l. The local Government would be important to look after the rubbish
    m. because everyone would have diseases.

The original text is written in the local community's variety of spoken English and would be perceived by most teachers as having problems with what is referred to as "punctuation, grammar and usage". It is easy to demonstrate however that "correcting" the text with respect to these difficulties does little to transform it into a mature piece of academic writing. The text is re-worked into "written" English along these lines as [6:21] below. Subsequently its selections for Theme and unmarked New are outlined. It is assumed for the purpose of analysing New that the tonic falls on the final salient syllable of each clause; the domain of the New is restricted to the group or group complex whose last salient syllable is tonic. Table 6.9 reveals that most of the meanings realised in Theme and New are congruent ones; the exceptions are *necessary* (congruently a modal verb like *must*) and the nominalisations *vandalism* and *fighting*.

[6:21]   ("WRITTEN ENGLISH" VERSION; revising "grammar, punctuation & usage")
    a. I think Governments are necessary
    b. because if there weren't any
    c. there wouldn't be any law:
    d. people would be killing themselves.
    e. They help keep our economic system in order for certain things.
    f. If there weren't any Federal Government
    g. there wouldn't be anyone to fix up any problems that occur in the com-
       munity.
    h. It's the same with the State Government —
    i. if the State Government didn't exist
    j. there wouldn't be anyone to look after the schools;
    k. vandalism and fighting would occur everyday.
    l. The local Government is important to look after rubbish,
    m. because otherwise everyone would have diseases.

Table 6.9. Theme and unmarked New in text [6:21]

THEME	UNMARKED NEW
I	necessary
there	weren't
there	any law
people	would be killing
They [governments]	certain things
there	any Federal Government
there	the community
It	the State Government
the State Government	didn't exist
there	the schools
vandalism fighting	everyday
The local Government	rubbish
everyone	diseases

Good writing is not simply a question of 'accent'; and so transforming the text from spoken to written usage does not substantially improve it. Real inprovements necessarily involve changes in texture, for example re-organizing Themes and internal conjunction. Both Theme selection and internal conjunction have been re-worked in [6:23] below. The government string is realised as unmarked Theme in clauses [6:23b,d,g] and [6:23e] and would have been Theme in all the others save [6:23h] were it not for the modalising projection in [6:23a], the branching in [6:23c], the non-finiteness in [6:23f] and the marked Theme in [6:23i]. And as Table 6.10 reveals, grammatical metaphor is now being used to organise the text: *for a number of reasons* (New in [6:23a]) and *as a result of these factors* (Theme in [6:23i]).

[6:22] (RE-ORGANISED VERSION; revising THEME and CONJUNCTION)

    a. I think Governments are necessary at *different levels* for **a number of reasons**.

    b. They make laws, without which people would be killing themselves,

    c. and help keep our economic system in order.

    d. To begin, the Federal Government fixes up problems that occur in the community.

    e. **Similarly**, the State Government looks after schools,

    f. preventing vandalism and fighting.

    g. **Finally** the Local Government is important to look after rubbish:

    h. otherwise everyone would have diseases.

    i. **As a result of these factors**, Governments at *several administrative levels* are necessary.

Table 6.10. Theme and unmarked New in text [6:22]

THEME	UNMARKED NEW
I	a number of reasons
They [governments]	would be killing
the Federal Government	in order
the State Government	the community
the Local Government	schools
Governments	vandalism and fighting
as a result of these factors	diseases
	necessary

The text is now on its way to becoming an effective piece of academic writing. The basic scaffolding for the genre has been erected (see Martin 1985b, 1989 for further discussion). The next step is to elaborate the second, third and fourth paragraphs. But the text is still a long way from exploiting grammatical metaphor to package information. In order to complete secondary school the student in question and his peers will have to face text-book English of the following kind, which does exploit grammatical metaphor in this way. In this kind of writing grammatical metaphors abound.

[6:23] (TEXT-BOOK ENGLISH; topical Themes in bold face, marked topical Themes underlined, unmarked New in italics)

a   **Wars** are *costly exercises.*

b   **They** cause *death and destruction*

c   and put resources to *non-productive uses*

d   but **they** also promote *industrial and economic change.*

e   **This benefit** does not mean that war is a good thing, but that it sometimes brings *useful developments.*

f   **The Second World War** further encouraged *the restructuring of the Australian economy towards a manufacturing basis.*

g   **Between 1937 and 1945** the value of industrial production *almost doubled.*

h   **This increase** was faster than otherwise *would have occurred.*

i   **The momentum** was maintained in *the post-war years*

j   and **by 1954-5** the value of manufacturing output was three times that of *1944-5.*

k   **The enlargement of Australia's steel-making capacity, and of chemicals, rubber, metal goods and motor vehicles** all owed something to *the demands of war.*

l   **The war** had acted as *something of a hot-house for technological prog-ress and economic change.*

m   **The war** had also revealed *inadequacies in Australia's scientific and research capabilities.*

n   **After the war** strenuous efforts were made to improve *these.*

o   **The Australian National University** was established *with an emphasis on research.*

p   **The government** gave its support to *the advancement of science in many areas, including agricultural production.*

q   Though it is **difficult** to disentangle the effects of war from *other influences,*

r   it is **clear** that future generations not only enjoyed *the security and peace won by their forefathers but also the benefits of war-time economic expansion.* (Simmelhaig & Spenceley 1984:121)

The function of grammatical metaphor in expository writing of this kind is critical. First of all the "Theme" of the exposition as a whole (its Thesis in generic terms) and its "New" (its Reiteration in generic terms) are both heavily metaphorical. The ideational metaphors in [6:23e & r] are highligh-

Table 6.11. Unmarked Theme and unmarked New in text [6:23]

UNMARKED THEME	UNMARKED NEW
Wars	costly exercises
They	death and destruction
they	non-productive uses
This benefit	industrial and economic change
	useful developments
The Second World War	the restructuring of the...
This increase	almost doubled
The momentum	would have occurred
The enlargement of Australia's...	the post-war years
The war	1944-5
	the demands of war
	a hot house for technological...
The war	inadequacies in Australia's...
The Australian National University	these
The government	an emphasis on research
	the advancement of science...
	other influences
	the security and peace...

ted with bold face below and unpacked into congruent spoken English in square brackets.

THESIS (the "theme" of the exposition)

e.   This **benefit** does not **mean** that war is a good thing, but that it sometimes **brings useful developments**.

[When people fight wars they change their industry and economic systems around; now I'm not arguing that war is therefore a good thing but simply pointing out that during wars people sometimes change things around in ways they can use later.]

REITERATION (the "point" of the exposition)

r.   it is clear that future generations not only enjoyed the **security** and peace **won** by their forefathers but also the **benefits** of war-time **economic expansion**.

[you can see clearly that future generations not only felt happy and secure because they weren't fighting wars because their forefathers had fought wars for them but also benefited because people had expanded the economy during the wars]

Turning from the text as a whole to its clause structure, grammatical metaphor can also be seen to function as a powerful tool for packaging information as Theme or New. Grammatical metaphor is exploited by Themes in the second paragraph to consolidate information presented in preceding Rhemes:

g   Rheme   (the value of industrial productions almost doubled)
h   Theme   This **increase**

h   Rheme   (was faster than would otherwise have occurred)
i   Theme   The **momentum**

j   Rheme   (the value of manufacturing output was three times that of 1944-5)
k   Theme   The **enlargement** of Australia's steel-making capacity, and of chemicals, rubber, metal goods and motor vehicles

In the third paragraph grammatical metaphor is exploited mainly by New to present examples (in [6:23o & p]) of the point of the paragraph (in [6:23m & n]):

m   New   **inadequacies** in Australia's scientific and research **capacity**
n   New   these [presuming the New in m]

o   New   an **emphasis** on **research**
p   New   the **advancement** of science in many areas, including agricultural **production**

The meaning of Theme and New will be further explored in 6.3 below. The point here is that the flexibility built into the grammar as far as the text forming resources of THEME and INFORMATION are concerned is exponentially enhanced by the productivity of grammatical metaphor as a tool for packaging meaning. Strings and chains may be integrated in complex ways before being realised as Subject, Theme, New or as one or another TRANSITIVITY function.

Grammatical metaphor, like interaction patterns, will be interpreted as a process here, rather than as a synoptic system taking its place alongside the text forming systems proposed for English above. Metaphorically speaking, it is part of the conversation that must go on among text forming systems across strata if meanings are to be integrated in contextually effective ways (see Matthiessen 1988b for a model of realisation as dialogue across strata). This process of negotiation will be further examined in 6.2 and 6.3 below. The gatekeeping function of grammatical metaphor is incorporated as part of *English Text*'s classification of text forming resources in Table 6.12.

Table 6.12. Grammatical metaphor as a texturing interface

Discourse Semantics			Lexicogrammar	Phonology/ Graphology
NEGOTIATION			SUBSTITUTION & ELLIPSIS	
IDENTIFICATION	GRAMMATICAL METAPHOR		THEME	INFORMATION
CONJUNCTION & CONTINUITY				TONE CONCORD & TONE SEQUENCE
IDEATION			COLLOCATION	

6.1.5. *Textual meaning*

With notable exceptions (e.g. Halliday 1984a) Halliday's work on English content form has generally assumed an unstratified system/structure cycle organised by rank and metafunction. Within this model, cohesion is treated as a set of non-structural resources located within the textual metafunction.

The following function/rank matrix from Halliday (1978a: 132) makes this alignment clear.

Table 6.13. *Functional complements (Halliday 1978: 132)*

	IDEATIONAL		INTERPERSONAL		TEXTUAL	
	LOGICAL	EXPERIENTIAL				(COHESION)
		STRUCTURAL				NONSTRUCTURAL
Complexes at all ranks (clause complex etc.)		(1) *Clause structure*				
	expansion identity	clause: transitivity, modulation: polarity	clause: mood, modality		clause: theme	reference substitution/ellipsis
	projection (paratactic	verbal group: types of process; tense	verbal group: person; polarity	connotations of attitude etc.	verbal group: voice; contrast	conjunction lexical cohesion: reiteration
	& hypotactic)	nominal group: types of participant; class, quality, quantity etc.	nominal group: person ('role')		nominal group: deixis	collocation
		adverbial group, prepositional group: types of circumstance	adverbial group: prepositional group: comment		adverbial group: prepositional group: conjunction	
			(2) *Information structure*			
			information unit: key		information unit: information distribution and focus	

Considered from the point of view of an unstratified content plane, this allocation of cohesion to the textual metafunction makes sense; cohesion is about relating ideational and interpersonal meanings to each other, intergrating them as text. Compared with systems such as PROCESS TYPE, CIR-CUMSTANTIATION, MOOD, MODALIZATION, MODULATION, POLARITY, VOCATION, TENSE and so on, cohesion is a textual resource.

Considered from the perspective of a stratified content plane however, this metafunctional interpretation of cohesion is not appropriate. Semantic systems in the model assumed here deal with meanings that are both more abstract and bigger in size than grammatical ones. And it follows from setting up a text-focussed discourse semantics of this kind (as opposed to a speech act-focussed pragmatics or a proposition-focussed semantics) that systems on this stratum will be concerned with text integrating relations. This does not mean that all discourse systems need therefore to be treated as metafunctionally textual. The grammatical systems that discourse systems are abstracted with respect to need to be taken into account. In addition, the relation of discourse systems to register variables is an important consideration.

Interpreted as an interface between context and grammar, discourse semantics can be seen to have its own metafunctional organisation, reflecting both the organisation of the lexicogrammatical resources realising its meanings as well as the organisation of context into the register variables tenor, mode and field (see Chapter 7 below). NEGOTIATION is realised through the interpersonal grammatical systems of MOOD (alongside MODALIZATION, MODULATION and ATTITUDE); taking interpersonal metaphor into account, these systems are all strongly correlated with the register variable tenor. IDEATION, as was noted in Chapter 5, is realised through experiential grammatical systems (including the LOGICO-SEMANTICS of the clause complex) and is strongly correlated with field. IDENTIFICATION is abstracted from nominal group DEIXIS, and alongside the lexicogrammatical systems of SUBSTITUTION and ELLIPSIS is a powerful measure of contextual dependency and thereby

Table 6.14. Register and metafunction in relation to discourse semantic and lexicogrammatical systems

REGISTER	DISCOURSE SEMANTICS	LEXICOGRAMMAR
Tenor	*interpersonal* -	
	NEGOTIATION	clause: MOOD (MODALIZATION, MODULATION, POLARITY, VOCATION, TAGGING)
Mode	*textual* -	
	IDENTIFICATION	nominal group: DEIXIS SUBSTITUTION & ELLIPSIS
		INTERDEPENDENCY
Field	*logical* -	
	CONJUNCTION	clause complex:
	experiential -	
		LOGICO-SEMANTICS
	IDEATION	clause: TRANSITIVITY (including lexis as delicate grammar); group rank experiential grammar; collocation

strongly associated with mode. CONJUNCTION was presented in Chapter 4 as the semantics of the clause complex and is oriented to activity sequences in field. The way in which CONJUNCTION is realised however (between clause complexes, within clause complexes or within clauses) is very sensitive to mode. Beyond this, ideational metaphor in general is a powerful measure of a text's level of abstraction and is another mode determined variable. This projection of metafunction across the content plane in correlation with register is outlined in Table 6.14, which illustrates the way in which interpreting cohesion as discourse structure re-organises its metafunctional address.

6.1.6 *Context*

Text is semantic choice in social context, and so texture needs to be contextualised in any comprehensive model of a culture's text forming resources. It is for this reason that Hasan and Halliday supplement cohesion with notions of register and text structure whenever defining text or text unity. For Halliday, register is the term used to describe the meanings at risk in a context of situation; more technically it is an alignment of probabilities in systems comprising the content plane (see Thibault 1987:610). These probabilities redound with field, mode and tenor, which collectively comprise a text's **context of situation**.

Halliday (1978a:142-143) defines these three components of the context of situation as follows:

> Field — the social action:
> that which is 'going on', and has recognizable meaning in the social system; typically a complex of acts in some ordered configuration, and in which the text is playing some part, and including 'subject-matter' as one special aspect;
>
> Tenor — the role structure:
> the cluster of socially meaningful participant relationships, both permanent attributes of the participants and role relationships that are specific to the situation, including the speech roles, those that come into being through the exchange of verbal meanings;
>
> Mode — the symbolic organisation:
> the particular status that is assigned to the text within the situation; its function in relation to the social action and the role structure, including the channel or medium, and the rhetorical mode.

Hasan (1985a:55) points out that each of these components "can be thought of as a variable that is represented by some specific value(s)" — as systemic potential in other words. The particular values that are selected in a specific context of situation she refers to as that situation's **contextual configuration**. The contextual configuration then makes predictions about text structure:

(i)   what elements must occur;
(ii)   what elements can occur;
(iii)   where must they occur;
(iv)   where can they occur;
(v)   how often can they occur (Hasan 1985a:56)

The notion of context will be developed in somewhat different directions in Chapter 7 below, where context of situation and context of culture will be construed as a series of connotative semiotics (named register, genre and ideology). At this stage however all that needs to be stressed is that contextual systems are a critical component of any culture's text forming resources. The notion of text cannot be understood unless linguistic text forming resources are interpreted against the background of (or better, as redounding with) contextual ones. From the point of view of functional linguistics texture can never be anything other than texture in context. *English Text*'s model of language (as a denotative semiotic) in relation to context (its connotative semiotics) is outlined in Fig. 6.3.

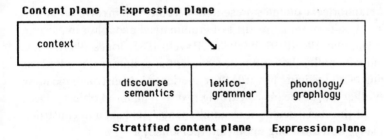

Fig. 6.3. Language as a denotative, context as a connotative semiotic

6.2 Grammatical metaphor

Like discourse systems, grammatical metaphor is sensitive to metafunction
and it is possible to recognize different types of metaphor according to the
kinds of meaning they interface. Examples of ideational (logical and experiential), interpersonal and textual metaphors have been introduced at various points in *English Text*; an example of each type of metaphor is presented in Table 6.15. The role of each in interfacing discourse semantics
and lexicogrammar is taken up in more detail below.

Table 6.15. Examples of grammatical metaphor across metafunctions

METAFUNCTION	**congruent**	**metaphorical**
ideational:		
logical		
conjunctive relation	therefore	reason
experiential		
process	advance	advancement
interpersonal		
assessment	might	possibility
textual		
reference	he	this point

All of the metaphorical examples presented in Table 6.15 involve nominalisation, the predominant semantic drift of grammatical metaphor in modern
English (see Halliday 1967d/1977b, 1985b; Ravelli 1985; Jones 1988). Since
nouns are fundamentally the output of experiential grammar this entails as
well a skewing of all meaning towards the experiential. Construing meaning
as a thing in other words means construing text as a material object — as a
material part of the social reality it is simultaneously engaged in constructing (ideationally) and intruding upon (interpersonally).

6.2.1 *Ideational metaphor*

Logical and experiential metaphor are in principle independent of each
other. Conjunctive relations may be realised metaphorically without neces-

sarily involving metaphorical processes, qualities or participants as well. The first clause in text [6:22] nominalises cause (*a number of reasons*) with no repercussions for grammatical metaphor in the rest of the clause (cf. *I think there should be Governments for several reasons*). It is internal conjunctive relations that lend themselves to "independent" metaphorical realisation in this way.

> [6:22:a] I think Governments are necessary at different levels for **a number of reasons**.

Conversely, experiential meaning may be realised metaphorically with no neccesary effect on conjunctive relations. Clause g-j in text [6:23] all have incongruent Subjects at the same time as temporal relations between the clauses are realised congruently as circumstantial phrases (i.e. setting in time: *between 1937 and 1945, in the post-war years, by 1954-5*).

> [6:23] g   Between 1937 and 1945 the **value of industrial production** almost doubled.
> h   This **increase** was faster than otherwise would have occurred.
> i   The **momentum** was maintained in the post-war years
> j   and by 1954-5 the **value of manufacturing output** was three times that of 1944-5.

Logical and experiential metaphors interact as what might be termed ideational metaphors when external conjunctive relations, typically consequential ones, are realised metaphorically. This interaction produces a high level of abstraction in text, making it inaccessible to large sections of the community (see Martin et al 1988, Martin 1990a on "secret English"). A good example of this process is found in [6:23k]. There, two experiential metaphors, *the enlargement of Australia's steel-making capacity* and *the demands of war* are causally connected by the logical metaphor *owed*.

> [6:23:k] The **enlargement of Australia's steel-making capacity**, and of chemicals, rubber, metal goods and motor vehicles all **owed** something to the **demands of war**.

Re-coded congruently as a clause complex, this clause translates as follows:

> [6:24] a. α   Australia could make more steel, chemicals, rubber, metal goods and motor vehicles
> b. β   partly because (people) had demanded them
> c. γ   to fight the war.

6.2.1.1 *Logical metaphor*

Metaphorical realisations of conjunctive relations were discussed in detail in Chapter 4 above (Section 4.2.1) in connection with the diversified realisation of this discourse system. A simplified outline of the scope of this diversification is outlined in Table 6.16.

Table 6.16. Congruent and metaphorical realisations of CONJUNCTION

Conjunctive relation:		CONSEQUENTIAL	TEMPORAL
CONGRUENT	cohesive conjunction	therefore	next
	paratactic conjunction	so	then
	hypotactic conjunction	because	before
METAPHORICAL	phrasal Process	due to	on
	Process	cause	follow
	Thing	reason	sequel

Text [6:22] is further revised to highlight metaphorical internal conjunctions as [6:25] below. Internal relations are realised four times as nouns (*for a number of reasons, another example, as a final point, as a result of these factors*) and once as a verb (*to begin*).

[6:25] (METAPHORICAL INTERNAL CONJUNCTION)

a. I think Governments are necessary at different levels for **a number of reasons**.

b. They make laws, without which people would be killing themselves,

c. and help keep our economic system in order.

d. **To begin**, the Federal Government fixes up problems that occur in the community.

e. **Another example** is that the State Government looks after schools,

f. preventing vandalism and fighting.

g. **As a final point** the Local Government is important to look after rubbish:

h. otherwise everyone would have diseases.

i. **As a result of these factors**, Governments at several administrative levels are necessary.

Winter's (1977) Vocabulary 3 items include a large number of these metaphorical realisations of internal conjunctive relations. Comparative and consequential relations are noted in the following list, reprinted from Chapter 5:

action	event	reason (consq)
cause (consq)	expect (consq)	result (consq)
compare (comp)	fact	situation
conclude (consq)	kind	solution (consq)
condition (consq)	manner (consq)	specify (comp)
contrast (comp)	point	thing
differ (comp)	problem	way (consq)

When combined with experiential metaphors, incongruent conjunctive relations are realised across a variety of TRANSITIVITY structures. Note the following variations on [6:23f]:

[6:23f]   MATERIAL PROCESS
The Second World War further **encouraged** the restructuring of the Australian economy towards a manufacturing basis.

[6:26]   CIRCUMSTANCE OF CAUSE
Because of the Second World War the Australian economy was restructured towards a manufacturing basis.

[6:27]   CIRCUMSTANTIAL ATTRIBUTE
The restructuring of the Australian economy towards a manufacturing basis was **due to** the Second World War.

[6:28]   VALUE
The **cause** of the restructuring of the Australian economy towards a manufacturing basis was the Second World War.

[6:29]   CIRCUMSTANTIAL PROCESS
The restructuring of the Australian economy towards a manufacturing basis **resulted from** the Second World War.

6.2.1.2 *Experiential metaphor*

Experiential metaphor is a complex process, which cannot be examined in detail here. Some of the more common types of grammatical metaphor associated with actions, qualities and participants are outlined in Table 6.17. Note that incongruence can flow against the nominalising semantic drift which characterises much abstract discourse in English; fields like personal computing for example contain a number of verbalised participants as

Table 6.17. Congruent and metaphorical realisations of experiential meaning

Action:			
congruent	finite Process	use	deceive
	non-finite Process	using	deceiving
metaphorical	Thing	use	deception
	Epithet	useful	deceitful
Quality:		(EXPERIENTIAL)	(ATTITUDINAL)
congruent	Epithet	quick	sad
metaphorical	Adjunct	quickly	sadly
	Thing	speed	sadness
	Process	quicken	sadden
Participant:			
congruent	Thing	disaster	computer
metaphorical	Epithet	disastrous	
	Process		computerize

technical terms: *computerize, boot, format, log on, paginate, scroll, tab* and so on.

Metaphorical qualities and actions are illustrated in the following clauses from [6:23]. Their function there is mainly to package experiential meaning for realisation as New.

[6:23]   m.   The war had also revealed **inadequacies in Australia's scientific and research capabilities**.

n.   After the war **strenuous efforts** were made to improve these.

o.   The Australian National University was established with an **emphasis on research**.

p.   The government gave its **support** to the **advancement of science** in many areas, including **agricultural production**.

It is important to note that grammatical metaphor is a "recursive" process; a number of the "congruent" unpackings in the table above can themselves be unpacked. *Capable* for example is really an incongruent assessment of ability, realised congruently as *can do*. Seen from an encoding perspective, the modulation of ability is first skewed from modal verb (*can*) to adjective (*capable*), which is in turn nominalised as *capabilities*. Similarly *inadequate* can be further unpacked as a negative phoric numerative *not enough*; *emphasize* can be rendered *say to be important*; *advance* can be

Table 6.18. Unpacking experiential metaphors in text [6:23:m-p]

	METAPHORICAL [6:23:m-p].	CONGRUENT [unpacked]
QUALITY	inadequacies capabilities	inadequate capable
PROCESS	efforts emphasis research support advancement production	try to do emphasize research support advance produce
PARTICIPANT	scientific agricultural strenuous	science agriculture strain

related to *make better*; and *strenuous* is related to the noun *strain* which itself construes an action as a thing. This means that abstract text, especially that textured by ideational metaphor, is often best unpacked in steps, up to the point where the analysis is sufficient for the deconstruction in which the analyst is engaged. One such unpacking strategy involves first unpacking logical metaphors and any experiential metaphors necessary to render them, then moving on the unpack the remaining experiential metaphors and finally turning to any interpersonal ones (textual metaphors will be taken up in 6.2.3). This strategy is illustrated below for [6:23k].

[6:23k] The **enlargement of Australia's steel-making capacity**, and of chemicals, rubber, metal goods and motor vehicles all **owed** something to the **demands of war**.

(i) UNPACKING IDEATIONAL METAPHOR
(rendering logical metaphors as conjunctions and unpacking any experiential metaphors necessary to accomplish this)

α   Australia's steel-making capacity enlarged, alongside that of chemicals, rubber, metal goods and motor vehicles
β   partly **because** war **demanded** it.

(ii) UNPACKING REMAINING EXPERIENTIAL METAPHORS

α   Australia's capacity to **make** steel **got bigger**, alongside that of chemicals, rubber, metal goods and motor vehicles
β   partly because war demanded it

(iii) UNPACKING INTERPERSONAL METAPHORS

α   Australia **could** make more steel, chemicals, rubber, metal goods and motor vehicles
β   partly because **people said**
γ   **"Give us materials**
δ   **so that³ we can fight** the war"

6.2.2 Interpersonal metaphor

Interpersonal metaphors were introduced in Chapter 2 in connection with congruent and metaphorical realisations of SPEECH FUNCTION in MOOD. Assessments of probability, usuality, inclination and obligation also display a range of diversified realisation. Some examples of interpersonal grammatical metaphors are reviewed in Table 6.19 (see Halliday 1985a:332-340 for further discussion).

Unlike ideational metaphors, interpersonal metaphors are not so much concerned with packaging information as Theme or New as with what Halliday has described as modal responsibility (1985a:76-78, 1984b/1988:39-45) — they arrange the Mood functions which are appropriate for particular interacts. Because of its ineffability this interpersonal texturing needs to be explored in context. Text [6:30] has been written by a sitting member to a new constituent in his electorate and makes use of interpersonal metaphor to focus modal responsibility on the member himself. Subject and Finite functions in ranking non-dependent clauses appear in bold face in [6:30] to foreground this pattern, which is explicitly announced in [6:30g] — *my responsibility is...* .

[6:30]   — 'I AM MODALLY RESPONSIBLE'
    a.   α   **I have** been advised
    b.   'β   that you have recently become one of the constituents in the Electorate of Mitchell.
    c.   ˣβ 1   Whether you have recently moved,
    d.   ⁺2   or whether you have reached the age that gives you full voting rights,
    e.   α   **may I** as your Federal Member of Parliament welcome you as a new constituent.

Table 6.19. Congruent and metaphorical realisations of interpersonal meanings

		PROBABILITY	USUALITY
MODALIZATON:			
congruent	Modal verb	*may*	*will*
metaphorical	Modal Adjunct	*possibly*	*usually*
	Epithet	*possible*	*usual*
	Thing	*possibility*	*tendency*
	relational Process	*(suggest)*	*(predict)*
	projecting Process	*(I) reckon*	*(I) predict*
	conjunction	*if*	*provided that*
		INCLINATION	OBLIGATION
MODULATION:			
congruent	Modal verb	*may*	*must*
metaphorical	Verb complex	*be allowed to*	*be obliged to*
	causative Process	*allow (x) to...*	*oblige (x) to...*
	Epithet	*permissable*	*necessary*
	Thing	*permission*	*necessity*
	projecting Process	*(I) recommend*	*(I) insist*
	conjunction	*in case*	*so*
MOOD			
PROPOSITION:			
congruent	statement	declarative	*He's here*
	question	interrogative	*Is he here?*
metaphorical	statement	probability	*It may be that...*
	question	usuality	*Is it usual that...*
	statement	projection	*I reckon...*
	question	projection	*Don't you think...*
PROPOSAL:			
congruent	command	imperative	*come here*
	offer	*Shall/can I..............*	*come over*
metaphorical	command	obligation	*you should...*
	offer	inclination	*I would...*
	command	projection:desire	*would you like...*
	offer	modulated reaction	*I'd love...*

f.   **We are** privileged to live in such a pleasant part of Australia.

g.   **My responsibility is** to make sure that the life style we enjoy is maintained and improved.

h.   ˣβ   Should you wish to contact me on any matter which is concerning you, either day-to-day or national importance,

i.   α   please **do** not hesitate to do so.

j.   ˣβ   If you are uncertain whether your problem is one affected by Commonwealth, State or Local Government,

k.   α   **we should** be able to advise you promptly.

As can be seen from the Mood and clause complex analysis provided, the new constituent appears as sole Subject in only one ranking independent clause (the imperative *please do not hesitate to do so*), and as joint Subject in f: *we are privileged...* — in the contexts of opportunity and flattery respectively. The effect can be highlighted by stripping the text of its interpersonal metaphors as in [6:31] below; adjusted and now congruent realisations of interpersonal meaning are in bold face.

[6:31]   — '**You** ARE MODALLY RESPONSIBLE'

a   **Apparently** you have recently become one of the constituents in the Electorate of Mitchell.

b   1   You **may** have recently moved,

c   ⁺2   or you **may** have reached the age that gives you full voting rights -

d   whichever the case, **my new constituent, welcome**.

e   α   We are **fortunate**

f   'β   that we **can** live in such a pleasant part of Australia.

g   α   I **must** work

h   ˣβ   so that the lifestyle we enjoy **can (only)** be maintained and improved.

i   You **may** want to contact me on any matter which is concerning you, either day-to-day or national importance -

j   You **can certainly** do so.

k   Your problem **may** be one affected by Commonwealth, State or Local Government.

l   α   We should be able to advise you promptly

m   "β   which it is affected by.

A comparison of Subject and Finite functions in ranking non-dependent clauses is outlined in Table 6.20. In the interpersonally congruent version of the text, the constituent assumes responsibility more often than the member. The interpersonal message is no longer 'what **I** can do for you' but rather 'what **you** can do'.

Table 6.20. Congruent and metaphorical positioning in texts [6:30] and [6:31]

SUBJECT & FINITE IN RANKING NON-DEPENDENT CLAUSES

metaphorical version [6:30]	congruent version [6:31]
I have	you have
may I	you may
we are	you may
my responsibility is	we are
(you) do not	I must
we should	you may
	you can
	your problem may
	we should

Table 6.21. Congruent realisations of interpersonal metaphors in [6:30]

	METAPHORICAL [6:30]	CONGRUENT [6:31]
modalization as condition:	whether you have... should you... if you are ...	you may you may you may
modalization as Attribute:	uncertain	may
modulation as Value:	my responsibility is	I must
modulation and modalization as Event complex:	hesitate to do so	can certainly
Mood Adjunct (presumption) as projection:	I have been advised	apparently
Greeting as Offer:	may I welcome you ...	welcome

The interpersonal metaphors which have been unpacked in [6:31] are itemised in Table 6.21. The notion of modal responsibility will be taken up again in Section 6.3.4.

6.2.3 *Textual metaphor*

The possibility of textual grammatical metaphor is not introduced in Halliday (1985a). However, as has been introduced in Chapters 2, 3, 4 and 5, discourse systems can be used to construe text as "material" social reality. From the point of view of lexical relations Winter's (1977) Vocabulary 3 items and Francis's (1985) A-nouns (e.g. *reason, example, point, factor*) organise text, not field. Similarly, text reference identifies facts, not participants, and internal conjunction orchestrates textual not activity sequences. NEGOTIATION can also be exploited to construe monologic text as dialogue. Good examples of meta-proposals/propositions were considered from a different perspective in Chapter 4 (see also 6.3.4 below): the imperative realisation of internal elaboration in [4:187j] — *Let's be clear*, and the interrogative realisation of internal concession as [4:188a] — *What if you're having to clean floppy heads too often?* These proportionalities are summarised below:

ORGANISING SOCIAL REALITY:	ORGANISING TEXT AS SOCIAL REALITY::
message part relation:	meta-message relation::
participant reference:	text reference::
external conjunction:	internal conjunction::
negotiating dialogue:	negotiating texture

Textual metaphors are illustrated in the following revision of [6:22]; in this text all of the textual metaphors are logically oriented — they provide resources for metaphorical realisations of conjunctive relations:

META-MESSAGE RELATION	reason, example, point, factor, pointing out
TEXT REFERENCE	this
NEGOTIATING TEXTURE	let me begin by...
INTERNAL CONJUNCTION	a number of reasons, for example, let me begin by, another example, as a final point, as a result of these factors

[6:32] (REVISED VERSION: illustrating textual metaphor)

    a   I think Governments are necessary at different levels for **a number of reasons**.

    b   **For example**, they make laws, without which people would be killing themselves,

    c   and help keep our economic system in order.

    d   **Let me begin by pointing out that** the Federal Government fixes up problems that occur in the community.

    e   **Another example** is that the State Government looks after schools;

    f   **this** prevents vandalism and fighting.

g   **As a final point** the Local Government is important to look after
    rubbish:
h   otherwise everyone would have diseases.

i   **As a result of these factors**, Governments at several administrative
    levels are necessary.

Textual metaphors are not however tied to logical meaning. They are commonly interpersonally oriented as well, deployed particularly for expressing an interlocutor's attitude to meanings being made:

META-MESSAGE RELATION	That **point** is just silly!
TEXT REFERENCE	**That**'s ricidulous!
NEGOTIATING TEXT	**What a** stupid point you just made!
INTERNAL CONJUNCTION	**Indeed**, she made a complete mess of it.

6.3 Interaction patterns

The interpretation of grammatical metaphor as a processing interface opens up the question of what the interface is for. This can be answered from above, with respect to register variation — interpersonal metaphor is sensitive to tenor, ideational metaphor to mode. The relationship between field, mode and tenor and grammatical metaphor will be taken up in Chapter 7 below. Here the problem of interfacing will be approached from below by asking questions about the function of packaging information as Theme, New, Subject and experiential clause and group functions.

6.3.1 *Cohesive harmony*

Cohesive harmony analysis is a technique for examining the interaction of reference chains, lexical strings and experiential grammar which has been developed by Hasan, initially as part of her study of children's narrative during the late 1960's. This work was undertaken in the Sociological Research Unit at the University of London's Institute of Education in connection with Bernstein's interest in language, socialisation and education. Sadly, the results of this study have never been published, and it was not until Halliday and Hasan (1980), Hasan (1984a) and Hasan (1985b) that Hasan's work extending the (1976) *Cohesion in English* framework became known.

Cohesive harmony is basically designed to measure coherence in text, although it needs to be kept in mind that the measure is only a partial one. As noted in 6.1, no measure of textual unity is complete without taking into account consistency of register (field, mode and tenor) and genre (text structure); and as Hasan (1985b:94) points out the technique needs to be refined to bring logical and interpersonal meaning into the picture (it does not in other words deal with organic relations — CONJUNCTION and NEGOTIA-TION, nor with the interaction of componential cohesion and MOOD or clause complex functions). Nevertheless, cohesive harmony does rank texts in ways which correspond to interlocutors' intuitions about relative coherence (see Rochester and Martin 1979 and Hasan 1984a for studies correlating such intuitions with text analysis).

Hasan's technique will be demonstrated here with respect to [6:33], a narrative written by a student in Year 7 (the first year of junior secondary school in NSW; 12-13 years old). The student's migrant background is reflected in her adaptation of the traditional tale.

[6:33] a. Once upon a time there lived a little girl named Snow White,
        b. she lived with her Aunt Mary and Uncle Tom in a castle.
        c. She lived with her Aunt and Uncle
        d. because her parents were dead.
        e. One day she heard her Uncle and Aunt talking about leaving Snow White in the castle because they wanted to go to America and didn't have enough money to take Snow White.
        f. Snow White did not want her uncle and Aunt to do this
        g. so she decided
        h. it would be best if she ran away.
        i. The next morning she ran away from home
        j. when her Aunt and Uncle were having breakfast.
        k. She ran away into the woods,
        l. She was very tired and Hungry.
        m. Then she saw this little cottage,
        n. she knocked
        o. and no-one answered
        p. she went inside
        q. and fell asleep.
        r. Meanwhile the seven dwarfs were coming home from work
        s. they went inside.
        t. There they found Snow White sleeping,
        u. Then Snow White woke up
        v. she saw the dwarfs.
        w. The dwarfs said

x. what is your name.
y. Snow White said
z. "My name is Snow White."
aa. Doc said
bb. if you wish
cc. you may live here with us.
dd. Snow White said
ee. Oh could
ff. Thankyou
gg. Then Snow White told the dwarfs the whole story
hh. and Snow White and the 7 dwarfs lived happily ever after.

Hasan's starting point is that coherence is not directly a function of the number of cohesive ties found in a text (the same point is made in Rochester and Martin 1979). More important is the way in which strings and chains interact systematically with each other as participant, process and circumstance. The first step in this analysis is to establish a text's strings and chains. Hasan's uses the term similarity chain for *English Text*'s taxonomically based lexical strings (where lexical strings are based on lexically rendered texts) and identity chain for *English Text*'s reference chains (excluding relevance phoricity). Hasan's definition of similarity and identity chains suggests a stratified approach to discourse semantics very like that proposed by *English Text*. Identity chains are based on co-referentiality, which is realised through pronominal cohesion, instantial equivalence, the definite article and demonstratives (or lexical repetition if the reference is generic); similarity chains are based on co-classification or co-extension, which are realised through substitution and ellipsis, lexical repetition and relations of synonymy, antonymy, hyponymy and meronymy. Discourse systems however, underlying these semantic chain structures, are not articulated.

One apparently unresolved problem with Hasan's technique is that there is often considerable overlap between some strings and chains, especially where pronouns are lexically rendered. For example, both the team and the boat strings analysed for [5:36] in Chapter 5 overlap with reference chains distinguishing the Australians from the Americans and Liberty from Australia II. Rendering substitution and ellipsis, but not pronominal reference would reduce the amount of overlap, but not eliminate it. For reasons that are not made explicit however strings and chains do not overlap in Hasan's diagrams, possibly because reference chains are given priority, with lexical strings composed only of items not already included in refer-

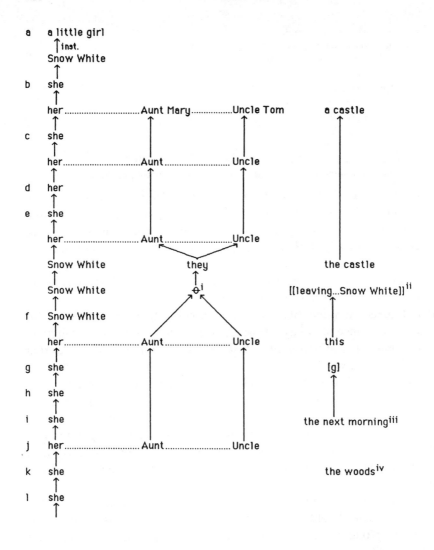

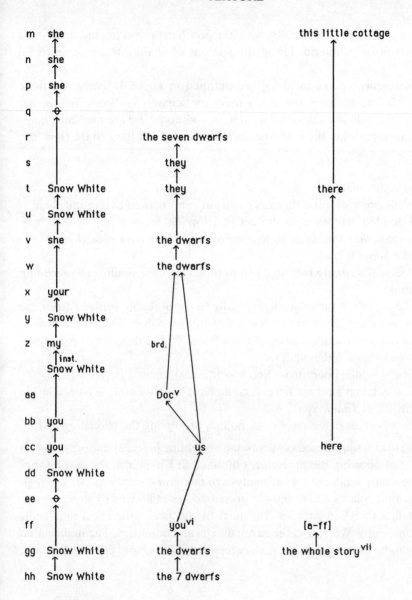

Fig. 6.4. Reference chains in text [6:33]

ence chains. A strategy for resolving the problem of overlapping strings and chains will be proposed during the analysis of chain interaction in [6:33] below.

Reference chains in [6:33] are outlined in Fig. 6.4. There are three major chains, realising the text's main participants — Snow White, her Aunt and Uncle and the seven dwarfs. In addition there are two short housing chains, realising the castle (*a castle-the castle*) and the cottage (*this little cottage-there-here*).

Notes on the analysis:

(i) Participants ellipsed through branching are marked as θ in the chain.

(ii) Extended reference to the act of [[*leaving Snow White in the castle because they wanted to go to America and didn't have enough money to take Snow White*]]

(iii) *The next morning* is bridged from time reference implicit in preceding clause.

(iv) *The woods* is introduced phorically here, probably bridged from the castle in [6:33e], though this is not shown in analysis; *the seven dwarfs* is similarly introduced, bridged from Snow White, though not connected to her chain in the analysis.

(v) *Doc* is bridged here from Snow White, last realised in [6:33z].

(vi) *You* is taken a phoric here; it could have been ignored as frozen inside the idiom *Thank-you*.

(vii) *the whole story* is a phoric "A-noun", presuming the preceding text.

Lexical strings based on taxonomic relations in [6:33] are presented in Fig. 6.5. Following the procedures outlined in Chapter 5, the text has not been lexically rendered for the analysis of taxonomic relations. Strings realising people, places and things are presented first, followed by strings associated with actions and qualities. The main "participant" strings deal with family relations, Snow White and the seven dwarfs and domiciles. The main action strings have to do with residence, perception, talking and coming & going.

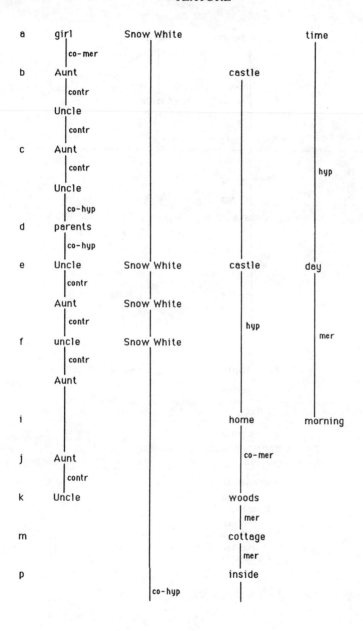

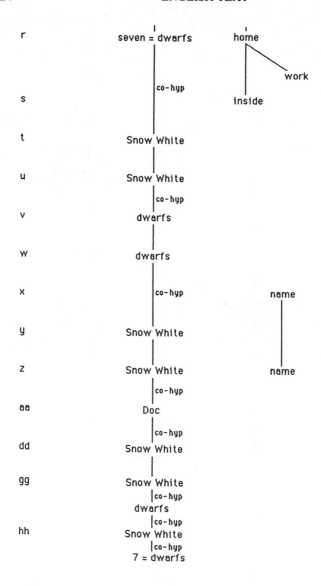

Fig. 6.5. People, places and things strings in [6:32]

Note on analysis:

(i) *home* and *work* are taken as places in this analysis to show their relationship to the domicile string; they could just as well have been treated as elaborations of the Process *coming* (*home* is so treated in the action strings below).

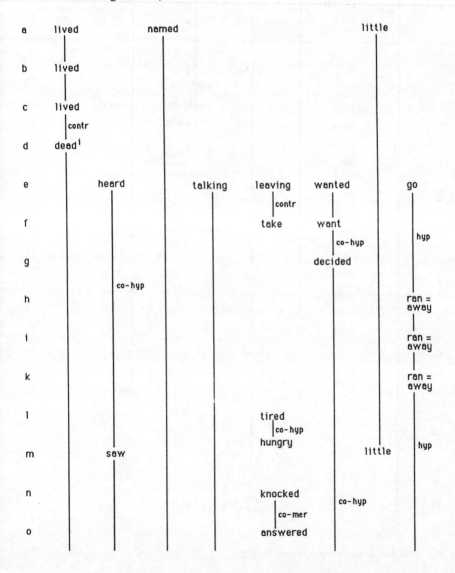

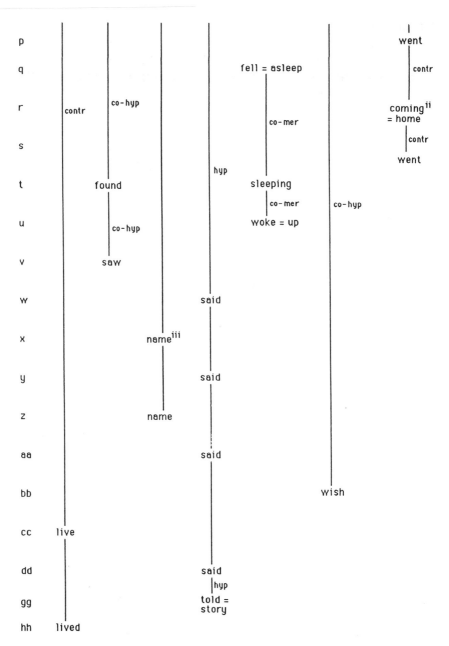

Fig. 6.6. Action and quality strings in [6:33]

Notes on the analysis:
(i) *dead* is taken as a metaphorical realisation of the action "die", and so worked into the "living" string here.
(ii) *home* is treated as a locative elaboration of the Process *coming* (cf. its treatment as a place in the place string above).
(iii) *name* is taken as a metaphorical realisation of the action "name", and so taken a repetition of *named* in [6:33:a].

The analysis of strings and chains makes it possible to distinguish what Hasan refers to as **peripheral** from **relevant** tokens. Peripheral tokens are potentially cohesive items which do not participate in lexical strings or reference chains. There are only five potentially cohesive items in [6:33] which do not enter into strings or chains: *having = breakfast, America, money, best* and *happily* (assuming that *the woods* is bridged from *castle* as suggested above, and that *happily* is not taken as an antonym of *tired and hungry*). Hasan (1985b:93) predicts that the lower the proportion of peripheral tokens to relevant ones, the more coherent the text. On this basis it might be predicted that [6:33] would be rated as relatively coherent by native speakers.

The next step in the analysis is consider the interaction between strings, chains and experiential grammatical functions. The problem of overlapping strings and chains can be illustrated with respect to the domicile string in [6:33] which overlaps with two distinct reference chains, one identifying the castle and the other the cottage:

DOMICILE STRING:
castle-castle-home-woods-cottage-inside-home-inside

DOMICILE CHAINS:
a castle-the castle-the woods
this little cottage-there-here

The strategy adopted here to overcome this difficulty will be to analyse cohesive harmony from the point of view of reference chains as far as people, places and things are concerned and from the point of view of lexical strings for actions and qualities. This strategy it must be noted has strong effects on the kind of string/chain interaction recognised for a text. The relation of the domicile string to Medium and Process roles is outlined in Table 6.22, alongside the relation between the domicile chains and their Medium and Process roles.

Table 6.22. *"Domicile" strings and chains in relation to* TRANSITIVITY *roles in text [6:33]*

Medium	Process	Circumstance of location	Range
DOMICILE STRING:			
she	lived	in a castle	
Snow White	leaving	in the castle	
she	ran away	from home	
she	ran away	into the woods	
she	saw	this little cottage	
she	went	inside	
the seven dawrfs	coming	home	
they	went	inside	
DOMICILE CHAINS:			
she	lived	in a castle	
Snow White	leaving	in the castle	
she	ran away	into the woods	
she	saw		this little cottage
they	found	there	
you	live	here	

Hasan defines string/chain interaction as occurring when more than one member of a string/chain is in the same experiential relationship to more than one member of another string/chain, basing clause rank experiential relationships on transitive (e.g. Actor˙Process˙Goal as below) rather than ergative roles (Agent˙Process˙Medium as above). The domicile string thus interacts with the coming & going string (Process˙Circumstance of location — 5 times) and the Snow White chain (Actor˙Circumstance of Location — 5 times). The domicile chains on the other hand display a very different pattern of interaction. The cottage chain does not interact at all; and the castle chain interacts with the Snow White chain as Circumstance of Location to Actor (3 times). Hasan defines **central** tokens as relevant tokens which interact and suggests that the higher the proportion of central tokens to non-central ones, the more coherent a text will be judged. As has just been demonstrated (see also Table 6.23) this ratio is sensitive to how the problem of overlapping strings and chains is resolved.

Following the strategy proposed above for sorting out strings and chains, cohesive harmony will be analysed with respect to the following strings and chains; these represent an exhaustive listing of the 105 relevant

Table 6.23. Interaction for domicile string vs domicile chain

Actor	Process	Circumstance of location
DOMICILE STRING:		
she		castle
Snow White		castle
she	ran away	home
she	ran away	woods
she	went	inside
the seven dwarfs	coming	home
they	went	inside
DOMICILE CHAIN:		
she		castle
Snow White		castle
she		woods

tokens in [6:33] (ellipses have not been rendered for purposes of this count):

REFERENCE CHAINS (60 tokens):
Snow White (*a little girl-Snow White-she-her-she-her-her...* 34 items)
her Aunt and Uncle (*Aunt Mary-Aunt-Aunt-they...* 11 items)
the seven dwarfs (*the seven dwarfs-they-they-the dwarfs...*10 items)
the castle (*a castle-the castle*)
the cottage (*this little cottage-there-here*)

LEXICAL STRINGS (45 tokens):
time (*time-day-morning*)
size (*little-little*)
disposition (*tired-hungry*)
residence (*lived-lived-lived-dead-live-lived*)
perception (*heard-saw-found-saw*)
naming (*named-name-name*)
talking (*talking-said-said-said-said-said-told=story*)
abandonment (*leaving-taking*)
calling (*knocked-answered*)
sleeping (*fell=asleep-sleeping-woke=up*)
desire (*wanted-want-decided-wish*)
moving (*go-ran=away-ran=away-ran=away-went-coming=home-went*)

Of these chains and strings, the following enter into string/chain interaction:

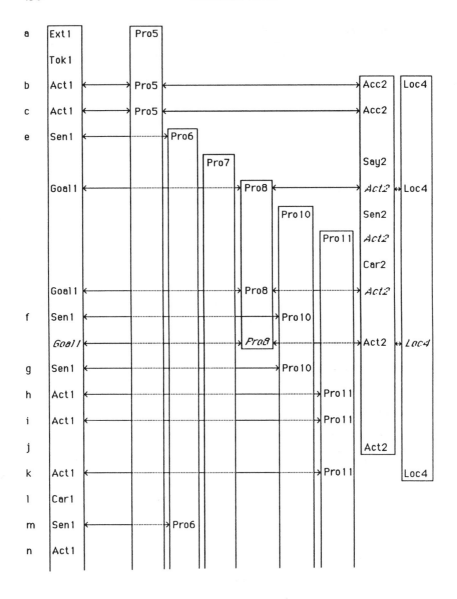

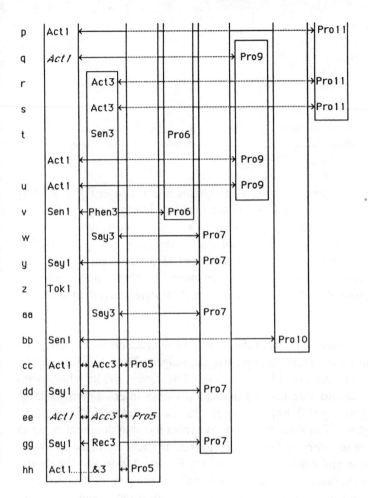

Fig. 6.7. Chain/string interaction in [6:33]

key:
italics (rendered function in elliptical or non-finite clause)

Actor	**Rec**eiver
Process	**Sen**ser
Goal	**Phen**omenon
Accompaniment	**Tok**en
Location	**Exist**ent
Sayer	**Car**rier

1, 2, 3...11 (indexes clause function to relevant string or chain)

1. Snow White
2. her Aunt and Uncle
3. the seven dwarfs
4. the castle
5. residence
6. perception
7. talking
8. abandonment
9. sleeping
10. desire
11. moving

Interaction among these 11 strings and chains is outlined in Fig. 6.7. Only central tokens have been included in the analysis. The TRANSITIVITY function of each member of these strings and chains is presented clause by clause; horizontal lines connect the central tokens of interacting strings and chains. This analysis recognises 54 central tokens, out of 105 relevant ones, a ratio which compares favorably with those uncovered by Hasan in her research on spoken narratives by younger children that were judged coherent by native speakers.

Hasan's final measure of coherence with respect to cohesive harmony analysis has to do with breaks in the picture of interaction — the fewer the breaks, the more coherent the text will be judged. Text [6:33] displays a fairly continuous pattern of interaction. The Snow White chain runs through the text and a number of the action strings interact across a large domain (residence [6:33b-hh], perception [6:33e-v], talking [6:33e-gg] and desire [6:33e-bb]). The main breaks derive from the abandonment string in the first part of the story and the sleeping string in the second, and from the Aunt and Uncle and castle chains in the story's orientation and the dwarfs chain in its resolution. The text thus reflects both the continuity associated with texture and the discontinuity associated with a developing narrative "macro-structure".

In summary then, Hasan's (1985b:94-95) definitions of peripheral, central and relevant tokens and suggestions as far as using cohesive harmony analysis as a measure of coherence are as follows:

TYPE OF TOKEN:

peripheral — tokens which do not particpate in strings or chains
relevant — tokens which do participate in strings or chains
central — relevant tokens which interact

MEASURES OF COHERENCE:

1.   The lower the propotion of the peripheral tokens to the relevant ones, the more coherent the text is likely to be.

2.   The higher the proportion of the central tokens to the non-central ones, the more coherent the text is likely to be.
3.   The fewer the breaks in the picture of interaction, the more coherent the text.

The limitations of this procedure should perhaps be stressed again at this point. First, cohesive harmony is a measure of texture, which is just one aspect of textual unity; it does not account for unity deriving from register and genre. Second, cohesive harmony is a measure of experiential texture; it has not been developed to the point where it takes into account the interaction of strings and chains with interpersonal, textual and logical structure. Third, cohesive harmony focusses on componential cohesion; it does not treat organic relations realising CONJUNCTION and NEGOTIATION. All this means that it is in principle possible to take a text and re-arrange it in any of the following ways without affecting cohesive harmony:

(i)   Change the order of any two elements of generic structure.
(ii)   Weave the strings and chains realised as Subject or Theme into Residue or New.
(iii)   Reverse the sequence of selected pairs of messages or moves.

Any of these disintegrating manoeuvres would affect interlocutors' intuitions about the coherence of a text, which is simply to underscore the linguistic (as opposed to contextual), experiential (as opposed to interpersonal, textual and logical) and componential (as opposed to organic) bias of cohesive harmony analysis.

As a final caveat the reasons for developing a measure of textual coherence need to be cautiously examined. One might argue from the perspective of formal linguistics that just as the goal of the grammarian is to account for speakers intuitions about which sentences are grammatical, so the goal of the textlinguist is to account for intuitions about which texts are coherent. But just as a functional grammarian would reject this delimitation of the goals of grammatical theory, so a functional discourse analyst might view accounting for speaker's intuitions about coherent text with some suspicion. Alternatively, one might pose questions about the effectiveness of a text in achieving it's interlocutors' social purpose. This rhetorical perspective is likely to prove more appropriate as far as functional linguistics is concerned. Or one might ask questions about a text's role is sustaining culture as a dynamic open system. These points will be taken up again in Chapter 7 below.

6.3.2 *Method of development*

Halliday (1985a:38) describes the grammatical function Theme as the element of clause structure which "serves as the point of departure of the message; it is that with which the clause is concerned." In English, Theme is realised through initial position (unlike say Tagalog where it is marked with the particle *ang* and typically appears in clause final position; see Martin 1983a). Halliday is careful to distinguish Theme from Given, assigning distinct Theme ^ Rheme (realised by constituent sequence) and (Given)'New structures (realised by intonation) to the English clause. This is an essential step in understanding the difference between **method of development** (this section) and **point** (Section 6.3.3 below); without this distinction no adequate account of English texture can be provided.

Conflation of the notions of Theme and Given in English appears to derive from work on functional sentence perspective in Prague School linguistics. Firbas (1964:268) for example translates Mathesius's proposed definition of Theme as follows:

> "[the theme] is that which is known or at least obvious in the given situation and from which the speaker proceeds."

Halliday's suggestion is that for English, the critical notion is "that from which the speaker proceeds", which may or may not be known (cf. the nonphoric Themes in [6:34i, j], [6:23a, r] and [6:36h, k, l, r] below). In this respect English contrasts typologically with languages like Tagalog whose Themes are next to categorically "given" (in the sense of being definite; see again Martin 1983a).

The most important work interpreting Theme as point of departure from a discourse perspective has been accomplished by Fries (1981/1983, forthcoming). In essence Fries' argument is that the way in which lexical strings and reference chains interact with Theme is not random; rather the pattern of interaction realises what he refers to as a text's method of development:

> (a) the lexical material placed initially within each sentence of a paragraph (i.e. the themes of each sentence of a paragraph) indicates the point of departure of the message expressed by that sentence, and (b) the information contained within the themes of all of the sentences of a paragraph creates the method of development of that paragraph. (Fries 1983:135)

Fries (1981/1983) illustrates this point with respect to a number of texts, one of which is reproduced as [6:34] below. Topical Themes are in bold face in this text, and marked topical Themes are underlined (in English declaratives, unmarked topical Theme is conflated with Subject, whereas marked topical Theme precedes it). In [6:34] Theme has not been analysed in hypotactically dependent clauses (non-finite b, c, p and finite q) nor in branched paratactic clauses with Subject ellipsis (h and l).

[6:34] TOPICAL THEMES (underlined)

a **The English Constitution — that indescribable entity** — is a living thing,

b growing with the growth of men,

c and assuming ever-varying forms in accordance with the subtle and complex laws of human character.

d **It** is the child of wisdom and chance.

e **The wise men of 1688** moulded it into the shape we know,

f but **the chance that George I could not speak English** gave it one of its essential peculiarities — the system of a cabinet independent of the crown and subordinate to the Prime Minister.

g **The wisdom of Lord Grey** saved it from petrification,

h and set it upon the path of democracy.

i Then **chance** intervened once more.

j **A female sovereign** happened to marry an able and pertinacious man,

k and it seemed **likely** that an element which had been quiescent within it for years — the element of irresponsible administrative power — was about to become its predominate characteristic

l and change completely the direction of its growth.

m But **what chance gave** chance took away.

n **The Consort** perished in his prime,

o and **the English Constitution**,..., continued its mysterious life

p dropping the dead limb with hardly a tremor

q as if he had never been. (Fries 1983:123-124)

The interaction pattern Fries focusses on here is that between the lexical strings associated with "wisdom" and "chance" and Theme selection. This

Table 6.24. Theme and method of development in [6:33]

"Wisdom"	"Chance"
The wise men of 1688	
	but the chance that George I...
The wisdom of Lord Grey	
	chance
	likely
	what chance gave

pattern is outlined in Table 6.24 and has been forecast by [6:34d] — *It is the child of **wisdom** and **chance***. Note that grammatical metaphor has been drawn on to weave these particular strings through Theme and to formulate the appropriate "hyper-Theme" predicting this interaction pattern. *Wisdom* is a nominalised quality (congruent *wise*, as in [6:34e]) and *chance* a nominalised modalization (congruent *might*) in [6:34d]; the modalization is dressed up as a quality in [6:34k] — *likely*.

This interaction of lexical strings and Theme is itself associated with [6:34]'s internal conjunctive structure. The text justifies the claim that the English constitution is the child of wisdom and chance with two examples ([6:34e-f] and [6:34g-q]). The Themes in [6:34e+f] and in [6:34g+i] scaffold this rhetorical structure. This three-way pattern of interaction (conjunctive relations, lexical strings and Theme) is outlined in Fig. 6.8.

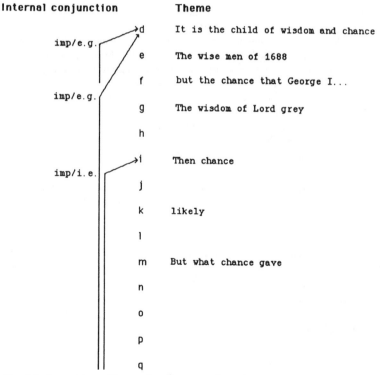

Internal conjunction   **Theme**

imp/e.g.

>d   It is the child of wisdom and chance

e   The wise men of 1688

f   but the chance that George I...

imp/e.g.

g   The wisdom of Lord grey

h

imp/i.e.

>i   Then chance

j

k   likely

l

m   But what chance gave

n

o

p

q

Fig. 6.8. Interaction of internal conjunction, lexical strings and Theme in [6:34]

Daneš (1974:118-119) suggests a number of ways in which strings, chains, Themes and Rhemes may interact in text. In some texts Themes typically relate to immediately preceding Rhemes, in others to immediately preceding Themes. Of special interest is the pattern suggested by Daneš whereby successive Themes are related to a single preceding Theme (or hyper-Theme as he terms it). This is the pattern that [6:34] would have displayed had wisdom and chance been made thematic in clause [6:34d] (e.g. *Wisdom and chance gave birth to the English Constitution*). As [6:34] stands however, Themes are predicted by clause [6:34d]'s New, not its Theme.

The important point here however is that [6:34d] stands in a predictive relationship to the interaction between lexical strings and Theme selection. It thus functions as what would be termed a Topic Sentence in school rhetoric — as the Theme of the paragraph in other words, rather than as the Theme of a clause. Danes's term hyper-Theme will be extended here to refer to paragraph Themes of this kind. For *English Text* then, a **hyper-Theme** is an introductory sentence or group of sentences which is established to predict a particular pattern of interaction among strings, chains and Theme selection in following sentences — *It is the child of wisdom and chance* is the hyper-Theme of [6:34]. On the basis of this definition of hyper-Theme, the term **macro-Theme**[4] can be defined as an sentence or group of sentences (possibly a paragraph) which predicts a set of hyper-Themes; this is the Introductory paragraph of school rhetoric. The proportionalities being set up here as as follows:

```
macro-Theme:text::
hyper-Theme:paragraph::
Theme:clause
```

In writing, the use of macro-Themes to predict hyper-Themes, which in turn predict a sequence of clause Themes is an important aspect of texture; and texts which do not make use of predicted patterns of interaction in this way may be read as less than coherent. As an example, consider the following written text, from a traumatic brain injured patient (from Prigatano et al. undated). Topical Themes are underlined, marked topical Themes underlined in all clauses (for further discussion of this text see Martin 1985c).

[6:35] (written mode)

a   What would you like to do at the end of your rehabilitation program?

b   My first choice is to go back to work at the hospital.

c **This** would be hard for me to do
d because **they** have hired someone to take my place.
e **I** liked the work.
f **I** was there for over 5 years.
g **I** also would like to go to a sheltered workshop.
h **This** would be good,
i but **it** has to have transportation to the place and to home.
j **The transportation** would have to be a bus
k because **I** do not have a driver's license.
l **I** was to have it renewed last year,
m but **that** was not done.
n **To get a driver's license,**
o **I** will need to take the written and the driver's exam.
p **The workshop** will help me control my temper,
q **which** is bad for me.
r **I** get mad easily
s and **this** is because of my brain injury.
t **All I can recall** is that I was knocked out for 3 weeks.
u **I** did my recovery at Mercy ICU.
v **I** had the car accident on my way to the hospital for a personnel directors meeting.
w **The workshop** might have been in Austin, Texas.
x **This** means I will be away from home,
y **which** I would miss very much.
z **I** miss not being at home.
aa **I** would like to work in the yard
bb and work on the cars,
cc especially washing and wax(ing) them.
dd **This** I have not done for years.

The obvious candidate for macro-Theme in a writing exercise of this kind is the question: *What would you like to do at the end of your rehabilitation program?* And *like to do* does predict the hyper-Themes of the reply:

My first choice is to go back to work at the hospital.
I also would like to go to a sheltered workshop.

The second of these clauses could have been more clearly highlighted as a hyper-Theme by making use of metaphorical incongruent internal conjunction instead of the CONTINUITY marker *also* (e.g. ***my second choice*** *would be…*); in this respect CONJUNCTION and the interaction of lexical relations and Theme selection are not reinforcing each other.

More problematic for text [6:35] is the fact that these two hyper-Themes do not consistently predict interaction patterns in the text which follows them. The first hyper-Theme, [6:35b] for example is followed by four referential Themes, identifying three different participants (*this, they, I, I*):

b	My first choice is to go back to work at the hospital.
c	**This** (*to go back to work at the hospital*)
d	because **they** (*the hospital*)
e	**I**
f	**I**

The second, less clearly signalled hyper-Theme introduces the sheltered workshop chain, which is realised thematically in clauses [6:35h, i, p, w & x]. This might not be a problem if [6:35h/i, p & w/x] themselves functioned as a further layer of hyper-Themes, predicting their own patterns of Theme selection (although internal conjunction would be necessary to co-ordinate their relation to their hyper-Theme). But as can be seen below, they do not. Instead, the text develops locally, from clause to clause, with Themes by and large picking up information from preceding Rhemes. One striking aspect of this localised development in [6:35] is the use of extended and text reference in [6:35c, h, m, s, x & dd] (*this, this, that, this, this, this*) to comment on a preceding clause; taken in conjunction with the agnate elaborating β clauses introduced by *which* in [6:35q & y], the text exhibits a very local method of development indeed (apparently pathologically so). The three frustrated hyper-Themes are dotted underlined in the Theme analysis below; the workshop chain is in small caps.

FRUSTRATED HYPERTHEMES

g	**I also would like to go to** A SHELTERED WORKSHOP.
h	**This** would be good,
i	but IT has to have transportation to the place and to home.
j	**The transportation**
k	because **I**
l	**I**
m	but **that** (*to have my driver's license renewed*)
n	**To get a driver's license**,
o	**I**
p	THE WORKSHOP will help me control my temper,
q	**which** (**my temper**)
r	**I**
s	and **this** (*the fact that I get mad easily*)
t	**All I can recall**
u	**I**
v	**I**

w	THE WORKSHOP might have been in Austin, Texas.
x	**This** (*the fact that the workshop might have been in Austin, Texas*)
y	**which** (*home*)
z	**I**
aa	**I**
bb	
cc	
dd	**This** (*washing and waxing cars*)

The lack of integrating interaction patterns in [6:35] contrasts sharply with the interaction of conjunctive relations, reference chains and marked Themes in [6:36], another of Fries' (1983:129-130) examples. The interaction pattern is clearly predicted by a hyper-Theme: *Although the United States participated heavily in World War I, the nature of that participation was fundamentally different from what it became in World War II* (as can be seen, Vocabulary 3 items like *difference* are critical features of hyper-Themes; see Winter 1977). Topical Themes are in bold face and marked Themes underlined in [6:36] below; β clauses appearing before their α are taken as marked Themes, and Theme is not analysed in the following α. The text's hyper-Theme is dotted underlined.

[6:36] (higlighting method of development and marked Themes)

a	**Although the United States participanted heavily in World War I**,
b	the nature of that participation was fundamentally **different** from what it became in World War II.
c	**The earlier conflict** was a one-ocean war for the Navy and a one-theatre war for the Army;
d	**the latter** was a two-ocean war for the Navy and one of five major theatres for the Army.
e	**In both wars** a vital responsibility of the Navy was escort-of-convoy and anti-submarine work,
f	but **in the 1917-1918 conflict** it never clashed with the enemy on the surface;
g	whilst **between 1941 and 1945** it fought some twenty major and countless minor engagements with the Japanese Navy.
h	**American soldiers who engaged in World War I** were taken overseas in transports
i	and landed on docks or in protected harbours;
j	**in World War II** the art of amphibious warfare had to be revived and developed,
k	since **assault troops** were forced to fight their way ashore.
l	**Airpower**, in the earlier conflict, was still inchoate and almost negligible;
m	**in the latter** it was a determining factor.

n   **In World War I** the battleship still reigned queen of the sea,
o   as **she** had in changing forms, since the age of Drake.
p   and **Battle Line** fought with tactics inherited from the age of sail;
q   but **in World War II** the capital naval force was the air-craft carrier taskgroup,
r   for which **completely new tactics** had to be devised.

Hyper-Theme:
a   <u>**Although the United States participanted heavily in World War I**</u>,
b   the nature of that participation was fundamentally different from what it became in World War II.

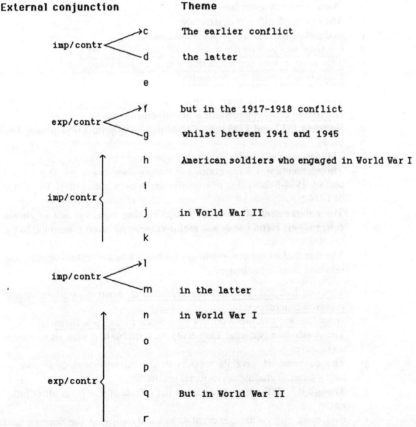

Fig. 6.9. Interaction of external conjunction, reference chains and marked Theme in text [6:36]

The interaction of contrastive conjunctive relations, reference chains and Theme selection is outlined in Fig. 6.9. This text highlights the significance of marked Themes as a resource for scaffolding a text's method of development (the conjunctive relations shown are external, although modelled to the left of the event line for display purposes in this analysis).

Text [6:36] is an excellent example of predictive relations between a hyper-Theme and clause Themes. Predictive relations between a macro-Theme and its hyper-Themes can be illustrated from text [6:23]. This text is represented below, with its macro-Theme double underlined, its hyper-Themes single underlined and topical[5] Themes in its remaining clauses in bold face.

[6:23] (illustating macro- and hyper-Themes)

    a   **Wars** are costly exercises.

    b   **They** cause death and destruction

    c   and put resources to non-productive uses

    d   but **they** also promote industrial and economic change.

    e   This benefit does not mean that war is a good thing, but that it sometimes brings useful developments.

    f   The Second World War further encouraged the restructuring of the Australian economy towards a manufacturing basis.

    g   **Between 1937 and 1945** the value of industrial production almost doubled.

    h   **This increase** was faster than otherwise would have occurred.

    i   **The momentum** was maintained in the post-war years

    j   and **by 1954-5** the value of manufacturing output was three times that of 1944-5.

    k   **The enlargement of Australia's steel-making capacity, and of chemicals, rubber, metal goods and motor vehicles** all owed something to the demands of war.

    l   **The war** had acted as something of a hot-house for technological progress and economic change.

    m   The war had also revealed inadequacies in Australia's scientific and research capabilities.

    n   After the war strenuous efforts were made to improve these.

    o   **The Australian National University** was established with an emphasis on research.

    p   **The government** gave its support to the advancement of science in many areas, including agricultural production.

    q   **Though it is difficult to disentangle the effects of war from other influences,**

    r   it is **clear** that future generations not only enjoyed the security and peace won by their forefathers but also the benefits of wartime economic expansion. (Simmelhaig & Spenceley 1984:121)

The first of [6:23]'s hyper-Themes is developed through a 'growth' string; the second is developed through an 'agencies' one. Note again that grammatical metaphor is critical in forming appropriate macro-Themes and hyper-Themes and in creating the appropriate strings to weave through clause Themes.

d   but they also promote industrial and economic change.

e   This benefit does not mean that war is a good thing, but that it some-times brings useful developments.

f   The Second World War further encouraged the restructuring of the Australian economy towards a manufacturing basis.

['growth']

h   **This increase**

i   **The momentum**

k   **The enlargement of Australia's steel-making capacity, and of chemicals, rubber, metal goods and motor vehicles**

m   The war had also revealed inadequacies in Australia's scientific and research capabilities.

n   After the war strenuous efforts were made to improve these.

['agencies']

o   **The Australian National University**

p   **The government**

Clearly, in longer texts, this pattern of macro-Themes predicting hyper-Themes can be extended, with hyper-Themes themselves functioning as macro-Themes in their own right (as might have happened in a better tex-tured version of [6:35] above). Once texts develop to this level of internal complexity, titles, sub-titles, headings and subheadings are commonly deployed to keep track of the composition structure being erected (as in this chapter for example; see also the discussion of Matthiessen & Halliday in press in 6.3.3 below). Schematically, the thematic relationships being introduced here are outlined in Fig. 6.10, with the proviso that a text may

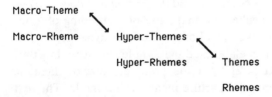

Fig. 6.10. Solidarity across levels of Theme

be organised thematically around more than the three levels shown. As noted above, the lowest level hyper-Themes in a text are referred to traditionally as Topic Sentences and the highest level "macro"-Themes as Introductions.

Text [6:32] is revised as [6:37] below, by developing a heavily nominalised macro-Theme which explicitly predicts hyper-Themes for each of its potential paragraphs. As above, the macro-Theme is double underlined and its hyper-Themes single underlined; experiential metaphors in the macro-Theme appear in bold face.

[6:37]   (REVISED VERSION: illustrating macro-Theme)
   a   I think Governments are necessary for a number of reasons.
   b   These have to do with the special duties of Governments at different administrative levels.
   c   These include the Federal Government's **concern with general problems that occur in the community**, the State Government's **interest in education** and the Local Government's **responsibility for waste disposal**.

   d   Let me begin by pointing out that the Federal Government fixes up problems that occur in the community...

   e   Another example is that the State Government looks after schools;
   f   this prevents vandalism and fighting...

   g   As a final point the Local Government is important to look after rubbish:
   h   otherwise everyone would have diseases...

   i   As a result of their concern with general problems, education and waste disposal, Governments at several administrative levels are necessary. (cf. Martin 1986b)

The interaction patterns considered to this point have focussed on written text; the compositional scaffolding discussed depends for its development on a degree of consciousness not associated with spontaneous spoken monologue (note how the interlocutor falters in [4:2] below in her attempts at written scaffolding: *the reason being is...* and *the first thing it does is...*) — although professional public speakers do make use of scaffolding of a not unrelated kind. Spontaneous spoken text however unfolds dynamically; it is not configured as a thing, with an elaborated part/whole structure. It is thus important to re-examine text [4:2] from the point of view of thematic development, to see what point of departure means in this mode. The text is re-presented below, with topical Themes in bold face and marked

Themes underlined (Theme has been analysed in dependent clauses with Subjects and β clauses have been interpreted as marked Themes where they are realised before their α, ignoring Themes in this α as above; Predicators in imperative and non-finite clauses are not treated as Themes, following Halliday 1985a).

[4:2]   Question:
    1.a.   **What** do you have to do in the showing area,
      b.   with **the dog** on the lead?

    Response:
    2.c.   Well, **you** always walk
      d.   with **the dog** on the left-hand side,
      e.   **the reason being** is [[the judge is standing in the centre of the ring]].
    3.f.   So, therefore, **you** need to get yourself between your dog and the judge.
    4.g.   **The dog** (!) must be able to see the dog at all times.
    5.h.   So, usually **when a class is going into the ring**,
      i.   the first thing it does is:
      j.   **the judge** is standing in the centre of the ring,
      k.   **the people** sort of walk the ring, with their dogs,
      l.   and then...**we** sort of wait.
    6.m.   **With the Dachshund**, a Dachshund is tabled.
    7.n.   **That's** [[because it's a low dog]],
      o.   and **the judge** goes over that.
    8.p.   **With the bigger breeds of dog**, they're stood on the ground,
      q.   because it's **easier** [[for the judge to handle them]].
    9.r.   **With the smaller breeds of dog such as Corgis, all the Toy- breeds, Dachshunds and this type of thing** we — as our turn comes,
      s.   **we**[6] stand our dog on the table,
      t.   **we** stand it in show stance,
      u.   with **the lead**, the lead held up,
      v.   hoping
      w.   that **our dog** will stand like a nice statue,
      x.   so as **the judge** can come.
    10.y.   **The judge** handles it,
      z.   and **this** is [[where I'm telling you, temperament plays a big part]].
    11.aa. **The judge** has to be able to look into the dog's mouth
      bb.   to see
      cc.   that **it's teeth** are perfect.
    12.dd. Usually then **he** feels down the neck, along its body,
      ee.   and **he** can sort of feel conformation
      ff.   by doing this,
      gg.   so **you**'re hoping all the time

hh. that **your dog** will stand nice and steady
ii. so **the judge** can do this
jj. and **it** doesn't hamper him
kk. handling the dogs.
13.ll. **After the judge has handled and gone over the dog**,
mm. then, you really do whatever the judge tells you.
14.nn. Basically **it** is always the same.
15.oo. **He** usually says,
pp. or **she** usually says,
qq. "Walk your dog in a triangle."
16.rr. Now, **as I told you already**,
ss. the dog is always walked on the left-hand side.
17.tt. So, **if your judge is standing here**,
uu. we walk away from him that way.
18.vv. **That** is [[so the judge can get the hind movement of your dog]].
19.ww. Then **we** usually walk sideways like that
xx. so as **he** can see [[the dog moving all over]]
yy. and then **we** walk back to the judge
zz. so as **he** can see the front movement.
20.aaa. **After that** he usually tells you
bbb. to wait over there.
21.ccc. **He** proceeds to do that with every dog.
22.ddd. Then **he** will say,
eee. "Line your dog up."
fff. or "Get the best out of your dog."
ggg. and **he** will sum them all up
hhh. and put them in first, second or third.

Being a procedural text, most clauses in [4:2] take people as their point of departure: the handler chain (9 tokens) and the judge chain (16 tokens). In addition the dog string appears as Theme in 8 clauses; the only other participant appearing as Theme is the lead, which can be related to the dog string. The remaining unmarked topical Themes include an incongruent conjunctive relation (*the reason being is*) and four instances of extended or text reference (*that, this, it, that*), each of which refer locally to the immediately preceding clause.

UNMARKED THEMES in [4:2]:
handler (9)
judge (16)
dogs (8)
the lead
the reason being
that [*the fact that a Dachshund is tabled*]

this [*the judge handling the dog*]
it [*whatever the judge tells you*]
that [*the fact that we walk away from him that way*]

Congruent unmarked Themes, then, are favoured in this spoken text. Unmarked topical Theme selection is not deployed to scaffold [4:2]'s staging or development (although it does reflect its genre). Instead marked Themes, both phrasal and clausal, are used to stage the dog showing procedure. Each of the four activity sequences recognised in 5.4.2.3 above is highlighted in this way:

MARKED THEMES in [4:2]:
when a class is going into the ring,
[walking the ring...]

With the Dachshund,
With the bigger breeds of dog
easier
With the smaller breeds of dog such as Corgis, all the Toy-breeds,
Dachshunds and this type of thing
[handling...]
After the judge has handled and gone over the dog,

[movement...]

as I told you already,
if your judge is standing here,
[movement demonstration...]

After that
[evaluation...]

This pattern of marked Themes in [4:2] is the dynamic equivalent of the synoptic metaphorical hyper-Themes discussed above. But in spoken mode the marked Themes punctuate rather than predict, annotating the text in episodes as it unfolds rather than scaffolding it as a macro-constituent structure that is in some sense preconceived. Seen in this light hyper-Themes can be interpreted as a further category of textual metaphor: a hyper-Theme is an metaphorical marked Theme.

Finally, it needs to be kept in mind that the discussion of strings, chains, Themes and conjunctive relations has to this point focussed experientially on topical Themes. Theme selection however is also an important interpersonal resource and was so deployed in [6:30] above. This text is represented below with interpersonal Themes dotted underlined and topical Themes in bold face (Theme is analysed in all ranking clauses). Considered from the perspective of group rank as opposed to clause rank meanings, all of the topical Themes in [6:30] are in fact 'interpersonal' ones: first and second person pronouns (*I, you, you, you, I, we, you, you, we*) and the metaphorical modulation *my responsibilities*. So the method of development of this text is an interactive one: the sitting member is concerned to **engage** his constituent. The association of unmarked Theme and Subject in English means that these interpersonal considerations are better pursued during the discussion of modal responsibility in 6.3.4 below. It is important to note at this point however that a pattern of Theme selection which foregrounds interpersonal meaning will not lend itself to the experientially oriented macro-Theme, hyper-Theme, Theme interaction reviewed above. It is for this reason that school rhetoric has long cautioned against writing in the first person (although it has also long forgotten why this is so).

[6:30] a   α   **I** have been advised

b   'β   that **you** have recently become one of the constituents in the Electorate of Mitchell.

c   ˣβ 1   Whether⁷ you have recently moved,

d   ⁺2   or whether **you** have reached the age that gives you full voting rights,

e   α   may **I** as your Federal Member of Parliament welcome you as a new constituent.

f   **We** are privileged to live in such a pleasant part of Australia.

g   **My responsibility** is to make sure that the life style we enjoy is maintained and improved.

h   ˣβ   Should **you** wish to contact me on any matter which is concerning you, either day-to-day or national importance,

i   α   please do not **hesitate** to do so.

j   ˣβ   If *you* are uncertain whether your problem is one affected by Commonwealth, State or Local Government,

k   α   **we** should be able to advise you promptly.

6.3.3 *Point*

Halliday (1985a:277-278) characterises Theme ˆ Rheme organisation in the clause as speaker-oriented (the Theme being what the speaker is on about) and Given ̇New structure as listener-oriented (the New being news to the listener). It follows from this that Theme and New should interact with discourse semantics in quite different ways; and this does turn out to be the case.[8] The difference between Theme and New selection can be illustrated with respect to the following text, analysed for intonation in Halliday 1985b:60. Text [6:38] is first analysed for topical Theme below (bold face), and following this Halliday's analysis of tonic prominence is presented. The text has more News than Themes because just over half the clauses are realised over two tone groups (see Halliday 1967c, 1970b, 1985a:271-286 for the analysis of intonation presented here).

[6:38]   (TOPICAL THEME underlined)

a   **The only real accident that I've ever had** was in fog and ice,
b   and **there** was a big truck parked on the side of the road, about three feet away from the side of the road,
c   and **it** was very thick fog,
d   and **a mini** had gone into this truck -
e   well **the mini** had just touched the offside of the truck with its nearside wing
f   and so **it** meant
g   **when I came along**
h   my side of the road was completely blocked,
i   and unfortunately **I** went into a four wheel skid
j   before coming up to this mini,
k   and at the time **I** didn't know
l   how to deal with a four wheel skid
m   and so **I** went into the mini.
n   - **You** hit it sideways on.
o   - **About twelve cars** went into me
p   and then **a friend of ours** came along
q   and **he** decided to try and overtake the lot
r   and so **he** went into each one,
s   sort of banging them sideways as it were,
t   and oh **this** was in daylight.
u   - Because of the fog.
v   - Needless to say **I** treat fog with great respect now.
w   - Yes, **I** know.
x   **They** they keep happening these multiple collisions in the fog.
y   Were **you** all right as a result of this?
z   - Oh yes, oh yes.
aa **There** was no-one injured.

[6:38]   (TONIC syllable in bold-face)
i   //4   the only real **acc**ident that //
ii   //4   I've ever **had** was //
iii   //1   in fog and **ice** //
iv   //1   there was...a //

v	//13	big **truck** parked on the side of the **road** a //
vi	//1	bout...three **feet** a //
vii	//1	**way** from the side of the road and it was //
viii	//1	very **thick** fog //
ix	//4	and a **mini** had //
x	//1	gone into this **truck** //
xi	//4	well the **mini** had just //
xii	//1	touched the **off**side of the truck with its //
xiii	//1	nearside **wing** and so it //
xiv	//4	meant when **I** came along //
xv	//4	**my** side of the road was com //
xvi	//1	pletely **blocked** and //
xvii	//4	un**fort**unately I //
xviii	//1	went into a four wheel **skid** be //
xix	//4	fore coming up to this **mini** and //
xx	//4	at **that** time I //
xxi	//1	didn't know how to **deal** with a four wheel skid and //
xxii	//4	so I went into the **mini** //
xxiii	//1	you hit it sideways **on** //
xxiv	//3	about twelve cars went into **me** and //
xxv	//3	then a friend of **ours** //
xxvi	//3	came **along** and //
xxvii	//1	he decided to try and overtake the **lot** and so he //
xxviii	//1	went into each **one** sort of //
xxix	//1	banging them **side**ways as it were and //
xxx	//1	oh this was in **day**light //
xxxi	//1	because of the **fog** //
xxxii	//4	needless to **say** I //
xxxiii	//4	treat **fog** with //
xxxiv	//13	**great** respect **now** //
xxxv	//1	**yes** I //
xxxvi	//1	**know** they //
xxxvii	//53	they keep **hap**pening these multiple collisions in **fog** //
xxxviii	//2	were you all **right** though as a result of this//
xxxix	//1	oh **yes** //
xxxx	//1	oh **yes** there //
xxxxi	//4	there was no-one **in**jured //

Where the tonic falls on the final salient syllable in a tone group, the domain of the structural function New is indeterminate; in principle it extend may leftwards from the tonic syllable until the initial salient syllable in the tone group is reached. Where the tonic falls on other than the final salient syllable of the tone group, then all information following the tonic syllable is Given. In order to simpify the interpretation of New presented here, only the minimal domain of the New will be considered; this will be taken as the highest ranking clause constituent (usually a ranking group or phrase) the tonic syllable falls on the final salient syllable of. This principle determines the following minimal News for [6:38], which can be contrasted with the selections for marked and unmarked Topical Theme in the right-hand column.

MINIMAL NEW in [6:38]

the only real accident
've ever had
in fog and ice
a big truck...on the side of the road
about three feet
away
very thick
a mini
into this truck
the mini
the offside
with its nearside wing
I
my
completely blocked
unfortunately
a four wheel skid
up to this mini
that
to deal
into the mini
sideways on
into me
a friend of ours
along
the lot
into each one
sideways
in daylight
the fog
needless to say
fog
great...now
yes
know

UMNARKED TOPICAL
THEME in [6:38]

driver (6)
friend (3)
mini (2)
accident (3)
there (2)
fog
it [e]
about twelve cars

MARKED TOPICAL
THEME in [6:38]

when I came along

keep happening...in fog
allright
yes
yes
no-one injured

The main contrast is in the range of meanings woven through Theme and New. Only a few of the text's participants and processes are selected as unmarked topical Theme, with far greater variation in New. The Themes focus on the major participants involved in the anecdote, while the News tell the story. Putting this in more general terms, Themes angle in on a given field, reflecting a text's genre; News elaborate the field, developing it in experiential terms.

This contrast in functions operates across text types and can be illustrated for exposition with text [6:36]. In a written text the domain of the New is even less clear than in writing. But information structure remains an important aspect of texture in writing, even though intonation is not explicitly realised. Taking New as the final clause constituent in [6:36] displays the same difference in the range of realisations noted for the spoken text considered above. The Theme grounds the genre, anchoring it to just a few meanings and the News articulate the field (topical Themes are in small caps in this example to distinguish them more clearly from News; marked Themes are underlined).

[6:36] (New interpreted as final ranking clause constituents)

a   ALTHOUGH THE UNITED STATES PARTICIPATED HEAVILY IN WORLD WAR I,

b   the nature of that participation was fundamentally different from what it became **in World War II**.

c   THE EARLIER CONFLICT was a one-ocean war for the Navy and a one-theatre war **for the Army**;

d   THE LATTER was a two-ocean war for the Navy and one of five major theatres **for the Army**.

e   IN BOTH WARS a vital responsibility of the Navy was **escort-of- convoy and anti-submarine work**,

f   but IN THE 1917-1918 CONFLICT it never clashed with the enemy **on the surface**;

g   whilst BETWEEN 1941 AND 1945 it fought some twenty major and countless minor engagements **with the Japanese Navy**.

h   AMERICAN SOLDIERS WHO ENGAGED IN WORLD WAR I were taken overseas **in transports**

i   and landed **on docks or in protected harbours**;

j   IN WORLD WAR II the art of amphibious warfare **had to be revived and developed**,

k since ASSAULT TROOPS were forced to fight their way **ashore**.
l AIRPOWER, in the earlier conflict, was still **inchoate and almost negligible**;
m IN THE LATTER it was **a determining factor**.
n IN WORLD WAR I the battleship still reigned **queen of the sea**,
o as SHE had in changing forms, **since the age of Drake**.
p and BATTLE LINE fought **with tactics inherited from the age of sail**;
q but IN WORLD WAR II the capital naval force was **the air-craft carrier taskgroup**,
r for which COMPLETELY NEW TACTICS **had to be devised**.

Theme selection in [6:36] is mainly restricted to the two World Wars alongside an army/navy/airforce string (*assault troops, airpower, she, Battle Line*). The text's method of development in other words narrowly circumscribes its selection of Themes. Choices for New are not restricted in this way; they open up the field of naval history, a small portion of which is being constructed in this text.

MINIMAL NEWS in [6:36]	TOPICAL THEMES in [6:36]
in World War I	World War I (4)
in World War II	World War II (5)
for the Army	both wars
for the Army	participation
escort-of-convey and	assault troops
anti-submarine work	airpower
on the surface	battleship
with the Japanese Navy	Battle Line
in transports	new tactics
on docks or in protected harbours	
had to be revived and developed	
ashore	
inchoate and almost negligible	
a determining factor	
queen of the sea	
since the age of Drake	
with tactics inherited from the age of sail	
the air-craft carrier task-group	
had to be devised	

The pattern of hyper- and macro-Themes recognised in 6.3.2 above raises the question of whether a similar symbolic pattern arises based on New. Reviewing text [6:23] it can be seen that hyper- and macro-New are also important aspects of texture, particularly in abstract writing. The function of hyper-New is illustrated in [6:23l] below; this clause pulls together and summarises the information build up in the rest of the paragraph. This complementarity of hyper-Theme predicting a text's method of development and hyper-New accumulating its point is outlined in Fig. 6.11.

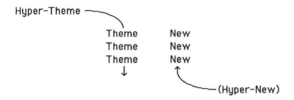

Fig. 6.11. Complementarity of hyper-Theme & hyper-New

The next paragraph is not pulled together in this way; instead, [6:23r] functions as a macro-New, summarising the text as a whole. As with hyper- and macro-Theme, grammatical metaphor is critical in pulling together the experiential meanings which have accumulated. Hyper-New is single underlined and macro-New double underlined in the following representation of [6:23]; the minimal News of remaining clauses appear in bold-face.

[6:23] (illustating New, hyper-New and macro-New)
  a   Wars are **costly exercises**.
  b   They cause **death and destruction**
  c   and put resources **to non-productive uses**
  d   but they also promote **industrial and economic change**.
  e   This benefit does not mean that war is a good thing, but that it sometimes brings **useful developments**.

  f   The Second World War further encouraged the restructuring of the Australian economy **towards a manufacturing basis**.
  g   Between 1937 and 1945 the value of industrial production almost **doubled**.
  h   This increase was **faster than otherwise would have occurred**.
  i   The momentum was maintained **in the post-war years**
  j   and by 1954-5 the value of manufacturing output was **three times that of 1944-5**.
  k   The enlargement of Australia's steel-making capacity, and of chemicals, rubber, metal goods and motor vehicles all owed something **to the demands of war**.

l   The war had acted as something of a hot-house for technological progress and economic change.

m   The war had also revealed **inadequacies in Australia's scientific and
research capabilities**.

n   After the war strenuous efforts were made to improve **these**.

o   The Australian National University was established **with an emphasis
on research**.

p   The government gave its support **to the advancement of science in
many areas, including agricultural production**.

q   Though it is difficult to disentangle the effects of war **from other influences,**

r   it is clear that future generations not only enjoyed the security and
peace won by their forefathers but also the benefits of war-time
economic expansion. (Simmelhaig & Spenceley 1984:121)

This pattern of interaction in [6:23] is outlined below, listing the text's
News, hyper-New and macro-New. The News of the introduction are listed
(in plain face) but do not participate in this pattern; they participate instead
in the complementary function of predicting the text's method of development reviewed above:

[costly exercises
death and destruction
to non-productive uses
industrial and economic change
useful developments]

towards a manufacturing basis
doubled
faster than otherwise would have occurred
in the post-war years
three times that of 1944-5
to the demands of war
The war had acted as something of a hot-house for technological progress
and economic change.

inadequecies in Australia's scientific and research capabilities
these (*inadequacies*)
with an emphasis on research
**to the advancement of science in many areas, including agricultural produc-
tion**
from other influences
it is clear that future generations not only enjoyed the security and peace
won by their forefathers but also the benefits of war- time economic
expansion.

Public speakers (and even writers, at a time when composition was taught in schools) are commonly advised: "tell your audience what you're going to say, say it, and then remind them what you've said". The generally cited Introduction ˆ Body ˆ Conclusion formula for expository texts makes the same point (as does Orientation ˆ Complication/Resolution ˆ Coda for narrative). What this wise counsel represents is the tendency for whole texts in English to symbolise the Theme ˆ Rheme and Given ˆ New structure of the English clause. Macro-Theme, hyper-Themes and clause Themes project forward, scaffolding the text with respect to its rhetorical purpose (i.e. its genre); macro-New, hyper-News and clause News on the other hand look back, gathering up the meanings which have accumulated to elaborate a text's field. The result is a textured sandwich in which texts project both forward and back as they unfold. Texture of this kind, which is a tendency in writing (by no means a categorical rule), is outlined schematically in Fig. 6.12.

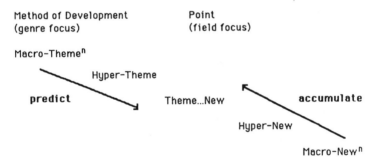

Fig. 6.12. Sandwich texture in abstract written discourse

Importantly, macro-News are not simply a replay of macro-Themes; they draw together new meanings which could not have been predicted by macro-Theme because they had not yet been made. This difference can be illustrated by considering the macro-Theme and macro-New of a recent paper by Matthiessen and Halliday (in press). The macro-Theme appears as the text's second paragraph and outlines the paper's major sections, which are also scaffolded with a Table of Contents[9] (the text's "super-Theme"):

[6:39]   **Macro-Theme** (Matthiessen & Halliday's paper)
Before we start the presentation of systemic functional theory, we will raise the question of what constitutes a theory of grammar here (Section 0). We will then explore one conception of grammar, grammar as a resource, and indicate how it emerges early in language development (Section 1). Having set the scene, we will map out the theoretical space of systemic functional grammar (Section II), presenting its dimensions and categories. Next, we will elaborate on one aspect of this account, the theory of metafunctions (Section III), and extend the account in two directions (Section IV). The final two sections are concerned with applications of the theory (Section V) and its relationship to other frameworks (Section VI). (Matthiessen & Halliday in press).

The major headings in the Table of Contents are organised around the hyper-Themes predicted by this macro-Theme:

0.   Theory of Grammar
I.   Conception and emergence of grammar
II. Scales and categories of systemic functional theory
III. Metafunctions again: modes of organisation
IV. Extending the grammar
V.   Grammar and the consumer: research applications
VI. SFG and other frameworks

This generic scaffolding contrasts with the paper's macro-New, which reviews the point of the paper in terms of what the systemic conception of grammar as a resource enables linguists to do. The macro-New has its own hyper-Theme (double underlined) and hyper-New (double underlined); note that the hyper-Theme strongly predicts Theme selection in this text, and that the hyper-New accumulates the main points amassed.

[6:40]   **Macro-New** (of Matthiessen & Halliday's paper)
HYPER-THEME (of the paper's macro-New)
Several themes run through the discussion, including stratification and metafunctional diversification. Let's just consider briefly the systemic theme — the theme we introduced in Section 1.1 in terms of the conception of grammar as resource — and what it enables us to do.

Themes and News
(i) The systemic intepretation of grammar (i.e, the intepretation of grammar in terms of systems) allow us to discern the continuity of language development from protolanguage into adult language: the systemic organisation is present from the very beginning, in the protosemantic systems, but structure appears only later as a means of realizing complex systemic selections.

(ii) The systemic interpretation of grammar allows us to see and to represent the simultaneous metafunctions manifested in the system as principles of organisation. This is related to the first point since the continuity between protolanguage and adult language is a functional one.

(iii) The systemic interpretation of grammar allows us to explore and represent the probabilistic nature of the overall grammatical system, i.e. the probabilities of the various options in the systems and of the combination of options. This is the kind of bridge needed to relate the system to its history and change (both in its historical evolution and instantially in texts) and to interpret registerial variation.

(iv) The systemic interpretation of grammar makes it possible to discern the contintuity between grammar and lexis and to bring them together into lexicogrammar. Lexicogrammatical selections may be realised lexically or structurally, but there are many interdependencies and the realization distinction is not a basis for stratifying (or modularizing) lexis and grammar as two different systems.

(v) The systemic interpretation of grammar paves the way for the recognition of systems such as tense and modality where there is a realizational "spread", i.e. where realisations span more than one structural type (e.g. verb and adverb or verb and suffix).

(vi) The systemic interpretation of grammar relates the level of grammar upwards, towards semantics in the first instance, and towards higher-level cultural systems of meaning, and we can begin to explore the relationship between 'profiles' in grammatical systems and in these higher orders of meaning.

(vii) The systemic interpretation of grammar provides the basis for systemic comparison and typology; for the exploration of systems of transitivity, mood, theme, etc. across languages.

HYPER-NEW (of the paper's macro-New)
These, then, are seven themes based on the systemic interpretation of grammar. And these themes relate to different ways of explaining the grammatical system in functional terms: developmental, semantic-discoursal, metafunctional, cultural, and so on.

The consideration of macro-Theme and macro-New in Matthiessen and Halliday's paper points to the difference between what are often referred to as an abstract and a summary. As abstract is essentially a dislocated macro-New (typically "Theme marked" at a text's beginning or published elsewhere); it presents the essence of what can be learned by reading the text the abstract functions as macro-New for. A summary on the other hand is more like a dislocated macro-Theme (often "Rhematic" at the end of a text or published elsewhere); it provides an outline of what can or has been read, re-scaffolding by way of review. Matthiessen and Halliday's summary of their paper is as follows (cf. the paper's macro-New above):

[6:41]   We have sketched systemic functional theory of grammar (Section II),
elaborated on the theory of metafunction (section III), and indicated how
the general theory can be extended to deal with grammatical metaphor and
lexis (Section IV). We have also exemplified the use of the theory (Section
V) and pointed to its typological neighbours among contemporary functional theories (Section VI). (Matthiessen and Halliday in press)

Hyper- and macro-News, like hyper- and macro-Themes are more
prominent in written than spoken English. However, just as marked
Themes were shown to functional in parallel ways to hyper-Themes in spoken mode, so extended reference can be shown to function in parallel ways
to hyper-News. Two excerpts from text [4:2] are re-presented below to
illustrate this point. *This* in [4:2ff & ii] and *that* in [4:2aaa & ccc] are used
to accumulate the actions in the activity sequences that have gone before in
a way which complements their scaffolding with marked Themes as discussed in 6.3.2. Extended reference is in other words to hyper-New as marked
Theme is to hyper-Theme:

> **Synoptic:Dynamic::**
> (WRITTEN:SPOKEN::)
> hyper-Theme:marked Theme::
> hyper-New:extended reference

[4:2]   (Examples of extended reference as HYPER-NEW)
    10.y.   The judge handles it,
       z.   and this is where I'm telling you, temperament plays a big part.
    11.aa.   The judge has to be able to look into the dog's mouth
       bb.   to see
       cc.   that it's teeth are perfect.
    12.dd.   Usually then he feels down the neck, along its body,
       ee.   and he can sort of feel conformation
       ff.   by doing **this**,
       gg.   so you're hoping all the time
       hh.   that your dog will stand nice and steady
       ii.   so the judge can do **this**
       jj.   and it doesn't hamper him
       kk.   handling the dogs.

       mm.   then, you really do whatever the judge tells you.
    14.nn.   Basically it is always the same.
    15.oo.   He usually says,
       pp.   or she usually says,
       qq.   "Walk your dog in a triangle."
    16.rr.   Now, as I told you already,
       ss.   the dog is always walked on the left-hand side.

17.tt. So, if your judge is standing here,
uu. we walk away from him that way.
18.vv. That is [[so the judge can get the hind movement of your dog]].
19.ww. Then we usually walk sideways like that
xx . so as he can see [[the dog moving all over]]
yy. and then we walk back to the judge
zz. so as he can see the front movement.
20.aaa. After **that** he usually tells you
bbb. to wait over there.
21.ccc. He proceeds to do **that** with every dog.

Returning to text [6:37], it can now be seen that its main remaining weakness has to do with the fact that its macro-New is not related to preceding hyper-News; and the reason for this of course is that the "Body" of the essay consists mainly of hyper-Themes. The essay's field has not been elaborated, so there is nothing for hyper-News to accumulate and pass on to the essay's conclusion, its macro-New. The essay now has a method of development, but no "point".

[6:37] (NEW as clause final constituents)
d Let me begin by pointing out that the Federal Government fixes up **problems that occur in the community**...

e Another example is that the State Government looks after **schools**;
f this prevents **vandalism and fighting**...

g As a final point the Local Government is **important to look after rubbish**:
h otherwise everyone would have **diseases**...

i As a result of their concern with general problems, education and waste disposal, Governments at several administrative levels are necessary.

In Chapters 1 and 5 it was noted that one essential interpretation of "A realises B" in functional linguistics is that A is **symbolically** related to B — relationships between levels (beyond that between content and expression form) are natural. The discussion of Theme and New in clauses, paragraphs and texts presented to this point in Sections 6.3.2 and 6.3.3 illustrates clearly the symbolic way in which text can be said to be realised by clause. Clause grammar is a metaphor for text structure; patterns of interaction between discourse semantics and lexicogrammar echo the textual organisation of the clause. It is in this sense that a functional grammar is a critical resource for textlinguistics.

6.3.4 *Modal responsibility*

Halliday (1984b/1988:43-45; 1985a:76-78) stresses the fact that Subject is a meaning making function in the English clause, alongside the textual functions Theme and New or experiential functions such as Actor and Goal. The meaning of Subject is glossed in terms of **modal responsibility**. This meaning is most transparent in proposals, where regardless of voice, the Subject is the constituent responsible for seeing that goods are exchanged or a service performed (as outlined in Table 6.25).

Table 6.25. Modal responsibility in proposals

		RESPONSIBLE PARTICIPANT
OFFER (speaker responsible)		
I'll get myself appointed, shall I?/	[passive]	I
I'll appoint you, shall I?	[active]	I
COMMAND (addressee responsible)		
Get appointed, won't you?/	[passive]	(you)
Appoint her, won't you?	[active]	(you)

The concept of modal responsibility is less obvious in propositions, and the meaning of Subject is hard to isolate because of the fact that in English declaratives and interrogatives Subject conflates with unmarked topical Theme. However, it is clear in contexts where marked Themes are used to scaffold a text's method of development that Subject selection is in principle independent of Theme selection. The following clauses from text [6:36] all offer a choice of Subject based on voice following the marked Theme, and the passive is deployed in [6:36e, j & q] to make the Navy and the capital naval force modally responsible (Subject/Value instead of Subject/Token in [6:36e & q], and Subject/Goal instead of subject/Actor in [6:36j]).

> [6:36] e   In both wars **a vital responsibility of the Navy** was escort-of-convoy and anti-submarine work,
>
> f   but in the 1917-1918 conflict **it** never clashed with the enemy on the surface;
>
> g   whilst between 1941 and 1945 **it** fought some twenty major and countless minor engagements with the Japanese Navy.

j   in World War II **the art of amphibious warfare** had to be revived and developed,

q   but in World War II **the capital naval force** was the air-craft carrier taskgroup,

The challenge here is to interpret the meaning of Subject from a discourse perspective, by looking at the way in which discourse structures interact with Subject selection. The best context for examining this interaction is dialogue, since negotiation provides the appropriate interpersonal context. As noted in Chapter 2, in the unmarked case, negotiation is aimed at closure; interlocutors work around an obligatory K1 or A1 move which will resolve the exchange. It follows from this that the interlocutor initiating an exchange will arrange propositions and proposals in such a way that they can be "naturally" resolved. The most efficient way of doing this is to set up the Residue as a kind of constant and realise meaning at risk in the Mood. The Mood element can then be used to close the exchange, ellipsing the Residue (see Table 6.26)

POLARITY, MODALITY and TENSE are the meanings most at risk; as Halliday (1985a:335) has suggested, POLARITY and MODALITY can in fact be interpreted as a scale of graded meanings associated with probability, usuality, inclination and obligation (see Fig. 2.5).

Table 6.26. Mood and Residue as "variable" and "constant"

Mood "variable"	Residue "constant"	Mood "variable"	Residue "constant"
PROPOSITION (giving)		(demanding)	
Ben has	won.	Did Carl	lose?
- Oh has he	θ?	- Yes he did	θ.
PROPOSAL (giving)		(demanding)	
I'll	go.		Get going.
- Would you	θ?	- Okay I will	θ.

Kress (1977) has suggested treating primary tense as a related scale, with past related to high, present to median and future to low probability.

These scales allow interlocutors to fine-tune proposals and propositions without disturbing their transitivity structure:

[6:42] POLARITY/MODALIZATION at risk
        Is that Flo?
        — It is/must be/would be/may be/isn't.

[6:43] POLARITY/MODULATION at risk
        Finish it.
        — I will/must/would/could/won't.

[6:44] TENSE at risk
        Is this helping?
        — It already has/is/soon will.

Next at risk is the Subject itself. A text's major taxonomic strings will weave themselves through this position, as alternative participants are made modally responsible. The notion of alternatives is critical here — the Subject is at risk precisely because there are other taxonomically related candidates for modal responsibility around. Aside from negotiating POLAR-ITY, MODALITY or TENSE the next most economical way of resolving an exchange is by substituting the Subject:

[6:45] SUBJECT at risk
        Did Ben win?
        — No, Carl did.

Finally, the Residue itself may need adjusting, although because of the meaning of Subject, this is a marked option which is taken up when additional taxonomic alternatives are available.

[6:46] RESIDUE at risk
        Did Carl win in Rome?
        — No, but he eventually did in Seoul.
        — Oh did he?

Barring this, the initiating proposition or proposal may need to be completely replaced, and negotiation started afresh:

[6:47] EXCHANGE at risk
        Did Flo win in Rome?
        — No, Rome wasn't on her schedule.
        — Oh, wasn't it?

These various types of negotiation are reviewed in Fig. 6.13, using examples from text [6:48] below (except for the Subject substitution exam-

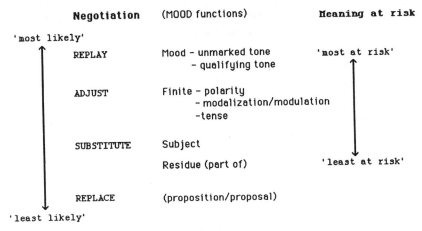

Fig. 6.13. Negotiation, risk and Subject selection

ple which is from [6:49]). Seen in these terms negotiation involves resolving an exchange by replaying its Mood function (possibly fine tuning through tone), adjusting its POLARITY, MODALITY or TENSE, or substituting its Subject or part of its Residue; alternatively the initiating proposal or proposition has to be replaced and negotiation started over again. The interlocutor initiating the exchange tries to facilitate this by centering meanings at risk in the Mood; it is this facilitation process that explains the pattern of Subject choice in dialogue — the Subject, in other words, is what is at stake.

Examples:

			SUBJ	FINITE
[replay Mood]				
	dd	if I argue with you,	I	(do)
	ee	I must take up a contrary position.	I	must
A	ff	— Yes —	(you)	(must)
[adjust POLARITY]				
	b	This isn't an argument.	This	isn't
B	c	— Yes it is!	it	is
A	d	— No it isn't.	it	isn't
[adjust MODALITY]				
A	v	— Well an argument isn't just contradiction.	arg.	isn't
B	w	— It can be.	it	can
A	x	— No it can't.	it	can't

[substitute Subject]

P	c	- You were the last one to use it yesterday.	you	were
J	d	— No, I wasn't.	I	wasn't
	e	Andrew was.	And.	was

[substitute part of Residue]

A	s	— I came here for a good argument.	I	(did)
B	t	— No you didn't.	you	didn't
	u	You came here for an argument.	you	(did)[10]

[replace proposition]

| B | u | You come here for an argument | you | (did) |
| A | v | — Well an argument isn't just contradiction. | arg. | isn't |

Interpersonal resources for negotiation are foregrounded in the following sketch from Monty Python's first movie*. Interlocutor A has paid for an argument, which he defines in ideational terms: *An argument is a connected series of statements intended to establish a proposition*; what he receives instead is simply interpersonal — contradiction: *the automatic gainsaying of any statement the other person makes*. This underlines the fact that negotiation is more than interaction; it is about interlocutors accommodating ideational meaning. Considered in these terms negotiation itself is continually frustrated in [6:48].

[6:48]

			SUBJ	FINITE
A	a	Well look —	(you)	(do)
	b	This isn't an argument.	This	isn't
B	c	— Yes it is!	it	is
A	d	— No it isn't.	it	isn't
	e	It's just contradiction!	it	's
B	f	— No it isn't.	it	isn't
A	g	— It is!	it	is
B	h	— It is not.	it	is
A	i	— Look —	(you)	(do)
	j	you just contradicted me!	you	(did)
B	k	— I did not!	I	did
A	l	— Oh you did.	you	did
B	m	— No, no, no!	(I)	(didn't)
A	n	— You did just then!	you	did
B	o	— Nonsense!	(that)	(is)
A	p	— Oh look —	(you)	(do)
	q	This is futile.	This	is
B	r	— No it isn't.	it	isn't
A	s	— I came here for a good argument.	I	(did)
B	t	— No you didn't.	you	didn't
	u	You came here for an argument.	you	(did)

*Reprinted from Chapman et al. Monty Python's Flying Circus - just the words, Vol. 2, pp. 87-88, by permission of Methuen London and Python Productions Ltd. London.

A	v	— Well an argument isn't just contradiction.	arg.	isn't
B	w	— It can be.	it	can
A	x	— No it can't.	it	can't
	y	An argument is a connected series of statements intended to establish a proposition.	arg.	is
B	z	— No it isn't.	it	isn't
A	aa	— Yes it is.	it	is
	bb	It's not just contradiction.	it	's
B	cc	— Look —	(you)	(do)
	dd	if I argue with you,	I	(do)
	ee	I must take up a contrary position.	I	must
A	ff	— Yes —	(you)	(must)
	gg	but that's not just saying, "No it isn't."	that	's
B	hh	— Yes it is!	it	is
A	ii	— No it isn't!	it	isn't
	jj	Argument is an intellectual process.	arg.	is
	kk	Contradiction is just the automatic gainsaying of any statement the other person makes.	contr.	is
B	ll	— No it isn't.	it	isn't
A	mm	— Yes it is.	it	is
B	nn	— Not at all.	(that)	(is)
A	oo	— Now look!	(you)	(do)

The text is divided into exchanges below with adjustments to modality and substitutions of Residue in bold face. The Subject and Finite functions of each clause are listed to its right; conflated Finite functions (e.g. Finite/Predicator — *contradicted*) and the "understood" Subject and Finite of imperatives are enclosed in parentheses. The text organising proposals (meta-proposals) realised by the imperative *look* are formatted in italics to distinguish them from the frustrated negotiation per se; each of these heralds a new proposition, punctuating the customer's growing frustration.

	[6:48]		SUBJ	FINITE
A	a	*Well look —*	*(you)*	*(do)*

[new **proposition**]

	b	This isn't an **argument**.	This	isn't
B	c	— Yes it is!	it	is
A	d	— No it isn't.	it	isn't

[new RESIDUE]				
	e	It's just **contradiction!**	it	's
B	f	— No it isn't.	it	isn't
A	g	— It is!	it	is
B	h	— It is not.	it	is
A	i	— *Look* —	*(you)*	*(do)*
[new **proposition**]				
	j	you just contradicted me!	you	(did)
B	k	— I did not!	I	did
A	l	— Oh you did.	you	did
B	m	— No, no, no!	(I)	(didn't)
A	n	— You did just then!	you	did
B	o	— Nonsense!	(that)	(is)
A	p	— *Oh look* —	*(you)*	*(do)*
[new **proposition**]				
	q	This is futile.	this	is
B	r	— No it isn't.	it	isn't
[new **proposition**]				
A	s	— I came here for a **good argument**.	I	(did)
B	t	— No you didn't.	you	didn't
[new RESIDUE]				
	u	You came here for an **argument**.	you	(did)
[new **proposition**]				
A	v	— Well an argument isn't just contradiction	arg.	isn't
[new FINITE]				
B	w	— It **can** be.	it	can
A	x	— No it can't.	it	can't
[new RESIDUE]				
	y	An argument is a **connected series of statements intended to establish a proposition.**	arg.	is
B	z	— No it isn't.	it	isn't
A	aa	— Yes it is.	it	is
[new RESIDUE]				
	bb	It's not just **contradiction**.	it	's
B	cc	— *Look* —	*(you)*	*(do)*

[new **proposition**]

	dd	if I argue with you,	I	(do)
	ee	I must take up a contrary position.	I	must
A	ff	— Yes —	(you)	(must)

[new **proposition**]

	gg	but that's not just saying, "No it isn't."	that	's
B	hh	— Yes it is!	it	is
A	ii	— No it isn't!	it	isn't

[new **proposition**]

| | jj | Argument is an intellectual process. | arg. | is |

[new **proposition**]

	kk	Contradiction is just the automatic gainsaying of any statement the other person makes.	contr.	is
B	ll	— No it isn't.	it	isn't
A	mm	— Yes it is.	it	is
B	nn	— Not at all.	(it)	(is)
A	oo	— *Now look!*	*(you)*	*(do)*

A real negotiation, as oppose to a frustrated one, is illustrated in [6:49] below. Its interlocutors do not resolve the negotiation on their own however, but are taken to arbitration in [6:49r]. One of the three brothers, Jeffrey, Phillip or Andrew is selected as Subject in all but a handful of the clauses; of the three other reference chains (the softball mit, the shoes and the whistle) only a single token appears as Subject — the mit, as part of their mother's intervention:

SUBJECT PARTICIPANTS	RESIDUE PARTICIPANTS
Jeffrey	P's mit (except [6:49dd])
Phillip	shoes
Andrew	whistle
	Mum
	laundry
	washing machine
	school
	pig

	[6:49]		SUBJ	FINITE
P	a	Jeffrey, where did you put my mit?	you	did
J	b	— I haven't got it.	I	haven't
P	c	— You were the last one to use it yesterday.	you	were

J	d	— No, I wasn't.	I	wasn't
	e	Andrew was.	And.	was
P	f	— You were so.	you	were
J	g	— Andrew was.	And	was
	h	He took it from me.	he	(did)
P	i	— Bull.	(that)	(is)
	j	You better find it now	you	(had)
	k	because I've got training today.	I	've
J	l	— No.	I	(won't)
	m	I didn't lose it	I	didn't
	n	so why should I look for it?	I	should
P	o	— I'm telling Mum on you.	I	'm
J	p	— I don't care.	I	don't
P	q	— I hate you.	I	(do)
M	r	— What's this bickering about?	bick.	is
P	s	— Jeffrey lost my softball mit.	Jeff.	(did)
J	t	— Phillip,	he...	he ...
	u	I did not.	I	did
M	v	— That's enough.	that	's
	w	One at a time.	(you)	(do)
	x	Jeffrey.		
J	y	— Phillip blamed me	Phil.	(did)
	z	because he lost his softball mit.	he	(did)
P	aa	— He was the last one to use it yesterday.	he	was
J	bb	— I was not.	I	was
M	cc	— Stop it.	you	(do)
	dd	The mit is in the laundry on top of the washing machine.	mit	is
p	ee	— I bet you put it there Jeffrey.	you	(did)
	ff	Didn't you?	you	didn't
J	gg	— I did not.	I	did
M	hh	— That's enough.	that	's
	ii	Stop arguing now	(you)	(do)
	jj	or you'll both be in trouble.	you	'll
	kk	Now, hurry yourselves up	(you)	(do)
	ll	or you'll be late for school.	you	'll
P	mm	— Get the shoes.	(you)	(do)
J	nn	— I'm not going to get them.	I	'm
	oo	It's your turn to carry them.	it	's
P	pp	— All right then, I'll carry them	I	'll
	qq	but I'm not taking yours.	I	'm
J	rr	— I don't care	I	don't
	ss	but you give me back my whistle.	you	(do)
P	tt	— I need it today.	I	(do)

J	uu	— Bad luck.	(that)	(is)
	vv	Give it back.	(you)	(do)
P	ww	— No.	(I)	(won't)
	xx	You said I could use it today.	you	(did)
J	yy	— Well I've changed my mind.	I	've
P	zz	— Well, bad luck to yourself.	(that)	(is)
	aaa	I'm not giving it back.	I	'm
J	bbb	— You're a pig.[11]	you	're

Text [6:49] is re-presented, divided into exchanges below, with substitution of Subject and Residue noted. Otherwise the notation is as for [6:48] above, except that attitudinal responses to preceding moves are also formatted in italics (*bull*, *I don't care*, *I don't care*, *bad luck*). Note that the arguments is 'resolved' by the boy's mother in [6:49rr] precisely by making the mit rather than the brothers modally responsible.

[6:49]   SUBJ   FINITE

[new **proposition**]
P   a   Jeffrey, where did you put my mit?   you   did

[new **proposition**]
J   b   — I haven't got it.   I   haven't

[new **proposition**]
P   c   — You were the last one to use it yesterday.   you   were
J   d   — No, I wasn't.   I   wasn't

[new SUBJECT]
     e   Andrew was.   And.   was

[new SUBJECT]
P   f   — You were so.   you   were

[new SUBJECT]
J   g   — Andrew was.   And   was

[new RESIDUE]
     h   He took it from me.   he   (did)
P   i   — *Bull*.   (that) (is)

[new **proposal**]
     j   You better find it now   you   (had)
     k   because I've got training today.   I   've
J   l   — No.   I   (won't)

[new Residue]
     m   I didn't lose it   I   didn't

[new Residue]
   n   so why should I look for it?   I   should

[new **proposition**]
P   o   — I'm telling Mum on you.   I   'm
J   p   *— I don't care.*   I   don't

[new **proposition**]
P   q   — I hate you.   I   (do)

[new **proposition**]
M   r   — What's this bickering about?   bick.   is

[new **proposition**]
P   s   — Jeffrey lost my softball mit.   Jeff.   (did)
J   t   — Phillip,   he...   -
     u   I did not.   I   did

[new **proposal**]
M   v   — That's enough.   that   's

[new **proposal**]
     w   One at a time.   (you) (do)

[new **proposal**]
     x   Jeffrey.   -   -

[new **proposition**]
J   y   — Phillip blamed me   Phil.   (did)
     z   because he lost his softball mit.   he   (did)

[new **proposition**]
P   aa — He was the last one to use it yesterday.   he   was
J   bb — I was not.   I   was

[new **proposal**]
M   cc — Stop it.   you   (do)

[new **proposition**]
     dd The mit is in the laundry on top of the   mit   is
          washing machine.

[new **proposition**]
p   ee — I bet you put it there Jeffrey.   you   (did)
     ff Didn't you?   you   didn't
J   gg — I did not.   I   did

[new **proposal**]
M   hh — That's enough.   that   's

[new **proposal**]				
	ii	Stop arguing now	(you)	(do)
	jj	or you'll both be in trouble.	you	'll

[new **proposal**]				
	kk	Now, hurry yourselves up	(you)	(do)
	ll	or you'll be late for school.	you	'll

[new **proposal**]				
P	mm	— Get the shoes.	(you)	(do)
J	nn	— I'm not going to get them.	I	'm

[new **proposal**]				
	oo	It's your turn to carry them.	it	's
P	pp	— All right then, I'll carry them	I	'll

[new RESIDUE]				
	qq	but I'm not taking yours.	I	'm
J	rr	— *I don't care*	I	don't

[new **proposal**]				
	ss	but you give me back my whistle.	you	(do)

[new **proposition**]				
P	tt	— I need it today.	I	(do)
J	uu	— *Bad luck.*	(that)	(is)

[new **proposal**]				
	vv	Give it back.	(you)	(do)
P	ww	— No.	(I)	(won't)

[new **proposition**]				
	xx	You said I could use it today.	you	(did)
J	yy	— Well I've changed my mind.	I	've

[new **proposition**]				
P	zz	— Well, bad luck to yourself.	(that)	(is)

[new **proposal**]				
	aaa	I'm not giving it back.	I	'm

[new **proposition**]				
J	bbb	— You're a pig.	you	're

The notion of meaning at risk is clearly illustrated by a number of the substitutions for Subject and Residue in [6:49]. The basic argument has to do with the nuclear structure Agent x Process + Medium (who does what to what) with the brother string woven through the Agent/Subject and the mit chain held constant as Medium/Complement; in addition an action string reflecting the activity sequence of borrowing and possibly losing the mit is woven through the Process/Predicator (*take-use-put/lose-look for-find*). The realisations of these interacting strings and chains are listed below.

a	Jeffrey	x	put	+	mit		
b	Jeffrey	+	have	=	mit		
c	Jeffrey	x	use	+	mit		
d	Jeffrey	x	use	+	mit		
e	Andrew	x	use	+	mit		
f	Jeffrey	x	use	+	mit		
g	Andrew	x	use	+	mit		
h	Andrew	x	took	+	mit	x	Jeffrey
i	Andrew	x	took	+	mit	x	Jeffrey
j	Jeffrey	x	find	+	mit		
l	Jeffrey	x	find	+	mit		
m	Jeffrey	x	lose	+	mit		
n	Jeffrey	+	look=for	+	mit		
s	Jeffrey	x	lost	+	mit		
u	Jeffrey	x	lost	+	mit		
z	Phillip	x	lost	+	mit		
aa	Jeffrey	x	use	+	mit		
bb	Jeffrey	x	use	+	mit		
ee	Jeffrey	x	put	+	mit		
ff	Jeffrey	x	put	+	mit		

Substitution for the Subject within an exchange draws on the brother string, as in [6:49c-g] below; before the proposition initiating this exchange is replaced, part of its Residue is also substituted for:

ALTERNATION:
Subject — *Jeffrey-Andrew*
Residue — *use-take*

			SUBJ	FINITE
[new **proposition**]				
P	c	— You were the last one to use it yesterday.	you	were
J	d	— No, I wasn't.	I	wasn't
[new SUBJECT]				
	e	Andrew was.	And.	was
[new SUBJECT]				
P	f	— You were so.	you	were
[new SUBJECT]				
J	g	— Andrew was.	And	was

[new RESIDUE]

	h	He took it from me.		he	(did)
P	i	— *Bull*		*(that)*	*is*

Examples of substitution in proposal exchanges are found later in the text, drawing on the strings *find-lose-look for* and *carry-take*. In spoken mode it is more difficult to weave process strings through the Subject than in writing (since actions tend to be realised congruently as verbs), even though alternative actions may well be the meaning at risk, especially in goods and services exchanges; this is less of a problem in writing, since the actions can be nominalised, and once "thingized" are natural candidates for Subject position.

ALTERNATION:
Residue   — *find-lose-look for*

[new **proposal**]

	j	You better find it now		you	(had)
	k	because I've got training today.		I	've
J	l	— No.		I	(won't)

[new RESIDUE]

	m	I didn't lose it		I	didn't

[new RESIDUE]

	n	so why should I look for it?		I	should

ALTERNATION:
Residue   — *carry shoes-take shoes*

[new **proposal**]

J	oo	It's your turn to carry them.[12]		it	's
P	pp	— All right then, I'll carry them		I	'll

[new RESIDUE]

	qq	but I'm not taking yours.		I	'm
J	rr	— *I don't care*		*I*	*don't*

Although it is harder to unpick the meaning of Subject in written monologue from the meaning of Theme and Given, texts such as [6:36] above which realise their method of development through marked Themes demonstrate the significance of modal responsibility in this mode. The interaction of conjunction, Theme and Subject selection in [6:36] is out-

lined in Fig. 6.14: distinct, though partially overlapping strings are woven
through Theme and Subject.

a   Although the United States participated heavily in World War I,
b   the nature of that participation was fundamentally different from what it became in
     World War II.

		Theme	Subject
contr	c	The earlier conflict	The ealier conflict
	d	the latter	the latter
	e	In both wars	a vital responsibility
contr	f	but in the 1917-1918 conflict	it (the Navy)
	g	whilst between 1941 and 1945	it (the Navy)
contr	h	American soldiers who engaged in World War I	American soldiers...
	i		
	j	in World War II	the art of amphibious..
	k	assault troops	assaudt troops
contr	l	Airpower	airpower
	m	in the latter	it (airpower)
contr	n	in World War I	the Battleship
	o	as she	she (the Battleship)
	p	and Battle Line	Battle Line
	q	But in World War II	the capital naval force
	r	for which completely new tactics	completely new tactics

Fig. 6.14. Interaction of external conjunction, Theme and Subject in text [6:36]

Unlike Theme, Subject selection in [6:36] does not reflect the text's contrastive method of development. The Subjects of each of the text's five exemplificatory differences are listed below; only the first pair are contrastive taxonomic oppositions:

ORIGINAL SUBJECTS in [6:36]
(i)   the earlier conflict-the latter
(ii)   a vital responsibility of the Navy-it-it (*the Navy*)
(iii)   American soldiers-assault troops
(iv)   airpower-it (*airpower*)
(v)   the Battleship-the capital naval force

Instead the Subject codes the modally responsible participants (including the metaphorical interpersonal "participant" *a vital responsibility* and two further nominalisations *the earlier conflict-the latter*); these are at risk not because they contrast with each other but because they are alternatives to potential Subjects in the Residue. The argument can be changed completely by promoting these to Subject position, as outlined below. The main result of this transformation is that the success of the propositions no longer depends on the American armed forces; these are demoted from modal responsibility and no longer seen to be at risk. This however is not the kind of argument that is likely to appropriately engage students of US naval history, and its lack of continuity is likely to disturb most readers.

TRANSFORMED SUBJECTS in [6:36]:
(i)   the Navy-the Army-the Navy-the Army
(ii)   escort-of-convoy and anti-submarine work-the enemy-the Japanese Navy
(iii)   transports-docks and harbours-strategists-the enemy
(iv)   very little influence-the main factor
(v)   the queen of the sea-Drake-tactics inherited from the age of sail- the aircraft carrier task group-strategists

TRANSFORMED SUBJECT AND RESIDUE SELECTION IN [6:36]:
the Navy was deployed on one ocean
and **the Army** fought in one theatre
the Navy was deployed on two oceans
and **the Army** fought in five major theatres

escort-of-convey and anti-submarine work was a vital responsibility of the navy
the enemy was never engaged on the surface
the Japanese Navy was engaged in twenty major and countless minor battles

transports took American soldiers overseas in World War I
and **docks and harbours** protected them on arrival

strategists had to revive and develop the art of amphibious warfare
the enemy forced assualt troops to fight their way ashore

very little influence was felt from the air
the main factor was airpower

the queen of the sea was still the Battleship
and **Drake** would have recognised her role;
tactics inherited from the age of sail determined the fighting strategy of Battle Line
the aircraft carrier task group was the the capital naval force
strategists devised completely new tactics

To this point modal responsibility has been considered in texts which do not foreground interpersonal metaphor. Assessments of probability, usuality, inclination and obligation have for the most part been realised congruently, with the result that the Mood function in a clause is easy to determine. Interpersonal metaphor may however make the analysis of modal responsibility less straight forward. In [6:49ee] for example, a median assessment of probability is expressed through a projecting clause *I bet* rather than through a modal adjunct (*probably*) or modal verb (*would*). Thus the delayed tag *didn't you*, which has been treated as a separate move [6:49ff], comes out as *didn't you* not *didn't I*; and the appropriate contradiction is *I did not (put it there)* not *you did not (bet I put it there)*. The underlined interpersonal metaphor in [6:49ee] is unpacked in the example below, more congruently as *probably* (bold face), then more congruently still as a modal verb *would* (small caps); this unpacking notation will be used in the examples considered below.

METAPHORIAL MODALITY			SUBJ	FINITE
p	ee	**[Probably** — you WOULD have]		
		— I bet you put it there Jeffrey.	you	(did)
	ff	Didn't you?	you	didn't
J	gg	— I did not.	I	did

Text [6:50] is taken from Halliday's (1982a) analysis of de-automatization and interpersonal metaphor in Priestley's *An Inspector Calls*. The text is rich in interpersonal metaphor, which is unpacked as the text is re-presented below. The participants at risk in [6:50] include the Inspector and members of the Birling family (Mrs Birling, Birling, Sheila) except Gerald, but not the woman they have wronged. Taking the congruent unpacking of interpersonal metaphor outlined in Table 6.27 as a base line, the woman wronged is made modally responsible on four occasions ([6:50r, s, nn, qq] — and [6:50nn,qq] are dependent clauses); she is realised four times as often in the Residue. The family (except Gerald) and the Inspector on the other hand are modally responsible as often or more often than not.

Table 6.27. Distribution of modal responsibility in [6:50] (based on congruent reading)

	AS SUBJECT [modally responsible]	AS RESIDUE [not modally responsible]
Inspector	d,e,f,g,h,i,y,aa,bb,cc,dd,hh,ii,jj,yy	t,u,x,z,bb,cc
Gerald	rr,ss	c,d,e,f,g,rr,tt
Mrs Birling	j,k,l,m,n,o,p,q,t,u,v,w,x,uu,ww,xx	k,l,v,uu,vv,ww
Birling	z,ee,mm	ff,hh,ii,jj
Sheila	oo,pp,vv	kk
[we 'Birlings']	a,b,c,ll,ll	
[you 'parents']	zz	zz
woman	r,s,nn,qq d,e,f,g,h,i,o,p,q,	mm,nn,rr,ss,uu,ww

The modal responsibility of each member of the family, including Gerald, is reviewed in turn in Sheila's monologue at the end of the text; modal responsibility is mapped onto experiential responsibility (i.e. Subject conflates with Agent) in this passage, symbolising the family's social responsibility for what has happened by way of contribution to the theme of Priestley's play.

[6:50]   (from Priestley *An Inspector Calls*)
Mrs Birling a   I think we've just about come to the end of this
                wretched business —
Gerald   b   — I don't think so.
           c   Excuse me.
                (He goes out. They watch him go in silence. We
                hear the front door slam.)
Sheila   d   (to Inspector) — You know, you never showed him that photograph of
                her.
Inspector e   — No.
           f   It wasn't necessary.
           g   And I thought it better not to.
Mrs Birling h — You have a photograph of this girl?
Inspector i   — Yes.
           j   I think you'd better look at it.

Mrs Birling	k	— I don't see any particular reason why I should.
Inspector	l	— Probably not.
	m	But you'd better look at it.
Mrs Birling	n	— Very well.
		(He produces a photograph and she looks hard at it.)
Inspector	o	(taking back the photograph) — You recognize her.
Mrs Birling	p	— No.
	q	Why should I?
Inspector	r	— Of course she might have changed lately.
	s	but I can't believe she could have changed so much.
Mrs Birling	t	— I don't understand you, Inspector.
Inspector	u	— You mean you don't choose to, Mrs Birling.
Mrs Birling	v	(angrily) — I meant what I said.
Inspector	w	— You're not telling the truth.
Mrs Birling	x	— I beg your pardon!
Birling	y	(angrily to Inspector) — Look here,
	z	I'm not going to have this, Inspector.
	aa	You'll apologise at once.
Inspector	bb	— Apologise for what — doing my duty?
Birling	cc	— No,
	dd	for being so offensive about it.
	ee	I'm a public man —
Inspector	ff	(massively) — Public men, Mr Birling, have responsibilities as well as privileges.
Birling	gg	— Possibly.
	hh	But you weren't asked to come here and talk to me about my responsibilities.
Sheila	ii	— Let's hope not.
	jj	Though I'm beginning to wonder.
Mrs Birling	kk	— Does that mean anything, Sheila?
Sheila	ll	— It means that we've not excuse now for putting on airs and that if we've any sense we won't try.
	mm	Father threw this girl out
	nn	because she asked for decent wages.
	oo	I went and pushed her out further, right into the street,
	pp	just because I was angry
	qq	and she was pretty.
	rr	Gerald set her up as his mistress,
	ss	and then dropped her
	tt	when it suited him.
	uu	And now you're pretending that you don't recognise her from that photograph.
	vv	I admit I don't know why you should,
	ww	but I know jolly well you did in fact recognize her, from the way you looked.

Table 6.28. Modality: type and orientation (Halliday 1985a:336)

	Subjective: explicit	Subjective: implicit	Objective: implicit	Objective: explicit
Modalization: probability	I think [in my opinion] Mary knows	Mary'll know	Mary probably knows [in all probability]	it's likely that Mary knows [Mary is likely to]
Modalization: usuality		Fred'll sit quite quiet	Fred usually sits quite quiet	it's usual for Fred to sit quite quiet
Modulation: obligation	I want John to go	John should go	John's supposed to go	it's expected that John goes
Modulation: inclination	(I undertake for Jane to help)	Jane'll help	Jane's keen to help	it's a pleasure for Jane to help

> xx   And if you're not telling the truth,
> yy   why should the Inspector apologize.
> zz   And can't you see both of you, you're making it worse.

Table 6.28 (from Halliday 1985a:336) summaries some of the congruent and metaphorical variations on the realisation of assessment relevant to the unpacking of [6:50] below (for further discussion of interpersonal metaphor see 6.2.2 above).

These realisations are bandied about in various ways to shift modal responsibility away from the participant that would otherwise be Subject in congruent realisations. For example, the Inspector first accepts responsibility, then ducks it and finally re-instates himself as part of a metaphorical modulation in [6:50d-g] below:

	MOOD FUNCTION	MOOD TAG (potential)
ACCEPT	No, (I didn't),	[*did I*]
REMOVE	It wasn't necessary (for me to),	[*was it*]
RE-INSTATE	I thought it better not to,	[*didn't I*]

Sheila   d   (to Inspector) — You know, you never showed him
                that photograph of her.
Inspector   e   — No.
            f   [**I wasn't obliged** to — I NEEDN'T have]
               <u>It wasn't necessary</u>.
            g   [**I wasn't keen** to — I WOULDN'T]
               And <u>I thought it better not to</u>.

In the face of these metaphors, interlocutors may choose to reply to either the congruent or metaphorical reading (or both). Mrs Birling ignores the Inspector's *I think* in replying to [6:50j]: *you'd better — I Should*; the Inspector however responds directly to her metaphorical modality *I don't see any reason why: I don't see any particular reason why — probably not*. It thus takes him an extra step to get back to the proposal at hand, and Mrs Birling then complies: *But you'd better look at it — Very well.*

Inspector	j	**[Probably** you **should]** I think you'd better look at it.
Mrs Birling	k	**[Undoubtedly I shouldn't]** — I don't see any particular reason why I should.
Inspector	l	**[you wouldn't]** — Probably not.
	m	**[you should]** But you'd better look at it.
Mrs Birling	n	— Very well.

Modality, as well as modal responsibility, can be adjusted metaphorically; the Inspector for example introduces a modulation of (dis)inclination through the mental process *choose* in [6:50u], to which Mrs Birling takes great offense.

Mrs Birling	t	— I don't understand you, Inspector.
Inspector	u	**[you aren't willing** to — you WON'T]** — You mean you don't choose to, Mrs Birling.

Interpersonal metaphors in [6:50] are unpacked below, using the conventions introduced above.

Mrs Birling	a	**[Probably** we've — we WILL have]** I think we've just about come to the end of this wretched business —
Gerald	b	**[Probably** not — we WON'T have]** — I don't think so.
	c	Excuse me. (He goes out. They watch him go in silence. We hear the front door slam.)
Sheila	d	(to Inspector) — You know, you never showed him that photograph of her.
Inspector	e	— No.
	f	**[I wasn't obliged** to- I NEEDN'T have]** It wasn't necessary.
	g	**[I wasn't keen** to — I WOULDN'T]** And I thought it better not to.

Mrs Birling	h	— You have a photograph of this girl?
Inspector	i	— Yes.
	j	[**Probably** you **should**]
		I think you'd better look at it.
Mrs Birling	k	[**Undoubtedly** I shouldn't]
		— I don't see any particular reason why I should.
Inspector	l	[you **wouldn't**]
		— Probably not.
	m	[you **should**]
		But you'd better look at it.
Mrs Birling	n	— Very well.
		(He produces a photograph and she looks hard at it.)
Inspector	o	(taking back the photograph) — You recognize her.
Mrs Birling	p	— No.
	q	Why should I?
Inspector	r	— Of course she might have changed lately.
	s	[she **certainly** hasn't — she CAN'T have]
		but I can't believe she could have changed so much.
Mrs Birling	t	— I don't understand you, Inspector.
Inspector	u	[**actually** you aren't **willing** to — you WON'T]
		— You mean you don't choose to, Mrs Birling.
Mrs Birling	v	(angrily) — I meant what I said.
Inspector	w	— You're not telling the truth.
Mrs Birling	x	— I beg your pardon!
Birling	y	(angrily to Inspector) — Look here,
	z	[I'm **determined** not to — I WON'T]
		I'm not going to have this, Inspector.
	aa	You'll apologise at once.
Inspector	bb	— Apologise for what — doing my duty?
Birling	cc	— No,
	dd	for being so offensive about it.
	ee	I'm a public man —
Inspector	ff	(massively) — Public men, Mr Birling, have responsibilities as well as privileges.
Birling	gg	[They **may**]
		— Possibly.
	hh	But you weren't asked to come here and talk to me about my responsibilities.
Sheila	ii	[**Possibly** not — he MAY not]
		— Let's hope not.
	jj	[**Possibly** so — he MAY]
		Though I'm beginning to wonder.
Mrs Birling	kk	— Does that mean anything, Sheila?
Sheila	ll	[we are **required** not to — we MUSTN'T]
		— It means that we've no excuse now for putting on airs

[we aren't **obliged** to — we SHOULDN'T]
and that if we've any sense we won't try.
mm Father threw this girl out
nn because she asked for decent wages.
oo I went and pushed her out further, right into the street,
pp just because I was angry
qq and she was pretty.
rr Gerald set her up as his mistress,
ss and then dropped her
tt when it suited him.
uu And now you're pretending that you don't recognise
    her from that photograph.
vv [**admittedly**]
    I admit I don't know why you should,
ww [you **surely** did — you MUST have]
    but I know jolly well you did in fact recognize her,
    from the way you looked.
xx And if you're not telling the truth,
yy why should the Inspector apologize.
zz [**obviously**]
    And can't you see both of you, you're making it worse.

This text is also organised by means of meta-proposals and meta-propositions which refer explicitly to the ongoing negotiation (functioning like the *look* proposals in [6:48] above). The adjusted modulation just considered was part of a propositional exchange of this kind:

[new meta-**proposition**]
Mrs Birling t   — I don't understand you, Inspector.
Inspector   u   — You mean you don't choose to, Mrs Birling.
Mrs Birling v   (angrily) — I meant what I said.

Meta-proposals are also found, as when Birling insists on an apology:

[new meta-**proposal**]
             aa   You'll apologise at once.
Inspector   bb   — Apologise for what — doing my duty?
Birling   cc   — No,
             dd   for being so offensive about it.

These meta-proposals and meta-propositions could be interpreted as a type of textual metaphor (the dynamic equivalent of Francis's 1985 A-nouns). This would however be to argue that verbal processes are fundamentally metaphorical in nature, rather than an ongoing classification of verbal behaviour as part of the experiential world. When used to orchestrate rather than report on dialogue, this intepretation does not seem too far-fetched.

Text [6:50] is re-presented, broken into exchanges below, with meta-propositions and meta-proposals noted.

[6:50]

[new **proposition**]

Mrs Birling a   I think we've just about come to the end of this wretched business —

Gerald   b   — I don't think so.

[new **proposal**]

    c   Excuse me.

(He goes out. They watch him go in silence. We hear the front door slam.)

[new **proposition**]

Sheila   d   (to Inspector) — You know, you never showed him that photograph of her.

Inspector   e   — No.

[new metaphorical Mood]

    f   It wasn't necessary.

[new metaphorical Mood]

    g   And I thought it better not to.

[new **proposition**]

Mrs Birling h   — You have a photograph of this girl?

Inspector   i   — Yes.

[new **proposal**]

    j   I think you'd better look at it.

[new metaphorical RESIDUE]

Mrs Birling k   — I don't see any particular reason why I should.

Inspector   l   — Probably not.

[replay proposal]

    m   But you'd better look at it.

Mrs Birling n   — Very well.

(He produces a photograph and she looks hard at it.)

[new **proposition**]

Inspector   o   (taking back the photograph) — You recognize her.

Mrs Birling p   — No.

[new **proposition**]

    q   Why should I?

[new **proposition**]

Inspector   r   — Of course she might have changed lately.

[new metaphorical MOOD]
> s   but I can't believe she could have changed so much.

[new meta-**proposition**]
Mrs Birling t   — I don't understand you, Inspector.

[new metaphorical MOOD]
Inspector   u   — You mean you don't choose to, Mrs Birling.
Mrs Birling v   (angrily) — I meant what I said.

[new meta-**proposition**]
Inspector   w   — You're not telling the truth.
Mrs Birling x   — I beg your pardon!

Birling   y   (angrily to Inspector) — Look here,

[new **proposition**]
> z   I'm not going to have this, Inspector.

[new meta-**proposal**]
> aa   You'll apologise at once.

Inspector   bb   — Apologise for what — doing my duty?
Birling   cc   — No,
> dd   for being so offensive about it.

[new **proposition**]
> ee   I'm a public man —

[new **proposition**]
Inspector   ff   (massively) — Public men, Mr Birling, have
> responsibilities as well as privileges.
Birling   gg   — Possibly.

[new **proposition**]
> hh   But you weren't asked to come here and talk to me
> about my responsibilities.

[new metapohorical MOOD]
Sheila   ii   — Let's hope not.

[new metaphorical MOOD
> jj   Though I'm beginning to wonder.

[new **proposition**]
Mrs Birling kk   — Does that mean anything, Sheila?

[new **propositions**]
Sheila   ll   — It means that we've no excuse now for putting on
> airs and that if we've any sense we won't try.
> mm Father threw this girl out

nn because she asked for decent wages.
oo I went and pushed her out further, right into the street,
pp just because I was angry
qq and she was pretty.
rr Gerald set her up as his mistress,
ss and then dropped her
tt when it suited him.
uu And now you're pretending that you don't recognise her from that photograph.
vv I admit I don't know why you should,
ww but I know jolly well you did in fact recognize her, from the way you looked.
xx And if you're not telling the truth,
yy why should the Inspector apologize.
zz And can't you see both of you, you're making it worse.

Finally the interplay between taxis and modal responsibility needs to be briefly considered. To this point modal responsibility has been discussed as if Subjects in embedded, dependent ranking and non-dependent ranking clauses were all equally at risk. Subjects in embedded clauses are not however modally responsible, as can be seen from the fact that embedded clauses cannot be tagged or queried. Both the tag and the response in [6:51] for example refer unambiguously to the test, not the drug.

[6:51] (embedding)
The test proved [[the drug killed her]], didn't it?
— Yes it did.

With hypotaxis, the situation is more equivocal; the tag and response in [6:52] may refer to either the test or the drug, although the tag is much more likely to refer to the α clause than the β:

[6:52] (hypotaxis)
The test suggested that the drug may have killed her, didn't it?
— It did.

So while hypotatically dependent clauses are still negotiable, their Mood element is less likely to be replayed than that of an α clause, and their Subject can accordingly be considered less at risk than those of ranking a clauses. This interplay of embedding, taxis and mood was exploited in text [6:30] to focus modal responsibility on the sitting member, as analysed above. Note however that both α clause Subjects realising the member alone are metaphorical:

METAPHORICAL	CONGRUENT
I have been advised	apparently
may I...welcome you	welcome

As a congruent Subject the member is realised collectively as *we*:

> We are privileged to live in such a pleasant part of Australia.
> we should be able to advise you promptly.

So while the member is textured as modally responsible, he is never experientially responsible. Where he could be, in the congruent version of [6:30g] for example, he is realised as the possessor of a nominalised modulation:

> My responsibility is to make sure that the life style we enjoy is maintained and improved.
> (— Is it?)

As the query shows, this shifts the argument from one about what to member has to do to one about what his responsibilities are, about which his staff will be happy to inform constituents, according to the final paragraph. Mapping interpersonal responsibility onto experiential responsibility (i.e. agency) as in the congruent version of [6:30g] places the member rather more at risk:

> I must make sure that the life style we enjoy is maintained and improved.
> (— Must you?)

It is for this political consideration that the text is structured as an interpersonal massage, rather than an experiential message. The text is re-presented below to highlight this interaction of taxis, embedding, interpersonal metaphor and modal responsibility.

[6:30]

a	α	I have been advised
b	'β	that you have recently become one of the constituents in the Electorate of Mitchell.
c	ˣβ 1	Whether you have recently moved,
d	⁺2	or whether you have reached the age [[that gives you full voting rights]],
e	α	may I as your Federal Member of Parliament welcome you as a new constituent.
f		We are privileged [[to live in such a pleasant part of Australia]].
g		My responsibility is [[to make sure [[that the life style [[we enjoy]] is maintained and improved]]]].
h	ˣβ	Should you wish to contact me on any matter [[which is concerning you, either day-to-day or national importance]],
i	α	please do not hesitate to do so.

j $^{x}\beta$ If you are uncertain [[whether your problem is one [[affected by Common-
              wealth, State or Local Government]]]],
k   α   we should be able to advise you promptly.

The way in which modal responsibility is mapped onto agency may well
be a life and death matter, as text [6:53] shows. Superintendent Harding is
explaining why an innocent Aboriginal man has been shot to death during
a commando style police raid (in connection with a search for a suspect who
has wounded two policemen). In contrast to the paper's headline, the
Superintendent textures the gun as responsible for the killing (cf. Trew
1979a).

'Uptight' police kill man in raid
[6:53]   (Superintendent Harding)
         a   A struggle took place
         b   and the officer was reacting
         c   to keep the peace
         d   and stop himself or others being hurt.
         e   **The gun** then discharged. (Sonya Zadel 1989: 1 & 7)

6.4 Texture and context

In this chapter a brief sketch of some of the ways in which discourse semantics interacts with lexicogrammar and phonology has been presented. The
problem addressed is a fundmental concern of modular models of semiosis
— namely, once modules are distinguished, how do they interface? What is
the nature of the conversation among components?

The basic strategy adopted to explore this question was to look closely
at the interaction of reference chains and lexical strings with specific
lexicogrammatical and phonological variables — specifically TRANSITIVITY
roles, Theme, New and Subject. The texture deriving from these four types
of interaction was discussed under the headings of cohesive harmony,
method of development, point and modal responsibility.

Looked at from the point of view of field and embracing the ineffable,
the semantics of these texturing processes can be glosssed, albeit metaphorically, as follows. Cohesive harmony locates a text within a particular field
or sub-field. As a measure of coherence cohesive harmony argues that the
more meanings are experientially related to each other in a text in similar
ways, the more coherent the text is. A maximally coherent text is thus
defined as one in which the same event is repeated over and over again, as

in a recount of the operation of a robot on a factory floor. Since this kind of activity sequence is not worth talking about, the experiential texture associated with coherence never amounts to simple repetition. But in some sense, the more focussed the field, the more coherent cohesive harmony analysis will show a text to be.

Method of development takes these harmonising meanings, and finds a peg to hang them on — it establishes an angle on the field. This angle will be sensitive to a text's generic structure where this is realised in stages. Method of development is the lens through which a field is constructed; of all the experiential meanings available in a given field, it will pick on just a few, and weave them through Theme time and again to ground the text — to give interlocutors something to hang onto, something to come back to — an orientation, a perspective, a point of view, a perch, a purchase.

Point is the discourse complement of method of development. Where Theme ties the text down, point elaborates it, developing it as news. A much greater range of meanings will be realised in New than Theme, though not a random set. A text's principle strings and chains will still be there, constrained by cohesive harmony; but there will be lesser strings and chains and odds and ends as well. A text is never hermetically sealed; a text, like the system behind it, is a dynamic open process — and point is a source of openness: a resistance to the closure predicated on cohesive harmony and method of development.

In short, method of development is where a text is coming from; point is where it's going to. Theme is how a speaker looks at things; New is where she takes the listener to. Hyper-Theme is what a speaker's going to say; hyper-New is what a listener's learned. Macro-Theme is their way in; macro-New is where they've been. A text is a trip: method of development is the route taken, while point is why you went there in the first place — what you've seen/learned/experienced/taken away. Method of development is the plan; point is the holiday.

Finally modal responsibility accommodates the interlocutor, making ongoing assessments of meaning at risk. Vulnerable meanings are woven through the Mood functions of a text's ranking clauses, constructing a constrained resource for openness — for interplay, as interlocutors negotiate the resolution of exchange. What is going on here is that meanings that can be shared without risk are not worth being made; there has to be some difference involved to make a text worth meaning. At the same time, a text is not worth meaning if it cannot be shared. And so the openness associated with point is delimited by the need to organise messages into interactive events in which certain meanings are taken for granted and others are the stakes. Where interlocutors cannot agree, these stakes may be very high. In summary, Residue is what interlocutors are judged to have in common; Mood is what they may not share.

Text is a dialectic, a semiotic rally. But the ball that comes back may be slightly different from the ball you've just played. And the ball has two parts — a bit you thought might come back different and a bit you assumed would stay the same. When the ball comes back unchanged, you throw it away and get a new one; and sometimes it doesn't come back at all — in which case you may choose another ball or stop playing altogether (or decide to find a new partner for the next round). Monologue is hitting up against the backboard; the tension is still there — choosing Subjects is important. But you negotiate against yourself; you can't hit the same shot twice, and someone might be watching anyhow. So the monologue is a dialogue. Text is a rally you aren't trying to win; it's a game you're trying to share.

The main resource facilitating all this interaction is grammatical metaphor. It is the scrambler — it processes meaning in natural and unnatural ways, depending on what texture demands. It orchestrates the many to many relationships among discourse and lexicogrammatical meanings, thereby indefinitely expanding the scope of the content plane as a meaning making resource. It provides the technology needed to predict and accumulate meanings. It makes a text like a clause; it makes a clause like a text. It thingizes and naturalises, it dissembles and reveals.

Because of this, grammatical metaphor is linguistics' most important tool for understanding discourse semantics as research is developed beyond the systems and patterns of interaction proposed here — and for understanding the relationship between texture and context. It is thus the key to understanding text in context — to contextualising the ineffable. This depends in part on developing a theory of context to complement this survey of the linguistic resources contributing to textual unity. And this in turn means asking questions about what this unity is for. It is to these and related problems that Chapter 7 will turn.

Grammatical metaphor then is the meta-process behind a text. It co-ordinates the synoptic systems and dynamic processes that give rise to text. It is the technology that let's the modules harmonise. It is their medium, their catalyst, the groove of their symbiosis, their facilitator, their mediator. It is the re/source of texture.

Taking grammatical metaphor as an orchestrating metaprocess, a summary of the texturing resources reviewed here can be outlined as Table 6.29.

Table 6.29. Texturing resources in English

Metaprocesses

GRAMMATICAL METAPHOR:	ideational	- logical
		- experiential
	interpersonal	
	textual	

Linguistic systems and processes

SYNOPTIC SYSTEMS	DYNAMIC PROCESSES
negotiation	modal responsibility
identification	method of development
conjunction	point
ideation	cohesive harmony

NOTES

1. The category of meronymy appears to have been inadvertantly omitted from the table.

2. In the context *She desperately wanted to win the gold medal in Seoul and win it she did.*

3. The conjunction *so that* has been selected here since it codes the meaning of inclination; see Chapter 4 above.

4. Macro-Themes may themselves be predicted by "super-Themes", super-Themes by "ultra-Themes" and so on, depending on the number of layers of structure in a text.

5. The topical Theme *clear* in r is metaphorical (experiential) realisation of an interpersonal Theme (congruently *clearly*).

6. Theme is analysed in these α clauses since *as our turn comes* was not treated as Theme in 9.r.

7. The modalised conjunctions *whether*, *whether* and *if* have been treated as interpersonal Themes in this analysis.

8. Fries (1981/1983:135) complements his notion of method of development with that of **point**, which he sees as realised through Rheme; his point is reinterpreted as "pattern of news" here.

9. Note that a Table of Contents is to macro-Theme as an Index is to macro-New; thus the close relationship between a Table of Contents and planning writing as opposed to an Index and looking things up.

10.   Compare: [A   s   — I came here for an argument.   I   (did)
                  B   t   — No you didn't.   you   didn't
                       u   You came here for a good argument.   you   (did)]

11.   I am indebted to Julie Choy, whose younger brothers are arguing, for this text.

12.   Congruently this amounts to *You carry them this time*, which reading is the source of the
      reply *All right then I'll carry them.*

7. Context

Register, genre and ideology

7.1 Context

As emphasised in Chapters 1 and 6 above, texture is a function of text in context; texts are social processes and need to be analysed as manifestations of the culture they in large measure construct. This means that alongside a theory of language, functional linguistics has to take some responsibility for a theory of the contexts in which language plays a part. This chapter is concerned with sketching out a few of the basic parametres along which a language based theory of context might evolve.

Following Halliday (1978a) context will be developed here from a sociosemantic perspective. This involves construing the context of a text as a semiotic system (or systems) manifested in whole or in part through language. Following Hjelmslev, context will be treated as a connotative semiotic which has language as its expression plane (see Barthes 1967, 1973). The levels of semiosis articulated by this process of realisation (context and language) will be referred to as communication planes.[1] This Hjelmslevian articulation of language and context is outlined in Fig. 7.1 (see also Fig. 6.3).

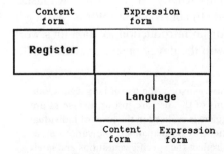

Fig. 7.1. Modelling context as the content plane of language

The sociosemantic organisation of context has to be considered from a number of different angles if it is to give a comprehensive account of the ways in which meanings configure as text. Seen from the perspective of language, context can be interpreted as reflecting metafunctional diversity. Projecting experiential meaning onto context giving **field**,[2] interpersonal meaning giving **tenor** and textual meaning giving **mode**, Halliday (1978a:122) outlines the semiotic structure of context as follows:

> The semiotic structure of the situation is formed out of the three sociosemiotic variables of field, tenor and mode. These represent in systematic form the type of activity in which the text has significant function (field), the status and role relationships involved (tenor) and the symbolic mode and rhetorical channels that are adopted.

Halliday's intrinsic theory of language function is thus projected onto context as an extrinsic theory of language use. The realisation relationship between context and language is treated as a symbolic one, with language a metaphor for social reality at the same time as social reality is a metaphor for language. The relevant proportionalities are as follows:

> METAFUNCTION:CONTEXT::
> experiential:field::
> interpersonal:tenor::
> textual:mode

Seen from the perspective of culture on the other hand, context can be alternatively interpreted as a system of social processes. This for example is the perspective that underlies much of Bakhtin's writing on genre. While acknowledging metafunctional diversity in terms strikingly similar to those developed by Halliday, Bakhtin places emphasis as well on the integration of these meanings as speech genres which evolve and differentiate themselves in different spheres of human activity. This more "wholistic" perspective on text-type Bakhtin (1986:60) constructs as follows (writing in 1952-1953; see Todorov 1984:75-85 for an introduction to Bakhtin's work on genre which converges strikingly with the development of genre studies in systemic theory):

> All the diverse areas of human activity involve the use of language. Quite understandably, the nature of forms of this use are just as diverse as are the areas of human activity...Language is realised in the form of individual concrete utterances (oral and written) by participants in the various areas of human activity. The utterances reflect the specific conditions and goals of each such area not only through their content (thematic) and linguistic

style, that is the selection of the lexical, phraseological, and grammatical resources of the language, but above all through their compositional structure. All three of these aspects — thematic content, style, and compositional structure — are inseparably linked to the *whole* of the utterance and are equally determined by the specific nature of the particular sphere of communication. Each separate utterance is individual, of course, but each sphere in which language is used develops its own *relatively stable types* of these utterances. These we may call *speech genres*.

The tension between these two perspectives will be resolved in this chapter by including in the interpetation of context two communication planes, genre (context of culture) and register (context of situation), with register functioning as the expression form of genre, at the same time as language functions as the expression form of register. Register can then itself be organised with respect to field, tenor and mode, reflecting metafunctional diversity in its expression form, leaving genre to concentrate on the integration of meanings engendered by field, tenor and mode as systemically related social processes. This three plane model can be outlined as in Fig. 7.2.

Any configuration of this kind then needs to be qualified with respect to cultural diversity (cf. dialogism and heteroglossia in Bakhtin 1981). Clearly, meaning potential is not evenly distributed across a culture (any more than material resources are). Access to genre, register and language as semiotic resources is mediated through discourses of ethnicity, class, gender and generation, which discourses are in a continual process of negotiation with each other (see Cranny-Franics 1990, Kress 1985/1989). Not only is this process of negotiation manifest in all text, but it functions as well as the

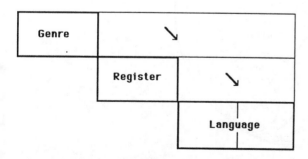

Fig. 7.2. Stratifying context as language's content plane

source of semogenesis, both contextual and linguistic. It is for this reason that a fourth communicative plane, ideology, will be articulated here, with genre, and hence register and language as its expression form.

An alternative form of projection, incorporating this fourth plane, is presented as Fig. 7.3. (from Martin and Matthiessen 1991). In this projection metaredundancy (Lemke 1984) is reflected through the metaphor of concentric circles, with larger circles recontextualising smaller ones; the size of the circles also reflects the fact that the analysis tends to focus on larger units as one moves from phonology to ideology. Thus the tendency at the level of phonology to focus on syllables and phonemes, at the level of lexicogrammar to focus on the clause, at the level of discourse semantics to focus on an exchange or "paragraph", at the level of register to focus on a stage in a transaction, at the level of genre to focus on whole texts and at the level of ideology to focus on discourses manifested across a range of texts. More in the spirit of Firth than Hjelmslev, this projection lends itself to a reading whereby meaning is constructed on all levels, backgrounding the form/content dualities structuring Fig.'s 7.1 and 7.2.

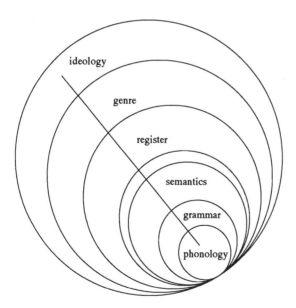

Fig. 7.3. Language and its semiotic environment

In the following section the development of theories of context within systemic linguistics will be briefly reviewed as background to developing the semiotic interpretation of context just outlined.

7.1.1 *Register theory*

Systemic approaches to context derive from the work of Malinowski (1923, 1935) who argued that texts have to be understood in relation to their context of situation and context of culture. Malinowski developed these ideas with respect to the problem of translating specific texts in particular contexts, leaving it to Firth (1950, 1957b, 1957c) to develop context more abstractly as a level of language. For Firth, context was one of a number of levels of analysis (alongside grammar, morphology, lexis, phonology and phonetics) required for linguistics to make statements of meaning about text (Firth 1935/1957a:33).

Firth's interest in the "generalised actual" led him to the following framework for analysing context of situation (elaborated by Halliday from Firth 1950/1957a:182 and Firth 1957/1968:177[3]):

- the PARTICIPANTS in the situation: what Firth referred to as persons and personalities, corresponding more or less to what sociologists would regard as the statuses and roles of the participants;

- the ACTION of the participants: what they are doing, including both their VERBAL ACTION and their NON-VERBAL ACTION;

- OTHER RELEVANT FEATURES OF THE SITUATION: the surrounding objects and events, in so far as they have some bearing on what is going on;

- the EFFECTS of the verbal action: what changes were brought about by what the participants in the situation had to say. (from Halliday 1985/1989:8)

Halliday (1961) similarly includes context as a level of language concerned with the relationship between form and extra-textual features of the situation. This is glossed as semantics in Fig. 7.4 (from Halliday, McIntosh and Strevens 1964:18), although it is important to keep in mind that Halliday (1961) recognises both formal and contextual meaning, with contextual meaning "an extension of the popular — and traditional linguistic — notion of meaning" (1961:245). As Halliday clarifies in Thibault (1987:614), "the whole system is meaning-creating. Meaning is the product of the interrela-

Subject concerned:	Phonetics		Linguistics		
Level (*general*):	SUBSTANCE (phonic or graphic)	relation of form and substance	FORM	CONTEXT (relation of form and situation)	situation (non-linguistic pheno-mena)
Level (*specific*):	PHONETICS	PHONOLOGY	GRAMMAR & LEXIS (vocabulary)	SEMANTICS	
	SCRIPT	'GRAPHOLOGY' (writing system)			

Fig. 7.4. Levels for linguistic description. Reproduced from M.A.K. Halliday, A. McIntosh & P. Strevens The Linguistic Sciences and Language Teaching, p.18. London (1964), Longman.

tions among the parts"; it is a mistake in other words to make "too close a tie-up between 'meaning' and the notion of a specifically 'semantic' level."

The more "specific" phonology-lexicogrammar-semantics labelling is the one generally developed in Halliday's writing after 1964, with the level of semantics given a contextual orientation through the concept of register (the term is taken from Reid 1956). Register is defined as "the configuration of semantic resources that the member of the culture associates with a situation type. It is the meaning potential that is accessible in a given social context" (Halliday 1978a:111).

Defining register in these terms pushes considerations of context such as those addressed by Malinowski and Firth one level up, to what Halliday refers to as context of situation — presumably what is referred to as *situation (non-linguistic phenomena)* in Fig. 7.4. Context of situation is then organised metafunctionally into field, tenor and mode as described above. The following quotation clarifies Halliday's use of the terms **register** and **context of situation** (the term register will be developed differently below):

> I would see the notion of register as being at the semantic level, not above it. Shifting in register means re-ordering the probabilities at the semantic level...whereas the categories of field, mode and tenor belong one level up. These are the features of the context of situation; and this is an interface. But the register itself I would see as being linguistic; it is a setting of probabilities in the semantics. (Thibault 1987:610)

A number of related frameworks were developed by Halliday's colleagues. The term **tenor** in fact comes from Spencer and Gregory (1964) (replacing Halliday, McIntosh and Streven's **style**). Gregory (1967) divides Halliday's tenor into personal tenor and functional tenor, giving four contextual categories instead of three. Ure and Ellis (1977) also recognise four variables — field, mode, formality and role (also found in Ellis and Ure 1969); as does Fawcett (1980) — subject matter, channel, relationship purpose and pragmatic purpose. Martin (1984a:63) attempted to bring out the relationships among these different systems as outlined n Tabe 7.1[4] (the correspondances are not of course exact):

Table 7.1. Five models of context compared

Halliday et al. (1964)	Gregory (1967)	Ure & Ellis (1977)	Halliday (1978a)	Fawcett (1980)
field	field	field	field	subject matter
mode	mode	mode	mode	channel
tenor	personal tenor	formality	tenor	relationship purpose
	functional tenor	role		pragmatic purpose

Unfortunately there is no space here to explore these different frameworks in detail (for an extended discussion see Young 1985). Instead, taking Halliday's (1978a) model as a base line, the problem of purpose will be explored, since it bears critically on the relationship between genre and register to be further developed below. Halliday's 1978a characterisation of field, mode and tenor was presented in Chapter 6 above. His closely related (1985/1989) description is reproduced here:

FIELD — **the social action**: 'what is actually taking place'
refers to what is happening, to the nature of the social action that is taking place: what is it that the participants are engaged in, in which the language figures as some essential component (1985/9:12)

TENOR — **the role structure**: 'who is taking part'
refers to who is taking part, to the nature of the participants, their statuses and roles: what kinds of role relationship obtain among the participants, including permanent and temporary relationships of one kind or another,

both the types of speech role that they are taking on in the dialogue and the whole cluster of socially significant relationships in which they are invovled (1985/9:12)

MODE — **the symbolic organisation**: 'what role language is playing' refers to what part language is playing, what is it that the participants are expecting the language to do for them in the situation: the symbolic organisation of the text, the status that it has, and its function in the context, including the channel (is it spoken or written or some combination of the two?) and also the rhetorical mode, what is being achieved by the text in terms of such categories as persuasive, expository, didactic, and the like (1985/9:12)

At a first glance what would appear to be going on here is that Halliday includes under the heading mode what other frameworks interpret as functional tenor, role or pragmatic purpose. Gregory (1967:186) for example refers the didactic element in lecturing to functional addressee relationships; similarly Ure and Ellis (1977:200) include didactic under the heading role.[5]

At the same time however it is important to note the uncertainty in Halliday's writing as to whether mode is meant to cover genre. At times this connection is explicitly made (e.g. "mode covers roughly Hymes' channel, key and genre" 1978a:62). Elsewhere Halliday would appear to disassociate genre from any one contextual variable (e.g. "In the most general terms there are two other components of texture. One is the textual structure that is internal to the sentence: the organization of the sentence and its parts in a way which relates it to its environment. The other is the 'macrostructure' of the text, that establishes it as a text of a particular kind — conversation, narrative, lyric, commercial correspondence and so on" Halliday & Hasan 1976:324). Gregory and Carroll in fact take Halliday to task for the former reading:

The present authors cannot, however, completely agree with Halliday...whose more abstract use of the term mode as the 'rhetorical channel' (seeming to subsume within it what is here dealt with as functional tenor) leads him to assign most considerations of *genre* to this particular dimension. We prefer to characterise *genre* in terms of all the dimensions of language variety. (1978a:44-45)

Their position is one however with which Halliday at times appears to agree:

The concept of genre discussed above [i.e. the rhetorical concepts of expository, didactic, persuasive, descriptive and the like — JRM] is an aspect of what we are calling the 'mode'. The various genres of discourse, including literary genres, are the specific semiotic functions of text that have social value in the culture. A genre may have implications for other components of meaning: there are often associations between a particular genre and particular semantic features of an ideational or interpersonal kind, for example between the genre of prayer and certain selections in the mood system. Hence the labels for generic categories are often functionally complex: a concept such as a 'ballad' implies not only a certain text structure with typical patterns of cohesion, but also a certain range of content expressed through highly favoured options in transitivity and other experiential systems... (1978a:145)

Overall it would appear that "rhetorical purpose" is the wild card in contextual description, being variously categorised under field (Halliday 1965), tenor (Gregory 1967), mode (Halliday 1978a, 1985/1989) and as a separate contextual variable in its own right (Firth 1950 — effects, Ure & Ellis 1977 — role, Fawcett 1980 — pragmatic purpose). The main reason for this is that purpose is difficult to associate with any one metafunctional component of the lexicogrammar or discourse semantics. The effect of a text is the result of all components of its meaning. This makes associating the notion of rhetorical purpose with Bakhtin's more global notion of speech genres an attractive one (cf. Gregory 1982). The advantages of this conceptualisation will be explored in 7.1.2 below.

7.1.2 *Communicative planes: register, genre and ideology*

In broad terms the development of work on register and context reviewed above can be interpreted in terms of a gradual de-materialising and concomitant semioticising of frameworks for relating language to situation (see in particular Hasan's 1977, 1979, 1985/1989 use of contextual features to generate text structure). The characterisation of contextual variables such as field, mode, tenor and genre as a semiotic resource remains however at a nascent stage, which makes it difficult to argue about levels of context — the degree of explicitness and formalisation required to argue convincingly about levels has not yet been attained. A number of reasons for distinguishing register and genre as levels have however been uncovered in preliminary work. These will now be reviewed.

Before beginning however, it is important to note that *English Text* extends the use of the term register as defined by Halliday. Halliday uses the term simply to refer to language as context's expression plane — the linguistic meanings (entailing their expressions) at risk in a given situation type. *English Text* extends the notion to cover in addition part of context's content plane; **register** is used in other words to refer to the semiotic system constituted by the contextual variables field, tenor and mode. As outlined above, in the model of context developed here, register is the name of the metafunctionally organised connotative semiotic between language and genre. This means that instead of characterising context of situation as potential and register as (context's) actual, *English Text* treats register as a semiotic system in its own right, involving notions both of system and process.[7]

	POTENTIAL (system)	ACTUAL (process)
Halliday (1978a)	context of situation:	register::
English Text	register:	language

The different place of register in the two models is outlined in Table 7.2.

Table 7.2. Different uses of the term register in Halliday 1978a and English Text

Halliday (e.g. 1978a)	*English Text*
CONTEXT OF SITUATION:	REGISTER:
	[as connotative semiotic]:
field	field
tenor	tenor
mode	mode (excluding rhetorical mode)
REDOUNDING **with (i.e. symbolising, construing and construed by)**	
LANGUAGE:	LANGUAGE:
semantics (register as meanings at risk)	discourse semantics
lexicogrammar	lexicogrammar
phonology/graphology	phonology/graphology

As noted above, the fact that notions of purpose and effect do not correlate with any one metafunctional component in language and have been associated at one time or another with different variables in the development of register theory suggests that a teleological perspective on text function might be better set up as superordinate to — rather than alongside or incorporated in — field, mode and tenor. The register variables field, tenor and mode can then be interpreted as working together to achieve a text's goals, where goals are defined in terms of systems of social processes at the level of genre. It should be stressed here that bringing telos into contextual theory at this point in no way implies that text is being interpreted as the realisation of speakers' intentions; genres are social processes, and their purpose is being interpreted here in social, not psychological terms. Nor does the model imply that the cultures as a whole are goal-directed, with some over-riding purpose governing the interaction of social processes. Social processes negotiate with each other and evolve, as noted above in the motivation for a level of ideology superordinate to genre and register. The metaphor of intentionality, in other words, is just as inappropriate for explaining why a culture has the social processes it does as for explaining why an individual speaker produces certain kinds of text. With these qualifications in mind, the notion of telos is a useful one for glossing systemic relations between combinations of field, mode and tenor choices at the level of genre (cf. Thibault 1989).

Approaching genre from a teleological perspective is also useful in accounting for the way in which texts typically move through stages to a point of closure and are explicitly treated by speaker/listener as incomplete where closure is not attained (having mentioned closure it is important to stress that genre, like all semiotic systems, is a dynamic open system (see Lemke 1984) and so in constantly evolving; in Bakhtin's 1986:60 terms: "The wealth and diversity of speech genres are boundless because the various possibilities of human activity are inexhaustible, and because each sphere of activity contains an entire repertoire of speech genres that differentiate and grow as the particular sphere develops and becomes more complex." Mitch-

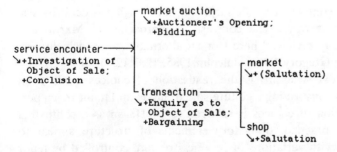

Fig. 7.5. Ventola's systemic formulation of Mitchell (1957/1975) on service encounters in Cyrenaica

ell's (1957) application of Firth's framework to the language of buying and selling in Cyrenaica for example involved setting up text structures for each of the three contexts he examined: market auction, market transaction and shop transaction. Ventola (1987:15) has systemicised this work along the lines of Fig. 7.5.

Mitchell makes the point that these stages are ordered (i.e. in a structural relationship with each other) but may be realised in different sequences. Taking this reservation into account, canonical structures for the market service encounters were proposed as follows (as Ventola's network shows, shop transactions differed only with respect to the optionality of the Salutation stage):

MARKET AUCTION:
Auctioneer's Opening ˆ Investigation of Object of Sale ˆ Bidding ˆ Conclusion

MARKET TRANSACTION:
Salutation ˆ Enquiry as to Object of Sale ˆ Investigation of Object of Sale ˆ Bargaining ˆ Conclusion

Mitchell's work was not followed up within systemic linguistics for almost a generation. But mainly influenced Hasan 1977[8], investigation of the stages associated with different text types and their realisation has been focal in more recent systemic work (see for example Sinclair and Coulthard 1975, Hasan 1977, 1979, 1984b, 1985a/1989, Ventola 1979, 1983, 1984, 1987, Martin 1985a, 1985b, Martin and Peters 1985; closely related work has also been undertaken in other models — for example Pike 1967 on church services, and Labov and Waletzky 1967 on narrative).

Given the strong teleological orientation of systemic work on text structure alongside the uncertainty about how to deal with rhetorical purpose in models of context, it is not surprising that staging is dealt by systemicists in different ways. The contrasting approaches of Martin and Hasan will be briefly reviewed here (for an alternative approach through phasal analysis see Gregory 1985, Malcolm 1985, 1987:123-130).

For Hasan, text structure is the realisation of choices made from among the options constituting a culture's field, mode and tenor (each permissable combination of choices is referred to by Hasan as a contextual configuration). In practice, obligatory elements of structure appear to derive from field, with variations in generic structure controlled by tenor and mode. This means that there is a very strong association between field, text structure and genre. As Hasan (1985/1989:61) puts it:

> by implication, the obligatory elements define the genre to which a text belongs; and the appearance of all of these elements in a specific order corresponds to our perception of whether the text is complete or incomplete.

Martin's alternative proposal is that text structure be generated at the level of genre, as in Ventola's systemic formulation of Mitchell's work above. Genre networks would thus be formulated on the basis of similarities and differences between text structures which thereby define text types. As part of the realisation process, generic choices would preselect field, mode and tenor options associated with particular elements of text structure. Text structure is referred to as **schematic structure** in Martin's model, with genre defined as a staged, goal-oriented social process realised through register (see Martin 1984b, 1985a, 1985b, Martin, et al. n.d., Ventola 1987:63-66).

The common ground between the two models lies in the correlation proposed between schematic structure and field, mode and tenor options; for both Martin and Hasan staging redounds with social context. Keeping in mind that realisation is not theoretically directional in systemic models, there is nothing substantive in the fact that whereas for Hasan, choices in field, mode and tenor are realised by schematic structure, for Martin schematic structure is realised through choices in these same components of register. Where the models do differ substantively is with respect to Martin's suggestion that there is a network of relationships underlying register which relates text types to each other in ways they cannot be inter-related considered from the perspective of any one register variable. The advantages of formulating genre as a pattern of register patterns will now be briefly reviewed:

(i) Establishing genre as a level of semiosis which is not itself metafunctionally organised means that texts can be classified in ways which cut across metafunctional components in language. This strengthens Halliday's suggestion that field is strongly predictive of experiential choices, tenor of interpersonal choices and mode of textual ones without sacrificing the classification of texts into generic types such as narrative, exposition, procedure, report etc. (Gregory 1988:315 makes the same point in abandoning functional tenor, which has multi-functional realisation). Generic labels such as narrative or exposition are impossible to tie satisfactorily to any one type of meaning; their realisation cuts across metafunctions. For this reason, it is useful not to associate genre too closely with any one register variable (e.g. mode in Halliday's work or field in Hasan's).

(ii) Setting up genre as a pattern of register patterns makes it possible to account for the fact that in a given culture, not all combinations of field, mode and tenor variables occur. This is perhaps easiest to study from a cross-cultural perspective, noting the effect of western science and technology (new fields) or of media (new modes) for example on "developing" nations as social processes change dramatically in the face of imported medicine, industry, literacy, radio, television etc. But all thriving cultures are continually elaborating their meaning potential by combining old variables in new ways and by making new distinctions to combine. A distinct level of genre makes it possible to monitor this dialectic of constraints and possibilities.

(iii) Making genre rather than register variables responsible for generating schematic structure makes it easier to handle changes in experiential, interpersonal and textual meaning from from stage to another in a text. There are many text types where this occurs: a teacher may shift fields to explain a point by analogy; a salesperson will manipulate tenor in order to close a sale; sports commentators shift rhythmically from play by play description to critique and evaluation. Underlying register, genre can be used to predict these changes, stage by stage, while at the same time accounting for a text's overall coherence. Halliday and Hasan's (1976:23) observation about coherent texts being "consistent in register" cannot in other words be interpreted literally as "the same in register throughout"; rather the text must be motivated by its register, changes in which can in turn be motivated by genre.

(iv) Distinguishing genre and register makes it easier to account for differences between the sequential unfolding of text as process and the notion of activity associated with field. Depending on mode, texts may or may not unfold in the same sequence as the activities they accompany or discuss. Live commentary on a football match has a different structure to newspaper accounts of the game; the commentary starts at the beginning of the match, the news story with its result. The commentary and news story differ in staging, and therefore in genre; but they are alike in terms of field — they both reflect the sequence of activities which comprised the game. Unhooking field from staging makes it possible to show how texts of these kinds are alike and different at the same time.

(v) Finally, and critically, there is the question of genre agnation. The argument here is that social processes are related in ways which complement the valeur determined by looking at them from the perspective of field, mode or tenor alone. Combinations of field, mode and tenor choices in other words enter into relationships with each other which are more than the sum of their parts; to some extent, genres have a life of their own (see 7.3.2 below). This argument can only be pursued by formulating networks for field, mode, tenor and genre and demonstrating that the genre network consists of different kinds of opposition to the field, mode and tenor ones. Consequently, exemplification will be reserved until after the presentation of preliminary field, mode and tenor options below.

Introducing genre as a level of contextual semiosis with responsibility for integrating the diversity projected from the functional organisation of language onto register, makes it important to introduce diversity of a different kind, at a deeper level in order to keep the model from becoming too monolithic and rigidly deterministic. This is necessary because a culture's meaning potential is distributed unevenly across social groups and so constantly changing. Tension among the discourses of these groups means that to achieve metastablility, the system must evolve. It is to account for this dialectic of difference, systemic inertia and evolution that a fourth communicative plane, ideology, is proposed.

Viewed synoptically, ideology is the system of coding orientations constituting a culture. As suggested by Bernstein (1971a, 1973, 1975, 1990), coding orientations are realised through contextually specific semantic styles associated with groups of speakers of differing generation, gender, ethnicity and class. Recently these have been studied in some detail in the context of mother-child interaction by Hasan (see Hasan 1988, 1990, Cloran 1989). The system of coding orientations positions speaker/listeners in such a way that options in genre, register and language are made selectively available. Social power can be defined in these terms according to the range of options available, the extent to which options available can be used for control, submission or negotiation, and the degree to which options can be taken up to change the context making them available.

Viewed dynamically, ideology is concerned with the redistribution of power — with semiotic evolution. This is easiest to study when discourses actively contest with each other. Martin (1986a) examined ecological debates in an attempt to show the ways in which the semiotic resources of genre, register and language were marshalled to effect and resist social change. In contesting texts contratextuality foregrounds the social differences constituted by coding orientations. It should be noted however that tension among discourses is a feature of all texts — they are heteroglossic in Bakhtin's terms. Dynamic open systems evolve, with or without revolution — negotiation among coding orientations is a necessary feature of the system. Diversification at the level of ideology is as important to metastability as is the apparent homogeneity of systems articulated at the levels of genre, register and language.

In the sections which follow, the semiotics of register, genre and ideology will be briefly outlined. For reasons of space, the networks proposed will be exemplified in very limited ways. Exploring the semiotic resources of a culture is obviously an inexhaustible enterprise and the territory to be mapped out can only be explored very provisionally here. At worst, the contextual dimensions proposed should provide a number of useful parameters for collecting and sorting the texts upon which a better grounded interpretation of the culture might eventually be based. At best, the model is one that has proved effective in shedding some light on the ways in which progressive education naturalises social differences which might otherwise be more productive of change and how this benevolent inertia might be undermined (e.g. Painter and Martin 1986, Hasan and Martin 1989). To the extent that it facilitates further political interventions of this kind this provisional sociosemiotic sketch of context will have played its part in enabling linguistics as a form of social action — the raison d'etre of functional linguistics.[9]

7.2 Register

7.2.1 Mode

Mode refers to the role language is playing in realising social action. Within register, it is the projection of textual meaning, and so is realised primarily through the textual metafunction in language. Mode thus puts major systems such as TONALITY and TONICITY in phonology, and THEME and INFORMATION (clause), DEIXIS (nominal group), TENSE (verbal group) and SUBSTITUTION and ELLIPSIS (clause and group) in the grammar at risk, and because of their textual orientation impacts on all systems at the level of discourse semantics (NEGOTIATION, IDENTIFICATION, CONJUNCTION and IDEATION).

As with textual meaning in general, mode is concerned with symbolic reality — with texture. Since symbolic reality (i.e. text/process) has the function of constructing social reality, mode is oriented to both interpersonal and experiential meaning. It thus mediates the role played by language along two dimensions. Interpersonally, mode mediates the semiotic space between monologue and dialogue. Text [4:2] for example begins as a conversation (*What do you have to do... — Well...*), but unfolds as monologue [4:2c-hhh]. The interview genre in other words involves changes in mode — from dialogue to monologue and back to dialogue again. As is typical of textual meaning the changes manifest themselves as a kind of wave. Putting this in general terms, mode mediates NEGOTIATION.

[4:2]   Question:
    1.a.   What do you have to do in the showing area,
      b.   with the dog on the lead?
    Response:
    2.c.   Well, you always walk
      d.   with the dog on the left-hand side,
      e.   the reason being is [[the judge is standing in the centre of the ring]].
    3.f.   So, therefore, you need to get yourself between your dog and the judge.
    4.g.   The dog (!) must be able to see the dog at all times.
    5.h.   So, usually when a class is going into the ring,
      i.   the first thing it does is:
        ...

Experientially mode mediates the semiotic space between action and reflection. Exemplifying again from [4:2], for the most part this text is constitutive of its field, which it generalises as an abstract procedure. For this reason the processes are for the most part timeless (i.e. simple present tense in English) and the participants involve generic or generalised reference. From [4:17tt] however, through to [4:17bbb], the text shifts its mode and becomes dependent on another text — the imaginary representation of the showing area on the coffee table to which the speaker refers exophorically: *here, that way, like that, over there*. Correspondingly, the tense shifts as well, from simple present to present in present (*is standing*), as it has occasionally elsewhere in the text ([4:2e, h, j, z, gg]). The text in other words becomes more dependent on its context — more a part, and less purely constitutive of what is going on. Putting this in general terms, mode mediates contextual dependency — the extent to which a text constructs or accompanies its field.

17.tt.   So, if your judge **is standing here**,
uu.   we walk away from him that way.
18.vv.   That is [[so the judge can get the hind movement of your dog]].
19.ww.   Then we usually walk sideways **like that**
xx.   so as he can see [[the dog moving all over]]
yy.   and then we walk back to the judge
zz.   so as he can see the front movement.
20.aaa. After that he usually tells you
bbb.   to wait **over there**.

These two metafunctionally oriented dimensions of mode will now be explored in more detail.

7.2.1.1 *Monologue/dialogue*

In effect, mode is the semiotic construction of communication technology. As far as interpersonal space is concerned, what is critical is the way in which various channels of communication affect the kind of interaction that is possible between speaker and listener. This is conditioned by the kind of feedback that is possible, depending on whether or not the speaker and listener can see each other and at the same time whether or not they can hear each other.

As far as aural contact is concerned, there are three possibilities — no contact as in reading/writing, one-way contact as with radio and two-way contact as with telephone conversation. Two-way aural contact enables turn-taking, which is only possible when speaker and listener can hear each other (setting aside sign language, which has a visual expression form). One-way contact means that for the speaker the full range of turn-taking resources remains intact (including intonation, rhythm, voice quality and other "paralinguistic" systems) but that they cannot be used for negotiation. No contact restricts the system's meaning potential since graphology is a more limited expression form than phonology. Recently however word processing has considerably expanded graphological resources in the context of personal computing through formatting and various possibilities for interacting with written text.

Similarly for visual contact, there are three possibilities — no contact as in reading/writing, one-way contact as with television and two-way contact as with face to face conversation. Two-way visual context means that any attendant semiosis that is realised visually can be brought into play (kinesics, proxemics, the social action in which the speaker/listener dyad is engaged and so on). This increases the potential for a text to depend on its material context, as part of or an accompaniment to what is going on.

These two dimensions of contact are used to cross-classify various channels of communication below (the matrix is by no means exhaustive). Communication technology is constantly expanding meaning potential in this area.

Table 7.3. Aural and visual contact, cross-classifying mode

| | VISUAL CONTACT | | |
	none	**one-way**	**two-way**
AURAL CONTACT			
none	writing	silent movie, home movie, Big Brother (1984[10])	sign language, mime
one-way	radio, audio tape, record	television, movie, video	lip-reading (hearing/deaf dyad)
two-way	telephone, intercom, short-wave radio	HAL (2001), blind/seeing dyad, video intercom[11]	face to face conversation

The fact that more than one medium is involved in most cells means that further delicacy is required. Just two of the key cells, no visual/aural contact (writing) and two-way visual/aural contact (speaking) will be further developed here. As far as speaking is concerned, further distinctions can be proposed with respect to the amount of interaction a mode allows. Turn taking is relatively free in casual conversation,[12] but more restricted in public settings, especially where groups of speakers are involved in the role of audience. In some contexts there may actually be rules about who speaks when (debates, formal meetings, parliament) and participants with special responsibilities for adjudicating them (moderators, chairpersons, speakers). In other contexts the rules for turn taking may not have been codified, turn taking is nonetheless firmly controlled — by interviewers in what might be termed quasi-conversations, and by lecturers and tutors in quasi-monologues. Finer distinctions of this kind are closely related to tenor, and are probably better treated as gradient rather than discrete. Seen from the perspective of mode however, all involve the mediation of semiotic space in ways that affect the kind of interaction that is possible. It is thus appropriate to tune mode into tenor, as in Fig. 7.6.

With writing, finer distinctions can be made by taking into account the fact the almost all writing reflects turn taking in some respects — most writing is expectant of some kind of response, even though it may be some time coming, for example by post or in the form of a critical review. Letters for example display several interactive features. They are addressed and signed, begin with greetings and close with leave takings, demand information and goods and services of various kinds and reply in kind. Moving along this scale, bureaucratic "letters" (i.e. memos and circulars) display several of these features; they tend not however to be personally addressed or signed, and are more likely to give information and demands goods and services than to demand information or respond to demands for service. Books are even less personal, although instructional texts are noticeably interactive, involving the reader in general terms (*you* and *we*), asking questions, setting exercises and the like. Truly private texts are the exception rather than the rule; some people do keep diaries and journals for

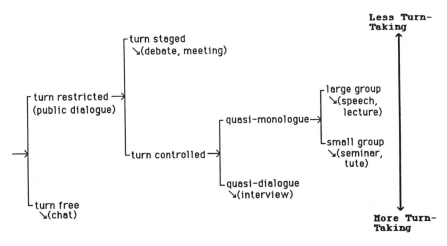

Fig. 7.6. Degrees of turn-taking in spoken mode

themselves, but even these sometimes take the form of letters (*Dear Diary, As for how I was feeling yesterday...*). Probably the only truly unaddressed texts are never heard, since they do not receive expression form (they are thought, not said) — except where they are constructed as stream of consciousness in novels. This dialogic[13] perspective on writing is outlined in Fig. 7.7.

Another dimension along which writing can be scaled has to do with composing — the way in which text is shaped as an object of meaning. In contrast with spoken language, where hearing is simultaneous with speaking, writing delays reading; and at the same time it renders meaning as an object which can be (self-)consciously acted upon.[14] The composing process may be indirect, as with dictaphones and dictation (talking writing) or direct. Direct composing may be done by hand or through a keyboard, either by typing or word processing. Assuming that composers are comfortable with the mode, these media can be scaled according to the (self-)consciousness they involve, which is related to fluency. Recording on a dictaphone is faster than short-hand, both of which are faster than composing

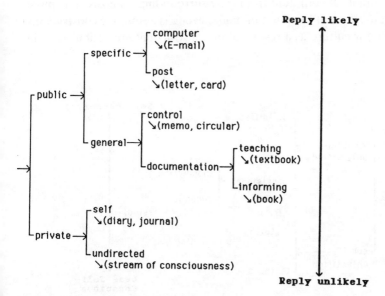

Fig. 7.7. Degrees of reply expectation in writing

directly in handwriting or print; this makes writing transcribed from tape more like speaking. At the same time, direct composition means that text manifests itself directly as an object to rework. This is easier on a word processor than by hand, and easier by hand than on a typewriter (which is why most writers reserve typing for a final drafts and are easily converted to word processing once the limitations of learning to use a keyboard and word processing package fluently are overcome). The process of writing is scaled according to the degree of (self-)consciousness involved below.

The mode systems developed here are displayed together in Fig. 7.9. The description, like all those to be developed in this chapter, is a very indelicate one. Research substantiating the oppositions suggested has in most cases only just begun and cannot unfortunately be illustrated here for reasons of space (for an application of quantitative methodology to semantic variation and context see Nesbitt & Plum 1988, Plum 1988).

Before moving on to consider the semiotic space between action and reflection, it is important to stress that the distinctions drawn here are semiotic, not material ones.[15] It is obviously just as possible to write dialogue (drama) as it is to sit monologuing with a friend; similarly both dialogue and stream of consciousness appear in books, but both types of meaning are radically different from their surrounding semiosis. The physical channel itself is not the point of mode. Mode is a semiotic construct and functions in our culture as a resource for constructing interaction. It is dif-

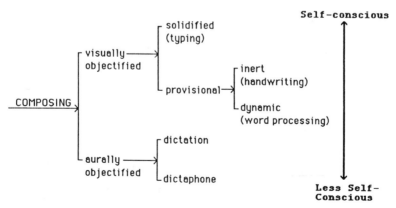

Fig. 7.8. Degrees of self-consciousness in 'writing'

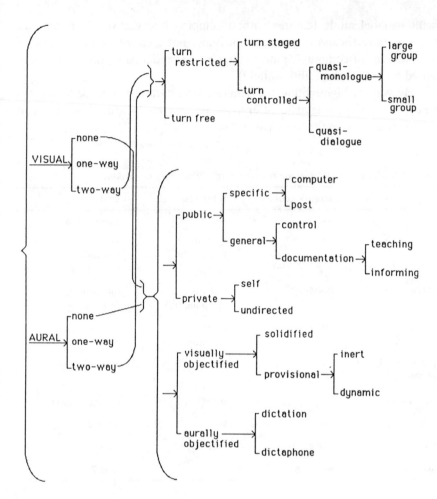

Fig. 7.9. Mode systems: speaking and writing focus

ficult to label mode features without slipping into realism. The network above is nevertheless a system of meaning, not a classification of modern technologies of communication (which in the model being developed here would be the responsibility of field).

By way of highlighting the semiotic orientation of interpersonal distance, some of the linguistic differences between monologue, interview and chat contexts are outlined in Table 7.4.

Table 7.4. Mode — aspects of the realisation of "interpersonal" distance

	monologue	interview	chat
CONTINUITY	—	—	more common
NEGOTIATION	—	synoptic interaction	synoptic & dynamic interaction
SPEECH FUNCTION	initiating	initiating (responding)	initiating & responding
IDENTIFICATION	endophoric	endophoric/ 1/2 exophoric	1/2 exophoric
SUBTITUTION & ELLIPSIS	—	some	more common
TAGGING	—	some	more common
VOCATION	—	some	more common
MOOD	declarative	indicative	varied
TONE	—	—	tone 2

7.2.1.2 Action/reflection

Experientially mode mediates the degree to which language is part of or constitutive of what is going on. In text [4:2] for example, most of the meanings are made verbally (excepting the exophoric reference discussed above). At the dog show itself however, language would have a much smaller role to play in the showing area, where most of the meaning is realised through action, not words. The judge has just a few things to say to organise the goings-on (small caps below), most of which are reported or quoted in [4:2]; for example:

20.aaa. After that he usually **tells** you

     bbb. TO WAIT OVER THERE.

21.ccc. He proceeds to do that with every dog.

22.ddd. Then he will **say**,

     eee. "LINE YOUR DOG UP."

     fff. or "GET THE BEST OUT OF YOUR DOG."

And people mean to themselves (projected ideas in small caps in the example below):

    gg. so you're **hoping** all the time

    hh. THAT YOUR DOG WILL STAND NICE AND STEADY

    ii. SO THE JUDGE CAN DO THIS

    jj. AND IT DOESN'T HAMPER HIM

    kk. HANDLING THE DOGS.

Showing a dog and describing how a dog is shown are in other words very different modes.

One way to scale texts along this action/reflection dimension of mode is to take the **activity sequences** aspect of field as a base line and see to what extent texts are structured with respect to these sequences. Texts can then be divided into those organised primarily with respect to activity sequences (iconic texts) and those organised along different lines (non-iconic texts). Labeling these text types field-structured and genre-structured is potentially misleading;[16] it needs to be kept in mind that in referring to the iconic texts as field-structured, what one is saying is that for this group of texts it is difficult to distinguish genre and field — looking from the perspectives of social process (genre) and activity sequence (field) amounts to very much the same thing (in other words the model of context developing here overdetermines the classification of these text types). With genre-structured texts on the other hand, the organisation of the text is very different from the organisation of activity sequences to which the text may refer. With this reservation in mind, a preliminary grid can be established as in Table 7.5 — with exemplary texts noted (Hasan 1985/9:58 uses the opposition ancilliary/ constitutive to establish a closely related continuum).

This grid distinguishes field-structured from genre-structured texts and subclassifies field-structured texts according to how much of the social action is constructed by language. Texts in which most of the social action is realised

Table 7.5. Mode — determination of text sequence by field or genre

"Field-structured" (time/place):	
activity sequence realised by social action	-ancillary
activity sequence realised by text	- monitoring [2:3]
	- reconstructing [3:88]
	- generalising [4:2]
"Genre-structured" (semantic space):	
review	[Martin 1985b:92]
theoretical	[4:3]

non-verbally are referred to as **ancilliary**; texts in which most of the social action is realised linguistically are further divided into those in which the language **monitors** what is going on (e.g. sports commentary), those in which it **reconstructs** what has gone on (e.g. biography) and those in which the language **generalises** about what goes on (e.g. recipes). Genre-structured texts are divided into those which **review** field-structured texts (e.g. movie reviews), and so are partially determined by their activity sequences, and **theoretical** texts which are not organised around a sequence of events in any respect (e.g. editorials). This scale arranges texts with respect to iconicity and the amount of ideational meaning that needs to be made explicit to realise the field.

It is important not to confuse the semiotic space under construction here with either of two independent dimensions: the interpersonal distinction between proposals and propositions, and the experiential distinction between activities and things. Pursuing the MOOD opposition first, monitoring texts for example can be 'imperative', telling someone what to do (e.g. aerobics class), or indicative, telling someone (e.g. a small child) what is going on (or is about to). Similarly reconstruction may be either an account of what someone was told to do or what they did, and generalising texts may be either macro-proposals (e.g. assembly manuals) or macro-propositions (e.g. accounts of how a product works). The same MOOD opposition is relevant to genre-structured texts, distinguishing hortatory ('so change your ways') from analytical ('so this is how things are') exposition (see Martin 1985b, Martin and Peters 1985). This crossclassification of mode by MOOD is outlined in Table 7.6.

Table 7.6. Degrees of abstraction for proposals and propositions

	PROPOSAL	PROPOSITION
MONITORING (present) (future)	guidance *Do.*	running commentary *We are doing.* *We'll just do.*
RECONSTRUCTING (past)	projected instruction *S/he told me to do.*	recount *I/we did.*
GENERALISING (timeless)	manual *You do.*	implication sequence *It does.*

Experientially, the distinction between texts which focus on activities and those which focus on things is also independent of the action/reflection dimension under construction here. Activity was taken as the base line in introducing this dimension of mode above, with organisation around sequence in time as the key variable. The same distinctions can however be applied to thing oriented discourse, with place (including composition and setting) rather the time the critical parameter. It is possible to comment (typically evaluatively) on people, places and things as one experiences them (monitoring); similarly one can reconstruct objects through description and generalise about them as generic classes in reports. The potential source of confusion here has to do with the fact that genre-structured texts tend to be heavily nominalised, and through grammatical metaphor con-

Table 7.7. Degrees of abstraction for activities and things

	ACTIVITY	THING
MONITORING	commentary *We are doing.*	evaluation *That's pretty.*
RECONSTRUCTING	recount *I/we did.*	description *It was pretty.*
GENERALISING	procedure *It does.*	report *They're attractive.*

struct fields as thing-like, whether referring to activities or not (see Martin 1991b). Abstract modes in other words interpret social reality through semiotic resources that in less abstract modes would be applied to things — texts are organised around semiotic space instead of experiential time or place. Keeping this in mind, the logical independence of action/reflection and activity/thing is outlined in Table 7.7.

The oppositions relevant to field-structured texts are elaborated systemically in Fig. 7.10. Texts accompanying a social process are distinguished from those constituting one. The accompanying texts are then distinguished according to whether the verbal action is that of participants in or observers of the social action. Participating texts may be either ancilliary, with minor clauses punctuating the social action (e.g. scoring and line calling during a tennis match) or monitoring, with present tense, here/now deixis, 1/2 person clauses providing a running account of what is going on (e.g. demonstrating a procedure). Commentary texts can be divided into those where speaker and listener are both observers (TV sports/parade/ wedding commentary) and those in which only one party is observing (radio commentary).[17]

Texts constituting a social process can be divided into those reconstructing a social process which has taken place and those constructing one

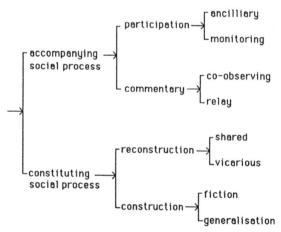

Fig. 7.10. Mode — degrees of abstraction

which has not (TENSE, DEIXIS and PERSON all shift to distanced values — past,[18] there/then, 3rd). Reconstructions may be based on shared or unshared experience, which affects how much of the social process has to be explicitly replayed. Constructions can be broken down into fiction and generalisation. Fictional texts are semiotically closely related to texts constructing unshared experience, but generally make fewer assumptions about what can be assumed. Generalising texts neutralise TENSE, DEIXIS and PERSON in order to construct social processes as potentials underlying and cutting across particular manifestations.

This network can be elaborated in various ways. Participation may allow room for the construction of an additional field if the activity sequence in which the speaker/listeners are involved is not too engaging (e.g. chatting while washing up). The notion of first (washing up) and second (what the chat is about) order field has been used for texts of this kind (Halliday 1978a:144).[19] Commentary texts are sensitive to the pacing of the activity being described; rugby for example is a much faster sport than cricket, making it difficult for language to keep up.

Field-structured texts constituting a social process are sensitive to the length of the time-line in focus. The longer the time-line, the more selective the coverage. These texts can therefore be crossclassified as episodic (e.g. biography) and primarily organised through setting in time (typically theme marked circumstantial adjuncts) or sequential (e.g. narratives) and primarily organised through sequence in time (typically by temporal conjunctions). Reconstructions of unshared experience can be further divided into vicarious (e.g. gossip) and personal (e.g. anecdote) experience. And fictional constructions can be broken into realistic (e.g. romance or detective fiction) and fantastic (e.g. science fiction); in fantastic texts, more has to be constructed as less can be assumed. These additional distinctions are incorporated into Fig. 7.11 below.

The final ideational consideration which has to be taken into account here has to do with projection. All of the text types considered to this point can be spoken or written directly; alternatively their verbalisation may itself be experientialised. Linguistically this is accomplished through behavioural, mental and verbal processes which explicitly construct meaning as doing (as in the examples from text [4:2] above). Alternative resources for projection include drawing (comics and cartoons), film and stage. Some examples of

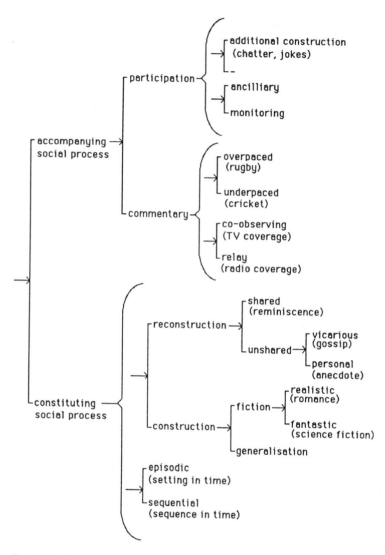

Fig. 7.11. Mode — more delicate degrees of abstraction

linguistically and pictorially projected texts across three modes are outlined in Table 7.8.

Table 7.8. Projection across modes

| | FIELD-STRUCTURED: | | GENRE-STRUCTURED |
	accompanying	(re-)constructing	
LINGUISTIC	simultaneous translation	narrative dialogue	quotations
PICTORIAL	comic strip dialogue	comic strip headers	figures, tables

With film and theatre projection is naturalised as real; this does not however take away from the fact that the language spoken has been scripted and is very different from the unprojected dialogue of everyday life. These projection systems are developed in Fig. 7.12 where they crossclassify the basic action/reflection mode options.

Some of the key realisations associated with experiential distance are reviewed in Table 7.9 for monitoring, reconstructing and genre-structured texts.

7.2.2 Tenor

Tenor refers to the negotiation of social relationships among participants. Within register, it is the projection of interpersonal meaning, and so is realised primarily through the interpersonal metafunction in language. Tenor thus puts major phonological and lexicogrammatical systems such as TONE, MOOD, KEY, POLARITY, MODALIZATION, MODULATION, COMMENT, TAGGING, VOCATION, PERSON (see Matthiessen 1992) and various attitudinal systems across ranks and permeating lexis at risk, as well as the system of NEGOTIATION at the level of discourse semantics. The model of tenor to be presented here is that developed by Poynton (1984, 1985, 1990a).

As with interpersonal meaning in general, tenor is concerned with the semiotics of relationships. It mediates these relationships along three dimensions, which will be referred to here as **status** (Poynton's power), **contact** and **affect**. Status and contact are closely related to Brown and Gil-

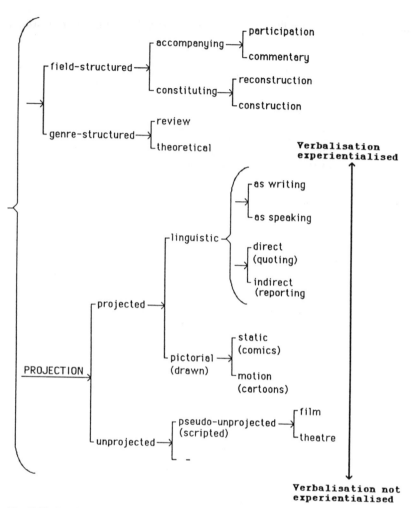

Fig. 7.12. Mode — action, reflection and projection

Table 7.9. Mode — aspects of the realisation of experiential distance

	field-structured: monitoring	reconstruction	genre-structured
CONJUNCTION	implicit; external; —	implicit & explicit; external; congruent	implicit & explicit; internal & external; incongruent
IDENTIFICATION	exophoric	anaphoric	generic
IDEATION	activity	nuclear & activity	taxonomic
NEGOTIATION	—	projected	quoted writing
CIRCUMSTANCE	setting in time (*soon*)	—	—
clause complex	—	intricate	—
grammatical metaphor	—	—	experiential
method of development	1st person	1/3 person	abstract
TENSE	present in present	past	present
INFORMATION	New only	—	—
TONALITY	—	—	marked

man's (1960) concepts of power and soldarity respectively. Status refers here to the relative position of interlocutors in a culture's social hierarchy while contact refers to their degree of institutional involvement with each other (Hasan 1977 appears to use the term social role for status and social distance for contact). Affect has been included to cover what Halliday (1978a:33) refers to as the "degree of emotional charge" in the relationship between participants.

The basic opposition as far as status is concerned is between equal and unequal depending on whether the social ranking of participants is comparable or not. Contact can be broken down into involved and uninvolved depending on a number of factors influencing the familiarity of participants with each other. Contact is logically independent of status, since seeing someone often does not in itself change one's ranking (senior administrators and their secretaries for example do not change rank because they see each other every day; they do however become more "involved" with each other). In many registers, for reasons of status, contact and genre, affect is not linguistically manifested (because participants scarcely know each other for example) — this is not to say that it is not immanent and cannot be realised in other ways; where language is emotionally charged, then the basic contrast is between positive and negative. Tenor, up to this point in delicacy, is outlined below (for a closely related perspective on social relations see Cloran (1987:95-98) who presents a much more delicate interpretation of tenor by Hasan).

Terminology in this area is clearly a problem, since there is no strong tradition of interpersonally oriented contextual studies in linguistics to draw upon and interpersonal meaning in general has tended not to be the focus of linguistic theory and description. The problem of how to use terms like status and power has already arisen and needs to be clarified here. Status-like relationships between participants can be interpreted from a number of perspectives, including mode, field, genre and ideology as well as tenor.

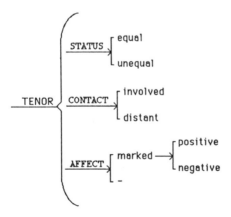

Fig. 7.13. Three dimensions of tenor

The term **prominence** will be used here to refer to the way in which various media construct public figures (mode), **authority** for the ways in which institutions position people through job classification and expertise (field), **control** for the way in which participants direct other participants to do things (genre) and **power** as the overarching term for the way in which ethnicity, gender, generation and class give participants differential access to status, prominence, authority and control. This set of terminology for situating social difference in the model of context being developed here is summarised below:

STATUS	- tenor (social hierarchy)
PROMINENCE	- mode (publicity)
AUTHORITY	- field (expertise & classification)
CONTROL	- genre (manipulation)
POWER	- ideology (access)

As noted by Halliday (1979) (see also Matthiessen 1988a), interpersonal meaning in grammar tends to be realised prosodically, rather than in particulate or culminative fashion. Similarly tenor has a non-discrete realisation in discourse. It is also possible to view interpersonal systems themselves as non-discrete, involving gradient rather than categorical distinctions (see Martin 1992) and in some cases dispersing themselves across systemic environments (e.g. TONE oppositions in relation to MOOD choices — i.e. KEY, TAGGING systems, resources for expressing attitude, Subject ellipsis and so on). In light of this it is more appropriate to consider the tenor systems proposed above in terms of clines and to study the relationships they construct with respect to an ongoing process of textual negotiation. A number of the finer distinctions proposed by Poynton will be reviewed below in order to foreground the systemic gradience at issue here and the question of the prosodic realisation of tenor will be taken up in more detail.

7.2.2.1 *Status*

One of Poynton's most critical contributions to the interpretation of tenor has been to identify the different realisation principles associated with status, contact and affect. For status, the key principle is **reciprocity** of choice (see McIntosh 1963/1966 on pronoun choice in *As You Like It*): equal status among interlocutors is realised by them taking up the same kinds of choices (e.g. *tutoyer*) whereas unequal status is realised by them taking up different ones (e.g. *tu/vous*). The unequal status in text [4:2] for example is signalled in part by the fact that the interviewer asks questions and listens while the interviewer answers questions and talks. This is not to argue that the interviewer is not in control; s/he is, but that is a matter of genre, not tenor — interviewers generally defer to interviewees as part of the social process of manipulating them (as do salespersons opening a sale in service encounters).

In order to explore the realisation of status it is useful to make a further distinction between dominance and deference in the context of unequal status between interlocutors. Not only are choices non-reciprocal in these contexts, but certain kinds of selections are associated with speakers of higher status and other kinds of choices with speakers of lower status — there is in other words a symbolic relationship between position in the social hierarchy and various linguistic systems, especially interpersonal ones. A preliminary attempt to survey some of the more important of these symbolic relationships is outlined by strata in Table 7.10. The realisation of status tends to foreground grammatical options.

As with register systems in general, tenor systems put certain types of meaning at risk and for the most part it is a pattern of interpersonal choices across a text which is meaningful, not the individual choices themselves. Indeed, the notion of reciprocity implies that a number of choices have to be examined from the perspective of different participants for tenor to be realised at all. The system of VOCATION (Poynton 1984) does however provide a number of indexical resources for marking status — once a speaker addresses another as Your Honour for example the dominance/deference dyad has been effectively revealed.

This survey of some of the realisations associated with unequal status, though incomplete, is still too extensive to discuss in detail here, let alone illustrate from a variety of texts. Poynton (1985/9:69-75) reviews the evidence for non-reciprocity in the context of women's speech; and Poynton (1984, 1990a) apply the framework to Australian naming practices. Beyond this the suggestions can be usefully tested against texts such as [6:49] and [6:50] in Chapter 6 above.

7.2.2.2 Contact

Whereas status addresses the concerns of social hierarchy, contact is concerned with the degree of involvement among interlocutors. This is determined by the nature of the fields speaker/listeners are participating in — how much contact they involve, how regularly, whether work or leisure

Table 7.10. Aspects of the realisation of unequal status

Unequal status NON-RECIPROCITY [grammar foregrounded]	dominate	defer
PHONOLOGY	tone certain (1,5) establish rhythm standard accent	tone uncertain (2,4) follow rhythm non-standard accent
GRAMMAR	no ellipsis polarity asserted modalization: high modulation: obligation attitude: manifested comment: presented vocation: familiar person: 1st tagging: inviting; agency: I /Agent	Residue ellipsis polarity matched modalization: low modulation: inclination attitude: concur comment: invited vocation: respectful person: 2nd tagging: checking; agency: I /Medium
LEXIS	explicit bodily functions swearing	euphemise tempered swearing
DISCOURSE SEMANTICS	negotiation: primary knower initiating challenging [not anticipate] turn controlling	primary actor responding tracking [anticipate] turn respecting
	initiate chains	elaborate chains (pronominal)
	initiate strings	elaborate strings (repetition)
interaction patterns	interpersonal congruence	interpersonal metaphor

activities and so on. Poynton's (1985/9:77-78) field oriented contact distinctions have been reworked slightly here; the notion of contact appears to be equivalent to what Hasan (1977:231-2, 1985a/9:57) refers to as social distance, which for her is determined by "the frequency and the range of previous interaction" (1977:231).

Following up the basic opposition between involved and uninvolved contact, involvement can be crossclassified with respect to two dimensions, one oriented to whether the social activity has to do with family, work or recreation and the other with whether the involvement is regular or occasional. This crossclassification is outlined in Table 7.11. Note that regular means different things in different contexts: a regular familial relationship involves daily contact, including weekends, whereas work excludes weekends and regular recreational relationships may be confined to them. As with contextual meaning in general there are no satisfactory labels for most options (for example *colleague*, *associate* and *off-sider* are all too specific for regular work involvement, as is *contact* for occasional work involvement); thus the oppositional meaning of the terms in their systems must be kept in mind.

Table 7.11. Cross-classification of contact by involvement and social activity

	FAMILY	WORK	RECREATION
REGULAR	immediate (father/child)	co-worker (lecturer/tutor)	friend (fixture partners)
OCCASIONAL	relatives (aunt/niece)	contact (writer/editor)	acqaintance (fixture opponents)

Uninvolved contact can be broken down into that involving phatic communion, as with neighbours and shopkeepers, and one-off contact with strangers — conductors, ushers, policemen, direction seekers and the like. Poynton makes the point that interlocutors may be involved with each other along more than one of these dimensions (her multiplex feature); this is a potential source of awkwardness (reviewing a co-worker's book for example). This "recursive" aspect of the system has not been built into Fig. 7.14. In addition Poynton's concern with the extent of the relationship — how much interaction the field involves over what period of time — has been omitted.

Somewhat ironically, the higher the degree of involvement as far as contact is concerned, the more exclusive the semiosis. A conversation between shopkeeper and client is far more predictable and thus easier to overhear than one between close friends on a bus or train. The extreme

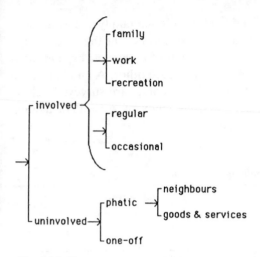

Fig. 7.14. Tenor — CONTACT systems

case of exclusive contact is the anti-language (see Halliday 1978a:164-182 on prison and criminal argot), which functions precisely to create an oppositional identity — a social reality defined in opposition to the reality shared by participants in the mainstream culture. The proliferation of distinctive lexis with a high attitudinal loading is a key feature of systems of this kind. Béal (1987) shows that colloquial spoken French differs from standard written French along similar lines far more dramatically than spoken English does.

The problem with adding too many field distinctions to the contact network has to do with motivating them in terms which have not already been defined for field — so the question of realisation is critical. Poynton's realisation principle for contact needs to be considered from the point of view of both system and process. From the perspective of system, the relevant principle is **proliferation**; the degree of contact determines the predictability of meanings at risk — the less contact the fewer the choices available and conversely, the more contact, the more options available to be taken up. Alongside this is the process oriented principle of **contraction**; less contact means that the realisation of the meanings selected has to be more explicit, whereas more contact means that more can be left unsaid. Contraction is easiest to illustrate from phonology, where various reduction processes may make the casual conversation of intimate friends and family almost unintelligible to outsiders. Proliferation is easier to illustrate at the level of discourse semantics, where choice of subject matter for example expands considerably the better more people get to know each other. A number of the key realisations for involved and uninvolved contact are surveyed below. Poynton (1984, 1990a) involve an extensive study of Australian naming practices in relation to these contact oppositions.

Table 7.12. Tenor — aspects of the realisation of contact

Contact PROLIFERATION/ CONTRACTION [phonology foregrounded]	involved	uninvolved
PHONOLOGY	Pre-tonic delicacy marked tonality marked tonicity varied rhythm fluent reduction processes native accent range of accents acronym	basic tone unmarked tonality unmarked tonicity constant rhythm hesitant full syllables standard accent single accent full form
GRAMMAR	minor clauses Mood ellipsis Mood contraction vocation range of names nick-name	major clauses no ellipsis no contraction no vocation single name full name
LEXIS	specialised technical slang general words	core non-technical standard specific words
DISCOURSE SEMANTICS	dialogue homophoric implicit conjunction	monologue endophoric explicit conjunction
interaction patterns	experiential metaphor	experiential congruence

7.2.2.3 *Affect*

As Poynton (1985/9:78) points out, affect differs from status and contact in that it is not manifested in all texts. It is much more likely to be realised in involved than uninvolved contact situations; and as far as status is concerned, it is more probable with equal than with unequal status — although it can of course be taken up at the discretion of participants in a dominance position. Poynton classifies affect as positive or negative and as permanent or transient. The latter distinction takes into account the fact interlocutors have long-term predispositions as well as more volatile short-term ones. This distinction will be developed here by suggesting that "transient" affect can be interpreted as a surge of "permanent" affect, with a long term low-key prosodic realisation bursting into an explicit and intense behavioural one: dislike erupting into telling someone off, sadness into tears, happiness into laughter and so on. In the grammar of TRANSITIVITY this correlates with the opposition between mental processes of reaction and behavioural processes. Accordingly, Poynton's system will be reworked with the features [surge] and [predisposition] here.

Poynton's (1984:25) network for affect, subclassifies positive and negative features, but the more delicate features are not discussed. Unfortunately at present there do not appear to be any obvious linguistic criteria for classifying types of affection. Feelings about oneself do seem to pair off with attitudes to someone else, and so a [self/other] system will be introduced here (for an alternative classification see Roget). Table 7.13 provides a provisional account of how affections might be classified along three dimensions: surge/predisposition, negative/positive and self/other. In addition the following proportionalities are suggestive:

> positive:negative::
> discord:satisfaction::   ['FEEL']
> insecurity:security::   ['BE']
> frustration:fulfillment   ['DO']

The basic realisation principle associated with affect is **amplification** (see Table 7.14). Like a stereo system, affect is something that can be turned on or off and balanced between speakers (both off, one on, both on) and whose volume can be adjusted to normal listening levels (predisposition) or turned on really loud when the occasion desires (surge). As far as content form is concerned, amplification is achieved largely through iteration — affectual meanings are repeated until the appropriate volume is reached. This interpersonal "taxis" is most striking in nominal groups (cf.

Table 7.13. Tenor — a provisional classification of affect

		SURGE	PREDISPOSITION	
		(behaviour)	(reaction)	
NEGATIVE:				
	DISCORD:			
	SELF	cry	sad	[misery]
	OTHER	tell off	dislike	[antipathy]
	INSECURITY:			
	SELF	loss of nerve	nervous	[disquiet]
	OTHER	terror	fearful	[apprehension]
	FRUSTRATION:			
	SELF	exasperation	tedium	[boredom]
	OTHER	demand	want	[desire]
POSITIVE:				
	SATISFACTION:			
	SELF	laugh	cheerful	[happiness]
	OTHER	embrace	affection	[care]
	SECURITY:			
	SELF	intrepid	confident	[confidence]
	OTHER	entrust	depend	[trust]
	FULFILLMENT:			
	SELF	excitement	interest	[engagement]
	OTHER	homage	respect	[admiration]

you lousy rotten stinking bastard you vs. *my lovely sweet little darling baby puppy dog*), where positive and negative attitude is replayed prosodically across Deictic, Epithet and Thing; but attitudinal interpolation of this kind is pervasive across a range of grammatical structures, irrespective of experiential constituency boundaries (e.g. swearing — **God damn** it I **fucking** *wish that* **shit** *of a un-***bloody***-grateful* **bastard** *would work his* **fucking** *problems out*; or modality — *I'm* **absolutely convinced** *that there* **certainly must** *be a solution* **right** *here,* **mustn't** *there?*). With expression form, parameters of pitch, rate, loudness, vowel length, aspiration and various paralinguistic features are stretched, providing additional resources for amplification; in involved contact situations these parameters may be dramatically reduced for cold clench-teethed realisations of suppressed surges of anger.

Table 7.14. Tenor — aspects of the realisation of affect

Affect [LOUD/SOFT] [lexis foregrounded]	system ITERATION	process AMPLIFICATION
PHONOLOGY		tone width voice quality rate pitch loudness phonaesthesia vowel length consonant aspiration
GRAMMAR	exclamative attitude comment minor expressive intensification repetition prosodic nominal groups diminuitives; mental affection manner degree	
LEXIS	attitudinal taboo swearing	
DISCOURSE SEMANTICS	no negotiation challenging	
INTERACTION PATTERNS	1/2 person modal responsibility	

The system network for affect developed in this section is presented in Fig. 7.15. As with system networks in general, the account is a purely synoptic one, glossing over completely the elaborate interplay that charges relationships between speakers. For this, a dynamic account needs to be constructed, drawing on a long tradition of theory and practice in clinical and social psychology. Regrettably, no attempt has been made to develop an interpersonal dynamics here (this concern will be raised again in 7.3.2.2 below).

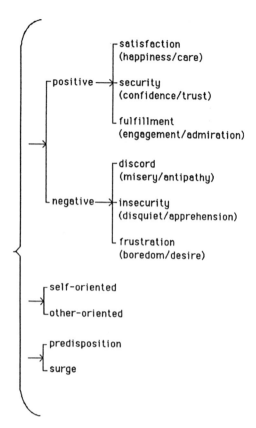

Fig. 7.15. Tenor — affect systems

7.2.3 *Field*

The semiotic system of field was introduced in Chapter 5 by way of contextualising the discussion of IDEATION. Field was introduced there in terms of sets of activity sequences oriented to some global institutional purpose (or more informally, field provides the semiotic interpretation of what counts as an answer to the question //1 *What do you do*// as put to strangers). Field is the contextual projection of experiential meaning and so alongside IDEATION puts at risk the clause rank systems TRANSITIVITY, CIRCUMSTANTIATION and AGENCY, as well as systems generating Numerative, Epithet, Classifier,

Thing and Qualifier in nominal group structure and various other group/ phrase systems, all of which need to be interpreted as embracing lexis as delicate grammar; in addition research into collocation patterns provides an important perspective on field's realisation (see Benson & Greaves 1981, 1992, forthcoming).

Benson & Greaves (forthcoming) for example show that the lexical item *hand* in an introductory bridge manual has left collocates oriented to the organisation of participants in field: *balanced hand*, *weak hand*, *first hand*; to the right however *hand* collocates with lexical items oriented to activity: *Take your tricks from the short **hand first**, Revalue your **hand using** dummy points, with a maximum **hand, opener** knows how high*. This organisation of fields as things and as activities will be briefly reviewed below; for the experiential realisation of field see Chapter 5 above.

7.2.3.1 Activity sequence

The notion of activity sequence has obvious affinities with various concepts developed in artifical intelligence and cognitive psychology (e.g. the frames, scripts, scenarios and schemata reviewed in Brown & Yule 1983:236-270). The most relevant articulation here however is that of Barthes (1966/1977:101-104), of whose earlier work Brown and Yule make no mention. Barthes's notion of sequence was developed in the context of studying the relations between story (alternatively *fabula* or *histoire*) and discourse (alternatively *sjuzhet* or *discours*) in narrative theory (see Toolan 1988:9-11), a context very similar to that in which the field/ genre distinction proposed here evolved in Australian educational linguistics. Barthes's sequence, which is equivalent to the notion of activity sequence used here, is defined as follows (his *nuclei* are roughly equivalent to the clause rank nuclear structures proposed in Chapter 5):

> A sequence is a logical succession of nuclei bound together by a relation of solidarity (in the Hjelmslevian sense of double implication: two terms presuppose one another):[20] the sequence opens when one of its terms has no solidary antecedent and closes when another of its terms has no consequent. To take another deliberately trivial example, the different functions order a drink, obtain it, drink it, pay for it, constitute an obviously closed sequence, it being impossible to put anything before the order or after the payment without moving out of the homogeneous group 'Having a drink' (Barthes 1977:101)

Barthes goes on to point out that sequences involve both expectancy and risk. Recognition of an activity sequence implies an expectation that one of its events will follow another, but the succession is not necessary. It is always possible for expectations to be countered, which creates the context for concessive conjunctive relations. Counterexpectation is a critical feature of narrative genre (and one that does not come naturally to young writers who generally fail to put succession at risk):

> However minimal its importance, a sequence, since it is made up of a small number of nuclei (that is to say, in fact of 'dispatchers'), always involves moments of risk and it is this which justifies analysing it. It might seem futile to constitute into a sequence the logical succession of trifling acts which go to make up the offer of a cigarette (*offering, accepting, smoking, lighting*), but precisely, at every one of these points, an alternative — and hence a freedom of meaning — is possible. ... A sequence is thus, one can say, *a threatened logical unit*, this being its justification *a minimo*. (1977:102)

Barthes continues by pointing out that activity sequences have names, and may be encapsulated by the name to form part of another sequence. This suggests in effect that the notion of constituency can be applied to compositional relations among activity sequences (and Barthes in fact provides an appropriate tree diagram for the first episode of Goldfinger):

> It (a sequence) is also founded *a maximo*: enclosed on its function, subsumed under a name, the sequence itself constitutes a new unit, ready to function as a simple term in another, more extensive sequence. Here, for example, is a micro-sequence: *hand held out, hand shaken, hand released.* This *Greeting* then becomes a simple function: on the one hand, it assumes the role of an indice (flabbiness of Du Pont, Bond's distaste); on the other, it forms globally a term in a larger sequence, with the name *Meeting*, whose other terms (*approach, halt, interpellation, sitting down*) can themselves be micro-sequences. (1977:102-103)

The meeting sequence in other words has as one of its nuclei another sequence — greeting:

> MEETING (greeting):
> approach ˆ halt ˆ interpellation ˆ (hand held out ˆ hand shaken ˆ hand released) ˆ sitting down

Focussing on narrative theory, Barthes does not take the step of theorising paradigmatic relations among activity sequences, for which the notion of field is developed here. A field such as linguistics for example involves a large number of sequences: lecturing, evaluation, supervising, writing, editing, meetings, committees, seminars, conferences, research activities, referee's reports, community work, administration and so on. More than one of these may well succeed another as a series of micro-sequences, but there is more to their interrelationships than this constituency analysis suggests. All are related to participation in the field of linguistics, sharing a large number of taxonomies of both the superordinate and compositional variety. Keeping in mind that the list of activities suggested above for the field of linguistics is not exhaustive and that the network below is a very indelicate one, systemic relations among activity sequences might be conceived for this field as outlined in Fig. 7.16 (there are unfortunately at present no obvious criteria for systemicising activity sequences within a field along these or similar lines):

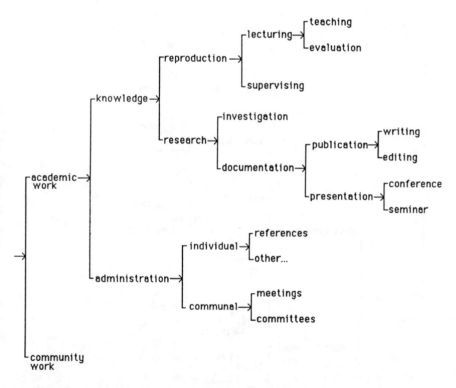

Fig. 7.16. Provisional classification of activity sequences for field of linguistics

7.2.3.2 Taxonomy

As noted in Chapter 5, alongside activity sequences, the participants involved in sequences are organised into taxonomies of two basic kinds: composition and superordination. The compositional taxonomy in Fig. 7.17 for members[21] of an Australian linguistics department for example

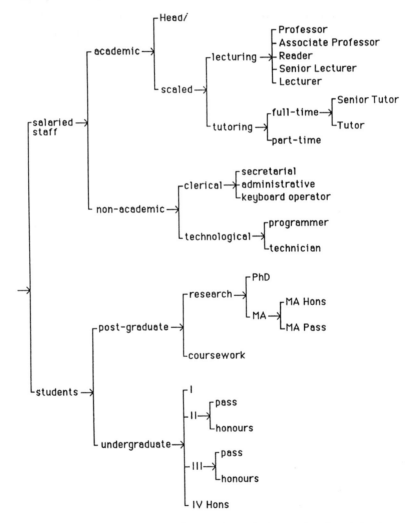

Fig. 7.17. Composition taxonomy for members of an Australian linguistics department

organises participants who play some part in all of the sequences reviewed above.

Similarly, the following superordination taxonomy constructs provisional relationships among the theories which inform teaching, research, community work and so on. The doings of a field cannot be interpreted without some understanding of the organisation of participants, both abstract and concrete, undertaking or undertaken by activities. Note that this taxonomy is uninflected for power, which rests for obvious reasons with theories that naturalise discourses of ethnicity, gender, generation and class by positing an arbitrary relation between form and meaning, thereby

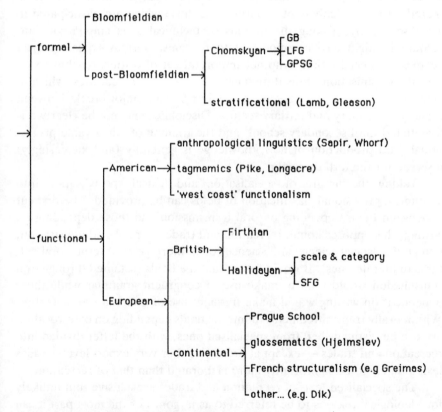

Fig. 7.18. Superordination taxonomy for theories of language

rendering language a transparent conduit through which these discourses are poured. Relationships between theories as far as ideology is concerned (see 7.4.2 below) would be different to those proposed in Fig. 7.18.

The taxonomic organisation and experiential realisation of field has already been considered in detail in Chapter 5 and will not be further reviewed here.

7.2.3.3 *Field agnation*

While criteria for organising activity sequences with respect to each other within a field need to be clarified, there are a number of factors which are suggestive as far as relations among fields are concerned. One of the most important is the distinction between core and non-core vocabulary reviewed in Chapter 5, which would appear to divide fields into those shared by most members of a culture and those which are participated in more selectively. Taking the notions of technical lexis and jargon into account it might also be important to recognise various types, or even degrees of specialisation. Another important set of distinctions has to do with the organisation of institutionalised learning across cultures, which in literate cultures generally begins at age 5 or 6, with major breaks between primary, secondary and tertiary sectors. Disciplines may not be clearly differentiated until secondary school, and the training of employable professionals and production of new knowledge is generally (and increasingly) reserved for the tertiary sector.

Taking the nature of socialisation and lexical specialisation into account, a provisional classification of fields can be provided. The first cut is between fields depending on oral transmission and those depending on writing; this opposes home, recreation and trades to public administration, humanities, social science and science (or in more general terms, oral cultures to literate ones). It would follow that the fields sustained through oral transmission would tend to make use of congruent grammar while those dependent on writing would make frequent use of grammatical metaphor. Within orally transmitted fields, domestic fields depending on core vocabulary can be distinguished from specialised ones, with the latter divided into recreation and trades — except at professional or very expert levels, trades lexis is likely to be significantly more elaborated than that of recreation.

The specialised lexis of recreation and trades is exclusive, but unlikely for ideological reasons to be referred to as jargon. For the most part it can be learned ostensively, as has core vocabulary in domestic fields, by pointing exophorically to something and saying what it is (*This is a ...*). Birders' recreational taxonomies for example differ from ornithologists' scientific ones along these lines — the criteria birders use to classify birds can be clearly perceived through a properly focussed eye and ear (see Wignell et al. 1987/1990).

Fields depending on written transmission require institutionalised learning. Mass education is a product of the needs of 19th century industry and public administration (exchanging goods and services); and the stratified education system in place in western cultures today functions as a response to the demands of 20th century science and technology (exchanging information). Administrative fields are not themselves always taught in secondary school (although commerce and business studies courses are on the increase in the curriculum); however the metaphorical grammar on which they depend is a feature of the science, social science and humanities disciplines that are typically taught. Most of the specialised lexis associated with these literacy dependent fields cannot be ostensively defined. It has to be learned through language, via Token·Value structures defining technical terms; and these definitions are stored in writing (in textbooks). The specialised language of bureacracy, the humanities, social science and science is commonly referred to as jargon — although it is not always clear whether it is technical lexis itself or the highly metaphorical grammar of these disciplines which is being dismissed. Science and social science tend to be more technical than humanities and public administration, although the discourse of the latter disciplines may be extremely abstract (more metaphorical in fact than scientific genres such as the explanation — see Martin 1991b).

The provisional network for field developed here is outlined in Fig. 7.19, graded from top to bottom along a scale of common/uncommon sense. The nature of the socialisation process whereby participants enter the various fields is glossed in parentheses below the features concerned.

This network glosses over the distinction between sequential and taxonomic aspects of field, so it is useful to briefly address these concerns separately here. As far as activity sequences are concerned, the degree of specialisation grades sequences along the following lines. Domestic sequences tend to be implicit — they are not usually written down, or taken notice of in any way by mature speakers, and are learned by doing, under the guidance of caregivers by children. The specialised activities of recrea-

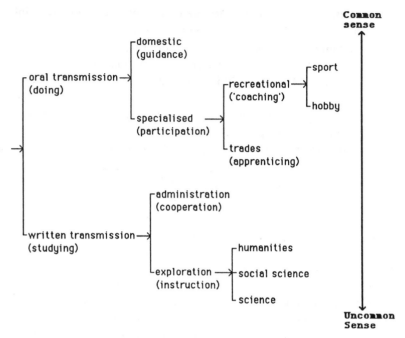

Fig. 7.19. A provisional classification of fields

tion and trades do now tend to be written down as part of the increasing professionalisation of sport (coaching) and trades (attending courses at technical colleges as part of an apprenticeship). While it might be argued that sports and trades can still be successfully transmitted orally, the relentless introduction of new technology in both fields means that some degree of literacy is required for accessing procedures in the latest manuals and brochures. Activity sequences in administration are heavily dependent on literacy since these are carefully documented as written procedures in any large organisation. Following these procedures correctly is essential for things to run efficiently, particularly with appointments and promotions, where conflicting discourses of ethnicity, gender, generation and class regularly produce tensions that have to be systematically negotiated. The activity sequences generated by the discourses of humanities, social science and especially science tend to be logical rather than sequential — *if/then* or *so then* rather than *and then*. It is for this reasons that scientific sequences (e.g. how it rains) are referred to as implication sequences in Wignell et al. (1987/1990), Shea (1988) and Martin (1990b).

As far as taxonomies are concerned, domestic taxonomies deal with the 'natural' order of things — the common sense construction of experience. The distinctive taxonomies of recreation and trades tend to be utilitarian in focus, organising in large part the special equipment and tools required and the Mediums they operate on. The distinctive taxonomies of public administration are also pragmatic, but tend to organise people (or better, subjects) rather than things (e.g. classification of personnel), and writing (e.g. files, legislation, minutes, manuals etc.) rather than experience. The linguistically constructed taxonomies of humanities, social science and science are the ones that are most appropriately referred to as technical since they function as distillations of common sense or less technical experience into uncommon sense classifications of the world. These gradings are summarised in Table 7.15.

Table 7.15. Technicality, activity sequence and taxonomy

	ACTIVITY SEQUENCES	TAXONOMIES
DOMESTIC (guidance)	implicit	"natural"
SPECIALISED (participation)	manuals	utilitarian (tools)
ADMINISTRATION (cooperation)	procedures	pragmatic (subjects)
EXPLORATION (instruction)	implication sequences	technical (things)

Any such scaling of fields with respect to degree of specialisation and technicality, alongside the scaling of oral and written (especially metaphorical) modes this implies, runs the risk of being misinterpreted as valuing different fields in different ways. This kind of ranking should not be read into the networks at the level of field. However it is obvious that fields are valued in different ways and so ranked by all cultures: in Australia, for example, being young, non-anglo, working class or female vastly restricts the meaning potential human cultures otherwise afford. Discourses of generation, gender, ethnicity and class channel subjects in very different ways according to the coding orientations they enjoy. It is the responsibility of the plane of ideology to make the nature of this channeling clear, deconstructing the momentum and inherent contradictions which allow it to evolve.

There is also the danger that the more domestic fields be misinterpreted as natural theories of experience with the more techincal ones treated as semiotic contruals of reality. This is not the case — all fields are semiotically constructed. For an interpretation of language development in the home as sociosemantic socialisation see Halliday (1975), Painter (1984).

7.3 Genre

The general issue of distinguishing register and genre as semiotic planes was introduced in 7.1.2 above. Hasan's association of obligatory elements of text structure with field makes it critical to consider the relationship between activity sequence (field) and schematic structure (genre) here. In this connection it is useful to compare three of Barthes's examples of sequences with three of Hasan's examples of text structure (only her obligatory elements will be considered here):

SEQUENCES (Barthes 1966/1977):
'telephone call':
telephone ringing ˄ picking up the receiver ˄ speaking ˄ putting down the receiver (1966/1977:101)

"having a drink":
order a drink ˄ obtain it ˄ drink it ˄ pay for it (1966/1977:101)

"offering a cigarette":
offering ˄ accepting ˄ smoking ˄ lighting (1966/1977:102)

TEXT STRUCTURES (Hasan 1977, 1984b, 1985a/9):
"medical appointment making":
Identification ˄ Application ˄ Offer ˄ Confirmation (1977:233)

"service encounter":
Sale request ˄ Sale compliance ˄ Sale ˄ Purchase ˄ Purchase closure (1985a/ 1989:60)

"nursery tale":
Initiating event ˆ Sequent Event^n ˆ Final Event^n (1984b:80)

At a glance it might appear that Barthes is analysing action whereas Hasan is analysing text (cf. Barthes's telephone call and Hasan's appointment making). But the opposition is by no means as simple as this. Most of Barthes's nuclei involve interlocutors speaking, and those which do not are easy to render linguistically in narration (as they have been in Barthes's own account). So a simple opposition between verbal and non-verbal action will not do.

More to the point is the fact that Hasan's elements of structure at times collapse several nuclei in Barthes's sequence: Identification for example in Hasan's appointment making covers Barthes's telephone ringing, picking up the receiver and speaking. At the same time, Hasan's elements may expand one of Barthes's nuclei, as Identification ˆ Application ˆ Offer ˆ Confirmation do for Barthes's speaking in potentially the same genre (although Barthes could of course have recognised a micro-sequence here). The point of these differences is that Hasan is placing boundaries at just those points where they are linguistically manifested, implying that the same sequences might be involved in very different genres (cf. Barthes's opposition of *histoire* and *discours*). A telephone call in a modern nursery tale for example might just be one of a number of acts comprising the Initiating Event (which for Hasan continues until the expectation set up by its main act is frustrated); in appointment making on the other hand the call itself needs to be broken down into the genre's structural formula.

This suggests that where language is constitutive of what is going on (mode) the relationship between activity sequence (field) and text structure may be quite divergent (genre); where language is ancillary on the other hand, there may be little difference between the two. The way in which the same activity sequence can be manipulated linguistically for different generic purposes will be illustrated in Section 7.3.2 below. The reason for separating field and genre as far as obligatory elements of text structure are concerned is to maintain inter-relationships among activity sequences and inter-relationships among text structures as distinct patterns of agnation regardless of mode (for further discussion of the notion of activity sequence in relation to genre see Lemke 1988b).

7.3.1 *Particle, wave and field*

Halliday (1978a, 1979) (see also Matthiessen 1988a, Matthiessen and Halliday in press) associates different types of structural realization with different metafunctions. These correlations are outlined in the Table 7.16.

In addition Halliday points out the correlation between these different metafunctional perspectives on realisation and Pike's work on particle, wave and field.[22] Pike (1982:12) represents the complementarity of these perspectives graphically as follows.

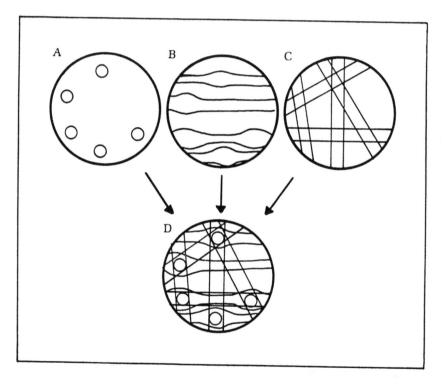

Fig. 7.20. Complementary of particle, wave and field (Pike 1982:12)

Table 7.16. Metafunction and types of structural realisation

METAFUNCTION	TYPE OF STRUCTURE Halliday (1978a:188)	Matthiessen (1988a); Matthiessen & Halliday (in press)
1 ideational		
(a) experiential	constituent [segmental]	constituency
(b) logical	recursive	interdependency [chain]
2 interpersonal	prosodic	prosody
3 textual	culminative	prominence [pulse]

Halliday correlates constituency realisation with the particulate perspective, culminative realisation with wave theory and prosodic realisation with field. The last of these correlations seems to be stretching a point since for Pike field theory is not so much concerned with non-discrete realisations as with "intersecting properties of experience" that "cluster into bundles of simultaneous characteristics which together make up the patterns" of experience (1982:13); Pike sums up his perspectives when introducing field as follows:

> We have discussed the way in which elements can be viewed by themselves as particles, or as waves smearing into some kind of continuum whose prominent parts make up nuclei. Now we turn to sets of relationships which occur when units are linked to one another by their presence in some larger system. A total set of relationships and of units in these relationships we call a field. (1982:30)

The component of systemic theory which would appear to correspond most closely to this articulation of field is system, not prosody. For this reason the discussion will be pursued here at the level of genre under the headings of particle, prosody and wave. The notion of text as an interdependency structure has already been explored when comparing *English Text*'s approach to conjunctive relations with that of Rhetorical Structure Theory (Chapter 4, section 8) and will not be further developed here.

7.3.1.1 *Particle*

Genre theory has tended to inherit from grammarians an experiential bias towards constituency representation, with teleologically driven stages working their way towards a goal (see Thibault 1989 for an extended critique). Mitchell's stages, Hasan's elements of text structure and Martin's schematic structures all share this orientation, which was however been qualified in various ways in their research. These synoptic perspectives on staging will be reviewed first, before turning to the dynamics of genre below.

7.3.1.1.1 *Synoptic perspectives*

While adopting a particulate perspective, genre theory from Mitchell onwards has recognised the need to distinguish sequence from order (see Firth 1957b/1968:186, Halliday 1961:250-251, 1976b:56-57, Palmer 1964), since the same functional relationship (order) may be realised in different sequences (or non-sequentially) and not all sequences are functional (i.e. realising order). Mitchell for example qualified his numbering of stages as follows:

> *Stage* is an abstract category and the numbering of stages does not necessarily imply sequence in time. Thus the auctioneer's [...] 'What am I bid?', may, in the instance, be uttered in the same breath as the opening [...]; nevertheless it is considered here as marking the opening of Stage 3, and has the effect of eliciting an opening bid. (1957:43)

Similarly Hasan (1977:239) points out that her Application element of structure may be surrounded by an Identification (I $^\#$ A $^\#$):

Identification	Dr Scott's clinic.
Application	— I wonder if I woud see Dr Scott today
Identification	the name is Mary Lee.

Hasan tackled this problem by formulating generic structure potentials, developing in a number of ways the kind of structural formula used in prosodic phonology (see also Halliday 1961:257-258 for examples of grammatical formulas). Waterson (1956/1970:175) for example expresses the basic structure of the Turkish monosyllabic word as follows: $^{y/w}$ (C) V C (C). The $^{y/w}$ superscript represents the relevant prosodies and parentheses indicate optional consonant margins. Hasan's more elaborated formulas for the service encounter and the nursery tale are presented below, along with a key to their interpretation.[23]

[(Greeting) (Sale Initiation) ˆ] [(Sale Enquiry^n) {Sale Request ˆ Sale Compliance}^{n} ˆ Sale ˆ] Purchase ˆ Purchase Closure (ˆFinis)

[($^\#$Placement$^\#$ ˆ) Initiating Event^n ˆ] Sequent Event^n ˆ Final Event [ˆ (Finale) (Moral)]

Key:
(X)	optionality
X ˆ Y	sequence
X Y	order
[X Y]	domain of order
X^n	iteration
{X ˆ Y}^{n}	enclosed elements proportionately iterative
$^\#$X$^\#$ Y	enclosed element interspersed/included in Y

For Hasan,[24] text structures are derived from generic structure potentials conditioned by choices in field, tenor and mode — with most of the optionality apparently determined by tenor and mode. This suggests that systemic relationships among different text structures are equivalent to relationships among field, mode and tenor options; and the question of systemic relationships among generic structure potentials does not arise. Challenging the first of these suggestions, and redressing the second, Martin (1985a) suggests reformulating generic structure potentials as system networks and realisation rules as with Ventola's (1987:15) reformulation of Mitchell above, proposing a speculative network and realisation rules for service encounters by way of illustrating how this might be done (Martin 1985a:253-254; Fig. 7.21 below).

To date, no empirical work has been done developing genre networks along these lines, and so the question of whether systemicising generic structure potentials leads directly to the two plane model of register and genre being developed here or not has not been fully resolved. The question of genre agnation will be taken up in 7.3.2 below.

7.3.1.1.2 *Dynamic perspectives*
In the same paper, Martin (1985a) cautions against another bias inherited by genre theory from grammarians — namely that towards a synoptic as opposed to a dynamic form of representation and interpretation. The basic problem here is that in order to attain generality, grammarians have tended in various ways to abstract away from linear progression (to divorce in other words functional order from sequence). Structure potentials such as those used by Hasan, and to an even greater extent the system/structure realisation cycle suggested by Martin, separate order and sequence in such

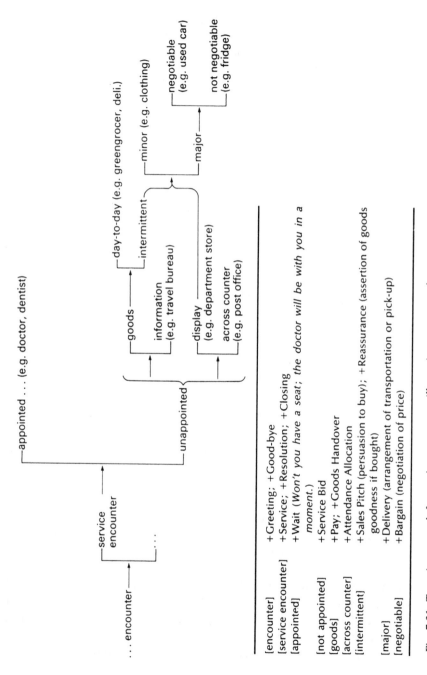

Fig. 7.21. Tentative network for service encounters, illustrating genre agnation

a way that choices leading to a particular text structure bear no direct temporal relation to the unfolding of that text in real time. To the extent that aspects of the unfolding of a text **are** conditioned by linear progression, this perspective breaks down. Martin suggests that generic structures display a number of features of this kind: variable sequential realisation of elements, iteration, systematic suspension and so on.

Ventola (1984, 1987, 1989) has followed up these problems in detail for service encounter genres and developed a flowchart notation for expressing genre as a dynamic potential from which schematic structures can be derived (see also Mak 1984 for an adaptation of Ventola's work in the context of the market places of Hong Kong). The advantage of the dynamic perspective is that choices can be conditioned by the point reached in a text's development. Keeping in mind Firth's comment that "The moment a conversation is started, whatever is said is a determining condition for what, in any reasonable expectation, may follow" (1935/1957a:31-32), this is an important perspective to keep in mind. The first two pages of Ventola's (1987:70-76) flowchart for the service encounters she examined is re-produced as Fig. 7.22 below; not only is this work the most detailed study of generic structure within a systemic functional framework but it complements in critical ways the synoptic orientation of work inspired by Hasan and Martin.

For alternative formulations of dynamic potentials, see Fawcett et al. (1988) who build temporal progression into their exchange network, in a sense re-fusing sequence and order (reviewed in Chapter 2, Section 5 above) and O'Donnell (n.d.) who presents a stratified account in which discourse choices modify context as part of an ongoing process of contextual realisation. For further discussion of synoptic and dynamic perspectives on text structure see Lemke (1988b).

7.3.1.2 *Prosody*

Beyond the problems of sequence and order reviewed above, the problem of non-discrete realisations which smear across rather than mapping onto elements of schematic structure needs attention. These have been as much ignored in grammar as in genre (see however Poynton 1990b), and so once again it is linguists' reliance on old tools for mapping new territory that stands in the way of progress (for a review of progress as far as prosodic realisation in grammar is concerned see Matthiessen 1988a). Linguists' uncertainty in this area is easiest to illustrate with respect to the work on narrative by Labov (Labov and Waletzky 1967, Labov 1972b, 1982).

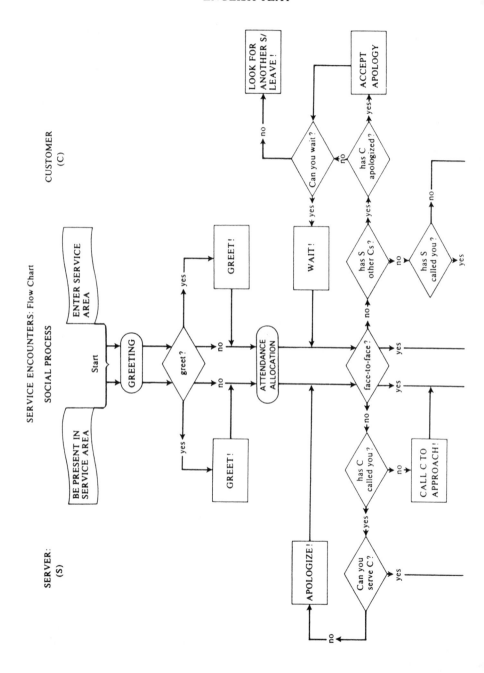

SERVICE ENCOUNTERS: Flow Chart

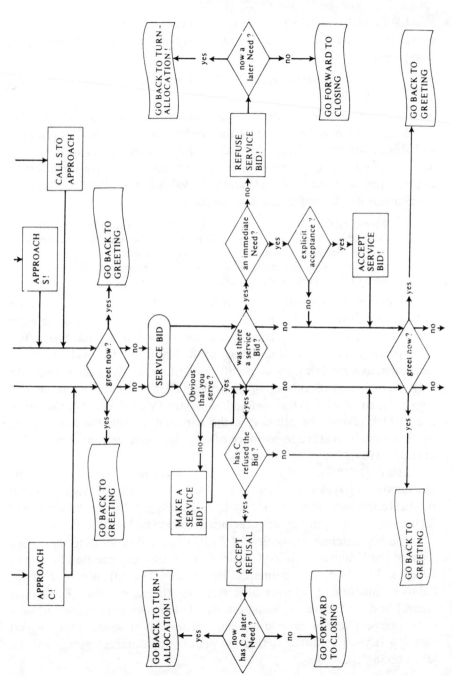

Fig. 7.22. Service encounters flowchart from Ventola 1987:70-71

Labov and Waletzky propose the following structure potential for narrative of personal experience (re-expressed here using Hasan's notational conventions):

(Abstract) ˆ [(#Orientation#) ˆ Complication] ˆ [#Evaluation# ˆ Resolution] ˆ (Coda)

Abstract, Orientation and Coda stages are optional; and both Orientation and Evaluation may be realised either before or as part of Complication and Resolution respectively. For Labov and Waletzky a narrative lacking an Evaluation is not a complete narrative ("Such a narrative lacks significance; it has no point." 1967:33) and the Evaluation is critical furthermore in distinguishing Complication from Resolution:

> We can establish the break between the complicating and resolving action by locating the placement of the evaluation. Thus the **resolution** of the narrative is that portion of the narrative sequence which follows the evaluation. If the evaluation is the last element, then the resolution section coincides with the evaluation. (1967:39)

Rather problematically for this definition of Resolution, the realisation of Evaluation turns out to be potentially non-discrete. There may be more than one Evaluation in a narrative, and not all Evaluations have the effect of suspending the temporal unfolding of the action — "the evaluation may be present as lexical or phrasal modification of a narrative clause, or it may itself be a narrative clause, or coincide with the last narrative clause" (1967:37). Evaluation is thus defined 'semantically' as the part of the narrative "which reveals the attitude of the narrator towards the narrative by emphasizing the relative importance of some narrative units as compared to others." (1967:37)

Labov (1972b) develops the prosodic realisation of Evaluation, treating the Labov and Waletzky stage as the "focus of waves of evaluation that penetrate the narrative". Labov and Waletzky's graphic representation of their narrative structure potential is thus amended by Labov as in Fig. 7.23.

The non-discrete realisation of Evaluation makes locating the major focus of the Evaluation difficult, which in turn calls into question the use of a localised Evaluation to define the Resolution. The difficulty here lies in Labov's equation of interpersonal meaning (language) with Evaluation (genre) and his failure to distinguish clearly between particulate and prosodic perspectives on generic structure. The way in which interpersonal meaning is used to inflect activity sequences for different genres will be taken up in 7.3.2 below.

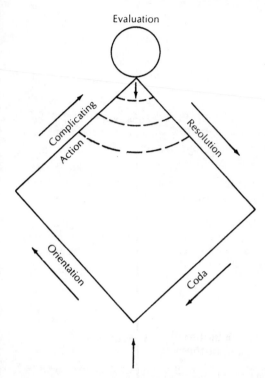

Fig. 7.23. Waves of Evaluation in narrative (Labov 1972b: 369)

Martin (1992) treats one aspect of interpersonal meaning at the level of genre as a kind of generic prosody (with high, median and low values) mapped onto a particulate structure of the kind reviewed in 7.3.1.1 above (see also Martin 1986a:247 on an attitudinal crescendo in hortatory exposition). Similarly Cranny-Francis and Martin (1991) treat the chorus of Bruce Springsteen's hit single 'Born in the USA' as an interpersonal prosody (see Fig. 7.24), whose meaning is recontextualised throughout the song to the point where it is amplified as a scream of anguish which provides the climax to the song's wording.[25] The interaction of the song's particulate and prosodic structure is critical. From a particulate perspective, the song is an Exemplum (see 7.3.2.2 below), telling the story of a young

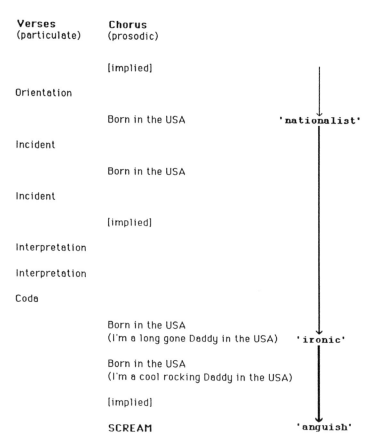

Fig. 7.24. Prosodic realisation of interpersonal meaning in Bruce Springsteen's 'Born in the USA'

working class American (Orientation), who is sent to Vietnam and returns home expecting a job and a hero's welcome but receives neither (Incident), who reflects on the futility of the war and the loss of a friend/brother (Interpretation), and who ends up in the hopeless subjectivity into which he was born (Coda). The first two times the chorus is sung (after the Orientation and first verse of the Incident), it can be read as nationalistic; and readers who cannot hear the following verses take this as the meaning of the song. But the next two times the chorus is sung it has been recontextualised by the Exemplum's Interpretation and Coda as deeply ironic — a deconstruction of the brutality of American class discourse. Finally words fail, and the prosody climaxes with a 'proto-linguistic' scream.

Given the subversion of Labov and Waletzky's Complication/Resolution distinction by the non-discrete realisation of Evaluation, recognising simultaneous dimensions of experiential and interpersonally oriented structure at the level of genre (as with Halliday's 1985a analysis of the English clause) seems a more promising approach than the unidimensional modelling undertaken by Labov.

7.3.1.3 *Wave (periodicity)*

The final pattern of realisation to be considered here is the culminative one, which in the grammar derives from the textual metafunction. As developed in Chapter 6, Sections 3.2-3, culminative patterns structure discourse at several levels beyond the clause. As Halliday puts this in Thibault (1987:612):

> Textual meanings typically give you the periodic movement which is so characteristic of discourse at all levels; everything from the smallest waves to the very large ones. In other words, there is a hierarchy of periodicity, and that comes from the textual metafunction.

The question of the hierarchy of periodicity is taken up in detail in Martin (in press a, b) (see also Martin & Peters 1985:85 on waves of abstraction in exposition and Martin 1986b:39 on Macro- and hyper-Theme) and will not be pursued here. Note in passing that wave patterns are very commonly reflected in the labelling given to beginning and end stages across genres, reflecting the peaks and troughs of prominence that open and close a text; a number of these are reviewed in Table 7.17.

Table 7.17. Culminative prominence and generic structure

	BEGINNING (initial prominence)	END (final prominence)
Mitchell (1957)	Auctioneer's Opening	Conclusion
Hasan (1977)	Greeting	Summary ^ Finis
(1985a)	Sale Initiation	Purchase Closure
(1984b)	Initiating Event	Finale
Ventola (1979)	Greeting	Leave-taking ^ Goodbye

Once posited as potentially divergent patterns of realisation, particulate, prosodic and periodic aspects of generic structure are not difficult to find. More problematic is the question of how to model and integrate them once observed. In particular this raises questions about the role played by genre in mapping field, tenor and mode choices onto each other in ways which capture teleological aspects of generic structure. Current formulations of genre as system do not resolve these issues, but are nevertheless pursued below.

7.3.2 Genre agnation

Linguists' concern with constituency at the level of genre has meant that questions of field, in Pike's sense of the term, have not been actively pursued. Hasan's notion of generic stucture potential does generalise across a range of text structures, determining their generic identity:

> The property of structure is what allows us to distinguish between complete and incomplete texts on the one hand, and between different generic forms on the other. With some oversimplification, the assumptions here can be stated as follows: associated with each genre of text — i.e. type of discourse — is a generalized structural formula, which permits an array of actual structures. Each complete text must be a realization of a structure from such an array. The generic membership of the text is determined by reference to the structural formula to which the actual structure can be shown to belong. (Hasan 1977:229)

But Hasan has not attempted to develop these structure potentials in the direction of system/structure theory; and as noted above, the question of systemic relations **among** structure potentials does not really arise.

Systemic relations of this kind have however been studied by tagmemicists, with Longacre's work probably the best known. Longacre (1976:202) uses the dimensions of +/− prescription and +/− chronological framework to crossclassify narrative, drama, procedural, expository and hortatory text types, subdividing [+chronological framework/−prescription] into monologic (narrative) and dialogic modes (drama). The resulting paradigm is reproduced in Table 7.18 (Longacre 1983:4 further develops this system, basically by adding a +/− projection system having to do with whether or not the text has to do with "a situation or action which is contemplated, enjoined, or anticipated but not realized"):

Table 7.18. Longacre's (1976) cross-classification of genres

	– prescription	+ prescription
+ chronological framework	NARRATIVE DRAMA	PROCEDURAL
– chronological framework	EXPOSITORY	HORTATORY

Working along lines of realisation suggested by Bakhtin in section 1 above, Longacre appeals to clusters of linguistic features to motivate his classification. Narrative for example is opposed to exposition as follows (1976:202):

NARRATIVE
1. 1/3 person pronouns
2. Agent/Experiencer as subject
3. Past tense/historical present
4. Head-tail & tail-head linkage

EXPOSITION
1. 3 person pronouns
2. Equative & descriptive clauses
3. Various tenses
4. By sentence topic & parallelism

Longacre does not appeal criterially to staging to motivate his system; but there is certainly no reason in principle why evidence from text structure could not be brought to bear on systemic relations across genres.

It is important to compare Longacre's features with those used by Hasan when classifying text structures with respect to contextual configurations. Two examples of Hasan's feature specifications for contextual configurations are reproduced below:

APPOINTMENT MAKING (Hasan 1977:231)
Field professional consultation: medical; application for appointment
Tenor client: patient-applicant, agent for consultant: receptionist; maximum social distance...
Mode aural channel; -visual contact: telephone conversation; spoken medium

SERVICE ENCOUNTER (Hasan 1985/1989:59)
Field economic transaction: purchase of retail goods: perishable food
Tenor Agents of transaction: hierarchic: customer superordinate and vendor subordinate; social distance: near maximum...
Mode Language role: ancillary; channel: phonic; medium: spoken with visual contact

Longacre's chronological dimension can be related to Hasan's field features, his prescription to her tenor and his dialogue/monologue opposition to her mode. In effect Longacre has selected features from different aspects of Hasan's contextual construct (i.e. field, mode and tenor variables) and integrated them into a single matrix in order to classify genres. This matrix is systemicised in Fig. 7.25, and could obviously be extended in delicacy and elaborated in various ways by drawing on additional register oppositions:

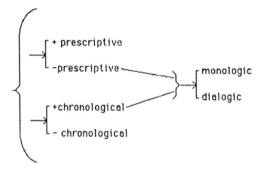

Fig. 7.25. Systemic formulation of Longacre's paradigm

English Text's suggestion is that in pursuing work of this kind, a very different system of valeur will be established than that developed when looking at field, mode or tenor variables alone (even though very similar oppositions might be used on the levels of register and genre). The reason for this is that no culture combines field, mode and tenor variables freely — all are selective. Thus the system of social processes constituting a culture at the level of genre will always differ from the systems of field, mode and tenor options it makes available in one or another contexts of situation.

7.3.2.1 *Factual genres*
Martin 1985b/1989, working along lines similar to Longacre's, developed a preliminary classification of "factual" genres drawing on field and mode. The basic field opposition was between texts which were focussing on activity sequences (e.g. narratives, recipes, manuals) and texts which were not (e.g. descriptions, expositions); the basic mode opposition was between texts which generalised across experience and those which referred to a specific manifestion of a culture. Generalised texts were further divided

into those which function to document information and those which explain. For examples of Description, Recount, Report, Procedure and Exposition genre see Martin (1985a/1989:3-16);[26] for examples of Explanation see Shea (1988), Martin (1989, 1990b, 1991b). In later work Martin and Rothery divided explaining texts into those which considered more than one point of view, Discussions and Explorations, and those which presented only one position, Exposition and Explanation. This genre matrix is outlined in Table 7.19.

Table 7.19. Cross-classification of factual genres

	-generalised	generalised: document	explain: resolve	debate
− activity structured	DESCRIPTION	REPORT	EXPOSITION	DISCUSSION
+ activity structured	RECOUNT	PROCEDURE	EXPLANATION	EXPLORATION

Martin (1985b/1989) and Martin & Peters (1985) further divided expository writing into analytical and hortatory varieties, depending on whether the text outlined an argument (macro-proposition) or tried to persuade listener/readers to undertake a particular course of action (macro-modulated proposition), a distinction related to Longacre's +/− prescriptive opposition. The inter-relationships proposed for these factual genres are formulated systemically in Fig. 7.26 (for further delicacy see Peters 1985). Significantly, the network is comprised of ideational, interpersonal and textual features and thus cuts across register variables to bring out the oppositions between the genres:

IDEATIONAL VARIABLES	+/− activity structure, document/explain
INTERPERSONAL VARIABLES	resolve/debate, analytical/hortatory
TEXTUAL VARIABLES	+/− generalised

7.3.2.2 *Narrative genres*

Certainly the best studied set of texts as far as genre theory is concerned is that generally referred to as narrative (see Toolan 1988 for a comprehensive review of this research). Most of the work however has focussed on deconstructing narrative structure rather than typological considerations. The problems faced by Labov and Waltezky with respect to the prosodic realisation of Evaluation, recursive Complication Resolution structures, conflated elements (e.g. Evaluation/Resolution) and optional staging have proved troublesome, not to mention the question of the longer literary artifacts (short story and novel) that have received so much theoretical attention. Recently Plum (1988), working in cojunction with Joan Rothery (1990), a specialist in children's narrative, has produced groundbreaking work on oral narrative which will be briefly reviewed here.

Plum's basic strategy is to break down Labov's narrative of personal experience into four related narrative genres: recount, anecdote, exemplum and narrative;[27] the distinction between recount and narrative is taken from Martin and Rothery's research into children's narrative (for a review of the genres established in their research see Martin 1984c). These "stories" are alike in that they are built up around a set of narrative clauses (an activity sequence in terms of the field theory developed here); in addition they share basic structural elements at their beginning and ends — for example Abstract, Orientation and Coda (Plum in fact makes some finer distinctions here). Where the stories differ is with respect to their "mid-

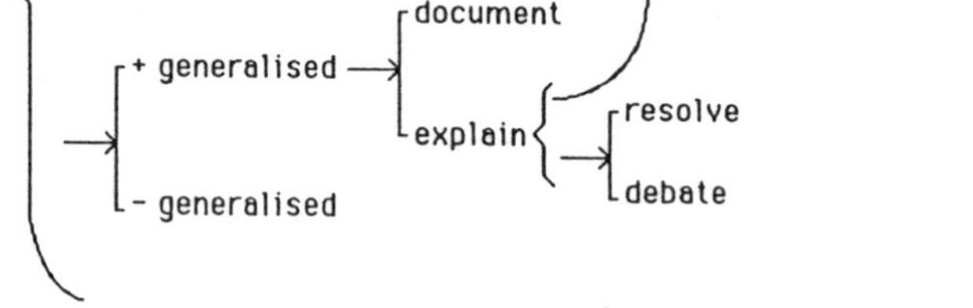

Fig. 7.26. Systemic formulation of agnation for factual genres

dles"; Plum's (1988:225) distinctive staging for the middle sections of each genre is reproduced below:

RECOUNT	Record		
ANECDOTE	Crisis	Reaction	
EXEMPLUM	Incident	Interpretation	
NARRATIVE	Complication	Evaluation	Resolution

For Plum, as in Martin and Rothery's work, the recount is a relatively iconic rendering of an activity sequence (the Record stage); Plum extends this by pointing out that for mature speakers, in the spoken mode, the recount will tend to be prosodically evaluated — to make it worth telling — although this "evaluation" does not constitute a distinct stage. Recounts differ from the other story genres in that nothing goes significantly wrong (anything that does go wrong is treated as unremarkable); in anecdotes, exemplums and narratives on the other hand the experiential focus is on something remarkably out of the ordinary. Expectancies about how an activity sequence will unfold are countered, with ensuing events departing from the norm in some significant way.

Anecdotes, exemplums and narratives then differentiate themselves according to the way in which this counterexpectancy is interpersonally rendered. With anacdotes, the Crisis stage is simply reacted to — with a surge of affect (discord, insecurity, frustration, satisfaction, security or fulfillment as in 7.2.2.3 above); with exemplums, the Incident makes a point — the story functions as a macro-modulation on how the world should/ shouldn't be; with narrative the Complication creates a problem which suspends action to allow time for Evaluation and then has to be overcome (the Resolution). Plum puts these distinctions as follows:

> While both narrative and anecdote are focussed on a crisis, narrative alone creates a balanced movement of rising tension, sustained suspense and falling tension, i.e. the classic generic structure of Complication, Evaluation, and Resolution. An anecdote, on the other hand, creates a Crisis but does not resolve it explicitly — in the well-told anecdote, the resolution is a cathartic outburst of laughter, a shocked (but audible!) silence, a gasp, etc. The narrator's explicit, and linguistically realised Reaction emphasises the critical nature of the events told in the Crisis, often by reiteration. And the exemplum downgrades the tellable events to a mere Incident whose only function is to serve as the raw material for the making of a point that lies totally outside the text. This it does via an Interpretation of the Incident. (1988:225)

Texts 7.1-4 have been constructed below to illustrate these genres as interpersonal manipulations of the same activity sequence (while attested examples of each genre are not difficult to find, and exemplums and anecdotes in particular abound in casual conversation, collecting a full paradigm based on the same activity sequence is a much more problematic task).

[7:1] RECOUNT

Orientation
Just another one of those days. The neighbours a couple of houses down had a party last night; they came and warned us and it wasn't too bad really. Woke Jane up a couple of times.

Record
Anyhow we got up the next day and packed up the car to take Jane back but when we opened the gate there was a car blocking half of our driveway - not surprising given the sound of things the night before. What a bugger. I checked with the neighbours but they didn't know whose car it was so I phoned the cops. When they came they said they couldn't do anything except give it a ticket. Completely useless. In any case we managed to fill in between the road and curb with rubble and just sneaked the car through - bit of a pain, but no too bad. Finally we got Jane back to her mother's and came home to do some work.

Reorientation
Bloody car is still there too.

[7.2] ANECDOTE

Abstract
I had an embarrassing moment this morning.

Orientation
The neighbours a couple of houses down had a party last night; they came and warned us and it wasn't too bad really. Woke Jane up a couple of times.

Crisis
Then this morning there was a car parked across our driveway. I figured it must have been someone from the party and so went down to knock on their door. I knocked and knocked but no-one came. I figured they were hung-over and sleeping in so I kept on banging really loudly — door, window, everthing within reach. Finally this guy crawls out of bed and opens the window. I explained the problem but it turned out it wasn't his party. The house was divided into flats and it was the people out the back.

Reaction
He wasn't too pleased, especially after having been kept up half the night by his neighbours!

Coda
I still don't know whose car it is.

[7:3] EXEMPLUM

Abstract
I had a crazy experience this morning.

Orientation
The neighbours two houses down had a party last night; they came and warned us and it wasn't too bad really. Woke Jane up a couple of times.

Incident
Then this morning there was a car parked across our driveway. I figured it must have been someone from the party and went down to knock on their door; but it wasn't anyone they knew. I tried a few other houses and then phoned the cops, thinking they'd come by and tow it away. Anyhow, they came quickly enough but when they got there they said all they could so was give it a ticket; they couldn't tow it away because it wasn't in a tow-away zone.

Interpretation
That seemed just crazy to me; I mean someone can park in your driveway and block your car in for days and there's nothing you can do about it. You just have to wait until they come back and drive away. If you open their car to move it you're breaking in! Crazy.

Coda
Bloody car is still there too.

[7:4] NARRATIVE

Abstract
We had a bit of a struggle getting Jane back this morning.

Orientation
The neighbours two houses down had a party last night; they came and warned us and it wasn't too bad really.

Complication
Then this morning there was a car parked across our driveway. I figured it must have been someone from the party and went down to knock on their door; but it wasn't anyone they knew. Then I tried the cops, who came quickly enough but when they got there they said all they could do was give him a ticket; they wouldn't tow him away and couldn't legally break into his car to move it — and neither apparently could I.

Evaluation
I thought "Bugger. This is ridiculous." Our car could be parked in here for bloody days waiting for the guy to come back for it.

Resolution

Anyhow, then we got the idea of going down the sidewalk a little and driving over the curb. The plumber had been doing some work so we collected bricks and pipes and filled in between the road and the curb and then we got some planks from out back to put over the top. I drove out a carefully as I could - there was just room to sneak past. And we managed to get over the curb without damaging the car or getting a flat tire on the rubble we'd put.

Coda

All we needed with all the work we have to do.

The ways in which interpersonal meaning inflects activity sequences to construct these four story genres is summarised in Table 7.20. As noted above, anecdotes, exemplums and narratives are built up around unusual sequences while recounts construct business as usual. Anecdotes take something unexpected and react to it in various ways, thereby highlighting lexicogrammatical resources for expressing affect. Exemplums are a kind of protest genre, dealing in objections to the moral order; they thus foreground modulations of obligation and negative affect. In narrative, unusuality frustrates the inclinations of key protagonists, who then struggle to turn adversity into a happier and restored equilibrium; narratives thus foreground modulations of inclination and transformations of negative to positive affect.

Table 7.20. Interpersonal meaning across story genres

	INTERPERSONAL: MODALIZATION	MODULATION	ATTITUDE
RECOUNT	usuality		prosodic affect
ANECDOTE	unusuality;		varied affect
EXEMPLUM	unusuality;	obligation	negative affect
NARRATIVE	unusuality;	inclination	negative to positive affect

Obviously much more work on these and related story genres is required before a workable approximation to their generic inter-relationships can be constructed. Three provisional systems are presented in Fig. 7.27 by way of encouraging this articulation. The first opposition distinguishes recount genres, which deal unproblematically with activity

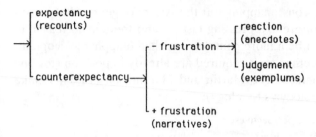

Fig. 7.27. Provisional classification of story genres

sequences, from other story genres which depend on counterexpectancy. Then narratives, which make use of counterexpectancy to frustrate the inclinations of key protagonists are separated from exemplums and anecdotes where what goes wrong is not 'predicted' in this way. The third systems opposes anecdotes, which focus on reaction, to exemplums, which deal in judgements.

There are many avenues available for extending a network of this kind. Recounts for example can be subclassified with respect to the time scale involved (my day, last week-end, it's been quite a month, annual reports, biographies, history etc.). Cross-classifying +/− frustration with reaction/judgements makes room for fables (+frustration/+judgement), parables and other moral tales. Anecdotes need to be related to jokes, and possibly comedy of various kinds. And narrative, needless to say, has to be indefinitely extended if it is to do justice to the centuries of composing and research that has elaborated such a significant portion of our culture. Of this work, *English Text* has offered the barest glimpse.

7.3.2.3 *Genre as system*
To this point *Engish Text* has glanced at only three of the lines of agnation which might be followed up: service encounter, factual and story genres. Another obvious candidate for attention is the set of macro-proposals: procedures (manuals, instructions, recipes etc.; e.g. text [4:2]), advertisements (e.g. text [4:200]), appeals (e.g. the ZPG text in Martin 1992) and so on, which might be divided into consumer benefactive (procedures) and composer benefactive (advertisments and appeals) sets. But this is just one line of inquiry; and there are many more.

For ideological reasons, mapping out the system of genres that constitutes our context of culture is a pressing task — and there is no reason in
principle to expect it to be a more complex one than mapping lexicogrammar. Most of the theoretical tools required are already in position (for one
further important dimension see Martin and Matthiessen (1991), Lemke
(forthcoming a) on typology vs topology):

> synoptic/dynamic perspectives
> system/process
> realisation: manifesting/construing/reconstruing/symbolising
> covariate/univariate/multivariate
> particle/wave/prosody
> rank/strata/plane
> metafunction
> delicacy
> etc.

Probably the main theoretical weakness as far as modelling is concerned
lies in interpreting both system and process as what might metaphorically
be referred to as "negotiation". This stems in part from a fundamental
weakness in the dynamic modelling of the exchange; but it projects from
there onto difficulties in dealing with tenor (the ways in which interlocutors
treat in status, contact, affect), with genre (the interplay through which participants consummate, frustrate or abandon a genre) and on to ideology
where tension among coding orientations vies with power, deprivation and
systemic inertia to engender evolution. As Halliday comments in Thibault
(1987):

> I would interpret the power relations in a particular situation, when we
> represent that situation in terms of field, tenor and mode, by building into
> our representation that fact that the situation may be different things for
> different interactants. The total picture is obviously going to bring in all
> angles; but in any typical context of situation in which there is a power
> relationship of inequality, then the configuration embodied in that situa-
> tion is different from the way it is seen from either end. This means, of
> course, that the register that is being operated by the interactants will be
> bifurcated, although we may choose to characterise the register of the situ-
> ation as a whole by building in both strands. (1987:620-621)

It remains to develop ways of building in "both strands" that show how text
negotiates with system, and different systems with each other; lacking a
model of this metasystemic dynamism, contextual theory remains danger-
ously incomplete.

The major stumbling block to overcoming this obstacle and deploying the tools that are already developed is unwieldiness. The text structures realising genre are large and thus time-consuming to analyse, and compared with examples of syllable and clause structures agnate texts are hard to find. As an institution linguistics is organised to frustrate work on systems of text — most of the generic slots available for presenting work (papers, seminars, theses etc. are too short to be equal to the task), appointment and promotion is based on individual, not group work (thereby encouraging revolution in place of evolution), and funding is directed to applications rather than research development (at the same time as applied work has low status within the discipline itself). All of this manifests an ideologically motivated naturalisation process that will be taken up in 7.4 below.

7.3.3 Genre and register

Before turning to the plane of ideology, the question of distinguishing register and genre as semiotic planes will be taken up once again with reference to the work of Halliday, Hasan and Longacre, none of whom "stratify" context along these lines. Their models can each be shown however to involve additional complexity that the genre and register model here avoids.

For Halliday, the complication has to do with introducing the concept of first and second order contexts, with first order field and tenor oriented to situation and second order field, tenor and mode defined by reference to language. Table 7.21 sums up his (1978a:143-145) position:

Table 7.21. First and second oder register in Halliday (1978)

	FIRST ORDER	SECOND ORDER
FIELD	social action	subject matter
TENOR	social roles	speech function roles
MODE	-	medium, rhetorical genre

First and second order tenor would be dealt with as the difference between register (tenor) and discourse semantics (NEGOTIATION) here; and Halliday's second order opposition of medium to rhetorical genre is *English*

Text's opposition between genre and mode. The distinction between first and second order field is presented as follows:

> In a discussion about a game of football, the social action is the discussion and the verbal interaction among the participants is the whole of this interaction. Here the game constitutes a second order of 'field', one that is brought into being by that of the first order, the discussion... (1978a:144)

English Text would model a context of this kind by treating it as discussion at the level of genre, and as simultaneously involving two fields at the level of register — one field realised through language in action mode (the discussion), and the other realised reflectively (the subject matter). Keeping in mind that as far as text structure is concerned genre and field give convergent accounts as texts approach ancillary mode, *English Text*'s approach to this context would amount in practice to treating the genre as discussion and the field as the game discussed.[28]

Mode also impinges on Hasan's model of context and text structure, since for her only texts where the role of language is ancillary and whose environment is pragmatic can be derived from contextual configurations (in her discussion she is opposing text types such as service encounters to the nursery tale; Hasan 1984b:76). Since for constitutive modes, context cannot predict text structure, Hasan suggests that for these texts what matters most is "the array of existing conventions" (1984b:78). Hasan's model then is one which derives text structures in two fundamentally different ways, depending on mode (see Harris 1987:36-37 for a related critique).

English Text's preferred position is to treat mode differences simply as differences in mode and to derive all text types from genre networks elaborated along the lines illustrated above. These networks are in a sense systemic formulations of what Hasan's refers to as a culture's "array of existing conventions". The model suggests however that these arrays are relevant for all genres, not just those constitutive in mode. This avoids the problems inherent in Hasan's apparently materialist reading of context, which leads her to derive some texts from their context of situation and others with respect to their cultural heritage. The ancillary/constitutive opposition is in any case a cline, which creates considerable uncertainty about how to model context for texts in 'middling' modes.

Finally Longacre proposes distinguishing between deep and surface structure genre. The distinction appears to be based in part on delicacy, with surface structure genre a finer grained taxonomy (1976:198), and partly on realisation, with surface structure genre specified in more grammatical terms. The difference between Longacre's deep and surface genre oppositions is unclear; he does however specify the realisation of the genres classified by these oppositions in different ways as illustrated in Table 7.22.

Table 7.22: The realisation of deep and surface structure genre in Longacre (1976)

Deep structure genre (Longacre 1976:200)

NARRATIVE	EXPOSITION
[−projected/+succession]	[−projected/−succession]
1. 1/3 person	1. No necessary person reference
2. Agent oriented	2. (Subject matter oriented)
3. Accomplished time	3. Time not focal
4. Chronological linkage	4. Logical linkage

Surface structure genre (Longacre 1976:202)

NARRATIVE	EXPOSITION
[−prescription/+chronological framework]	[−prescription/−chronological framework]
1. 1/3 person pronouns	1. 3 person pronouns
2. Agent/Experiencer as subject	2. Equative & descriptive clauses
3. Past tense/historical present	3. Various tenses
4. Head-tail & tail-head linkage	4. By sentence topic & parallelism

The general point here is that single plane models tend to introduce additional complexity to handle the contextual variables distributed among field, tenor, mode and genre by *English Text*. So the cost of recognising two connotative semiotics instead of one is not as high as it might initially appear.[29]

7.4 Ideology: discursive power

The first principle of linguistics is to distinguish between *system* and *structure*. ... The statement of structures and systems provides, so to speak, the anatomy and physiology of texts. It is unnecessary, indeed perhaps inadvisable, to attempt a structural and systemic account of a language as a whole. Any given or selected restricted language, i.e. the language under description is, from the present point of view, multi-structural and polysystemic. (Firth 1957b/1968:200)

As this and similar passages illustrate, Firth's concern with meaning as function in context made him wary of abstractions which generalised across contexts; thus for example his refusal to identify a consonant entering into different oppositions in syllable initial and final position as the same sound (i.e. phoneme; see Palmer 1970) and his interest in restricted languages as far as making statements of meaning was concerned. In general terms Firth privileged text over system (see Halliday's comments in Thibault 1987:603) and it was left to Halliday to develop system/process theory in a way that placed potential and actual on an equal footing, related through the dialectic of realisation. Firth died in 1960 only the day before Halliday was planning to show him "Categories of the theory of grammar" (Halliday 1961:242), and probably settled more easily into the after-life that he might have after December 15. It is nevertheless appropriate, some 30 years later, to reconsider Firth's concern with the multi-structural and polysystemic nature of language, especially in the context of the now current appreciation of the work of Bakhtin.

Setting aside for a moment the problems of formalising realisation as a dialectic, *English Text* has for the most part followed Halliday's lead in refusing to privilege either system or process. The attention paid to system however does run the risk of being read as involving a over-deterministic interpretation of language, register and genre as homogeneous systems. This (mis)reading needs to be seriously addressed.

The first point that needs to be made is that the interpretation of language and context developed here is indeed multi-structural and polysystemic. System/structure theory has been re-involved in the description on a number of different levels — rank, stratum and plane — most of which involve metafunctional diversity and so can be analysed simulatneously as particle, wave and prosody; in addition, synoptic and dynamic perspectives on text as system and text as process have been introduced. Any text then is interpreted as manifested in a multi-dimensional semiotic space and analysis relates it systemically to meanings that might have been along several complementary lines of agnation. In principle the multiplicity of meanings recognised is limited only by the delicacy of the networks on different levels from which the text is derived.

Within semiotic theory the notion of intertextuality has been developed out of the work of Bakhtin (1981, 1986) to deal with simultaneous inter-relationships of this kind (see Todorov 1984:60-74). Like Firth, Bakhtin was interested in the heterogeneous nature of speech communities (for which he developed the notion of heteroglossia); and like Firth he saw this heterogeneity manifested in all texts (for which he developed the notion of dialogism[30], using the metaphor of dialogue to capture the sense in which different voices converse as texture). The register and genre theory reviewed and developed above represents systemic theory's attempts to model heteroglossia and dialogism; it does this by formulating register and genre as social semiotic systems realised through text, thereby providing an account not simply of how one text relates to another (cohesion across products) but in addition of how one text relates to all the texts that might have been (product in relation to system). Systemicists' socio-semantic model is arguably the most powerful account of inter-textual relations proposed to date within either functional linguistics or semiotic theory in general (for further discussion of convergence in systemic and semiotic theory see Threadgold 1986a, 1986b, Lemke 1985, 1988a, 1989a, forthcoming b, c, d).

The interpretation does however need to be qualified in two important respects — namely heterogeneity in the speech community and semogensis (i.e. semiotic change). In their interpretations of language, register and genre as semiotic systems, systemicists have generally attempted to model cultures as a whole — to generalise meaning potential across all imaginable texts (Halliday himself it should be noted has remained rather Firthian in character as far as semantics is concerned, preferring register specific descriptions and cautioning against premature attempts to describe the semantic system as a whole — e.g. 1988a:3; needless to say *English Text* has nowhere heeded this caution). The problems with this are: 1. as noted above, this meaning potential is not evenly distributed across participants in a culture; and 2. for a culture to survive, this meaning potential has to evolve. These two problems are in fact closely related; it is the tensions produced by the unequal distribution of meaning potential that forces a culture to change. This brings social semiotic theory face to face with the central problem of marxist theory: what is the nature of the dialectic between base and superstructure that facilitates and at the same time frustrates social change? Even more to the point, from the perspective of a theory of linguistics as social action, how is it possible to intervene in a dialectic of this kind? These are the questions that the communicative plane of ideology has been articulated to address.

7.4.1 *Coding orientation: ideology as system*

The notion of heterogeneity in the speech community has already been introduced in the discussion of contact above with reference to Halliday's study of antilanguages, where hegemonic and antilanguage discourses are polarised within the limits of what can be recognised as a single community. Retreating somewhat from polarisation of this kind, it remains the case that in all known speech communities meaning-making is unevenly distributed according to what in semiotic theory are referred to as the discourses of class, gender, ethnicity and generation (see Cranny-Francis 1990). For Bernstein, the most important of these discourses is class (e.g. "Without a shadow of a doubt, the most formative influence upon the procedures of socialisation, from a sociological point of view, is social class." 1971b/ 1974:198), presumably since class conditions the way in which meanings are distributed according to gender, ethnicity and generation. Privileging the discourse of social class in this way is common practice in marxist theory, but may in itself be gendered or otherwise biassed by privileging agencies and has been so challenged by feminists. From the perspective of social semiotics, whether or not any one of these discourses needs to be foregrounded should perhaps remain an open question at this time.

This query aside, Bernstein's theory remains the most relevant sociological theory as far as the sociosemantic interpretation of heteroglossia is concerned (for a useful introduction see Atkinson 1985) — his focus on socialisation provides a framework for interpreting the problem of systemic inertia and change, and somewhat uniquely among sociologists language occupies a central place in his theory (in marxist terms, for Bernstein, as for Halliday, culture seems to function as superstructure and contextualised language as base). Equally significant has been Bernstein's concern with education, which according to Althusser (1971:152) is the dominant ideological state apparatus in mature western capitalist social formations. Bernstein's theory of codes addresses the semiotic nature of this apparatus and forms the basis for the synoptic articulation of ideology to be developed here.

Basically Bernstein's suggestion (see Bernstein 1971a, 1973, 1975, 1990; Bernstein 1982, 1987 provide useful retrospectives on the development of code theory) is social class positions subjects[31] to make meaning in distinctive ways depending on context. Taking up Halliday's (Thibault 1987:620) terms quoted above, code "bifurcates" register, with the result that speakers from different classes (or generations, ethnicities and genders) construe context in different ways. In Bernstein's own terms:

> ... I shall take the view that the code which the linguist invents to explain the formal properties of grammar is capable of generating any number of speech codes, and there is no reason for believing that any one language code is better than another in this respect. On this argument, language is a set of rules to which all speech codes must comply, but which speech codes are realized is a function of the culture acting through social relationships in specific contexts. (1971b/1974:197)

Without an interpretation of these divergent speech codes, or better, **fashions of meaning**, contextual theory does indeed run the danger of over-determining, homogenising and thereby reifying semiotic communities. The notion of 'fashions of meaning' which has been used to relativise context here is based on work by Whorf who differentiated languages and cultures on the basis of different fashions of speaking — divergent constellations of meaning or configurative rapports (for the development of Whorf's work on semiotic relativity see Hasan 1984c on Urdu and Martin 1988b on Tagalog). Bernstein's work on coding orientations was influenced in part by Whorf's thinking; Bernstein however has as he puts it 'relativised' Whorf (see Bernstein 1971a/1974:143-144) by proposing divergent ways of meaning as an inherent feature of socially stratified speech communities.

Any theory which challenges the naturalised discourse of liberal humanism in this way is certain to be publicly discredited and stands every chance of being completely effaced. To argue that "deep down" groups of people are sociosemantically different is simply not thinkable in western capitalist society, which "deep down" wants to believe that everyone is very much the same, except for individual differences, which they should of course be encouraged to express. Predictably, Bernstein's views have been constructed as controversial ones (see Atkinson 1985, Halliday 1988a, Hasan 1988 for instructive reviews of these debates). Ironically,[32] but again quite predictably, one of the worst offenders in this process has been the American sociolinguist William Labov who has pursued a lengthy campaign of misrepresentation, taking care at all times not to document his objections to Bernstein's research in writing. The nearest he comes to a written critique is the following:

> The most extreme view which proceeds from this orientation — and one that is now being widely accepted — is that lower-class black children have no language at all. The notion is first drawn from Basil Bernstein's writings

that "much of lower-class language consists of a kind of incidental 'emotional' accompaniment to action here and now." (Jensen 1968:119). Bernstein's views are filtered through a strong bias against all forms of working-class behaviour, so that middle-class language is seen as superior in every respect — "as more abstract, and necessarily somewhat more flexible, detailed and subtle." (1969/1972:204)

This is such an obvious misprepresentation of Bernstein's views at any stage, let alone 1969, that Labov was forced to publicly apologise in a letter to *The Atlantic* published in 1972 (Labov 1972c). Labov however carried on his campaign in the oral culture, referring for example in a seminar at the University of Hawaii in July 1977 to "Basil Bernstein's idea that if you teach children more complicated grammar, that makes them smarter", provoking derisive laughter among most of the American graduate students involved; similar behaviour in public forums was attested during his visit to Australia later in the year. Given the predominant folk-wisdom that Labov has refuted Bernstein, it seems likely that his campaign carried on well beyond this point in time. Clarifications by Bernstein (1971/1974:257-278, 1982, 1987), Hasan (1973, 1988), Adlam (1977), Atkinson (1985), Halliday (1978a, 1988a) and so on have all been systematically ignored by Labov.[33]

Labov and his colleagues also worked theoretically, this time in writing, to forestall investigation of semantic variation across speakers. Critical here was Labov's conceptualisation of all sociolinguistic variation in terms of alternative ways of expressing the same referential meaning. Labov (1978) defends this notion against Lavendera's (1978) challenge (see also Romaine's 1981 critique); and Weiner & Labov 1983 suggest on the basis of a study of the active/passive opposition in English that syntactic variation in general is not socially conditioned.

Research however has vindicated Bernstein. In a series of studies focussing on semantic variation systemic linguists have demonstrated empirically that interlocutors construe contexts differently depending on sanity (Martin & Rochester 1979), age (Martin 1983c), gender and class (Plum 1988) and all of generation, gender and class (Plum & Cowling 1987, Hasan 1986, 1988, 1990, Cloran 1989, Hasan & Cloran 1990). The largest of these studies has been directed by Hasan, some of whose results will be briefly reviewed here.

Hasan's basic strategy has been to adapt the methodology developed by variation theorists to the study of semantic variation, implementing their concern with naturalistic data, a socially stratified sample and quantitative methods. Her data set consists in part of mothers' interactions with pre-school children in the home, which provides an excellent basis for studying some of the fashions of meaning associated with the discourses of generation (mother/child), gender (male/female children) and class (middle/working) in critical socialising contexts; additional data follows up the experiences of some of these children upon entering infants school. Hasan's major innovation has been to base her study on semantic variables, essentially by conceptualising system networks as variable rules (see Nesbitt & Plum 1988) and coding her data on the basis of selections from delicately elaborated discourse semantic networks she devised. Cloran 1989 reports on some of the results manifesting discourses of gender and class in the home; these will be used to illustrate Hasan's findings here (for a comparison of coding orientations at home and at school see Hasan 1988).

Cloran's results are based on the coding of approximately 20,000 messages, each of which was described in terms of an average of 50 semantic selections from Hasan's networks; 24 mother/child dyads were involved in the study, evenly divided by gender and class into four cells. One of the fashions of speaking located by applying principal components analysis to the coded data had to do with mothers' control style. Cloran's characterisation of this style is as one in which mothers habitually tend:

> 1. to demand goods and services by using exhortative commands (realized typically by the imperative forms, e.g., *Don't do that*, or by using high-value models such as *must, have to, gotta*, etc.) rather than the more discretion-giving consultative or suggestive type (realized by interrrogatives, e.g., *Would you do it?* or *How about doing it?*);
> 2. to give rationalizations by appeal to bribes or threats [e.g., *You do it again and I'll whack you.* in the example below; JRM] rather than to consequences inherent in an act (e.g., *if you touch the hot stove, you'll burn yourself*);
> 3. to demand information using how/why questions rather than specification-seeking questions (e.g., *What happened?*) or confirmation-seeking ones (e.g., *Did you cut yourself?*);
> 4. not to announce the commencement of some activity (e.g., *I'll just go and hand out the washing*) or its completion (e.g., *I've finished my lunch now*). The significance of this negative loading appears to be such that a speaker is not overtly concerned with involvement of the addressee in the ongoing activity.

Cloran (1989:134) suggests that mothers favoring this fashion of meaning allow their children little discretion when responding to commands and back up these proposals with bribes and threats. Furthermore *how/why* questions were used rhetorically by these mothers or to counter children's utterances. Cloran's example of behaviour of this kind is as follows (note that the question *What's funny about that?* is rhetorical; an answer is not expected):

> [7:5] Mother: Don't do that...Now look, you'll get it all over me
>   Peter: (Laughs)
>   Mother: It's not funny. What's funny about that? You do it again and I'll whack you.

As Cloran points out this example nicely illustrates the variable nature of semantic styles as tendencies, not rules; the mother in 7:5 appeals to both an inherent consequence (*You'll get it all over me*) and a threat (*I'll whack you*) to control her son (the text is in Bakhtin's terms, dialogic — it realises more than one voice; his dialogism can thus be seen as a natural implication of any text based theory of semantic variation). Statistically, this method of control, referred to as **imperative** by Bernstein (1971a/1974:180), is used significantly more by mothers of boys rather than mothers of girls, and significantly more by working class as opposed to middle class mothers. Interestingly enough, in light of earlier criticism of Bernstein's own data, these results show a positive correlation between what children suppose controlling agents would say in an experimental situation (Turner 1973) and what their mothers do in fact say. The question of valuing this fashion of meaning will be taken up in 7.4.3 below.

Interpreting a number of socially organised configurative rapports of this kind, Hasan (1988:84-85) arrives at the following convergent articulation of Bakhtin's heteroglossia:

> – should material conditions of social life differ markedly either across cultures, or across strata within the same culture, then the form of social interaction will also differ;
> – if social interaction differs across segments of the same society, then different forms of consciousness will arise;
> – since consciousness is central to carrying out social functions, different forms of consciousness will find expression in (amongst other things) different orientations to meaning; in such societies semantic variation is logically predicted;
> – communication between speakers with distinct semantic orientations will give rise to problems, for the words of the one will be filtered through the divergent view point of the other.

What are the implications of Hasan and Bernstein's work for the interpretation of ideology as system? This is a question which is in some respects premature. Work on mapping out the fashions of meaning constituting a culture at the level of ideology has only just begun (most of Hasan's own work in this area remains unpublished as of 1989). Hasan's results do suggest that fashions of meaning can be generalised as coding orientations along the lines suggested by Bernstein and will eventually be articulated as the discourses of class, gender, generation and ethnicity permeating and giving rise to all texts in our culture. It needs to be kept in mind however that the level of abstraction involved will be extremely high; Bernstein's own glosses (e.g. personal/position, public/private, elaborated/restricted, universalistic/particularistic and so on) have all proved valuable attempts to grapple with the ineffable. But at the same time all have been misunderstood and exploited by liberal humanists who take their dictionary definitions as defining and on the basis of this notional fallacy develop misrepresentations and supposed critiques Bernstein's work. All of this is compounded by the fact that fashions of meaning and the more abstract notion of coding orientation need always to be interpreted in context — that is, with respect to the genre and register through which they are manifested. Given our present understanding of these planes, this is a challenging task; and certainly not one for which even a provisional network of oppositions can be provided at this time.

Perhaps the most that can be said at this stage is that from a synoptic perspective, ideology is a system of coding orientations which makes meaning selectively available depending on subjects' class, gender, ethnicity and generation. Interpreted in these terms, all texts manifest, construe, renovate and symbolically realise ideology, just as they do language, register and genre. Because coding orientations are variably realised, ideology will never be a question of this or that but one of more and less; and because these coding orientations distribute discursive power unevenly, there will always be semiotic tension in the community. The variable realisation of ideology provides the dynamic openness through which this tension can be resolved — it is a necessary condition for the system to evolve. Something of the textual dynamics of this tension will be taken up in 7.4.2 below.

7.4.2 Contratextuality: ideology as process

As noted with respect to text [7:5] above, variable realisation implies in a sense that all texts are multi-voiced. There is in other words a certain tension in the system, which manifests itself in semiotic processes. For the most part this dissonance is scarcely heard; certain habitual configurations of meaning dominate others and the disharmony goes unnoticed. At times however the tension among voices explodes. This happens when an **issue** brings the uneven distribution of discursive power into focus and participants in a community try to act consciously on this distribution with a view to re-allocation. The semiotic struggle over redistribution then becomes a fruitful site for the study of ideology, and is especially rewarding with respect to the problem of sociosemantic change.

The most relevant work in this area of inquiry derives from the East Anglia school of critical linguistics (Fowler et al. 1979, Kress & Hodge 1979; for developments from this model see Kress 1985/1989, Kress and Hodge 1988, Hodge 1988 and the 1987 retrospective by Fowler). Trew in particular (1979a, 1979b) examined newspaper reports focussing on two semiotic explosions — the 1977 Notting Hill Carnival and the June 1975 massacre of African demonstrators in Harare. By examining conservative, liberal and radical readings of these events over a period of days Trew was able to deconstruct the ways in which lexicogrammar was deployed to construct and successively modify a range of interpretations. The ideological spectrum provided formed the basis of Martin's (1986a) study of a recurrent ecological debate.

There Martin suggested as part of a model for dealing with ideology in crisis a system involving two axes: protagonist/antagonist and left/right. **Antagonists** were characterised as interlocutors who are interested in creating issues, **protagonists** as interlocutors attempting to dissolve them; the term **left** was used to refer to those who had semiotic power to gain through the ensuing debates, the **right** for those with power to lose. On the basis of these distinctions a power profile can be developed around specific areas of tension in ideological systems, always keeping in mind that particular group's association with one or other position on the profile changes over time and from issue to issue (although there are obviously recurrent associations which can be generalised). In general terms the systemic oppositions are outlined below; as far as the dynamics of ideology are concerned these are best treated genuine oppositions, not simply as alternative choices within a system.

This model can be exemplified for the field of linguistics with respect to tension in Australian appointments proceedings during the 1980's. The role of right protagonist is taken up by Government and Binding theory, deriving from the work of Chomsky and his more recent graduate students. This

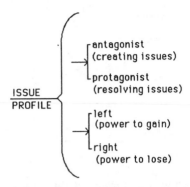

Fig. 7.28. A dynamic perspective on ideological tension

group is hegemonically positioned in the discipline and works within a framework that dualises form and meaning, posits an arbitrary relation between the two, defines **the** goal of linguistics in terms of stating neurological limitations on possible grammars, focusses on universals and uses intuitions as data to achieve this, works on meaning from the point of view of lexis, if at all, preferring in general to stratify in terms of a syntax/semantics/pragmatics hierarchy and so on. GB is opposed by left protagonists who try to beat them at fundamentally this same game, including large numbers of Chomsky's less recent graduate students; during the 1980's this position is filled by Lexical Functional Grammar and Generalised Phrase Structure Grammar, whose practitioners have high status within the discipline, are considered 'real' linguists alongside Government and Binding theorists and are eminently appointable.

Flanking these to the left and right are antagonists. The right antagonists are comprised largely of older Chomkyans who view the emergence of issues influenced by the left with some concern. They work hard to eliminate these issues, often favoring the dismissal genre developed by Postal in the 1960's; for examples see Stockwell in 1980, Newmeyer (1980) on Hymes and Fought (1975/1981), Levinson (1983) on systemic approaches to conversational structure, Huddleston (1988) on Halliday's *Introduction to Functional Grammar* etc. To the left sit the west coast functionalists who present a radical challenge to certain hegemonic tenets such as the claim that syntax and discourse are arbitrarily related (e.g. Thompson, Chafe[34] and Givón). Neither of these groups are eminently

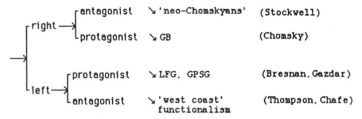

Fig. 7.29. Hegemony and opposition in theoretical linguistics

employable; but they are still linguists (beyond the margins of this profile on the other hand sit systemic, stratificational and tagmemic *linguists*, whose status as such provokes considerable suspicion; and beyond them semioticians and post-structuralists about whom there can be no doubt). This profile is outlined in Fig. 7.29 and can be usefully compared with the field network for theories developed in 7.2.3.2 above; whether one agrees with the two networks in detail or not, and disagreement can only be discursively arbitrated, the critical point remains that the oppositions among theories are quite different from the perspectives of field and ideology.

The influence of this profile on appointments, as on every aspect of the discipline, is immense. Publications are evaluated in terms of the journals in which they appear, with journals controlled by right protagonists having highest status; protagonists' referee reports weigh more heavily than those of antagonists, and of course special significance is attached to a right protagonist's praise; the right aligns itself on committees with allied exponents of liberal humanism across the faculty, the charm of their theory being the transparent role it assigns language where questions of ideological tension are concerned (effacing language is critical to the naturalisation processes whereby the uneven distribution of meaning potential is legitimised; see section 7.4.4 below). This matrix of forces is hard to beat, and renegade departments do not survive for long.

While the profile developed above certainly recurs across a number of issues, it is important to note that as issues change, so may the role played by linguists in the oppositions. With applied linguistics appointments for example, systemic linguists might well find themselves positioned as left protagonists, instead of completely effaced; and where questions of national language policy arise, linguists of many persuasions have often found themselves allied. Similarly with literacy issues, while educational linguists in Australia have been generally concerned with changing schools in ways that radically redistribute control of written genres, the teaching methodology (visible pedagogy in Bernstein's terms) they recommend aligns them in some respects with the New Right. Only an issue by issue profile can deal with shifting allegiances of this kind.

The range of texts deriving from issue profiles of the kind illustrated here is of course immense, even though only a minority of texts foreground dissonance in this way. Martin 1986a introduces the term **contratextuality** for texts which directly oppose each other from different positions and this idea has been extended in delicacy by Lemke (1988a:48). Contratextuality is critically related to semogenesis in ways that are only beginning to be investigated (for a revealing study of the semiotic subversion of genre fiction by feminist writers see Cranny-Francis 1990) and it is probable that work in this area will be among the first to shed light on the vexing question of how text renovates system as dynamic open systems evolve, thereby affirming their metastability.

7.4.3 *Prejudice*

Returning at this point to text [7:5], and the coding orientation it illustrates, it is clearly impossible, as a member of our culture, not to react. Is this mother a good mother? Is this the right way for her to treat her son? Isn't there a better way to behave? And so on. Sensitive to reactions of this kind, liberal humanists, following Labov's lead, have generally tried to discredit studies focussing on semantic variation, to dismiss their results as incidental and to imply that studies of this kind are better not undertaken in the first place since they serve simply to legitimize existing prejudice. Hasan (1988:85) quotes a typical response of this kind from Wells (1977):

> those who wish to show that the language of lower-class children is differ-
> ent, will always find evidence to prove their point, but it does not follow
> that those differences necessarily put those children at an educational dis-
> advantage — unless they trigger off expectations that all too easily become
> self-fulfilling.

The last objection is the most telling, since it argues that it doesn't matter that Bernstein (1971b/1974:197) writes that "there is no reason for believing that any one language code is better than another in this respect." Nor does it matter that Cloran suggests, following Bernstein, that each semantic style "has both positive and negative consequences for the child." (1989:137) It argues on the contrary that simply documenting social differences of this kind plays into the hands of prejudice, further damaging the lot of those already discursively depowered (e.g. women, children, workers, migrants and the like).

This is not the place to debate the demerits of this position, although there can be no doubt whose interests this intellectual ostrichism serves (see Hasan 1988:85-87 for discussion). What is important here is the conviction with which this concern is held. It is based on reactions to fashions of meaning and is itself a reaction to fashions of meaning; it demonstrates that the profile of oppositions around issues discussed in 7.4.2 above, and more generally the coding orientations associated with class, gender, ethnicity and generation focus attitudes in systematic ways. Affect is in other words ideologically addressed (see Martin 1986a on the orientation of attitude in ecological debates) and exploring this projection of interpersonal meaning is an important dimension of semiotic space.

Linguistic work in this area, as with interpersonal meaning in general, is at a nascent stage. Poynton (1985/1989) examines the way in which gender conditions the ways in which Epithets focus differentially on men and women, noting in passing that the large scale collocational studies required in this area have not yet been undertaken. Beyond this studies are needed on the inter-relationships between affect and morality (between ATTITUDE and MODULATION to put this grammatically): *I like/dislike* clearly conditions *you should/shouldn't* in ways that have barely been broached (see Martin 1992). Work in narrative theory is likely to prove revealing in this regard, especially with reference to the interpretation of moral tales (the exemplum discussed above, alongside jokes, fables, parables and other stories with a "message"). Hasan's current studies of mothers' reaction to mothers' talk should also help penetrate this important frontier.

7.4.4 *Naturalisation (inertia)*

As developed in Sections 7.4.1-3 above, the very uneven distribution of meaning potential across a culture sustains ongoing tensions, many of which are prone to erupt — and the negative affect deriving from these tensions continually gives rise to violent action of an often horrific order (for example rape, murder, suicide, assault, revolution and war to name but a few of the more obviously brutal forms). At the same time the distribution of power remains remarkably stable — something in the system facilitates it.

It is read, when it is read at all, as **natural**. In Althusser's terms:

> caught in this quadruple system of interpellation as subjects...the subjects 'work', they 'work by themselves' in the vast majority of cases, with the exception of the 'bad subjects' who on occasion provoke the intervention of one of the detachments of the (repressive) State apparatus. But the vast majority of (good) work all right 'all by themselves', i.e. by ideology (whose concrete forms are realised in the Ideological State Apparatuses). They 'recognize' the existing state of affairs (*das Bestehende*), that 'it really is true that it is so and not otherwise', and that they must be obedient to God, to their conscience, to the priest, to de Gaulle, to the boss, to the engineer, that thou shalt 'love thy neighbour as thyself', etc. Their concrete, material behaviour is simply the inscription in life of the admirable words of the prayer: *'Amen — So be it.'* (1971:181)

Althusser goes on to address the liberal humanist articulation of this process of naturalisation which depends on the subject being the author of and responsible for her/his actions at the same time as s/he submits to a higher authority and is "thereby stripped of all freedom except that of freely accepting his submission" (1971:182). It is this insistence that the powerless be left free to submit which motivates the actions of those seeking to efface the study of semantic variation, since studies of this kind destroy the illusion of freedom on which the naturalisation process depends.

So — texts are coherent, cultures are not. Where does this leave linguistics which is articulated as a form of social action?

Clearly one important job, which has already begun (inspired by the critical linguistics of the East Anglia school and developed in Chilton 1985, Threadgold et al. 1986, Fairclough 1989), lies in deconstructing the naturalisation process. Systemic functional linguistics has always adressed this concern, and *English Text*'s development of discourse semantics and contextual theory was undertaken with this goal explicitly in mind. What seems crucial here is a model which displays the way in which language inflects and is inflected by contextual systems; one model of this kind has been provided. What is missing is a deeper understanding of facilitation — the realisation process whereby choices configure across levels in ways which are hard to disassociate. Much more work is needed on the way in which these fashions of meaning resonate across systems and are inhospitable to change.

Where critical linguistics has fallen short of evolving into a form of social action lies in its observer as opposed to an intruder role. Even in educational contexts critical linguists have tended to stand back and let teachers and consultants do the work of changing educational transmissions (see Hasan & Martin 1989:3), being somewhat reluctant to shunt themselves between theory and practice. As far as linguistics as social action is concerned this is not adequate. The theory has to be developed to the point where it informs interventions in political processes — where critical linguists take charge for example of public relations for the ANC or intervene directly with education ministers in curriculum debates. This involves developing appropriate theories of semiotic subversion — How can critical linguists de-automate facilitation?,[34] How can they fill in disjunctions (i.e. ideologically motivated gaps in the ways in which field, mode and tenor combine)?, How can they evolve genres which challenge power?, How can they distribute them?

Answering questions such as these takes linguists far from the liberal humanist paradigm that has informed their work throughout most of the development of their theories in this century. The answers form the basis for a neo-marxist theory of language and culture in which language functions as base and connotative semiotics as sociosemantic superstructure. Given the genesis of systemic contextual theory in work by marxist linguists during the McCarthy era in Britain, this seems a cheering note on which to end this discussion of register, genre and ideology. Or perhaps better, in Hjelmslev's words:

Humanitas et universitas

NOTES

1.   The term *plane* is taken over for these levels from Hjelmslev, who used it to refer to what are termed strata in this volume.

2.   Halliday is inconsistent as far as the question of whether ideational (i.e. experiential and logical) meaning projects field (1978a:116, 125) or whether the projection is from experiential meaning alone (1978a:143, 189, 1985b:9:26). This uncertainty has probably arisen because while the logico-semantics of logical meaning (expansion and projection; see also the discussion of nuclear relations in 5.3.3 above) is field oriented, taxis itself (grammatical intricacy) is very sensitive to mode.

3.   Firth's actual (1957b) system is: 1. The participants: persons, personalities and relevant features of these. (a) The verbal action of the participants. (b) The non-verbal action of the participants. 2. The relevant objects and non-verbal and non-personal events. 3. The effect of the verbal action.

4. Firth's original schema can be tied in with a four term system such as Gregory's as follows: participants with personal tenor, action with field, other relevant features with mode and effects with functional tenor.

5. Halliday himself, writing in (1965:14), slips didactic, explanatory, consolation and so on into field.

6. Gregory (1988) revises his (1967) framework, doing away with functional tenor, bringing his system more closely into line with Halliday (1978a) and with *English Text*.

7. This was originally simply a misunderstanding on Martin's part of Halliday's model (cf. Thibault 1987:610); since it has now appeared in so many publications, it seemed more appropriate to extend Halliday's notion than undo the misinterpretation here.

8. Halliday's (1961) analysis of meals is suggestive, but does not focus on the language involved.

9. Compare Halliday (1985e:5): "From Bernstein I learnt also, for the second time in my life, that linguistics cannot be other than an ideologically committed form of social action."

10. Orwell's book is based on Zamyatin's *We*, originally published in 1924; *We* reflects the less developed technology of Zamyatin's time, making use of glass walls, doors and ceilings in place of "camera" monitoring.

11. The one-way visual, two-way audio systems used for security purposes.

12. This is not to imply that turn-taking in casual conversation is not systematic, as documented by ethnomethodology.

13. Dialogic is used here in opposition to monologic referring to the extent to which the text involves turn-taking. This is not to be confused with Bakhtin's use of the term to refer to texts as heteroglossic, weaving together several discourses.

14. False starts and rewordings are of course found in the spoken mode; but the editing is much less frequent and severe than with written text.

15. Hasan (1985a/1989:58) distinguishes between medium (semiosis) and channel (substance) to make a closely related point.

16. The distinction does **not** divide texts into those realising field and those realising genre; **all** text realise both field and genre in the model of context developed here. The argument is rather that with field-structured texts, field (activity sequence) and genre (schematic structure) overdetermine text organisation.

17. Technologically this is the same distinction that was introduced as far as feedback and interaction was concerned above; it is reintroduced here because of its effect on ideational as well as interpersonal meaning.

18. For quantitative study of tense in relation to the model of context developing here, see Plum & Cowling (1987).

19. It has also been used for distinguishing the field of a review (first order) from the field of the text being reviewed (second order), which is a different distinction involving what can be conceived of metaphorically as projection. *English Text's* distinction between genre and field makes it unnecesary to use the concepts of first and second order field to distinguish a discussion (genre) about a football game from the game itself (field:activity sequence).

20. The relation is in other words a covariate one.

21. The role of Head is typically conflated with that of Professor, but the position may be filled by other senior staff.

22. The term *field* as used by Pike is obviously very different from the term *field* in systemic register theory.

23. Halliday's (1961:257) [n] superscript for recursion is used here in place of Hasan's backward looping arrow.

24. For studies exploring Hasan's model of generic structure see especially Ventola (1979), Cloran (1987), Harris (1987).

25. The scream accompanies footage of Arlington cemetary in John Sayles' video of the song.

26. The term *Explanation* is used differently in Martin (1985b/1989) than in subsequent work, where it is reserved for activity structured scientific accounts of natural phenomena (e.g. why it rains); the term will be reserved for this scientific genre here.

27. And observation, which is far less activity structured than the other, and so will be passed over here.

28. Halliday (1978b:26) introduces an alternative complication, involving the notions of inner and outer situation; this framework is applied to the analysis of curriculum genres in Christie (1989) and Rothery (1990).

29. Compare also Gregory's (1967:185) opposition between contextual and situational categories, his later (1988) distinction between generic situation and register and Ure and Ellis's (1977:202) contrast between a situational dimension and language patterning: register.

30. The distinction between heteroglossia and dialogism in Bakhtin's writing is unclear; here heteroglossia is associated with system and dialogism with process. Bakhtin himself however did not work with the Hjelmslevian notion of system and process, and was unlikely to have developed an opposition of this kind in light of his objections to Saussure's opposition of *langue* and *parole*.

31. Althusser's legally derived metaphor helps to focus on the ideological subjugation of interlocutors.

32. Since Labov's results make no sense apart from a sociosemantic sociological theory of the kind Bernstein has evolved.

33. And wilfully ignored at that, as they have been drawn to Labov's attention on more than one occasion privately and in public forums by various scholars.

34. Li, Thompson, Chafe, Dubois and others have recently formed a linguistics department at Santa Barbara dedicated to challenging hegemonic orthodoxies; one measure of their success will be whether or not this orientation survives their collective retirements — without caseful planning it certainly will not.

35. The reference here is to the Prague school's concept of de-automatization (or less aptly foregrounding); what is needed is a model of subversion which intentionally de-automates across texts, whether verbal artifacts or not.

References

Adlam, D.S. (with the assistance of G. Turner & L. Lineker) 1977. *Code in Context*. London: Routledge & Kegan Paul (*Primary Socialisation, Language and Education*).

Alexander, R.J. 1984. "Fixed Expressions in English: reference books and the teacher". *English Language Teaching Journal* 38(2). 127-134.

Althusser, L. 1971. "Ideology and Ideological State Apparatus". L. Althusser, *Lenin and Philosophy and other Essays by Louis Althusser*, 127-188. London: Monthly Review Press.

Atkinson, P. 1985. *Language Structure and Reproduction: an introduction to the sociology of Basil Bernstein*. London: Methuen.

Bakhtin, M.M. 1981. *The Dialogic Imagination*. [translated by C. Emerson & M. Holquist] Austin: University of Texas Press.

Bakhtin, M.M. 1986. "The Problem of Speech Genres". M.M. Bakhtin, *Speech Genres and other Late Essays* [translated by V. McGee], 60-102. Austin: University of Texas Press.

Barthes, R. 1966. "Introduction to the Structural Analysis of Narratives". *Communications* 8. 1966. [reprinted in Barthes 1977, 79-124].

Barthes, R. 1967. *Elements of Semiology*. New York: Hill & Wang.

Barthes, R. 1973. *Mythologies*. London: Paladin.

Barthes, R. 1977. *Image, Music, Text*. London: Fontana.

Bateman, J.A. 1989. "Dynamic Systemic-Functional Grammar: a new frontier". *Word* 40(1-2). 263-286. (*Systems, Structures and Discourse: selected papers from the Fifteenth International Systemic Congress*).

Beaman, K. 1984. "Coordination and Subordination Revisited: syntactic complexity in spoken and written narrative discourse". D. Tannen [ed.] *Coherence in Spoken and Written Discourse*, 45-80. Norwood, N.J.: Ablex (*Advances in Discourse Processes XII*).

Béal, C. 1987. *Social Relations through Grammar: some key realisations of tenor in the French Language*. MA Thesis. Department of Linguistics, University of Sydney.

Becker, J. 1975. "The Phrasal Lexicon". R. Schank & B. Webber [eds] *Theoretical Issues in Natural Language Processing*. Cambridge: Cambridge University Press.

Beekman, J. 1970. "Propositions and their Relations within a Discourse". *Notes on Translation* 37. 6-23.

Beekman, J. & J. Callow 1974. *Translating the Word of God*. Grand Rapids, Michigan: Zondervan.

Belsey, C. 1980. *Critical Practice*. London: Methuen.

Bennett, D.C. 1968. "English Prepositions: a stratificational approach". *Journal of Linguistics* 4. 153-172.

Benson, J.D., B. Brainerd & W.S. Greaves. 1986. "A Quantificational Approach to Field of Discourse". E. Brunet & M. Juillard [eds] *Actes du Colloque ALLC de Nice*.

Benson, J.D. & W.S. Greaves 1981. "Field of Discourse: theory and application". *Applied Linguistics* 2(1). 45-55.

Benson, J.D. & W.S. Greaves. 1992. "Collocation and Field of Discourse". W.A. Mann & S.A. Thompson [eds] *Discourse Description Diverse Analyses of a Fund Raising Text*. Amsterdam: Benjamins.

Benson, J.D. & W.S. Greaves. forthcoming. "Using Narrow-Span Collocations in Parsing Lexico-Grammatical Output of Field in a Natural Language Text". Paper presented at International Systemic Congress, Helsinki, June 1989.

Benson, J.D., B. Brainerd & W.S. Greaves. 1986. "A Quantificational Approach to Field of Discourse". E. Brunet & M. Juillard [eds] *Actes du Colloque ALLC de Nice*.

Bernstein, B. 1971a. *Class, Codes and Control 1: theoretical studies towards a sociology of language*. London: Routledge & Kegan Paul (*Primary Socialisation, Language and Education*). [republished with an Appendix added by Palladin, 1974]

Bernstein, B. 1971b. "Social Class, Language and Socialisation". A.S. Abramson et al. [eds] *Current Trends in Linguistics* 12. The Hague: Mouton. [reprinted in Bernstein 1971a/1974, 193-213]

Bernstein, B. [ed.] 1973. *Class, Codes and Control 2: applied studies towards a sociology of language*. London: Routledge & Kegan Paul (*Primary Socialisation, Language and Education*).

Bernstein, B. 1975. *Class, Codes and Control 3: towards a theory of educational transmissions*. London: Routledge & Kegan Paul (*Primary Socialisation, Language and Education*).

Bernstein, B. 1982. "Codes, Modalities and Cultural Reproduction". M.W. Apple [ed.] *Cultural and Economic Reproduction in Education: essays on class, ideology and state*, 304-355. London: Routledge & Kegan Paul.

Bernstein, N. 1986. "On Pedagogic Discourse". J.G. Richardson [ed.] *Handbook for Theory and Research in the Sociology of Education*. New York: Greenwood Press.

Bernstein, B. 1987. "Elaborated and Restricted Codes: an overview 1958-85". U. Ammon, K. Matthier & N. Dittmar [eds] *Sociolinguisitics/Soziolinguistik*. Berlin: De Gruyter.

Bernstein, B. 1988. "A Sociology of the Pedagogic Context". L. Gerot, J. Oldenburg & T. van Leeuven [eds] *Language and Socialisation: home and school*, 13-24. (Proceedings from the Working Conference on Language in Education, Macquarie University 17-21 November 1986). Sydney: Macquarie Unversity.

Bernstein, B. 1990. *Class, Codes and Control 4: the structuring of pedagogic discourse*. London: Routledge.

Berry, M. 1977a. *Introduction to Systemic Linguistics: 1, structures and systems*. London: Batsford.

Berry, M. 1977b. *Introduction to Systemic Linguistics: 2, levels and links*. London: Batsford.

Berry, M. 1979. "A Note on Sinclair and Coulthard's Classes of Act Including a Comment on Comments". *Nottingham Linguistic Circular* 8(1).

Berry, M. 1981a. "Systemic Linguistics and Discourse Analysis: a multi-layered approach to exchange structure". Coulthard & Montgomery, 1981, 120-145.

Berry, M. 1981b. "Polarity and Propositional Development, their Relevance to the Well-Formedness of an Exchange". *Nottingham Linguistic Circular* 10(1). 36-63.

Berry, M. 1981c. "Towards Layers of Exchange Structure for Directive Exchanges". *Network* 2. 23-32.

Berry, M. 1987. "Is Teaching an Unanalysed Concept?" M.A.K. Halliday & R.P. Fawcett [eds] *New Developments in Systemic Linguistics Vol. 1: theory an description*, 41-63. London: Pinter.

Berry, M. 1989. "They're All Out of Step Except Our Johnny: a discussion of motivation (or the lack of it) in systemic linguistics". *Occasional Papers in Systemics Linguistics* 3. 5-68. Department of English Studies, University of Nottingham.

Biber, D. 1985. "Investigating Macroscopic Textual Variation through Multi-Feature/Multidimensional Analysis". *Journal of Linguistics* 23. 337-360. (*Special Issue on Computational Tools for Doing Linguistics*).

Biber, D. 1986. "Spoken and Written Textual Dimensions in English: resolving the contradictory findings". *Language* 62(2). 384-414.

Birch, D. & M. O'Toole [eds] 1988. *Functions of Style*. London: Pinter.

Brazil, D. 1981. "The Place of Intonation in a Discourse Model". Coulthard & Montgomery, 1981, 120-145.

Brown, G. & G. Yule. 1983. *Discourse Analysis*. Cambridge: Cambridge University Press (*Cambridge Textbooks in Linguistics*).

Brown, P. & S. Levinson. 1978. "Universals in Language Usage: politeness phenomena". E. Goody [ed.] *Social Markers in Speech*, 56-311. Cambridge: Cambridge University Press.

Brown, R. & A. Gilman 1960. "The Pronouns of Power and Solidarity". T. Sebeok [ed.] *Style in Language*, 253-276. Cambridge, Mass.: MIT Press.

Burton, D. 1980. *Dialogue and Discourse*. London: Routledge & Kegan Paul.

Burton, D. 1981. "Analysing Spoken Discourse". Coulthard & Montgomery, 1981, 146-157.

Butler, C.S. 1984. "What can/has Systemic Functional Linguistics Contributed to an Understanding of Spoken Text?" B. Bartlett & J. Carr [eds] *Language in Education Workshop: a report of proceedings*, 1-21. Centre for Research & Learning, Mount Gravatt Campus, Brisbane CAE.

Butler, C.S. 1985a. *Systemic Linguistics: theory and applications*. London: Batsford.

Butler, C.S. 1985b. "Discourse Systems and Structures". J.D. Benson & W.S. Greaves [eds] *Systemic Perspectives on Discourse vol. 1: selected theoretical papers from the 9th Internatinal Systemic Workshop*, 213-228. Norwood, NJ: Ablex.

Butler, C.S. 1987. "Communicative Function and Semantics". M.A.K. Halliday & R.P. Fawcett [eds] *New Developments in Systemic Linguistics Vol. 1: theory and description*, 212-229. London: Pinter.

Butler, C.S. 1988. "Politeness and the Semantics of Modalised Directives in English". J.D. Benson, M.J. Cummings & W.S. Greaves [eds] *Linguistics in a Systemic*

Perspective, 119-154. Amsterdam: Benjamins (= *Current Issues in Linguistics Theory* 39).

Callow, K. 1970. "More on Propositions and their Relations within a Discourse". *Notes on Translation* 37. 23-27.

Callow, K. 1974. *Discourse Considerations in Translating the Word of God*. Grand Rapids, Mich.: Zondervan.

Carter, R.A. 1982. "A Note on Core Vocabulary". *Nottingham Linguistic Circular* 11(2). 39-50.

Carter, R.A. 1986. "Good Word: vocabulary, style and coherence in children's writing". J. Harris & J. Wilkinson [eds] *Children's Writing: a linguistic view*, 91-120. London: Allen & Unwin.

Carter, R.A. 1987. *Vocabulary: an applied linguistic guide*. London: Allen and Unwin.

Chafe, W. 1976. "Givenness, Contrastiveness, Definiteness, Subjects, Topics, and Point of View". C. Li [ed.] *Subject and Topic*, 27-55. New York: Academic Press.

Chapman, G., J. Cleese, T. Gilliam, E. Idle, T. Jones & M. Palin. 1990. *Monty Python's Flying Circus: just the words*, vol. 2. London: Mandarin.

Chilton, P. 1985. *Language and the Nuclear Arms Debate: nukespeak today*. London: Pinter (*Open Linguistics Series*).

Christie, F. 1989. *Curriculum Genres in Early Childhood Education: a case study in writing development*. Ph.D. Thesis. Department of Linguistics, University of Sydney.

Christie, F. [ed.] 1991. *Social Processes in Education: proceedings of the First Australian Systemic Network Conference, Deakin University, January 1990*. Darwin: Centre for Studies of Language in Education, Northern Territory University.

Clark, H.H. & S.E. Haviland 1974. "Psychological Processes in Linguistic Explanation". D. Cohen [ed.] *Explaining Linguistics Phenomena*. Washington, D.C.: Hemisphere.

Clark, H.H. & S.E. Haviland 1977. "Comprehension and the Given-New Contrast". R.O. Freedle [ed.] *Discourse Production and Comprehension*, 1-40. Norwood, N.J.: Ablex.

Cloran, C. 1987. "Negotiating New Contexts in Conversation". *Occasional Papers in Systemic Linguistics* 1. 85-110. Department of English, University of Nottingham.

Cloran, C. 1989. "Learning through Language: the social construction of gender". Hasan & Martin, 1989, 111-151.

Connell, R. 1988. "Social Power, Language and Education". L. Gerot, J. Oldenburg & T. van Leeuven [eds] *Language and Socialisation: home and school*, 25-35. (*Proceedings from the Working Conference on Language in Education, Macquarie University 17-21 November 1986*). Sydney: Macquarie Unversity.

Concise Oxford Dictionary. London: Oxford University Press. 1964.

Coulthard, M.C. 1977. *An Introduction to Discourse Analysis*. London: Longman (*Applied Linguistics and Language Study*).

Coulthard, M.C. & M. Montgomery. [eds] 1981. *Studies in Discourse Analysis*. London: Routledge & Kegan Paul.

Cranny-Francis, A. 1988. "The Moving Image: film and television". Kress, 1988, 157-180.

Cranny-Francis, A. 1990. *Feminist Fiction: feminist uses of generic fiction*. Cambridge: Polity.

Cromack, R.E. 1968. *Language Systems and Discourse Structure in Cashinawa* (= *Hartford Studies in Linguistics* 23) Hartford, Conn.: Hartford Seminary Foundation.

Daneš, F. 1974. "Functional Sentence Perspective and the Organisation of the Text". F. Daneš [ed.] *Papers on Functional Sentence Perspective*, 106-128. The Hague: Mouton.

van Dijk, T.A. 1977a. "Connectives in Text Grammar and Text Logic". T.A. van Dijk & J. Petöfi [eds] *Grammars and Descriptions*. Berlin: De Gruyter.

van Dijk, T.A. 1977b. *Text and Context: explorations in the semantics and pragmatics of discourse*. London: Longman.

Doyle, A.C. 1981. "The Valley of Fear". *The Penguin Complete Sherlock Holmes*, 769-868. Harmondsworth: Penguin.

Du Bois, J.W. 1980. "Beyond Definiteness: the trace of identity in discourse". W.L. Chafe [ed.] *The Pear Stories: cognitive, cultural and linguistic aspects of narrative production*, 203-274. Norwood, N.J.: Ablex.

Dutch, R.A. 1966. *Roget's Thesaurus of English Words and Phrases*. London: Longman.

Eggins, S. 1990. *Conversational Structure: a systemic-functional analysis of interpersonal and logical meaning in multiparty sustained talk*. Ph.D. Thesis. Department of Linguistics, University of Sydney.

Ellis, J. 1965. "Linguistic Sociology and Institutional Linguistics". *Linguistics* 19(5). 5-20.

Ellis, J. 1971. "The Definite Article in Translation Between English and Twi". M. Houis [ed.] *Actes du Huitieme Congres de la Societe Linguistique de l'Afrique Occidentale 1969, Vol. 1*, 367-380. Abidjan.

Ellis, J. & J. Ure. 1969. "Language Varieties: register". A.R. Meetham [ed.] *Encyclopedia of Linguistics: information and control*, 251-259. Oxford: Pergamon.

El-Menoufy, A. 1988. "Intonation and Meaning in Spontaneous Discourse". J.D. Benson & W.S. Greaves [eds] *Systemic Functional Approaches to Discourse*, 1-26. Norwood, NJ: Ablex.

Evans, I. 1986. *The Federation House: a restoration guide*. Sydney: The Flannel Flower Press.

Fairclough, N. 1989. *Language and Power*. London: Longman (Language and Social Life).

Fawcett, R. 1980. *Cognitive Linguistics and Social Interaction: towards an integrated model of a systemic functional grammar and the other components of an interacting mind*. Heidelberg: Julius Groos.

Fawcett, R.P. 1988a. "The English Personal Pronouns: an exercise in linguistic theory". J.D. Benson, M.J. Cummings & W.S. Greaves [eds] *Linguistics in a Systemic Perspective*, 185-220. Amsterdam: Benjamins (= *Current Issues in Linguistic Theory* 39).

Fawcett, R.P. 1988b. "What Makes a "Good" System Network Good? — four pairs of concepts for such evaluation". J.D. Benson & W.S. Greaves [eds] *Systemic Functional Approaches to Discourse*, 1-28. Norwood, N.J.: Ablex.

Fawcett, R.P., A. van der Mije & C. van Wissen. 1988. "Towards a Systemic Flowchart Model for Discourse Structure". R.P. Fawcett & D. Young [eds] *New Developments in Systemic Linguistics, Vol. 2: theory and application*, 116-143. London: Pinter.

Fillmore, C. 1968. "The Case for Case". E. Bach & R. Harms [eds] *Universals in Lingusitic Theory*, 1-88. New York: Holt, Rinehart and Winston.

Firbas, J. 1964. "On Defining the Theme in Functional Sentence Perspective". *Travaux Linguistiques de Prague* 1. 267-280.

Firth, J.R. 1935. "The Technique of Semantics". *Transactions of the Philological Society* [reprinted in Firth, 1957a, 7-33].

Firth, J.R. 1950. "Personality and Language in Society". *Sociological Review* 42. 37-52. [Reprinted in J.R. Firth, 1957a, 177-189].

Firth, J.R. 1957a. *Papers in Linguistics 1934-1951*. London: Oxford University Press.

Firth, J.R. 1957b. "A Synopsis of Linguistic Theory, 1930-1955". *Studies in Linguistic Analysis* (= *Special volume of the Philological Society*), 1-31. London: Blackwell. [reprinted in Palmer, 1968, 168-205].

Firth, J.R. 1957c. "Ethnographic Analysis and Language with Reference to Malinowski's Views". R.W. Firth [ed.] *Man and Culture: an evaluation of the work of Bronislaw Malinowski*, 93-118. London. [reprinted in Palmer, 1968, 137-167].

Ford, C. & S.A. Thompson. 1986. "Conditionals in Discourse: a text based study from English". E. Traugott, J. Reilly & A. Termeulen [eds] *On Conditionals*, 353-372. Cambridge: Cambridge University Pres.

Fowler, R., B. Hodge, G. Kress & T. Trew. 1979. *Language and Control*. London: Routledge & Kegan Paul.

Fowler, R. 1987. "Notes on Critical Linguistics". R. Steele & T. Threadgold [eds] *Language Topics: essays in honour of Michael Halliday, Vol. 2*, 481-492. Amsterdam: Benjamins.

Francis, G. 1985. *Anaphoric Nouns*. (= *Discourse Analysis Monographs* 11). English Language Research, University of Birmingham.

Francis, G. 1989. "Thematic Selection and Distribution in Written Discourse". *Word* 40(1-2), 201-221. (= *Systems, structures and discourse: selected papers from the Fifteenth International Systemic Congress*).

Fries, P.H. 1981. "On the Status of Theme in English: arguments from discourse". *Forum Linguisticum* 6(1). 1-38. [republished in J.S. Petöfi & E. Sözer [eds] 1983 *Micro and macro Connexity of Texts*, 116-152. Hamburg: Helmut Buske Verlag [*Papers in Textlinguistics 45*.]]

Fries, P.H. forthcoming. "Patterns of Information in Initial Position in English". P.H. Fries & M. Gregory [eds] *Discourse in Society: functional perspectives*. Norwood, N.J.: Ablex (= *Meaning and Choice in Language: studies for Michael Halliday*).

Giblett, R. & J. O'Carroll [eds]. 1990. *Discipline — Dialogue — Difference: proceedings of the Language in Education Conference, Murdoch University, December 1989*. Murdoch, W.A.: 4D Duration Publications, School of Humanities, Murdoch University.

Givón, T. 1979. *On Understanding Grammar*. New York: Academic Press.

Gleason, H.A. Jr. 1968. "Contrastive Analysis in Discourse Structure". *Monograph Series on Languages and Linguistics* 21 (Georgetown University Institute of Languages and Linguistics). [reprinted in Makkai & Lockwood 1973, 258-276].

Goldsmith, J.A. 1976. "An Overview of Autosegmental Phonology". *Linguistic Analysis* 2(1). 23-68.

Goldsmith, J.A. 1990. *Autosegmental and Metrical Phonology*. Oxford: Basil Blackwell.

Goodman, K.S. 1987. "Determiners in Reading: miscues on a few little words". *Language and Education: an international journal* 1(1). 33-57.

Gregory, M. 1967. "Aspects of Varieties Differentiation". *Journal of Linguistics* 3. 177-198.

Gregory, M. 1982. "The Nature and Use of Metafunctions in Systemic Theory: current concerns". W. Gutwinski & G. Jolly [eds] *The Eighth LACUS Forum 1981*, 67-74. Columbia, S.C.: Hornbeam Press.

Gregory, M. 1985. "Towards Communication Linguistics: a framework". J.D. Benson & W.S. Greaves [eds] *Systemic Perspectives on Discourse, Vol. 1: selected theoretical papers from the 9th International Systemic Workshop*, 119-134. Norwood, N.J.: Ablex.

Gregory, M. 1988. "Generic Situation and Register". J.D. Benson, M.J. Cummings & W.S. Greaves [eds] *Linguistics in a Systemic Perspective*, 301-329. Amsterdam: Benjamins (= *Current Issues in Linguistic Theory* 39).

Gregory, M. & S. Carroll. 1978. *Language and Situation: language varieties and their social contexts*. London: Routledge & Kegan Paul.

Grimes, J.E. 1975. *The Thread of Discourse*. The Hague: Mouton.

Gutwinski, W. 1976. *Cohesion in Literary Texts: a study of some grammatical and lexical features of English discourse*. The Hague: Mouton (= *Janua Linguarum Series Minor* 204).

Halliday, M.A.K. 1961. "Categories of the Theory of Grammar". *Word* 17(3). 241-292. [reprinted in Halliday, 1976b, 52-72]

Halliday, M.A.K. 1965. "Speech and Situation". *Bulletin of the National Association for the Teaching of English: some aspects of oracy* 2(2). 14-17.

Halliday, M.A.K. 1966a. "The Concept of Rank: a reply". *Journal of Linguistics* 2(1). 110-118.

Halliday, M.A.K. 1966b. "Lexis as a Linguistic Level". C.E. Bazell, J.C. Catford & M.A.K. Halliday [eds] *In Memory of J.R. Firth*, 148-162. London: Longman.

Halliday, M.A.K. 1967a. "Notes in Transitivity and Theme in English: Part 1". *Journal of Linguistics* 3(1). 37-81.

Halliday, M.A.K. 1967b. "Notes on Transitivity and Theme in English: Part 2". *Journal of Linguistics* 3(2). 199-244.

Halliday, M.A.K. 1967c. *Intonation and Grammar in British English*. The Hague: Mouton.

Halliday, M.A.K. 1967d. *Grammar, Society and the Noun*. London: H.K. Lewis (for University College London). [republished in Halliday 1977b, 1-18]

Halliday, M.A.K. 1968. "Notes on Transitivity and Theme in English: Part 3". *Journal of Linguistics* 4(2). 179-215.

Halliday, M.A.K. 1969. "Options and Functions in the English Clause". *Brno Studies in English* 8. 81-88. [reprinted in Halliday & Martin, 1981, 138-145]

Halliday, M.A.K. 1970a. "Language Structure and Language Function". J. Lyons [ed.] *New Horizons in Linguistics*, 140-165. Harmondsworth: Penguin.

Halliday, M.A.K. 1970b. *A Course in Spoken English: intonation*. London: Oxford University Press.

Halliday, M.A.K. 1970c. "Functional Diversity in Language, as Seen from a Consideration of Modality and Mood in English". *Foundations of Language* 6(3). 322-361. [reprinted in Halliday, 1976b, 189-213]

Halliday, M.A.K. 1971. "Linguistic Function and Literary Style: an inquiry into the language of William Golding's 'The Inheritors'". S. Chatman [ed.] *Literary Style: a symposium*, 362-400. New York: Oxford University Press. [reprinted in Halliday, 1973, 103-140]

Halliday, M.A.K. 1973. *Explorations in the Functions of Language*. London: Edward Arnold.

Halliday, M.A.K. 1974. "Interview with M.A.K. Halliday". H. Parret [ed.] *Discussing Language*, 81-120. The Hague: Mouton (*Janua Linguarum Series Maior 93*).

Halliday, M.A.K. 1975. *Learning how to Mean: explorations in the development of language*. London: Edward Arnold (*Explorations in Language Study*).

Halliday, M.A.K. 1976a. "Anti-Languages". *American Anthropologist* 78(3). 570-584. [reprinted in Halliday, 1978, 164-182]

Halliday, M.A.K. 1976b. *Halliday: system and function in language*. G. Kress [ed.]. London: Oxford University Press.

Halliday, M.A.K. 1976c. "Types of process". G. Kress [ed.] *Halliday: system and function in language*, 159-173. London: Oxford University Press.

Halliday, M.A.K. 1977a. "Text as Semantic Choice in Social Contexts". T. van Dijk & J.S. Petöfi [eds] *Grammars and Descriptions*, 176-225. Berlin: De Gruyter (*Research in Text Theory*). [reprinted in Halliday, 1978, 128-153]

Halliday, M.A.K. 1977b. "Ideas about Language". M.A.K. Halliday *Aims and Perspectives in Linguistics*, 32-49. Applied Linguistics Association of Australia (*Occasional papers 1*).

Halliday, M.A.K. 1978a. *Language as a Social Semiotic: the social interpretation of language and meaning*. London: Edward Arnold.

Halliday, M.A.K. 1978b. "Commentary". M.A.K. Halliday & M. Poole *Notes on "Talking Shop: demands on language"*, 23-35. Sydney: Film Australia.

Halliday, M.A.K. 1979. "Modes of Meaning and Modes of Expression: types of grammatical structure, and their determination by different semantic functions". D.J. Allerton, E. Carney & D. Holcroft [eds] *Function and Context in Linguistics Analysis: essays offered to William Haas*, 57-79. Cambridge: Cambridge University Press.

Halliday, M.A.K. 1981a. "Text Semantics and Clause Grammar: some patterns of realisation". J.E. Copeland & P.W. Davis [eds] *The Seventh LACUS Forum*, 31-59. Columbia, S.C.: Hornbeam Press.

Halliday, M.A.K. 1981b. "Types of Structure". Halliday & Martin, 1981, 29-41.

Halliday, M.A.K. 1982a. "The De-Automatization of Grammar: from Priestley's 'An Inspector Calls'". J.M. Anderson [ed.] *Language Form and Linguistic Variation: papers dedicated to Angus McIntosh*, 129-159. Amsterdam: Benjamins.

Halliday, M.A.K. 1982b. "How is a Text like a Clause?" S. Allen [ed.] *Text Processing: text analysis and generation, text typology and attribution*, 209-247. Stockholm: Almqvist & Wiksell International.

Halliday, M.A.K. 1984a. "Language as Code and Language as Behaviour: a systemic-functional interpretation of the nature and ontogenesis of dialogue". R. Fawcett, M.A.K. Halliday, S.M. Lamb & A. Makkai [eds] *The Semiotics of Language and Culture, Vol. 1: Language as Social Semiotic*, 3-35. London: Pinter.

Halliday, M.A.K. 1984b. "On the Ineffability of Grammatical Categories". A. Manning, P. Martin & K. McCalla [eds] *The Tenth LACUS Forum 1983*, 3-18. Columbia, SC: Hornbeam Press. [reprinted in J.D. Benson, M.J. Cummings & W.S. Greaves [eds] 1988. *Linguistics in a Systemic Perspective*, 27-52. Amsterdam: Benjamins (= *Current Issues in Linguistics Theory* 39)].

Halliday, M.A.K. 1984c. "Linguistics in the University: the question of social accountability". J.E. Copeland [ed.] *New Directions in Linguistics and Semiotics*, 51-67. Houston: Rice University (*Rice University Studies*).

Halliday, M.A.K. 1985a. *An Introduction to Functional Grammar*. London: Edward Arnold.

Halliday, M.A.K. 1985b. *Spoken and Written Language*. Geelong, Vic.: Deakin University Press [republished by Oxford University Press 1989]

Halliday, M.A.K. 1985c. "Context of Situation". Halliday & Hasan, 1980/1985, 3-14.

Halliday, M.A.K. 1985d. "Dimensions of Discourse Analysis: grammar". T.A. van Dijk [ed.] *Handbook of Discourse Analysis, Vol. 2: dimensions of discourse*, 29-56. London: Academic Press.

Halliday, M.A.K. 1985e. "Systemic Background". J.D. Benson & W.S. Greaves [eds] *Systemic Perspectives on Discourse, Vol. 1: selected theoretical papers from the 9th International Systemic Workshop*, 1-15. Norwood, N.J.: Ablex.

Halliday, M.A.K. 1987a. "Language and the Order of Nature". N. Fabb, D. Attridge, A. Durant & C. MacCabe [eds] *The Linguistics of Writing: arguments between language and literature*, 135-154. Manchester: Manchester University Press.

Halliday, M.A.K. 1987b. "Spoken and Written Modes of Meaning". R. Horowitz & S.J. Samuels [eds] *Comprehending Oral and Written Language*, 55-82. New York: Academic Press.

Halliday, M.A.K. 1988a. "Language and Socialisation: home and school". L. Gerot, J. Oldenburg & T. van Leeuwen [eds] *Language and Socialisation: home and school*, 1-12. (*Proceedings from the Working Conference on Language in Education, Macquarie University 17-21 November 1986*). Sydney: Macquarie Unversity.

Halliday, M.A.K. 1988b. "On the Language of Physical Science". M. Ghadessy [ed.] *Registers of Written English: situational factors and linguistic features*, 162-178. London: Pinter (*Open Linguistics Series*).

Halliday, M.A.K. 1989. "Some Grammatical Problems in Scientific English". *Australian Review of Applied Linguistics* Series S, No. 6. 13-37.

Halliday, M.A.K. 1990. "New Ways of Meaning: a challenge to applied linguistics". *Journal of Applied Linguistics* (Greek Applied Linguistics Association) 6. 7-36. [*Ninth World Congress of Applied Linguistics Special Issue*].

Halliday, M.A.K. 1991a. "Linguistic Perspectives on Literacy: a systemic-functional approach". F. Christie, 1991.

Halliday, M.A.K. 1991b. "Towards Probabilistic Interpretations." E. Ventola [ed.] *Recent Systemic and other Functional Views on Language*, 35-62. Berlin: de Gruyter (*Trends in Linguistics: studies and monographs*).

Halliday, M.A.K. 1992. "Some Lexicogrammatical Features of the Zero Population Growth Text". W. Mann & S.A. Thompson [eds] *Discourse Description: diverse analyses of a fund-raising text*, 327-358. Amsterdam: Benjamins.

Halliday, M.A.K. in press a. "The Construction of Knowledge and Value in the Grammar of Scientific Discourse: with reference to Charles Darwin's *The Origin of the Species*". M. Gotti [ed.] *Atti del XI Congresso Nazionale dell'Associazione Italiana di Anglistica, Bergamo, 24 e 25 Ottobre 1988*.

Halliday, M.A.K. in press b. "So You Say 'Pass'..Thank You Three Muchly". A.D. Grimshaw [ed.] *What's Going on Here: complementary studies of professional talk*. Norwood: Ablex.

Halliday, M.A.K. in press c. "The Analysis of Scientific Texts in English and Chinese". H. Bluhme & Hao Keqi [eds] *Proceedings of the International Conference on Text and Language, Xi'an Jiaotong University, Xi'an, China, 29-31 March 1989*.

Halliday, M.A.K. in press d. "The History of a Sentence: an essay in social semiotics". R.M.B. Bosinelli [ed.] *Language Systems and Cultural Systems: Proceedings of the International Symposium on Bologna, Italian Culture and Modern Literature, University of Bologna, October 1988*.

Halliday, M.A.K. & R. Hasan. 1976. *Cohesion in English*. London: Longman (= *English Language Series* 9).

Halliday, M.A.K. & R. Hasan. 1980. *Text and Context: aspects of language in a social-semiotic perspective*. Sophia Linguistica VI. Tokyo: The Graduate School of Languages and Linguistics & the Linguistic Institute for International Communication, Sophia University. [new edition published as M.A.K. Halliday & R. Hasan 1985 *Language, Context, and Text: aspects of language in a social-semiotic perspective*. Geelong, Vic.: Deakin University Press [republished by Oxford University Press 1989]]

Halliday, M.A.K. & J.R. Martin [eds]. 1981. *Readings in Systemic Linguistics*. London: Batsford.

Halliday, M.A.K., A. McIntosh & P. Strevens. 1964. *The Linguistic Sciences and Language Teaching*. London: Longman (*Longmans' Linguistics Library*).

Harris, S. 1987. "Court Discussion as Genre: some problems and issues". Department of English, University of Nottingham. *Occasional Papers in Systemic Linguistics* 2. 35-74.

Hasan, R. 1973 "Code, Register and Social Dialect". Appendix to B. Bernstein, 1973, 253-292.

Hasan, R. 1977. "Text in the Systemic-Functional Model". W. Dressler [ed.] *Current Trends in Textlinguistics*, 228-246. Berlin: Walter de Gruyter.

Hasan, R. 1979. "On the Notion of Text". J.S. Petöfi [ed.] *Text vs Sentence: basic questions of textlinguistics*, 369-390. Hamburg: Helmut Buske (*Papers in Textlinguistics* 20(2)).

Hasan, R. 1984a. "Coherence and Cohesive Harmony". J. Flood [ed.] *Understanding Reading Comprehension: cognition, language and the structure of prose*, 181-219. Newark, Delaware: International Reading Association.

Hasan, R. 1984b. "The Nursery Tale as a Genre". *Nottingham Linguistic Circular* 13. 71-102. (*Special Issue on Systemic Linguistics*).

Hasan, R. 1984c. "Ways of Saying, Ways of Meaning". R. Fawcett, M.A.K. Halliday, S.M. Lamb & A. Makkai [eds] *The Semiotics of Culture and Language, Vol. 1: Language as Social Semiotic*, 105-162. London: Pinter.

Hasan, R. 1985a. "The Structure of a Text". Halliday & Hasan, 1980/1985, 70-96.

Hasan, R. 1985b. "The Texture of a Text". Halliday & Hasan, 1980/1985, 70-96.

Hasan, R. 1986. "The Ontogenesis of Ideology: an interpretation of mother child talk". Threadgold, Grosz, Kress & Halliday, 1986, 125-146.

Hasan, R. 1987 "The Grammarian's Dream: lexis as most delicate grammar". M.A.K. Halliday & R.P. Fawcett [eds] *New Developments in Systemic Linguistics, Vol. 1: theory an description*, 184-211. London: Pinter.

Hasan, R. 1988. "Language in the Processes of Socialisation: home and school". L. Gerot, J. Oldenburg & T. van Leeuven [eds] *Language and Socialisation: home and school*, 36-96. (*Proceedings from the Working Conference on Language in Education, Macquarie University 17-21 November 1986*). Sydney: Macquarie Unversity.

Hasan, R. 1990. "Semantic Variation and Sociolinguistics". *Australian Journal of Linguistics* 9(2). 221-276.

Hasan, R. forthcoming. "Offers in the Making: a systemic-functional approach". School of English and Linguistics, Macquarie University.

Hasan, R. & C. Cloran. 1990. "Semantic Variation: a sociolinguistic interpretation of everyday talk between mothers and children". J. Gibbons, H. Nicholas & M.A.K. Halliday [eds] *Learning, Keeping and Using Language: selected papers from the 8th World Congress of Applied Linguistics*, 67-99. Amsterdam: Benjamins.

Hasan, R. & J.R. Martin [eds] 1989. *Language Development: learning language, learning culture*. Norwood, N.J.: Ablex (*Meaning and Choice in Language: studies for Michael Halliday*).

Haviland, S.E. & H.H. Clark. 1974 "What's New? Acquiring new information as a process in comprehension". *Journal of Verbal Learning and Behaviour* 13. 512-521.

Hawkins, P. 1977. *Social Class, the Nominal Group and Verbal Strategies*. London: Routledge & Kegan Paul (*Primary Socialisation, Language and Education*).

Hill, T. 1958. "Institutional Linguistics". *Orbis* 7. 441-455.

Hjelmslev, L. 1961. *Prolegomena to a Theory of Language*. Madison, Wisconsin: University of Wisconsin Press.

Hodge, R. 1988. "Discursive Transformations and Strategies of Resistance". L. Gerot, J. Oldenburg & T. van Leeuven [eds] *Language and Socialisation: home and school*, 174-185. (*Proceedings from the Working Conference on Language in Education, Macquarie University 17-21 November 1986*). Sydney: Macquarie Unversity.

Hollenbach, Barbara. 1973. "A Preliminary Semantic Classification of Temporal Concepts". *Notes on Translation* 47. 3-8.

Hollenback, Bruce. 1975. "Discourse Structure, Interpropositional Relations and Translation". *Notes on Translation* 56. 2-21.

Hoey, M. 1983. *On the Surface of Discourse*. London: George Allen & Unwin.

Huddleston, R.D. 1984. *Introduction to the Grammar of English*. Cambridge: Cambridge University Press.

Huddleston, R. 1988. "Constituency, Multi-Functionality and Grammaticalization in Halliday's Functional Grammar". *Journal of Linguistics* 24. 137-174.

Hudson, R.A. 1967. "Constituency in a Systemic Description of the English Clause." *Lingua* 18. 225-250. [reprinted in Halliday & Martin, 1981, 101-121.]

Hudson, R.A. 1973. "An Item and Paradigm Approach to Beja Syntax and Morphology. *Foundations of Language* 9. 504-548. [reprinted in Halliday & Martin, 1981, 271-309.]

Hudson, R.A. 1974. "The English Noun Phrase: an argument for systemic grammar". University College, London. mimeo.

Hudson, R.A. 1976. *Arguments for a Non-Transformational Grammar*. Chicago, Ill.: Chicago University Press.

Hudson, R.A. 1980. *Sociolinguistics*. Cambridge: Cambridge University Press.

Hudson, R.A. 1987. "Daughter Dependency Theory and Systemic Grammar". M.A.K. Halliday & R.P. Fawcett [eds] *New Developments in Systemic Linguistics, Vol. 1: theory and description*, 246-257. London: Pinter.

Hymes, D. & J. Fought. 1975. T. Sebeok [ed.] *Current Trends in Linguistics* 13, 903-1176. The Hague: Mouton. [republished in 1981 as *American Structuralism*. The Hague: Mouton (= *Janua Linguarum, Series Maior 102*)]

Jones, J. 1988. *Grammatical Metaphor and Technicality in Academic Writing*. MA Long Essay. Department of Linguistics, University of Sydney.

Jones, S. & J. McH. Sinclair. 1974. "English Lexical Collocations". *Cahiers de lexicologie* 24. 15-61.

Kasper, R. 1988. "Systemic Grammar and Functional Unification Grammar". J.D. Benson & W.S. Greaves. [eds] *Systemic Functional Approaches to Discourse*, 176-199. Norwood, N.J.: Ablex.

Katz, J.J. & J.A. Fodor. 1963. "The Structure of a Semantic Theory". *Language* 39. 170-210.

Keenan, E.L. 1971. "Two Kinds of Presupposition in Natural Language. C.J. Fillmore & D.T. Langendoen [eds] *Studies in Linguistic Semantics*. New York: Holt, Rinehart & Winston.

Kress, G. 1977. "Tense as Modality". *University of East Anglia Papers in Linguistics* 5. 40-52.

Kress, G. 1985. *Linguistic Processes in Socio-cultural Practice*. Geelong, Vic.: Deakin University Press [republished by Oxford University Press 1989]

Kress, G. [ed.] 1988. *Communication and Culture: an introduction*. Sydney: New South Wales University Press.

Kress, G. & R. Fowler. 1979 "Interviews". Fowler, Hodge, Kress & Trew, 1979, 63-80.

Kress, G. & B. Hodge. 1979. *Language as Ideology*. London: Routledge & Kegan Paul.

Kress, G. & R. Hodge. 1988. *Social Semiotics*. London: Polity.

Kress, G. & T. Threadgold. 1988. "Towards a Social Theory of Genre". *Southern Review* 21(3). 215-243.

Labov, W. 1969. "The Logic of Non-Standard English". *Georgetown Monographs on Language and Linguistics* 22. Washington, D.C.: Georgetown University Press [repinted in Labov, 1972b, 201-240]

Labov, W. 1972a. "The Study of Language in its Social Context". P.P. Giglioli [ed.] *Language and Social Context*, 283-307. Harmondsworth: Penguin.

Labov, W. 1972b. "The Transformation of Experience in Narrative Syntax". *Language in the Inner City*, 354-396. Philadelphia: Pennsylvania University Press.

Labov, W. 1972c. "Letter to The Atlantic". *The Atlantic* 230. 5-45. November.

Labov, W. 1978. "Where Does the Linguistic Variable Stop? A response to Beatrix Lavendera". *Sociolinguistic Working Paper* 44. Austin: Southwest Educational Development Laboratory.

Labov, W. 1982. "Speech Actions and Reactions in Personal Narrative". D. Tannen [ed.] *Analysing Discourse: text and talk* (*Georgetown University Round Table on Language and Linguistics 1981*). Washington, D.C.: Georgetown University Press.

Labov, W. & D. Fanshel 1977. *Therapeutic Discourse: psychotherapy as conversation.* New York: Academic Press.

Labov, W. & J. Waletzky 1967. "Narrative Analysis". J. Helm [ed.] *Essays on the Verbal and Visual Arts*, 12-44. (*Proceedings of the 1966 Spring Meeting of the American Ethnological Society*). Seattle: University of Washington Press.

Lamb, S.M. 1964. "The Sememic Approach to Structural Semantics". *American Anthropologist* 66(3). 57-78.

Lamb, S.M. 1969. "Lexicology and Semantics". A.A. Hill [ed.] *Linguistics Today*, 40-49. New York: Basic Books.

Lavendera, B. 1978. "Where Does the Sociolinguistic Variable Stop?" *Language in Society* 7. 171-183.

van Leeuven, T. 1982. *Professional Speech: accentual and junctural style in radio announcing.* MA Hons Thesis. School of English and Linguistics, Macquarie University.

Lehrer, A. 1974. *Semantic Fields and Lexical Structure.* Amsterdam: North Holland.

Lemke, J. 1984. *Semiotics and Education.* Toronto: Toronto Semiotic Circle (= *Monographs, Working Papers and Publications* 2).

Lemke, J.L. 1985. "Ideology, Intertextuality and the Notion of Register". J.D. Benson & W.S. Greaves. [eds] *Systemic Perspectives on Discourse, Vol. 1: selected theoretical papers from the 9th International Systemic Workshop*, 275-294. Norwood, N.J.: Ablex.

Lemke, J.L. 1988a. "Discourses in Conflict: heteroglossia and text semantics". J.D. Benson & W.S. Greaves [eds] *Systemic Functional Approaches to Discourse*, 29-50. Norwood, N.J.: Ablex.

Lemke, J.L. 1988b. "Text Structure and Text Semantics". E. Steiner & R. Veltman [eds] *Pragmatics, Discourse and Text: explorations in systemic semantics*, 158-170. London: Pinter.

Lemke, J.L. 1988c. "Genres, Semantics and Classroom Education". *Linguistics and Education* 1(1). 81-100.

Lemke, J.L. 1989a. "Semantics and Social Values". *Word* 40(1-2). 37-50. (*Systems, Structure and Discourse: selected papers from the Fifteenth International Systemic Congress*).

Lemke, J.L. 1989b. "Social Semiotics: a new model for literacy education". D. Bloome [ed.] *Learning to Use Literacy in Educational Settings*, 289-309. Norwood, N.J.: Ablex.

Lemke, J.L. 1990. "Technical Discourse and Technocratic Ideology". J. Gibbons, H. Nicholas & M.A.K. Halliday [eds] *Learning, Keeping and Using Language: Selected papers from the 8th World Congress on Applied Linguistics*, 435-460. Amsterdam: Benjamins.

Lemke, J.L. 1991. "Text Production and Dynamic Text Semantics". E. Ventola [ed.] *Recent Systemic and other Functional Views on Language*, 23-38. Berlin: de Gruyter (*Trends in Linguistics: studies and monographs*).

Lemke, J.L. forthcoming a. "The Topology of Genre: text structure and text types".

Lemke, J.L. forthcoming b. "Ideology, Intertextuality and the Communication of Science". M. Gregory [ed.] *Relations and Functions within and around Language*. Norwood, N.J.: Ablex.

Lemke, J.L. forthcoming c. "Intertextuality and Text Semantics". M. Gregory & P. Fries [eds] *Discourse and Society: functional perspectives*. Norwood, N.J.: Ablex.

Lemke, J.L. forthcoming d. "Heteroglossia and Social Theory". New York Bakhtin Circle [eds] *M.M. Bakhtin: radical perspectives*. Minneapolis: University of Minnesota Press.

Levinson, S.C. 1983. *Pragmatics*. London: Cambridge University Press (*Cambridge Textbooks in Linguistics*).

Lockwood, D.G. 1972. *Introduction to Stratificational Linguistics*. New York: Harcourt, Brace, Jovanovich.

Longacre, R.E. 1974. "Narrative vs Other Discourse Genre". R. Brend [ed.] *Advances in Tagmemics*. Amsterdam: North-Holland.

Longacre, R.E. 1976. *An Anatomy of Speech Notions*. Lisse: Peter de Ridder.

Longacre, R.E. 1979. "The Paragraph as a Grammatical Unit". T. Givón [ed.] *Syntax & Semantics, Vol. 12: discourse and syntax*. New York: Academic Press.

Longacre, R.E. 1983. *The Grammar of Discourse*. New York: Plenum.

Lyons, J. 1977. *Semantics, Vol. 1*. Cambridge: Cambridge University Press.

Mak, S. 1984. *The Language of Buying and Selling in Hong Kong: a linguistic study of service encounters in Cantonese*. MA Thesis. Department of Linguistics, University of Sydney.

Makkai, A. & D. Lockwood. 1973. *Readings in Stratificational Linguistics*. University, Al: Alabama University Press.

Malcolm, K. 1985. "Communication Linguistics: a sample analysis". J.D. Benson & W.S. Greaves [eds] *Systemic Perspectives on Discourse, Vol. 1: selected theoretical papers from the 9th International Systemic Workshop*, 136-151. Norwood, NJ: Ablex.

Malcolm, K. 1987. "Alternative Approaches to Casual Conversation in Linguistic Description". *Occasional Papers in Systemic Linguistics* 1. 111-134. Department of English, University of Nottingham.

Malinowski, B. 1923. "The Problem of Meaning in Primitive Languages". Supplement I to C.K. Ogden & I.A. Richards *The Meaning of Meaning*, 296-336. New York: Harcourt Brace & World.

Malinowski, B. 1935. *Coral Gardens and their Magic, Vol. 2*. London: Allen & Unwin.

Mann, W.C. 1984. *Discourse Structure for Text Generation*. Marina del Rey, Ca.: Information Sciences Institute [*ISI Research Report ISI/RR-84-127*].

Mann, W.C. & C.M.I.M. Matthiessen 1985. "A Demonstration of the Nigel Text Generation Computer Program". J.D. Benson & W.S. Greaves [eds] *Systemic Perspectives on Discourse, Vol. 1: selected theoretical papers from the 9th International Systemic Workshop*, 50-83. Norwood, N.J.: Ablex.

Mann, W.C. & S.A. Thompson. 1985. "Assertions from Discourse Structure. *Proceedings of the Eleventh Annual Meeting of the Berkeley Linguistics Society*. Berkeley: Berkeley Linguistics Society.

Mann, W.C. & S.A. Thompson. 1986. "Relational Propositions in Discourse". *Discourse Processes* 9(1). 57-90.

Mann, W.C. & S.A. Thompson. forthcoming a. "Rhetorical Structure Theory: a theory of text organisation and its implications for clause combining". L. Polyani [ed.] *Discourse Structure*. Norwood, N.J.: Ablex.

Mann, W.C. & S.A. Thompson. forthcoming b. "Rhetorical Structure Theory: description and construction of text structures". [presented at the Third International Workshop on Text Generation, Nijmegen, Netherlands]

Martin, J.R. 1979. "Coherence in Student Composition". M.A.K. Halliday [ed.] *Working Conference on Language in Education: report to participants*, 14-31. Sydney: Sydney University Extension Programme & Department of Linguistics.

Martin, J.R. 1981. "CONJUNCTION and CONTINUITY in Tagalog". Halliday & Martin, 1981, 310-336. London: Batsford.

Martin, J.R. 1983a. "Participant Identification in English, Tagalog and Kâte". *Australian Journal of Linguistics* 3(1). 45-74.

Martin, J.R. 1983b. "CONJUNCTION: the logic of English text". J.S. Petöfi & E. Sözer [eds] *Micro and Macro Connexity of Texts*, 1-72. Hamburg: Helmut Buske Verlag (= *Papers in Textlinguistics* 45).

Martin, J.R. 1983c. "The Development of Register". J. Fine & R.O. Freedle [eds] *Developmental Issues in Discourse*, 1-39. Norwood, N.J.: Ablex (*Advances in Discourse Processes* 10).

Martin, J.R. 1984a. "Functional Components in a Grammar: a review of deployable recognition criteria". *Nottingham Linguistic Circular* 13. 35-70.

Martin, J.R. 1984b. "Language, Register and Genre". F. Christie [ed.] *Children Writing: reader*, 21-29. Geelong, Vic.: Deakin University Press.

Martin, J.R. 1984c. "Types of Writing in Infants and Primary School". L. Unsworth [ed.] *Reading, Writing, Spelling*, 34-55. (*Proceedings of the Fifth Macarthur Reading/ Language Symposium.*) Sydney: Macarthur Institute of Higher Education.

Martin, J.R. 1985a. "Process and Text: two aspects of semiosis". J.D. Benson & W.S. Greaves [eds] *Systemic Perspectives on Discourse, Vol. 1: selected theoretical papers from the 9th International Systemic Workshop*, 248-274. Norwood, N.J.: Ablex.

Martin, J.R. 1985b. *Factual Writing: exploring and challenging social reality*. Geelong, Vic.: Deakin University Press [republished by Oxford University Press. 1989]

Martin, J.R. 1985c. "The Language of Madness: method or disorder?" *Language and the Inner Life*, 4-35. Canberra: Faculty Military Studies, Duntroon (*Department of English, Occasional Papers* 4).

Martin, J.R. 1986a. "Grammaticalising Ecology: the politics of baby seals and kangaroos". Threadgold, Grosz, Kress & Halliday, 1986, 225-268.

Martin, J.R. 1986b. "Intervening in the Process of Writing Development". Painter & Martin, 1986, 11-43.

Martin, J.R. 1987. "The Meaning of Features in Systemic Linguistics". M.A.K. Halliday & R.P. Fawcett [eds] *New Developments in Systemic Linguistics, Vol. 1: theory and description*, 14-40. London: Pinter.

Martin, J.R. 1988a. "Hypotactic Recursive Systems in English: toward a functional interpretation". J.D. Benson & W.S. Greaves [eds] *Systemic Functional Approaches to Discourse*, 240-270. Norwood, N.J.: Ablex.

Martin, J.R. 1988b. "Grammatical Conspiracies in Tagalog: family, face and fate — with regard to Benjamin Lee Whorf". J.D. Benson, M.J. Cummings & W.S. Greaves [eds] *Linguistics in a Systemic Perspective*, 243-300. Amsterdam: Benjamins (= *Current Issues in Linguistic Theory* 39).

Martin, J.R. 1989. "Technicality and Abstraction: language for the creation of specialised texts". F. Christie [ed.] *Writing in Schools: reader*, 36-44. Geelong, Vic.: Deakin University Press.

Martin, J.R. 1990a. "Language and Control: fighting with words". C. Walton & W. Eggington [eds] *Language: maintenance, power and education in Australian Aboriginal contexts*, 12-43. Darwin, N.T.: Northern Territory University Press.

Martin, J.R. 1990b. "Literacy in Science: learning to handle text as technology". F. Christie [ed.] *Fresh Look at the Basics: literacy for a changing world*, 79-117. Melbourne: Australian Council for Educational Research.

Martin, J.R. 1991a. "Intrinsic Functionality: implications for contextual theory." *Social Semiotics* 1(1). 99-162.

Martin, J.R. 1991b. "Nominalisation in Science and Humanities: distilling knowledge and scaffolding text". E. Ventola [ed.] *Recent Systemic and other Functional Views on Language*, 307-338. Berlin: de Gruyter (*Trends in Linguistics: studies and monographs*).

Martin, J.R. 1992. "Macroproposals: meaning by degree". W.A. Mann & S.A. Thompson [eds] *Discourse Description: diverse analyses of a fund raising text*, 359-395. Amsterdam: Benjamins.

Martin, J.R. in press a. "Theme, Method of Development and Existentiality — the price of reply". *Occasional Papers in Systemic Linguistics* 6. [Department of English Studies, University of Nottingham]

Martin, J.R. in press b. "Life as a Noun: arresting the universe in science and humanities. M.A.K. Halliday & J.R. Martin [eds] *Writing Science: literacy as discursive power*. London: Falmer.

Martin, J.R., F. Christie & J. Rothery. n.d. "Social Processes in Education: a reply to Sawyer and Watson (and others)". I. Reid [ed.] *The Place of Genre in Learning: current debates*, 46-57. Geelong, Vic.: Centre for Studies in Literary Education (Typereader Publications 1). [more fully published in *The Teaching of English: Journal of the English Teachers' Association of New South Wales* 53. 1987. 3-22]

Martin, J.R. & C.M.I.M. Matthiessen. 1991. "Systemic Typology and Topology". Christie, 1991.

Martin, J.R. & P. Peters. 1985. "On the Analysis of Exposition". R. Hasan [ed.] *Discourse on Discourse* (*Workshop Reports from the Macquarie Workshop on Discourse Analysis*), 61-92. Applied Linguistics Association of Australia (= *Occasional Papers* 7).

Martin, J.R., P. Wignell, S. Eggins & J. Rothery. 1988. "Secret English: discourse technology in a junior secondary school". L. Gerot, J. Oldenburg & T. van Leeuven [eds] *Language and Socialisation: home and school* (*Proceedings from the Working*

Conference on Language in Education, Macquarie University 17-21 November 1986), 143-173. Sydney: Macquarie University.

Mathesius, V. 1964. On the Potentiality of the Phenomena of Language". J. Vachek [ed.] *A Prague School Reader in Linguistics*. Bloomington, Ind.; Indiana University Press.

Matthiessen, C.M.I.M. 1985. "The Systemic Framework for Text Generation". J.D. Benson & W.S. Greaves [eds] *Systemic Perspectives on Discourse, Vol. 1: selected theoretical papers from the 9th International Systemic Workshop*, 96-118. Norwood, N.J.: Ablex.

Matthiessen, C.M.I.M. 1988a. "Representational Issues in Systemic Functional Grammar". J.D. Benson & W.S. Greaves [eds] *Systemic Functional Approaches to Discourse*, 136-175. Norwood, N.J.: Ablex.

Matthiessen, C.M.I.M. 1988b. "Semantics for a Systemic Grammar: the chooser and inquiry framework". J.D. Benson, M.J. Cummings & W.S. Greaves [eds] *Linguistics in a Systemic Perspective*, 221-242. Amsterdam: Benjamins (= *Current Issues in Linguistic Theory* 39).

Matthiessen, C.M.I.M. 1989. "Review of M.A.K. Halliday's Introduction to Functional Grammar". *Language* 65(4). 862-871.

Matthiessen, C.M.I.M. 1992. *Lexicogrammatical Cartography: English systems*. Department of Linguistics, University of Sydney: Mimeo.

Matthiessen, C.M.I.M. forthcoming a. "Lexico(grammatical) Choice in Text Generation". Draft of paper presented at Fourth International Workshop on Language Generation, July 1988.

Matthiessen, C.M.I.M. forthcoming b. "Organising Text: rhetorical schemas and generic structure potential".

Matthiessen, C.M.I.M. & J. Bateman. 1991. *Text Generation and Systemic Linguistics: experiences from English and Japanese*. London: Pinter.

Matthiessen, C.M.I.M. & M.A.K. Halliday. in press. "Systemic Functional Grammar". J. Ney & F. Peng [eds] *Current Approaches to Syntax*. London & Amsterdam: Whurr & Benjamins.

Matthiessen, C.M.I.M. & J.R. Martin. 1991. "A response to Huddleston's Review of Halliday's Introduction to Functional Grammar". *Occasional Papers in Systemic Linguistics* 5. 5-74.

Matthiessen, C.M.I.M. & S.A. Thompson. 1988. "The Structure of Discourse and Subordination". J. Haiman & S.A. Thompson [eds] *Clause Combining in Grammar and Discourse*, 275-329. Amsterdam: Benjamins.

Mayer, M. 1974. *Frog, where are you?* London: Collins.

McIntosh, A. 1961. "Patterns and ranges". *Language* 37. 325-337 [reprinted in A. McIntosh & M.A.K. Halliday. 1966 *Patterns of Language: papers in general, descriptive and applied linguistics*, 183-199. London: Longman]

McIntosh, A. 1963. "'As You Like It': a grammatical clue to character". *A Review of English Literature* 4(2). 68-81. [reprinted in A. McIntosh & M.A.K. Halliday. 1966 *Patterns of Language: papers in general, descriptive and applied linguistics*, 70-82. London: Longman]

Mitchell, T.F. 1957. "The Language of Buying and Selling in Cyrenaica: a situational statement". Hesperis 26. 31-71 [reprinted in T.F. Mitchell. 1975. *Principles of Neo-Firthian Linguistics*, 167-200. London: Longman]

Mock, C.C. 1985. "A Systemic Phonology of Isthmus Zapotec". J.D. Benson & W.S. Greaves [eds] *Systemic Perspectives on Discourse, Vol. 1: selected theoretical papers from the 9th International Systemic Workshop*, 349-372. Norwood, N.J.: Ablex.

Monaghan, J. 1979. *The Neo-Firthian Tradition and its Contribution to General Linguistics*. Tubingen: Max Niemeyer.

Morgan, J.L. & M.B. Sellner. 1980. "Discourse and Linguistic Theory". R.J. Spiro, B.C. Bruce & W.F. Brewer. [eds] *Theoretical Issues in Reading Comprehension*, 165-200. New Jersey: Lawrence Erlbaum.

Nesbitt, C. & G. Plum. 1988. "Probabilities in a Systemic-Functional Grammar: the clause complex in English". R.P. Fawcett & D. Young [eds] *New Developments in Systemic Linguistics, Vol. 2: theory and application*, 6-38. London: Pinter.

Newmeyer, F.J. 1980. *Linguistic Theory in America: the first quarter-century of tranformational generative grammar*. New York: Academic Press.

Newmeyer, F.J. 1986. *The Politics of Linguistics*. Chicago: University of Chicago Press.

O'Donnell, M. n.d. "A Dynamic Model of Exchange". Department of Linguistics, University of Sydney.

Painter, C. 1984. *Into the Mother Tongue: a case study of early language development*. London: Pinter.

Painter, C. & J.R. Martin. [eds] 1986. *Writing to Mean: teaching genres across the curriculum*. Applied Linguistics Association of Australia (= *Occasional Papers* 9).

Palmer, F.R. 1964. "Sequence and Order". C.I.M. Stuart [ed.] *Report of the 15th Annual (First International) Round Table Meeting on Linguistics and Language Studies* (= *Monograph Series on Languages and Linguistics* 17), 123-130. Washington, D.C.: Georgetown University Press.

Palmer, F.R. [ed.] 1968. *Selected Papers of J.R. Firth 1952-1959*. London: Longman.

Palmer, F.R. 1970. [ed.] *Prosodic Analysis*. London: Oxford (*Language and Language Learning*).

Parsons, G. 1990. *Cohesion and Coherence: scientific texts - a comparative study*. Department of English Studies, University of Nottingham (*Monographs in Systemic Linguistics* 1).

Peters, P. 1985. *Strategies for Student Writers: a guide to writing essays, tutorial papers, exam papers and reports*. Milton, Qld.: John Wiley and Sons.

Pike, K.L. 1967. *Language in Relation to a Unified Theory of the Structure of Human Behaviour [2nd edition]*. The Hague: Mouton.

Pike, K.L. 1982. *Linguistic Concepts: an introduction to tagmemics*. Lincoln: University of Nebraska Press.

Pike, K.L. & E.G. Pike. 1983. *Text and Tagmeme*. London: Pinter.

Plum, G. 1988. *Textual and Contextual Conditioning in Spoken English: a genre-based approach*. Ph.D Thesis. Department of Linguistics, University of Sydney.

Plum, G. & A. Cowling. 1987. "Some Constraints on Grammatical Variables: tense choice in English". R. Steele & T. Threadgold [eds] *Language Topics: essays in honour of Michael Halliday, Vol. 2*, 281-305. Amsterdam: Benjamins.

Poynton, C. 1984. "Names as Vocatives: forms and functions". *Nottingham Linguistic Circular* 13 (*Special Issue on Systemic Linguistics*), 1-34.

Poynton, C. 1985. *Language and Gender: making the difference*. Geelong, Vic.: Deakin University Press [republished: Oxford University Press. 1989]

Poynton, C. 1990a. *Address and the Semiotics of Social Relations: a systemic-functional account of address forms and practices in Australian English*. PhD Thesis. Department of Linguistics, University of Sydney.

Poynton, C. 1990b. "The Privileging of Representation and the Marginalising of the Interpersonal: a metaphor (and more) for contemporary gender relations". T. Threadgold & A. Cranny-Francis [eds] *Feminine/Masculine and Representation*, 231-255. Sydney: Allen & Unwin.

Prakašam, V. 1987. "Aspects of Word Phonology". M.A.K. Halliday & R.P. Fawcett [eds] *New Developments in Systemic Linguistics, Vol. 1: theory an description* 272-286. London: Pinter.

Prigatano, G.P., J.R. Roueche & D.J. Fordyce. undated. "Nonaphasic Language Disturbances after Closed Head Injury". Presbyterian Hospital and Neurosurgery Section, University of Oklahoma. mimeo.

Propp, V. 1968. *The Morphology of the Folktale*. Austin: University of Texas Press.

Ravelli, L. 1985. *Metaphor, Mode and Complexity: an exploration of co-varying patterns*. BA Hons Thesis. Department of Linguistics, University of Sydney.

Reddy, M.J. 1979. "The Conduit Metaphor: a case of frame conflict in our language about language". A. Ortony [ed.] *Metaphor and Thought*, 284-324. Cambridge: Cambridge University Press.

Reed, A. 1977. "CLOC: a collocation package". *ALLC Bulletin* 5. 168-173.

Reed, A. 1984. "Anatomy of a Text Analysis Package". *Computer Language* 9(2). 89-96.

Reid, T.B.W. 1956. "Linguistics, Structuralism, Philology". *Archivum Linguisticum* 8. 28-37.

Robbins, M. 1989. "Police Hooliganism Clouds the North's Sunshine Image". *The Weekend Australian*. March 25-26 1989. 24.

Rochester, S.R. & J.R. Martin. 1977. "The Art of Referring: the speaker's use of noun phrases to instruct the listener". R. Freedle [ed.] *Discourse Comprehension and Production*, 245-270. Norwood, N.J.: Ablex.

Rochester, S. & J.R. Martin. 1979. *Crazy Talk: a study of the discourse of schizophrenic speakers*. New York: Plenum.

Rothery, J. 1990. *Story Writing in Primary School: assessing narrative type genres*. Ph.D. Thesis. Department of Linguistics, University of Sydney.

Romaine, S. 1981. "On the Problem of Syntactic Variation: a reply to Beatrix Lavendera and William Labov". *Sociolinguistic Working Paper* 82. Austin: Southwest Educational Development Laboratory.

Sale, C., B. Friedman, & G. Wilson. 1980. *Our Changing World, Book 1: the vanishing natural ecosystem*. Melbourne: Longman Cheshire.

Schegloff, E.A. & H. Sacks. 1973. "Opening up Closings". *Semiotica* 7(4). 289-327 [reprinted in R. Turner 1974 *Ethnomethodology: selected readings*. Harmondsworth: Penguin]

Shea, N. 1988. *The Language of Junior Secondary Science Textbooks*. BA Honours Thesis. Department of Linguistics, University of Sydney.

Simmelhaig, H. & G.F.R. Spenceley. 1984. *For Australia's Sake*. Melbourne: Nelson.

Sinclair, J. McH. 1966. "Beginning the Study of Lexis". C.E. Bazell, J.C. Catford & M.A.K. Halliday [eds] *In Memory of J.R. Firth*, 410-430. London: Longman.

Sinclair, J. McH. 1987. "Collocation: a progress report". R. Steele & T. Threadgold [eds] *Language Topics: essays in honour of Michael Halliday, Vol. 2*, 319-332. Amsterdam: Benjamins.

Sinclair, J. McH. 1988. "Sense and Structure in Lexis". J.D. Benson, M.J. Cummings & W.S. Greaves [eds] *Linguistics in a Systemic Perspective*, 73-87. Amsterdam: Benjamins (= *Current Issues in Linguistic Theory* 39).

Sinclair, J. McH. & R.M. Coulthard 1975. *Towards an Analysis of Discourse: the English used by teachers and pupils*. London: Oxford University Press.

Sinclair, J. McH., S. Jones & R. Daley. 1970. *English Lexical Studies (Report to OSTI on Project C/LP/08)* Department of English, University of Birmingham.

Solomon, C. 1977. *The Complete Asian Cookbook*. Sydney: Lansdowne Press.

Spencer, J. & M.J. Gregory 1964. "An Approach to the Study of Style". N.E. Enkvist, J. Spencer & M.J. Gregory. *Linguistics and Style*, 57-105. London: Oxford (*Language and Language Learning*).

Starosta, S. 1988. *The Case for Lexicase*. London:Pinter.

Steiner, E. 1985. "The Concept of Context and the Theory of Action". Chilton, 1985, 215-230.

Steiner, E. & R. Veltman [eds] 1988. *Pragmatics, Discourse and Text: explorations in systemic semantics*. London: Pinter.

Stennes, L.H. 1969. *The Identification of Participants in Adamawa Fulani (= Hartford Studies in Linguistics* 24) Hartford, Conn.: Hartford Seminary Foundation.

Stockwell, R.P. 1980. "Summation and Assessment of Theories". E.A. Moravcsik & J.R. Wirth [eds] *Current Approaches to Syntax (Syntax and Semantics* 13) New York: Academic Press.

Taber, C.R. 1966. *The Structure of Sango Narrative (= Hartford Studies in Linguistics* 17) Hartford, Conn.: Hartford Seminary Foundation.

Talking Shop: demands on language. 1978. Sydney: Film Australia.

Thibault, P. 1987. "An Interview with Michael Halliday". R. Steele & T. Threadgold [eds] *Language Topics: essays in honour of Michael Halliday, Vol. 2*, 599-627. Amsterdam: Benjamins.

Thibault, P. 1989. "Genres, Social Actiona and Pedagogy: towards a critical social semiotic account". *Southern Review* 22(3). 338-362.

Thibault, P. 1991. *Social Semiotics as Praxis: text, social meaning making and Nabakov's "Ada"*. Minneapolis: University of Minnesota Press (*Theory and History of Literature* 74).

Thompson, J.B. 1984. *Studies in the Theory of Ideology*. Cambridge: Polity.

Thompson, S.A. 1985. "Grammar and Written Discourse: initial vs. final purpose clauses in English". *Text* 5(1-2). 55-84.

Threadgold, T. 1986a. "The semiotics of Halliday, Voloshinov and Eco". *American Journal of Semiotics*. 43(4). 107-142

Threadgold, T. 1986b. "Semiotics, ideology, language". Threadgold, Grosz, Kress & Halliday, 1986, 15-59.

Threadgold, T. 1988. "The Genre Debate". *Southern Review* 21(3). 315-330.

Threadgold, T., E.A. Grosz, G. Kress & M.A.K. Halliday [eds] 1986. *Language, Semiotics, Ideology*. Sydney: Sydney Association for Studies in Society and Culture (= *Sydney Studies in Society and Culture* 3).

Todorov, T. 1984. *Mikhail Bakhtin: the dialogical principle*. Manchester: Manchester University Press (= *Theory and History of Literature* 13).

Toolan, M.J. 1988. *Narrative: a critical linguistic introduction*. London: Routledge (*Interface Series*).

Traugott, E.C. 1978. "On the Expression of Spatio-Temporal Relations in Language". J.H. Greenberg, C.A. Ferguson & E. Moravcsik [eds] *Universals of Human Language III: word formation*. Stanford: Stanford University Press.

Traugott, E.C. 1982. "From Propositional to Textual and Expressive Meanings: some semantic-pragmatic aspects of grammaticalisation". W.P. Lehmann & Y. Malkiel [eds]. *Perspectives on Historical Linguistics*. Amsterdam: Benjamins.

Trew, T. 1979a. "'What the Papers Say': linguistic variation and ideological difference". Fowler, Hodge, Kress & Trew, 1979, 117-156.

Trew, T. 1979b. "Theory and Ideology at Work". Fowler, Hodge, Kress & Trew, 1979, 94-116.

Turner, G.J. 1973. "Class and Children's Language of Control". Bernstein, 1973, 135-201.

Turner, G.J. 1985. "Discourse Structures: social class differences in answers to questions". J.D. Benson & W.S. Greaves [eds] *Systemic Perspectives on Discourse, Vol. 2: selected applied papers from the 9th International Systemic Workshop*, 258-281. Norwood, N.J.: Ablex.

Turner, G.J. 1987. "Sociosemantic Networks and Discourse Structure". M.A.K. Halliday & R.P. Fawcett [eds] *New Developments in Systemic Linguistics, Vol. 1: theory and description*, 64-93. London: Pinter.

Ure, J. 1971. "Lexical Density and Register Differentiation". G.E. Perren & J.L.M. Trimm [eds] *Applications of Linguistics: selected papers of the 2nd International Congress of Applied Linguists, Cambridge 1969*, 443-452. Cambridge: Cambridge University Press.

Ure, J. & J. Ellis. 1977. "Register in Descriptive Linguistics and Linguistic Sociology". O. Uribe-Villas [ed.] *Issues in Sociolinguistics*, 197-243. The Hague: Mouton.

Ventola, E. 1979. "The Structure of Casual Conversations in English". *Journal of Pragmatics* 3. 267-298.

Ventola, E. 1983. "Contrasting Schematic Structures in Service Encounters". *Applied Linguistics* 4(3). 242-258.

Ventola, E. 1984. "The Dynamics of Genre". *Nottingham Linguistic Circular* 13 (*Special Issue on Systemic Linguistics*), 103-123.

Ventola, E. 1987. *The Structure of Social Interaction: a systemic approach to the semiotics of service encounters*. London: Pinter.

Ventola, E. 1988a. "The Logical Relations in Exchanges". J.D. Benson & W.S. Greaves [eds] *Systemic Functional Approaches to Discourse*, 51-72. Norwood, N.J.: Ablex.

Ventola, E. 1988b. "Text Analysis in Operation: a multilevel approach". R.P. Fawcett & D. Young [eds] *New Developments in Systemic Linguistics, Vol. 2: theory and application*, 52-77. London: Pinter.

Ventola, E. 1989. "Problems of Modelling and Applied Issues Within the Framework of Genre". *Word*, 40(1-2), 129-161. (*Systems, structure and discourse: selected papers from the Fifteenth International Systemic Congress*).

Vittachi, T. 1989. "Leaving the Peasants in the Dark". *New Internationalist* 191. 10-11.

Waterson, N. 1956. "Some Aspects of the Phonology of the Nominal Form of the Turkish Word". *Bulletin of the School of Oriental and African Studies* 18. 578-591. [reprinted in Palmer 1970, 174-187]

Weiner, E.J. & W. Labov. 1983. "Constraints on the Agentless Passive". *Journal of Linguistics* 19. 29-58.

Wells, G. 1977. "Language Use and Educational Success: an empirical response to Joan Tough: The Development of Meaning". *Research in Education* 18.

Wignell, P., J.R. Martin & S. Eggins. 1987. "The Discourse of Geography: ordering and explaining the experiential world. *Writing Project: report 1987 (Working Papers in Linguistics* 5) Department of Linguistics, University of Sydney. [republished in *Linguistics and Education* 1(4). 1990. 359-392]

Winograd, T. 1983. *Language as a Cognitive Process, Vol. 1: syntax*. Reading, Mass.: Addison-Wesley.

Winter, E.O. 1977. "A Clause Relational Approach to English Texts: a study of some predictive lexical items in written discourse". *Instructional Science* 6(1). 1-92.

Young, D. 1985. "Some Applications of Systemic Grammar to TEFL or 'Whatever became of register analysis?'" J.D. Benson & W.S. Greaves [eds] *Systemic Perspectives on Discourse, Vol. 2: selected applied papers from the 9th International Systemic Workshop*, 282-294. Norwood, N.J.: Ablex.

Young, D.J. 1987 "Continuative and Inceptive Adjuncts in English". M.A.K. Halliday & R.P. Fawcett [eds] *New Developments in Systemic Linguistics, Vol. 1: theory and description*, 230-245. London: Pinter.

Zadel, S. 1989. "'Uptight' police kill man in raid". *Sydney Morning Herald*, Friday, April 26, 1989. 1&7.

Zamyatin, Y. 1972. (originally 1924) *We*. Harmondsworth: Penguin.

Index

A1, 47
A1f, 48
A2, 47
A2f, 47
A-event, 48-49
Abstract *see* narrative
accept, 53-54
Acknowledge Offer, 34, 38, 45
Acknowledge Statement, 34, 45
act
    macro-phenomenon, 40, 139, 236
    rank in exchange structure, 51-57
action, 47
    immediate, 48-49
    postponed, 48-49
activity sequence, 292, 293, 321-324,
    325, 517, 537-539
    & IDEATON structure, 337-338, 350-
      351, 367-369
addition, 125-126
additive conjunction, 171-73, 176, 179,
    205-206
    addition additive conjunction, 205-
      206
adjacency pairs, 34, 36-46, 45-46, 47,
    77-78, 383
adversative conjunction, 171-173, 176
affect, 523, 525, 533-536
affirmative, 44
AGENCY, 13
agnation, 507
    field agnation, 542-546
    genre agnation, 507, 560-569
alternation, 176
    alternation additive conjunction, 205-
      206

ambiguous reference, 125-126
amplification, 533
    see also affect
anaphoric, 123-124, 141
anaphoric nouns, 376-377, 416, 483
anecdote, 564-567
antagonist, 582-583
anticipate, 49
antonymy, 287, 288, 301-302, 304
attending, 44, 45, 49
attitude, 43, 568
    & exclamations 74
    see also affect
Attribute, 130, 164
attributive, 163, 170, 279, 319
authority, 527

B-event, 48-49
back-channel, 67, 70
Bid, 81
Birmingham School, 46, 48, 51-57, 58
bridging, 124-125, 126, 144
    & IDEATION 307-309

Call, 42, 45, 49-50, 55
calling, 44, 45, 48-49
cataphoric, 123-124, 143
causal conjunction, 171-173
    see also consequential conjunction,
      193-202
central token, 428, 432
challenging, 71-76
check, 67-68, 70
Circumstance, 278-279, 316
    Extent, 131, 154-155

Location, 131, 153-154
Manner, 154-155
Matter, 164
Role, 131
clarification, 68, 70
class, 6
see also social class
Classifier, 311-312
clause complex, 19, 23, 159-160, 162, 165
& Rhetorical structure theory, 256-257
co-classification, 384, 419
coding orientation, 576-581
co-extension, 384, 419
coherence, 27-28, 381-382, 432-433
see also cohesive harmony
cohesion, 19, 23, 26, 28, 56-57, 381
compared with discourse semantics, 387-390
cohesive harmony, 27, 370-372, 386, 417-433, 488-489
string & chain interaction, 371, 392, 427-432
see also peripheral, relevant & central tokens
co-hyponymy, 297, 301
collective, 306, 307
collocation, 275-277, 287, 288, 289, 290, 385
co-meronymy, 303-304
Command, 32, 33, 38, 45
comment, 53, 58
comparison, 102, 115-119
& generic reference, 104
difference vs similarity, 117
comparative conjunction, 171, 176, 179, 202-205
complementarity, 303, 304
Complication see narrative
componential relation, 383
composition, 295-296, 303-309, 540
concession, 176, 199
& activity sequences, 323
internal concession, 222

see also consequential conjunction
condition see consequential conjunction
confirmation, 68-70
congruence, 58-59
CONJUNCTION, 26, 27, 93, 96, 159-270
analysis exemplified, 243-249
cohesive conjunction, 163, 164, 165, 168, 170
external vs internal conjunction, 178-183, 226-230
Halliday's synoptic summary of expansion, 171, 174-175
in Halliday & Hasan, 171-173
structural analysis, 234-243
vs CONTINUITY, 230-231
connotative semiotic, 405, 493
consequence see consequential conjunction
consequential conjunction, 171, 176, 179, 193-202
consistency, 306, 307
constituency, 26
constitution, 307
contact, 523, 525, 528-532
content form, 7, 15
context, 26, 28, 404-405, 493-590
& metafunction, 494
for Firth, 497
for Halliday, 498
continuative, 164, 218
CONTINUITY, 230-234
contraction, 531, 532
see also contact
contrast, 176-177
contrast conjunction, 202-205
contratextuality, 585
control, 527
converse, 302, 304
core vocabulary, 289
covariate structure, 23-25, 26, 156, 332
Crisis see anecdote
critical linguistics, 2, 265, 587
culminative see periodic
cycle, 303, 304

Da1, 47
Dk1, 47
de-automatization, 386
declarative, 31-32, 41
definite article, 94, 99
Deictic, 111, 132, 134
delicacy, 5
demanding, 32, 35, 44, 45
demonstrative, 94, 99, 111
denotative semiotic, 405
dependency structure, 24
  & Rhetorical structure theory, 251-
   253
  daughter dependency analysis, 65-66
  in conversational analysis, 60-66
  in lexical strings, 332
  in reference chains, 140, 156
  in reticula, 240-241
dependent clause, 41-42, 486
dialogism, 495, 575
dictionary, 273
directive, 54, 56, 58
discourse semantics, 1, 26
discourse structure, 21-26, 95-96, 156-
  157, 265-269
discourse systems, 26-28
disjunction, 588
dynamic, 59, 60, 166, 491, 506, 570
  & CONJUNCTION, 262-264
  & genre, 551, 553, 554-555
  & IDENTIFICATION, 121-127, 137
  & method of development, 447
  & point, 459-460
  & tracking, 69-71
  exchange dynamics, 66-76
dynamic open system, 503

elaboration, 57, 159, 310
  & nuclear relations, 310-314, 317, 326
ELLIPSIS, 26, 33, 34, 373-375, 388-389
embedded clause, 41-42, 486
endophoric, 122-124
enhancement, 57, 159, 310
  & nuclear relations, 316-317
Epithet, 315

equal/unequal status see tenor, status
esphoric, 123-124, 143, 145
ethnicity, 495, 546, 576
ethnomethodology, 46, 76-77
Evaluation see narrative
event-line, 95-96
Ex, 49-50
exchange, 47
exchange structure, 46-59, 52
exchanging, 44, 45
Exclamation, 43-44, 45
exclamative, 43-44
exemplum, 557-558, 564-567
exophoric, 122, 142
expansion see elaboration, extension,
  enhancement
experiential meaning, 8, 9, 10
explicit conjunction, 183-184, 236-237
exposition, 560
expression form, 7, 15
extended reference, 139, 459
extension, 57, 159, 310
  & nuclear relations, 314-316, 317
external conjunction, 184-206, 236-237
  external additive, 205-206
  external comparative, 202-205
  external consequential, 193-202
  external locative, 206
  external temporal, 185-192
  see also CONJUNCTION

fact, 40, 139, 228, 236
factual genres, 562-563
fashion of meaning, 577, 586
field, 288-290, 291-292, 404, 494, 499,
  536-546, 561
  for Pike, 548-549
  specialised field, 542-543
  technical field, 543
field-structured, 517, 518
finite, 41, 170
Finite, 463-464
  see also Subject, Mood
follow-up, 47-48

foregrounding *see* de-automatization
function
  vs class, 6
functional grammar, 2

gender, 495, 546, 576, 586
general item, 287, 374
generalised reference, 119
generation, 495, 546, 576
generic reference, 102-105, 145-146
generic structure potential, 505-551, 560
genre, 26, 495, 503-505, 546-573
  & field, 547
  & mode for Halliday, 500
  for Longacre 560-561, 573
genre-structured, 517, 518
Given *see* New
giving, 32, 35, 44, 45
goods & services, 32, 35, 44, 45, 47
Gr, 49-50
gradable, 303
grammatical metaphor, 16-17, 406-417
  & CONJUNCTION, 165, 169, 229, 264-265
  & IDEATION, 327-328, 331
  & IDENTIFICATION, 138-140
  & MODALITY, 75, 477
  & mode, 519-520
  & texture, 393-401, 490-491
  experiential metaphor, 327-329, 409-412
  ideational metaphor, 406-407
  interpersonal metaphor, 39, 50-51, 412-415, 487
  logical metaphor, 408-409
  textual metaphor, 416-417, 483
  unpacking, 411-412
grammatical parrallelism, 386
greeting, 44, 45, 48-49
Greeting, 42, 45

heteroglossia, 495, 575, 576, 580
hierarchy of periodicity, 559
homophoric, 121-122, 124, 142
hyperonymy, 297, 299-300
hyponymy, 288, 297, 299, 300-301, 374

hypotaxis, 22, 24, 26, 42, 159, 165
  & expansion, 40, 159-160, 168, 170
  & projection, 40, 159-160

idea, 139, 159, 235
ideational meaning, 13
IDEATION, 23, 26, 27
  & comparative conjunction, 202-203
  analysis exemplified, 338-369
  Structure, 326-338
  see also taxonomic relations, nuclear relations, activity sequences
IDENTIFICATION, 23, 26, 27, 93-157, 106
  analysis exemplified, 127-129, 146-153
  & comparative conjunction, 202-203
identifying, 163, 170, 279-284, 319
identity chains, 419
  see also reference chains
ideology, 26, 495-496, 507, 573-588
  as process, 581-585
  as system, 576-581
imperative, 31-32, 41
imperative control, 580
implicit conjunction, 183-184, 236-327
Incident *see* exemplum
inclination, 38
indefinite article, 94, 99
independent clause, 41
indicative, 31-32, 41
information, 32, 35, 44, 45, 47
INFORMATION, 11, 434
initiating, 34-35, 44, 45
instantial reference, 136-137, 144-145
instantial lexical cohesion, 334-383
instantiation, 5
interaction patterns, 392-293, 417-488
interdependency, 26
  see also clause complex
internal conjunction, 207-230, 236-237, 377-378
  internal additive conjunction, 218-221
  internal comparative conjunction, 207-218
  internal consequential conjunction, 222-224

internal temporal conjunction, 224-226
see also CONJUNCTION
interpersonal meaning, 8-9, 11
Interpretation see exemplum
interrogative, 31-32, 41
wh, 34
intertextuality, 574-575
intonation, 76, 383, 384, 385, 386, 448-451
intricacy, 93
involved/uninvolved contact see tenor, contact
issue, 582

K1, 47
K1f, 48
K2, 47
K2f, 47
knowledge, 47

lexical cohesion, 286-288
& field, 288-290
see also IDEATION
lexical item, 290-291, 326
lexical rendering, 329-331
lexical strings, 331-332, 333
see also IDEATION: structure
lexis, 271
as delicate grammar, 277-286, 289, 290
list relation, 251-252
locative conjunction, 206
locution, 139, 159, 235
logical meaning, 12, 13
logico-semantic relations, 170-179, 309-310
see also expansion, projection

macro-phenomenon see act
major clause, 41-42
manner consequential conjunction, 193, 194, 199, 200-201
marker, 54
Medium, 314-315

meronymy, 287, 288, 303-306
message part, 294, 314, 325
metafunction, 7-13, 20-21
& context, 494
& discourse semantics, 390, 402-403
& structure, 10-13
& system, 8-9
metaphenomenon see fact, idea, locution
metaredundancy, 496
method of development, 434-448, 489
& interpersonal Theme, 448
minor clause, 41-42
modal responsibility, 412, 413, 415, 461-488, 489-490
analysis exemplified, 466-468, 470-474
& interpersonal metaphor, 477-488
modal verb, 36, 45
modality, 38
orientation, 74, 480
see also modalization, modulation
modalization, 3, 38-39, 41-42, 45, 46, 413, 480, 568
& challenging, 73-74
& CONJUNCTION, 194, 322
mode, 93, 404, 494, 500, 508-523, 561, 572
action/reflection, 516-523
& genre for Halliday, 500-501
monologue/dialogue, 510-516
modularity, 55-56, 90, 155-157, 178, 203, 265-266, 325, 383-385, 390-393, 560
modulation, 3, 38-39, 41-42, 45, 46, 413, 480, 568
& challenging, 71-72
CONJUNCTION, 194, 322
Mood, 33, 462, 464
Mood ellipsis, 33, 38
MOOD, 4, 9, 31-32, 35, 40-41, 44, 46, 50, 413
move, 34, 46-47, 59
move complex, 57-59
multivariate structure, 21-22, 46-47
& CONJUNCTION, 249-250

narrative, 560, 564-569
narrative of personal experience, 556-557
naturalisation, 584, 586-588
negotiation, 44, 45, 49
NEGOTIATION, 26-27, 31-91, 46-50, 63
  analysis exemplified, 78-90
neutralised reference, 119
New, 434, 449-451
  hyper-New, 453-456
  macro-New, 453-456, 457-459
  see also point
nominalisation, 138-139, 168
non-finite, 41-42, 170
non-referential nominal groups, 129
nuclear relations, 293, 294, 309-321
  & TRANSITIVITY, 318-319
  structure, 335-337, 344-350, 362-367
nucleus-satellite relation, 251-252

obligation, 38
Offer, 32, 37, 38, 40, 45
organic relations, 383
Orientation see narrative

particulate, 10, 22, 549, 550-553
parataxis, 22, 25, 26, 159, 165, 168, 170
participant identification, 95-96
  in Kâte, 95-96
  in Tagalog, 96-97
particle, 548-549, 556-558
peripheral token, 427, 432
periodic, 11-12, 22, 559-560
  see also wave
phoricity, 98-102, 134
  & nominal group structure, 134-135
  redundancy, 100-101, 135
  relevance, 100-101, 135, 144, 154
  reminding, 99, 101, 134-135
phrasal verbs, 312-313
plane, 493, 501-508
point, 434, 448-460, 489
POLARITY, 38
positive/negative affect see affect, tenor
possessive nominals groups, 132, 314

possession
  alienable & inalienable, 305
  Post-Head, 53
power, 527
Pre-Classifier, 133-134, 305, 313-314
Pre-Deictic, 133, 305, 313-314
Pre-Epithet, 133-134, 313-314
preface, 53, 58
Pre-Head, 53
Pre-Numerative, 133-134, 137-138, 305, 313-314
Pre-offer, 37
presenting, 102
  in detail, 105-109
presuming, 102
  in detail, 109-115
presumption, 101
presupposition, 101
primary actor, 48
primary knower, 48
probability, 38
process, 4
process type, 279
Proffer, 37
PROJECTION, 13, 21, 244
  impersonal, 130
proliferation, 531, 532
  see also contact
prominence, 527
prompt, 53
pronoun, 94, 99, 111
proper name, 94, 99, 110
proposal, 32, 36, 461, 462, 519
  metaproposal, 483
proposition, 32, 461, 462, 519
  metaproposition, 483
proportionalities, 4, 8
prosodic, 11, 22, 534, 553, 556-559
protagonist, 582-583
purpose see consequential conjunction

Question, 32, 46

Range, 130-131, 137, 311, 314
rank, 6, 20-21

in discourse semantics, 46-47, 50
in lexicogrammar, 7
in phonology, 7
lexical relations, 303, 304
RCall, 49-50
react, 54
reacting, 44, 45, 48-49
Reaction *see* anecdote
realisation, 4, 378-379, 460
realisation statements, 5
reciprocity, 527-528
Record *see* recount
recount, 564-567
reference *see* presenting, presuming, generic, specific, comparison, exophoric, endophoric, homophoric, esphoric, anaphoric, cataphoric, neutralised reference, generalised reference, instantial reference, extended reference, text reference, IDENTIFICATION
reference chain, 140-146
reformulation comparative internal conjunction, 208-214
register, 26, 28, 381, 496, 497-501
for Halliday, 498, 501-502
Halliday's first & second order register, 571-572
see also field, mode, tenor
relative clause, 40, 236
relational clause *see* attributive, identifying
relevant token, 427, 432
repetition, 286, 287, 288
replay, 70
Residue, 33, 462, 463
ellipsis, 33
see also Mood
Resolution *see* narrative
responding to, 34-35, 44, 45
Response Offer to Command, 34, 38, 45
Response Statement to Question, 34, 46
Response to Call, 42, 45
Response to Exclamation, 43, 45
Response to Greeting, 42, 45

reticulum, 95, 141, 234-235
REx, 49-50
RGr, 49-50
Rheme *see* Theme
Rhetorical structure theory, 249-264, 268, 549

scale, 303, 304
schematic structure, 505, 550-551
schizophrenic discourse, 386-387
secondary actor, 48
secondary knower, 48
semantic variation, 578, 585
semiotic distance, 509
semogenesis, 575, 585
series, 303
service encounter, 82-90, 503-504
Signal, 54
similarity, 176
similarity conjunction, 202-205
similarity chain, 419
see also IDEATION:structure
simultaneous temporal conjunction, 185-187, 191-192
social class, 495, 546, 559, 576
socio-semantics, 80, 576
specific reference, 102-105
SPEECH FUNCTION, 34-35, 44, 46, 50
stage *see* schematic structure
starter, 53, 56
Statement, 32, 45
status, 523, 525, 527-528
stratification, 1, 14-20, 20-21, 56, 373-390, 403, 498, 502
CONJUNCTION & clause complex, 168-170
context & language, 502
IDEATION & lexis, 290-294
IDENTIFICATION & nominal groups, 129-134
register & genre, 505-507, 571-573
SPEECH FUNCTION & MOOD, 33-35, 50
stratificational linguistics, 1, 95-96, 136, 234
Subject, 32, 461, 464

vs Theme, 475
SUBSTITUTION, 26, 33, 373-375, 388-389
subversion, 588
successive temporal conjunction, 185-192
summons, 54, 81
superlative, 112
superordinate, 287, 297, 299-300, 374
superordination, 295-296, 297-303, 541
superset reference, 112-114
synonymy, 286, 287, 288, 300-301
synoptic *see* dynamic
system, 4
system networks, 4-5
  componential, 283-284
  displayed network, 284
  taxonomic, 283
systemic flowchart, 60-61
system/structure theory, 4-5, 573-574

taxonomic relations, 294-309
  structure, 333-335, 340-344, 354-362
  see also superordination, composition
taxonomy, 289, 292, 293, 540-542
technicality, 545
telos, 503
temporal conjunction, 171-173, 176, 179, 185-192
tenor, 404, 494, 499, 499-500, 523-536, 561
  see also affect, contact, status
TENSE, 13
text, 17, 28

text reference, 139, 162, 267, 377, 416, 417
text structure, 504-505, 550-551
  see also schematic structure
textual meaning, 8-9, 12, 13
texture, 26, 381, 382-383, 488-491, 493
THEME, 9, 11, 434
  & CONJUNCTION, 436, 441
  hyper-Theme, 437-439, 442, 443, 444
  in Tagalog, 97
  Macro-Theme, 437-439, 442, 443, 444, 457-459
  marked Theme, 440, 461
  topical Theme, 435
  unmarked Theme, 446
  vs Subject, 475
  see also method of development
THEME PREDICATION, 130
thesaurus, 273-275, 288
Token, 280
tonic, 449-450
tracking, 67-71
TRANSITIVITY, 9

univariate structure, 21-22, 24, 26
usuality, 38

value, 280
variable rule, 579
vocabulary 3 items, 375-376, 409, 416

wave, 548-549
wh clause, 40, 236